PRICING,

DISTRIBUTION,

and EMPLOYMENT

Economics of an Enterprise System

PRICING, DISTRIBUTION, and EMPLOYMENT

ECONOMICS OF AN ENTERPRISE SYSTEM

REVISED EDITION

JOE S. BAIN

UNIVERSITY OF CALIFORNIA, BERKELEY

HENRY HOLT AND COMPANY · NEW YORK

PREFACE TO THE REVISED EDITION

In the present revision as in the first edition, this book has been written primarily for use as a text in a first or basic course in economic theory. It presupposes that the student will have had some survey course in economics, though not necessarily one from which he has gained any systematic appreciation of economic analysis. As such, its content might be designated as either "elementary" or "intermediate" economic theory. It may, depending on curricular plans, find use in undergraduate courses for juniors or seniors specializing either in economics or in business administration, or in elementary graduate courses in economic theory. Since the contents of prerequisite survey courses vary considerably from place to place, I have given some attention initially to the most elementary concepts in economic theory, and have then carried the analysis as far as seemed desirable for a first-year theory course.

The economic theory presented herein is essentially limited to the contemporary or modern analyses of price or value, of income distribution, and of the level of income and employment. In all cases the theories presented are of the conventional static or equilibrium variety, and no attempt is made to develop theories of process, growth, or change through time. In the present stage of development of economic theory it still appears expedient to regard these conventional equilibrium theories as fundamentals of economic theory in general, with which the student should become thoroughly acquainted before considering more difficult models for prediction and analysis.

The emphasis or orientation of the work also remains unchanged in this revision. That is, economic theory is not presented primarily as an elegant system of formal logic, or as a complex of analytical tools which might be useful in the solution of any of a number of practical economic problems. It is presented rather in its major role—as a system of thought which offers explanations and predictions of how the economy works, and normative evaluations (given some ethical judgments) of the predicted tendencies of behavior. The work is thus concerned to explain to the student the main content of a certain system of hypotheses which have been developed relative to the determinants, the character, and the social desirability of economic behavior within the modern enterprise economy. The formal aspects of economic theory have been emphasized sufficiently to enable the student to gain some critical appreciation of the method by which these hypotheses have been developed. It seems to the writer that this emphasis is appropriate both for the undergraduate taking what will in most cases be his terminal course in economic theory, and for the student with notions of becoming a professional economist who is taking the first of a long series of courses in the subject. In either case, imparting the general content of a system of economic theory has a priority over attempting to train the technician.

The following chapters therefore do not present an especially elaborate or advanced treatment of the formal apparatus of economic theory, nor do they attempt to develop a number of recently proposed extensions of the theory based on complex but as yet very tentative assumptions. What is presented is a simple version of theory, based on simple and conventional postulates, and developed on the formal level enough to show what in general economic theory has to say and how it arrives at its conclusions.

On the other hand, the work attempts to cover considerably more of the whole content of modern economic theory than some more formalistic treatments. The analysis of pricing and distribution is carried beyond the so-called particular equilibrium theories of the firm and industry to deal with the interrelated behavior of all firms and productive factors within the economy, or the "general equilibrium" implications of specific patterns of firm and industry behavior. Thus, the genuine importance of diverse pricing phenomena is emphasized by considering in some detail their impact on the level of employment and the allocation of resources among uses. Correspondingly, the effects of various sorts of predicted economic performance upon the general economic welfare are the subject of analysis throughout.

The plan of the work remains substantially unchanged; it considers successively commodity pricing, income distribution, and the level of income and employment. As before, the theory of employment is given a relatively synoptic treatment, whereas value and distribution theory are considered in greater detail. The theories of consumer choice and of production do not receive extensive formal development, but are introduced in the course of the analysis respectively of buyer demand and of varying costs and factor substitution. Within this plan, however, there has been considerable revision.

The work has been rewritten in large part, principally in order to enlarge the scope of the materials treated in many chapters, to simplify the exposition of some concepts, and to provide a fuller or less condensed presentation of intrinsically complex analytical arguments. At the same time, I have modified my treatment of a number of issues to reflect evolution in my own thinking, to recognize some contributions of the last few years, and to attain greater rigor and clarity. In consequence, this revised edition is substantially longer than the first, in the sections dealing with price theory and distribution theory.

The greatest changes in the treatment of price theory will perhaps be found in a more comprehensive chapter on demand (including added ma-

terial on the theory of consumer choice), in substantially extended evaluations of the welfare impacts of competitive and monopolistic pricing, in a
revised and extended analysis of oligopolistic pricing, and in a new chapter
on the theory of price discrimination.

The succeeding part of the work—on income distribution and employment—has been thoroughly reorganized and rewritten in the interest of
easier pedagogy. The conventional theory of income distribution, as developed on certain simple equilibrium assumptions, is now presented without
interruption in the three chapters following the section on price theory,
while the theory of income and employment, together with an analysis of
interest and other distributive shares under nonstationary conditions, follow.
This change of organization may assist the instructor who wishes to include
in a course some material on income distribution without becoming en-
tangled with the dynamics of interest and employment.

The discussion of monopolistic and monopsonistic influences on factor
pricing, to which all of Chapter 12 is devoted, has been revised and considerably extended, so that it now represents a unified and systematic analytical treatment of this essential range of problems. The analysis of the
characteristics of particular productive factors, contained in Chapter 13, has
likewise been extended. By contrast, the presentation of the theory of employment has been simplified and compressed in order to serve better the
needs of a basic year course in economic theory.

The economic theory or theories presented in this work are basically
not original, and in large part represent the conventional or accepted doctrines which have emerged, with borrowings from the Continent, from the
neo-classical and neo-Keynesian traditions. I have frequently found it necessary, however, to develop syntheses of related theories, to choose between
genuinely divergent theoretical arguments, to reformulate arguments which
seem heretofore to have been ambiguously stated, to introduce novel elaborations of received theory, or to develop explicitly certain conclusions which
follow readily from conventional theoretical arguments but which have not
been made plain before. Since much of this work consists of reducing preva-
lent oral tradition to systematic written form, and since the book is designed
primarily as a student text, I have made no attempt to designate lines between reproduction of received doctrines and novel extensions or elaborations of them. The end product may be regarded as my own interpretation
and elaboration of the elements of a certain body of conventional economic
theory.

The first ten chapters of the revised work (also published separately
under the title *Price Theory*) present a substantially self-contained discussion of price analysis, and as such may serve the needs of various semester
courses which deal principally with this subject. The complete work should

provide reading for the year course or intensive semester course which covers a wider range of economic theory.

In developing this revision, as in preparing the original manuscript, I have been assisted greatly by the comments and suggestions of many of my students and colleagues at the University of California. For detailed criticism and comment I am especially indebted to Professors Robert Dorfman, William Fellner, Roy Jastram, John Letiche, Earl Rolph, and Peter Steiner, and to Drs. Douglas Dowd and Frederick Moore. I am similarly grateful for the suggestions and comments made by many others who have read or used the work in the original edition. Finally, I have been immeasurably assisted by Professor Howard Ellis, who has read and criticized the entire manuscript of the revised edition.

J. S. B.

University of California, Berkeley
January, 1953

PREFACE TO THE FIRST EDITION

This book is written primarily for use in the first collegiate upper-division course in economic theory. It presupposes that the student will have had some survey course in economics but not necessarily one which goes very far with formal economic analysis. As such, I suppose it might be characterized as either "elementary" or "intermediate" economic theory. Recognizing that the content of the prerequisite survey course varies from place to place, I have begun on a rather elementary level and carried the subject as far as seemed desirable for undergraduate teaching.

As the student is introduced to economic theory, there is initially a serious question as to what should be emphasized. From one standpoint economic theory may be viewed as a system of formal reasoning that supplies certain analytical tools which can be applied to the solution of numerous practical problems. Correspondingly, the basic theory offering has often been constructed primarily as a "tool-box" course, emphasizing a technical training for the future economist. But economic theory may more broadly be viewed as a system of thought which offers an explanation of how the economy works and an evaluation of the tendencies that this system of thought discovers. The subject material is construed in the latter sense in this volume. My primary purpose is to explain to the student in some detail what theory tells him of the working of his economy and of the reasons this economy behaves as it does. Since the bulk of undergraduate "majors" in economics or business administration are obviously not going to become professional economists, it seems appropriate thus to reduce the emphasis on formal training and to focus attention mainly on the meaningful propositions which economic theory has developed.

Because they have been written with this emphasis, the following chapters do not present an especially intensive or advanced treatment of the formal apparatus of economic theory. The basic concepts and solutions are presented and discussed, but mainly as a means of showing what economic theory has to say and in general how it arrives at its conclusions. On the other hand, the work may be somewhat more comprehensive of the content of economic theory and of its implications than some more strictly formal treatments. The discussion of pricing and distribution, for example, is not limited to a consideration of the firm and industry (the particular equilibrium) but extends to cover a number of aspects of the interrelated behavior of all sectors of the economy (the general equilibrium). Thus pricing is considered not only as an individual industry problem but as a general phenomenon affecting the level of employment and the allocation of resources among uses.

The content of the volume includes a theory of price, in particular and general equilibrium aspects, a theory of the distribution of income, and a theory of the level of income and employment. Some of these matters have perhaps been more thoroughly explored than others. For example, the theory of employment is given only a synoptic treatment in connection with the discussion of capital and interest, and a course devoted primarily to income and employment should certainly seek much additional reading material. In general, however, I have attempted to prepare a primer covering a good deal of the content of modern economic theory. Certain exceptions to this may be noted. The theory of consumer choice is not developed but only referred to as an explanation of the observed system of demands for goods. The theory of production is not treated in great detail but is brought into the discussion mainly in the explanation of varying costs and of the inter-substitution of factors by the firm. These omissions are deliberate; if the instructor desires to emphasize these matters, a great many standard treatments of them are available.

Little of the basic theoretical content of this volume is original. I have, however, felt free to apportion emphasis to various lines of analysis in accordance with their empirical relevance and their pedagogical value. Thus the analysis of price is dominantly an analysis of monopoly price and primarily of pricing in oligopolistic situations. This would seem appropriate in view of the current structure of the American economy. I have discussed oligopoly pricing at considerably greater length than is customary in theory textbooks, in the belief that we should emphasize the pricing situations of the real world. The treatment of income and employment runs entirely in terms of a sequence analysis; some Keynesian ideas are put forward in a period-analysis format in order to bring them perhaps a bit closer to experience.

The materials contained herein have been mostly covered in the first semester of a year's course on theory—that devoted to pricing and distribution—and have served as an introduction to a second semester on income and employment. With appropriate selection and supplementation, I hope that they may be useful under various curricular arrangements.

My sincere thanks go to Professor William Fellner for his extremely helpful advice and criticism on many points throughout the manuscript. And I am deeply indebted to a number of my colleagues who have used a mimeographed version of the first nine chapters in teaching and have made many useful suggestions.

J. S. B.

University of California, Berkeley
February 10, 1948

CONTENTS

Part 1 PRICE THEORY

Part 2   THEORY OF DISTRIBUTION AND EMPLOYMENT

Part 1

PRICE THEORY

CHAPTER 1

THE NATURE AND FUNCTION
OF ECONOMIC THEORY

As this work is concerned with economic theory, it is perhaps best begun with a brief statement of what economic theory is and what it does.

THE MEANING OF AN ECONOMY

To understand the nature and function of such theory, we need first to grasp the idea of *an economy*. An economy is simply a society of people engaged in their main occupation of making a living. People all over the world are organized for the purpose of producing and distributing the things they want to use. All the people in the world, or in any continent or country, are members of a sort of army made up to provide useful output for consumption. Their economy embraces organized effort in agriculture and forestry, in mining and manufacture, in transportation and marketing, and in the arts and professions.

All such lines of endeavor, and the people following them, are essentially parts of a unified economic organization which provides a living for all. Although the individual coal miner or bricklayer or tobacco-shop proprietor may not be very acutely aware of the fact, he is a member of a huge team which counts as members all workers in the society. The actual existence of a unified economic organization with a central purpose is quite clear in a completely socialized country, where there is a government which places great emphasis on the fact and undertakes a sort of central management of all economic activity. But the organization is equally present in a private-enterprise society like our own, even though there is little or no central planning or management, and though the pattern of economic effort emerges from the activities of a large number of independent persons, each of whom is guided mainly by his pursuit of individual gain.

The main difference is that under socialism the over-all economic accomplishment is largely premeditated, whereas in a free enterprise system it just emerges as it will, automatically or by accident, and controlled mainly by competition. This has, at any rate, been generally true under American capitalism, except when in times of special stress the government has imposed certain direct regulations on the economy to assure a certain type of performance.

MEASURING THE PERFORMANCE OF AN ECONOMY

Capitalistic, socialistic, or otherwise, any economy performs in some way, and its performance can be measured and appraised. There are several aspects of the performance of an economy which, among others, seem important to most people:

1. *The amount of goods produced.* It is important to know what the output of an economy is, in the aggregate and per capita, every year—what its *productivity* is and, inferentially, its ability to employ available labor and resources.
2. *The efficiency of production.* What are the costs, in terms of human effort and physical resources, which are incurred per unit of output relative to the lowest attainable costs?
3. *The pattern of income distribution,* or the manner in which the goods produced are distributed among the population.
4. *The pattern of allocation of resources among alternative uses.* It is important to know the proportions in which the economy produces the various goods useful to the population and how well this proportion corresponds to that which would best satisfy consumers.
5. *The progressiveness of the economy.* How rapidly on the average does the output of the economy increase over time?
6. *The stability of the economy.* To what extent do the output of the economy and also its allocation and income-distribution patterns fluctuate over time?

These are the major aspects of the performance of an economy within the realm of the provision of material goods—they are in effect the main determinants of the aggregate *material welfare* of the populace. The acceptability to a society of the working of an economy, needless to say, does not turn solely on how well it enhances material welfare. The individual's status in his occupation, his freedom to shift jobs, quit work, or go fishing, and the general sort of political system which is coordinate with his economic system, may all be important additional determinants of the total welfare of the society. These facts can hardly be overemphasized. But the performance of an economy in the more strictly material respects previously mentioned is nonetheless very important in any society. It is with the evaluation and analysis of such material performance that economics generally, and conventional economic theory in particular, is mainly concerned, and upon this we shall therefore focus our attention.

Six aspects of material performance of an economy have been listed above. In each case most people have an idea of what is desirable. Large output and employment are generally preferred to small, at least up to some margin of overwork. Most of us also want low costs per unit of output, a composition of total output which best serves consumer needs, and freedom from excessive economic instability. There may be more difference of opinion on the best type of income distribution and the best degree of progressiveness in our economy, but some majority sentiment on these matters can be established.

Everyone has a vital interest in how well his economy performs in these respects. How close does it come to ideal or desirable behavior? Does it provide as much material welfare as is reasonably possible? The answer to these questions will reveal how satisfactory an economic organization we have, and it also will indicate whether public action is needed to improve the working of the economy. It is, therefore, important to make actual measurements of how our economy has been performing in the respects indicated. It is equally important to *explain why* an economy performs as it does and to be able to *predict* the sort of performance it will give under various circumstances.

Measuring economic performance is not essentially difficult. A great many statistics on employment, output, income distribution, and so forth have to be collected, compiled, and interpreted, but once this is accomplished their significance is readily understood. We have on hand from private and public agencies manifold statistics on such things as production, employment, cost, composition of output, and income distribution within our economy. These statistics give us some idea of how well our economy has performed and where improvement might be desired.

But measurement is not enough. In the first place, if we find that our economy has been performing in a certain way for the past several years, we shall want to know whether this performance (bad, good, or indifferent) should be expected to continue or not. Is the observed performance inevitable, or is it accidental? Or, more generally, is it the necessary outcome of some identifiable *determinants* of economic performance? In the second place, if we find the going performance of the economy somewhat unsatisfactory, we may wish to change it. But to develop a policy which will alter economic performance, we need to understand its causes. We must know what leads to what in the realm of economic performance before we can devise alterations in the organization which will improve its working. Thus, it is obviously necessary to develop not only a *measurement* of how the economy works but also an *explanation* of why it works as it does. Only in this way will we be able to *predict* how our economy is likely to perform and to devise policies to improve its performance.

THE FUNCTION OF ECONOMIC THEORY

Economic theory, or at any rate a good part of it, provides such an explanation. It attempts to explain how an economy works, why it works as it does, and, perhaps also, how it should work. It ordinarily begins by analyzing certain basic conditions which influence any economic activity, such as the character of consumers' desires for goods, the nature of production techniques, the relative supplies of human and natural resources, and the motivations of the persons engaging in or directing productive activity. It then proceeds to develop an explanation and prediction of how an economy will perform in certain circumstances.

The "certain circumstances" proviso is important since no explanation of economic performance exists which is good for all times and places. The character of economic performance is heavily conditioned by the political and institutional framework within which activity is organized, and as a result any detailed explanation of performance is likely to refer primarily to what happens in some particular institutional framework. The most highly develoepd variety of economic theory at present is concerned mainly with the explanation of action within a capitalist economy. Certain parts of it would be useful in building a correspondingly detailed theory of the performance of a socialized economy, but by no means all of it. Actually, we need various economic theories corresponding to the variety of basically different institutional settings within which economic activity occurs. Whatever the setting referred to, however, the basic explanatory function of economic theory remains.

Since the economy of the United States is of a capitalistic or free-enterprise type and since its problems are the major economic concern of most of us, we shall center attention in this book on the theory of the working of a capitalist economy. This theory attempts to explain how a capitalist economy behaves, what sort of results it tends to give, and why it gives these results. In so doing we shall, of course, not be covering "all" of economic theory. We shall, however, be studying the elements of the most highly developed version or form of such theory, and in so doing we may be prepared to move easily to the study of other forms.

In passing it should also be noted that we have to this point construed the content of economic theory quite narrowly—as a system of explaining how a given economy performs. To be sure, the bulk of current economic theory is devoted to explaining the functioning of a given *contemporary economy;* to analyzing how our going economy performs at present or over historically very brief intervals of time. It is, moreover, to such economic theory that we shall devote our entire attention in this book. More broadly, however, economic theory may also comprehend the explanation of other phenomena. In particular, it may deal with the development or evolution of economic behavior over historically medium or long time intervals and with the pattern of institutional evolution over such periods. This sort of economic theory is much less fully developed than the type to be studied here, but it is potentially no less significant. Only limitations of space preclude a survey of its general scope and subject material in this volume.

CHARACTERISTICS OF A FREE-ENTERPRISE ECONOMY

The analysis of the working of a free-enterprise economy, or any similar economic analysis, must begin with a consideration of the nature of human wants and the character of production techniques. To understand the functioning of any economy we must first establish the governing pattern of consumer desires for a variety of goods and the basic relations of effort expended to output secured in producing various goods. The basic psychological and physical laws influencing the operations of all economies must be established. But our free-enterprise analysis must reflect with equal clarity the institutional characteristics of modern capitalism which determine the type of performance such an economy gives.

The salient characteristics of modern capitalism may be loosely labeled as free enterprise, free consumption, and free labor. Although we are so accustomed to all of these institutions that we take them for granted, it may be useful, briefly, to review their general meaning.

To begin with the consumer, or more generally the buyer of any goods, let us see what "free consumption" means. Under our system it is generally true that any individual consumer or other buyer, after receiving an income, has relatively unrestricted free choice as to where, when, and for what he will spend his income. He can spend it all, save it all, or divide it between spending and saving as he desires. So far as he spends it, he can spend it on goods for immediate consumption or on productive assets according to his own desires. And he may choose among various alternative consumption and capital goods as he wishes. The essence of this system is sometimes expressed by saying that "the consumer is sovereign" or that we have *consumer sovereignty.*

The word sovereignty implies one notion already mentioned—that the consumer is independent and free of outside restriction in spending the income he receives. But it also implies more. Since the great bulk of all income under our system is paid into the hands of independent persons who have unrestricted power of disposal over it, consumers as a whole are also in a sense supreme rulers of economic systems. This is true so far as by independently determining whether and when to spend their incomes, and for what, they largely determine the total flow of income through time and also determine the composition of the total output produced by the economy. Production, in other words, is largely guided by or oriented to the independently expressed desires of individual consumers or buyers. This institutional arrangement is sharply different from one, for example, wherein the volume and composition of output are largely set by some central governmental authority.

To be sure, this is a rule subject to important exceptions. So far as income is diverted from individuals by taxes and spent by governmental bodies, we are shifting from individual-consumer sovereignty to collective decision making regarding spending through governmental agencies. A fourth or more of our total income is now subject to such diversion and control, and to the extent that it is, the individual yields his sovereignty over his income to some collective decision-making body. But it is still fair to say that our economic system is governed dominantly by the individual preferences of consumers as expressed in spending their incomes.

An equally important characteristic of modern capitalism is that it rests on *free enterprise*. Productive activity is conducted largely by private concerns operated primarily or directly for the advantage of the private individuals who own them. Such an arrangement is based essentially on a political system which recognizes a substantially universal exercise of the private ownership and operation of land, resources, and the physical equipment for production. Through the institution of private ownership private individuals are able to own and control productive organizations of every type and to guide their operations in such a fashion as to enhance individual gains. Owning the physical means for production and having relatively full powers of control over them, they can secure the human labor needed for production by hiring labor at a wage established under a general system of free contract for human services. The governmental authority, on the other hand, generally regards the function of organizing and carrying out productive activity as reserved to private property owners and undertakes this function itself only under limited and exceptional circumstances. As a result, productive activity in a capitalist economy is organized and carried on mainly by a rather large number of private individual owners or organizations of owners in private business firms or corporations.

The activity of these private organizations is not generally guided by any direct regulation or by any social responsibility to produce more or less or this instead of that. Private enterprises in our system are expected to, and do, direct their actions in such a way as to make individual profits—perhaps the largest possible individual profits. It follows that the prime decisions as to what and how much to produce, how much labor and resources to employ, and what to charge the public are made by individual firms. These decisions turn mainly on their effects on enterprise profits. There is, moreover, no central agency for coordinating individual profit-seeking decisions. They become coordinated only indirectly through the complicated mechanisms of the markets for goods and services.

Individuals and firms, of course, do not produce primarily for use or barter: they produce goods and services to sell for money. Individuals sell their labor or the services of their property for a money price, thereby receiving money incomes. Productive firms buy labor, materials, and equipment for money, and in turn they sell their outputs for money. The money received upon sale of their outputs flows from the incomes of labor and of resource owners and from enterprise profits, thereby completing the circle. So much is elementary. Ours is a money-exchange economy, where activity is immediately related to the flows of money expenditure seeking to purchase various goods and services. It follows that the pursuit of profit by enterprises is precisely the pursuit of a monetary profit—of a difference between money income and money expenditure.

In deciding, with an eye to profit, how much and what to produce and how many to employ, private enterprises are necessarily guided by the general volume of money purchasing power seeking goods. They are also guided by the relative prices that buyers offer for various different goods. Production naturally follows the aggregate money demand for goods and the composition of this demand. It, thus, appears that in seeking profits the productive system of private enterprises is in a sense necessarily guided or ruled by the desires of independent consumers as expressed in their income expenditures.

The third pillar of the system has been labeled as free labor. This refers not only to the fact that labor is free and sovereign—not being subject either to slavery or feudal obligations—but also to the fact that the individual is free to refuse employment generally or in particular occupations, to shift from job to job as he desires and employment is available, to refuse work at what he regards as insufficient wages, to defer working while extending his education, and so forth—all, of course, within the limits of his ability to obtain a sufficient income to support himself. In addition, laborers are permitted to organize in unions for concerted action to accomplish their ends. Similar freedom (except for that of collective organization) is generally enjoyed by the owners of property providing productive services—they are relatively unrestricted in their disposal of these services. Laborers and owners of other productive services are, of course, guided in their actions by the character and composition of the demands for their services by enterprises, but they are free to react to these demands as they will. Similarly, enterprises in securing labor and other services with which to produce are influenced by the prices at which these services are held by their owners in general or in particular occupations.

In a capitalist economy we thus have a very large number of independent decision-making units whose dealings with each other ultimately determine the course of aggregate economic activity. Consumers offer their money incomes to enterprises for various goods and thus offer an incentive for enterprises to produce an aggregate output of some size and composition. Enterprises deal with consumers by setting prices at which they will supply consumer demands, and they deal with laborers and other resource owners by making money offers for their services or by buying certain amounts of their services at set prices. Laborers and resource owners, in turn, deal with enterprises by offering to sell their services at offered prices or by establishing the prices at which they will sell their services. Thus, they receive the incomes which, with enterprise profits, make up the purchasing power consumers offer for goods. From this complex of decisions and dealings by a large number of individuals seeking their own advantage, as they interact and are coordinated in the markets for goods and services, the over-all performance of the capitalist economy emerges.

This is a brief description of the framework of action in a capitalist economy. A task of economic theory is to explain what course this action takes and what results it tends to have.

THE CONTENT OF ECONOMIC THEORY

The economic theory of the working of a capitalist economy falls into two principal parts which, though related, are readily distinguished.

One part of such theory attempts to explain what determines for a capitalist economy the size and course through time of the aggregate flow of money expenditure, production, and employment. In an economy like ours productive activity and employment are elicited by a flow of money purchasing power or demand for goods. The rate of output and employment which will be brought forth depends dually on the size of this flow of purchasing power and on its relation to the general level of the prices of goods and of productive services which are used in making goods. A larger money demand at given prices will tend to induce enterprises to produce more; higher prices with a given money demand will mean less can be bought and less will be produced. It follows that a major task of theory is to investigate what determines the rate of flow of money purchasing power and its relation to the general level of prices for the economy as a whole. By explaining the determination of aggregate purchasing power, the price level, and their relationship, theory may strive to predict under what circumstances a capitalist economy will give full employment, when it will give only partial employment, and according to what patterns over-all production and employment may be expected to fluctuate.

An important part of economic theory is now directly concerned with this general problem of income, employment, and economic fluctuations. It attempts to show how the level and movement of aggregate money income, employment, and production are determined by individual behavior in spending money income, by business decisions respecting investment, by

price movements, and by the character of our financial and banking institutions.

An equally important task of the theory of economic behavior under
capitalism is to explain how the allocation of resources among uses and the
distribution of income are determined. Within our economy there is clearly
a complex process of competition, bargaining, and selection of alternatives—
engaged in by consumers, enterprises, and resource owners—which eventually determines how the economy performs in several major respects.
These include: (1) how much of each good will be produced compared with
others—for example, the ratio of automobiles to beefsteak to mechanical
pencils; (2) what proportion of resources will be used in basic production
and what in distribution and "selling"; and (3) what shares of income will
go to labor, to land and resource owners, to loan and investment capital,
and to enterprise profits.

In the analysis of the process of competition and bargaining which determines these things, we find that prices play a leading role. The decisions
of buyers as to how much and what to buy depend on the absolute and relative prices of the things offered them; the decisions of sellers as to how much
and what to produce and sell depend upon the prices they can get for various
goods and various amounts of given goods they might produce. Similarly,
the absolute and relative prices of labor and land will determine how much
of them will be offered for employment and what shares of income they will
receive. The system of prices is, thus, a sort of determinant or governor of
individual actions which will ultimately determine allocation and income
distribution in a capitalist economy. At the same time, individual prices and
the price system in general are determined by, or behave in response to, the
various price-oriented decisions just mentioned. The price system not only
governs but also is ultimately determined by the interacting complex of individual decisions regarding the purchase and sale of goods and services. In
reacting to, and thus ultimately determining the nature of, a system of
prices buyers and sellers thus collectively determine the character of resource
allocation and income distribution in an enterprise economy.

If we analyze the determination and working of a price system, therefore, we shall necessarily analyze the major determinants of allocation and
income distribution. The branch of economic theory which undertakes to
analyze these matters is thus appropriately known as *price economics* or
price analysis or *price theory*. It undertakes to explain how the interacting
decisions of buyers and sellers in markets eventually codetermine a system
of prices, a pattern of resource allocation, and a pattern of income distribution. At the same time, in analyzing the responses of enterprises to market
and price situations it casts some light on the determination of productive
efficiency and on the progressiveness of the economy in technique and

product. So understood, price analysis is a second major sector of economic theory devoted to the explanation of the working of a capitalist economy.

ORGANIZATION OF THIS WORK

In this work we shall try to cover the basic elements of both branches of economic theory mentioned above—the theory of income and employment and price theory. Taken together, these theories attempt to give an explanation and prediction of the performance of a capitalist economy in the six respects listed on page 2.

Our first concern will be price analysis, in its two main subdivisions—*commodity*-price analysis and *factor*-price analysis. Price analysis undertakes to explain primarily the allocation of resources among uses and the distribution of income among the various factors of production.

Commodity-price analysis, to which we turn first, is broadly concerned with how the profit-seeking and competitive activity of enterprises—producing goods and selling them in markets—operate to allocate resources among uses, or, in other words, to determine what goods and services will be produced and in what proportions. In general, how does an enterprise system respond to a complex of demands for goods by a multitude of consumers and other buyers? This analysis inquires into the general nature of buyer demands for a variety of goods and the determination of the prices and outputs of individual goods. It considers also the determination of the quality or design of such goods, their costs of production, and the amounts expended in promoting their sales. It involves further the analysis of the relations among the prices and outputs of all goods and of the adjustment of these prices to costs of production.

Commodity-price analysis is simplified if at first we determine what tends to occur or would occur if there were some given constant flow of money purchasing power demanding commodities as a whole and also if there were fixed and given money prices for the factors of production, so that the prices of those things which make up the costs of production were fixed. This arbitrarily simplified analysis enables us to ascertain how commodity prices, outputs, and so forth *tend to adjust* to any going situation of money income and factor prices. It also enables us to predict the tendency of allocation of resources in any given situation. The analysis may then be made somewhat more realistic and general by relaxing the arbitrary assumption of given factor prices and by inquiring what would happen if, money income still being constant, the average level of factor prices were free to adjust to this flow of income. By so doing we may ascertain not only the tendency in the allocation of resources, but also the adjustment of prices to costs throughout the economy.

The second main step in the development of economic theory leads us into factor-price analysis. Assuming that every factor price—wage, rent, or interest—is free to adjust in relation both to commodity prices and to other factor prices, this analysis attempts to ascertain the manner of determination of the prices of the various factors relative to each other and to commodity prices at any given level of employment. To simplify the exposition and to defer for the time being the analysis of the determination of the general level of employment, this analysis may first be conducted on the assumption that there is a given constant flow of money purchasing power.

The preceding defines the general scope of price analysis to be treated below. Price analysis essentially inquires what would happen in the realm of resource allocation and income distribution with a given constant flow of money purchasing power. This, as we shall see, is equivalent to assuming some given level of employment. (The explanation of the determination of the level of employment is deferred.) A further task in this work, therefore, will be to develop the analysis of the level of employment and its movement through time. This analysis abandons the arbitrary assumption of given money purchasing power; it recognizes the flow of such purchasing power to be flexible and interrelated with the average level of prices. It inquires into the determinants of the ratio between the flow of money purchasing power and the price level, and thus of the level of employment of labor and other productive resources. Such an analysis is needed to explain the possibility of chronic or periodic unemployment in the economy, the emergence of inflation, and cyclical and other fluctuations in income and employment.

SOME REMARKS ON THEORETICAL METHOD

The task of economic theory, as suggested above, is to provide an explanation of how a certain type of economy will perform, in general or in a particular set of circumstances. The economic theory we shall be studying attempts to explain the performance of a capitalist economy in such respects as the level and fluctuation of employment, the allocation of resources among uses, and the distribution of incomes. This explanation in effect involves an identification of the major ultimate and proximate determinants of economic performance and the description of the process by which these determinants interact to produce a given type of performance. It also should show how an alteration in the character of certain determinants should lead to an alteration of performance.

Theory should, therefore, enable us to explain why our economy has been performing in a certain observed way in the past and perhaps to identify the crucial elements which caused it to perform that way rather than another. It also should enable us to predict how the economy is likely to perform in given circumstances in the future. Finally, it should enable us to identify those crucial determinants a purposive alteration in the character of which should enable government agencies to influence the future course of behavior.

The method which economic theory uses to develop such an explanatory system may be rather unfamiliar to the student novice. It is essentially a method of establishing certain premises or assumptions concerning the determinants of economic performance, then of drawing logical deductions which predict the performance that these determinants will lead to, and finally of checking the predicted performance against actual performance to test the validity of the explanatory system which has thus been developed. If the explanation or prediction seems unsatisfactory, then the theory may be reworked by examining the validity of the basic premises or the adequacy of the deductive logic. Economic theory, as we know it today, benefits from many re-examinations and revisions; it is, at any rate, much more adequate than formerly.

It is important to note that, since economic theory as we know it operates basically by deducing conclusions from stated premises, its whole validity hinges on the validity and adequacy of these premises or assumptions. It is, therefore, also important to realize that these premises or assumptions are not just made up out of thin air or casually invented for the occasion. They are essentially statements about observed facts or empirical generalizations concerning the character of certain presumably crucial determinants of economic performance. Thus, a theory of pricing a particular good may be developed from the assumptions (1) that consumers will buy more of it as its price is reduced, and vice versa; (2) that its costs per unit of output will rise after its output is increased beyond a point; (3) that there is just a single seller of this good; and (4) that he sets his price and output so as to maximize his profit. Each of these assumptions is essentially an empirical generalization about a given market situation or category of such situations, and everything depends on the factual accuracy of such generalizations. If these and similar generalizations are accurate, and if we make enough of them to cover the major determinants of the performance being examined, then careful deductive logic should enable us to predict this performance—in this case, pricing of a good by a monopolist—and to explain the type of performance in question. We may be able to arrive at an appraisal of the validity of a theory by checking actual performance against predicted performance in situations of the sort the theory identifies.

The procedure of economic theory is thus to develop adequate empirical generalizations about presumptive determinants of economic behavior, which then enter into *assumptions* in a logical system; to deduce the results or performance to which their determinants should give rise and the process by which they do so; and then to check the predictions against experience to test the validity of the theory thus developed. It is at this last point, however, that economics, like any social science, encounters difficulties. Economics essentially treats the behavior of human beings. Moreover, it treats just one fraction or aspect of that behavior. Even this fraction of behavior is so complex that it is difficult to explain or analyze all at once— we can seldom do better than to tackle it bit by bit. And it is substantially impossible to isolate the economic behavior of people, or more particularly small parts of it, for examination under controlled conditions which might permit us to arrive at really conclusive verification or testing of various parts of economic theory. In other words, we cannot put economic behavior within the confines of a sterile laboratory for the type of controlled experiments that permit relatively conclusive testing of theories in chemistry or physics.

As a result, no economic theory is ever really verified or conclusively proved right or wrong under controlled experimental conditions. It is thus perhaps safer to refer to economic theory as a body of tentative *hypotheses* which offer an explanation and prediction of economic performance. Does this mean that they are useless or, in any event, rather unreliable? Not in general. In the first place, since we do not possess and are not likely ever to have conclusively verified theories of economic behavior, these hypotheses we do have are quite a bit better than nothing. They furnish, at least on a tentative level, a reasoned analysis of economic activity and a very useful guide to governmental policy measures which might otherwise have to proceed on the basis of pure guesswork. In the second place, though not conclusively verified, much of economic theory may be reasonably reliable. If the empirical generalizations which it draws are reasonably accurate and adequate and if its deductive logic is unassailable, its predictions are bound to be valid. Through continued development over many years economic theory has thus become fairly reliable and may be applied usefully so long as its intrinsic characteristics and limitations are well understood.

In any event, economic theory is by no means completely untested. Although controlled laboratory experiments are not feasible, economists have for a long time been engaged in checking on the validity of predictions by drawing upon statistical measurements and other observations of economic behavior to determine if given theoretical predictions are sustained by fact. The results of this testing seldom result in conclusive proof of a theory, but they do permit one to see if actual behavior is consistent with a theory. As a result, economic theory has been continually improved through time. Although in this volume we shall devote our attention primarily to the hypotheses of economic theory and give little attention to the results of detailed empirical testing, the body of hypotheses we examine already benefits from the lessons of much past testing.

The fact that economic theory has been developed by establishing empirical generalizations as assumptions and then deducing their implications accounts for two of its characteristics which deserve brief mention. First, economic theorists, in making a reasoned attack on a great complex of economic phenomena, have ordinarily chosen to treat various individual phenomena or sectors of economic behavior in a sort of logical isolation from others. They have inquired in effect or attempted to explain what *would* happen in a given area of economic behavior *if* behavior in other respects were of a certain type. For example, we have previously mentioned the analysis of commodity pricing as it would be *if* there were a constant flow of money purchasing power and fixed prices for the factors of production. Much of the body of economic theory is thus made up of parts and pieces analyzing what would occur in a given area of behavior "all other things being equal," or, more accurately, if all except a few proximate determinants of behavior were fixed and unchanging in a certain way. Many of the component hypotheses of economic theory thus have a decidedly provisional, or "iffy," character. This is not really too serious a shortcoming; for treating various smaller problems such provisional hypotheses are ordinarily quite adequate—in fact, easier to understand and apply than if they were made more complex. For treating larger problems a less restricted type theory is needed, and, in general, we have it. On the higher levels of economic theorizing, explanatory systems are developed which deal directly with the interdependence of various sectors of economic behavior and abandon provisional assumptions which would destroy the explanatory value of such theory. Economic theory which treats of one narrow phenomenon in isolation is often called "partial" or "particular"; that which comprehends broad ranges of interrelated phenomena is frequently called "general."

A further characteristic of conventional economic theory, which may be noted briefly, concerns its treatment of time. The phenomena with which economics treats are aspects of human behavior as it evolves and changes through time. Explanation of a whole process of development of behavior through time by means of assumptions and deductive logic is of course very difficult, particularly so far as the determinants of behavior may progressively change through time. Much of economic theory as we know it today has been designed to simplify the explanatory task by inquiring mainly into what performance would be with some given and fixed set of determinants, after some sort of stable balance or regular pattern of behavior had been reached in such a given situation. It does not investigate very much the implications of changing determinants, or the reasons for their change, nor does it emphasize the process through which a stable balance would be reached with given determinants. The "end result" of the response of behavior to given determinants is what is underlined. This sort of theory is often referred to as "equilibrium" theory—referring to the final equilibrium result of given determinants. Having this characteristic, it, of course, is not satisfactory for explaining certain processes of change. But in suggesting where we are tending to arrive in a given set of circumstances, it emphasizes perhaps the most important single sort of information we desire to have. Economic theory treating with the character of behavior processes through time is as yet relatively undeveloped, and for the moment we have to lean heavily on the aid the "equilibrium" variety of theory can give us. Since we are dealing here with the basic elements of theory, we will confine our attention largely in this work to theory of the equilibrium variety.

A BEGINNING POINT IN ECONOMIC ANALYSIS

Economic theory today comprises a very large and complex body of generalization and analysis, and one of the student's problems is to know how to begin learning about it. This can best be done by first biting off a little bit. As we have indicated above, our first concern will be with the theory of the pricing of commodities.

The best starting point in the analysis of commodity pricing is the analysis of the operation of the individual business enterprise. In a capitalist economy such enterprises make the crucial decisions as to what to produce, how much to produce, what to charge, and so forth. The eventual behavior of prices and outputs for the entire economy emerges from their decisions and from the interactions of these decisions through a competitive and bargaining process. We shall, therefore, first be concerned with the "economics of the firm"—an investigation of the principles which govern certain srtategic decisions made by the individual enterprise. This leads naturally into the analysis of the interactions of the decisions of related firms, in "industry" groups and for the economy as a whole and the analysis of the manner in which the processes of competition impose some systematic law of behavior on individual prices and outputs, allocation of resources, income distribution, employment, and related aspects of performance.

Though the firm is our initial focus, we shall, of course, very early have to give attention also to the behavior of the individuals or economic units with which it deals. Thus, in analyzing commodity pricing, we must consider concurrently the behavior of consumers in the market and the nature of their *demands* for commodities.

SUPPLEMENTARY READINGS

ALFRED MARSHALL, *Principles of Economics* (8th ed.), New York: The Macmillan Company, 1930, Book. I.

LIONEL ROBBINS, *The Nature and Significance of Economic Science* (2d ed.), New York: The Macmillan Company, 1935.

JOSEPH SCHUMPETER, "The Nature and Necessity of a Price System," *Economic Reconstruction,* New York: Columbia University Press, 1934.

W. SOMBART, "Capitalism," *Encyclopedia of the Social Sciences,* Vol. III.

THORSTEIN VEBLEN, *The Theory of Business Enterprise,* New York: Charles Scribner's Sons, 1932, Chaps. 1-4.

2 THE DEMAND FOR COMMODITIES

The first branch of economic theory to be examined analyzes the general area of commodity pricing. It tries to explain how, under given conditions of demand for goods and of costs of production, the price and output of an individual commodity will be determined. It also analyzes how the relative prices and outputs of all commodities are determined under such given conditions, what pattern of price and outputs tends to result, and how well this serves society. Although prices and outputs are emphasized the most, it also analyzes strategic aspects of the determination of such things as the relative efficiency of production, the quality of products, and the size of sales promotion costs.

A. SOME BASIC CONSIDERATIONS

HOW ENTERPRISE SALES POLICIES ARE DETERMINED

Since commodity prices and outputs are proximately determined by enterprises selling goods, the analysis is best begun by considering the nature of the decisions or choices made by the individual firm. In a money-exchange economy, an enterprise operates by buying and selling. It purchases materials, equipment, land, and labor, combines them in a finished product, and sells this to a buyer. In so doing it presumably attempts to "buy cheap and sell dear" or, more exactly, to maximize the difference between income and outgo over the time interval for which it makes advance calculations.[1] This is fairly obvious. The question is—to what does the firm look in determining the precise course of action which will produce the maximum profit, or difference between receipts and expenses? To discover this it is necessary to analyze the character of the controlling conditions to which the firm looks and which govern its activities in the pursuit of a profit.

At least five things are of immediate concern to such a firm—the prod-

[1] The assumption that the firm attempts to *maximize* profits is generally accepted as the best rough description of the actual central motive of firms in general. Much subsequent analysis explicitly rests on this assumption, and its validity depends on the accuracy of the assumption.

uct it will produce, the price at which it will sell, the quantity to be produced, the cost of producing it, and the amount of selling cost to be incurred in soliciting buyers. The firm must decide what to produce, both
generally and precisely—whether to produce cigarette lighters or fishing
poles, and, if it is fishing poles, what type and what quality of poles. It
must calculate what its chosen product will sell for, or the alternative selling
prices of each of a range of alternative products. It must decide how much
to produce of the finally selected product. It must calculate how much this
product will cost to produce, and how much to spend on advertising and
other sales promotion. Out of these considerations it may decide what to
produce, how much of it, what to spend, and what to charge to its customers.

As we consider this complex problem, two points stand out. First, the
various determinants of enterprise action, such as price, output, product,
and cost, are not independent of one another, but rather interdependent.
Second, none of these is single-valued or invariant—any of them, such as
price, may assume different magnitudes as other determinants, such as output or product, are varied. In effect, each of the five determinants mentioned is a *variable* which depends upon other variables.

It follows that the firm is not simply interested in price, output, product
cost, selling cost, and product—which for convenience we may designate
respectively $p, q, c, s,$ and ϕ, but in the relationships of each of these variables to the others.[2] In fact, each variable is in a complex or multiple relationship to the others—thus, price p depends on (or is a function of) quantity
q, production cost c, selling cost s, and product ϕ. The problem may be,
and often is, simplified, however, by considering the strategic relationships
between certain pairs of the variables which determine the actions of firms.

The most significant relationships appear to be the following:

1. The relation of selling price p to output produced and sold q—the
relation of sales receipts to the amount offered for sale. This can be calculated or estimated for any given product, selling cost, and production cost,
and is ordinarily known as the *demand* relation. It is precisely the relation
of p to q, when ϕ and s are held constant at chosen values. We will consider this relation at length in this chapter.

2. The relation of cost of production c to output q for any given product. (Price and selling cost will presumably not influence this relationship.)
This measures the response of production cost to variations in output, sub-
suming a choice of production technique.[3]

[2] Some arbitrary simplification is involved in regarding product as a single variable
represented by a single symbol, ϕ, since product may be varied in numerous directions
or dimensions.

[3] The shape of this relationship for any given product will depend generally on
the *technique of production* available to the firm (it will presumably seek the most

3. The relation of price p (or quantity q) to selling cost s, when the product and quantity (or price) are given. This measures the response of sales receipts or demand to variations in selling cost.

4. The relation of product ϕ to price (quantity being given) or quantity (price being given)—in effect the relation of product to demand—with given selling cost.

5. The relation of product ϕ to production cost c at any given output (selling cost and price presumably having no influence on this relationship).

In deciding what and how much to produce, what to sell for, and how much selling cost to incur, the firm will presumably take into account all these relationships. So doing, it will presumably seek that *combination* of product, price, output, production cost, and selling cost which will yield the greatest possible profit. In succeeding chapters we shall explore the character of those calculations.

The analysis of commodity pricing in general begins by considering how the firm makes this complex calculation and what results ensue. Before this task can be tackled directly, however, as it is in Chapters 4 through 9, it is necessary to establish the general character of these relationships which govern the actions of firms. That is, we need to know *how,* in general, price is related to quantity of sales, cost is related to output, selling cost to sales volume, and so forth. Therefore, we shall consider in some detail the two leading relationships—the relation of price to quantity sold, or the *demand relationship,* and the relation of cost to output produced. In this chapter the demand relation faced by the firm will be set forth. Concurrently the whole structure of buyer demands from which this relation emerges will be considered.

THE DEMANDS FOR THE OUTPUTS OF FIRMS

Each firm has a primary interest in the demand for its own output. It wants to know how much it can sell in a certain period of time at various alternative prices. This information can be summarized in a firm's *demand schedule.* Such a schedule should show the amount of output per month or per year which the firm can sell at each of a number of alternative prices.

The firm's demand schedule shows the *relation* of the price it charges to the quantity it can sell. But the quantity that can be sold, or the demand for its output, is obviously dependent on other things in addition to its price—the type of product the firm is producing and its general design and quality. *A firm's demand schedule, therefore, obviously refers to some given product which is the output of the firm.* Each different product will have potentially

economical one) and on the level of prices of productive factors which enter into its costs. Although it may not ordinarily have control over such factor prices, it does thus have a further choice to make—that of a technique of production.

a different demand schedule. It must also depend on the extent to which the firm promotes its sales by advertising or other means; any single firm's demand schedule refers necessarily to the relation of price to quantity of sales which corresponds to some given rate of sales-promotion expenditures. We can thus legitimately speak of a given demand schedule for a firm's output only with reference to some given product and some given rate of selling costs.

Given the firm's product and its selling costs, there are still other determinants on which the quantities it can sell at various prices depend. Very important among these is the total volume of money purchasing power which buyers have to offer for all outputs of all firms. When buyers have more to spend, they will tend to buy more of everything, or if there is no more to buy, to pay higher prices for what there is. The quantities which a firm can sell at various prices will, therefore, generally depend heavily on the general level of purchasing power. It will have a *given* demand schedule for its output only at some given level of purchasing power, and different demand schedules at different levels. Thus, we see that a given demand schedule for a firm refers to a given product, given selling costs, and given purchasing power.

And this is not all. The disposition of buyers to take a particular firm's output will depend on what else is available, both of products which are good substitutes for that produced by the firm and of products in general, and on what the prices of these other items are. If there is a greater number of attractive substitutes for its output at given prices, the firm can sell less at any price. If the prices of such substitutes become higher, it can sell more at any price. The quantities the firm can sell at various prices depend on the character and quality of all other goods and on their prices. If we could legitimately assume that all other products and prices in general remained given while the individual firm varied its price, we could say that each firm had a given demand schedule for its output, which showed the quantities that it could sell at various prices, given its product and its selling costs, given total purchasing power, and given the character, quality, and prices of all other products. The shape of this demand schedule would obviously be fixed by the character of buyer preferences among all goods at any particular time.

Actually, there is one more complication to be taken into account. It is not always legitimate to suppose that the prices of other goods will tend to remain unchanged while a single firm changes its price. Most firms produce outputs for which there are close substitutes or competing goods, and it is quite possible that a change in price by a given firm will induce a change in prices of these competing goods. If this occurs, the induced response in competitive prices will influence the quantities the firm can sell at various prices—that is, the shape of its own demand schedule. Whether or not there will be induced responses in competitive prices when one firm changes its price is likely to depend mainly, as we shall see below, on whether or not other goods exist which are close competitors with its output and on how many such competitors there are. However this may be, it appears that the character or shape of the demand schedule for the output of the individual firm will be contingent not only on the character of all other goods available and on the level of all other prices as of the time it might vary its price to influence its quantity of sales, but also on whether and to what extent any other prices will be altered as the result of its own price change.

In summary, a demand schedule for the output of an individual firm shows the quantities it can sell of its output at various alternative prices, given its product and selling cost, given total purchasing power, given the character and quality of all other products available to buyers, and given the initial prices of all such other products as of the time that it contemplates charging a series of alternative prices. Under these given circumstances it reflects what the firm will be able to sell at various alternative prices as the result of buyers shifting to or from his product as he lowers or raises his price, and additionally as the result of any changes in other prices which are induced by its own price changes.

The preceding defines the demand schedule for a firm's output. At any time the firm will, obviously, wish to have an idea of what this demand schedule is. If it is selling a given line of electric toasters at $12.50 each and experiencing monthly sales of 10,000 units, it will want to know what its monthly sales would be if instead it were to charge $14.00, $13.50, $13.00, $12.00, $11.50, or $11.00. It will also want to know other things—such as how its sales will change if total purchasing power rises or declines, if it increases selling cost, if it redesigns its product, if its competitors change their prices, and so forth. That is, it will wish to know how its demand schedule will *move* in response to such other changes. But the shape of its current demand schedule, showing its price-sales relationship in any going situation, will be of primary importance to it in arriving at its sales policies. Let us, therefore, concentrate on the character of this demand schedule. Is there anything in general that may be said about the character of such schedules, which would apply to those of all firms or to large groups of them? If there is, it will be important since it will give us a clue to the nature of one strategic determinant of enterprise behavior.

This inquiry brings us to a general consideration of the nature of buyers' demands for goods, and in particular of the way in which they respond to changes in the prices of the things they buy. The question posed so far is essentially how buyers will react to a change in the price of a single firm's output, either with other prices being given or with other prices responding as they will to the initial change. This is only one of several related questions involving spheres of economic activity progressively broader than that of the firm.

In the first place, firms, or the outputs of firms, do not make up for the whole economy a sort of undifferentiated aggregate, each output within which is in equally close competition with every other. Firms or their outputs instead occur commonly in groups of such a character that the outputs of a group are relatively close substitutes for each other in the view of buyers whereas they are relatively poor substitutes for the outputs of other groups. The outputs within any such group, or *industry,* generally have prices which are similar and move more or less together. There is, thus, some interest in the demand schedule for the combined output of each group or industry, showing the relation of the total sales of firms in the industry to the general price charged for its several component outputs. Investigation of this industry demand schedule is in fact essential to a full understanding of the firm's demand schedule, the character of which depends in some degree on the demand schedule for the industry of which the firm is a member. A related matter to be studied first is thus the character of the demand schedule for the output of an industry or the combined output of a group of firms producing close substitutes.

In the second place, the demands for the outputs of all industries (and all component firms) are obviously interrelated. The demand for any industry output at various prices for that output depends on the prices of all other industry outputs, and this is true of each in turn. In effect, there is an economy-wide family of industry (and firm) demand schedules which are mutually interdependent, this interdependence reflecting the behavior of buyers in choosing among a variety of goods, each of which has a potentially variable price. The significance of an individual industry demand schedule is not really understood until its place in this complex is comprehended. A second additional task is, therefore, to analyze the nature of this interdependence of all demand schedules for all outputs. This essentially involves some analysis of the character of buyers' behavior in disposing of a total income for a wide variety of goods.

Thus, we have three matters to analyze: (1) the character of the single firm's demand schedule; (2) the character of the individual industry's demand schedule; and (3) the character of the interrelated complex of the demand schedules of all industries and firms. These are essentially interrelated aspects of the general problem of demand. As we approach the study of demand relationships in general as they influence production and pricing, it is simplest to begin with the analysis of the demand for the output of an individual industry, turning later to the interrelationships of all demands and to the demand for a single firm's output.

B. DEMAND FOR INDUSTRY OUTPUT

DEFINITION OF AN INDUSTRY

In analyzing demand the first question we pose concerns the general nature of an industry demand schedule. That is, in a situation of given products, selling costs, aggregate purchasing power, and other prices, what will be the relation of the general price charged by firms in an industry to the quantity of its output buyers will take?

First, let us decide exactly what is meant by an industry. Unfortunately, there is not always a precise or neat definition. The primary basis for the delimitation of industries is the good or commodity. One group of sellers is frequently set apart from another because they produce distinctly different goods, which fulfill different needs of buyers generally and are regarded by buyers as rather imperfect substitutes for each other. All kinds of goods are substitute sources of satisfaction. But as refrigerators and watches are not at all close substitutes to any buyers, they are different commodities, and their respective producers are in different industries. Thus, initially we have as rough categories a steel industry, an aluminum industry, a breakfast food industry, a ladies' dress industry, and others to a number of several hundred. Within each industry is a group of producers, few or many, whose individual products or outputs are very close substitutes for each other, but whose aggregate output is a much more distant substitute for the outputs of other industries. Correspondingly, the demands for the products of the member firms of an industry are closely interrelated, but they are more distantly related to the demands for products of other firms.

This will do for a first approximation, but it is not precise. What do we do, for example, if a firm produces two distinct products which are not close substitutes for each other at all, like electric light bulbs and spark plugs—is it in one industry or two? And how close substitutes do two products have to be before they fall in a single industry?

Ideally, an industry is a group of products of firms which are perfect substitutes for each other to a common group of buyers and which are very poor substitutes for all other products in the economy. (As far as each firm involved produces a single uniform product, the industry is also ideally a group of firms producing such a group of perfect substitute products; if the firm produces two nonsubstitute products, it operates in two different industries.) Products within a group are perfect substitutes for each other if they are regarded as absolutely identical and interchangeable by buyers (are in effect a single uniform commodity), if they are sold to a common group of buyers, and if, therefore, a price for any one product in the group which is lower than those of the others will tend to attract all buyers of the commodity the industry produces. They are poor or distant substitutes for all other products if any change in their price will have no perceptible effect on the quantity of any other product which is sold at given prices and if changes in the price of any other product will not perceptibly affect their sales. If a group of products are perfect substitutes *inter se* and distant substitutes for all others—in the sense defined—they plainly constitute a distinct industry. The industry is, thus, basically defined by price-sales inter-relations among products of different firms. It includes products whose prices have the strongest possible influence on each other's sales; it excludes products whose sales are not perceptibly influenced by any price changes of included products and vice versa.

If we could suppose that the total output of the economy were composed of a number of standard commodities, that between every pair of such commodities there were no perceptible price-sales interrelation, and that all outputs of each given commodity were perfect substitutes sold to a common group of buyers, then each commodity would be coextensive with a distinct and clear-cut industry, and every individual firm's product would fall in some such industry. Unfortunately for analytical purposes, actual industrial organization is not so simple. Three types of complications are found in fact, and the definition of an industry must be elaborated to take account of each of them.

A first complication is that the products of various firms producing a given sort of commodity are in most cases not identical or perfect substitutes. There are instances where their outputs are in fact practically identical or homogeneous, as in the case of farmers producing wheat of a given grade and specification. In most instances, however, the outputs of firms producing the same sort of good are somewhat imperfect substitutes in the eyes of buyers, being *differentiated* one from another by design, quality, packaging, advertising, or direct sales promotion. Thus the various makes of automobiles are *differentiated products,* as are the various brands of cigarettes, the brands of soap, and so forth.[4] When this is the case, the output of one seller of cigarettes is related to another cigarette output in the same way in which it is related to another firm's automobile output— it is an imperfect substitute for either of them. The relationship of Camels to Chesterfields and the relationship of Camels to Buicks are different only in degree—Camels are a close substitute for Chesterfields and a distant substitute for Buicks.

This phenomenon requires an adaptation in the definition of an industry. Each seller of a slightly different good should not be put in a separate "industry" when his price changes in fact tend strongly to influence

---

[4] See Edward H. Chamberlin, *The Theory of Monopolistic Competition,* 5th ed. (Cambridge: Harvard University Press, 1946), Chap. 4, for the principal original discussion of product differentiation.

the sales of a number of close substitute products. The definition of the industry is thus conveniently expanded so that an industry may include not only identical or perfect substitute products but alternatively close substitute products. The general criterion for inclusion of products in an industry then becomes close substitutability, of which perfect substitutability is a special and extreme case. A group of products are close substitutes if a reduction in the price of any of them will significantly or noticeably affect the quantity purchased of the others at given prices—if a significant portion of the buyers of the others may be "stolen" by such a move. The industry includes a range of close-substitute products so defined; it excludes any product the demand for which is not significantly influenced by the industry's price changes.[5]

Using this definition, we can discover many clearly defined industries in spite of product differentiation. But there is necessarily some lack of precision and some overlapping of industries, as where one or more products will be fairly close substitutes for each of two otherwise unrelated groups of products. Thus, products A, B, and C may constitute an industry and products F, G, and H another distinct industry, but products D and E may be closely related by substitutability to both groups. The phenomenon of overlapping or imprecisely limited industries requires careful analytical treatment. Recognizing this potential difficulty, however, we may define an industry as a group of either identical or close-substitute products, set apart from other products the sales of which will not respond significantly to changes in the industry price.

A second complication is that we shall occasionally find two groups of products each of which qualifies in part as a separate industry under the preceding definition but with some significant interrelation of the two groups. That is, there is a *close* substitution relation within each group and a *more distant* but still significant substitution relation between the two groups. As a result, a change in either group price somewhat affects the demands for the outputs of the other group. When this occurs, the two industries are, of course, not strictly independent, but the respective groups of products may, nevertheless, be recognized as quasi-separate industries. The analysis of price determination in such cases should take account of the interaction of the related group prices.

The third major complication in defining an industry stems from the fact that not all the firms producing a given range of potentially close-

[5] The criterion of close substitutability suggested is that the seller of any product of a close substitute group will be able to attract a significant portion of buyers of the other products by reducing his price. It may be extended to include cases where any one seller would thus attract relatively few buyers from each of many competitors, but where concurrent price reductions by a considerable number of sellers of such substitutes would significantly reduce the sales of the remaining sellers of the group.

substitute products will necessarily sell to a common market or group of buyers. The world market for most goods is broken up into continental submarkets by the force of transport costs, and further into national markets by political boundaries, tariffs, trade restrictions, and so forth. The European and American producers of many goods, for example, sell to largely exclusive groups of buyers. Within the United States, moreover, the sellers of many locally produced or hard-to-transport items supply local groups of buyers which are not reached by sellers located in other states or regions. An industry, for analytical purposes, should include a group of close substitute products which are sold in common to a single group of buyers. It should exclude products available only to an entirely different group of buyers. An industry thus has geographical or market limits as well as a commodity limit. These geographical limits are seldom precise; overlaps are very common. In practice we must be content to recognize an industry as including a group of close-substitute products which are sold in large part to a common group of buyers and only in small part to buyers not supplied in common. Thus, the outputs of automobile manufacturers of the United States constitute an industry for practical purposes because they all offer the bulk of their outputs on a nation-wide basis to all potential American buyers, and ship only a small fraction of their outputs into the foreign market (thus overlapping a bit with the European automobile industry). Precisely an industry is a group of close-substitute products each of which is sold entirely to a common group of buyers. (It is this simplified conception of an industry which we will employ immediately below.) In practice, an industry is any workably close approximation to this logical ideal.[6]

An industry being thus defined, we may provisionally view every firm as being a member of some industry (or a member of two or more industries if it produces two or more nonsubstitute products). Its product is a close substitute for others in the same industry and is a more distant substitute for those outside the industry. (Overlaps and in-between firms are, of course, allowed for.) For the aggregate output of each industry there is

[6] See Joe S. Bain, *Economics of the Pacific Coast Petroleum Industry* (Berkeley: University of California Bureau of Business and Economic Research, 1944), Part I, pp. 10-11, for a further discussion of the definition of an industry; also George J. Stigler, *The Theory of Price* (New York: The Macmillan Company, 1946) pp. 280-283.

In the preceding discussion we have, in general, assumed that when two products are placed in different industries because a reduction in the price of the first will not perceptibly affect the sales of the second, this relationship is reversible, so that a reduction in the price of the second will likewise not affect the sales of the first. This symmetrical situation is undoubtedly by far the most common. Where an asymmetrical relation exists, so that A's price reduction affects B's sales but B's price reduction does not affect A's sales, we need further adaptation in the industry definition. Such products might be considered as making up a special variety of single industry, or as constituting quasi-separate industries.

at any time some demand, or schedule of amounts the firms of the industry can sell at various common prices. We shall investigate next the character of this demand for the output of an industry.

THE DEMAND FOR THE OUTPUT OF AN INDUSTRY

To investigate the nature of the demand for the output of a single industry, let us take the simple case of what we will assume to be a clearly defined industry of identical or homogeneous products whose producers sell entirely to a common group of buyers. We will assume a single good—let us say sulfuric acid—produced by a number of firms and sold entirely in a single market, that of the continental United States. The demand for sulfuric acid will thus refer to the demand in this specific market alone. It must also refer to some specific time interval—let us say the amount to be bought in some certain month. We will further assume, perhaps somewhat inaccurately, that changes in sulfuric acid prices will not perceptibly affect the quantity sold of any other product and that changes in any other product price will not perceptibly affect sulfuric acid sales. This sets the sulfuric acid industry clearly apart from every other and simplifies the case. Our problem is to analyze the demand for the sulfuric acid industry of the United States for a time period of one month. What are the essential properties of such a demand?

The amount of a commodity which buyers will take in a given month will depend upon the choice pattern of these buyers as between this good and others, the volume of money purchasing power buying goods in general, the prices of other goods, and the price of the good in question.[7] Each of these circumstances will influence the quantity of the good which buyers take. Let us center attention first, however, on the relation of the price of a good—sulfuric acid—to the quantity of it which buyers will take. To do this, we shall suppose that buyers' choice patterns, total purchasing power, and the prices of all other goods are given and fixed at certain levels, either absolutely constant or sufficiently invariant to have no perceptible effect on the demand for sulfuric acid. All of these assumptions are legitimate so far as price changes for sulfuric acid by definition would not *induce* any of these other things to change. We simply rule out independent changes in them. We shall investigate only the relation of the price of sulfuric acid to its sales—the extent to which the number of units of sulfuric

[7] By assumption, no *one* other product price will perceptibly affect sulfuric acid sales. But a general change in the prices of all or most other products might do so, as a very large number of very small effects on acid sales were aggregated. The amount of sales-promotion expense on this and other goods, and the design and quality of each, may be taken provisionally as given.

acid bought would be influenced by variations in its price within this given situation.

The leading aspect of this relation is that, all other things being equal, the amount bought will hinge on the price charged and will become larger as the price becomes lower. *For the output of any industry there is ordinarily an inverse relationship between sales volume and price.* At any one price, such as $1.25 per unit, a certain number of units, such as 672 million, may be bought. If the price *instead* were $1.30, fewer units would be bought; if it *instead* were $1.20, more units would be bought. At each specific *alternative* price there should be a specific corresponding sales volume, which tends to become larger as price becomes lower. Such a relationship of price to sales volume would be observed not only for sulfuric acid but also for nearly every product.

THE INDUSTRY DEMAND SCHEDULE

This relationship of sales volume to price may be illustrated in a *demand schedule*. A demand schedule shows, for a given market and time interval, the volume of purchases which would take place at each of several alternative prices. Such a schedule might look as follows:

Price of acid (per unit)	Sales volume of acid (millions of units)
$1.30	661
1.29	662
1.28	663
1.27	665
1.26	668
1.25	672
1.24	676
1.23	680
1.22	684
1.21	688
1.20	692

The schedule could be extended to include any range of prices, but we should ordinarily be interested in a short range of prices which might be experienced within the chosen time interval. The schedule shows how many units all of the industry's purchasers would buy in the given month if the price were alternatively each of those shown. Thus, if the price were $1.28, buyers would take 663 million units per month; if *instead* it were $1.22, they would take 684 million units, etc.

The schedule is drawn on the assumption of a given and unchanging purchasing power throughout the month and of a given state of buyers' wants. We have also assumed to be temporarily unchanging any other things which might influence the sales volume of sulfuric acid. These include the prices of other goods as a group. In effect, the demand schedule shows the *net* relationship of the price of sulfuric acid to its sales volume, assuming that all other things influencing sulfuric acid sales are for the moment unchanging.

This idea may be made more precise by employing mathematical notation. We have before us several *variables* (a *variable* is a quantity which assumes various successive sizes). Two of these variables are the price of sulfuric acid and the sales volume per month of this acid in a given market. We may denote them as p_s (for the price) and q_s (for the quantity of sales). Now p_s is related to (or is "a function of") q_s in a certain specific way. When p_s changes, q_s undergoes a definite corresponding change. We wish to know the exact relationship of the two variables. But q_s is *also* related to several other variables—to buyers' income (I), let us say, and to other prices in general, from p_a to p_n—and probably changes in response to changes in these.[8] To obtain the *net* relationship of q_s to p_s—that is, to get the variation of sulfuric acid sales in response to variations in sulfuric acid price *alone* and uninfluenced by variations in prices p_a to p_n and in I— we assume that prices p_a to p_n and I are constant at given levels (that they are sufficiently invariant to have no perceptible effect on q_s), and *isolate* the effect of p_s on q_s. It is this isolated effect that the demand schedule should show us.

This "ceteris paribus" (other-things-being-equal) demand schedule is a meaningful conception if in fact no other price nor income will change *in response* to changes in the sulfuric acid price enough to influence the acid demand. Suppose, however, that some prices will so change and will, thereby, affect the demand for sulfuric acid. If this change follows no determinate pattern, no determinate independent relation of sulfuric sales to price can be found. If, however, the other variables respond in a determinate and predictable fashion to sulfuric acid prices, then a determinate demand schedule for sulfuric acid can be defined on the assumption of predictable covariations in those variables. Such a demand schedule—a so-called *mutatis mutandis* schedule—is the alternative to the *ceteris paribus* schedule in such cases. For simplicity in the succeeding argument, however, we will view industry demand curves as being of the simpler *ceteris paribus* variety. They must be so if the group of products in question conforms fully to the theoretical definition of an industry.

Statisticians have attempted to find industry demand schedules for various products, such as potatoes, steel ingots, and automobiles, and have

[8] If the sulfuric acid industry conforms to our definition of an industry, q_s will not change perceptibly in response to a change in any other single price, but it may change perceptibly in response to simultaneous changes in a great many other prices.

arrived at numerical results generally showing inverse net relationships of price and quantity for given goods. They encounter difficulty, of course, in eliminating properly the effect of the "other variables" such as prices of other products. Whatever the difficulties of statistical measurement, however, the idea of a demand schedule relating price and sales volume for the output of a given industry is evidently useful and valid.

THE INDUSTRY DEMAND CURVE

The *demand schedule* for the output of an industry, in summary, shows the net relationships of the price of that output to the amount of it which

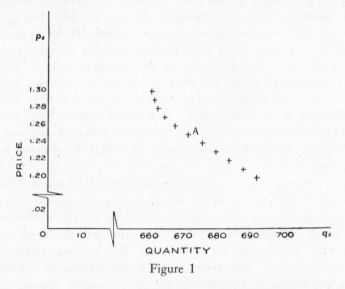

Figure 1

buyers will take. Such a schedule may be represented graphically on a pair of coordinate axes as in Figure 1. This graph presents the same information contained in the table on page 28. The price of sulfuric acid is measured along the vertical axis and the quantity (bought) along the horizontal. There are eleven points for the eleven prices in the table, and each point is a *coordinate* showing the quantity from the table which corresponds to one price. Point A, for example, lies a vertical distance of 1.25 from the zero point on the price scale and a horizontal distance of 672 from the zero point on the quantity scale; it thus shows that the quantity 672 corresponds to (would be bought at) the price $1.25. Other points show similar relationships. The advantage of this graphic presentation is that when we observe the relation of one coordinate point to another we get a vivid idea of the way in which the quantity bought *responds* to changes in price. In the preceding example a moderate reaction is noted.

It is but a short step in graphic analysis to consider these successive coordinate points as connected up with a line, or, more conveniently, to suppose that we have a series of successive price changes each of which is indefinitely small so that the succession of points makes up a practically continuous line. In this way we pass from a graph of successive discrete points, showing discrete quantities for discrete prices (Figure 1), to a continuous line, showing the relation of quantity to price for every con-

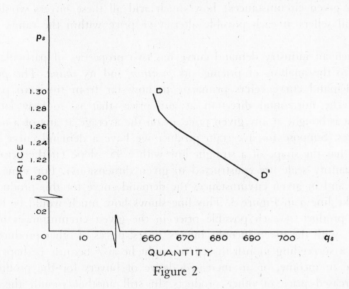

Figure 2

ceivable price. This line is called a *demand curve;* the one in Figure 2 is drawn from the same data shown in Figure 1. The demand line or curve (which we label *DD'*) shows the general relation of price to quantity bought for sulfuric acid. Because it is a continuous line, it shows the quantity for each and every possible price down to the millionth or smaller fraction of a cent. To derive such a curve in practice, we necessarily work with a number of discrete prices and interpolate between them, or "fit" a line to them, ordinarily by some statistical regression technique.

The student may well inquire what purpose there is in getting a continuous line for every conceivable shading of price. Admittedly, the businessman is interested only in a series of discrete prices, at perhaps one-cent —or even five-cent—intervals. The justification for setting up a continuous demand curve is twofold. First, a continuous line is more susceptible to analysis than a series of discrete points. Such a line, without in any significant way distorting the picture, enables us to think about pricing problems more effectively. Second, fitting such a line statistically is an expedient way of eliminating random deviations in the actual data which would otherwise confuse the problem.

The demand curve shown above, representing the net relationship of price to quantity bought of the output of an entire industry, is an *industry or market demand curve*. If the market should be supplied by a single seller—a monopolist—it would also be an individual seller's demand curve. Otherwise it is the common demand for the outputs of the several or many sellers who supply the market. In the example we have chosen, it is the demand by all buyers in the United States for sulfuric acid and shows (under given circumstances) how much acid all these buyers would take from all sellers at each possible alternative price within the range of the curve.

Such an industry demand curve has two properties of particular relevance to the analysis of pricing—its *position* and its *shape*. The *position* of a demand curve refers primarily to how far from the zero point it lies in the horizontal direction at any price—that is, to how large an amount is bought at any given price, or on the average at any of a number of prices. Suppose for a certain product we have a demand curve which always has the shape of a straight line with a 45° slope (if the price scale and quantity scale are constructed to given dimensions). For some given month and in given circumstances the demand curve for this product will look like line *a* in Figure 3. This line shows how much would be bought of the product at each possible price in the given circumstances of that month—with the given income, buyers' tastes, prices of other products, etc. But in a succeeding month the curve might lie at *b* because perhaps of an increase in income, or an increased desire of buyers for the product, or an increased price of other products. In still another month the curve might shift to *c* because of smaller income, decreased buyer desires, or lower prices of substitutes. The curves *a*, *b*, and *c* represent the market demand curve for a single product in different positions or show how a demand curve may *shift* from position to position with changes in the surrounding circumstances. When a demand curve shifts, ordinarily a different quantity will be bought at every price than was bought before it shifted. It is not necessary, however, that a demand curve should retain the same shape as it shifts.

It will be inferred that when we employ a demand curve in analysis the effect of the changes of the price of a product on its own sales is shown by the shape of the curve—that is, by moving along a given curve —but that the effect of all other changes on the sales of the product are shown by shifts in the curve—by changes in its position. The position of the industry demand curve is, of course, a dominant consideration in price determination, and the succeeding discussion of the shape of the curve should not be allowed to obscure this fact.

The shape of an industry demand curve involves the *direction* in which it slopes, the steepness of its slope, and characteristics of change of slope such as degrees and directions of curvature. A substantially uniform property of the shape of all industry demand curves is that they slope "downward to the right," or are *negatively* sloped. That is, quantity sold increases as price decreases (if other prices, buyers' tastes, and total purchasing power are unchanged) so that the price change is negative when the quantity change is positive, and vice versa. Some curves may slope steeply and others gradually, but nearly all of them presumably slope

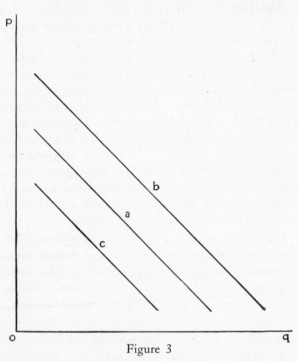

Figure 3

negatively at one rate or another. Since this general characteristic of industry demand curves is of the greatest importance, we may defer any further consideration of the shape of such demand curves until we have examined the basis for believing that practically all such curves are negatively sloped.

WHY INDUSTRY DEMAND CURVES HAVE A NEGATIVE SLOPE

The assertion that demand curves slope negatively rests mainly on observation and analysis of buyers' psychology. For goods bought for direct consumption, such as shoes, these observations and analysis run somewhat as follows: The consumer ordinarily has limited means; he cannot acquire all he wants of every good. There is available to him an assortment of desirable goods, which are, in general, substitute sources of satisfaction, but the amounts of them the buyer can acquire are restricted by the limitation of his purchasing power. His problem is to apportion his spending among all available goods in such a way as to maximize the aggregate satisfaction he receives from his total purchases. Given the prices for all goods, therefore, he will try to juggle the relative desirability (to him) of various goods against their relative costliness until he arrives at that pattern of expenditures which seems to give him "the most for his money."

Arriving at such a determinate spending pattern is made possible by the fact that the various goods available are not perfect substitutes as sources of satisfaction to him. They provide a variety of satisfactions, and each is an imperfect substitute for others in its particular role. Therefore, as the consumer considers acquiring more and more of any one good (in place of other goods), additional increments to his purchases of that good become relatively less desirable. Additional units of any good add successively less to the consumer's satisfaction, as compared with units of other goods, as he acquires more of that good. The marginal satisfaction—that is, the addition to satisfaction provided by the last unit of every good acquired—declines comparatively for every good as more and more of it is added to consumption. Conversely, the marginal satisfaction becomes greater as less and less is used.

Now if this is the case and if the prices of various goods are given to the consumer, the consumer can obtain the maximum possible satisfaction from all goods if he adjusts his purchases of them just so that the marginal satisfaction provided by the last unit of each good purchased has a ratio to its price the same as the ratio for every other good. Or, the ratio of the addition to satisfaction made by the last unit of any good A acquired to the addition to satisfaction made by the last unit of any good B should be the same as the ratio of the price of A to the price of B. If good A costs \$2 and good B costs \$4, the consumer should buy the two goods in such proportion that the last unit of B acquired gives him twice as much satisfaction as the last unit of A acquired. In other words, he should apportion his expenditures among goods in such a way that the last dollar spent on every good yields him an equal increment to his satisfaction. If he does this, it is easily demonstrated that he will obtain the greatest possible aggregate satisfaction from his total expenditure. For if he reaches a buying pattern wherein the last dollar spent on each good yields an equal increment to his satisfaction, any shift of a dollar of spending to one good from another will then add less to his satisfaction than it takes away, since the satisfaction added by a further dollar's worth of any one good diminishes and is smaller than the satisfaction he loses by taking away a dollar's worth of any other good.

It has long been held by many economists that consumers' choice patterns are such that successive unit additions to the quantity purchased of each good add successively less to a consumer's satisfaction and that the consumer, in view of this, apportions his expenditures among various goods in such a way as to maximize his satisfaction. These are essentially empirical generalizations drawn from intuition and from observation of consumer behavior. It is generally also postulated that any consumer regards the prices at which he buys as given to him and beyond his influence —a reasonable assumption, as there are a great many relatively small consumers. If these three assumptions are all correct, the deduction is certainly correct that the consumer buys goods in such proportions that the added satisfaction obtained from the last dollar's worth of each is the same. Many economists accept the assumptions and the deduced conclusion as a good approximate description of actual consumer behavior.

This theory of consumer behavior has very broad application in evaluations of the working of the price system, and we shall refer to it at many points later. At the moment though, we are immediately interested in its implications for the slope of the industry demand curve.

These implications are easily seen. With any given set of prices all consumers supposedly have adopted a pattern of purchases of all goods such that the ratio of the marginal satisfaction from the last unit of a good to its price is the same for every good. Then if any one price is reduced, the consumer is no longer in a satisfaction-maximizing balance. He seeks a new balance—where the last dollar spent on each good will again yield equal satisfaction—by adding to his purchases of the cheapened good until the marginal satisfaction from the last unit of it acquired diminishes to a ratio with its lowered price the same as obtains for all other goods he buys. Or, if the price of a certain good rises, he will restrict his purchases of it sufficiently to maintain a satisfaction-maximizing pattern of purchases. In effect, the consumer adds to or subtracts from his purchases of a good as its price falls or rises in order to maintain himself in a position of maximized satisfaction—to bring the diminishing or increasing marginal satisfaction from the last unit of the good into balance with its changed price.

The effect of a price reduction for a good on a consumer's purchases should in fact be potentially twofold. First, he *substitutes* the cheapened good for other goods in general in his consumption pattern, in order to maintain a satisfaction-maximizing balance. Second, if he spends much of his income on this good, the reduction of its price frees a significant amount of his purchasing power for expenditure both on this good and on goods in general. These two effects of a price reduction on the purchases of a good are commonly known as a substitution effect and an income effect. Both effects in general tend to increase a consumer's purchases of a good as its price is reduced. The obverse holds for price increases.[9]

According to the preceding argument, each individual consumer should have his own demand schedule for the good produced by any industry, showing the amounts he will buy at various prices. As we have seen, this should show increased purchases at lower prices. The demand schedule for the output of the industry will be simply the summation of all the individual demand schedules of individual consumers for its output—totaling at each price all the amounts individual consumers will buy. It likewise will, therefore, show increased purchases at a lower price—the industry demand curve will slope downward to the right.

The preceding argument applies to consumer's goods, the purchase of which depends mainly on the satisfaction to be realized from these goods by their buyers. Many goods, however, are not bought by final users but are acquired by manufacturers for processing or use in production or by middlemen for distribution. The purchase of these goods does not turn directly upon the satisfaction they could give to their buyers but upon the profit to be gained in producing with them or reselling them. Nevertheless, the demand curves for such *producer's goods* should also be negatively sloped—that is, the quantity purchased should increase with price reductions and vice versa. This is because the demand for a producer's good is necessarily *derived* from the demand for some ultimate consumer's good, and the *derived demand* will ordinarily have the same general slope as the *primary demand*.

The demand for steel by automobile manufacturers, for example, is derived from the demand for automobiles by consumers. (The demand curve for automobiles is presumably sloped negatively for reasons mentioned above.) A price reduction in steel will stimulate the demand for steel if it induces the automobile manufacturers to make more automobiles, and it will do this so far as it leads to a reduction of automobile costs and prices, which in turn should stimulate automobile sales. A steel price reduction will thus tend to increase steel purchases by automobile makers, although perhaps not by very much, by giving rise to lower automobile prices and increased automobile sales. (A steel price increase should have the reverse effect.) A steel price reduction may also stimulate steel use so far as it induces automobile manufacturers to substitute steel for other metals in making automobiles or to use more steel per automobile. This tendency also causes the derived-demand curve to slope in the same direction as the primary-demand curve. But since the outlay for any one producer's good is ordinarily only a minor part of the cost of the final product

---

[9] See J. R. Hicks, *Value and Capital* (London: Oxford University Press, 1939), Part I, for an extended discussion of the theory of consumer choice and the derivation of demand curves.

in the production of which it is used, the industrial buyer of such a producer's good will ordinarily not react very strongly to moderate changes
in its price.[10] As a general rule, therefore, the industry demand curve for
a producer's good—a derived demand—will be negatively sloped like the
primary-demand curves from which it derives, but the quantity of the
good which buyers take will be less responsive to price changes than it is
in the case of primary goods.[11]

The preceding support of the idea that industry demand curves are
negatively sloped proceeds largely from general observations concerning
buyers' psychology and behavior and from a series of logical deductions
drawn from assumptions which are based on these observations. This particular conclusion about negatively sloping demand curves squares fairly
well with the experience of most of us. It is fairly well verified by statistical
measures of the industry demand curves for many products.[12] If we choose
any product and set out to find the statistical net relationship over a period
of time between price charged and quantity sold, we ordinarily shall find
a negatively sloping demand curve.

On the other hand, many critics have felt that the underlying theory
which supports this conclusion is unrealistic or poorly substantiated, particularly so far as it postulates the existence of rational consumers who
more or less consciously attempt to maximize their satisfaction from a
variety of goods. These criticisms are potentially important so far as this
theory of consumer behavior has applications much more general than
simply supporting the idea of negatively sloped demand curves. However,
many economists feel that the theory, although it attributes to consumer
behavior a sort of mathematical precision which such behavior does not
in fact possess, does identify the principal broad tendencies which guide
consumer activity.

THE DEMAND SCHEDULE AND THE NUMBER OF BUYERS

In the preceding discussion of the demand schedule or curve we have seen
that a demand schedule represents essentially a series of alternative offers

[10] The main exception to this would occur if one producer's good could be extensively substituted for another if its price fell enough. Aluminum is probably a
case in point.

[11] Precisely, the elasticity of a derived demand for any good A depends on the
elasticity of the primary demand (from which it is derived), the proportion of the
cost of the primary good which is spent on good A, the substitution conditions between
good A and the other goods or factors used in making the primary good, the supply
conditions for substitute goods or factors, and the response of the price of the primary
good to changes in its costs.

[12] See, for example, Henry Schultz, *The Theory and Measurement of Demand*
(Chicago: University of Chicago Press, 1938).

by a group of buyers to take various amounts of a good at various alternative prices. We have also seen that such a schedule of alternative offers arises in a market setting where each of the buyers of any good accepts any of a number of prices which emerge for the good as given to him and beyond his influence and he adjusts his purchases of it to any given price so as to receive maximum satisfaction from his spending. At each different price which may emerge he will purchase a different amount, but at every price in turn he adjusts his purchases on the legitimate supposition that variations in the quantity of these purchases will not cause that price to change. This must evidently be because each individual buyer takes so small a proportion of the total amount sold at any price that by varying it he will not influence the sales of sellers sufficiently to cause them to change from the going price. Therefore, each price, in turn, is simply a "given" to the single buyer; he adjusts his quantity of purchases to it on the supposition that he alone can do nothing to cause it to change.

When the individual buyer behaves on this supposition (which is quite correct so long as buyers are many and small), each of them essentially puts forth a demand schedule for any good representing offers to purchase different specified amounts at different given prices. When we "add up" the demand schedules of many individual buyers for a given good, we have the market demand schedule or industry demand schedule for that good. And this schedule is quite independent of the *conditions of supply* for the good—independent, that is, of the relation of the total quantity sold to the price at which sellers would be willing to produce it. No buyer "looks through" to this relationship because no one buyer takes enough to induce sellers to change their price even by refusing to buy entirely. Therefore, we have a schedule of offers to buy at various prices, quite independent of supply conditions, and this is the demand schedule.

The preceding is emphasized at length because there will really be a demand schedule for a good *only* when each buyer simply sets his purchases at any given price without trying to influence price—or, in effect, only when there are many small buyers. The very notion of a given demand schedule for a good, independent of supply conditions for the good, presupposes that the number of buyers is large and that no one of them buys a significant proportion of the total amount of the good bought. For if the individual buyer can influence, or, at the extreme, set the price at which he buys, it is evident that he will no longer simply adjust his purchases to any going price as if it were given to him, but he will in effect select or set one of a range of available prices and will do so with an eye to how much supply he can obtain from sellers at various prices. It is also evident that in this case he then will put forth no true demand schedule of alternative offers at alternative prices but simply will fix *a* price and *a* quantity of sales most advantageous to him. Although the same implicit schedule of added satisfaction from added units of the good still exists, it will no longer express itself in a corresponding demand schedule—it will simply enter into the buyer's calculation of what price to fix. This is quite clear in the hypothetical case where one buyer takes the entire output of an industry (buyer's monopoly or monopsony). But it is true in a degree of any situation where the individual buyer takes enough of the industry output to permit him to influence the price at which sellers will sell. In all such cases the demand schedule per se gives way essentially to either (1) administration of price by the buyer or (2) setting of price by bargaining between buyers and sellers. The demand schedule really exists as such only for situations where no buyer can set or influence price, and buyers cannot bargain for a price.

This does not mean that the demand curve is a concept of limited usefulness. For substantially every consumer good, for the bulk of producer goods, and to a lesser degree for productive factors, we find markets with many buyers, none of which can perceptibly influence price. Here the demand schedule is an accurate representation of the essential nature of buyer behavior. It follows that in the analysis of commodity pricing we make no great error for purposes of a simplified approximation if we speak as if every good had a market with many buyers. On the other hand, we must recognize the other case—an exceptional case in the instance of commodity markets but less so in that of factor markets—where buyers are few. Here the analysis of demand cannot employ the demand curve in the usual sense, and a special form of analysis must be employed.

For the present (throughout this chapter and in subsequent chapters on price determination through Chapter 7) we shall assume that all markets are of the many-buyer type and have true demand schedules. This is at any rate expedient since the developed analysis of demand and pricing within contemporary economic theory rests ordinarily on this supposition. In Chapter 8 we shall consider the modifications in the analysis of demand and pricing which are necessary when it is recognized that there are at least some market situations marked by fewness of buyers.

It should be re-emphasized, however, that here and subsequently, throughout this and succeeding chapters, wherever we speak of a demand schedule for the industry output, or for the output of the individual seller, or for that of any other unit, it is explicitly presupposed that that unit is selling to many buyers. We thus refer to what may be regarded as the normal market situation, but we do not take into account the exceptions.

C. ELASTICITY AND CROSS-ELASTICITY OF DEMAND

ELASTICITY OF DEMAND

A general property of industry demand curves, as we have seen, is that they all slope downward to the right, evidencing an inverse relationship between price and quantity. This is about all that various different market demand curves have in common, however. For although a series of price

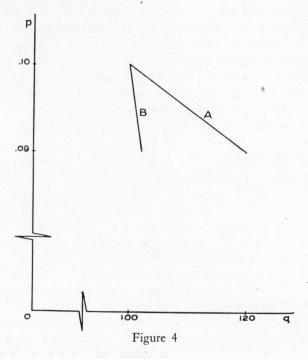

Figure 4

reductions for any good will ordinarily elicit a corresponding series of increases in quantity bought (tastes, purchasing power, and other prices remaining unchanged), the rate at which quantity responds to price may vary widely. A 10-percent reduction in the price of one good might bring about a 20-percent increase in its sales, whereas for another good a 10-percent price reduction might be accompanied by only a 2-percent increase in sales. The demand for the first good is much more responsive to price change than that for the second.

Suppose that of good *A*, 100 pounds is bought at 10 cents and 120 pounds at 9 cents; but that of good *B*, 100 pounds is bought at 10 cents and 102 pounds at 9 cents. The two demand curves will differ as shown in Figure 4. It is ordinarily said that the demand for which the response of percentage change in quantity to percentage change in price is the larger (for good *A*) is *more elastic* than that of the less responsive demand (for good *B*).

We will return to this idea of *elasticity* in a moment but may indicate meanwhile that the slope of a curve (on arithmetic scales) does not indicate the ratio of *percentage* quantity change to *percentage* price change and that the relation of the slope of two curves is not always an indicator of the relation of these ratios. Slope measures the ratio (inverted) of absolute changes in quantity and price, which is per se less significant than the corresponding ratio of percentage changes.

Demand curves may also differ in shape according to whether they are *linear* or *curved*. A *straight-line* demand curve shows that a series of successive price changes of constant amount will elicit a series of quantity changes of constant amount; this would be true, for example, if for every price reduction of 1 cent an increase in sales of 20 pounds took place. A *curved-line* demand curve shows that a series of successive price changes of constant amount will elicit a series of quantity changes of varying amount—thus five successive price reductions of 1 cent might elicit quantity increases of successively 2, 3, 4, 5, and 6 pounds. To illustrate this let us suppose the following two demand schedules for the two goods *A* and *B*:

Price of *A*	Quantity of sales of *A*	Price of *B*	Quantity of sales of *B*
10	100	10	100
9	120	9	102
8	140	8	105
7	160	7	109
6	180	6	114
5	200	5	120

If we plotted these schedules as demand curves, the demand for *A* would be a straight line, and that for *B* a curve. Demand curves will, thus, differ in degree of curvature as well as in steepness of slope. Some of them may also be irregular in shape.

The most significant thing about a demand curve, however, is that it shows the exact relation of each price change to the corresponding change in quantity bought. It also shows, inferentially, the effect of changes in price, *p*, on the *total revenue* from sales (*p* multiplied by *q*).

Suppose we have a demand curve *F* which shows sales of 1,000 units at the price of $1 and sales of 1,100 at the price of $0.99; a demand curve *G* which shows sales of 1,000 at the price of $1 and sales 1,010.1 at the price of $0.99; and a demand curve *H* which shows sales of 1,000 at the price of $1 and sales of 1,005 at the price of $0.99. These data may be tabulated as follows:

Price of F	Quantity of sales of F	Price times quantity
$1.00	1,000	$1,000
.99	1,100	1,089

Price of G	Quantity of sales of G	Price times quantity
$1.00	1,000	$1,000
.99	1,010.1	1,000

Price of H	Quantity of sales of H	Price times quantity
$1.00	1,000	$1,000
.99	1,005	994.95

In addition to the fact that quantity is most responsive to price in *F*, less so in *G*, and least so in *H*, we may note a crucial respect in which these curves differ. *In curve* F *total expenditure on the good increases as price is reduced.* Thus, at the price of $1 total expenditure is $1,000, but at the price of $0.99, buyers will spend $1,089. A price reduction increases total expenditure, and conversely a price increase will reduce total expenditure. *In curve* G *a price change leaves total expenditure unchanged* (to a very close approximation in this example—exactly in conception). Total expenditure is $1,000 at $1 and also $1,000 at $0.99. Finally, *in curve* H *a price reduction results in a curtailment of total expenditure.* At $1 the total expenditure is $1,000, but at $0.99 it is only $994.95. These curves differ generally in that price reductions result in, respectively, increase, no change, and reduction of total expenditure. The direction of this effect may be ascertained for any demand curve by multiplying together the price-quantity combination at each of a succession of prices.

The direction and rate of response of total expenditure on a good to change in its price are indicated by the *elasticity* of its demand. Where total expenditure increases with a price reduction (or decreases with a price rise)—curve *F*—the demand is called *elastic.* When total expenditure is constant in spite of a price change, the demand is called *unit elastic* (curve *G*). When total expenditure decreases with a price reduction or increases with a price increase, the demand is called *inelastic* (curve *H*). This is a rough tripartite classification of elasticity. But it is obvious that among *elastic* demands there are those which are "more elastic" than others. In some a small price reduction might elicit a rather small increase in total expenditure; in others a small price decrease might cause a very large increase in total expenditure. Some measure not only of the *direction* of change, but of the *degree* of responsiveness of total revenue to price change is useful.

A PRECISE MEASURE OF ELASTICITY

An accurate measure of the direction and degree of response of total revenue to price change may be obtained by dividing the proportionate change in quantity of sales by the corresponding proportionate change in price for an infinitesimally small price change at any point on a demand curve. This corresponds to the percentage change in quantity divided by the corresponding percentage change in price when the changes are *very small*. Thus, in Figure 5 we have a demand curve and an initial price p and

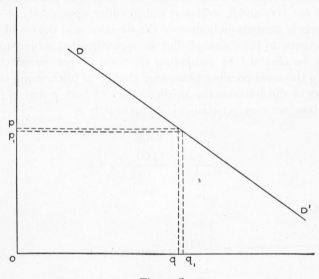

Figure 5

quantity q. To measure the elasticity of the demand curve at the point, let us suppose a very small price reduction to p_1 by the amount of Δp. This is accompanied by an increase of quantity to q_1 by the amount of Δq. These changes are so small that the difference between p and p_1, or between q and q_1, may be neglected in calculation. Then the elasticity of demand is measured as

$$e = \frac{\dfrac{\Delta q}{q}}{\dfrac{-\Delta p}{p}} = \frac{\Delta q}{-\Delta p} \cdot \frac{p}{q},$$

where Δ stands for "a small change in."

Now when elasticity e, thus measured, is exactly -1 (the sign is necessarily negative if price and quantity change in opposite directions), total revenue will remain unchanged in response to a price change. If e is greater than -1 (-2, -3, -10, etc.), total revenue increases with a price reduction and in greater degree as e is greater. If e is smaller than -1 (-0.7, -0.5, -0.2, etc.), total revenue decreases with a price decrease and in greater degree as e is smaller. The direction of response of total revenue is thus indicated by whether e at a point is greater or less than -1. The degree of response is indicated by the size of e.

Elasticity of a given demand is precisely the ratio of proportionate change in quantity to proportionate change in price *at a point* on a demand curve. When this ratio is taken for *discrete changes* in price and quantity, which are not very small, so that p and p_1 differ significantly, it does not give a precisely accurate indication of the direction and degree of response of total revenue to price change. But an approximation subject to a small error may be obtained by computing the ratio of percentage change in quantity to the corresponding percentage change in price, using in the denominators of the fractions the smaller values of both p and q. Thus, in curve F above we may get elasticity approximately as

$$e = \frac{\dfrac{\Delta q}{q}}{\dfrac{-\Delta p}{p_1}} = \frac{\dfrac{+100}{1,000}}{\dfrac{-.01}{.99}} = -9.9$$

In curve G,

$$e = \frac{\dfrac{+10.1}{1,000}}{\dfrac{-.01}{.99}} = (\text{approx.}) -1$$

In curve H

$$e = \frac{\dfrac{+5}{1,000}}{\dfrac{-.01}{.99}} = -0.495$$

The convenience either of the precise point measure or of the approximate "arc" measure is apparent. When the demand curve is shaped so that expenditure increases with price reductions, e is greater than -1 (since proportionate quantity change exceeds proportionate price change). When expenditure is constant in spite of price change, e is -1 (since proportionate quantity change is equal to proportionate price change). When expenditure falls with price reductions, e is less than -1 (since proportionate quantity change is less than proportionate price change). By the size of e, we can tell approximately how elastic or inelastic demand is. Thus, an elasticity of -50

would indicate a very elastic demand, one of -2 a moderately elastic demand, one of $-.003$ a very inelastic demand, and so forth.[13]

Two explanatory comments should be added to the preceding remarks. Since elasticity is measured by $\frac{\Delta q}{\Delta p} \cdot \frac{p}{q}$, it is clear that elasticity is related to the *slope* of the demand curve, which is measured by the inverse of $\Delta q / \Delta p$—a ratio of absolute changes in q and p. But elasticity is not simply the inverse of slope. It is this multiplied by p/q. Thus, although a steeply sloped demand curve is generally evidence of inelasticity and a gradually sloped one evidence of elasticity, the slope must be related to the relative magnitudes of p and q at the point where elasticity is measured in order to get the precise measure of elasticity.

Further, elasticity is a precise concept only as it refers to a *point* on a demand curve—that is, to an indefinitely small change in price at that point. Elasticity may obviously differ from place to place on a demand curve (and ordinarily does); each point has potentially a separate elasticity. Thus, for a straight-line demand curve, such as that shown in Figure 5, we would find a different elasticity at every point, as $\Delta q / \Delta p$ remained constant at all points and p/q varied, so that elasticity decreased for successively lower prices.

For purposes of further analysis in this volume we need not labor the mathematical niceties of elasticity. We may be content to understand what it measures and why it is important. It is a precise measure of the "shape" of a demand curve at any point, and it is primarily important as an indication of the reaction of total expenditure to price change on a given demand curve.

PROPERTIES OF VARIOUS INDIVIDUAL INDUSTRY DEMANDS

The preceding discussion has been concerned with the demand curve for the output of a single industry, specifically for the assumed instance of a precisely defined and neatly delimited group of sellers of identical outputs. For such an industry we have analyzed the relation of the quantity sold by the industry to the price which all firms within it charge, when there are given buyer tastes, given total purchasing power, and given prices for all other industries. It is established that for the output of such an industry under these conditions, there is a definite industry demand curve with a negative slope and with some shape which gives rise to a certain elasticity or complex of elasticities.

As we turn to the actual industries in the American economy, is there anything more that can be said of the demands for their products? That is,

---

[13] See Stigler, *op. cit.,* pp. 51-54, for a further discussion of elasticity.

do we know more than that the demand curve for substantially any industry slopes negatively and that it has at every point some elasticity or other?

In considering this question, we must realize that the actual "industries" of our economy do not fully conform to the precise model mentioned above. Most of them are marked by some degree of product differentiation—the products of their member sellers are close but not perfect substitutes. As a consequence, the industry demand curve cannot refer to the necessarily single price for a single homogeneous commodity and the response of sales of this commodity to changes in this price. It must refer instead to the response of the combined sales of the member firms to concurrent changes in all of their prices by similar amounts or proportions. Further, many actual "industries" are not completely isolated groups of sellers, whose outputs are extremely distant substitutes for those of all other sellers. A group of products which for rough-and-ready purposes we would be ready to identify as an industry may frequently have some noticeable substitution relation with other groups. Changes in their prices will thus have some influence on the sales of other such groups and may induce minor responses in other prices. If so, the industry demand curve is appropriately drawn to recognize the effects of these induced price responses. Recognizing such variations in the meaning of an industry demand curve, we may turn to the properties of various demand curves of this sort.

Each industry has some demand curve for its output, and together these industry curves constitute a family of demand curves for all output with each curve representing, in a prevailing situation, the quantities of a specific commodity salable over a range of prices for that good. These demand curves will in general be negatively sloped—that is, they will show increasing sales with decreasing price. But they may obviously differ with respect to *position* and to *elasticity*. The character of these differences, the reasons for them, and some of their consequences deserve comment.

The relative position of an industry demand curve—that is, the absolute amounts bought over the usual range of prices and the corresponding share of all purchasing power which the industry commands—depend upon the current state of productive techniques, the state of consumer preferences, and the corresponding importance of the good in the production and consumption scheme of the economy. Thus, the demand for wheat flour may be quite large at every practically conceivable price, whereas the demand curve for fishermen's rubber hip boots may reflect by its position a very small demand at every price. The various positions of different industry demand curves is a simple matter but one of great importance in a free-enterprise economy. Any individual demand curve reflecting buying power seeking a particular good tends to attract business enterprises to supply that good up to some point consistent with the costs of making it and with the firms' calculations of maximum profit opportunities. Thus, a very large demand for gray cotton yarn tends to elicit a large investment and the employment of a large labor force in making it; a small demand for precision barometers elicits a small investment and small employment in making barometers.

Looking at the matter more broadly, the relative or comparative sizes of the various demands for all goods (together with the relative costs of producing them) tend to apportion or allocate productive effort among various goods roughly according to the relative spending power buyers are prepared to offer for them. Business enterprises are not permanently wedded to the production of certain goods; over long periods they shift willingly from one product to another according to the money demand for it and the profit opportunities it offers. New enterprises will be brought into being, moreover, to supply new or developing demands. The complex family of individual demands for goods tends, therefore, to guide the apportionment or allocation of resources into various lines of production. We must consequently keep it in mind that any seller, though immediately faced by the market demand for the good he is currently producing, is in his long-range planning faced by a family of demands for all goods, the relative attractiveness of which he must keep in mind in considering his profit opportunities. This observation will appear to be of fundamental importance when we later consider the function of the economy as a whole.

Industry demand curves may also differ a good deal with respect to elasticity. Thus, the demands for many goods are quite inelastic, or unresponsive to price change, whereas others are moderately elastic and still others quite elastic. A change in the price of cigarettes will probably have little effect on cigarette sales; the demand for automobiles was once calculated to be of about unit elasticity (a 1-percent price reduction would induce about a 1-percent increase in quantity sold); the demand for aluminum has been held to be quite elastic within customary price ranges. Also, demand for a given good may have significantly different elasticities at different levels of price. Thus, the demand for coal has tended to be relatively inelastic to downward price reduction when there was no important lower-priced substitute fuel; but if its price were substantially higher relative to those of substitute fuels, its demand at that point would probably be much more elastic. The elasticity of particular industry demand curves is obviously a matter of importance to sellers therein. It is important whether a price reduction will lead to larger or smaller total revenue for the sellers of the industry, by how much sales will be restricted by a price rise, and so forth.

Why do different industry demand curves have different elasticities? The reason is found largely in the difference in the substitutability of their outputs for other goods. As we have seen, various industry outputs are generally imperfect substitutes for each other as sources of satisfaction to buyers. As a result, the buyer finds that successive additional units of any one good provide successively smaller additions to his satisfaction compared to the satisfaction provided by other goods which they may replace. When the price of a particular good falls, the buyer will extend its purchases only to the point where the last unit purchased makes an addition to his satisfaction per dollar spent on it equal to the satisfaction provided by the last dollar spent on every other good. When the ratio of its price to other prices becomes lower, he tends to substitute it for other goods down to, but only to, such a point.

But although they all may be imperfect and not very close substitutes for other outputs, some industry outputs may be better substitutes than others for other goods. That is, industry outputs may replace other goods more or less readily as sources of satisfaction to buyers. For those which are relatively better substitutes for other goods, successive increases in their purchases will be accompanied by relatively moderate declines in the satisfaction added by additional units. For those which are poorer substitutes for other goods, the satisfaction added by additional units will decline more rapidly. Therefore, a given price decline will cause the buyer to increase his purchases of the former in greater proportion than those of the latter in order to reach the satisfaction-maximizing point where the last dollar spent on every good adds an equal amount to his satisfaction. Therefore, the demands for industry outputs which are better rather than worse substitutes for other goods will be the more elastic, and elasticity of demand will tend to increase as substitutability increases. In common-sense terms, the better a substitute a given good is for other goods, the more readily buyers will move in the direction of buying it in place of other goods as its price falls.

All of this talk about substitution may make it seem that when the price of any one good is reduced and its sales increased, this *must* mean that the purchases of other goods are actually reduced and that the question is just how much. This would be strictly true for the effect of a reduction in the ratio of one price to others, which, nevertheless, left buyers with no more *real* purchasing power or income than before, but the effect of an actual price decrease is more complicated. It not only reduces the relative price of the good in question, but also increases the purchasing power of buyers with a given amount of money to spend. For example, if a buyer has been taking 300 packages annually of cigarettes at 20 cents a pack and spending $60 a year for them, a drop of cigarette price to 15 cents a pack gives him 300 packages for $45 and essentially releases $15 a year to be spent on all goods and with which to increase his real income. It does not necessarily follow that the buyer, therefore, will spend just exactly this $15 of released money on additional cigarettes—he may spend more or less. With the price decline for cigarettes (or any good) the buyer will undoubtedly make some addition to his cigarette purchases, thus in some virtual sense substituting them for other goods, but the extent of this increase may be insufficient to maintain his expenses on cigarettes at $60. In this case his demand for cigarettes is inelastic, and a cigarette price cut will actually increase the demand for other goods. It is also possible that the buyer's tendency to substitute the cheapened goods for others will be strong enough to keep his expenditures on it constant (giving rise to a unit-elastic demand) and that it will be so strong as to lead to increased expenditures with price cuts (elastic demand). The general principle is that since any price cut for some given good has this income-releasing effect in addition to a substitution-inducing effect and since added income *may* be shifted to other goods, the price cut may either increase, leave unchanged, or decrease the demands for other goods. Which it will be depends on the substitutability of the given good for others.

For this to be true it is not necessary that any large part of the buyer's budget be spent on the good in question—it applies to hairpins as well as to housing. It may be true in addition that the amount spent on the good and the income released by a price cut are large relative to the buyer's total income. Then elasticity of demand for the good and the effects of its price cuts on demands for other goods will also depend on the relative responsiveness of the various demands to significant changes in income. Such "income effects" on its demand or on demands for other goods may be of significant size in such cases.

Various industry demands may thus have various elasticities, even though in no case is an industry output a very close substitute for any other. This is mainly because there are many grades or degrees of distant substitutes. One industry may produce an output which is so distant a substitute for others that a cut in its price will lead to a decline in total expenditure on it and some increase on expenditure on other goods, though probably an imperceptible increase for any one other good. Another may produce an output which is a sufficiently good substitute for others that a reduction in its price leads to significantly increased expenditure on it and an imperceptible reduction in the demands of each of a large number of other goods—which imperceptible "shavings" from other demands, nevertheless, add up to quite a sum. Another may attract still hardly perceptible but larger shavings from other demands and have a still more elastic demand.

Of course, so far as product groups which we popularly identify as industries are not precisely delimited but face a number of outside substitutes sufficiently close that a change in industry price will have a small but, nevertheless, perceptible effect on the sales of such substitutes, the elasticity of demands for them may be quite high. Such groups are really only quasi-separate industries, or subindustries, but the elasticity of their separate demand curves may be significant for many purposes of analysis. At the extreme we encounter the subgroup of close-substitute products which are sufficiently close substitutes for other groups that a change in the group price will affect the sales of other groups sufficiently to induce a considerable response in their prices. Consider the case of theater admissions and night-club entertainment, the demand for each of which is significantly influenced by the price of the other. Groups of this sort are in theoretical concept subdivisions of a single industry. In these cases if a demand curve is constructed for a subgroup, it cannot validly be drawn on the assumption that the prices of related product groups are given, but it should instead show the response of the subgroups' sales to its price, given any systematically induced covariation in competing prices. A unique demand curve can be constructed only if there are predictable, more or less automatic, responses of such prices to the group's own price change.

THE INTERRELATIONS OF INDUSTRY DEMANDS—CROSS-ELASTICITY OF DEMAND

We now see that a change in the price of any one industry output not only influences the quantity bought of that industry output, but also may have some slight influence on the quantities bought of other outputs—in general or particular ones. The effect of a given industry price change on the sales of any one other good may be measured by a ratio known as *cross-elasticity of demand*.

The elasticity, or "own-elasticity" of demand for a particular good, it will be remembered, measures the ratio of the proportionate change in the quantity bought of a good to the proportionate change in its own price which induces it, ordinarily on the assumption of all other prices being given. Thus, the elasticity of a good A may be expressed as

$$\frac{\dfrac{\Delta q_a}{q_a}}{\dfrac{\Delta p_a}{p_a}}$$

Cross-elasticity of demand between any two goods, on the other hand, measures the ratio of the proportionate change in the quantity purchased of one good to the proportionate change in the price of the other good which induces it. Suppose there are two goods A and B.

We may imagine a small change—for example, a reduction—in the price of good A. We also suppose that the price of good B is given. The sales of B may be affected by the price change in A. Now cross-elasticity of the demand for B in terms of the price of A is measured, under these assumptions, as:

Proportionate change in quantity purchased of B
───
Proportionate change in price of A

Or,

$$\frac{\dfrac{\Delta q_b}{q_b}}{\dfrac{\Delta p_a}{p_a}}$$

Suppose an initial price of good A of \$1 and an initial price of good B of \$5 and an initial sales volume of B of 1,000 units. Suppose that when the price of A falls by 1 cent, the sales of B decline to 996. Then the cross-elasticity of the demand for B in terms of the price of A is calculated approximately as:

$$\frac{\dfrac{-4}{1,000}}{\dfrac{-.01}{0.99}} = +.396$$

A 1-percent change in p_a induces about a $\frac{4}{10}$ths of a percent change q_b. It will be noted that where one good in effect replaces the other (a negative change in its price results in a negative change in the sales of the other) the sign of the cross-elasticity is positive. Precisely defined, it should be noted that cross-elasticity measures simply the tendency of buyers to shift from one good to another when the price of the latter changes, regardless of the ability or disposition of the sellers of the latter to supply them.

Cross-elasticities of demand between various pairs of goods may, of course, have various magnitudes, reflecting the various interrelations of various demands and prices. A first use to which we may put the concept of cross-elasticity is the clarification of our previous definition of an industry. What we said on pages 23 to 26 above was essentially that an industry was a group of products among which there were high cross-elasticities of demand but which had very low (but not generally zero) cross-elasticities of demand with all other products. This definition may require some clarification so far as among a large group of close substitutes the cross-elasticity between any pair may have a different value for price increases than for price decreases (in which case the price-decrease measure provides the central guide), but it will suffice for the moment.[14] This complication will

---

[14] The principal situation in which cross-elasticity of demand between a pair of products will differ greatly for price increases and price decreases is that in which there is a large group of products each of which is a close substitute for all the others and in which the initial output of each is a small proportion of the group output. Then any seller by a price decrease may tend to attract many buyers from each of the others; there is a high cross-elasticity of demand for the output of any other seller in

be considered below when we analyze the character of cross-elasticities among close substitutes within industries of various structure.

The concept of cross-elasticity may also be used in devising a simplified special and somewhat restricted definition of "substitute" products. Any two goods may be designated as "substitutes" when the cross-elasticity of demand between them is positive in sign—that is, a decrease in the price of one induces at least some decreases in the sales of the other. The magnitude of such a positive cross-elasticity indicates the degree of substitutability. A low cross-elasticity indicates poor substitutes; a high cross-elasticity indicates close substitutes. Between perfect substitutes the cross-elasticity of demand approaches the value of infinity for a price cut in either. When substitutability is defined and measured in this way, it should be noted that it is defined and measured in terms of the *total* effects of a price change for one good on the demand for another—that is, virtual "substitution" effects due to change in relative prices and "income" effects due to absolute price change.

Although such a substitute relation of products within an industry is the rule, and may be common (though more distant) among the outputs of different industries or subindustries, an opposite relation may also hold between various outputs. That is, the decrease in the price of one output may lead to some increase in the sales of others—the cross-elasticity of demand may be negative in sign. Such a relationship becomes strong where two goods are used jointly or complement each other in production or in consumption. For example, phonograph records and record players are used together in consumption, or hardwood flooring and plumbing fixtures in the production of houses. Such pairs of goods are designated as *complementary goods* and the relation between them as *complementarity;* the condition is associated with a substantial negative cross-elasticity of demand. A fall in the price of flooring, so far as it stimulates building by reducing its cost, also stimulates the demand for plumbing fixtures. Such groupings of interrelated demands are fairly common. Where the negative cross-elasticities between goods are large, their respective "industries" are thus linked together, and this relationship must be recognized in analysis. Where a change in the price of one good induces a significant price change for a complementary good, the effects of this induced price change must be reflected in the demand curve for the first good.

terms of his price when it is decreased. But if he raises his price, even though he loses most or all of his customers to sellers of close substitutes, he may tend to lose only a few customers to each rival, adding but little to each of their sales, since his rivals are many and his initial output is a small portion of total group output. In this case, there is a low cross-elasticity of demand for the output of any other seller in terms of his price when it is increased. When such a situation is encountered, only cross-elasticity as measured for price cuts is a good indicator of the degree of substitutability of outputs.

So much for the measurement and classification of the relations among prices and sales of different industries or among outputs generally. It is obvious that the change in any industry price is likely to have some influence on the demands for other industry outputs. It is also obvious that this influence will generally be small. Subject to the exceptions of subindustries closely related by the perceptible substitutability or complementarity of their outputs, we have an economy made up of a large number of relatively independent industries. The demand curve for any one of them may be drawn on the assumption that the prices of other goods are given and unchanging, or, more precisely, on the assumption that no other price will change enough in response to a change in this industry's price to influence the sales of this industry perceptibly. Substitutability and complementarity between industry outputs are in general not close because they are not close substitute sources of satisfaction and because most industries secure a relatively small proportion of the total purchasing power expended on all goods. In general, a change in one industry price will not affect the demand for any one other industry output very much. On the other hand, it is evident that a similar change—let us say a reduction—in the prices of all industries but one would have a noticeable effect on the demand for the output of the remaining industry. The addition of the individually negligible effects of many individual price reductions would ordinarily add up to a substantial total effect. This is simply to say that the position of the demand curve for any one industry output depends upon the prices of all other goods taken together, although it may depend insignificantly on the price of any one other industry output. Thus, there is a complicated family of interdependent demand curves and prices for all goods, the nature of which deserves some analysis.

THE FAMILY OF DEMANDS FOR ALL OUTPUTS

Let us consider this conception of an interrelated family of demands for industry outputs. At first we conclude that for any industry output there is at any time a demand curve showing how sales will vary with change in price, on the legitimate supposition that all other prices will remain unchanged as the industry price varies. This demand curve will be one primary determinant of its price. But we then conclude that the position of each industry demand curve in turn depends precisely on the level of all other prices. Thus, we hold essentially that the prices of and the positions of demand curves for all goods are mutually determined. A demand curve for any one industry output is simply an expression of the price-sales relation for it in a going situation of all other prices. As prices in general adjust or move, all demand curves shift. They reach stable resting positions only when all prices become stable because of a general balance of demands and supplies.

If this makes the individual demand curve seem a little bit like a will-o'-the-wisp, it should because that is what it is. Its true character may be made clearer by examining buyer behavior toward all goods at once. If we have a large number of (let us say n) goods available, each at a given price, buyers with given incomes to spend will purchase a determinate amount of each. The various amounts should be determined according to the principle of obtaining the same added satisfaction or benefit from the last dollar spent on each. Let us begin then with n goods and n prices for them, to which correspond n particular quantities demanded. For the price of each good, p_a, there is a quantity demanded, q_a. Now in this situation, we can construct a demand curve for each good in turn which shows the extent to which buyers will increase purchases of it if its price falls and decrease them if its price rises, other prices remaining unchanged. Every good has such a demand curve which shows just this, and this is all it shows. Its position and shape demonstrate, in a given situation, the reactions of buyers to its price change alone in order to maintain a position where the last dollar spent on every good yields an equal satisfaction or benefit.

At any moment, with n goods and n going prices, sellers of the goods are faced with n such demand curves. They are not likely to look much beyond such demand curves since their individual price changes cannot change the broader surroundings much. They, therefore, adjust their outputs, directly or indirectly, to these demands. If these adjustments result in prices and outputs generally different from the original ones, all the demand curves shift as buyers readjust to the new prices, and sellers adjust again. By thus following their demands they may eventually reach a combination of prices and quantities which is stable or in balance—where the amount sellers wish to supply of each good is equal to the amount buyers wish to take. Then prices as well as demand curves would tend to hold still. The importance of the individual industry demand curves is, thus, not that they are fixed beacons in a complicated economy but that they are potentially shifting relationships to which at any one time the activities of the various groups of sellers are oriented. The importance of their interrelation is that as the position of each responds to other prices, sellers so oriented are, in general, led to adjust their outputs to the currently expressed needs of buyers. The manner in which a stable adjustment of outputs to demands develops is a matter for analysis in later chapters.

EFFECTS OF INCOME ON DEMAND

The preceding is concerned largely with the relation of the demand for an industry output to its price and with the interrelations of all such demands and prices. Such relationships are conveniently analyzed on the assumption of some given level of buyers' total purchasing power, thus isolating the effects of price on demand from those of income on demand.

It must of course be recognized that demands in general and the position of every demand curve depend upon the size of the aggregate flow of purchasing power seeking all goods. For most goods a larger general purchasing power means a larger demand. Most demand curves shift to the right as money incomes expand during the upswing of the business cycle and to the left with the decline in general purchasing power which characterizes business recessions.[15] The over-all volume of purchasing power is, consequently, a strategic determinant of the incentive for enterprisers to produce in any line.

Not all demands, of course, respond to shifts in general purchasing power in the same proportion. The demands for luxuries and for durable goods increase most rapidly with increases of general income and fall off most heavily as income declines. The pattern of relative demands for all goods thus shifts systematically with shifts in the general level of income.

The responsiveness of the demand for any good to changes in buyer purchasing power may be measured by its "income-elasticity." This is defined as the ratio of a proportionate change in the quantity bought of a good to the proportionate change in buyers' income which induces it, all prices remaining unchanged.

So far in the immediately preceding discussion, we have generally assumed that within each industry the member firms sell identical outputs at a necessarily identical price. This has allowed us to speak of the industry as having at any one time a single commodity and a single price common to all sellers, and thus has enabled us to construct a simple industry demand curve. The argument is made more complex, although its fundamental conclusions are not significantly altered, when we recognize that within many industries the outputs of various member firms are not identical but differentiated and that their prices are thus not necessarily identical. Thus, in the soap industry one seller may price his product at 40 cents a pound, another at 38 cents, another at 42 cents, and because of brand preferences all may succeed in selling soap at the same time. Where such product differentiation occurs, it is not possible in strict logic to construct an industry demand curve relating *the* price of the industry to the total output. There may be more than one price, and the outputs do not add to a strictly homogeneous total. It is nevertheless possible to construct a provisional or working demand curve for the industry which represents the change in the aggregate amount (neglecting

---

[15] There are certain exceptional ("inferior") goods the demand for which may decline as income increases. This is said to be true of bread in countries of low income. Poverty forces people to subsist on little else when income is low, but other foods may be substituted for it rapidly as income increases.

nonhomogeneity) which all firms can sell if, starting with any given set of interfirm price differentials, they concurrently change their prices by identical proportions. Some such approximation must stand in lieu of a more satisfactory industry demand curve in such cases. It is in fact a relatively satisfactory substitute, since the product differentiation within industries is usually not so great as to make summation of different outputs unreasonable, and since in most cases the member firms will be held by competition to very similar if not identical prices. The industry demand curve in such industries is, thus, a slightly arbitrary concept, but it is, nevertheless, quite valid and in no wise upsets the generalizations heretofore drawn concerning the relation between different industry demands. Further implications of product differentiation will be discussed as we turn to the demand curve for the output of the individual firm.

D. DEMANDS FOR THE OUTPUTS OF FIRMS

THE DEMANDS FOR INDIVIDUAL SELLERS' OUTPUTS

The industries the demand curves for which have been discussed above are, of course, nothing more than groups of firms whose prices are closely related because they sell close substitute outputs to a common group of buyers. Such industry demand curves show how much all buyers from the industry will take at each of a range of alternative prices during a given time interval. As such, it is the demand which all the firms in the industry face together—the common demand for their combined output. If there are 75 sellers in an industry, and the industry demand curve shows sales of 10,000 at the price of $1 and of 11,000 at $0.95, this means that if the combined offerings of all 75 sellers are 10,000 units, the price for their output will be $1 per unit, but if their combined offerings are 11,000, the price will fall to $0.95.

If an individual seller of a good knows the industry demand curve for this good—or makes an estimate of it on which he depends—it gives him the answer to one question: If (under given circumstances of buyer income, etc.) the total supply of the product is any amount q, what will the market price be? If the seller now wants to estimate future market supply, he can in turn estimate the price which he and his competitors will get for their outputs. Knowledge of market demand curves may thus be useful to individual sellers, and in some types of industry individual sellers may take direct account of the industry demand in making their decisions regarding price and output.

The industry demand curve for a commodity, however, does not necessarily allow the individual seller to answer a second question: What will his own selling price be if his output is alternatively the amounts x_1, x_2, x_3? In short, it does not necessarily relate the individual seller's output to the price he will receive. Yet, every seller should be primarily interested in a curve which will give him just this information. He wants to know his *individual seller's demand curve,* which may be defined as a curve showing how much output the individual firm can sell at each possible price.

Why doesn't the industry demand curve give the seller this information? The reason, in general, is that he does not supply the entire output of the industry. He may supply a considerable fraction of it, or only a small portion of it, but single-firm, or monopolistic, supply of an industry output is rare. If he supplies only a part of it, the resulting situation is such that his own price-sales relation may deviate from that indicated by the industry demand curve. First, since his product is then a close or perfect substitute for those of a number of rivals, his price changes will tend to induce buyers to shift between them and himself, provided his rivals do not respond to his price change, thus potentially giving him a much more elastic demand than the industry demand. Whereas the industry demand curve reflects the shift of buyers' expenditure between industries as industry price changes, the seller's demand may thus also reflect the shift of buyers within the industry among rival sellers. This may give rise to a different price-sales relation for the seller than obtains between industry price and output.

Alternatively, if a seller's rivals make prices so as to hold their outputs constant while he changes his price, thus precluding any shift of buyers among sellers, his own price changes may, nevertheless, have a magnified proportionate effect on his sales volume, as he thus would gain or lose all buyers added to or subtracted from the entire industry demand by this price change. Other possibilities are open, and the precise character of the seller's demand curve will be contingent on whether and how the seller's rivals respond to his price or output changes. This, in turn, will depend on the structure of the industry. But in any event, there is obviously no necessary correspondence between the seller's demand curve and his industry demand curve. Since it is the seller's rather than the industry demand curve which will directly affect enterprise action, the possible sorts of demand curves individual sellers may face must be investigated.

In general, we may say that the demand curve for the individual seller's output is in some way related to his industry demand curve, but that the character of this relation as well as the general character of his demand curve depends on the competitive relations between this seller and other sellers producing identical or close substitute products. Common-sense observation tells us, moreover, that there are a number of distinctly different sorts of competitive situations and that the character of the seller's demand (and the way it is related to governing industry demand) may thus differ considerably from industry to industry. In fact, the firm's calculation of its own demand may be of several distinct types, and a first step in considering how firms calculate the demands for their products (and eventually their price and output policies) is to construct *a classification of industries*.

THE CLASSIFICATION OF INDUSTRIES

Industry or market classifications may be simple or complex, depending upon the number of differences among industries which we recognize. For beginning purposes we may distinguish five classes, as follows: [16]

1. Industries with one seller.
2. Industries with many sellers.
   a. Where the products of all sellers are identical.
   b. Where the products of various sellers are "differentiated."
3. Industries with a few sellers.
   a. Where the products of all sellers are identical.
   b. Where the products of various sellers are "differentiated."

It will be noted that in this classification markets are distinguished according to only two characteristics: the number of sellers—many, few, or one; and the relation among the outputs of the sellers in an industry—whether they are identical or differentiated. The meaning of a "one-seller" industry is evident when we have defined an industry. By "many" sellers is meant a large enough number that each is so small that he controls an insignificant proportion of the total industry output or little enough that any probable change in his output will add or subtract so little from the total industry output as not perceptibly to affect the industry price. By "few" sellers is meant a small enough number that one or more sellers controls a significant proportion of industry output so that moderate changes in his output may add or subtract enough from industry output perceptibly to affect the industry price. The simplest version of fewness of sellers is found where there is a small number of firms (for example two, ten, or twenty) of approximately equal size so that each controls a significant share of industry output.

The meaning of product differentiation has already been discussed. In some industries the outputs of competitive sellers will be substantially identical so that buyers make no distinction or choice among the products offered by different sellers. In others the outputs of the various firms, although close substitutes to buyers, are not perfect substitutes, being distinguished by design, quality, packaging, "firm name" or branding, or sales promotion.

It will appear that these two characteristics of industries are probably the most important in determining the character of an individual firm's demand and its relation to that of the industry of which it is a member. The

[16] Cf. Fritz Machlup, "Monopoly and Competition," *American Economic Review,* September 1937, pp. 445-451.

number of sellers is significant because it determines the extent to which individual sellers can influence over-all industry performance and thus will take direct account of the industry demand and of the possible reactions of their competitors in determining their own prices and outputs. The degree of product differentiation is important because it determines to what extent the firm enjoys some potential independence in pricing its product and some means of directly influencing or maintaining its own volume of sales.

There are, of course, other characteristics of the industry with a significant influence on the individual firm's demand—among them the degree of concentration of output among sellers (proportions of industry output controlled by the several sellers) and the degree of durability in use of the output.[17] The number of buyers demanding output from the industry may also be of great significance. For the moment we will deal throughout with all industries on the assumption of the usual situation of many small buyers, no one of whom can perceptibly influence his buying price. A whole new set of subcategories is required for the case of one or a few buyers, since here the very notion of an objective demand curve faced by sellers gives way. These special cases will be considered in Chapter 8 below. For the moment we shall concentrate attention on the significance of the number of sellers and the degree of product differentiation, assuming many buyers throughout.

SINGLE-FIRM MONOPOLY

Let us consider the character of the seller's demand curve in each of the structural situations identified above. The firm's view of the relation of its sales volume to the price it charges is perhaps simplest in an industry with one seller—in a so-called "single-firm monopoly." A single-firm monopoly is most easily defined as the case in which one firm has an output for which there are no close substitutes. Cross-elasticity of demand with every other output is very small. There are no other output changes in the price of which can perceptibly affect the demand for the firm's output, or the demand for which can be perceptibly affected by changes in the firm's price. When there is a significant cross-elasticity with another product, we do not have single-firm monopoly. If one can imagine the case of a limited group of substitute products with small but perceptible cross-elasticities between each pair of products where, nevertheless, concurrent changes in the price of most of, or all but one of, the products will significantly affect the demand for any one product, the firm in this situation is likewise not classified as a single-firm monopolist.

It follows that the single-firm monopolist faces no substitute the price of which will respond to his price changes enough to affect his demand and

[17] See E. S. Mason, "Price and Production Policies of Large-Scale Enterprise," *American Economic Review,* Supplement, March 1939, pp. 61-74.

that his demand is not perceptibly affected by changes in the price of any other output or limited group of outputs. To this condition of no close substitutes may be optionally added the one that at no price which the monopolist may find it advantageous to charge will there be any threat of entry by a new seller to compete with him. The single-firm monopoly category is relatively rare in our economy, but several industries, including cash registers, basic aluminum, and telephone communications are, or once were, practically monopolized.

The relation of the sales volume to the price of a single-firm monopolist is evidently shown by an industry demand curve for his product—his own "seller's" demand curve is an industry demand curve for an entire commodity. The characteristics of demands for the outputs of such monopolists are therefore those of industry demand curves generally, as regards both direction of slope and elasticity; and they may differ from monopoly to monopoly according to the varying patterns of buyers' desires for the various products. The demand for a single-firm monopolist's output of a certain product might appear as in Figure 5.

The fact that a single-firm monopolist, in calculating the effect of each possible price change on his sales volume, can refer to the industry demand for an entire product is important in two principal ways. First, the monopolist faces a demand schedule for his output which, subject only to his finding it out, is relatively stable and is free from the effects of price changes, induced or otherwise, in competing goods. To be sure, the monopolist's demand curve will shift with changes in buyers' income or in response to a simultaneous change in most or all of the other prices in the economy. But it will be practically insensitive to changes in the price of any one other product or limited range of products—it is not influenced by the action of any competitor or limited group of competitors. Likewise, the monopolist can vary his price over a wide range without engendering any reaction in competitive prices which would in turn perceptibly influence his sales. He can in effect freely select each of a large number of prices with the expectation that a definite sales volume will correspond to each and that this price-sales relation will not be altered by the price responses or other price adjustments of close competitors.

The single-firm monopolist, to summarize our first point, has a definite and relatively stable demand schedule for his own output. The second significant property of this monopolist's demand schedule is that, like any industry demand curve, it slopes downward to the right. This means, from the monopolist's standpoint, that under given circumstances (of general purchasing power and the like) an increase in the output he offers to buyers will result in a reduction of price; a decrease in output should cause an increase in price. The monopolist's revenue per unit of output tends to fall as output increases. As a result, the monopolist, even if his output cost him nothing, would have some tendency to restrict his production below the maximum, seeking that combination of price and output which promised the greatest *aggregate* profit. In short, the monopolist has a definite demand curve for his output, with some degree of slope downward to the right; he is, therefore, in a position to exploit the given relation of price to output to his maximum advantage. In effect, he can deliberately select a *price policy* of his own.

The manner and the extent to which the monopolist exploits the demand for his product, of course, will depend upon its elasticity. If he has a very elastic demand, output may be extended with very small sacrifice in price, and there will be less tendency to restrict output. With a very inelastic demand, on the other hand, where total revenue is greater the smaller the output, there may be a tendency to restrict output indefinitely or until the demand finally becomes elastic.

The preceding is a partial analysis of the demand for a single-firm monopolist's product. To understand its full significance we must consider how such a monopolist balances the cost of his output against this demand to select a definite price and output which will maximize his net profit. Before turning to this (see Chapter 5), however, we should consider the relation of price to output as it is viewed by firms in other categories of markets.[18]

PURE COMPETITION

Monopoly, in the sense of full-fledged single-firm monopoly, is rare in the American economy. Only somewhat less rare are industries at the opposite extreme, with many sellers, all of whom sell a homogeneous (identical) product, often characterized as industries in *pure competition*. An industry in pure competition has enough sellers, all relatively small, that no one of them produces a significant portion of the total market supply. No seller, either by extending his own output even by a large percentage or by withdrawing it entirely, can perceptibly influence the market price of his product. The product of every seller, moreover, is in the minds of buyers quite indistinguishable from that of every other in the industry.

Ordinarily a hundred or more small sellers, none of whom produced more than 1 or 2 percent of the market output, would be required to fulfill approximately the condition regarding numbers; all would have to produce some single commodity sold at specified grades and quite undifferen-

---

[18] It may be noted that so long as the monopolist is defined as immune from the threat of entry by new sellers at any price he finds it advantageous to charge, all relevant ranges of the industry demand curve correspond to the demand for his output. If, however, he will attract entry above some relevant price, then the industry demand curve above that price will not in effect be his own demand curve but one shared with entering rivals.

tiated by quality, advertising, packaging, or branding. We find a fair approximation to pure competition in agricultural markets for certain grain crops and in the industrial field in the cotton gray-goods industry. But the practical instances of pure competition are relatively few. It may, nevertheless, be instructive to observe the contrast between the single seller's demand curve in pure competition and in monopoly.[19]

The seller in pure competition, since he produces a very small and indistinguishable portion of a large aggregate supply, has no perceptible control over the price of his output. There will be at any time some going market price for the good he makes (for example, gray cotton yarn), at which all outputs of the single homogeneous good must sell. The individual seller, since he supplies a very small proportion of the total volume of the good being produced at this price, will not be able to influence this price perceptibly by expansion or contraction, within considerable limits, of the amount he supplies. That is, if he withdraws his entire supply, the total industry supply will be reduced by such a small fraction that the industry price will rise by an imperceptible amount. He can extend his output substantially (up to double or perhaps a much larger multiple of its going size, for example) without adding a large enough proportion to total industry supply to cause more than an imperceptible fall in industry price. Variations in the output the individual seller produces and offers for sale, from zero to a point substantially beyond his going output, will thus result in no *perceptible* variation in the industry price at which he can sell. Therefore, we may say that his situation very closely approximates one in which the industry price is simply given to him and will not vary in response to substantial output variations of his own.

To look at it another way, he can sell nothing at any price perceptibly above the market price; he can sell up to some multiple of his present output substantially at the market price; consequently, he has no reason to sell (within this output range) below the market price.

If we diagram the resulting relationship of his output to his selling price, we find that (for a substantial range of output variations) *the demand*

[19] The cross-elasticity conditions of pure competition are as follows: The cross-elasticity of demand between any pair of outputs within the industry, as measured for a price cut for one output (the prices initially having been identical) will approach infinity, as all buyers tend to seek the lowest price for a given standard good. This is the condition of homogeneity of products. On the other hand, a price increase for one output will give a much lower cross-elasticity with any other output within the industry, since the single seller, though losing all his buyers by a price increase, will lose a negligible number to any one of his many competitors. And a small percentage change in the output of any one seller will have an approximately zero effect on the industry price, or price of any other seller in the industry. This is the condition of large numbers.

curve for a single seller's output in pure competition very closely approxi-
mates a horizontal straight line at the level of market price. Such a demand
curve is shown in Figure 6. In effect, as the seller views demand, changes
in his output sold anywhere in the neighborhood of going output have no
influence on price. He can vary his output over a wide range without perceptibly influencing his selling price.

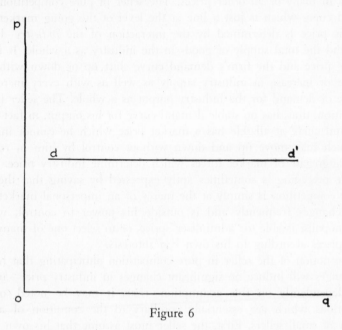

Figure 6

In purely competitive industries we shall usually discover firms limited
by cost or other conditions from extending their individual outputs sufficiently to influence industry price. Therefore, this approximately horizontal
demand curve will include all relevant price-sales combinations available to
the firm. Recognizing this, let us compare the demand situation faced by
the seller in pure competition with that faced by the monopolist.

These two demand situations differ in two significant ways. First, the
competitive seller has no perceptible control over price and no possibility
of adopting a price policy. He can at the most select the output he wants
to produce at the going price. Since increases in his own output do not tend
perceptibly to reduce his price, he does not have the virtual tendency that
the monopolist does to restrict his output.[20] Only the rise in his costs with
increases in his output will limit his production. In short, he is not in any

[20] A horizontal demand curve is "perfectly elastic," or has elasticity equal to infinity, since there is indefinite increase in quantity with zero decrease in price.

position to exploit for his own ends the slope of the industry demand curve for the good he produces.

A second peculiarity of the demand situation of the seller in pure competition is that his own demand curve is much less stable than that of the monopolist. A monopolist faces a given relation of price to quantity of sales which in general shifts only in response to changes in buyers' incomes or changes in many or all other prices. The seller in pure competition has a demand curve which is just a line at the level of the going market price, and this price is determined by the interaction of the *industry* demand curve and the total supply of goods in the industry as a whole. It follows that the price and the firm's demand curve shift up or down with every decrease or increase in industry supply as well as with every increase or decrease of demand for the industry output as a whole. The seller in pure competition, thus, has no stable demand curve for his output, in fact hardly a demand curve at all. He has a market price which he cannot influence but which may move up and down without control by him in response to the aggregate of market forces which determine industry price.

The preceding is sometimes aptly expressed by saying that the seller in pure competition is simply at the mercy of an impersonal market price, which changes frequently and is outside his power to control, whereas the monopolist is able to "administer" price, or to select one of many alternative prices according to his own best interests.

The notion of the seller in pure competition anticipating that his output changes will induce no significant changes in industry price—and acting independently on this assumption—rests, it may be noted, on two assumptions which are essentially corollary to the condition of a large number of small sellers. First, the seller must assume that his own output adjustments will elicit no response from any competitor—no competitor will retaliate against his output increases or "go with him" in output restriction. This is a reasonable assumption since in the many-seller situation he cannot influence price enough directly to induce any reaction and since sellers in general will be so doubtful of the possibility of spontaneous concerted action to restrict output that none of them will lead off in it. This is fundamentally because every seller in turn could fail to follow such a concerted movement to his advantage and without inducing retaliation. Second, there must be no possibility of effective collusion among sellers to regulate outputs or set prices in concert. This is a reasonable assumption again because of the difficulty of organizing collusion among so many and because each seller in turn can gain by violating any collusive agreement and can do so without eliciting retaliation. Both assumptions, in short, follow reasonably from the condition of a large number of small sellers—independent action disregarding the possibility of competitive responses is logically inferred.

MONOPOLISTIC COMPETITION

Neither single-firm monopoly nor pure competition is especially common in the American economy; these categories represent mainly extreme cases between the limits of which most real markets lie. In practice the situation in an industry is very frequently that there is neither *one seller* nor *very many small sellers;* moreover, the products they sell, regardless of their numbers, are usually not identical but differentiated in some degree. Thus, we find that the three remaining categories of our market classification are factually more important than those already mentioned. These three categories are:

1. Industries with few sellers [21] selling identical products, or *pure oligopoly.*
2. Industries with few sellers selling differentiated products, or *differentiated oligopoly.*
3. Industries with many sellers and differentiated products, or *monopolistic competition.*[22]

Of these, the second is probably the most common, but there are numerous industries which have the approximate characteristics of each category. Let us investigate the character of a seller's demand curve in each case, beginning with monopolistic competition.

An industry in monopolistic competition has many sellers with differentiated but close-substitute products. By "many sellers" we mean that the sellers are many and small enough that no one of them controls a significant proportion of the total market output; no firm by extending or reducing its output within considerable limits will affect the sales of any other seller enough to induce a direct reaction. (This would be true, for example, if there were 100 small sellers. Then the aggregate effect on other sellers of a substantial gain in sales by any one would tend to be divided 99 ways, with no one effect being noticeable.)

[21] "Few sellers" is here a shorthand term referring either to the case where the total number of sellers is few, or where one or more controls a significant proportion of industry output.

[22] "Monopolistic competition" is used here to refer to a somewhat restricted market category. It may also be used to refer to all pricing where there is product differentiation within the industry. Chamberlin, in his *Theory of Monopolistic Competition,* in fact uses the term in this way, and since he was the first of modern theorists to develop formally the problems both of differentiated oligopoly and of differentiated "many-seller" markets, this convention might well be followed. We use the term "monopolistic competition" here to identify only "many-seller" cases because of the preponderant identification of the word "competition" with a large number of sellers in theoretical literature.

The products of the various sellers are relatively *close substitutes* for each other (as one brand of cigarettes for another), but they are not *perfect substitutes*. Monopolistic competition is thus distinguished from pure competition, where the products of all the sellers in the group are perfect substitutes. Since an individual seller in monopolistic competition has a product which no other seller duplicates, at any rate exactly, he is in a sense a *monopolist*. The practical difference between his position and that of the single-firm monopolist, described above, is that the seller in monopolistic competition has a product for which there are many close substitutes, whereas the product of the single-firm monopolist has no such substitutes. Consequently, the demand for the monopolistic competitor's product will be much more sensitive to a relatively small range of prices than that of the single-firm monopolist.

The meaning of the "close-substitute" relation in such a situation, however, or generally the condition of cross-elasticity of demand among differentiated products, is potentially subject to a variety of interpretations. Two principal interpretations may be considered. First, it is possible that each product in the industry is a close substitute for each other one in the sense that there is a high cross-elasticity of demand between each pair of products. Therefore, a small proportionate price reduction for any one product would reduce the sales volume of every other product by a relatively large proportion, attracting many buyers of each rival to the cheapened product. Second, it is possible that there is a small (but not imperceptible) cross-elasticity of demand between each pair of products so that a small proportionate price reduction by any one would reduce the sales volume of every other product by a small proportionate amount. In either case, the cross-elasticity between pairs of products would not *necessarily* read the same for price increases in one product as for price decreases since the price cutter might gain a certain unit amount from each rival with a given price cut, but he might lose only the same unit amount, *to be split among many rivals,* with an equivalent price increase.

We cannot know precisely what the substitution conditions among products in such an industry are without knowing a good deal more than we now know about the character of buyer preferences as among a large number of physically similar goods which, nevertheless, are differentiated one from the other in some manner. To avoid undue complexity at this stage, we shall consider mainly what seems likely to be the most usual situation—namely, that there is a relatively large cross-elasticity of demand between each pair of products in the industry although it is a cross-elasticity which may or may not be larger for price cuts than for price increases. That is, each seller may substantially reduce the sales of his rivals by a relatively small price cut, their prices remaining unchanged, and by an equivalent price rise he will increase their sales either just as substantially or somewhat less substantially, possibly depending on his initial price.

In this situation what will the demand curve for the individual seller's output show in monopolistic competition? In the first place, it will tend to be very elastic but not perfectly so. By reducing his price slightly, other sellers' prices remaining unchanged, the individual seller will add greatly to his sales by attracting some buyers from each of many rivals, but not all of their buyers. By increasing his price slightly he will tend to lose many of his buyers to his rivals, but not all of them. For example, suppose that there are 101 sellers, each supplying 100 buyers initially, and suppose that by a price decrease of 1 percent any seller is able to attract one buyer (or 1 percent of the buyers) from each of his 100 rivals. Then by a price cut of 1 percent he would increase his own sales by 100 percent. If similarly by a price rise of 1 percent he would lose 1 percent of his buyers to each of his 100 rivals, he would reduce his sales by 100 percent by such a price rise. In this case his own demand curve would have an elasticity of -100 and would be very elastic—so elastic indeed that it would be hard to distinguish practically from one of perfect elasticity.

In the second place, this demand curve may be drawn on the legitimate supposition that the sales of his rivals will not be enough affected by his price-output changes in the neighborhood of his going output that their prices will be adjusted in response.

This is simply because he initially supplies a very small proportion of the industry output. Therefore, a price increase sufficient to lose him all of his customers will add imperceptibly to the sales of each of his many rivals, and a price decrease sufficient to increase his sales by a large proportion (up to some limit) will involve taking a similarly imperceptible amount away from the sales of each of his many rivals. So far as he is limited by cost or other conditions from increasing his output beyond some small multiple of his current output, therefore, he will never be led independently to vary his price sufficiently to affect the sales of any rival very much. Within such limits his very elastic demand curve shows a variation of his sales with his price which may occur without inducing any price reaction from his rivals.

In the third place, the *position* of his demand curve is extremely sensitive to the prices charged *by his rivals as a group*. His own demand curve shows an extremely narrow range of prices at which he can sell anything at all. Being very elastic, it includes only a narrow range of prices, above which he can sell nothing and below which he need not go to sell any amount he is practically able to produce. The level at which this range of prices is found is, in general, the level of the prices of all of his competitors; his price cannot be much different from theirs, since their products are all close substitutes for his. This level of price is, in turn, simply determined by the relation of the industry demand to the aggregate output of all sellers in the industry. Any single seller's demand curve simply reflects his narrow range of choice as to prices at the general level of price so determined. It follows that simultaneous increases in output by all or most of the sellers in such an industry will cause the general level of industry price to fall and the demand curve of each seller to shift downward to this level; simultaneous restrictions of output will have the reverse effect. As in pure competition, the seller's demand curve in monopolistic competition is pri-

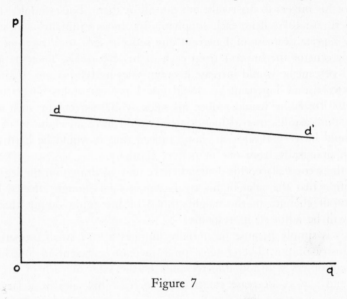

Figure 7

marily a line at the level of the going market price. But instead of being perfectly elastic (horizontal), it is slightly sloping—highly elastic but not perfectly elastic. The general character of any such seller's demand curve, with somewhat exaggerated slope, is illustrated in Figure 7.

This curve shows the reaction of the seller's sales to his independent price changes, at a given level of competitors' prices and with those prices remaining unchanged, or alternatively the reaction of his selling price to independent changes in the supply he offers to buyers, in the same circumstances. From the preceding discussion it is clear that a curve which showed the reaction of the seller's sales to his price changes when all of his competitors changed their prices identically (or of his price to his output changes when all sellers changed their outputs identically) would be much less elastic and would in a sense represent some fraction of the industry demand curve. But the seller will not look to such a curve, since he may legitimately suppose that his independent price and output variations will elicit no response from his competitors.

Why is the market situation thus described designated as one of monopolistic competition? It is because there are similarities both to monopoly and to pure competition. The closer similarity is to pure competition. The individual seller has a demand curve which is simply an extremely elastic line at the level of the going market price. And it shifts about as this price shifts about as the total industry supply varies relative to industry demand.. His situation differs from that of the seller in pure competition in that his demand curve is slightly less than perfectly elastic; he can raise his price slightly without losing all of his customers, and to increase his sales he must cut his price slightly. It is in this respect that he is similar to a monopolist—his demand curve departs somewhat from perfect elasticity so that he has some discretionary control over price and so that sales increases are associated with price reductions and vice versa. Moreover, he may initiate price changes without inducing a response from any rival. But his situation obviously differs from that of the monopolist in that his demand curve is much more elastic (reflecting less discretionary control over price and correspondingly less incentive to output restriction) and in that it shifts about widely in response to simultaneous changes in the prices of a group of close substitute products.

From this it is apparent that our monopolistic competitor seems a good deal more like a competitor than like a monopolist. This similarity to pure competition is reduced, however, by the fact that *by varying his product,* or changing the nature of its differentiation from others, the individual seller may cause his demand curve to shift, obtaining an advantage in sales or price over his rivals. He thus has open an added avenue for competition, which is not open if all sellers' products are homogeneous and invariant.

So far we have not inquired in detail about the relative effects of price increases and decreases on the individual firm's sales in monopolistic competition. By drawing his demand curve in Figure 7 as a continuous smooth line, we have momentarily implied that their effects will be comparable— that is, a 1-percent price increase will subtract about the same percentage from a firm's sales as a 1-percent price decrease adds to them. This would also suppose that the cross-elasticity of demand with any rival (or with the "average" rival) was identical for price increases or decreases. Although this is a possibility, it is no more probable than alternative situations. An equally possible situation may be one where, from some given initial price, the firm will gain more by a price reduction than it loses by a price increase of equivalent magnitude. In this case its demand curve will have a "kink" and will be less elastic above this price than below this price. Another qualification is as follows: As the cross-elasticities of demand among various pairs of products become lower, the demand curve of the individual seller, obviously, becomes less elastic. Monopolistic competition, thus, could include situations in which the single seller has a significant degree of discretionary control over price.

OLIGOPOLY

The individual seller's situation in each of the three classes of industries discussed so far is the same in two respects. First, in each case the seller faces a unique and definite schedule representing the relation of his price to his sales volume. Second, the price and output variations represented in this schedule may be undertaken on the legitimate supposition that there will be no induced or responding variation of other prices. In other words, the seller can expect that for each output he offers, there will be one definite selling price corresponding and not a range of possible prices any one of which might be experienced. And he can vary his price or output without inducing *retaliatory* changes in the prices of substitute products. The first condition more or less follows from the second since as soon as retaliatory changes are encountered, uncertainty as to the nature of these changes introduces a corresponding uncertainty as to the character of the seller's demand curve.

In the case of single-firm monopoly the seller's demand situation is of the type described because there is no substitute product "close enough" to have its sales significantly affected by the monopolist's price changes. In pure or monopolistic competition it is thus because the competing sellers are so numerous and small that no one of them commands a significant proportion of the total market of the industry and thus cannot influence industry output or the price or sales of any one rival perceptibly. In any event, no seller in any of these three categories has a demand which will shift about more or less unpredictably in response to competitive price *retaliations* if he changes his own price or output.

The demand situation of the seller is definitely otherwise in those important market categories in which the sellers are *few* in number—"pure oligopoly" and "differentiated oligopoly."

In its simplest form oligopoly is found in an industry in which the competing firms (producing either close or perfect substitute outputs) are several, but are few enough and large enough so that each controls enough of the total industry output that a moderate extension of its output will reduce the sales of rival firms by a noticeable amount. This is definitely the case if from two or three up to perhaps two dozen firms control an entire industry output with each controlling enough to affect rivals by its output changes. The condition obtains until the number of sellers is large enough and the individual share of industry output small enough, that one seller's output adjustments will not have a noticeable (or noticed) effect on others' sales.

In a more complex form oligopoly is found when each of several of the sellers in an industry controls a significant proportion of industry output but when the remainder of industry output is supplied by a number of small firms with very small individual shares of this output. This situation is strictly "oligopoly with a competitive fringe," but for purposes of initial classification we may include it under the general heading of oligopoly.

In an important proportion of our industries there is "fewness of sellers" in one of these two senses. Either the entire output of an industry is controlled by from two to perhaps a dozen firms, or a sizeable share of the industry's output (say from 40 to 90 percent) is controlled by a few large firms, while the remaining output is spread among 20 or 30 or 100 "small fry." In either event, the market structure is dominantly oligopolistic in that the leading pricing decisions are made by a few large firms, the individual demands for whose products are closely dependent on each of the others' prices and outputs.

The importance of this sort of market structure is, of course, a reflection of the high degree of concentration in a large portion of American industry, which in turn stems in part from the widespread organization of business firms for the exploitation of mass-production and mass-distribution techniques. Among the "pure oligopolies" (concentrated industries producing practically homogeneous products) we would count the steel, copper, aluminum, lead, cement, industrial alcohol, sulfur, and many other industries. Oligopolies producing differentiated products include the automobile, rubber tire, electric appliance, cigarette, soap, and many other industries. Oligopolistic industries account for substantially more output than all other types combined in the general area of manufacturing.[23] They are of considerable importance in other areas such as those of the distributive trades, contract construction, transportation, and finance. It would probably be safe to estimate that well over half of the value of all private-enterprise production in the United States emerges from industries where there is some evidence of oligopolistic structure.

In oligopoly the dominant feature of the individual seller's demand curve—or relation of his price to sales volume—is that it is at least potentially uncertain, uncertain because his own output adjustments will induce significant repercussions in rivals' prices or outputs which are not uniquely predictable. Each seller controls enough of the industry output so that a

[23] For data on number of sellers and concentration within industries see *Hearings* before the Subcommittee on Study of Monopoly Power, Committee on the Judiciary, House of Representatives, 81st Congress, 1st Session, Serial No. 14, Part 2-B (1950), pp. 1436-1456.

moderate change in his output will tend to elicit changes in his rivals' prices and outputs sufficient to affect his own sales. These induced changes or repercussions are not uniquely predictable according to any general rule. Each seller will logically respond to a rival's price or output change in a way which depends on his *conjectures* concerning the further responses by all of his rivals which will be induced either by the initial price or output change or by his response to that change. To carry the matter a step further, his reaction will logically depend upon his conjecture about the conjectures of his rivals, which guide them as they react to any initial or induced change. This is true of each seller in turn.

This dependence of rivals' reactions, and therefore of the individual seller's demand curve, upon a complex system of "crossed conjectures," provides the setting for basic uncertainty as to the character of this demand curve. The reason that no necessarily unique pattern of reactions (and therefore no certain sellers' demand curve) emerges from this complex of conjectures is that each seller, in reacting to rivals' price-output changes, is in a sense dually motivated. In part he is moved in the direction of co-operating with his rivals to reach a joint monopoly price and maximization of profits, but in part he tends in the direction of taking from them and for himself as much of the market as possible. So long as it is impossible for any seller to know to what extent each rival in turn will be guided in his reactions by each of these conflicting motives, it is obvious that no certain pattern of reactions to an initial price change may be expected and that no certain seller's demand curve emerges. The problem does not arise in monopoly, where there are no rivals, or in pure or monopolistic competition, where the price-output adjustments of each seller, whatever his motivation, induce no reactions by competitors.

The negative aspect of the seller's demand situation in oligopoly is thus that he does not necessarily have a definite demand curve for his own output. In any given situation, to be sure, he presumably has some going sales volume which depends upon his going price and those of his rivals, but at possible alternative prices there is potential uncertainty as to what his sales volume will be.

On the positive side, it is apparent that every seller's *estimate* of his probable demand curve is conditioned by the fact that the character of this curve depends upon the price reactions of his rivals. The several prices and outputs in oligopoly are *mutually interdependent* in a very direct way. Moreover, this mutual interdependence is *recognized* by all sellers, and its recognition by others is presumably recognized by all. Each seller acts on the supposition that others will react and on the supposition that in doing so they will look to the repercussions to their reactions. This notion is summarized by the term *mutually recognized interdependence,* which characterizes all oligopoly. It is thus not impossible that under various special circumstances some particular pattern of rivalrous reactions may become established which permits the individual oligopolists to feel rather certain about their own demand curves.

So long as the individual oligopolist acts independently, to be sure, and so long as in addition he is unsure of his various rivals' specific motivations or has no long basis of experience with his rivals which would reveal these motivations, he has no unique demand curve relating his price to his sales volume. Logically there is a number of possible provisional or conjectural demand curves he might imagine.[24] Even here, however, the number of major possibilities is limited. In differentiated oligopoly, for example, where each seller may quote a separate price, a price cut by one seller may be met by no price reaction, by a smaller price cut by rivals, by an equivalent cut, or by a retaliatory price cut of larger magnitude. A similar range of possibilities exists for reactions to a price increase. For each principal possibility a provisional demand curve may be constructed by the individual seller, and the number of principal possibilities is not indefinite. It should be noted, moreover, that, with the exception of possible retaliatory price cuts—as when a rival might meet a five-cent price cut with a ten-cent cut and possibly a price war—the range of possibilities lies effectively between a "competitive" and a "monopoly" limit. At one extreme the rivals of a seller might not react at all to his price changes, in which case his demand curve would be—for pure and differentiated oligopoly—of the same order as that of the seller in pure or monopolistic competition, although less elastic. At the other extreme (barring retaliation) the rivals might just match price changes, in which case his demand curve would appear as a share of the industry demand curve or like that of a single-firm monopolist. Or his demand curve might lie between these limits. Its character may be complicated by the fact that rivals react differently to price cuts than to price rises. But generally it may be said that, barring retaliatory cuts or price-warring tactics, the oligopolist's demand curve (for upward or downward price movements) is neither more elastic than in competition (pure or monopolistic) nor less elastic than in monopoly. It may still be quite uncertain within this range.

Experience may greatly reduce or even eliminate the range of uncertainty about rivals' reactions. In an oligopoly with a stable membership of firms over a period of years experiment with price changes may lead to the establishment of a normal or generally expected pattern of reactions to price or output changes, and given this, all sellers have a fairly certain estimate of their own demand curves. Prolonged and fairly meticulous observance of such a pattern by all firms in an industry may lead to what is effectively a *tacit understanding* among rivals which all observe and accept. Such a pattern may be of various types. A commonly observed pattern is that where

[24] See Chamberlin, *op. cit.,* Chap. 3; also R. F. Kahn, "The Problem of Duopoly," *Economic Journal,* March 1937.

all sellers recognize a *price leader,* one who assumes the initiative in raising and lowering price and whose price changes are always promptly matched by the other firms in the industry. Emergence of such a pattern suggests tacit acceptance by all of a "live and let live" policy of sharing the market at a single price and presumably of allowing one seller to lead the price to the most advantageous level. In this case the oligopoly tacitly becomes a quasi-unified group of sellers who view the industry demand curve for their combined outputs as a *shared* demand curve to be cooperatively exploited, possibly as a monopolist would exploit it. The individual seller's demand curve in this case—when he changes price—becomes a fraction of the industry demand curve, with elasticity similar to that of the industry curve. Other patterns of reaction, however—reflecting more emphasis on interfirm antagonism and less on joint exploitation of the industry demand—may and do emerge.

Since oligopolistic uncertainty may stand in the way of profitable price adjustments, there is a natural desire on the part of sellers to eliminate it. Experience or experiment over time may accomplish this end, and in satisfactory fashion. But there is unquestionably a tendency to take care of it more conclusively by forming agreements among oligopolists as to price and output. These agreements may permit collusive exploitation of the industry demand after the fashion of a monopolist and award to each seller what is effectively a predetermined share of the industry demand at every price charged in common by the agreeing partners. Such agreements are illegal in the United States under the antitrust laws, and, moreover, the inherent antagonisms among sellers may frequently forestall their adoption, but they are not unknown. Under such agreement a fairly definite demand situation for the individual oligopolist emerges, or, to put it another way, all may look past their individual demand curves toward the industry demand curve and its joint exploitation by the agreeing firms.

To summarize this discussion, there are several major alternative possibilities regarding the shape of the individual seller's demand curve in oligopoly or his estimate of his price-sales relationship:

1. Simple uncertainty about the net effects of changing his price or output. This means there is no method of choice among a range of alternative conjectured demand curves.
2. More or less complete certainty that all rivals will match prices and tacitly share the market, perhaps under the guide of a price leader. This means joint exploitation of the industry demand curve, or what amounts to a given share of the industry demand curve for each seller for concurrent price changes with his rivals.
3. Approximately the same result from a collusive agreement among the rival sellers.

4. Some other predicted pattern of rivals' reactions which would lead to a particular estimate of the seller's demand curve but not necessarily that found with price leadership or collusive agreement.

The sellers in a given oligopolistic industry may have individual demand curves reflecting any of these situations, or possibly others. In a given oligopoly, moreover, the sellers may shift from one sort of demand situation to another over time.

The preceding remarks about sellers' demand curves apply in general to any oligopoly, whether "pure" or "differentiated." In pure oligopoly the demand curve of any seller will reflect the fact that, whatever the pattern of price and output reactions, all sellers' prices for the single homogeneous product must in general become identical. In differentiated oligopoly the individual sellers of imperfect substitute products may charge somewhat different prices while all attract customers, and their demand curves may reflect their ability to make very small independent price changes without eliciting automatic reactions from rivals. In the main, however, the alternative demand situations available to the sellers in pure and differentiated oligopoly are very similar. The principal distinctions between the two sorts of oligopoly result from the differing importance of selling costs and will be discussed later.

All of the discussions above have referred implicitly to the demands for the outputs of sellers in oligopolistic industries whose market shares are large enough that their price-output adjustments affect rivals perceptibly. There must be some such sellers in any oligopoly. But there may also be some small sellers with insignificant market shares. Demand curves for the latter sorts of sellers will, of course, tend to be like those of sellers in pure or monopolistic competition, depending upon whether the oligopoly is pure or differentiated. This will, in any event, tend to be true unless the large sellers "police and coerce" the small sellers by explicitly threatening reaction to their individual price-output adjustments. Where a number of small sellers coexist in an industry with several large sellers, price analysis must consider the essential differences in their individual demand curves and the resulting effects upon their policies.

THE DEMANDS FOR INDIVIDUAL SELLERS' OUTPUTS—SUMMARY

We have just surveyed the character of the individual seller's demand curve in each of five main classes of industry—single-firm monopolies, pure and differentiated oligopolies, and industries in pure and monopolistic competition. The economy includes industries in all these classifications; therefore, we shall find sellers faced with demand situations characteristic of each class.

As we have seen, the demand for the seller's output may differ quite distinctly from class to class.

Why are these differences among sellers' demand schedules important? Their principal importance is that they reflect varying degrees of ability on the part of the seller to influence or control his price. In monopolistic or pure competition the individual seller has little or no control over price— he either faces (in the latter case) a given market price or has available to him (in the former) a narrow range of possible prices in the neighborhood of the prices of his competitors. In single-firm monopoly he has a very wide choice of prices, which is reflected in the fact that his demand curve (an industry demand curve) is far from perfectly elastic. In oligopoly his effective control over price may be at or near either of the extremes just mentioned, or somewhere in between, depending on the pattern of behavior which emerges from the situation of oligopolistic interdependence.

Another way of putting this is to say that the variety of sellers' demand curves reflect varying degrees to which individual sellers will be influenced by or take into account the elasticity of the industry demand curve. To what extent is any one seller, in contemplating a given percentage change in his output, influenced by the percentage change in the industry price which will occur if all sellers in the industry (as they commonly may) make the same percentage output change concurrently? And to what extent does each seller disregard this relationship and look only to a somewhat different reaction of price to quantity which would hold if he and only he varied his output?

The individual seller's demand curve, and its relation to the industry demand curve, answers this question. The single-firm monopolist looks directly to the industry demand curve, since it is also his own demand curve, and is fully influenced by the effects of industry output change on industry price. Sellers in pure and monopolistic competition, on the other hand, are scarcely aware of the industry price-output relation. Since each supplies a negligible fraction of industry output, his view is that his output variations influence price very little if at all, and he is, therefore, uninfluenced by the sort of response of price to output which will occur if he and all his competitors make independent but simultaneous adjustments of output. Sellers in an oligopoly may, because of interdependence, be variously influenced by the elasticity of the industry demand curve for their combined outputs.

The significance of this difference among sellers is that they will, therefore, tend to behave differently with respect to determining prices and outputs. The monopolist, looking directly to the industry demand curve, has a maximum incentive to restrict output (to some most profitable point) in order to raise price. In pure or monopolistic competition, on the other hand, each of a large number of competitors overlooks what happens to price if they all extend or restrict output together, and acts as if his own output has little or no effect on price. A group of such sellers, all acting independently, therefore, evidences little aggregate incentive to restrict industry output in order to raise price. In so doing the competitive group as a whole, with a given industry demand curve, will be led to produce a larger aggregate output than would a monopolist. The position of oligopolistic sellers in this regard is "somewhere in between"—at or near the monopoly pole or perhaps tending in the competitive direction.

The significance of differences in sellers' demand curves is thus that they reflect differing degrees to which sellers will take into account in setting their own prices and outputs the relation between industry price and output which ultimately governs their welfare as a group. The major reason for such differences is found in differences in the number of sellers in the industry or, more generally, in differences in the number and size distribution of sellers. It is this which primarily determines the extent to which the seller may independently influence industry price and will thus be led to consider the elasticity of the industry demand curve. For this reason industries are classified primarily on the basis of the number of sellers. The degree of product differentiation within the industry is also significant, so far as it determines the degree of independent discretionary control over the relation of his price to that of his rivals which the seller enjoys. Since such discretionary control is likely ordinarily to be slight, however, the major significance of product differentiation does not lie in its effects on the *shape* of the individual seller's demand curve. It is found rather, and very significantly, in the fact that by altering the pattern of differentiation—either by varying his product or by varying his sales-promotion activities—the individual seller may substantially affect the *position* of his own demand curve in relation to others. Analysis of the implications of this ability and its exercise will be developed in later chapters.

The preceding emphasizes the differences among industries with respect to the demand curves envisaged by individual sellers and, hence, with respect to the type of response which the sellers will make to a given industry demand. These differences are important. Nevertheless, a basic similarity among industries in this regard should not be overlooked. As a matter of degree, to be sure, different industries may respond somewhat differently to their industry demands by virtue of differences in structure and corresponding differences in the sellers' demand curves. On the other hand, every industry is guided more or less directly by its industry demand curve. It tends to respond to the expressed demands of buyers for the sort of good it produces in any of a variety of ways, which are in any case likely to produce some rough correspondence of the cost of production to price. Overlooking for the moment the variations among industries with respect to the exact character of this adjustment, therefore, it is true that the interrelated family of demands for all goods serve in a rough sense as a guide to the production of various sorts of goods and, thus, to the allocation of resources among uses. To be sure, the existence of monopolistic situations at many points tends to impair the perfection with which the price system might otherwise work to allocate resources, but it must be recognized that it still tends to work, though in impaired fashion, in a very definite sense.

E. THE DEMAND FOR COMMODITIES—SUMMARY

Let us now consider as a whole the foregoing analysis of the demand for commodities. This analysis was begun by an inquiry into the nature of the demand curve for the output of the individual seller—of his view of the relation of the price he charges to his sales volume. At the outset it appeared that to understand the nature and significance of this relation we must understand something about the demands for goods in general and their inter-relationships.

The analysis of demands in general was begun by recognizing the existence of an extremely wide variety of individual firm outputs available for the satisfaction of the wants of buyers. These outputs are in a general way substitute sources of satisfaction to buyers. However, we find that the *substitution relation* among pairs of such outputs is not always the same. Some pairs of outputs are close substitutes to buyers—they provide similar sources of satisfaction and easily replace each other in satisfying buyers' wants. Other pairs of outputs are poor or distant substitutes to buyers—they provide distinct sources of satisfaction, and one does not readily replace the other in satisfying a buyer's wants, so that successive unit additions of one matched by successive unit subtractions of the other in his budget would tend to lessen the total satisfaction he received from goods in general. The substitution relations of the outputs of various firms are usually found (or to a reasonably good approximation) to be such that these outputs fall into a large number of groups of close substitutes of such a character that the outputs within each group are generally close substitutes for each other but distant substitutes for all others. Each of these groups may be called an "industry," and the combined output of the industry may be designated as a commodity or a good.

Thus, buyers have available a large number of industry outputs or goods, each of which is a relatively poor substitute for every other. Because these goods are poor substitutes, any buyer will find that successive increments in the amount purchased of any one—virtually in the place of others—will add successively smaller increments to his total satisfaction, either absolutely or as compared to the increments to satisfaction provided by the last additions to (or subtractions from) his purchases of other goods. If he wishes to maximize his satisfaction, therefore, he will not spend all of his income on any one good, but he will seek a balance where the incremental satisfaction provided by the last unit added of each good is sufficient to justify the satisfaction he foregoes by not spending his money on other goods instead. He will find a position of maximum satisfaction where his purchases are so designed that the proportion of the increments-to-satisfaction-of-the-last-unit (or of the "marginal utilities") of every pair of goods is the same as the proportion of their prices.

If this is the rule of buyer action, a number of conclusions follow. *First,* the quantity purchased of any good at a given price depends on the prices of all other goods; or, in general, all price-quantity combinations for all goods make up a mutually interdependent family. The demand for any good at a given price depends not only on buyer income but also on the level of all other prices. We cannot know the *position* of any one demand without knowing all other prices. *Second,* buyers will react to a reduction in the price of any one good by increasing their purchases of it in order to bring the marginal satisfaction from it again into the satisfaction-maximizing balance with price. This means that the demand curve for any good or industry output will be sloped negatively, indicating larger purchases at lower prices. *Third,* various industry demand curves may have various elasticity or responsiveness of quantity purchased to price, depending upon the general substitutability of their outputs for other goods.

Fourth, as long as we are speaking of industry outputs, the price adjustments described by the demand curve for any one industry may be made without eliciting any perceptible reaction in any other price, since there are no close substitutes for the industry output. *Fifth,* the position of each demand curve is, nevertheless, substantially affected by the level of all other prices in general (though insignificantly by the level of any one). Thus, it is found that any one industry demand curve represents no more than the price-quantity combination for any one good in a given situation of income and other prices. It is seen also that all industry demand curves are an interdependent family, each shifting in response to general price changes for all other industries. Yet, the sellers in any industry are likely to look no further than, if as far as, this industry-demand-curve relation in deciding upon profit-maximizing prices.

The above gives us an over-all idea of the familial interrelationship of the prices and quantities bought of all goods or industry outputs as determined by buyers' choice patterns and satisfaction-maximizing behavior. It also reveals the character of the response of quantity bought to the price of any one good, other prices remaining substantially unchanged. It further provides the setting for understanding the relation of any individual firm's price to its quantity of sales.

The individual seller may ordinarily be viewed as providing either part or all of the output of any industry but not more.[25] The manner in which he views his relation of output to price is a matter of importance since it strongly influences the quantity of output he tends to produce. If every seller viewed as his demand curve a curve of elasticity identical to that of the industry demand curve, this would be very significant. Such a curve would show a distinct departure from perfect elasticity, or, in other words, a rather important response of price to moderate variations in quantity of sales. It would thus give the seller a significant incentive to restrict output in order to raise the price up to some point. However, such a view on the seller's part is automatically encountered only in the case of a single-firm monopoly, where one seller supplies the entire industry output. In other situations, where the seller supplies only part of the industry output, this may or may not be true. In oligopoly—with few sellers—the mutually recognized interdependence of sellers may lead them to act effectively as one or as if each had a demand curve of elasticity similar to that of the industry demand curve. But it may not, and this will require analysis.

In competitive industries—pure or monopolistic—however, we have seen that the individual sellers may disregard their individual effects on industry price and determine output on the supposition that price is exactly or approximately given. Each views his demand curve as perfectly elastic or very elastic. Thus, the price-output relation shown by the industry demand curve is disregarded by each; therefore, the aggregation of many similar independent output adjustments may bring about an effect on industry price which no one of them feels responsible for, takes account of in decision making, or can control. Their *competition* may lead to a much different adjustment of output to industry price than would occur with a single-firm monopoly. It is because of the significance of these differences in sellers' demand curves that we have been led to inquire in detail into their nature in various categories of industry.

As we have seen, the primary determinant of their character is the number and size distribution of sellers in the industry, although the degree of product differentiation within the industry also has some bearing. More generally, the seller's demand curve within any industry (other than a single-firm monopoly) reflects the fact that the several products are close or perfect substitutes, among which buyers shift easily or with no resistance, the existence or absence of interdependence of sellers depending upon the share of the industry supply controlled by each. It also reflects the fact that the group of products are together distant substitutes for any other good. Thus the character of the individual seller's demand curve is logically explicable in

[25] If a seller produces outputs sold in two or more industries, we may treat his operations in each separately in analyzing his demand curves.

terms of the same theory of consumers' choice which explains the character of the complex of industry demands.[26]

How may this analysis of demand be employed in the general analysis of the determination of prices and outputs and of the allocation of resources among uses? First, having blocked out the nature of the complex of demands for all goods, we may on the most general level proceed to analyze how the responses of all firms in all industries to this complex of demands tend to adjust the composition of total output to the needs of buyers as expressed in this complex. Second, in order to do so, we shall need initially to determine how each industry in turn, considered separately, adjusts its output to any going demand curve (thereafter considering the cross-adaptation of various individual industry adjustments). Here the concept of the industry demand curve will be extremely useful. Finally, in order to analyze the adjustment of industry output to demand, we shall need to analyze the response of the individual firm in each category of industry to its own demand and the manner in which the combination of such responses to individual firm demands leads, in each category, to an adjustment of industry output to industry demand. Here the analysis of individual firm demand curves in industries of different structures will play a primary role.

The preceding states the applications of demand analysis in the order of their general importance. As a matter of procedure, we shall necessarily move through these applications in the reverse order—looking first to the adjustment of the firm to its demand in each of the several categories of industry, second, to the industry adjustment of the complex of firms to industry demands, and third, to the interaction of all industry prices and outputs to determine the composition and pricing of total output. Before we can enter fully into these inquiries, however, we must consider a second sort of determining calculation which sellers make—that of the relation of their outputs to their costs of production.

[26] Some writers, bothered by the lack of logical nicety involved in the use of the "industry" concept in a world where industries tend to overlap or have indefinite boundaries, would place less initial emphasis in analyzing demand upon industry groupings of firms. Instead they would emphasize principally the demand for the output of the individual firm and the relation of each firm's demand to the prices of other firms' outputs (measured by the cross-elasticity of demand). This approach, by attempting less than the "industry" approach, avoids the use of precisely defined concepts which lack *exact* counterparts in the economy we actually have. As such a demand analysis is employed in analyzing price determination, however, it must eventually refer to closely interdependent groups of firms, or provisional "industries." Careful and critical employment of either approach should lead to satisfactory and similar results. For a discussion of the alternative approach mentioned, see Robert Triffin, *Monopolistic Competition and General Equilibrium Theory* (Cambridge: Harvard University Press, 1940).

SUPPLEMENTARY READINGS

ALFRED MARSHALL, *Principles of Economics* (8th ed.), Book III.

EDWARD H. CHAMBERLIN, *The Theory of Monopolistic Competition* (5th ed.), Cambridge, Mass.: Harvard University Press, 1946, Chaps. 3-4.

J. R. HICKS, *Value and Capital,* Oxford University Press, London, 1939, Part I.

HENRY SCHULTZ, *The Theory and Measurement of Demand,* Chicago: University of Chicago Press, 1938.

ROBERT TRIFFIN, *Monopolistic Competition and General Equilibrium Theory,* Cambridge: Harvard University Press, 1940.

GEORGE J. STIGLER, *The Theory of Price,* New York: The Macmillan Company, 1946, Chaps. 4-6.

RUBY TURNER NORRIS, *The Theory of Consumer's Demand,* New Haven: Yale University Press, 1941.

3 THE PRODUCTION COSTS OF THE FIRM

The decisions of individual firms regarding quantity of output and selling price, which are the primary determinants of the composition of total output, turn in part on the demand curves for their outputs. But they also depend on what it costs to produce the various products and on the relationships, firm by firm, of production cost to the rate of output. We have surveyed the conditions of demand for the outputs of individual firms and of industries and have analyzed their origins and their significant characteristics. Next we should examine, initially for the firm, the character and the determinants of costs and of the relation of cost to output.

A. FUNDAMENTAL CONSIDERATIONS

THE DEFINITION OF COSTS OF PRODUCTION

To decide fairly precisely what should be meant by the term "costs of production" is an initial necessity. Such costs may initially, and for most purposes of analysis, be defined in the way most familiar to all of us. That is, costs of production may be understood to be the amounts of money paid out or contracted to be paid or otherwise sacrificed by the firm in order to secure the productive services with which to produce output. The costs of production of any particular aggregate or unit of output, thus, may refer to the monetary sacrifice of the firm in securing productive services used in producing that output. This, in turn, will represent that proportion of all money payments or other sacrifices in securing such services—past, present, or future—which the firm considers to be allocable to the production of that output.

In a general way this corresponds to the amounts of money the firm actually pays or contracts to pay to purchase the productive services needed to produce a given output. But not exactly. This is primarily because the firm may use some productive services which it does not purchase or "pay for" directly but in the using of which in production it implicitly makes a monetary sacrifice. Such is true when the services of an owner of the firm are used in management without payment of anything called a salary, or when owners' invested funds are used without direct payment of interest as such, the implicit interest return being included in "profits." These services are not purchased or paid for as such, but their use in production subjects the firm to a financial sacrifice. This sacrifice is equal to the payments which these services could secure in their most remunerative alternative employment—in general, their market value as determined by other uses. It is thus necessary in arriving at the full cost of production to add to payments made or contracted for purchased services an *imputed value* of nonpurchased services used in production, an amount sometimes called the "opportunity price" of these services. The cost of production of any output then may be defined as either the purchase price or the imputed value of all productive services used in producing the output and is equivalent to the total monetary sacrifice of the firm made to secure it.[1]

This cost of production, or measure of such cost, refers evidently to the sacrifices made by the firm as measured in money terms. Therefore, it is appropriately termed the *private* (money) *cost* of production. It is the cost, and the only cost, which the firm will presumably take into account in decision making. It may be distinguished from "social cost," which applies to the cost to society of producing a given output.

The private money cost to the firm of producing any output evidently depends upon (1) the physical quantities of actual resources or services therefrom used in production and (2) the prices which the firm pays for or imputes to these resources or resource services. The private money cost of producing a ton of steel depends upon the quantities of iron ore, limestone, coal, blast-furnace use, etc. used in its production and upon the prices of these resources or resource services. To arrive at the money cost we need to multiply the quantity used of each resource by its price and to add up the resulting arithmetical products. The quantities of resources or their services consumed in producing a given amount of output are sometimes called the "real costs" of the output; the total money value of these resources or services, as defined, is ordinarily the private cost in money terms.

As already indicated, it is this private money cost which will matter to the firm and which, therefore, will enter directly into the analysis of firm behavior. It is interesting to inquire also, however, what are the costs to society or to persons in general other than the owners of the firm, of producing a given output? Superficially, it is simply the amounts of physical re-

---

[1] This definition is at all ambiguous only if the firm is able to purchase some productive services at a price less than their market value in some alternative use, in which case the higher value is a more consistent measure of the cost of producing the given output than is the actual purchase price. In such a case the firm would have a certain difference between outlays for production and costs of production which would represent a gain logically separate from that earned in the given line of production. Such instances are presumably rare.

sources used in production, which we have referred to as "real costs." More fundamentally, we may identify two other meanings of social cost. First, the cost to society of producing a given output may be regarded as the *value of the output foregone* in other lines by producing in the output line in question. It is what we do without elsewhere in order to have a particular thing or the value of the alternative output we could produce with the physical resources used to produce the given output. Thus, if it takes a ton of steel to produce a military tank, the social cost of the steel used is the value of the steel as represented in dishpans, automobiles, refrigerators, and so forth. Cost then is regarded always as an alternative value of real resources used. In the case of labor costs leisure may constitute an "alternative occupation" to be included and valued with the rest. Second, the "social" (or "real") cost of producing any output may be defined in terms of the amount of "pain," or unpleasantness, or real human sacrifice spent in production—for example, the amount of dissatisfaction resulting from a day's labor. This may work out (although on shaky psychological grounds) for human labor, but it is hard to extend it to inanimate resources used in production. We shall, therefore, define "social cost" only in terms of alternative values foregone. "Real cost" will be used arbitrarily to refer simply to the quantity of physical resources or their services used in getting output.

For the moment the preceding constitutes simply a sort of philosophical digression on the "true meaning" of costs. At a later stage the concepts of real and social costs will be quite useful in analysis. It may be noted that private money costs are not always or in general a precise or entirely accurate measure of social costs so far as the prices firms pay for productive services may be variously related to the prices of the goods they could produce in other lines. They tend to become so only under special circumstances of market organization and enterprise behavior. This conclusion will emerge from subsequent analysis. At present we shall be entirely concerned with the private money costs of firms producing outputs—and it is these we shall refer to for the moment simply as the costs of production.

THE LEVEL OF PRODUCTION COSTS

The costs of production which firms incur in producing various different goods are important because, taken in conjunction with demands for such goods, they determine the quantities of goods to be produced and sold and their prices. As we turn to the analysis of production costs of various goods by various firms, two matters seem important. First, the general level of cost of producing any good is significant—that is, the general range within which the cost in dollars per unit of output will fall. This, with the demand for the good, will tend to set the range within which price and output will fall, provided prices are at least roughly tied to costs. Similarly, the differences in the levels of cost among different goods, taken in relation to the various demands, will dominantly influence the proportions in which various goods are produced. A second matter of importance is *the relation of cost to output* for each good—the manner in which its aggregate or unit costs vary as its output is progressively extended—since this also obviously will influence pricing and output.

This variation of cost with output may be investigated both for the single firm and for the industry of firms (possibly variable in number) as they change output together. We shall concentrate in this chapter primarily on the variation of cost with variation in the output of the individual firm.

First, however, let us consider the matter of the general level of cost. The general level of cost of producing any good evidently depends upon (1) the amount of productive services—labor, machine hours, and so forth— used in producing any unit amount of the product and (2) the money prices of these productive services paid or imputed by the firm. That is, it depends on the real cost in resources and the going prices of the resources.

The general level of real costs (and, consequently, of money costs) per unit of output for a product depends upon what type of product it is, and it varies greatly from one product to another, depending on the size and complexity of the good. Thus, automobiles are quite costly in real terms; refrigerators require fewer man and machine hours and materials; hairpins are much less costly in real terms. Such real costs are not immutably given for any good, however. They are contingent also on the technique of production used and on the efficiency of the productive services employed. Consequently, the general level of real cost for any good is given only as of some currently available technique and level of efficiency of productive services. Under such given conditions, however, there will be wide differences in the level of real costs among various goods.

Given the levels of real costs for various goods and given the prices of the productive services which comprise the real costs, a corresponding money cost for each good automatically emerges. The *relevant* cost to the firm, of course, will be the lowest attainable cost of producing any given output, which implies a corresponding selection of the most economical techniques. All other possible costs to the firm are usually irrelevant and may be neglected. The differences of money costs between two goods are quite simply explained by real costs alone if they both use precisely the same types of productive services since then the same set of prices for such services is involved in each case. For example, if a trash can costs 20 pounds of steel and an hour of labor, and an ashtray costs half a pound of steel and 6 minutes of labor, we can see readily that if steel is 4 cents a pound and labor $2 an hour (for whatever reason), then a trash can will cost $2.80 and an ashtray $0.22. Where different resources are used in producing different goods, we are drawn for the explanation of money cost differences inevitably into an explanation of differences in the prices of different resources. Thus, an atomic bomb costs more than a TNT bomb of equivalent weight of explosive not because it contains more plutonium than the other bomb contains TNT, but because the price of plutonium is substantially higher. To explain the difference in money cost we must explain this difference in prices. For the moment we may observe simply that differences in the prices of various resources are based largely on the relative scarcity of their supply and the relative intensity of the demands for them. Given such price differences of the resources so determined, the money cost to the firm of any product follows directly from its real costs. The price determination of resources may be considered at a later point.

As with real costs, the general levels of the money costs of various products differ widely, and this difference in level is of primary importance in determining the composition of total output. Having underlined this obvious but important fact, let us turn to the manner in which the cost of any product may vary with variation in its output.

THE VARIATION OF COST WITH OUTPUT

The analysis of pricing would be much simpler if there were, with given productive techniques, some invariant cost per unit of output for every good regardless of the amount produced. This would be true, for example, if, with a certain production technique, steel ingots would cost $60 per ton to produce regardless of whether the production per month were one ton, 100 tons, 10,000 tons, or 1,000,000 tons, and if, under similar circumstances, beef cattle cost $15 per 100 pounds to raise regardless of whether the annual output were 50 steers, 50,000,000 steers, or anywhere between. But we rarely find such an invariant relation of unit cost to output. Some systematic variation of cost with output is ordinarily found, and the character of this variation must be considered in analyzing price determination.

As we make an initial survey of the possibilities of cost variation, it appears that for any particular good or industry output the variation of cost with output may be analyzed for productive "units" of various scope. Primarily, we may distinguish as units the individual firm and the industry. That is, the individual firm may vary its output over a considerable range, and the industry of many firms may vary its output over a wider range through the concurrent variations of its members. Or, in effect, the output variation on which we may focus attention might be, let us say, the increase of the rubber tire output of the Top Century Tire Company by 10 percent, or 1,000,000 tires per month, or the increase of the tire output of the whole tire industry of the United States by 10 percent, or 7,000,000 tires per month. For various reasons the pattern of variation of cost with output may not be exactly the same in the two cases. Some principal reasons for this, even if the possibility of different cost variation patterns for different firms in the industry are overlooked, are (1) that various member firms may contribute to an increase in industry output in a variety of different possible proportions, (2) that industry output changes, being large, may induce changes in the prices of productive service that the individual firm's output changes, being smaller, would not induce, and (3) that industry output increases may in certain settings be accomplished by adding new firms to the industry rather than by adding to the output of any one of them. Thus, it is necessary to analyze in turn the variation of cost with output first for the firm and then for the industry.

In this chapter we shall study primarily the variation of cost with output within the individual firm since it is this which bears most proximately on the firm's price-output decisions.

As the firm varies its output (or the industry, for that matter), it is evident that there are two distinguishable sources of variation in its money costs per unit of output. First, the real costs per unit of output—that is, the physical quantities of productive services used to produce a unit of output—may vary. It may take different amounts of labor, plant, materials, and so forth to produce a unit of output at one rate of output than at another. With given prices of productive services this will potentially lead to a resulting variation in money costs per unit of output. Second, the prices of the productive services used may be induced to vary as more or less of them is demanded by the firm as it has larger or smaller output. Such variation will also obviously have an effect on money cost variation.

The individual firm may ordinarily use such a minor fraction of the total supply of any productive service that its output variations (and corresponding variations in the use of such services) will have no perceptible effect on the prices of the productive services it buys. Therefore, the sole source of cost variation for the firm may typically be regarded as variation in real costs, simply reflected in a corresponding money cost variation at any going level of prices for productive services. Exceptions to this rule, however, must be recognized. When we analyze industry output variation, on the other hand, induced variations in the prices of productive services may play a significant role in the total variation of costs.

DIFFERENT WAYS OF VARYING OUTPUT—LONG AND SHORT PERIOD

Let us now turn directly to the relation of cost to output for the firm. The question posed is what happens to a firm's cost per unit of output when, with a given technique, it extends its output progressively from zero to some indefinite limit? The question may be simplified and yet remain realistic if we impose the supposition that the prices it pays for productive services are given and invariant regardless of its output. The phrasing of the main question, it may be noted, indicates a hope that there are some things about cost-output relations which may be said equally of every firm in the economy, regardless of its product.

An initial consideration of this question suggests that how the firm's costs respond to its output variations will depend somewhat on *how* it accomplishes its output variation. In general, a firm may vary output either (1) by holding a "plant" or plants—that is, an aggregation of relatively long-lived facilities such as factory buildings and machinery—in fixed amount and varying the rate of use of such plant; (2) by varying the size or scale of the productive plant (by building more or retiring some) while only adapting the rate of use of plant to take best advantage of the changing scale, or (3) by some combination of the two measures—for example, by building more plant and by using both this and the previous plant more intensively. To simplify the analysis we will emphasize only the two extreme possibilities. That is, the firm may vary output either by *variations in scale* of plant (with adaptations of utilization) or by *variations in utilization* of plant. Output variations accomplished either way may influence the cost of production per unit of output, but the influence may be significantly different in the two cases. Therefore, it will be necessary to distinguish the relation of cost to output with variation in utilization from that with variation in scale.

Both relations are emphasized because the firm may be able to vary output only in one way in some settings and in either way in others. The prime determinant of the options in this respect is the length of the period of time within which the output variations must be made. If the period is so short that fixed plant cannot be varied in size, then only variations in the rate of utilization of plant can be used to vary output within such a period. If, on the other hand, the period is long enough to permit unrestricted variation in the size of plant (or in the quantities of *all* productive services used), variation in scale is available as a method of output adjustment as well, and, since it will generally be the more efficient method of output variation, will be used. This leads us to an analytical distinction in the treatment of cost variation between the *short period* and the *long period* (sometimes also designated as *short run* and *long run*), distinguished by whether or not their duration is sufficient to permit free variation in the size of fixed plant by the firm.

To analyze price determination, it is thus necessary to determine the general characteristics of the relation of cost to output for the firm both with variation of rate of use of plant in the short period and with variations in the scale of plant (with adaptations of utilization) in the long period. We will turn first to cost-output relations for the firm in the short period. The firm, of course, does not make decisions only with respect to the rate of output with given product and given technique of production. It must at least intermittently decide exactly what product to produce and what technique or design of plant to use, and this with an eye to the effect of product and of technique on the cost of production. Given these decisions, however, and given also the prevailing efficiency of productive factors, it will be positively concerned with the relationship of the money cost of production to the rate of output.

B. SHORT-RUN COST VARIATION

DEFINITION OF THE "SHORT PERIOD" AND OF FIXED AND VARIABLE COSTS

The "short-period" relation of cost to output necessarily refers to a somewhat arbitrarily defined time interval. Ordinarily we consider it an interval during which certain productive factors employed by the firm, such as the building, heavy machinery, and permanent supervisory staff, are present in fixed or invariant amounts and during which the aggregate quantity of other factors, such as labor and materials, is potentially variable in amount. Yet there is no clear-cut distinction in practice between "fixed" and "variable" factors. In effect, the longer a time period we contemplate, the more factors are potentially variable and the fewer are fixed. In formal logic, therefore, the short period to which we shall refer is no especial chronological time interval uniformly applicable to all sorts of firms, but a sort of "operational period," arbitrarily defined as of such length that buildings and long-lived equipment are invariant in quantity and that labor and materials are freely variable in quantity. The common-sense counterpart of this interval for most manufacturing enterprises would perhaps be from six months to two or three years from any beginning date. For other types of enterprise it might be longer or shorter.

In this short period the firm has (by definition) certain "fixed factors" and certain "variable factors"—plant and equipment, let us say, on the one hand, and labor and materials on the other. It can increase or decrease its output in this period by varying the aggregate amount of variable factors it uses, or, in effect, by varying the *proportion* between fixed and variable factors.

Correspondingly, the firm in the short period finds that its costs fall into two general categories—*fixed costs* and *variable costs*. *Fixed costs* are those which in the short period are in the aggregate absolutely invariant to changes in output; in precise terms, they are the aggregate amount of costs the firm would incur at a *zero* output. The *variable costs* are costs which in the aggregate vary with output, or, in effect, any costs added as a result of any increase of output above zero. In general, the fixed costs will also be the costs of fixed factors and will include depreciation of plant, interest cost on investment, and salaries of permanent managerial staff. Similarly, the *variable costs* will ordinarily be the costs of variable factors, such as wages and material costs. But the categories are not necessarily fully congruent, and there may be some fixed-factor costs which are variable and some variable-factor costs which are fixed. The distinction between fixed costs and variable costs is, therefore, an independent one.

The content of fixed costs for a chosen interval is sometimes obscure, and an additional comment may be in order. Fixed costs for an interval will ordinarily include, first, costs incurred in the past—before this period—and allocated to the period regardless of its output. These are amortizations of past costs, like depreciation of the cost of equipment on hand which will occur even at zero output, although such allocations may be intrinsically arbitrary. Such costs are already "sunk" and cannot be lessened by any stratagem. Second, fixed costs will include current outlays, made during this period, which will in any event be made at zero output. It will be noted that the second category of fixed cost, though fixed for the current short period, are evidently made in anticipation of operations in a future period. Although currently fixed, therefore, they are—for a *longer* period of calculation—essentially variable costs the future recovery of which is anticipated. It may also be noted that economic fixed costs and accounting overhead costs are not identical. The latter include any costs which are allocated by formula against different lots or units of output and may include variable as well as fixed costs.

THE SHORT-RUN RELATION OF COST TO OUTPUT—AGGREGATE COST

Given this dichotomy of the firm's short-run costs into fixed and variable costs, we may next inquire how such costs respond to variation in the firm's output.

The relationship of cost to output (with given product, technique, and efficiency) can be represented in a *cost schedule* for the firm, which shows the alternative costs of production at which various alternative outputs can be produced. The same information can be shown diagrammatically in a *cost curve,* which plots the variation of cost with output. Such a cost schedule or cost curve can be either for the *short run* or for the *long run*. In either case the cost schedule and curve should represent a net relation cost c to output q, in the sense that it shows only those variations in cost which occur because of or directly in response to variations in the output in question. Costs may in general be influenced by or vary in response to not only output variations, but also independent variations in the prices of productive services, and possibly variations in other variables. The cost schedule or curve, however, shows only the response of cost to output alone, under the assumption that all other things influencing cost are given, except so far as they themselves may be directly induced to vary by variations in output. Thus, if cost is influenced not only by output but by the prices of productive services, the cost schedule or curve will be drawn on the assumption that such prices are given at a certain level, except so far as these prices are induced to vary by variation in output. To the extent that they are, this induced variation will be reflected in the net variation of cost with output.

The usual situation for the firm, as a small purchaser from a large supply of each productive service, is that variations in its output (and use of such services) will induce no response in their prices. Therefore, the cost schedule or curve for the firm is generally drawn on the legitimate assumption that prices of all productive services are constant at given levels—legitimate in the sense that although such prices may vary independently, they will not respond to the firm's output variations and therefore do not affect the net relation of cost to output. In this typical case the cost variation shown by the cost schedule or curve is solely attributable to variations in real costs with output. In the more unusual case, where productive service prices respond to output, the cost curve must not assume given prices, but it must reflect the effects of the induced variation in such prices. In this chapter we shall deal entirely with cost-output relations where productive-service prices are given; the more unusual relation will be discussed in Chapter 8.

Output	Aggregate cost
0	$ 50
1	58
2	65
3	71
4	76
5	81
6	87
7	94
8	102
9	111
10	121
11	132
12	144
13	157
14	171
15	186
16	202

Is any typical relation of cost to output found among firms in the short period? Investigation has indicated that there is, in a rough sense at least, a pattern of response of cost to short-run output variation which is found in all enterprise. The nature of this pattern is suggested by the "aggregate" cost schedule above, the first column of which shows various alternative outputs for a firm per some unit of time (say a day) and the second column of which shows the *aggregate* cost of producing each of these outputs. It may be read as follows: to produce no units of output per day the firm would sustain an aggregate cost of $50; to produce one unit per day, an aggregate cost of $58; to produce two units per day an aggregate cost of $65, etc. If this cost schedule is translated diagrammatically into a continuous curve (called an *aggregate cost curve*), it appears something like that in Figure 8.

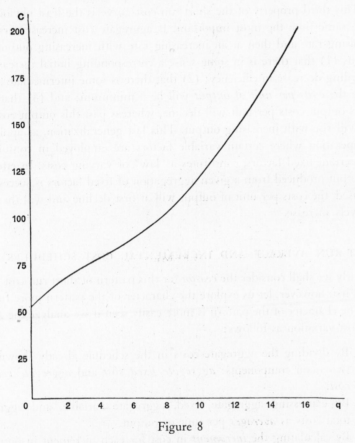

Figure 8

At first glance, this schedule and curve may seem to reveal little, but careful examination of them will reveal several important tendencies.

First, as we have observed already, there is some positive fixed cost at the zero output level. This is reflected in the fact that the aggregate cost curve has a positive origin on the vertical axis.

Second, the aggregate cost—that is, the total amount it costs the firm to produce—increases with increasing output. This is obvious and is evidenced by the fact that the aggregate cost curve slopes continually upward to the right.

Third, the aggregate cost increases *at varying rates* in response to given variations in output. Specifically, it first increases *at a decreasing rate,* and then it begins to increase *at an increasing rate* as output is progressively extended. This is evidenced by the fact that the aggregate cost curve becomes progressively less steep in slope up to the output of 4, but becomes progressively steeper in slope after the output of 5 is passed.

This third property of the short-run cost curve is the least obvious and at the same time the most important. If aggregate cost increases first at a decreasing rate and then at an increasing rate with increasing output, it is obvious (1) that there is in some sense a corresponding initial increase and succeeding decrease in efficiency; (2) that there is some intermediate output where the *costs per unit of output* will be a minimum; and (3) that short of this output costs per unit will decline, whereas past this output costs per unit will rise with increasing output. This last generalization, as applied to any operation where certain variable factors are employed in conjunction with certain fixed factors, constitutes a "law" of varying costs. In effect, as the output produced from a given aggregation of fixed factors is successively increased, the costs per unit of output will at first decline and will then progressively increase.

SHORT-RUN AVERAGE AND INCREMENTAL COST SCHEDULES

Presently we shall consider the *reason* for this pattern of short-run cost variation. First, however, let us explore the character of the pattern more fully.

The character of the pattern is more easily seen if we analyze the aggregate cost variation as follows:

1. By dividing the aggregate costs in the schedule already shown into two main components: *aggregate fixed cost* and *aggregate variable cost.*
2. By expressing aggregate fixed, aggregate variable, and aggregate total costs as *averages* per unit of output.
3. By calculating the *increment* in cost for each increment in output.

The results of those calculations, applied to the cost data from page 92 are expressed in the table on page 95.

Careful examination of this table reveals the principal properties inherent in the sort of aggregate cost variation we have characterized as typical. The following points may be noted:

1. Aggregate cost variations.
   a. *Aggregate fixed cost,* as shown in column (3), is, of course, constant for all levels of output—in this case at $50.

SHORT-RUN COST VARIATION

(1) Output	(2) Aggregate total cost	(3) Aggregate fixed cost	(4) Aggregate variable cost	(5) Average total cost *	(6) Average fixed cost *	(7) Average variable cost *	(8) Increment in cost
0	$ 50	$50	$ 0				
							$ 8.00
1	58	50	8	$58.00	$50.00	$8.00	
							7.00
2	65	50	15	32.50	25.00	7.50	
							6.00
3	71	50	21	23.67	16.67	7.00	
							5.00
4	76	50	26	19.00	12.50	6.50	
							5.00
5	81	50	31	16.20	10.00	6.20	
							6.00
6	87	50	37	14.50	8.33	6.17	
							7.00
7	94	50	44	13.43	7.14	6.29	
							8.00
8	102	50	52	12.75	6.25	6.50	
							9.00
9	111	50	61	12.33	5.55	6.78	
							10.00
10	121	50	71	12.10	5.00	7.10	
							11.00
11	132	50	82	12.00	4.55	7.45	
							12.00
12	144	50	94	12.00	4.17	7.83	
							13.00
13	157	50	107	12.08	3.85	8.23	
							14.00
14	171	50	121	12.21	3.57	8.64	
							15.00
15	186	50	136	12.40	3.33	9.07	
							16.00
16	202	50	152	12.62	3.12	9.50	

* Averages are computed only to the nearest cent. This obscures some details of the average cost variations.

b. *Aggregate variable cost,* as shown in column (4), is calculated as the difference between aggregate total cost and aggregate fixed cost (column 2 minus column 3). This aggregate variable cost contains all the variations to which aggregate costs are subject.

2. Average cost variations.

a. *Average fixed cost,* or fixed cost per unit of output (column 6), is calculated by dividing each aggregate fixed cost (from column 3) by the corresponding output (column 1). Average fixed cost declines monotonically, of course, as a constant amount is spread over more and more output.

b. *Average variable cost,* or variable cost per unit of output (column 7), is calculated by dividing each aggregate variable cost (column 4) by the corresponding output (column 1). Average variable cost at first declines with increasing output, reaching a low of $6.17 per unit at the output of 6, and thereafter it increases with increasing output. This variation reflects the general law of varying costs already referred to.

c. *Average total cost,* or total cost per unit of output (column 5), is calculated either by adding the average variable and average fixed cost at each level of output (column 6 plus column 7), or by dividing each aggregate total cost (column 2) by the corresponding output (column 1). It will be noted that average total cost also first declines with increasing output, reaches a minimum, and then increases. The minimum average total cost, $12, is reached at a larger output than the minimum average variable cost—at an output of 11 instead of at 6—because of the influence of declining average fixed costs. The variation in average total cost thus reflects the same law as variable cost but is complicated by the variation in average fixed cost.

3. Increments to aggregate cost.

The increment in aggregate cost per unit of output is shown in column 8. This represents the increase in aggregate cost for each increase in output. Thus, when the output moves from 0 to 1, the increment in cost is $8; when output moves from 1 to 2 units, the increment in cost is $7. The successive decrease and increase of increments to aggregate costs as output increases is corollary to the fall and rise of average variable costs.

It will be noted that the incremental cost is necessarily less than the average variable cost while the latter is falling, and greater than the average variable cost while it is rising. It bears the same relationship to the average total cost. If output is varied continuously rather than by discrete increments, incremental cost is necessarily equal to either of these averages at that output point where the average reaches its minimum. This is because each increment in cost enters into and influences (either upward or downward) the preceding average cost.

Viewed as a whole, this tabular breakdown of a typical aggregate cost variation makes clear the structure of costs for a firm in the short period. The firm finds that its costs vary in response to variations in output in such fashion that, as output is extended, variable costs per unit of output at first decline and then increase, ordinarily at an increasing rate. Similarly, the increment to aggregate cost per unit of output first declines and then progressively increases as output is increased. Average fixed costs decline with increasing output, but at a decreasing rate, as the fixed "overhead" is spread over more and more units of output.

After the output for which average variable costs are a minimum is exceeded, average total costs will still fall for an interval with increasing output because the decline of average fixed costs will exceed the rise in average variable costs. But as some rate of output is reached, the rise of average variable costs just counterbalances the dwindling decline of average fixed costs, and here the minimum average total cost is reached. This output for which average total cost is a minimum has been called *the short-run optimum output* for the firm, or the optimum rate of utilization for its given fixed plant. (It is, indeed, the output which allows of lowest unit costs for a given short period. As we shall see below, however, this output may not be especially sought after by the firm, and only under certain fortuitous circumstances will it be the most desirable output from a social standpoint.)

SHORT-RUN COST CURVES

The cost relationships just described may be illustrated more clearly by using a diagram, such as Figure 9, in which each cost component is expressed as a continuous curve. Thus, for the numbers in the average fixed cost schedule we substitute a continuous curve, AFC, which shows the level of average fixed cost for every conceivable gradation of output. Similarly, average variable cost is shown as a continuous curve, AVC, as is average total cost, ATC. In place of the schedule of cost increments, we substitute a *marginal cost curve, which shows the rate of increment of aggregate total cost per increment in output*. All these curves are derived directly from the original aggregate cost data shown in the table on page 95.[2]

[2] Thus let TC = aggregate total cost; VC = aggregate variable cost; FC = aggregate fixed cost; X = output. Of course $TC = FC + VC$. Also $ATC = TC/X$; $AVC = VC/X$; $AFC = FC/X$; and $AVC + AFC = ATC$. Further $MC = \dfrac{d(TC)}{dX}$ = the rate of change of TC in response to change in X.

The cost variations shown in the table appear about as in Figure 9 when translated into continuous cost curves. The pattern of cost variation thus illustrated has, as we have indicated before, several characteristics which are thought to be typical of short-run cost curves generally. Diagrammatically,

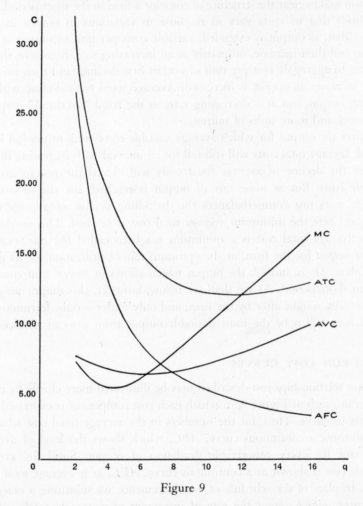

Figure 9

these appear as (1) an average variable cost curve which has some sort of a U or "dish" shape, falling to a minimum and then rising (the rise would presumably continue with increasing steepness if we showed further output increases); (2) an average fixed cost curve which declines monotonically at a progressively decreasing rate; and (3) an average total cost curve which, as the sum of the first two curves, also is U or "dish" shaped, declining to a minimum (at an output greater than that for which average variable cost is minimized) and then rising. The marginal cost curve typically falls for initial increases in output and thereafter rises continually.

The mechanical formal properties of such a family of cost curves are clear from our discussion above. The curve MC necessarily intersects AVC and ATC at their respective minima; the minimum of ATC lies at a larger output than the minimum of AVC; the curve AFC is in every case of a given fixed shape—a so-called rectangular hyperbola.

The full significance of these cost variations to an enterprise must be explored in succeeding chapters. It should be clear, however, that the cost curves are drawn to summarize certain information of importance to the firm: (1) the movement of total cost per unit of output with variation in output (ATC); (2) the corresponding variation of average variable costs (AVC); (3) the corresponding variation of average "overhead" or fixed cost (AFC); and (4) the *additions* to aggregate cost for given additions to output (MC). Considering such variations in conjunction with the price variations shown by his demand curve, the entrepreneur should be able to select the price or output which will maximize his profit.

This representation of the variation of cost with output in the short run and with given plant is drawn on the supposition that the prices of the productive services which the firm employs are given at certain levels and do not vary by reason of variations in the firm's output. Wage rates, for example, are $2 per hour regardless of output, and the same is true of material prices and machine costs. This is because the firm's employment of factors is supposed to be so small that variations in it will not influence factor prices. As a consequence, the variation in average and marginal costs shown reflects only varying efficiency due to varying proportions of fixed to variable factors and *not* to any variations in wage rates or other factor prices. Where the prices of factors vary systematically because of variations in the firm's output, the behavior of the cost curve is more complicated. Such situations will be discussed in Chapter 8.

THE CAUSES OF SHORT-RUN COST VARIATION

The preceding sections set forth what is regarded as the typical pattern of cost variation with output for firms in the short period. The questions may now be advanced, first, as to how we know that this is the typical pattern and, second, as to what are the reasons for it.

Let us first review briefly what essentially is stated about this pattern and is to be explained. Only two basic generalizations are involved. First, in any short period there is an aggregate of fixed cost, which when spread over an increasing output gives rise to a progressively decreasing fixed cost per unit of output. Second, the progressive increase in output is accompanied by an increase in aggregate variable cost first at a decreasing and then at an increasing rate, and this is reflected in (1) a variable cost per unit of output which at first declines and then increases as output is extended and (2) a marginal cost which likewise at first declines and later increases as output is extended—both the average and marginal cost variations being reflections of the variation in aggregate variable cost.

The generalization about fixed cost is too obvious to require detailed justification or explanation. As long as there is an aggregate of cost which would be incurred even at zero output—and is thus fixed for the short period—it is simple arithmetic that as it is divided among successively larger outputs, the fixed cost per unit must decline in a certain pattern.

The generalization about variable cost is perhaps less obvious. In the first place, how do we know that, in general, average variable cost successively decreases and increases as output is increased? In part this knowledge is based on empirical studies of actual cost variation, although these lead to some refinements of the generalization which will be discussed in the next section. In part also, however, the generalization is based upon observations of the response of output to successive increments in the quantity of variable productive services (or factors) used in connection with a given quantity of fixed factors—that is, on investigations of the basic *physical* relations between short-period "inputs" of factors and the resulting "outputs" of goods, which must ultimately determine the pattern of short-run cost variation.

The nature of the basic findings just mentioned is suggested by certain tendencies implied but not directly shown by the cost table on page 95. By reading column 7 (average variable cost) we observe that as output is successively increased from 0 to 16 units, the variable cost per unit of output, in dollars, first declines and then increases. It starts at $8 with 1 unit, declines to $6.17 with 6 units, and rises to $9.50 by the time 16 units are reached. Yet this cost variation is by definition one which takes place with *given* prices for productive factors—if labor is the variable productive factor, its wage is given (let us say) at $10 per day regardless of the output rate of the firm. The same applies to any other factor used. It follows that if variable costs per unit of output in money terms at first decline and then increase, *this must be because the variable real costs per unit of output first decline and then increase.* That is, it takes first successively fewer units of variable factors per unit of output and then successively more such units of variable factors per unit of output as output is increased. The variation of variable money cost is simply a reflection of a fundamental variation in variable real cost.

Suppose for example that the only factor entering into variable cost is labor and that the wage rate for labor is $10 per day. Then column 7 of the table on page 95 may be plainly read as a schedule of the variable real cost in labor-days per unit of output at various outputs—in this case by dropping the dollar sign and moving the decimal point one place to the left. It then says that with 1 unit of output, variable cost is 0.8 days of labor, with 6 units of output 0.617 days of labor, and so forth. The same applies to marginal cost. On the same supposition, we have reflected an early decline and later progressive rise of marginal real costs (see column 8) from 0.8 days of labor for the first unit, to 0.5 days of labor for the fourth unit, to 1.6 days of labor for the sixteenth unit. That is, marginal real costs at first decline and then increase (in given relation to variable real costs), and the variation of marginal costs in money terms simply reflects this.

Thus, it appears that our generalization about the pattern of variable cost variation has been all along fundamentally a generalization about variation in the physical quantities of variable factors required per unit of output and about the increments to their aggregate quantity required for successive additional units of output. Average variable costs in real terms first decline and then increase as short-run output is increased; marginal real costs do likewise in a certain relation to the average costs.

This is an interpretation of our initial generalization, but not a justification or an explanation. For justification of the statement we must turn primarily to empirical investigations mentioned above, of the response of physical outputs to successive increases in the quantities of variable factors employed (of variable inputs) with a given fixed plant or quantity of fixed factors. These investigations have been the source of the preceding generalization. They have shown that, in fact, variable costs per unit of output, in terms of physical quantities of factors employed, do at first decline and then increase as output is increased with a given fixed plant and that marginal costs in real terms behave accordingly. This pattern of response of real average variable and marginal costs to short-run output increases thus has standing as an empirically established "law."

This law might be referred to as a law of successively decreasing and increasing average real costs and marginal real costs. It has been conventionally stated, however, in inverted fashion. The conventional statement, instead of referring to the variation of real cost per unit of output, which is essentially input per unit of output (I/O) has referred instead to the variation of the reciprocal of this ratio—that is, output per unit of real cost, or output per unit of input (O/I). Similarly, instead of referring to marginal real cost (input) for each increment to output $(\Delta I/\Delta O)$, it has referred to marginal increment to aggregate output for each increment to input $(\Delta O/\Delta I)$. It may seem unnecessary to translate this law of short-run cost variation to these new terms, but the task is justified by the fact that in other reading one may encounter it in either form.

Thus translated, the basic relation of inputs (real costs) to outputs may be stated as follows. Suppose that in producing any good, certain factors of production are employed in fixed quantity and certain other factors in varying quantity. Then, as successive increments are made to the amount of the variable factor employed, the average product (average output) per unit of variable factor will at first increase and then decrease; similarly, the successive increments to variable factors employed will yield at first increasing and then successively decreasing increments to aggregate product. In a word, as variable factors are successively increased against a fixed factor, there is at first an increasing and then a decreasing *average product* per unit of variable factor and a similarly increasing and decreasing *marginal product*. This law is frequently called *the law of diminishing returns* or, alternatively, *the law of variable proportions*.

Such a variation in average product and marginal product is implied in our cost table on page 95. It may be revealed by a little arithmetic. In the table on page 103, reproduce from that cost table: output (column 1), aggregate variable cost (column 2), average variable cost (column 3), and marginal cost (column 4). However, on the simplifying supposition that labor is the only variable factor and that it cost $10 per day, let us state the aggregate variable, average variable, and marginal costs in terms of days of labor. The first four columns then give us output, aggregate variable real cost, average variable real cost, and marginal real cost.

Given these data, the output per unit of variable input, or average product per labor hour, may be simply calculated at each output by taking the reciprocal of the corresponding item in column 3. This is the same as dividing the aggregate output by the aggregate variable real cost (column 2). (In effect, if the cost per unit of output at the output of 5 is 0.620 days of labor, we know that the output per day of labor is 1/.620 or 1.61). The variation of output per labor hour at various outputs, thus calculated, is shown in column 5. This column indicates the variation of average product per unit of variable input which is predicted by the law of diminishing returns. Average product at first rises and then falls as inputs are increased.

Similarly, the increments to aggregate product per unit increment to variable input may be calculated as the reciprocals of the column (4) cost increments. This approximation to marginal product, thus calculated, is shown in column 6. It reveals the sort of successive rise and fall of marginal product per unit of input as inputs increase which the law of diminishing returns predicts. It will be observed that this marginal product bears the same generic relation to average product which marginal cost bears to average cost. That is, it lies above average product while average product is rising and below average product when average product is falling, and with continuous variation it would equal average product where average product reached its maximum.

If we were to plot the variation described in curves on a diagram, we would find that average product is described by a curve that first rises and then falls with increasing output, and marginal product by a similar curve,

VARIATION IN COST AND PRODUCT

(1) Output	(2) Aggregate variable cost * (in days of labor)	(3) Average variable cost † (in days of labor)	(4) Increment in cost ‡ (in days of labor)	(5) Output per unit of variable input § (average product)	(6) Increment in output ‖ (for unit increment of input)
0					
			0.8		1.25
1	0.8	0.800		1.25	
			0.7		1.43
2	1.5	0.750		1.33	
			0.6		1.67
3	2.1	0.700		1.43	
			0.5		2.00
4	2.6	0.650		1.54	
			0.5		2.00
5	3.1	0.620		1.61	
			0.6		1.67
6	3.7	0.617		1.62	
			0.7		1.43
7	4.4	0.629		1.59	
			0.8		1.25
8	5.2	0.650		1.54	
			0.9		1.11
9	6.1	0.678		1.48	
			1.0		1.00
10	7.1	0.710		1.41	
			1.1		.91
11	8.2	0.745		1.34	
			1.2		.83
12	9.4	0.783		1.28	
			1.3		.77
13	10.7	0.823		1.21	
			1.4		.71
14	12.1	0.864		1.16	
			1.5		.67
15	13.6	0.907		1.10	
			1.6		.63
16	15.2	0.950		1.05	

* Items from column 4 of table on page 98, each divided by $10, the assumed price per day of labor.

† Items from column 7 of table on page 95, each divided by $10.

‡ Items from column 8 of table on page 95, each divided by $10.

§ Reciprocals of items in column 3 above.

‖ Reciprocals of items in column 4 above.

which rises higher, begins its decline at a smaller output and intersects the average product curve at the latter's maximum. That the variations represented by such curves would describe exactly the same phenomenon of real-cost variation shown in the cost-curve diagram on page 98 would be revealed by the fact that they would also be generally the shape of a dish but with the dish turned over, bottom side up.

In summary, the law of diminishing returns, whether stated in terms of declining and then rising real costs per unit of output, or in terms of rising and then declining output per unit of variable factors employed—always where there is an invariant factor—lies at the base of our generalization about short-run cost variation for the firm. This law has further and more general applications, however, and we will have occasion to refer to some of them at a later point.

Perhaps, we may still inquire, if this pattern of variation in the relation of cost to output does demonstrably occur as a general rule, why does it occur? What is the logic of the law of diminishing returns? The deepest our answer can go is to say that evidently as a variable factor is used in conjunction with a fixed factor to produce a good, there are proportions which give larger and smaller outputs per unit of variable factors. As the quantity of the variable factor is increased, the output per unit of variable factor increases up to a point where it reaches a maximum; thereafter a higher proportion of variable to fixed factors causes the output per unit of the variable factor to decrease.

As a final note to the preceding discussion, we have assumed for simplicity in analyzing the variation in real cost and in product that the firm uses only one variable factor (labor) and thus is concerned in the short run only with the variation in output as the quantity of this factor is varied. In actuality, of course, it will ordinarily use several variable factors and, in addition, will have to decide in what proportions to combine these with each other, presumably choosing that combination which will minimize the variable cost of each output. The principles affecting such a cost-minimizing choice will be further explored in Chapter 11; for the moment we will assume the composition of the variable-factor increment to be chosen by such principles. Given this, the response of output to successive composite increments in variable factors should follow the same path described by our cost analysis or by the law of diminishing returns.

THE SPECIFIC SHAPE OF THE AVERAGE VARIABLE COST CURVE

The preceding sections establish the generalizations that the average variable cost curve in the short run is generally of a U or dish shape, and that average fixed costs decline with output increase. Figure 9 indicates the general character of the predicted unit cost variation. But it does not purport to describe exactly in every respect the short-run cost variation experienced by all firms and industries. It is typical in that it reflects (1) the inclusion of at least some fixed cost, and (2) the incidence of some initial decline of marginal and average variable costs, followed by some upward variation of these costs as output increases beyond a certain point. From firm to firm, and more particularly from industry to industry, however, there are very significant differences in (1) the proportion of variable to fixed costs, and (2) the shape of the variation in average variable costs.

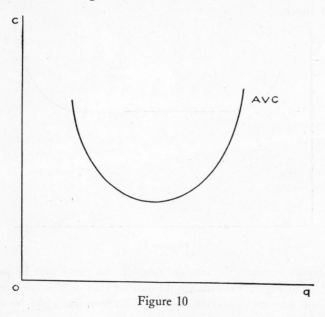

Figure 10

In the example we have given, for instance, the proportion of fixed to variable costs is fairly high, and the variation of average variable and of marginal cost is comparatively gradual (although at some output larger than we have shown average variable and marginal costs would necessarily rise steeply as the physical capacity of the plant was reached). This gradual variation of costs, reflected in a rather flat or shallow U shape in the average variable and average total cost curves, and in an only moderately sloping marginal cost, indicates that the plant in question could be used fairly efficiently over a rather wide range of output. The *rate of utilization* of plant could be varied widely with rather moderate variations in unit cost.

Cost variation for firms in other industries, however, might be very different. Textbook examples often favor a family of cost curves which shows the average variable cost curve with a decided U shape, as in Figure 10. Here, average variable costs rise rather steeply as output moves in either direction from the minimum so that there is only a small range in the rate of plant utilization which gives reasonable efficiency. Such cost behavior might characterize plants with certain technical peculiarities. But it is equally possible that the pattern of cost variation may, within the general limits of the law of varying costs, fall anywhere between wide extremes. At one extreme the average variable cost curve may be a very wide and flat-bottomed U, showing no cost variation over a considerable range of output, as in Figure 11. Here, the rate of utilization could be varied from possibly 20 percent to 90 percent of maximum capacity without influencing variable costs very much.

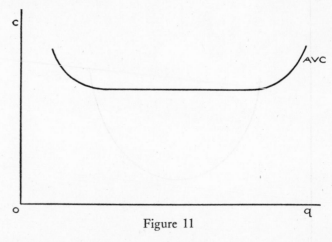

Figure 11

At another extreme, the average variable cost curve may be practically V-shaped, as in Figure 12. This would indicate that only at one critical rate of utilization was any reasonable approach made to the attainable efficiency of the plant. Various instances found, in fact, may lie anywhere between those extremes, and may also show peculiar variations of their own.

The reason for substantial differences in cost behavior among different firms is evident in the basic reason for short-run cost variation. In the short run, variable and marginal costs at first fall and then rise with increasing output because of the changing proportions of variable to fixed factors—of labor and raw materials to plant. Inherent in the technical design of any plant will be a ratio or coefficient between labor and materials on one hand and machinery and equipment on the other which allows lowest variable unit costs. Production at such a rate that this ratio is just maintained gives minimum average variable costs; production at lower or higher rates will cause such costs to increase. But the degree to which these costs respond to variations in output may differ widely among plants.

In the first place, the technical character of plants may differ considerably. In some plants the ratio of variable to fixed factors may be technically inflexible so that output cannot be had at all without a given "dose" of labor and materials per plant unit and cannot be increased much by adding more variable factors per plant unit. This might be true, for example, of a mechanical punch press operated by one man—it needs one man and only one, and consumes no less or more than so much material per hour. In other plants the ratio of variable to fixed factors may be technically variable away from their lowest-cost proportion with only a moderate disadvantage in cost. Thus a mining company with given fixed equipment might employ from a few dozen to several hundred men (up to the final limit of overcrowding) with only moderate variations in variable unit cost. The more varia-

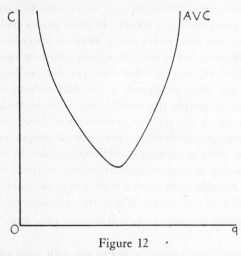

Figure 12

bility in the ratio of variable to fixed factors that the technique and design of a plant allow, the shallower and flatter the U-shaped variable cost curve will tend to be.

A more potent consideration affecting the pattern of short-run cost variations in a plant is the *divisibility* of the plant. If all of a plant must be operated at once in order to run at all, then employing a small proportion of the normal work force will greatly affect the working proportion between labor or other variable factors and fixed plant. But if the plant is divisible into identical fractions or parts, each of which may be operated separately while the other parts are closed down, it will be possible to maintain the same working proportion of variable to fixed factors while employing widely different amounts of variable factors. Thus, if a steel plant consists of a single technical unit—let us say one Bessemer converter—any considerable variations in work force or amount of materials used will seriously affect costs. But if an iron-making plant is made up of ten largely independent blast furnaces, any number of which can be operated at a time, the work force might vary from 10 percent to 100 percent of the maximum without greatly influencing the average variable cost of producing iron. In the latter case the average variable cost curve might be almost horizontal over most of its length, with the U-shapedness appearing only at extremely small or large outputs, as in Figure 11. In short, divisibility of the plant into numerous identical subdivisions tends to lessen cost variability and to result in wide flat-bottomed U-shaped cost curves—up to capacity. Technical indivisibility of plant is associated with more distinct variability of short-run average variable costs.

Nonvariability of average variable costs is also favored where a plant may be operated for any fraction of the working week or month. A short-run cost curve shows variation in unit cost in response to variation in output per some unit of time, such as a month. In most plants such a variation in the rate of output does not involve using more or fewer variable factors in a plant at any one time, but it may be accomplished by operating more or fewer days per month or more or fewer shifts per day. As long as the number of shifts worked per week or month is variable without significant additional costs, the rate of output per month, which can be varied widely without affecting very much the physical proportion of labor to plant, will not much influence average variable costs over a wide output range. Wherever the technique and other governing conditions are such as to facilitate relatively costless variation in time worked, therefore, we tend to find relatively constant average variable costs over a wide range of output, reflected in a flat-bottomed U-shaped cost curve. Where the technique is such that inter-mittency of operations is costly, costs will tend to vary more with variations in output.

In short, although any enterprise operating with fixed plant will experience some variation of average costs in response to varying output, and although unit costs will ultimately rise as physical capacity is reached, the degree of variation in average variable and marginal costs may differ greatly from case to case. In some cases, where intermittent plant operation is costly and where the plant is an indivisible technical unit, the average variable cost curve may be a very steep U, with unit costs falling greatly as a certain rate of utilization is approached and rising quickly as it is surpassed. In many others, where the plant characteristics are otherwise, average variable cost will tend to be relatively constant over a wide range of output, and significant cost variations will occur only at extreme outputs.

In American manufacturing industry, where plants are often very large, where a single enterprise may operate several similar plants, and where intermittent operation is often feasible, the phenomenon of *constant average variable costs* (except at extreme outputs) has been frequently noted. For this type of business enterprise, at least, statistical studies lead us to believe that the typical pattern of cost variation is represented in a wide flat-bottomed U shape for the average variable cost curve and in constant or unvarying marginal costs over a wide range of output. This may be significant in price determination.[3]

Although the variability of average variable costs in the short run is of primary importance, considerable significance is also attached to the relative size of fixed and variable costs. In certain industries fixed costs are very large, amounting to as much as 50 percent of the total unit cost at capacity output; in others they are relatively insignificant. The relative size of the aggregate fixed cost is important because fixed costs per unit of output always decline in a set pattern with the extension of output. If fixed cost is a very large proportion of total cost, this decline of average fixed cost is likely to dominate the whole pattern of total unit cost variation; whether variable unit costs are constant or noticeably variable, the average *total* cost of production will fall significantly over a relatively wide range of output. In a plant with big fixed costs great economies attach to full production because of the connected opportunities for "spreading overhead" over large outputs. In a plant with small fixed costs the pattern of variation of variable costs will dominate the variation of average total cost.

SHORT-RUN COST VARIATION—SUMMARY

Our discussion of costs so far has centered about the variation of production costs in response to variation in output by the firm, where the output variation is effected by varying the rate of utilization of a given fixed plant. We have thus emphasized the short-run cost variation with which a firm is concerned in making decisions over time periods which are too short to permit it to vary the size of its plant. This so-called short-run cost variation is thus ordinarily relevant to price-output decisions which affect the next month, six months, or year. Before another type of cost variation is discussed, two additional comments on the short-run cost curves may be added.

First, it should be re-emphasized that the characteristic pattern of short-run cost variations discussed above, which features a successive fall and rise in average variable costs and an uninterrupted decline in average fixed costs as output is increased, is a reflection of the existence of fixed factors which are invariant in amount over the period for which output variations are contemplated. The existence of such factors gives rise not only to fixed cost, but also to the varying proportionality of factors which accounts for changing average variable costs. The short-run cost pattern would not be characteristic of situations where all factors were variable and where the proportions of all factors could thus be kept constant at different levels of output.

[3] For an example of the empirical study of cost behavior, see Joel Dean, *The Relation of Cost to Output for a Leather Belt Shop* (New York: National Bureau of Economic Research, 1941). A general discussion of cost behavior appears in *Cost Behavior and Price Policy* (New York: National Bureau of Economic Research, 1943).

Second, the formal properties of short-run cost curves are such that they show the *net relationship* between variation in output and variation in costs. Movements along the cost curve show only those changes in costs which occur directly in response to changes in output; they do not show cost changes which are due to independent changes in wage rates or material prices or due to independent variations in the quality of factors. Since the typical assumption is that the latter variables will not vary in response to the firm's output variations, but only independently, the cost curve is typically drawn on the assumption that wage rates, etc. are constant, as above. We consider cost c, as one variable, which is specifically related to several other variables, including output q, the wage rate W, material prices M, and so forth. Cost may vary in response to changes in q or W or M or all of them. The cost curve, however, typically shows only the net relationship of c to q, assuming that all other variables which influence c remain constant as output varies. *Variations in cost which are caused by independent changes in wage rates and material prices are shown not in movements along our cost curves but in shifts of these curves.* In the less typical case where wage rates and material prices vary systematically in response to variations in the firm's output, the effect of such connected variations is reflected in movements along average and marginal curves. (See Chapter 8.) But any *independent* variation in factor prices is still reflected in shifts in the curves.

C. LONG-RUN COST VARIATION

MEANING OF THE LONG RUN

Short-run cost calculations, since they show how a firm's costs will vary in response to variation in output within the limits of a given amount of fixed plant, are relevant so long as the firm is concerned with a short future time period within which it cannot greatly expand or contract its plant. But the firm will also be concerned with the relationship of cost to output for successively longer periods, including intervals long enough for it to vary the size of its plant factors freely. A simplified version of this relationship is the theoretical "long-run" relation of cost to output, calculated on the assumption that there are no fixed factors, or no given amount of plant.

The *long-run cost curve* of a firm is correspondingly one which shows the variation of cost in response to variation in output for a period long enough that all factors of production, including plant and equipment, are freely variable in amount. The "long" period in question, like the "short" period, thus has no certain chronological limits but is functionally defined. But it is fairly approximated in intervals of three to ten years over which firms may calculate their plans for long-run expansion (or contraction).

In precisely what decision-making context would a firm have reference to such a long-run cost curve? It will refer to it in determining the rate of output for a period which (1) begins far enough from now that the firm will have time fully to adjust the quantity of its plant to the necessities of that period, and (2) lasts long enough after its beginning that all durable goods acquired for use in the period can be fully used up or worn out during the period and that their costs can be fully amortized in accordance to plan. The long-run cost curve, appropriately referred to as a "planning curve," is applicable in deciding the relation of the firm's scale to an average situation of demand for its output over a future period of considerable length.

THE LONG-RUN COST CURVE

A long-run cost curve for any firm, like a short-run curve, shows the net relation of cost to output. Like a short-run curve, it can represent average

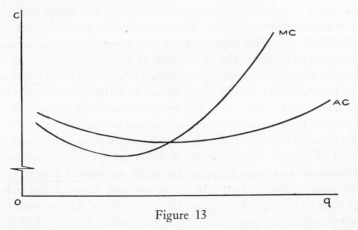

Figure 13

costs or marginal costs. The principal formal difference is that *in the long run there are no fixed costs*. All costs are variable. The family of cost curves will therefore consist only of an average total cost curve and a marginal cost curve. If long-run average costs followed the same sort of U-shaped variations as short-run average costs, therefore, the long-run average and marginal costs of a firm would appear as in Figure 13. The absence of any distinction between fixed and variable costs will be noted.

In drawing any long-run average cost curve, like that illustrated, it is supposed that plant, equipment, and all other factors are freely variable. At the same time, the rate of utilization of any chosen quantity of plant factors is also freely variable. The drawing of the long-run average cost curve thus assumes that the scale of the firm and the rate of use of any plant factors are coordinated and simultaneously adjusted so as to produce any chosen output at the lowest possible cost. Any cost amount from a long-run average cost curve which corresponds to a specific output is thus the lowest cost at which that output can be produced, *scale and rate of utilization of plant factors being coordinately chosen.*

Does the long-run average cost curve also have a typical shape which is found with some uniformity in all sorts of business enterprise? The answer to this question is not entirely certain, although investigations of the relation of cost to scale in a large number of industries give us some basis for generalization. Speaking very broadly, it is possible to say that the long-run average cost curve is typically U-shaped—that as the scale of the firm is progressively extended, the cost per unit of output at first declines, then becomes constant, and finally increases. Thus the "typical" long-run average cost curve has some U or "dish" shape, one version of which is illustrated in Figure 13.

Empirical studies of industrial costs seem to support this statement. In most industries a very small firm is quite inefficient; as the firm becomes larger, it tends to become more efficient, reaching a minimum cost per unit of output at some particular scale. Thereafter, further expansion up to some still larger scale may have little effect on unit costs, which remain constant with increases in capacity. But if the scale of the firm is made still larger, it is thought that a point tends to be reached where unit costs begin to rise.

The rationalization of this phenomenon in terms of the common sense of engineering and organization has been extensively developed. It is suggested that in most industries there are certain *economies,* or cost savings, available through expansion of scale up to a certain point. These include the economies of greater *specialization of labor,* of greater *specialization of capital equipment,* of *large* as opposed to *small mechanical devices,* of *large-scale distribution,* and so forth. As a firm becomes larger, it can reduce its average costs by taking advantage of those economies. The economies ordinarily emphasized here are "real" economies of using factors priced at given levels, although there may also be pecuniary economies due to decline of factor prices with increasing scale. The range of alternative scales over which the firm can so reduce average costs is referred to as a stage of *decreasing costs* in response to increasing scale. The extent to which further and further expansion of scale will result in falling average costs will differ from industry to industry according to techniques employed. After scale has been extended to some critical point in each case, however, the economies of increasing scale will have all been fully exploited, and further additions to the size of the firm will not result in further reduction of unit cost. On the other hand, there is apparent no automatic tendency for costs to rise with still greater scale. Once all economies of increasing scale have been exploited, costs should tend to remain constant in the face of further expansion unless some other factor intervenes.

It may be noted that this tendency of average costs to fall as the firm extends its scale of operations may inhere dually in (1) the cost advantages of larger single factories or other aggregations of plant factors on a single site or in a single technical unit and (2) the further cost advantages of enlarging the firm so as to include two or more such factories or technical units. The observed tendency to decreasing cost with increasing scale evidently reflects both of these influences. Thus, the scale curve for the firm may include outputs which may be produced by several factories or technical units of disparate location.

It is quite possible that the scale curve might continue to register declining costs even after it had become large enough so that there were no further economies of enlarging a single factory but where there were further economies to a firm large enough to operate several factories. If there are economies of large firms other than those of large single plant units, however, they are evidently restricted to either (1) real economies of large-scale management or distribution or (2) pecuniary (and nonreal) economies, resulting, for example, from ability to bargain for lower factor prices. Many economists are unconvinced that there are real economies of large-scale management or distribution which permit a firm to lower its real costs per unit of output after it reaches a large enough output to exploit fully the economies of the large plant unit. If this were so, the unit real costs of output would tend, *ceteris paribus,* to remain constant with expansion beyond the capacity of one optimal-size plant unit. Or, if these economists are wrong (we lack the information to permit final decision on this point), real costs per unit of output might decline beyond such an output point. In either event, unit money costs could well decline because of strictly pecuniary economies. However this may be, the firm's scale curve reflects declines of unit costs with increased scale for all reasons combined, whether a single plant unit or multiple plant units are involved, up to the point where no further economies of scale are encountered. Thereafter, there may very possibly be no change in unit costs for some further extension of scale and output.

The reason that average costs eventually tend to rise with further increases in scale, it is held, is found in an additional factor—the *diseconomies* of very large-scale management. If a firm becomes large enough, the argument goes, the burden of administration becomes disproportionately great; "red tape" tends to proliferate; and total costs per unit of output tend to rise. Thus, we get a terminal stage of increasing costs with increasing scale which adds the last leg to the U-shaped long-run average cost curve.

All the preceding is probably true in a general sense as applied to many firms and industries. It should be emphasized, however, that within this general pattern there are big differences in long-run cost behavior among industries. In certain industries economies of increasing scale are realized for expansion of the firm up to such a point that the whole market would be fully supplied by a single firm before it had reached its lowest-cost or optimum size. Such an industry may be called a "natural monopoly," and the firm in question may never grow big enough to encounter the ultimate up-turn in its long-run average cost curve. In other industries the optimum scale of firms may be large enough that only a few firms of such scale can be supported by the market. In still others a very small firm may be able to exploit the economies of scale fully, and the market may be able to sup-port many firms of the most efficient size. One of the reasons that in many of our industries there are very few firms is that in numerous lines of manu-facture the economies of large-scale production are great and costs are re-duced by concentrating production in a few hands.

It should also be emphasized that the firm's scale curve, although gen-erally of a U shape, may take on various specific shapes consistent with the general rule. In particular, it may be a U with a big flat bottom, reflecting declining unit costs with initial increases in scale, then approximately con-stant unit costs over a rather wide range of scales, and finally some distinct upturn in unit costs as diseconomies of big management are ultimately en-countered. Empirical investigations very tentatively suggest that such is the case in many fields of manufacturing.

The variation of a firm's production costs in response to varying output in the long run, in sum, tends to be such that the cost curve relating average cost to output is of some general U shape, evidencing successive fall and rise of unit cost as output is extended. Correspondingly, the firm's long-run marginal cost curve, showing increments in cost with increasing output, will usually first fall and then rise, always intersecting the average cost curve at its lowest point, as in Figure 13.

In terms of such a relationship of unit cost to rate of output (considered in conjunction with the demand for its product), any business firm will de-cide how large to make its long-run scale of operations. We may anticipate here a later discussion by remarking, first, that it is not at all inevitable that the firm will select the "optimum scale"—that is, the long-run rate of output which gives the lowest unit cost—and, second, that it is only under special conditions of market structure that production by firms at exactly this "optimum" scale will necessarily be most desirable from the standpoint of society. From a social standpoint it is important that the output of any in-dustry be related to that of other industries in an "ideal" fashion (yet to be defined) and that the resulting industry output be produced at the lowest attainable aggregate cost. If this output cannot conceivably be produced with firms operating at optimum scales, then any necessary departure from these scales is consistent with maximum social welfare.

THE REASONS FOR LONG-RUN COST VARIATION

The rule that the usual firm's cost per unit of output is a minimum at some determinate scale of operations and becomes higher if the scale is made smaller or larger than this, has so far been supported only by referring to certain "economies of large-scale production" and to "diseconomies of very large-scale management." Although such economies and diseconomies are found in practice, reference to them does not put the explanation of varying long-run costs on the same footing as that of varying short-run costs. In fact, it leaves unsettled a clear implication of our earlier discussion to the effect that, with all factors freely variable, we might expect no variation at all in long-run average costs in response to varying scale.

In the discussion of the short period it was pointed out that the tendency of short-run unit costs first to fall and then to rise as the rate of utilization of a fixed plant is increased results from the changing *proportion* of variable to fixed factors. The optimum rate of utilization is struck at only one rate of output, where this proportion permits the lowest average total cost. This is because, in the short run, a part of the factors of production is fixed instead of being freely variable.

But if all factors are freely variable in amount, as they are in the long run, it would seem that at any rate of output the lowest-cost proportion of factors could be maintained at any output, that it would be the same proportion at any output, and that, therefore, the long-run rate of output or scale of operations should have no effect on unit costs. Unit costs should remain constant at a minimum level for any scale of operations. How may this logic be reconciled with our observations concerning the economies and diseconomies of increasing scale?

The key to this apparent dilemma is simply that there are concealed limitations on the free variability of all factors in the long run. Although all factors of production, excepting perhaps management, are freely variable in amount, *the various factors* (capital equipment, labor, and resources) *are not, in specific forms, indefinitely divisible into small units.* Thus, although it is possible for a firm to use more or less capital equipment within wide limits, it is not always possible to use more or less equipment in the specific forms it is needed. It must use a whole belt conveyor for its assembly line, or none at all—it cannot use $\frac{1}{100}$ of a belt conveyor. Similarly, although it can use more or less labor within wide limits, it cannot use the various specialized forms of labor in fractional units. A big plant may be able to use one production control statistician to advantage; a small plant cannot ordinarily use $\frac{1}{10}$ of a statistician. Moreover, it is a general tendency for the several factors of production to become more efficient per unit of output as they are used in these specialized and "lumpy" forms.

If such indivisibilities of specialized forms of resources are encountered and if the highly lumpy forms of given resources are potentially more efficient, two conclusions follow. First, the firm may find it uneconomical at small scales to use basic resources in their potentially most efficient forms (such as highly specialized machines or highly specialized workers) because in their potentially most efficient forms they are available only in "lumps" so large, or with such a large output potential, that their use on small outputs would result in sufficient *underutilization* that costs per unit of output would be quite high. Therefore, the firm may produce small outputs with "inferior" forms of basic resources, which give higher unit costs than "superior" forms would at larger outputs but which have a net cost advantage at smaller outputs. The economies of using resources in their most efficient forms can be realized only at large outputs; hence, long-run costs decline as output increases. Second, although the firm reaches an output where a given lump of specialized resource may economically be employed, this may still be an output which underutilizes the lump, and costs may be further reduced as output increases up to the point of its full utilization. This "spreading" of the cost of the indivisible unit is a further source of decline of long-run average costs with increasing output. Moreover, variation in the proportion of other factors to the "lump" may result in a similar decline of average costs.

The cause of the downward variation of average costs with increased output for the firm in the long-run is thus really not found in the fact that one aggregate of factors is fixed in quantity while another is varied against it. It is found rather in the fact that in various specialized forms the productive factors occur in indivisible units or are lumpy; as a result, the firm can realize the maximum potential economies of using them in their most efficient forms only at rather large outputs. The phenomenon is based on varying proportionality only so far as attainment of the true optimal proportion among resources in their most efficient forms requires an output large enough to eliminate the cost disadvantages potential in the lumpiness of specialized forms of resources.

In brief, *the recognized economies of large-scale production are essentially a reflection of a technical indivisibility of factors of production within given patterns of technique.*

The explanation of the ultimate rise in unit costs after the firm reaches a certain size has similarities both to the "fixed factor" argument and the "changing form of factor" argument. The phenomenon observed is that of inefficiencies of large-scale management—that as output is extended, the management factor cannot be indefinitely expanded without increases in cost of management per unit of output. This might be reduced to saying that management is in some sense a "fixed" or "imperfectly variable" factor and that diminishing returns to other factors are encountered as other factors are expanded against it. It is probably as true to the facts to say, however, that the management factor per se must change form as the enterprise becomes larger (accumulating more bureaucracy, more red tape, and longer "chains of command") and that management costs, therefore, simply rise if the organization passes a certain size point. This puts the explanation of the "up leg" of the U-shaped long-run cost curve on the same grounds as the explanation of the "down leg."

The preceding offers an explanation of the U shape of the long-run cost curve for the firm. Since the output at which diseconomies of large-scale management are encountered may be well beyond that at which the economies of large-scale production are fully exploited, it is clear that this U-shaped curve may in many cases have a long flat bottom, representing a substantial range of output over which unit costs are invariant.

Throughout the preceding discussion of long-run cost curves, we have generally assumed that the factor prices paid by the firm do not vary in response to variations in the firm's output, and so we constructed the curve on the assumption of given factor prices. The economies and diseconomies referred to are thus entirely real economies and diseconomies, and they alone cause long-run costs to vary. Where the firm becomes very large, however, there may in addition be systematic variations in factor prices in response to variations in the firm's output, giving rise to strictly pecuniary economies or diseconomies of large scale. Where these are encountered, they should be reflected in the shape of the long-run cost curve. This special phenomenon is neglected below, but it will be considered in Chapter 8.

THE RELATION OF LONG-RUN TO SHORT-RUN COST CURVES FOR THE FIRM

To this point we have considered the character of the short-run and the long-run cost curves for the firm. Let us now take up their relationship, which is most easily seen as a relationship of the short-run average total cost curve to the long-run average cost curve.

In order to see this relationship, let us first consider what these curves show. The long-run cost curve indicates the response of average total cost to output as output is varied by simultaneously varying the "scale of plant" —that is, the quantity of all quasi-permanent facilities or staff which would be fixed in a short period—and the utilization of such "plant" so as to reach the lowest attainable cost of each output. It is relevant to the firm's output plans over long future periods, and it shows costs attainable with a hypothetically continuous range of different "plant" sizes (where "plant" is used to refer to quasi-permanent facilities, staff, etc., which the firm employs), each size of plant being used to produce only that one output which it can produce more efficiently than any other size. The short-run average total cost curve, on the other hand, shows for some particular size of plant the variation of total unit costs with variation in the rate of utilization of that plant.

At any one time the firm has some size of plant and some particular corresponding short-run cost curve. But, in general, there is a *different* short-run cost curve for each possible different size of plant—or a hypothetical family of such curves. At any moment the firm is "stuck" with one. But over time, as it adjusts plant scale, guided by the opportunities of the long-run cost curve—as it "moves along the long-run cost curve"—it passes from one short-run curve to another, finding a different one at each point on the long-run curve.

The formal relation of the long-run cost curve to the short-run cost curve is, therefore, really a relation of the long-run curve to a family of short-run curves. The character of this relation is suggested by the remark that the long-run average cost curve is defined as showing for each possible output the lowest cost of producing that output, size of plant and rate of use of plant being covaried to obtain the best result. If this is so, three things are obvious about the relationships of the short- and long-run curves. First, so far as costs may be kept down by changing scale at least somewhat with each long-run output change, each average cost on the long-run cost curve refers to a cost attainable with some different size of plant. Therefore, to every point on the long-run cost curve there corresponds a different short-run cost curve. Second, any point we find on the long-run cost curve is just one point out of all the points on the particular short-run average cost curve of the plant built to produce the indicated output in the long run. All other points on that short-run cost curve (and on each short-run curve in turn) do not lie on the long-run average cost curve because other outputs may be obtained more economically in the long run with other plant sizes. All other points on any short-run curve, aside from the one which lies on the long-run curve, thus lie above the long-run curve. Third, the point on each short-run curve which does lie on the long-run curve represents the one output which the corresponding size of plant can produce with greater efficiency than any other plant.

The long-run average cost curve thus simply passes through a succession of such points on a continuous family of short-run curves—each point representing the one output which a particular size of plant can produce more efficiently than any other. The character of its relationship to a family of alternative short-run curves is such that it passes through one point on each of an indefinite succession of such curves, just touching the lower edge of each one. It is sometimes referred to as an "envelope curve," enveloping a family of short-run curves in the manner indicated.

Thus, in Figure 14, $SRAC_1$, $SRAC_2$, and $SRAC_3$ represent the short-run average total cost curves attached to each of three successive scales of operation. The curve $LRAC$ is the long-run average cost curve which generalizes the long-run relation of cost to output shown by the movement from one short-run curve to another. The U shape of the long-run curve implies that the short-run curves for successively larger plants permit lower and lower average costs up to a certain "optimum" scale and thereafter higher and higher average costs. Since we draw the long-run cost curve as a continuous line, we assume that plant may be increased in size by indefinitely small gradations. Every point on *LRAC* is a point of tangency with some short-run cost curve which it envelops; although only three such short-run curves are actually shown on the diagram.[4]

What is the significance of these relationships from the standpoint of the firm? In making its long-run plans, the firm is guided by its long-run cost curve, which shows the lowest unit cost at which each alternative average rate of output can be produced over long periods. Thus, looking also to demand, it may be led during any interval to select a certain rate of output to

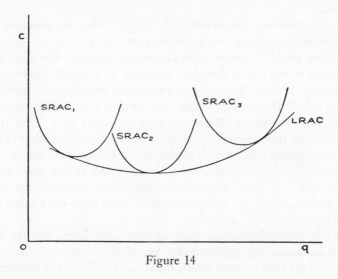

Figure 14

produce through time, and it may build plant of the best size to produce it, thus obtaining the lowest attainable cost for that output. If it does then produce this output in succeeding intervals, it will in a sense be "on" a point on its long-run average cost curve and a corresponding point on a short-run curve where it touches the long-run curve. If, however, having once built this size of plant, the firm encounters a smaller or larger demand

[4] It will be noted that the *LRAC* curve does not intersect the minimum-cost points of any of the short-run curves except the lowest. This is because at scales short of the optimum scale the lowest cost for any output is to be had by "underusing" a plant with a capacity slightly larger than the output needed—by operating a certain size of plant at an output short of that for which its own average total costs are a minimum. With costs declining in response to increasing scale, the output for which the plant's average total costs are a minimum can be produced more cheaply with a slightly larger plant operated at slightly less than the larger plant's minimum-cost output. Past the optimum scale it is conversely most economical to "overuse" plant with a capacity slightly smaller than the needed output. (The capacity of plant here refers to the output of a given size of plant which gives it its own minimum unit-cost rate of utilization.) For further discussion of the envelope curve, see Stigler, *op. cit.,* pp. 138-142.

than anticipated (because of fluctuations of demand around some average or of misestimation of demand), it will find that for short periods—that is, until it can again adjust capacity—it can vary output only along the lines shown by the short-run cost curve which corresponds to its present plant. If it faces a persistently different demand than it had built for, it will again begin adjusting scale and moving along its long-run cost curve. The short-run cost curves thus show simply the immediate cost-output alternatives facing the firm which has made some particular adjustment of scale. The long-run cost curves show its alternatives when more time-consuming adjustments can be completed.

In this connection, the student will recognize that the arbitrary dichotomy of cost-output relations into a "short run" and a "long run" is a drastic simplification made for purposes of elementary analysis. The firm in practice, starting at any given date and adjusting to demand conditions, considers many successively longer "short runs," each including the previous and extending a little further into future time until it reaches one long enough to permit variation of all factors and thus to qualify as a "long run." Its decision-making process must in essence consider the relationship of a series of such overlapping time periods extending up to the "time horizon" of its anticipations. When we speak of what the firm does in "the short run" and "the long run," we draw an extremely simplified picture of the decision-making process, albeit one which may shed much light on a more complicated reality.

It is further worth emphasis that the firm's cost curves, like the demand curve for its output, are operationally derived from *estimates* made by the firm. The cost-output relation which influences its decision is an *anticipated* relation, just as is its price-sales volume relation. Such estimates are probably drawn from past experience, but they are, nevertheless, estimates and subject to uncertainty. Where the uncertainty is great, the firm may have a rather sketchy knowledge of its strategic cost and demand curves, or it may try to find ways of compensating for its lack of substantial knowledge of these determinants.

D. FURTHER ASPECTS OF COST VARIATION

SHIFTS IN COST CURVES

We have so far discussed the relation of cost of production to output for business firms and have discovered certain typical patterns of cost variation which are likely to influence all price determination. But in so doing we have centered attention on only one of the changes which can cause a firm's production costs to vary—namely, the variation in its output of a given good. As we have specifically indicated already, independent changes in wages or in the prices the firm pays for its materials are not reflected in our cost curves, although these changes can be readily represented by shifts in these curves. Thus, the average and marginal cost curves of a firm when wages were $5 an hour and materials and equipment were at some specific price might appear as AC_1 and MC_1 in Figure 15. These curves typically show the variation of cost in response to change in output, given the stated level of

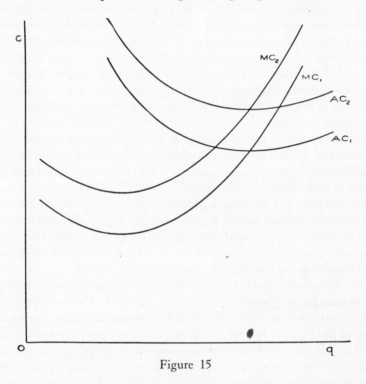

Figure 15

wages and material prices and positing no response of wages and material prices to output. If wages rise—for example, to $7 an hour—and materials to some corresponding higher level, we would register the resulting change in production costs by a shift of both cost curves to the new positions AC_2 and MC_2. The new cost curves would show the relation of cost to output, given the new wage-price level. The effect of independently changing wages and material prices on costs is thus shown in the shift from one curve to another (and also in any change in the shapes of the cost curves, resulting from disproportionate changes in wages and material prices, which might cause the firm to use different proportions of the various factors). Where wages and material prices respond to changes in the firm's output, of course, the effect of such responses must be reflected in movements along the cost curve. This is discussed further in Chapter 8.

There are obviously also other changes influencing costs which we have temporarily neglected in emphasizing the net relationship between cost and output. Two of these are changes in product and changes in the technique of production. In drawing our conventional cost curve we assume that the firm is producing a given definite product; the cost curve shows us the relation of cost to output for that specific product. Variations in the design or quality of such product may well affect costs, but such effects are not shown in a given cost curve, which specifically applies to one unchanging product. If the product is changed in quality or design, this must also be reflected in a shift to a new cost curve, as from AC_1 to AC_2 in Figure 15. Both the position and the shape of the cost curves may, of course, be affected. The shift of costs in response to variation of product may be just as significant to the firm in deciding its policy as is the cost-output relation shown by the shape of any one curve.

The same may be said of changes in technique; the cost-output relation represented in any cost curve is linked with and reflects a specific technique of production. Changes in cost resulting from change in technique must be reflected in shifts between cost curves.

The advantage of showing separately in a cost curve the simple net relation of cost to output, and of representing any other independent changes in cost by shifts in cost curves, is that it enables us to consider the variables which cause costs to change one at a time, and thus to simplify the problem. It also enables us to describe cost variations on a simple two-dimensional diagram, rather than having to use multidimensional mathematical equations. It must be recognized, however, that the cost of production for a firm is jointly and simultaneously influenced by the rate of output, the type and quality of product, the type of technique, and the wage-price level at which it hires and buys. The firm in practice must take simultaneous account of all such variations, and of their effect on costs. It does not choose a rate of output *in vacuo,* or a technique *in vacuo.* It must make a joint decision on the technique to use, the quality and design of product to produce, and the rate of output to maintain. It must also consider the combined effect on cost of the various aspects of its total decision. This must be kept clearly in mind when we employ cost curves in analyzing price determination.

OTHER VARIABLES INFLUENCING FIRM POLICY

Let us look back at this point and see how much we have learned concerning the variables and relationships which control the firm's price and output policy. In Chapters 2 and 3 we have discussed two principal intervariable relationships which will in general influence all firms—the relation of price to sales volume (the demand curve) and the relation of production cost to output (the cost curve). We have also referred to the relation of consumer income to demand and to the relation of product, technique, and money factor prices to production cost. But we have not discussed other relationships to which the firm must be sensitive, especially those of product to demand and of selling cost to demand for a product.

In particular, we have been concerned only with the costs to the firm of producing goods and making them available; we have not considered or included the costs of inducing people to buy them. Advertising, sales promotion, and allied expenses are selling costs. It is useful to distinguish them for two reasons. First, the importance of selling costs varies greatly from industry to industry and firm to firm; they may be negligible in some cases and important in others. Second, although there is a fairly clear relation between output and production cost for most firms (represented in the U shapes of average cost curves) there is no such predictable relation between output and selling cost. Sales promotion is not a stable technique which gives rise to predictable regularities in the relation of output to cost. In fact, selling costs are related to output only indirectly via their relation to the demand for the firm's product. It is, therefore, appropriate that they should be given separate treatment in the course of analyzing price determination. We will therefore turn at once to problems of price determination and discuss selling costs as those problems are analyzed.

VARIATION OF COST WITH INDUSTRY OUTPUT

We have until now been concerned mainly with the variation of production cost in response to variation in the output of the firm. We have inquired, for example, what happens to the cost per unit of output of a firm as it extends its output, either in the short run or the long run, from zero out to any limit. (For the firm, some limit ordinarily seems to be imposed either by the fact that its unit costs progressively rise after some output is passed or by the fact that the market will absorb no more.) This variation of the firm's cost with its output is of primary relevance to the firm in making decisions on price and output, and thus, it is pertinent to the analysis of enterprise behavior. From a broader viewpoint, however, we may also be interested in what happens to the average cost of production when an industry of several or many firms varies its output—in the response of cost to industry output variation.

This is a different question essentially because industry output variation involves either (1) the *simultaneous* variation of the outputs of a number of firms or (2) an addition to or subtraction from the number of firms producing. In either case the aggregate change in output which corresponds to a given percentage change in the base amount is larger when the base is industry output rather than firm output, and thus the increase in the demand for productive factors is greater and more likely to influence factor prices. Thus, induced factor-price change is more likely to have to be taken into account in analyzing the response of costs to industry output variation. Further, if industry output is varied by varying the number of firms rather than by varying the output of any firm, the response of industry costs to industry output variation is not necessarily the same as the response of firm costs to firm output variation. The variation of industry costs with industry output thus requires further analysis.

The character of the variation of industry cost with industry output is rather easily read from the corresponding variation for the firm in those cases where (1) the number of firms is fixed, so that industry output variation can be accomplished only by simultaneous output variations by member firms and where (2) industry output variations induce no changes in the prices of productive factors. In this case the shape of the curve showing relation of industry average or marginal cost to industry output must simply reflect the shapes of the average and marginal cost curves of the member firms of the industry. It can be precisely defined only on given suppositions regarding the manner in which various firms share in the increase or decrease in industry output, but given these, we can derive a curve showing the relation of industry average and marginal costs to industry output by some process of summation of the corresponding curves for the member firms. Here the industry cost variation will simply reflect the underlying firm cost variations and also the manner in which the fixed number of firms share in output changes for the industry. Such a relation of the industry cost variation to the firm's cost variation will ordinarily prevail approximately in the short run, where change in the number of firms in existence is not possible, if in addition industry output variations do not induce factor-price changes. This sort of relation will be initially discussed on pages 136 to 139 below, in the analysis of purely competitive pricing.

The relation of industry cost to output will be of a different shape from that of firm cost to output, however, if either (1) industry output changes induce factor-price variations which variation in the output of any one firm will not induce, or (2) industry output variation is accomplished by variation in the number of firms. It is quite possible, to take the first point, that, whereas any firm produces such a small output and thus hires so few factors that its output variation induces no factor-price change, variation of industry output by simultaneous output variation by many firms (or by variation in the number of firms) will perceptibly affect the prices of productive factors. If this is so, industry output variation produces *shifts* in the cost curves of all firms upward or downward as factor prices are induced to rise or fall. In this event the shape of the industry cost curve (average or marginal) reflects the effects of these shifts, as well as the effects of any movements along the cost curves of member firms, and, thus, the curve may have a different shape from any one of them. If, for example, factor prices to the industry are induced to rise as its output is extended, the industry cost curves will be made steeper in slope thereby. Such influences on the shape of industry cost output relations will be considered in Chapter 4 below, and subsequently elsewhere.

In addition, industry output variation may be accomplished in the long run not by variation in the outputs of firms but by variation in the number of firms. If this is the case, the shape of the industry cost-output relation is not at all affected by the shapes of the firm cost-output relations but will reflect simply the *level* of costs at which all firms are producing various industry outputs. If there are no induced factor-price changes as industry output varies, this means that the industry average cost curve will be a horizontal straight line. If there are induced factor-price variations, the industry cost curve will reflect simply the *shifts* in the level of cost caused by factor-price variation induced by industry output changes. So in this circumstance the shape of the industry cost-output relation will be only remotely related to the shapes of firms' cost-output relations. This also will be discussed further in Chapter 4.

In summary, the shape of the industry cost-output relation and its relationship to the firm cost-output relation will be strongly influenced by (1) whether the period being considered is short or long, (2) if it is long, whether there is free *entry* and *exit* of firms to and from the industry to facilitate output variations by such entry and exit, and (3) whether industry output variations induce factor-price variations which individual firm output variations will not induce. The preceding constitutes simply a sketchy introduction to the subject of industry cost variation. The matter will be discussed further in subsequent chapters on price determination.

Having made some analysis of demand conditions for the outputs of firms and industries, and some corresponding analysis of costs and cost variation with output, let us turn directly now to the analysis of the determination of prices and outputs.

SUPPLEMENTARY READINGS

JACOB VINER, "Cost Curves and Supply Curves," *Zeitschrift für Nationalökonomie,* III, 1932.

ALFRED MARSHALL, *Principles of Economics* (8th ed.), Books IV and V.

E. A. G. ROBINSON, *The Structure of Competitive Industry,* London: Nisbet, 1935.

CONFERENCE ON PRICE RESEARCH, *Cost Behavior and Price Policy,* New York: National Bureau of Economic Research, 1943.

KENNETH E. BOULDING, *Economic Analysis,* New York: Harper & Brothers, 1941, Chaps. 22-23.

4 PRICE DETERMINATION
IN PURE COMPETITION

Since the purpose of price analysis is to determine how a price system functions to allocate resources and distribute income, the nature of demands for and costs of products are not essentially important matters in themselves; a detailed knowledge of demands and costs, however much it is buttressed by mathematical refinement, has a distinctly limited usefulness. Demand and cost are important mainly because they are essential to the explanation of how the price system works.

Price formation begins with the individual firm, whose pricing decisions turn primarily upon the demand for its product and the cost of producing it. Let us now consider, in a simplified case, how such a firm makes decisions concerning price and output. From this we may proceed to an analysis of industry price-output determination and of the determination of the composition of aggregate output.

A. PRELIMINARY MATTERS

PRICE DETERMINATION FOR VARIOUS TIME INTERVALS

The most important problem concerns the function of the price system over time intervals long enough that the rate of production of goods can be varied and can thus become adjusted to the current levels of demand and of cost. We are thus concerned with price determination by the interaction of production costs and buyers' demands, an interaction which requires a sufficient passage of time for rates of output to change and for both demands and costs to make themselves felt. We will not consider at any length price determination in *very* short periods, during which the rate of production cannot be varied, and for which, in effect, costs of production are less important in price determination than the size of stocks or inventories on hand.

We have already mentioned two sorts of time intervals for which cost variations may be analyzed: (1) the long period, during which the firm may vary output through free variation in the quantities of all productive factors employed, and (2) the short period, during which output can be varied through variation in quantities employed of only a part of the factors of production, certain "plant factors" being fixed in quantity. In either of these periods costs of production interact with demand to determine price and output. For long-period planning expected long-run average and marginal costs interact with the anticipated long-run average level of demand to determine a long-run central tendency for price and output. During short periods short-run average and marginal costs interact with the currently prevailing (and changing) levels of demand to determine specific price tendencies for these shorter periods. A series of short-period prices, following a fluctuating

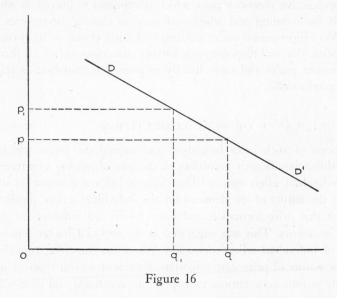

Figure 16

demand, may have as their central tendency the long-run price just mentioned.

There is, however, an even shorter interval, which we will simply call a *"very short" period,* short enough that for its duration output cannot be varied at all. For such a period price depends mainly on immediate demand and on the amount of stocks on hand. If demand fluctuates during such periods, price movements will depend on the amount of inventories on hand and on the rate at which the owners of such inventories are willing to dispose of them. Such very-short-period prices may tend to fluctuate on either side of short-run prices.

The theory of very-short-period pricing will not be expounded in much detail. In a very short period there will be for any good a given industry demand, showing the amounts buyers are ready to take at various prices. There will also be a certain stock of the good available or on hand over a time interval during which existing stocks of finished output cannot be supplemented. Dealers in the good may decide to put the entire stock on the market during this very short period, in which case price will find a corresponding level on the demand curve, or they may decide to withhold part of it, in which case the price will be higher. Thus, if in Figure 16 the demand for a good is DD' for a very short period, and the stock on hand is oq, offering of the entire stock will result in a price of op. But if sellers offer only oq_1, withholding the amount q_1q, the price will be op_1. Various suppositions concerning the tendency of sellers to withhold stocks may be developed. By and large, however, their tendency to withhold will be governed by the prospective *short-run* price which is expected to prevail as additional output is forthcoming and which will rule as existing inventories are replaced. Very-short-period prices are thus tied fairly closely to short-run prices and to costs. We will dispense with further discussion of special theories of very-short-run prices and turn directly to price determination as related to costs of production.

THE SIGNIFICANCE OF PURE COMPETITION

The process of such price formation and indeed the prices which result from it differ significantly according to the sort of market structure within which individual sellers operate. The characteristics of this market structure influence the nature of the demand for the individual sellers' product, with the result that price formation and price results are different for different types of industries. This was suggested at the end of Chapter 2 in our discussion of individual sellers' demands. We must, therefore, consider separately the nature of price determination in each of several types of industry —initially in pure competition, monopoly, differentiated and pure oligopoly, and monopolistic competition.

We begin with industries in pure competition—where there are many small sellers, all of whom produce identical products. Several markets for agricultural crops, especially the grains, reasonably approximate purely competitive conditions. That is, a given crop is produced by several thousand farmers, no one of whom controls a significant proportion of the total output. Their various outputs, moreover, being reduced to standard specifications or grades, are viewed as identical by all buyers. In the field of industrial production purely competitive market structures are unusual because ordinarily the sellers are few and their products are often differentiated. Two industrial markets which give fair approximations to pure competition, however, are that for cotton gray goods and that for bituminous coal. Cotton gray goods are produced by about 600 small firms, without any very significant differentiation among their outputs. Soft coal is produced by over a thousand small mining companies, and the output is substantially undifferentiated. In other areas, like that of the distributive trades, markets with many small sellers are more common, but product differentiation ordinarily places them in the category of monopolistic rather than pure competition. For the American economy as a whole the purely competitive market or any close approximation to it is an exceptional case.

Some explanation, therefore, is required for treating this rather special case before turning to the more common market situation where sellers are few and products significantly differentiated. Pure competition is considered first for four reasons. First, the analysis of pricing in pure competition is relatively simple and uncomplicated; consequently, it serves as a useful introduction to more complicated phases of price analysis. The range of pricing and allied decisions which must be made by a seller in pure competition is ·much narrower than that facing sellers in monopolistic and oligopolistic markets. There is thus less for analysis to take account of, and certain fundamentals common to all markets may be made to stand out more clearly.

Second, the price behavior and results which emerge from purely competitive markets serve as a convenient measuring rod or standard for appraising the price results in other (and more common) sorts of markets. The price results associated theoretically with pure competition are often held to possess certain *normative* properties or to represent a sort of ideal in capitalist pricing behavior. In any event, many of the traditional justifications for a *laissez-faire* economy, which argue that a capitalist economy is through its price system automatically self-regulating toward ideal results, refer explicitly or implicitly to a world of purely competitive markets or, at any rate, of markets not *significantly* different in their operation from markets in pure competition. This is true of Adam Smith (*The Wealth of Nations,* 1776) and of Friedrich Hayek (*The Road to Serfdom,* 1944). Without prejudging the normative merits of pure competition, we recognize here that the analysis of purely competitive markets may provide tentative standards by which other more common sorts of behavior may be measured.

Third, it is likely that at least certain categories of industries other than the purely competitive may behave quite similarly to purely competitive industries. This may be true, for example, of industries in monopolistic competition and possibly of others. Although the extent of this similarity remains to be evaluated, its existence adds to the significance of the highly simplified predictions which emerge from the analysis of purely competitive price. Finally, of course, there are enough purely competitive markets in the modern economy to make investigations of this type practically important. We will, therefore, consider at once the operation of the firm, the industry, and the economy when governed by pure competition.

B. SHORT-RUN PRICING IN PURE COMPETITION

OUTPUT DETERMINATION BY THE FIRM

The basic characteristics of a market in pure competition are (1) that the various sellers in the market produce a single identical product and (2) that they are so many in number and so small that no one of them can perceptibly influence the price of this product. From the large number and relative smallness of these sellers there may also ordinarily be inferred a third market characteristic. It is quite easy for additional sellers to enter the market if they so desire; there is *ease of entry*.[1] In such a market, how may price and output be expected to behave, and how may the force of competition be expected to govern productive activity?

There are in general two ways of seeking an answer to this question. One is to find some markets with a purely competitive structure, observe what happens in them, and then make some generalizations concerning their behavior. Another is to postulate the relevant conditions which control the operation of enterprise in such a market and to work out deductively the sort of behavior which logically should emerge from the postulated circumstances. The latter method is that of conventional price analysis and that which we shall investigate at present. It is certainly not a substitute for inductive investigation, which should always supplement and test the conclusions of the more abstract theory, but it does offer by far the most facile and accessible means of developing a general idea of what the significance of any market situation is.

Our first inquiry will concern how the individual firm in a purely competitive industry decides upon its short-run price and its output. Suppose, for example, there are 600 small sellers of gray cotton yarn. Let us consider the price-output decisions of one of them—first for a short period. Here we

---

[1] The full conditions for "easy" or "free" entry may be defined as follows: (1) The investment necessary to establish a firm is small enough that many potential entrants can obtain sufficient funds to establish a firm; (2) the increment to industry output resulting from the entry of one additional firm is so small as to have no perceptible effect on industry price, and thus the potential entrant is not deterred by fear of changing the existing price situation; (3) all potential entrants have free access to all resources or factors needed for production, at competitive market prices, since there is no monopolization of resource ownership or control by established firms; (4) there are no other artificial impediments to entry; and (5) new entrants can produce outputs identical to those of established firms. Where all these conditions are observed, we have the ultimate in ease of entry, or purely competitive free entry. In markets outside the purely competitive category, however, there may be *relatively* easy entry, where some but not all of these conditions are observed. "Easy" entry in oligopoly, for example, might observe all conditions except the second, and possibly the first and fifth.

have a firm with a given product (a standardized grade of yarn) and a given fixed plant, which for the course of the short period it cannot vary in size. As a small buyer of factors, it will also be faced with given money prices for the factors of production which it purchases and which enter into its cost of production. How does it decide how much to produce and what price to charge for the next short-run (for example, six-month) interval?

Presumably the firm will calculate (1) the prospective selling price it can receive for its goods and any variations of this price with variations in its own output and sales volume, and (2) the prospective cost of producing goods for sale and any variation of this cost with variations in its rate of output. In other words, it will refer to the demand curve for its own output and to its short-run cost curves.

The demand curve for the output of a seller in pure competition approximates a horizontal straight line at the level of going or anticipated market price. That is, he can sell any output he can reasonably produce without causing the market price to change perceptibly, and can sell nothing above that price.[2] The seller in pure competition has no price decision to make. He will simply accept or estimate market price and choose the rate of output which, in the light of the relationship of the production costs to output, seems to him most profitable.

The nature of his problem may be illustrated by considering the going price of his product in conjunction with the short-run cost curves for his given plant in a single diagram, as in Figure 17. Here dd' is the demand curve for the firm's own output—in effect a "price line" showing the going market price at which it can sell any output. The various cost curves show how its average total cost, average variable cost, average fixed cost, and marginal cost of production vary with varying output, given the prevailing factor prices. The usual motive of a business firm, we have assumed, will be *to choose that output which will maximize its aggregate profit for the period under consideration.* The firm, supposedly, seeks the output which, for the short period at hand, will allow it to make the largest possible aggregate profit or smallest possible aggregate loss.

In Figure 17 it is apparent that the firm can make some sort of profit at any output between q_1 and q_2 (at which limits price is equal to average total cost) though at outputs smaller than q_1 or larger than q_2 it would make a net loss. To choose the output (between q_1 and q_2) which will

[2] This is the case certainly where there are many small buyers for the industry output and, thus, a conventional industry demand schedule for industry output. It *may* also be the case where there is one buyer or a few, who simply announce a buying price. Attention will be centered generally in this chapter, however, on the usual many-buyer market.

maximize its aggregate profit, the firm will refer directly to its *marginal cost of production* and the *marginal receipts from its sales.*[3]

The *marginal cost* of production, shown by the line *MC*, is the addition to aggregate cost for any unit addition to output. The *marginal receipts* is now defined correspondingly as *the addition to aggregate receipts for any*

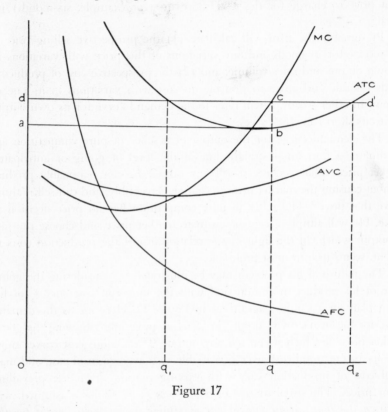

Figure 17

unit addition to output (and sales). In pure competition, where price remains invariant as the individual seller increases his output, his marginal or additional receipts from any unit added to output are the same as the price of that unit of output. Thus, if a firm's demand schedule shows the following purely competitive relation—

[3] To maximize aggregate profit the firm wishes to find that output at which there is the greatest difference between aggregate receipts and aggregate total cost (definitionally the same as the output where there is a maximum difference between aggregate receipts and aggregate variable cost). This is essentially also the output where the profit per unit of output times the quantity of output is a maximum. It is most easily *identified* by comparing marginal cost and marginal receipts at successive outputs.

p	q	Total receipts $p \cdot q$	Marginal receipts (change in $p \cdot q$)
10	12	120	—
10	13	130	10
10	14	140	10

it is apparent that marginal receipts are always the same as price. The firm's demand curve, dd', is, therefore, also its *marginal receipts curve,* showing additions to total revenue per unit of additions to output.

To find the most profitable output the firm will logically add to its output as long as the marginal cost of additional output is less than the marginal receipts of that output. But it will not extend output when the marginal cost of additional output becomes greater than the marginal receipts. It is then evident that the firm will maximize it profits at the output for which marginal cost just equals marginal receipts. In pure competition, where the marginal receipts earned by any unit of output are the same as its price, the firm will evidently extend output exactly to the point where marginal cost equals price. This is the output oq in Figure 17.

At this output the price is measured by the distance qc, the total cost per unit by the distance qb, and the profit per unit of output by the distance bc. The *aggregate profit* is measured by the rectangle $abcd$ (the profit per unit, bc, multiplied by the quantity of output, ab). This is necessarily the largest profit which can be earned during the short period in question. It is suggested that the student reconsider the preceding four paragraphs until he understands the argument thoroughly.

The general rule which the firm follows to maximize its short-run profit is to select the output at which marginal cost is equal to marginal receipts, which in the case of pure competition also means that marginal cost is equal to price. If the market price at which the firm can sell changes during a short period, the firm will change its output sufficiently to bring marginal cost into equality with the new price.

In Figure 18 we suppose that a firm, with the same costs shown in Figure 17, is faced successively with the prices p_1, p_2, p_3, and p_4. As the market price changes from one level to another, the competitive firm's demand curve, a horizontal line, simply shifts to a new level. It is evident from our preceding argument that at the price p_1 the firm will produce q_1; at p_2 it will produce q_2; at p_3 the quantity q_3; at p_4 the quantity q_4. That is, it will adjust its output so as to *equate* marginal cost to each new price. In this way it will earn the largest profit or incur the smallest loss obtainable at any particular price.

It is not necessary that the firm make a profit in excess of full costs, or that it break even, to induce it to remain in business for the short period. (The average total costs of the firm, represented in the *ATC* curve, are defined as inclusive of a normal return on capital and of wages of manage-

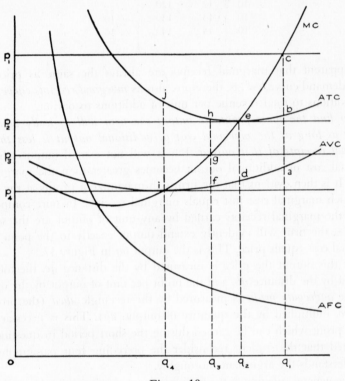

Figure 18

ment—or, in effect, of a normal profit.) Whether the firm makes more or less than costs including this normal profit in a given short period simply depends upon where market price happens to lie. If market price is high, as at p_1, the firm makes an excess profit at its most profitable output, in the amount *bc* per unit. If price falls just at p_2, the firm can just recover full costs (average total costs equaling price), but it can make no excess profit. If price is p_3, the firm makes a net loss in the amount *gh* per unit. If price is still lower at p_4, it makes a larger net loss of *ij* per unit. Any of those results might ensue in the short period. Higher prices ordinarily character-ize prosperous times and lower prices depression periods.

It is easily evident that the firm should be willing to produce at the prices p_1 or p_2, where it either makes an excess profit or recovers full costs.

But it may at first appear surprising that the firm should continue to po-
duce at a net loss, at prices p_3 or p_4. The logic of such a procedure is evident,
however, if we recall that short-period costs are partly fixed and partly
variable and that the fixed costs would be incurred at zero output. If the
firm refuses to produce at all, it will incur a net loss equal to its total fixed
costs. It should, therefore, be willing to accept any price which will enable
it to reduce this loss or, in other words, any price in excess of the average
variable (or out-of-pocket) cost of production. If it does this, it will find
that production at a net loss per unit enables it to minimize its total loss for
the short period by recovering some proportion of the otherwise lost fixed
cost.

Thus, in Figure 18 the firm is willing at the price p_3 to produce the
output q_3 (making a net loss per unit of gh) because this enables it to make
a return per unit *above average variable costs* in the amount fg. This return, though not enough to defray all fixed costs, at least recovers a part
of them and thus makes production worth while. We may, therefore, generalize that the firm will produce in the short run (at an output where
marginal cost equals price) as long as price exceeds the average variable
cost of output. Thus, the minimum price which would induce the firm to
produce in Figure 18 is p_4, where price just equals average variable cost.
At lower prices the firm would presumably shut down.[4]

The excess above variable costs which the firm is able to earn in a
short period is often referred to as the *quasi-rent* earned by the fixed plant
in that period. Thus, in Figure 18 at the price p_1 the quasi-rent per unit of
output is ac; at p_2 it is de; at p_3 it is fg; and at p_4 it is zero. The rule is
that the firm will produce in the short period as long as it can earn any
positive quasi-rent.

It should also be evident, since the competitive firm always adjusts
its output in accordance with the variation in its marginal cost of production, that the firm's rising short-run marginal cost curve may be regarded
also as its *short-run supply curve*—that is, it is the curve which indicates
the amount of output forthcoming at any particular price. This is precisely
true for the range of the firm's marginal cost curve wherever it lies above
average variable cost. The reason for this is obvious on a little reflection.
The marginal cost curve shows *explicitly* the marginal cost at each quantity
of output (that is, the added cost of the last unit at each quantity of out-

---

[4] How far the firm will see price drop below its full cost before shutting down
depends upon the fraction of its full costs which it considers fixed for such a period.
This proportion is partly a technical matter, depending upon the relation of equipment costs to labor and material costs. But it also depends upon the length of the short
period for which the firm calculates. The longer a short period it takes into account,
the fewer of its costs will appear fixed.

put). But the firm, to maximize profits, always acts so as to produce a quantity of output for which marginal cost equals price. Therefore, the firm always is in a position such that marginal cost equals price (for any output where marginal cost exceeds average variable cost). If this is true, price may be *substituted* for marginal cost at each point, and the marginal cost curve then shows the output which the firm will supply at each price. This is precisely what a firm's supply curve is—a curve showing the relation of price to output supplied. It may be emphasized, however, that the generalization holds only where the firm does equate marginal cost to price, as where it maximizes profits in pure competition, and not more generally.

Thus far we have described the way in which in the short run a firm in pure competition should adjust its output to the going market price. Such a firm has no control over price and therefore no "price policy." It necessarily accepts the going or estimated market price as given and beyond its own control, and it devotes itself to selecting that output which offers the largest short-run quasi-rent and profit. This output is necessarily defined as that for which the firm's short-run marginal cost of production equals price. The firm will produce so long as price, at this output, is greater than average variable cost.

PRICE AND OUTPUT FOR THE INDUSTRY

Although our analysis suggests how a single firm should respond to a given market price, it does not yet tell us how this market price is arrived at. The next question, therefore, is this: How in a purely competitive market do the aggregated reactions of individual firms determine the industry price? We consider this question first for the short run, during which *the number of firms* and *the sizes of their respective plants* cannot be changed.

A purely competitive market is composed of a large number of firms producing a single product. For our purposes let us study a market of 700 firms producing gray cotton yarn. On a certain date the market price of their good is *op* per unit. At this price each firm produces some output *oq*, at which its own short-run marginal cost equals this price, as in Figure 19. What happens in the market as a whole? For the entire market an *aggregate supply* equal to the sum of all the individual *oq*'s of the several hundred firms is produced. If there are 700 firms, the aggregate supply may be defined as:

$$Q = (q_1 + q_2 + q_3 + \cdots q_{700}),$$

or, in effect, the sum of the individual outputs chosen by all firms.

This aggregate supply, together with the *industry demand* for the product, should establish a market price. The industry demand for gray cotton yarn might appear as *DD'* in Figure 20, showing the amounts of yarn which buyers as a whole are prepared to take at each market price. The price scale in Figure 20 is the same as that shown for the individual seller's

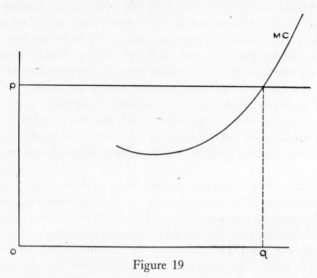

Figure 19

demand line. The quantity scale runs in much larger quantities. Thus, the output *oq* of one seller is represented by a very small distance, whereas the combined output of 700 sellers is the much longer distance *OQ*.

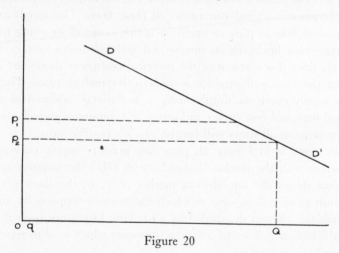

Figure 20

In the example in Figure 20 we began by supposing a provisional price op_1 (similar to *op* in Figure 19) for the good. At this price sellers react and produce a combined output *OQ*. Now the process of market price determination is under way. The output OQ will sell at some specific price but not necessarily at the provisional price op_1 which brought it forth. In the example above it will sell at a lower price, op_2, and the market price will consequently fall to this level. But with this price drop each seller will produce a little less (reducing output to a point where marginal cost again equals price). As a result the aggregate output will be reduced to somewhat below OQ, and the price will rise above op_2. By a process of successive adjustment the market will arrive at some price, op_e, intermediate between op_2 and op_1, *at which the aggregate amount buyers are willing to take just equals the aggregate amount sellers are willing to supply.*

Thus, it is clear that the aggregate of adjustments of supply undertaken by many small firms, interacting with the market demand, determines a short-run "equilibrium" price at which industry demand and supply are in balance.

This explanation is accurate enough as far as it goes, but it is unnecessarily cumbersome. The determination of short-run market price in pure competition may be characterized more concisely as follows. The demand conditions affecting price are evidently represented in the industry demand schedule for the good, DD', showing the amount which all buyers will take at each price. The short-run supply conditions for the market as a whole may be represented in a corresponding *industry supply curve SS'*, which shows the amounts of goods all sellers will offer at each price. *This short-run industry supply curve is evidently the aggregate of the short-run supply curves of all the individual firms in the market, or, in effect, the sum of the short-run marginal cost curves of these firms.* The supply curve of the individual firm in pure competition is that range of its rising marginal cost curve which lies above its intersection with the firm's average variable cost curve, since this segment of the marginal cost curve shows the amount of output the firm will produce at each corresponding price. To get the industry supply curve we simply make a "horizontal" addition of all such individual marginal cost curves and arrive at a summation which shows the aggregate amount all firms will furnish at each possible price.

If we now, as in Figure 21, place this industry supply curve, SS', in juxtaposition with the market demand curve, DD', the intersection of the two curves shows the equilibrium market price. In the short period the equilibrium price will be op_e, at which the amount supplied by all sellers just equals the amount demanded by all buyers. Departure from this price in either direction will set in course adjustments which tend to return price to the equilibrium level.

The preceding construction of the short-run industry supply curve assumes that variable factor prices paid by firms in the industry do not change in response to a change in industry output. The supply curve thus is a simple summation of firms' marginal cost curves, each drawn on the assumption of given factor prices, and its slope reflects only movement along such curves. If, however, factor prices change in response to changes in *industry* output—though not to changes in any firm's output—thus causing the cost curves of all firms to shift as industry output varies, then the industry supply curve must be drawn to reflect such induced shifts in firms' marginal cost curves as well as movements along them.

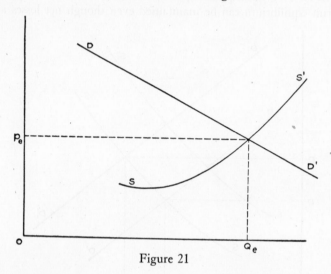

Figure 21

The equilibrium found where the short-run industry supply curve intersects the industry demand curve has two essential properties. First, price is such that the aggregate amount sellers are willing to produce just equals the amount buyers are willing to take. The price thus tends to be maintained rather than to be departed from, so long as demand and supply conditions are unchanged. Second, each seller is in individual short-run equilibrium, producing just such an amount that his marginal cost equals market price. This is, of course, essential if the price is an equilibrium price.

Although each seller regards price as outside his control and simply adjusts his output to whatever the going price may be, it is thus clear that the combined actions of many such sellers unequivocally determine a definite market price at which the individual profit-seeking adjustments of all sellers can be maintained consistently with the aggregate desires of buyers. We see, first in the instance of short-run adjustments, that a market in pure competition is "automatically regulated" or "self-regulating" to a certain end. "An invisible hand," as Adam Smith described it, harnesses the essentially selfish adjustments of each of many sellers to produce a price result that none of them has planned.

PROPERTIES OF SHORT-RUN BEHAVIOR IN PURE COMPETITION

What is the character of this unplanned price result? For the short run it has relatively few properties. First, the equilibrium price is equal to the marginal cost of production of all sellers. Second, the short-run price may be equal to, greater than, or less than the average total cost of any or all producers. As long as all plant capacity and the number of firms are fixed, a short-run equilibrium can be maintained even though net losses are gen-

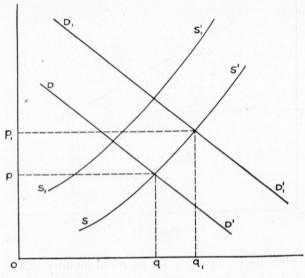

Figure 22

eral or highly attractive excess profits are generally being earned in the industry. Adjustments to correct for such conditions can occur only in the longer run. All that is required in the short run is that price shall be at least as high as the average variable costs of production of at least some sellers in the industry. In the short run price bears no necessary correspondence to average total cost of production.

These are the principal evident properties of purely competitive price in any given short-run situation. Certain other significant properties are observed, however, if we consider short-run adjustments to changes in demand or cost. As the economy moves through time, the level of demand for goods generally, or for any particular good, ordinarily fluctuates with changes in the volume of consumer purchasing power. Similarly, the level of industry costs fluctuates with changes in wage rates and material prices which are independent of the industry's output. Such fluctuations are reflected in systematic *shifts* in industry demand and supply curves, as shown in Figure 22. Thus, an increase in demand with the advent of more prosperous times would be reflected by a shift of the industry demand curve for a good from DD' to D_1D_1'. A rise in the level of costs independently of industry output would be registered in a shift of the industry supply (combined marginal cost) curve from SS' to S_1S_1'. When such shifts occur in a purely competitive industry, no seller can control price, and as a result there is an immediate and full adjustment of price and output to changes in demand or cost. Thus, if demand is DD' and supply SS', equilibrium price is op and quantity oq. But a shift of demand to D_1D_1' (supply remaining the same at SS') will automatically raise price to op_1 and quantity to oq_1. Other shifts in supply or demand will bring similarly immediate responses.

An important property of pure competition is thus that price is automatically responsive to changes in demand or cost, and tends to be very *flexible* over time if there are changes in these price-determining variables. The purely competitive price thus tends to perform an active regulatory function in adjusting output to changes in the surrounding economic situation. So far as it tends to rise and fall readily in response to controlling changes, moreover, it tends to dampen fluctuations in output, which thus can be more stable over time than it would be if price were more rigid.[5]

The preceding discussion has characterized the determination of price and output in pure competition for the short run—that is, for periods of six months to one or two years during which the amount of fixed plant available in such an industry is relatively inflexible. For such a period price and output observe certain systematic tendencies. In particular, they are readily adjusted to the marginal costs of producing with the given fixed plant. Otherwise, however, short-period price behavior follows no certain pattern. The volume of output, the size of profits, and the relation of attained to optimum (lowest-unit-cost) output varies with the relation of the amount of productive capacity to the current level of buyers' demand. But over longer periods, during which the size of plants and firms and the number of firms in the industry can be freely increased or decreased, we should expect that the force of competition would effect some more certain average relation of capacity to demand and place some limits on the average rate of profit or loss incurred by producing firms.

This is to say that, although with year-to-year fluctuations or other changes in costs or demands the immediate or short-term adaptation of the industry to new or nontypical situations may vary over the entire range of possible adjustments envisaged by the theory of short-run pricing, the adjustment which will develop over longer time periods to any customary demand and cost situation may be of a much more specific and limited

[5] For a general discussion of price flexibility, see Saul Nelson and W. G. Keim, *Price Behavior and Business Policy,* Temporary National Economic Committee, Monograph No. 1 (Washington, 1941), Chap. 2.

character. An industry price-output adjustment relative to a given situation of industry demand and cost which is stable or of equilibrium character as long as the number and plant capacity of firms is unchangeable may not constitute a stable adjustment as sufficient time passes (or when it already has passed) for the number and the scale of firms to be varied. The short-run analysis is thus primarily useful in predicting the range of possibilities open for relatively immediate adjustments to new or nontypical demand and cost situations or for period-to-period adjustments to fluctuating demand and cost conditions. We must look to long-run analysis to predict the ultimate tendency in adjustment to any given set of demand and cost conditions and to identify, therefore, the central or average tendency through time of the adjustment the purely competitive industry will make to given demand and cost conditions or to the "average" demand and cost situation over time.

C. LONG-RUN PRICE AND OUTPUT IN PURE COMPETITION

THE PROCESS OF ADJUSTMENT FOR THE INDUSTRY

For a long period as for a short one, the firm in pure competition is concerned with adjusting its rate of output to the going or anticipated level of market price. But in the long run it may vary its output not only by varying the rate of use of its existing plant, but also by simultaneously varying the size of this plant. The relationship of cost to output in which it is interested is described by its long-run cost curve, already discussed in Chapter 3. The firm will presumably set its long-run average and marginal costs against the expected long-run level of market price and choose that combination of plant size and rate of use of plant which it believes will afford it the greatest profit.

The firm's adjustment is seen in Figure 23. Its demand curve is a hori-zontal line at the expected long-run average market price. It considers its long-run average and marginal costs in conjunction with this price. Following the logic already developed, the firm will set its scale of operations at such a level that long-run marginal cost is equal to price (since this allows the maximum long-run profit) so long as price is equal to or greater than its minimum average cost for the long run. That is, at the price p_2 it will build to a scale to produce the output q_2—to a larger than lowest-cost scale. At the price p it will build to a scale to produce the output q—to lowest-cost scale. At any lower price, p_1, this firm will not produce at all; it will refuse to build any new plant or will begin to liquidate its existing plant.

It may be noted that, should the firm initially have made a short-run adjustment to a given market price (by equating short-run marginal cost to price), this would not remain an equilibrium adjustment with further passage of time unless the firm's scale was already such that long-run marginal cost also equaled price and that at this output price exceeded long-run average cost. Otherwise, the firm would make long-run adjustments according to the pattern just described—until its ultimate short-run adjustment was consistent with an optimal long-run adjustment.

So much for the reaction of the single firm to any anticipated long-run price, which is precisely the same order as its adjustment to a short-run price. The determination of the long-run price for the industry, however,

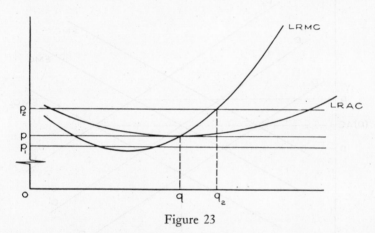

Figure 23

does involve a different element and a different result. The industry price will in effect be determined jointly by the aggregate output adjustments of an initial number of firms in the industry *and by the entry or exit of firms in response to excess profits or net losses.*

Suppose initially, as in Figure 24, that the long-run industry demand is DD', that ΣMC represents the summation of the long-run marginal cost curves of the existing firms in the industry, and that AC is the level of the minimum average cost (including normal profit) of every firm in the industry. (The reason for considering all firms equal in this respect will be discussed below.) In this event, the combined industry output will be OQ, the price, op, will be equal to AC, and all firms will be making just a normal profit at minimum cost. Each firm will be in a position indicated by the relation of p to $LRAC$ where $LRMC$ equals p in Figure 23. Since none will wish to leave and since additional entry would cut price below minimum average costs, the industry is evidently in long-run equilibrium.

Such an equilibrium would not ordinarily occur without adjustment, however, but would have to be approached by entry or exit. Thus suppose, alternatively, the number of firms and the conditions of cost being the same, that the demand for the industry is D_1D_1' (Figure 24). The initial number of firms (with combined marginal costs ΣMC) is now too large—that is, the price op_1, which results if all equate marginal cost to price, falls below minimum average costs (which are at the level of AC). Firms will begin to leave the industry, as each firm is in a position indicated by the relation of p_1 to $LRAC$ where $LRMC$ equals p_1 in Figure 23. Supply will be restricted, the ΣMC curve will shift leftward (as there are fewer $LRMC$ curves for individual firms to enter into the total, ΣMC), and price will rise. When

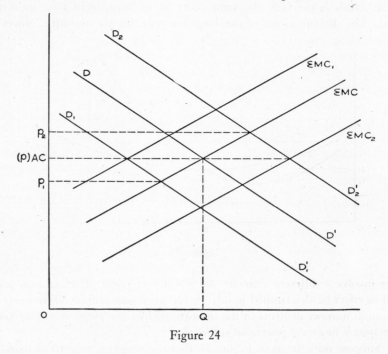

Figure 24

enough firms leave that it reaches the position ΣMC_1, price will equal op, equal to minimum average costs AC, and the industry will be in long-run equilibrium to the demand D_1D_1'. (Price will in effect be p from Figure 23.) In short, exit of firms takes place until total supply is such that price simultaneously equals the long-run marginal cost and minimum average cost of production of all firms (which they have all attained), and here exit stops.

Suppose, alternatively, that with the same minimum average costs, and with the initial aggregate marginal cost ΣMC, the industry demand is D_2D_2'. Now with the initial number of firms, price will be op_2, and above the average costs of all firms, in the position shown by the relation of p_2 to $LRAC$ where $LRMC$ equals p_2 in Figure 23. These firms will be content to remain and make excess profits, but additional firms will wish to enter the industry to get some excess profits also. (Investments in this industry promise to earn a profit in excess of the basic interest return they could command in the general market for funds, and thus if funds are freely available at that interest rate, they will be entered and invested here.) As they do so, the aggregate supply (ΣMC) will shift rightward, and price will fall. When sufficient firms have entered that it reaches ΣMC_2, price wil be op, equal to minimum average costs, AC (the minimum $LRAC$ from Figure 23), and the industry will be in equilibrium to the demand D_2D_2'. The entry of firms takes place until total supply is such that price equals minimum average costs, which all firms have attained. There it should stop.

Taking the preceding argument as a whole, it is evident that in the long run, and with unimpeded entry and exit of new firms, the scale and number of firms will adjust together to produce such an industry output that price equals the minimum average costs of production of all firms. This is the result of free and unrestricted pure competition.

THE LONG-RUN INDUSTRY SUPPLY CURVE

In arriving at this conclusion, however, we made certain simplifying assumptions—namely, that all firms in an industry have the same minimum average cost at any given industry output and that this minimum cost does not shift up or down as industry output is extended or restricted by entry to or exit from the industry. Where these conditions both hold, *the long-run supply curve for the industry* is in effect a horizontal line at the level of this minimum average cost—for example, the line extended from AC in Figure 24. That is, under free entry and exit firms are in the long run continually forced to produce at prices equal to their minimum average costs, and output will be extended or retracted at this uniform minimum cost-price level simply by adding to or subtracting from the number of firms until output is such that price equals this cost. Hence the locus of successive minima of the long-run average costs of the member firms (the line extended from AC in Figure 24) is the long-run supply curve for the purely competitive industry. Where the demand curve intersects this supply curve, we find the long-run price and output for the industry. Although each firm adjusts so as to produce where long-run marginal cost equals price, the pressure of entry and exit is such that it succeeds in producing only where minimum average cost is also equal to price. Since this minimum average cost is not altered as industry output is changed by entry or exit of firms, the industry has a perfectly elastic long-run supply curve at its level.

Let us now reconsider the simplifying assumptions concerning uniformity of minimum costs as among firms at any given industry output and the constancy of the minimum cost level in the face of change in industry output.

The proposition that all firms have identical minimum costs at any given industry output in the long run stems from the definition of costs. It is initially assumed for this argument that all firms can and do in the long run use the one most economical technique of production (this may be considered a corollary of free entry) and thus that their costs do not differ because of differences in technique. Given this, all firms must have identical minimum average costs in equilibrium as long as the units of any factor used by one firm have the same efficiency as those used by others and as long as each firm pays for or counts as the cost of any factor the same given market price that other firms do.

The latter will be true so far as they all acquire any factor from what is essentially a single market and at a single market price, and this is also implicitly assumed. If they use factors of differing efficiency, their minimum average costs will under this assumption be identical if each factor unit is paid or imputed a market value representing the full earning power corresponding to its particular efficiency. An *apparent* difference in costs among firms may result from the fact that some firms in calculating costs impute or pay to factors of given quality other than their market prices, or from the fact that they do not pay or impute to factors of superior efficiency the full market value of their superior efficiency. But when costs are defined to include a market value imputed to each factor unit which represents its full earning power (under conditions of competitive free entry)—as they should be—all firms in a competitive industry will have identical minimum average costs, which will equal industry price in long-run equilibrium. Costs will, of course, not include the earning power of impediments to entry, since these are assumed not to exist.[6] But it is of course understood that included in costs and covered by the equilibrium price are "normal profits"—that is, a basic interest return on owners' investment and the imputed value of any other services for which the firm does not make contractual payments.

The second assumption was that the minimum average costs of firms do not shift up or down as industry output is changed by firms entering or leaving the industry—that as firms are added, they will not have higher minimum costs than those already in, and that as firms leave, this will not result in the remainder having lower costs. Investigation of this assumption leads us to consider the relationship of expansion or contraction in one industry to the prices of productive factors used by the industry.

If all productive factors are available to a given industry in perfectly elastic supply—if any of them may be obtained in larger or smaller quantity without influencing its money price—then output can be expanded or contracted by the entry or exit of firms without influencing the money costs of any firm or the proportions in which various factors are employed. This

[6] See George J. Stigler, *The Theory of Price* (New York: The Macmillan Company, 1946), pp. 159-166, and Kenneth E. Boulding, *Economic Analysis* (New York: Harper & Brothers, 1941), Chap. 21, for further analysis of this somewhat complicated issue, which is treated only in elementary and simplified fashion here.

assumption of a perfectly elastic supply of all factors to the industry is thus the direct corollary of the assumption of a perfectly elastic long-run supply curve for the output of a purely competitive industry.

If, however, some or all employed factors are in limited supply to the industry so that their prices increase as entry takes place and more are used or decrease as exit occurs and less are used, then the money costs of all firms will shift up or down (*LRAC* for every firm will shift up or down) as entry or exit takes place and industry output changes. As a result, entry to eliminate excess profits will result in rising industry cost and exit to eliminate losses will result in falling costs. The long-run equilibrium for the industry will still be characterized by all firms producing with minimum *LRAC* equal to price. But the long-run industry supply curve (the locus of minimum *LRAC*'s at various outputs) will have an upward slope instead of being horizontal. Then industry price in the long-run must be expected to rise if demand increases and output is expanded by moving from one long-run equilibrium to another.

What is the expectation of the character of this long-run supply curve for actual industries? For a single small industry buying nonspecialized productive factors in large markets, expansion or contraction of its requirements will probably not influence factor prices much, and the long-run industry supply curve should be very elastic. For industries using a factor in limited supply or factors of the total supply of which the industry employs a considerable proportion, expansion of industry output will raise the price of such factors by significantly increasing the demand for them (as well as potentially inviting changed factor proportions), and the long-run industry supply curve will slope upward to the right. (It is also possible that an expansion of industry output could lead essentially to a decline of factor prices in some circumstances, in which event the industry supply curve would slope downward to the right. We shall not analyze this case.)[7]

The consideration which will basically determine whether the industry supply curve is horizontal or upward sloping is whether changes in the industry output result in a sufficient change in the total demand for any factor of production that, given the supply conditions for the factor, its price to the

[7] The causes of slope in the long-run industry supply curve have hardly been exhausted here. For a more extended discussion see Viner, "Cost Curves and Supply Curves," *Zeitschrift für Nationalökonomie,* III, 1932. See also Joan Robinson, *Economics of Imperfect Competition* (London: Macmillan & Co., Ltd., 1934), Chap. 10, for a further analysis of industry costs.

As we consider groups of industries together, it is apparent that general expansion of output, drawing on a supply of all factors which for the economy as a whole is definitely limited, may result in rising factor prices and costs unless there is a reserve of unemployed factors to draw upon. Any general expansion of output, in an economy where unemployed factors require higher than prevailing wages to induce them to work, will result in a general upward shift of costs and prices.

industry will thereby be changed. Thus if a small competitive industry—
let us say one producing ink bottles—buys glass, a certain grade of labor, and
machinery each in a large market wherein it takes perhaps 1 percent or less
of the supply of each factor, then a considerable expansion or contraction
of industry output will change the demand for glass, labor, or machinery so
little that their prices will not change perceptibly. Then the long-run industry supply curve will be horizontal. But if another industry—let us say one
producing bed sheets—buys significant proportions of the supply of basic
cotton goods and of the labor in a certain market, its output expansion may
result in a sufficient increase in the demand for these things that their prices
will rise, since the total supply of such factors will not be perfectly elastic.
(This possibility would be especially apparent in the case of labor, for
example, if there were a large number of special submarkets for labor and
if wages had to be increased to induce labor to move from one to another.
Then an industry would not have to be so very large in order to influence
the price in a given labor market and to cause wages to rise as it attracted
labor from other skills or other areas to its market.) In this case the long-
run industry supply curve may well slope upward to the right.

LONG-RUN INDUSTRY BEHAVIOR IN PURE COMPETITION

Returning to the equilibrium of the single industry in pure competition, it
is clear that several specific sorts of results tend to emerge from such an
industry in the long run. We have already shown that in the short-period
equilibrium the following tend to be true:

1. Firm output is always so adjusted that the short-run marginal costs
of all firms are equal to price.

2. Industry price and output tend to be automatically adjusted in accordance with the relationship of the short-run industry supply curve to
demand.

3. Price may be equal to, less than, or greater than the average total cost
of production of producing firms, but it may not be less than the average
variable cost of production of such firms.

In the long-run equilibrium it is apparent that the following should also
tend to be the average results:

1. Industry price tends to be at the level of the minimum average cost
of production of all firms. The firms of the industry thus earn no excess
profits, but only the normal profits—wages of management, interest on investment, etc.—which are included in costs.

2. Since all firms are operating with minimum average costs of production, competition has forced them to operate at their *lowest-cost scales*
and at their *lowest-cost rates of utilization*. The average costs per unit of

output at any output are thus the minimum attainable with going techniques.

3. There are no selling costs to be covered by price, since these are ruled out by the complete lack of product differentiation. (This is equally true of the short run.)

4. The output of every firm is such that its long-run marginal cost is equal to price—that is, the *firm's* long-run marginal cost equals price.

5. Since the aggregate and average private cost of every output is a minimum and since output is extended to where price equals average cost, the long-run industry output is the largest (with given factor prices, given demand, and given techniques) that can be secured subject to the condition of firms in the industry "breaking-even" or covering costs.

6. With industry average cost equaling price, it may be demonstrated that under most conditions there is a certain relationship to price of long-run *industry marginal cost* (the increment to cost induced by an increment to industry output, definitionally not the same as the firm's marginal cost) which is such that if repeated for all industries it would reveal a desirable composition of total output. This last point remains to be demonstrated in section E of this chapter below.

These are the principal properties of the price-output adjustment of the purely competitive industry in long-run equilibrium. All but the last property ((6) above) are evident from or may be immediately deduced from our preceding discussion. The last point will require some analysis, and we shall turn to it after discussing the significance of the others.

The preceding formal analysis, in effect, has given us a prediction of certain aspects of the behavior of a purely competitive industry (1) in the short-run *equilibrium,* and (2) in the long-run *equilibrium.* To what extent does it provide valid predictions of the actual behavior of actual purely competitive industries through time? And, so far as it does, is it the short-run theoretical model, or the long-run model, which will have the principal predictive value? The answers to these questions will evidently depend upon the extent to which actual performance through time conforms to an equilibrium performance and also, if there is some conformance, upon whether it is only to conditions of a short-run equilibrium or to conditions of a long-run equilibrium as well.

The short-run equilibrium adjustment which is predicted is one which could be reached by an industry over a relatively short time interval, a year or six months ordinarily, in which industry demand, productive techniques, and factor prices—as well as number and size of firms—were unchanging. Formally they would have to be entirely unchanging for full attainment of short-run equilibrium, but if they were approximately unchanging, short-run equilibrium could be approximated over a relatively brief time interval. Since in fact industry demands, factor prices, and so forth ordinarily change rather slowly through time, it would appear that actual industries may tend to approach short-run equilibrium conditions rather closely at most times —that is, to keep production adjusted to where short-run marginal cost about equals price. The short-run equilibrium model should thus supply a meaningful prediction of the possible variety of year-to-year adaptations of a purely competitive industry to going conditions of demand and cost, and also a prediction of the response which the industry will make to change or fluctuation in demand and cost if the change is viewed as transitory (thus not eliciting a long-run adjustment) or in any event over immediate intervals, pending a further or long-run adjustment. It does not provide, however, any very precise prediction of the adjustment which the industry will ultimately adopt relative to given demand and cost conditions if these conditions remain relatively stable through time, since it does not undertake to explain the adjustment of the size and number of firms which will take place relative to given cost and demand conditions. It thus fails to identify the *central-tendency* of successive short-run adjustments through time or the sort of short-run adjustment, relative to any given or average demand or cost conditions, which will be typical. It identifies a wide range of *possibilities* for short-run adjustment as new cost and demand situations emerge: it does not identify the central *probability* of adjustment relative to demand and cost conditions which are customary or which prevail on the average through time. For this prediction we turn to the theory of long-run price and output adjustment.

The long-run equilibrium adjustment which is predicted for an industry in pure competition is, in strict formal logic, one which would be reached relative to some given conditions of industry demand, productive techniques, and factor prices, provided that such conditions remained unchanging for a length of time sufficient for complete adjustment of the scale and the number of firms. In practice at least several years of unchanged demand and cost conditions would be necessary to permit the full attainment of such a long-run equilibrium. It might thus be argued that in a dynamic economy, where there are (1) continual fluctuations and (2) steady or sporadic secular changes in demands, factor prices, and productive techniques, long-run equilibrium will seldom if ever be fully attained, and that, therefore, the long-run equilibrium model has little predictive value.

The first part of this argument is essentially correct—that is, in a dynamic economy full long-run equilibrium will seldom be attained. But the second deduction does not follow from the first. For even if steadily changing or fluctuating conditions of demand and cost preclude full attainment of long-run equilibrium, there is nevertheless a tendency to *adjust toward* or to *pursue* a long-run equilibrium adjustment relative to evolving demand and cost data at all times. Although long-run equilibrium, relative to current demand and cost conditions, may never be precisely attained, it should always be approached or approximated. In the case of steady secular change—as, for example, steady increase in demand—the industry should tend to pursue a progressively changing or moving equilibrium position through time, which alters as demand data alters. In the case of fluctuating demand and cost conditions the industry should tend to make a long-run adjustment to some average over time of the year-to-year conditions of demand and cost. In either case, then, the results attributed to the industry in long-run equilibrium should provide a prediction of actual behavior to the extent that industries always tend to approach, pursue, or approximate a long-run equilibrium adjustment to some sort of average of anticipated future conditions of cost and demand. By identifying the goal continually approached by competitive adjustments, we identify important properties of the actual behavior of industries through time. The long-run equilibrium model predicts a tendency of adjustment—a goal which may never be reached but which is consistently approached. It follows that the typical short-run equilibrium situation to be predicted is one which is consistent with or subsumed by an approximation to long-run equilibrium adjustment. The major value of the short-run analysis is in predicting the character of immediate responses to change in the basic data of cost and demand.

The theory of purely competitive long-run equilibrium thus gives us the most valid simple prediction of the average tendency of adjustment through time to prevailing demand and cost conditions. It tells us "about how a purely competitive industry should tend to behave on the average." It is this theory, therefore, which provides the most meaningful general prediction concerning purely competitive industry behavior. On the other hand, it does not give us an account of the process of adjustment to change nor of the probable average discrepancy from full long-run equilibrium adjustment which will prevail through time under dynamic conditions. The theory of short-run pricing casts some light on these questions, but still more detailed theorizing, not yet developed, would be required to give a full account of these matters. In spite of the less than complete adequacy of long-run equilibrium theory as a picture of actual behavior through time, however, it does identify perhaps the most significant aspects of the average performance of purely competitive industry behavior through time. It is thus meaningful to inquire into the social desirability of purely competitive industry performance in terms of its long-run equilibrium tendencies—to inquire how desirable this performance is, *so far as it approximates* long-run equilibrium performance. This will be the task of the two succeeding sections. In a further section, we shall consider the aspects of behavior neglected while centering on equilibrium tendencies—namely, the process-of-adjustment characteristics of purely competitive industries under dynamic demand and cost conditions.

D. THE SOCIAL DESIRABILITY OF INDUSTRY
BEHAVIOR IN PURE COMPETITION

STANDARDS OF DESIRABLE BEHAVIOR

Let us now consider the extent to which the behavior of any purely competitive industry is socially desirable, so far as this behavior is identified simply with its long-run equilibrium tendency.

On pages 2 and 3 above we have indicated that the material welfare created by the economy as a whole is influenced by the level of employment and production, the efficiency of production, the pattern of income distribution, the composition of total output, the progressiveness of the economy in product and technique, and the stability of the economy. The behavior of any one individual industry cannot determine or be primarily responsible for the character of such over-all results for the whole economy. Nevertheless, the behavior of each industry contributes to or has some influence on such over-all results for the economy. Each industry through its behavior essentially makes some sort of *response* to the effective demand for its output. The character of this response will have some virtual influence on over-all economic performance. Thus, it is possible to evaluate the behavior of any type of industry from the standpoint of the relative desirability of its particular response to the effective demand for its output, as judged by the sort of impact this has on over-all economic performance. We may, in effect, attempt to establish an *ideal* or *normative* response for any industry and then try to judge a particular industry or category of industries according to how close the sort of response represented in their behavior comes to the ideal.

In setting such standards, however, there is a certain limit to be observed. As long as the standards are conceived as applicable to a free-enterprise, profit-seeking economy, they must, in effect, call only for behavior consistent with the retention and survival of such a form of economy. The precise limitation to be observed is that the ideal behavior must be the best attainable consistent with firms in any industry at least covering all costs or breaking even in the long run. Standards which would require persistent net losses would imply the collapse of enterprise production and are inconsistent with the retention of an enterprise system. We thus seek ideals or norms for an industry's response to effective demand, subject to this restriction.

The immediate question, therefore, is how the long-run tendency of the behavior of a purely competitive industry (its response to effective demand) compares to the best attainable response, the best attainable being which would most favor optimal employment, efficiency, progressiveness, etc., within the economy as a whole. We shall see, however, that the setting of a norm or standard for the behavior of an individual industry from the standpoint of its impact on some of the dimensions of over-all economic behavior is not possible without some further analysis. Thus, the standard for optimal industry behavior from the standpoint of its impact on over-all employment cannot be meaningfully established until we have analyzed the basic determinants of the level of employment for the economy as a whole. Similarly, we cannot establish a standard for optimal industry behavior from the standpoint of the composition of aggregate output in terms of the behavior of any one industry alone. Such a standard necessarily refers to the relationships between the responses of all industries in the economy to their respective demands. Nevertheless, some standards of behavior may tentatively be suggested at this time which are applicable to the individual industry and are understandable without further analysis. Where this is the case, and also in more complex cases, it has frequently been held that the long-run equilibrium behavior of the purely competitive industry corresponds so closely to the ideal that it is effectively the source of the standard itself—in other words, purely competitive behavior has been said to possess some important *normative properties*.

The extent to which the purely competitive industry in long-run equilibrium possesses such normative properties (so far as we are presently in a position to make this plain) may be indicated by considering the extent to which purely competitive industry behavior is conducive to the best over-all economic performance in each of the six dimensions outlined above—employment, efficiency, progressiveness, etc.

Before attacking these issues, let us consider just what should be meant by "a purely competitive industry" for purposes of such an evaluation. It is explicit that we mean an industry with many small sellers and no product differentiation. When we speak of the long-run equilibrium properties of such an industry, however, it is also implicit that we refer to an industry wherein these conditions of pure competition will survive into a long-run equilibrium—where in effect the very forces of competition will not necessarily destroy these conditions. In particular, it must be true that the pursuit of lowest-cost scale by all firms in the long run will not so reduce the number of firms that they are no longer many and small. That is, the size of an optimum scale firm must be small enough relative to the size of the market that there can be many firms of such scale in long-run equilibrium. By a purely competitive industry in the long run we must thus mean one where the purely competitive structure is "natural," in the sense that there is no inherent conflict between the economies of large-scale firms and an atomistic market structure. For if there were, the industry would not tend to be purely competitive in the long run.

Some, but by no means all, industries fulfill the conditions necessary to permit automatic maintenance of purely competitive conditions in the long run. When we speak of the merits of purely competitive behavior, the evaluation will refer to industries where atomistic structure is thus consistent with efficient firm scales. The evaluation will definitely not apply to the merits of atomistic structure per se as far as this might imply in many cases an artificial limitation on the size of firms which would prevent them from becoming efficient in scale. In such cases pure competition would not only tend to be self-destructive in the absence of arbitrary intervention, but if forced by such intervention, it would result in a degree of inefficiency which would tend to vitiate most of the virtual advantages such a market structure tends to have. In general, then, when we conclude that pure competition has this or that advantage, we mean that it has it so far as purely competitive structure is consistent with efficiency in scale of firms; we do not mean that pure competition would be equally advantageous if forced upon an industry where it would result in uneconomically small scales.

EFFECTS ON OUTPUT AND EMPLOYMENT

This being understood, let us first consider the impact of the long-run equilibrium behavior of a purely competitive industry on output and employment. What sort of impact does the long-run behavior of the individual industry in pure competition tend to have on aggregate output and employment? As indicated in point (5) on page 149 above, the purely competitive industry tends in the long run to produce any output at its minimum attainable aggregate and average private cost and to extend its output to the point where price (as determined by the industry demand curve) equals such minimal average cost. It is thus true that with (a) given industry demand, (b) given factor prices (or given response of factor prices to its output), and (c) given techniques of production the purely competitive industry tends in the long run to produce the largest output attainable within the limit of covering costs or breaking even.

It in fact does so, however, only so long as we may be sure that the purely competitive structure of the industry does not have offsetting disadvantages which lie concealed in the "givens" of the preceding statement. The generalization holds, in the first place, subject to given techniques which determine the general level of cost. In effect, the purely competitive industry, by equating its minimal average cost to price, necessarily produces the largest output attainable (given industry demand and factor prices) only if its techniques of production will tend to be just as advanced and efficient as would be attained with any different market structure. If there may be some systematic association of market structure to technological progressiveness, we must correspondingly qualify our conclusion that with a purely competitive structure output is as big as possible. For if monopolized industries, for example, tended to introduce much more efficient techniques, and thus have lower costs, then the relative technological backwardness of purely competitive industries might mean that they were not virtually maximizing output even though extending output to the point where average cost equaled price. An "artificial" monopoly might do better, provided it did not incur serious diseconomies of large scale. This indicates a possibility—not a conclusion.

The generalization holds, in the second place, subject to a given level of the industry demand curve and given factor prices or given response thereof to industry output. If we take the industry demand curve as given and also the industry cost curve (which implies given techniques *and* given factor price behavior), then certainly the purely competitive industry produces the maximum feasible output. The broader determinant of the level of output, however, is the *relationship* of aggregate money demand for goods, a fraction of which is represented in the industry demand curve, to the level of money factor prices, which fix the level of industry costs. Now if this relationship would be no different (or at any rate no less favorable to high employment) when influenced by the behavior of purely competitive industries than when influenced by the behavior of other sorts of industries, the original conclusion holds. But the ratio *may* be so influenced, as far as the distribution of income between profits and other distributive shares— which may differ between pure competition and other cases—influences the flow of money spending on consumer goods by individuals and on investment goods by business firms. Thus, we cannot be sure of the net impact on employment of purely competitive industry behavior (as opposed to alternatives) until we have analyzed the virtual impact of purely competitive profit behavior on the flow of money spending.

Finally, of course, the conclusion that there is a tendency to maximize output holds only for industries which are "naturally" of purely competitive structure—where attainment of optimal scale of firms is consistent with an atomistic market structure. In other cases, where pure competition could not be maintained except by artificial and inefficient restriction on the size of firms, industry output would not necessarily be maximized. In summary as regards pure competition and the volume of output and employment, pure competition tends to give maximal output "other things being equal," but we cannot be certain they are "equal" without careful analysis of several related matters.

Although we have established that, subject to certain assumptions, the purely competitive industry tends in the long run to produce the "largest possible output"—that is, the output where price equals minimized average costs—we have not established that this output is "ideal." What is ideal cannot in fact be decided by referring only to one industry. Full employment of resources (which presumably is desired) is actually attainable with all industries doing other than equating average cost to price. Given this, the "ideal" output for any industry can be established only as an ideal *ratio* of its output to other outputs—that is, as a corollary of the ideal composition of aggregate output. We shall turn to the further analysis of ideal output in the next section when we consider performance of the economy as a whole. For the moment, we can say only that the virtually maximized output of any one purely competitive industry provides a very tentative standard of behavior, subject to further analysis.

EFFICIENCY, INCOME DISTRIBUTION, AND SELLING COST

A second issue concerns the impact of purely competitive behavior on the efficiency of production. As already indicated, firms in pure competition are in the long run led naturally to equate marginal cost to price, and forced by the pressure of entry or exit to build plants of lowest-cost scale and to use them at the optimal rate. Thus, in a given state of techniques, pure competition tends in the long run to give the lowest attainable aggregate and average private money costs of producing any given output. As far as these are proportional to real and social costs, it also tends to give lowest attainable real and social costs.[8] This generalization is obviously subject to qualification as long as there might be a tendency to more efficient techniques under other market structures. It also obviously holds only where purely competitive structure is "natural," in the sense that the market can support a large number of firms of optimal scale.

A third issue concerns the impact of the pricing of a purely competitive industry on income distribution. Without insisting upon any unique standard for income distribution, we may note the following about income distribution under pure competition. In the long run, price under pure competition tends to be forced to the level of average cost. Thus, there is a systematic limit on the profits of enterprise and on the distribution of the income of the industry between ownership interests and employed factors such as labor. The owners of firms in such industries tend to realize only a normal interest return on investment plus managerial wages plus any reward of superior efficiency (all of these being included in cost as defined) while other factors of production tend to get the balance. In particular, any excessive profits from artificial limitation of supply are effectively ruled out. This means, in general, if it is true that profit receivers are in any event fewer and richer than others, that pure competition tends to produce a personal distribution of income *more equal* than if there were any excess profits. Given the basic inequalities of income distribution inherent in inequalities of property ownership and in

[8] There is a general tendency to correspondence of these various measures of cost. We shall not analyze the possibility of discrepancies here.

differences in the value of personal labor services, many persons would hold that such a tendency in the direction of reduced inequality of income distribution is desirable. There is no particular question but that this tendency is inherent in purely competitive conditions. There is a question, however, whether such a tendency on balance stimulates or dampens the flow of money spending relative to a given level of money factor prices, and thus the general level of employment and output. There is also a question as to whether the condition of zero excess profits in long-run equilibrium is the most favorable to technological progressiveness, since technical developments may be financed out of profits and profits may serve as an incentive to innovation.

A further issue concerns the size of "selling costs" or, more generally, the proportion of productive resources devoted to sales promotion as opposed to basic production. It is significant that in pure competition production occurs without any selling cost, since no seller has anything unique to advertise. Although the total absence of such costs is not necessarily ideal in every market situation, an absolute maximum of economy in this type of expenditure must be counted as a potentially advantageous property of pure competition. The significance of selling costs in other market situations must be discussed at a later point.

OTHER ASPECTS OF BEHAVIOR

The progressiveness of firms in purely competitive industries, as measured by the readiness with which they adopt new techniques, improve products, or expand plant to supply the needs of a growing market, cannot be conclusively assessed on a priori grounds. On the one hand, the freedom of entry to such markets, together with the improbability of any firm withholding developments for fear of adversely affecting industry profits, is definitely favorable to progress. Any innovation which by lowering costs or increasing price offers some temporary excess profits to the innovator should tend to be made. On the other hand, the individual seller's lack of control over the long-run relation of his market price to his cost may make any contemplated innovation which is not sure to be profitable seem more risky than it would, for example, to a monopolist, especially by shortening the interval over which the seller may earn excess profits to reward a successful innovation.[9] Also, very small sellers with low profits may lack adequate funds for research. Both of these factors tend to dampen progressiveness. The net effect of pure competition on progress depends on the relative force of these two sets of factors. We shall discuss this matter at length in the suc-

[9] See pp. 226-229 below.

ceeding chapter on monopoly.[10] Resolution of this question, it should be noted, is crucial to any final judgment regarding the effects of pure competition on efficiency, and it may also bear on its effects on the over-all level of employment.

The effects of purely competitive price behavior on the stability of the economy raise such a complex analytical issue that it would not be fruitful to deal with them fully at this point. Certain basic tendencies of individual industry price behavior which are relevant to this issue, nevertheless, may be noted. Purely competitive prices in general are flexible or responsive to changes in cost and demand. For any one industry price flexibility tends to make output more stable in the face of given fluctuations in purchasing power; for a number of industries it tends, when buying power fluctuates, to keep their relative outputs in a relationship governed by impersonal cost and demand conditions rather than by the relatively arbitrary decisions of individual enterprisers. Whether similar behavior by all industries, through indirect as well as direct effects, will in the net favor stability, poses an analytical issue with which we shall not deal at this point.

In the preceding paragraphs we have attempted a tentative evaluation of purely competitive industry behavior from the standpoint of its impacts on various dimensions of over-all economic welfare. It has been considered with reference to each of the principal dimensions of such welfare previously listed, with the exception of that of the composition of aggregate output or allocation of resources among uses. The impact of pure competition upon allocation cannot effectively be analyzed for the case of the single industry, since allocation is a phenomenon emerging from the comparative performance of all industries. We shall consider the effects of pure competition upon allocation below when we consider the normative properties of a purely competitive economy.

If we review our findings to this point on the normative properties of pure competition in the individual industry, several generalities emerge. First, the purely competitive industry provides a sort of provisional standard or norm for long-run equilibrium behavior in a number of respects—size of output with given demand and cost, efficiency with given technique, income distribution as between profits and other income shares, and selling costs. In each of these cases, however, there is a condition or an "if" attached to the identification of the norm. The output is very provisionally normative *if* the income distribution effects do not dampen the flow of money spending unduly and *if* techniques are the most efficient. The efficiency is normative *if* techniques will be as efficient. The income distribution is normative *if* it does not have serious dampening effects on spending. The selling costs are normative *if* it is demonstrable that no selling costs yield economic benefits.

[10] See pp. 218-231 below.

To pose these "ifs" is not to say that the normative properties are thus destroyed. But it is indicated that purely competitive behavior per se is normative only if these doubts are resolved favorably to it. To resolve them at all will require much further analysis. Finally, the merits of pure competition with respect to efficiency are merits only for industries where the purely competitive structure is consistent with attainment of all economies of scale by member firms. Pure competition gives provisionally good results (subject to the other "ifs") where we can have it with efficient scales. Where we cannot, it loses much of its tentative appeal.

The finding that does emerge positively from studying pure competition is that, whether pure competition can give them to us or not, the following general norms of long-run behavior for any individual industry may be accepted:

1. Maximum efficiency, as influenced both by scale of operations and by techniques, in the sense of lowest attainable aggregate cost of any output produced.
2. No excess profits except to the extent that these are justified as incentives to desirable innovation or to the flow of business spending.
3. No selling costs not specifically justified by a useful economic function.

We shall have occasion to employ these standards as we consider the behavior of other sorts of industries.

It appears that the purely competitive industry provides certain tentative norms for industry behavior *not* in the sense that the purely competitive structure is necessarily normative or most desirable in most cases—and this especially because of potential conflicts between efficiency in scale and atomistic structure—*but* in the sense that certain long-run behavior tendencies found in purely competitive industries would be desirable behavior tendencies anywhere. Even to these *standards of performance* provided by pure competition there are certain possible qualifications, but this is the general meaning of pure competition as a norm.

With respect to effects on progressiveness and on economic stability, it is not so clear that pure competition possesses even provisional normative properties. Its merits in these regards, as well as the precise nature of normative behavior for any industry, will be left as open issues for the moment. The condition that output will in the long run be a virtual maximum for every industry within any given situation of demand and cost—in the sense that price equals minimized average costs when techniques are optimal—cannot be accepted per se; the criterion of ideal output must emerge from the analysis of the ideal allocation of resources as among all industries. Although such output performance may be ideal in an economy of purely competitive industries, it is not generally applicable to all cases. This will appear in the succeeding discussion.

E. NORMATIVE PROPERTIES OF AN ECONOMY IN PURE COMPETITION

THE PURELY COMPETITIVE ECONOMY

There is thus one aspect of the over-all performance of the economy which has not been considered in the preceding discussion—the allocation of resources among uses or the composition of aggregate output. Correspondingly, we have not as yet attempted to establish a standard or norm of ideal performance with respect to allocation nor to assess the performance of the purely competitive industry in terms of such a standard. The reason that we have not done this is that economic performance with respect to allocation of the resources among uses is not a matter of the performance of the single industry; it is a mater of the *relative* performance in certain respects of all industries. We cannot say that the performance of a single industry from the standpoint of allocation is bad or good, since the very notion involved is the comparative performance of all industries in the economy. The standard of good allocation must thus refer to the comparative performance of a complex of industries. Similarly, the merits of pure competition from the standpoint of allocation would be found in the sort of allocation which would emerge from an economy which was made up entirely of purely competitive industries—from *universal* pure competition.

This is a reflection of the fact that the function of the price system generally, and the relative merits of its function under various sorts of market structure, cannot be fully revealed by analyzing the operation of one industry at a time. Perhaps the most important task of the price system is to guide the allocation of resources among different industries in accordance with relative cost and relative buyer demand. Analysis of how this task is performed requires that we examine certain results of the simultaneous adjustments of all industries at once. When we turn to this analysis, we must not only deal with the general process of the cross-adaptation of various individual industry adjustments, but also must recognize in so doing the similarities or differences among the market structures of the various industries. In the actual economy, of course, the various industrial markets are of divergent structural types. Some are monopolies; many are oligopolies or in monopolistic competition; some are in pure competition. In this mixed situation the function of the price system is quite complicated. For the moment, however, we are interested primarily in the normative properties of pure competition. It is thus logical, in our inquiry into these properties, to extend our analysis by inquiring into the function of a hypothetical economy *in which all of the industries are purely competitive*. This should enable us to ascertain the virtual merits of pure competition from the standpoint of resource allocation. It should also permit us to deal in the most simplified form with certain basic elements of the working of a price system.

Before undertaking this analysis, the same *caveat* must be entered with respect to the implicit supposition concerning the meaning of pure competition as that entered in the previous section on the single industry. That is, the purely competitive economy of which we shall speak is strictly a hypothetical economy in which every industry tends in the long run to remain purely competitive—where in no industry is there a fundamental conflict between atomistic structure and economies of scale. This assumption is more serious in this case, however. There are individual industries which fulfill this condition, whereas it is simply not fulfilled for all of the industries in any actual economy. The analysis of purely competitive allocation, and of the functioning of a purely competitive price system, thus, refers to a strictly imaginary situation. But the inquiry is worth while because (1) it is valuable in instructing us in the working of any price system and (2) because it provides a means of identifying and defining the conditions of ideal allocation. It does not provide a norm for industrial structure as far as economies of scale may conflict with atomistic market structure.

Let us consider first certain general aspects of the working of a price system involving the prices and outputs of many industries with primary reference to tendencies in long-run equilibrium. Suppose that we had an economy in which every industry was purely competitive—where in each industry there were many small sellers with a uniform product and where entry to all industry was free and easy. Suppose also that there was a given constant flow of money purchasing power seeking all goods, which was maintained invariant through time. (This latter assumption will enable us to assume away the problem of the determination of the level of employment by implicitly assuming it to be fixed at a given level and thus to concentrate on other aspects of the function of a competitive price system.) What then will be the accomplishments of a purely competitive price system as it reaches a long-run general equilibrium for all industries?

EMPLOYMENT AND INCOME DISTRIBUTION

We know already that we would expect each industry in turn to adjust to a certain long-run equilibrium relative to any given demand curve and with any given level of factor prices—an equilibrium such that price should equal the minimum average cost of production of all firms as well as their long-run and short-run marginal costs. If all industries followed this tendency simultaneously, the following additional phenomena would have to be taken into account. First, the position of each industry demand curve would shift in response to the movements of all other prices—expressing the adjustments of their purchases which buyers make to an evolving complex of prices. They would continue shifting (with corresponding responses by each industry) until a point was reached where in every industry simultaneously price was equal to the long-run average cost of production, and quantity produced was that quantity which buyers would take under the condition that all prices simultaneously equaled long-run average cost. Thus, we would have determined not simply a price and a quantity for each industry but a mutually consistent family of prices and quantities which would be such that the quantities were just those which sellers would be willing to supply when prices equal minimum average costs and also just those which buyers would be willing to buy at such prices. There would be a *general equilibrium* of all prices and quantities which had a content much broader than the *particular equilibrium* of any one industry relative to an arbitrarily given demand.

Second, it is implicit in the process described that entry into each industry and into production in general, being free and always attracted by any excess profit, would result in the bidding up of the general level of factor prices (if factors were already fully employed) or the reduction of commodity prices to a point where total revenues in the economy and in each industry would exactly equal total costs. For if there were any margin of excess profit anywhere, new firms would be induced to enter (the supply of enterprise would increase) and by so doing would increase either the prices for factors or the supply of goods until average costs equaled prices everywhere. That is, factor prices would tend to reach a level relative to commodity prices such that there were no excess profits. If factor prices were "too low" for this when full employment obtained, they would tend to be bid up. The possibility remains, however, that factor prices might initially be high enough relative to the general level of money spending that a price-equals-average-cost equilibrium for all industry would not result in full employment of factors. In this event factor prices would tend to fall (as unemployed factors competed with employed factors). If the money flow was then self-sustaining, while this adjustment took place, they would seek such a level that there would be full employment and simultaneously such that prices would everywhere equal average costs.

It should be noted that any tendency to reach an exact full-employment level, however, would not be essentially a property of pure competition per se, but rather of the free adjustability of factor prices *relative* to the flow of money spending. Pure competition per se assures only that prices will tend to equal average costs, but it admits of the possibility of underemployment if (1) factor prices should be rigid at too high a level relative to the flow of money purchasing power or (2) every fall in factor prices should induce a corresponding fall in money purchasing power. Conversely, full employment could be had without prices everywhere equaling average costs of production.

It is apparent that in a purely competitive economy the pursuit of profit by enterprising sellers would result in long-run equilibrium in (1) a certain relation of cost to price in every line such as eliminated all excess profits and (2) an allocation of resources among uses, or composition of aggregate output, such that the quantity of each good produced was just that which buyers wished to take when the price of every good was equal to its minimum average cost of production. To be sure, enterprise production under any probable sort of market structure will result in production in every line at least roughly proportionate to buyer demand, considerations of cost being taken into account. Thus, the money demands of buyers and the profit-seeking activities of sellers interact to accomplish some organization of resource use relative to buyers' wants. But in a purely competitive economy this equilibrium organization of resource use would take on a very precise character, and this would reflect the facts that no seller was large enough to influence any price and that entry to every field was free and without impediment.

In these circumstances it is evident that the organization of economic effort in the highest attainable degree would be automatically or impersonally regulated by the price system, and it would be dependent in the least attainable degree on the personal discretion of any individual or group, whether private or governmental. This aspect of a competitive enterprise economy appeals to many people because it implies the relative unimportance of personal power in the regulation of economic life, and it does not appeal to others because they would feel safer with some central planning than at the mercy of an impersonal market. We can hardly judge the merits of these relative positions solely by reference to the virtual accomplishments of a hypothetical purely competitive economy in long-run equilibrium, but it should, nevertheless, be pertinent to assess further one of these accomplishments.

THE ALLOCATION OF RESOURCES AMONG USES

One of the principal attractions of a hypothetical situation in which every industry is purely competitive is that in long-run equilibrium there would tend to be a virtually ideal allocation of resources among uses. A first step in demonstrating this is to define in simple terms the conditions for *ideal allocation,* or ideal composition of aggregate output, from the standpoint of consumer welfare. The general condition for ideal allocation is that the outputs of all goods should be such that no unit of resources could be shifted from the production of one good to another without decreasing the total satisfaction obtained by buyers. Until this point is reached, satisfaction could be increased by reallocation; when it is reached, satisfaction is by definition at its maximum. The composition of aggregate output for which this condition will be fulfilled is necessarily one for which the addition to buyer satisfaction provided by the goods produced by the last or marginal unit of any productive factor employed should be the same in each line of production or industry where the factor is employed. If labor is employed in producing shoes and neckties, the addition to buyer satisfaction provided by the addition to shoe output of the last hour of labor used in the shoe industry should be the same as the addition to buyer satisfaction provided by the addition to necktie output of the last hour of labor employed in the necktie industry.

This condition must hold for all pairs of industries simultaneously if we have ideal allocation. If it does not, then a shift of factors among industries will increase buyer satisfaction. For example, if the added buyer satisfaction from the necktie output of an hour's labor is less than the added satisfaction from the shoe output of an hour's labor, a shift of labor from necktie to shoe production will increase buyer satisfaction. If the condition does hold, however, any shift of a factor from one industry to another would reduce buyer satisfaction. This is because any shift of a unit of a factor from one line to another would then add a satisfaction in the augmented line smaller than the satisfaction taken away in the other line. This in turn is because the added satisfaction from further units of any good *diminishes* as its quantity is increased, whereas the satisfaction lost by taking away units of any good increases as its quantity is reduced. Thus, if the output additions of the last hour of labor in shoes and in neckties initially provide identical additions to buyer satisfaction, a shift of an hour of labor from shoes to neckties will (1) take away a given satisfaction from shoe output and (2) add a *smaller* satisfaction to necktie output, since the further addition to necktie output makes a smaller increment to satisfaction than the preceding addition and thus an increment to satisfaction smaller than the decrement suffered in shoes. Thus, we see that for ideal allocation the additions to buyer satisfaction made by the marginal unit of any factor must be the same in every line of production.

If only a single consumer were concerned, this should also mean that money price of the goods added by the marginal unit of a factor should be the same in every line of production. The consumer presumably adjusts to goods prices in such a way that the last dollar spent on every good yields the same increment to his satisfaction. Therefore, equal money values of incremental outputs of a factor in various lines should be indicative of equal increments to satisfaction to this single consumer. A difficulty is potentially encountered, however, when we recognize that the "buyer satisfaction" of which our original definition speaks is essentially the aggregated satisfaction of many buyers. To speak of this at all simply, we must suppose that various individual buyer satisfactions are intercommensurable—can be meaningfully added up into a single sum. (This is especially necessary as far as the gains from a given change in allocation may accrue preponderantly to one group of buyers and the losses to another.) But in what way—how are they reduced to values of a single variable? For a simple approximation we may assume that all satisfactions are measured on the same scale of money values—that a final dollar's worth of goods to Jones represents the same amount of satisfaction as a final dollar's worth of goods to Brown. If we accept this simplifying assumption, it will then generally be true that ideal allocation is found where the money price of the goods added by the marginal unit of any factor is the same in every line of production, regardless of the shifting identities of buyers. Thus if the last hour's labor employed in shoe production adds shoes for which buyers will pay $4, ideal allocation requires that the last hour's labor employed in necktie production adds neckties for which buyers will pay $4. The preceding gives us a very simplified version of the conditions of ideal allocation. It may be readily demonstrated that in long-run general equilibrium a purely competitive economy would tend to give this sort of allocation.

When a long-run general equilibrium was reached for such an economy, it would be true (among other things) that the composition of aggregate output was such that the quantity of each good produced was just that which buyers would take when the price of that good equaled, as it would, its minimum average cost of production. In every industry simultaneously output would be such that price equaled industry average cost or would be that where the industry demand curve intersected an industry supply curve which represented the minimum average cost of every possible output. In every industry in turn we would have an equilibrium price-output situation of the sort illustrated by the intersection of D_2D_2' and ΣMC_2 at the level of AC in Figure 24 (or by the intersection of DD' and ΣMC, or of D_1D_1' and ΣMC_1—some equilibrium where price equaled minimal industry average cost). This much is already evident.

The crucial question is what would be the relation of *marginal cost* to price. It is evidently true that the marginal cost of each firm would equal price, but this is not necessarily the *relevant* marginal cost since it shows increase in cost for increase in a firm's output, whereas industry output is commonly extended in the long run not by adding to any firm's output but by adding to the number of firms. Thus, there may be other versions of marginal costs—in particular, *industry marginal cost* or the addition to industry costs for any addition to industry output. And of industry marginal cost several measures exist. First, there is the *marginal real cost to the industry;* that is, the increment in quantities of factors used to produce another unit—so many hours of labor, for example. Second, there is the money value of this marginal real cost—that is, the values of the factors included in marginal real cost at their prices as prevailing at the point of the output increment in question. Third, there is the marginal money cost, or marginal outlay, to the industry for an increment in output—the increase in the amount of money spent on factors as a result of an increment to output. As long as factor prices do not change with output, this is obviously identical with the money value of marginal real cost. But if factor prices are induced to rise by an increase in industry output, it will exceed the money value of marginal real cost by an amount equal to the induced increase in payments to all factors employed prior to the increment.

Thus, suppose that an industry is producing 1,000 units of output per day by employing 5,000 hours of labor, and it increases its output to 1,001 units by employing 5 hours more of labor. Suppose that by so doing it raises the wage rate from $2 to $2.01 per hour and its aggregate cost thus from $10,000 (5,000 × $2) to $10,060.05 (5,005 × $2.01). Now the marginal real cost of the last unit is 5 hours of labor. The money value of marginal real cost is $10.05 ($2.01 × 5). The marginal money cost is $60.05 ($10,060.05 − $10,000). It exceeds the money value of marginal real cost by $50 because the industry now pays 1 cent more per hour for all labor, including the 5,000 hours it previously employed. Marginal money cost to the industry is the money value of marginal real cost plus this induced increase in the price of "inframarginal" factors.

We thus have three versions of industry marginal cost. The next thing to be noted is that, in general, the long-run industry average cost to which price is equated in pure competition corresponds to the money value of marginal real cost to the industry. This is obviously true so far as any long-run increment to industry output is made entirely by an addition of a firm, leaving the real costs of firms supplying the previous output unchanged. Then the average cost of the new firm, at factor prices prevailing after the increment, is obviously the money value of the full increment to industry real costs, and this is shown by the industry average cost curve at the new industry output. (Thus, if, in the preceding example, one unit of output is added by adding one firm which employs 5 hours of labor, and if the real cost of the preceding 1,000 units—namely, 5,000 hours of labor—is unchanged, the money value of marginal real cost is 5 hours of labor times the new wage rate of $2.01, or $10.05, and this is precisely the same as the industry average cost of $10.05 which now holds for all firms at the now prevailing level of factor prices.) Industry average cost also generally represents money value of marginal real cost in any case where extension of industry output does not result in a *shift* of the real costs of pre-existing firms unconnected with variation in their outputs. Demonstration of this proposition in all of its aspects would be a complex matter; it will not be undertaken here, so that we shall simply assert that, with the exception noted, industry average cost in pure competition will generally be the same as the money value of marginal real cost to the industry.

If this is true, our proposition that in the long-run general equilibrium the output of every industry would be such that price equaled the industry average cost reduces to the proposition that price would also equal the money value of marginal real cost to the industry. That is, in every industry buyers would be willing to pay for the output a price which equaled the money value of the real factors added in order to produce the last unit of that output.

Now if this were true—that money value of marginal real cost equaled price in every industry—it is demonstrable that the conditions for all ideal allocation, subject to one further assumption, would be exactly fulfilled. These conditions, it will be recalled, are that the marginal units of a factor employed in several or all industries should yield outputs of the same price or value in each of these industries. When money value of marginal real cost was equal to price in every industry, it would be true that the last dollar's worth of productive factors employed in each industry would be adding an output worth exactly a dollar—the price of the output being identical to its marginal cost, each dollar of marginal cost would just be matched by or bring forth an output priced at a dollar. Thus, if the money value of marginal real cost in the production of metal office chairs were $10 for the last chair added and the price of chairs $10 each and the money value of marginal real cost of ashtrays were $0.50 for the last ashtray added and the price of ashtrays were $0.50 each, it would be true that in both lines the last dollar of marginal cost, or dollar's worth of productive factors, brought forth an output worth one dollar. The last dollar's worth of factors employed in each line, therefore, would bring forth an output of the same price or value. And, so far as buyers adjusted their purchases so that the last dollar spent on every good yielded the same increment to satisfaction, then the last dollar's worth of factors employed in every line would be producing an output which yielded the same increment to satisfaction.

This is not yet quite the same as saying that the last *unit* of any factor would produce an output of the same value and satisfying power. Yet, if the last dollar's worth of factors in each line represented the same amount of factors, that would obviously follow. This would clearly be the case if only a single factor—for example, labor—were involved in all marginal real costs and if all industries paid the same price for that factor. Then the condition that the last dollar's worth of labor (money value of marginal labor cost) in each industry would produce an output worth the same amount reduces to the condition that the last unit of labor in each industry would produce an output worth the same amount. If, for example, the wage rate were $2 per hour in all industries, it would follow that the last half hour of labor employed in each industry yielded goods worth a dollar. The analysis is more complex if two or more factors enter into marginal real cost, but it could be demonstrated that the same conclusion would follow. If all industries paid the same amount for units of any factor (that is, so far as there was a perfect market for every factor or free mobility of each factor from industry to industry so as to equalize its price to all industries) then the share of the value of the marginal output imputed to the last unit of any factor would be the same in all industries.

It is thus concluded that under conditions of the long-run general equilibrium for a purely competitive economy and with free mobility for any factor sufficient to make its price the same to all industries, allocation would be ideal, in the sense that in every industry the last unit of any factor would add an output which had the same price and added the same amount to buyer satisfaction. When this was true, aggregate satisfaction could only be decreased by shifting factors from one industry to another. If the last hour of labor employed in every industry, for example, yielded an output worth just $2 to buyers, any shift of labor from one industry to another would only diminish total satisfaction. A further hour of labor employed in any industry would add goods worth less than $2 because of diminishing marginal satisfaction with increased supply, whereas $2 worth of satisfaction would be lost by subtracting the output of the hour of labor from any other industry (or, with further subtractions, more than $2 because of increasing marginal satisfaction with reduced supply). The same would be true for each factor in turn, and, thus, the allocation attributed to purely competitive equilibrium could not be improved.

A price system under universal pure competition, therefore, would tend to bring about the best possible allocation of resources among uses, or composition of aggregate output, from the standpoint of buyers' satisfaction. Shoes and houses and bread and beefsteak and automobiles would tend to be produced "in just the right proportions." The conclusion that this would be so, however, is subject to a number of assumptions which might not be completely fulfilled in practice even with universal pure competition (although the basic tendency would remain subject to corresponding exceptions). These assumptions include the following.

First, ideal allocation requires implicitly not only that money value of marginal real cost everywhere equal price, but also that the aggregate cost of each successive output—from which the marginal cost is calculated—be the minimum attainable aggregate cost for that output. Otherwise the marginal cost is not the most appropriate guide to allocation. This condition is fulfilled in pure competition so far as all firms are forced to produce every output in the long run at minimum average and aggregate costs attainable with the going techniques of production. But should it be demonstrable that techniques tended to be inferior under pure competition, a qualification to the "ideal-allocation" finding would have to be entered. Further, of course, the whole allocation advantage of an economy of purely competitive industries rests on the assumption that in each of these industries all economies of a large-scale firm can be had while maintaining a large number of firms—pure competition is supposed to be the "natural" structure. Thus, the advantages of a purely competitive economy are the advantages of a hypothetical economy in which atomistic market structures could be consistent with economies of scale—and not of an economy artificially forced to abandon such economies in order to have atomistic structure. This should be clearly understood to be implicit in the preceding evaluation of purely competitive allocation.

Second, the conclusion holds fully only so far as there would be sufficiently free mobility of each factor among industries to bring about a single uniform price for it in each industry—there would in effect have to be a single free competitive market for every factor. Impediments to factor mobility, which deter shifts from one occupation to another by units of factors even when they could receive more elsewhere, are impediments to ideal allocation. And the existence of pure competition in the selling market of every industry would by no means insure perfect factor mobility. If there can be persistent large differences in the wage rate for the same grade of labor in two industries, then equality of money value of marginal real cost to price in both cases would no longer be indicative of ideal allocation. A marginal unit of labor would be producing goods worth more in the high-wage industry. Thus, perfect factor mobility is a condition of ideal allocation; departures from it would distort the allocation pattern attributable to universal pure competition. Such factor immobility, however, distorts *any* allocation pattern, and if we cannot eliminate it, universal pure competition would, *ceteris paribus,* give better allocation than any other market structure arrangement.

Third, the industry average cost which is equated to price in pure competition is representative of the money value of marginal real cost to the industry only where an increment to industry output does not affect the real cost of producing all units produced prior to the increment. To be sure, this is ordinarily the case. But if the real costs of "inframarginal" units should change because of increase in industry output—as is not totally inconceivable—then the money value of marginal real cost will differ from industry average cost and will not equal price. In this case competitive allocation would diverge from the ideal. This is perhaps an unimportant exception since examples of this sort of divergence are hard to imagine.

Fourth, the proposition holds strictly only so far as the real costs counted by firms in the industry are identical with the real costs borne by the community in general. Included in the real costs which the firms count and pay for should be all relevant real costs to everyone. So far as the real costs, let us say, are simply labor, materials, and capital equipment, for which the firm pays, this condition would seem to be fulfilled. But if, for example, an industry creates a smoke nuisance or a pollution of streams, which involves a real cost or loss to the community for which its firms do not pay, it may be argued either that the money value of the real cost of production borne by firms "short-counts" the value of full real cost or that the net value of the industry's output is overvalued if we take it at selling price. Then equation of industry average (private) cost to price is not the same as equation of full marginal real cost to net increment in satisfaction. In this case allocation under universal pure competition would be distorted. The same conclusion applies if an industry receives an indirect public subsidy, such as the provision for its use of free public works, the cost of which is borne by taxpayers. This potential discrepancy between the value of real cost to society and the value of real cost borne by firms tends to distort the allocative functions of any price system, purely competitive or otherwise, so perhaps it is still true that, *ceteris paribus,* purely competitive pricing would tend to give relatively better results.

Fifth, the tendency to attain ideal allocation of employed resources is especially meaningful only if there is also a tendency toward full employment. An ideal composition of an insufficient aggregate output is a poor prize if 30 percent of the usable resources are unemployed. Truly ideal allocation should require also that there is no "involuntary unemployment" of factors (that is, no factors which wish to work at going factor prices but cannot find work). It should require further that the relation of factor prices to commodity prices should be such that marginal costs everywhere equal prices. This would imply that there was not only an ideal of allocation of employed resources among uses, but also an ideal allocation of employable resources—particularly labor—between work and leisure. Pure competition could guarantee approximate equality of price and marginal cost, but it could not (nor can other than purely competitive markets per se) guarantee full employment. Its allocation accomplishment would thus tend to be only virtual or partly realized unless full employment were obtained.[11]

SUMMARY

Let us now briefly summarize our conclusions with respect to the normative properties of long-run equilibrium in a hypothetical economy with pure competition in all its commodity markets. First, such an economy would not necessarily reach a condition of full employment. It would if factor prices were in effect freely adjustable *relative to* the flow of money purchasing power, but it might not if they were not. In this respect it would be basically no different from an economy with different market structures except so far as the income distribution and specific price relations it produced favored a better relation of aggregate spending to factor prices. Second, it would have in the long-run equilibrium a clear tendency, subject to some qualifications which may apply equally to other market structures,

[11] For a further analysis of competitive and ideal allocation, see Abba P. Lerner, *The Economics of Control* (New York: The Macmillan Company, 1944), Chaps. 1-9.

to bring about the best sort of allocation of resources among uses. In this respect it would tend to enjoy a virtual superiority over economies with other market structures. Third, it would clearly tend in the long-run equilibrium to bring about a distribution of income such that there would be no excess profits and so that the entire income of production would be distributed to the productive factors of labor, land, and capital. There would be no rewards simply to artificially induced shortage of supply, since such restriction of supply would be absent. This does not say anything, however, about the relative distribution of income as among land, labor, and capital, or its normative properties. This would depend upon (1) the structure of the markets for factors and (2) the distribution of abilities among workers and the distribution of land and capital ownership among persons generally. We shall defer consideration of the merits of competition in factor markets until Chapter 11 and succeeding chapters in the second part of this work.

The further evaluation of the merits of an economy with purely competitive industries throughout will simply reflect conclusions reached for the individual purely competitive industry, on pages 152 to 159 above. That is, efficiency of production would tend to be maximal unless other market structures would give birth to more efficient techniques (or unless a many-firm industry is inconsistent with getting economies of large-scale firms); selling costs would tend to be zero; progressiveness might or might not be optimal.

Thus, we establish a sort of scoreboard on which to rate the presumptive performance in long-run equilibrium of a hypothetical economy with all of its industries in pure competition. But it is certainly a hypothetical economy, and the question may legitimately be raised as to what good it does us to know the potential merits and shortcomings of such an economy. Certainly we do not have, never have had, and never will have an economy in which all or most of the industries are of purely competitive structure. Why then all this interest in an imaginary situation?

There are several pertinent answers to this question. First, as a matter of general interest, the belief that the *real* economy tends to be automatically self-regulating toward an ideal result frequently rests upon attributing to the real economy the properties of an economy with universal pure competition. It is interesting to observe the several doubts surrounding this belief even if the actual economy were purely competitive and also the basic questions raised by the fact that it is not. Second, although most of the industries in the economy are in fact not purely competitive, it is not impossible that most of them, even though their structures are different, may tend to behave in a fashion which approximates the behavior of purely competitive industries. Or perhaps by certain public policy measures they could be influenced so to behave. The extent to which this is true will require further analysis. But so far as it is true, the behavior properties of a hypothetical purely competitive economy may *approximate* the behavior properties of an actual or attainable real economy. Therefore, by analyzing the tendencies of this hypothetical and very uncomplicated sort of an economy, we may be able to determine with the least analytical effort the inherent tendencies of any price system governed by the same sorts of behavior and determine the extent to which the promotion of this sort of competitive behavior is socially desirable. As we have seen, behavior which closely approximates the purely competitive has a number of advantages, but there may also be some potential drawbacks.

Third, even though actual industries may not behave enough like purely competitive industries that the picture of a purely competitive economy has much practical descriptive power and even though most industries could not be forced into purely competitive structure without great losses of efficiency, the analysis of the behavior of a purely competitive economy leads to the development of norms or standards *of performance* which should be sought from any sort of industry by some policy means or other. Thus in the preceding section the analysis of the single industry in pure competition led to the tentative establishment of standards of performance with respect to efficiency, selling costs, and the existence of excess profits. Similarly, the analysis of allocation in a purely competitive economy establishes the fact that allocation is ideal when the money value of marginal real cost is equal to price in all industries. These standards of performance are applicable in the evaluation of any sort of industry or economy—purely competitive or not—in determining the extent to which social welfare is served. We shall have occasion to apply these standards as we turn to the analysis of economies made up of industries of different market structure.

In summary, our analysis of the normative properties of the performance of the purely competitive industry and the purely competitive economy in the long-run equilibrium has enabled us to do three things: (1) determine the extent to which actual industries in pure competition—where purely competitive structure is consistent with efficiency in scale—tend to contribute to good over-all performance in the economy; (2) establish certain standards of long-run performance applicable to any industry, whether or not of purely competitive structure; and (3) establish a standard of long-run performance for any economy relative to the composition of aggregate output or allocation of resources among uses. This list of standards is at this point of course incomplete—it does not specify ideal behavior for the industry or complex of industries from the standpoint of its impact on over-all employment or an economic stability or with respect to progressiveness. But it may serve as a working list for the moment, subject to later elaboration and revision.

F. PURE COMPETITION IN A WORLD OF CHANGE

LONG-RUN EQUILIBRIUM TENDENCIES AS INDICATORS OF PERFORMANCE

The preceding appraisal of the behavior of the purely competitive industry and economy and the suggested norms of desirable behavior for any industry or economy run largely in terms of long-run equilibrium tendencies. Our criteria of desirable behavior of the industry or complex of industries from the standpoint of employment, efficiency, income distribution, and allocation are in terms of the best adjustments to effective demand as a long-run equilibrium adaptation to such demand is reached by the industry or industries. Thus, we speak of the best relation of the long-run industry average cost to price, of the long-run industry marginal cost to price, and of the long-run scale of operations to lowest-cost scale. Similarly, the behavior of the purely competitive industry or economy which is appraised is that behavior which it would evidence once it reached a situation of long-run equilibrium adjustment to given conditions of demand.

We have previously indicated that for a long-run equilibrium to be reached in fact by any industry, it would be necessary that for a considerable period of time—a number of years at the least—there be no changes in the position of the industry's demand curve, no autonomous changes in factor prices, and no changes in techniques of production. For a general long-run equilibrium in an economy to be reached there would have to be no changes over a considerable period of time in the flow of money purchasing power and in buyers' tastes (which determine the complex of demands) and no changes in the supplies of productive factors or in productive techniques. For long-run equilibria to be closely approximated there would have to be no very great changes in these regards over a period of years. Experience tells us that it simply is not so that these basic determinants of economic equilibria ever remain unchanging for long enough to permit a very close approximation to a full long-run equilibrium by the typical industry or by the economy. Money purchasing power fluctuates and moves secularly through time; buyers' tastes change; factor supplies vary; techniques are continually developing. As a consequence, the basic demand and cost conditions to which industries respond are continually on the move, and a full long-run equilibrium is never reached by the usual industry or by the economy. Before a long-run equilibrium adjustment can be reached to the basic demand and cost data of any year 1, we are in year 2 with a somewhat different set of data, and the path of adjustment (in pursuit of equilibrium) is correspondingly altered. Thus, although the industry or economy may *pursue* a long-run equilibrium, this equilibrium itself is a continually moving target, which may be followed but is never really reached.

In view of the fact that the industry or economy thus simply never gets to a long-run equilibrium (although it may always in some sense be "chasing" a hypothetical moving equilibrium through time), the relevance to practical affairs of norms of behavior which run in terms of long-run equilibrium tendencies, though clear, is of a specific and restricted type. Although the long-run equilibrium is never reached, nevertheless, it is consistently pursued. For each year in turn through time there is a different set of determining "data" (that is, money purchasing power, buyers' tastes, techniques, etc.), and for this set of data there is a hypothetical long-run equilibrium adjustment which the industry or economy would tend to find. Moreover, the processes of market adjustment tend to lead the industry or economy in the direction of this long-run equilibrium at any moment. Before it is reached, the data have changed and the industry or economy alters the direction of its adjustment accordingly to pursue the new equilibrium position—and so forth ad infinitum through time. If this is true, it is also true that to some degree the industry or economy, by always pursuing the long-run equilibrium, tends approximately to reach it. The long-run equilibrium adjustment thus represents a tendency or direction in adjustment, although the tendency may never be fully developed in any case. The more slowly that the basic "data" change through time the more closely long-run equilibrium adjustments will be approximated; the more "dynamic" the economy is with respect to changing money flows, techniques, and so forth, the poorer the approximation. But in any event, long-run equilibrium with respect to given or evolving "data" always represents a tendency or direction or goal of adjustment by any industry or economy.

If this is so, it follows that criteria of the more beneficial long-run equilibrium tendencies by the industry or economy are quite meaningful—in the sense that they identify the more desirable sorts of tendency of adjustment to either given or evolving demand and cost conditions. When we say it is desirable that for each industry the money value of marginal real cost should equal price in long-run equilibrium, we mean for practical purposes that an industry should always be moving toward this goal rather than be moving toward some other. It also follows that the appraisal of a market structure like the purely competitive in terms of its long-run equilibrium tendencies is likewise a valid judgment of certain aspects of its actual performance under dynamic conditions, since it to some degree tends to approximate or pursues such long-run equilibrium adjustments through time. Thus, we have emphasized long-run equilibrium tendencies in purely competitive industries and norms for long-run equilibrium adjustment.

PROCESSES OF ADJUSTMENT TO CHANGE

At the same time, it is clear that if the industry or the economy is continually on the move in pursuit of new long-run equilibria, there are other aspects of its behavior to be taken into account than the goal it is pursuing. For it is then always in a *process of adjustment* to changing data, and the characteristics of this *process* through time also become a matter for concern. We should thus ultimately consider (1) norms of a desirable sort of adjustment process to changing data and (2) characteristics of this process under pure competition and under other market-structure conditions.

Economic theory is unfortunately not as yet developed to the point where it can either (1) provide reasonably unequivocal norms of a desirable process of adjustment to changing data by an industry or complex of industries or (2) predict in detail the time process of adjustment of firms and industries. Thus, we are limited at best to a few observations on certain behavior tendencies of the purely competitive industry which are suggested by the short-run analysis.

One of these, which may be suggested here, concerns the adaptation of the purely competitive industry or economy to a fluctuating demand or flow of money purchasing power, as is experienced in an economy subject to business-cycle fluctuations. Here the pursuit of long-run equilibrium tendencies is complicated by a continuing series of short-run adjustments to changing money demands and concurrent changes in money factor prices. It has already been observed that the purely competitive industry tends to adjust "automatically" to any going short-run demand by producing an output such that short-run marginal cost equals price. With cyclical shifts in either demand or cost, price and output will be coordinately adjusted so as to maintain this price-marginal cost equality. As a result there will be a freely moving and flexible price as money purchasing power and factor prices fluctuate through time and in some sense a maximal flexibility of price consistent with profit-maximizing behavior by the firms of the industry. This maximum of price flexibility, moreover, means a minimum of output flexibility, other things being equal, or a maximum stability of output.

Extending this argument from the single industry to the whole economy, it is clear that if all markets were purely competitive, the price system in general would be very responsive to fluctuations in income, with both absolute and relative prices reacting sensitively to changes in demand. It is not clear, however, that this would necessarily be an advantage to the economy. General price flexibility would *virtually* tend to stabilize output, provided that we could suppose that the fluctuation of purchasing power was itself uninfluenced by the flexible changes of price it induced. Then any given fluctuation of income, initiating shifts in the demands for various products, would effect a smaller fluctuation in output the more flexible prices were. But it is possible that any induced fluctuation in price in turn generates further fluctuation in income, and thus it intensifies any initial fluctuation in purchasing power. It may do this if, with any initial price change, buyers *speculate* on further price changes by buying in advance if prices are rising or withholding purchases if prices are falling. In this event price flexibility may be cumulative and may intensify instability. The case for a purely competitive economy or for maximal price flexibility in a world of dynamically fluctuating income, therefore, is by no means clear. We shall refer to the issue again in Chapter 10.

One further aspect of the process of adjustment of the purely competitive industry or economy to changing demand and cost through time may perhaps be emphasized. There are, as we have seen, continual changes through time in the form not only of fluctuating money income and factor prices (in business cycles) but also of secular changes in techniques of production, basic factor supplies, and buyers' tastes. Any industry, therefore, while in pursuit of a moving long-run equilibrium position, is more proximately engaged in making a related succession of short-run equilibrium adjustments to immediate situations with its temporarily given plant equipment. These adjustments, as we have seen, follow a given pattern in pure competition—output and price are set so that short-run marginal cost equals price so long as price may exceed short-run average variable costs. Are such period-to-period short-run adjustments normative?

ECONOMIC SECURITY

We have noted that it is open to question whether they are normative from the standpoint of impact on output stability through time. The same indecision must be expressed with respect to their impact on the general average level of employment because of uncertainty regarding the impact of resultant income-distribution effects on total spending. And it cannot be said that the effects on income distribution per se in the short run have peculiarly normative properties. Short-run excess profits or net losses may be incurred with fluctuating distortions in income-distribution patterns, and these are justified or desirable only as they are necessary to induce ultimately beneficial long-run tendencies of adjustment.

It is here, as a matter of fact, that we see plainly one "price" that must be paid by a society for the use of a really automatic market process. Under dynamically changing conditions the income positions of various individuals may be quite uncertain and precarious, and they may lack what they consider to be an adequate "security" in their lives. Pure competition, as the most impersonal and automatic of market systems, is perhaps the most ruthless from the standpoint of the individual in his income position. This is a major reason for progressive tendencies to temper the efficiency of impersonal regulation of activity by a market price system with the mercy of a good deal of government intervention to afford more security to individuals.

Because of these reasons it is especially difficult to develop unequivocal norms regarding the *process* by which ideal long-run adjustment tendencies should be approached. It is unreasonable to hold that any short-run adjustment process is fully justified simply if it contributes most directly to speedy approaches toward desirable long-run adjustments if, in fact, there are implicit disadvantages in such a process and if we are always in process of adjustment. On the other hand, it is difficult to strike the proper balance between speed and efficacy of adjustment in approaching goals, and the "side-effects" of the process of adjustment as the goals are pursued. Most doctors would probably prefer using miracle-drug A to cure a given disease if it took five weeks for the cure, killed none of the patients, and left some annoying chronic symptoms, to using miracle-drug Z, which effected one-day complete cures but killed 20 percent of the patients. But if we have a range of drugs between A and Z with varying properties in these regards, there might be some argument over choice. The same sort of reasoning applies to selecting a price mechanism which is the best, both process of adjustment and end tendencies being taken into account.

So far as the process-of-adjustment properties of purely competitive industries or economies may be assessed, the issue is of the following general sort. No definite judgment can be made as regards to the impacts on level of employment or on output stability for the whole economy. Short-run efficiency in producing given outputs tends to be optimal as long as techniques are optimal. Short-run allocation tendencies (with short-run marginal costs everywhere equal to price) are desirable. But the income-distribution tendencies with fluctuating or changing demands or costs, although they serve to speed desirable long-run adjustments, may make the market a rather hazardous place for individual participants. Consumers pay "extortionate" prices in periods of rapid income expansion or technological advance (as short-run excess profits emerge and prices equal marginal rather than average costs); producers suffer net losses in depressions and a number of them go bankrupt. Of course, this is true in a degree of any market-regulated system, but it is perhaps most acutely true of a purely competitive economy and of the purely competitive industries in any economy. This limitation upon otherwise normative tendencies of purely competitive market organization must be held in mind, and the problem reopened as we consider other sorts of market structure.

PROFITS IN A CHANGING ECONOMY

A prediction which emerges from the earlier analysis of purely competitive industries is that in the long-run equilibrium they will tend to have prices equal to average costs where these average costs include only a "normal" profit to the firm. In the long-run equilibrium this profit, which is included in cost, will equal simply the imputed market value of any factors employed by the firm which it does not purchase and pay for but rather which it owns from the outset. It is ordinarily conceived as including principally (1) any imputed wage of owner-managers who do not pay themselves salaries and (2) an interest return on capital invested by owners equal to the market rate of interest which such funds could earn in the money market if not invested here. Above such returns purely competitive long-run equilibrium would yield no extra return or excess profit.

Is any modification on this prediction necessary as applied to profits in purely competitive industries which, operating in a dynamic economy, are continually pursuing but never necessarily reaching a long-run equilibrium position? Evidently yes. First, if such equilibrium is always pursued but never quite reached, it is evident that the *average* profits over time should generally *approximate* or approach normal profits as defined, but they need not exactly correspond to them either for any one industry or on the average for a group of industries. Second, there may be systematic sources of fairly prolonged deviation from normal returns in individual industries. A secular series of increases or decreases in the demand for the output of an industry over time, with a somewhat lagging adjustment to them, may lead to excess profits or to net losses in the purely competitive industry over substantial periods of time—and over periods of time much longer than that necessary to adjust fully to any one shift in demand (any one "long period," as previously defined). Further, technological improvements which reduce costs for established firms may create excess profits over substantial intervals before the pressures of imitation and entry reduce price toward average cost again. In general, the individual purely competitive industry under certain circumstances of continued dynamic change may deviate for periods much longer than the theoretical short period from the zero-profit level, essentially because a succession of similar changes in demand or cost conditions may follow each other in time, each requiring a new process of adaptation. Third, with demand fluctuating, as in the business cycle, any tendency to earn normal profits on the average over time will be fulfilled by making excess profits in booms and net losses in depression—the long-run balance will be found in effect in an average of different short-run adjustments.

Fourth, the effect of faulty estimates and uncertainty must be taken into account. The demands and costs to which firms would adjust in a stable long-run equilibrium would be necessarily definitely known demands and costs, which reoccurred monotonously through time. In a changing economy, however, such demands and costs cannot be foreknown; they must be estimated, and the estimates upon the basis of which firms act, however rational their foundation, are subject to error. It follows that there will be cases in which for a certain interval demand is underestimated or cost overestimated and in which the adjustment will lead toward excess profits until the error is rectified. Conversely, there will be other cases where demand is overestimated or cost underestimated so that for a time net losses may result. These deviations of received returns from estimated returns essentially represent positive or negative *windfalls* attributable to uncertainty and error of estimate. They will result in some systematic *dispersion* of the average profit rate of competitive (or other) industries around a mean for any chosen time interval. The fact that they do occur is evidence of the fact that there is *risk* involved in investing in any line.

A question arises now whether or not, in the face of such risk, enterprises in purely competitive industries will so act in adjusting output to demand that the chance of loss is about equal to the chance of extra gain. Will they "gamble at even odds"? If they in effect do this, then on the average among industries positive windfalls or gains from risk taking should equal negative windfalls or losses from risk taking, and the *average* return or profit in competitive industries should tend toward a simple interest return on invested funds. Some people have argued, however, that businessmen will usually alter their actions in the face of risk, shortening the output relative to any given mean expected demand in such a way as to receive a net return for "risk bearing"—or, in effect, that they will act cautiously enough that for a group of industries positive windfalls will exceed negative windfalls consistently by some given "risk reward." This is by no means an evident fact, but investigations have not as yet resolved this issue one way or the other. However this may be, it is evident that uncertainty and resulting business adjustments based on erroneous estimates do impose a real cost or loss on society to the extent that resources are misapplied and that extra profits in some lines are necessary to induce investors to expose themselves periodically to financing losses in others.

ACTUAL CASES OF PURE COMPETITION

The preceding appraisal of the performance of purely competitive markets stems directly from an exploration of the logic of profit seeking within this market structure. The conclusions are deduced rather than inductively discovered. The student, therefore, is entitled to ask how these conclusions "square" with observed results in actual markets.

We should first re-emphasize that very few markets in the United States have structures closely approximating a purely competitive one. In mining, manufacture, transportation, and communications concentration has proceeded, with few exceptions, to the point where the number of sellers is small enough or some sellers large enough that individual sellers can at least somewhat influence the market price. Many of these markets are further complicated by differentiation among the products of rival sellers, which gives the sellers further direct control over their pricing. In the distributive and service trades the number of sellers in a market is ordinarily large, but product differentiation is important enough to cause a distinct departure from purely competitive conditions. Agriculture has ordinarily been cited as the stronghold of pure competition, since farmers are ordinarily many and their products highly standardized. But even here the growth of very large-scale farming in certain crops, coupled with the formation of producers' cooperatives in many others, has frequently resulted in the concentration of output in the hands of a few sellers. As a result, we find any close approximation to pure competition among sellers only in a relatively few industrial markets and in a part of the agricultural sphere.

In this limited area of the economy purely competitive markets seem to have at least some of the behavior tendencies which our theory would lead us to expect. The long-run average profits of enterprise are low, certainly lower than in many fields where strong monopoly elements are present. Prices tend to be very flexible over time, responding very strongly to cyclical changes in the level of buyers' demands, and the rate of output is correspondingly more stable over time than it is elsewhere in the economy. There is also incomplete evidence that output is generally adjusted to keep marginal costs of production close to price. Scales and rates of utilization of plant evidence no consistent average departure from the optima with going techniques.

An extended consideration of a number of such industries, such as those producing cotton gray goods, bituminous coal, and many agricultural crops, also reveals that certain anticipated difficulties of adjustment to dynamic change have been encountered with rather severe impacts upon enterprise and upon productive factors employed in these industries. First, in the absence of direct interference by the government to limit the working of competition, fluctuations of demand over the course of the business cycle have induced wide price fluctuations, and although these have permitted the output supplied and purchased to fluctuate relatively little—an advantage to consumers—they have meant that enterprises tend to alternate between periods of severe net losses and periods of profitable operation and that the income positions of those dependent on enterprise earnings, consequently, are very unstable over time. By the same token, consumers "get a bargain" in depressions but pay what seem to be exploitative prices in boom times, more or less as the result of the working of impersonal market forces. Further, cyclical price flexibility in these industries seems to have been encouraged by a corresponding wage flexibility, which reduces costs in depression and permits production to be maintained at very low prices, but likewise it makes the income of labor in these fields cyclically very unstable. The exceptional flexibility of wages and other factor prices in these areas may result from the exceptionally poor mobility of labor and other resources from these to other industries, but, whatever its cause, it tends to result in alternating feast and famine for all resources employed in such areas.

A second difficulty of adjustment is observed where these industries have been faced with long-term secular declines in demand, which require ultimate curtailment of industry output and a shift of resources from these industries to others. The theoretical long-run adjustment to a decline in demand should presumably involve an exit of firms from the industry as existing plant facilities wear out, and a corresponding exit of labor and other mobile resources, to the point where price again equals average cost and where the wages and other factor prices entering into average cost are the same in these as in other industries. In an interim "short run," of course, redundant capacity and net losses, and redundant labor forces and subnormal wages, might be expected. The trouble with industries like those in agriculture, coal, and cotton textiles is that, in a situation of declining demand, the long run has been a very long time in coming or conversely the short run has had great chronological duration. Thus, as much as two decades have passed in such industries with losses or subnormal profits, excess capacity, subnormal wages, and redundant work force and with little evident tendency for a sufficient exit of firms and work force to take place to permit approximate restoration of a desirable long-run equilibrium.

The basic difficulties giving rise to this type of prolonged maladjustment and thus to "distressed areas" in the economy are, given the inescapable fact of a reduced demand, (1) very long life of fixed plant in certain industries, which makes the "short run" last a long time if contraction of the industry is involved, and (2) lack of a mobility of labor out of these industries sufficient to permit its desirable reallocation when the pattern of buyers' demands changes adversely. Chronic low-wage and low-profit areas have thus emerged, and a long-run adjustment toward desirable allocation and normal profits has been a very long time coming. Now it may be argued that such basic difficulties are not the "fault" of purely competitive conditions and that given these difficulties a purely competitive pricing mechanism is doing as much as, or more than, any pricing system could do eventually to force the sort of readjustment of supply to demand which is socially desirable. And it may be argued that the human distress which accumulates during the prolonged adjustment process, if it is a fault, is a fault of market-regulated systems generally rather than one of pure competition in particular. On the other hand, it is clear that a purely competitive price system, by working impersonally and with maximum potential efficacy to reallocate resources when demands change, at the same time deals most unfeelingly and severely with the individuals involved when resources stubbornly refuse to move. A less "efficient" system, which permitted of monopolistic reduction of output and raising of price in such situations, although it might actually impede desirable long-run adjustments, would be bound to have an attractiveness as an expedient means of preserving resource incomes under conditions of reduced demand. This does not necessarily classify purely competitive market organization as an inferior type. It does suggest that its fully effective working under dynamic conditions requires a high mobility of resources among industries and that lacking this, there may be an understandable tendency to *compensate* for the basic difficulty by departing from competitive pricing instead of trying to remove the basic difficulty in order to make competitive pricing more desirable.[12]

THE DEVELOPMENT OF MARKET STRUCTURES

Since purely competitive industries generally tend to suffer from cyclical instability and since a number of them have suffered from long-term distress because of delayed adjustments to changed market conditions, it is not strange that pure competition is unpopular with the competitors involved in it. Minimal profits, unstable profits, and the hazard of prolonged periods of distress do not exactly represent the goals of profit-seeking enterprises. And enterprises exposed to pure competition are likely to be relatively unimpressed by the thought that they are contributing to the working of a market system which, according to theorists, favors ultimate economic efficiency.

Their plight seems all the worse to them in an economy where pure competition is far from universal—where many industries are of oligopolistic or concentrated structure, with competition restricted sufficiently to permit higher and more stable profits. Sellers subjected to the rigors of pure competition are likely to feel underprivileged. Their relative disadvantage is made more severe by the fact that entry into the favored oligopolistic spheres is difficult so that they have trouble shifting to more favored industries and by the fact that the purely competitive areas of easy entry tend to become overcrowded with small enterprise looking for a place to go. The fact that the basic trouble may be in the abnormal profits and restricted entry conditions in concentrated industries, and not in the minimal profits and easy entry of the competitive industries, offers little solace to sellers in the latter.

[12] For a discussion of problems of actual competitive industries see Lloyd G. Reynolds, "Cutthroat Competition," *American Economic Review,* December 1940; also Walter Adams, *The Structure of American Industry* (New York: The Macmillan Company, 1950), Chaps. 1-3.

As a consequence sellers in purely competitive industries have generally been unhappy in their lot, have decried as destructive, cutthroat, and murderous the competition to which they are subect, and they have sought special relief from the rigors of competition. This drive to escape pure competition has been basically responsible for producer cooperatives in agriculture, for the winning of government price supports in the same field, and for special price regulation for bituminous coal. There is probably an inherent tendency in capitalist enterprise to attempt escape from the consequences of pure competition by one device or another, and this in part explains the drive toward business combination in many fields around 1900 and the later endeavors to obtain governmental interference with competition in industries of atomistic structure. The latter tendency was accelerated when a great number of industries had attained the greater stability and higher profits ordinarily associated with more concentrated market structures.

In spite of several theoretical properties of pure competition which are attractive from the standpoint of over-all welfare, therefore, business enterprises are consistently motivated to escape it if possible. This drive to escape the strictures of pure competition seems in part responsible for the fact that unregulated purely competitive market organization is not very common now, and never has been in the history of industrial economies. The desire of the individual seller is naturally to get out of the position where he is at the mercy of an impersonal market price and where there is no organized control of industry output. From the standpoint of business enterprise there are several possible avenues of escape from pure competition. These include: (1) merger or combination of firms toward the point of monopoly or fewness of sellers, (2) formation of collusive agreements among sellers to restrict output and raise price, (3) governmental restriction of output or setting of price to accomplish the same ends, and (4) differentiation of products by individual sellers to give them some jurisdiction over their individual prices and some possibility of promoting their individual sales.

Activity directed along these avenues simply to restrict or alter the character of competition accounts in part for the comparative rarity of pure competition as a stable market structure. But it is by no means the only, nor necessarily the most important, explanation of the development of a variety of other market structures. The second major force accounting for this development is technology, particularly as it determines the optimal scale of a firm as related to the size of the market in which it sells. As previously emphasized, pure competition is a tenable market structure only in those cases where the lowest-cost scale of a firm comes at so small a rate of output that a large number of firms of this scale will be required to supply the total market demand. Where the optimum-scale output of the firm is so large that only a few firms of this scale will supply all the market will take at a price approximate to cost, pure competition is simply un-tenable unless there is governmental interference to preserve it. That is, the pursuit of long-run equilibrium adjustments by all firms (where the firm's long-run marginal cost equals price) will naturally result in the elim-ination of all but a few firms, and the industry simply will not remain purely competitive as long-run equilibrium is approached. Now the deter-minant of the optimal scale of firms in any industry, absolute and relative to the size of the market, is the specific technology available in that industry for organizing resources for production. In some industries techniques make available substantial economies to large-scale firms; in others they do not. It follows that, depending on specific techniques, there will be in some industries a "natural" tendency (aside from endeavors of sellers to restrict competition) toward the stable preservation of a competitive structure; in others there will be a "natural" tendency, through the very forces of com-petition, toward the development of concentrated or even monopolistic struc-ture. It also follows that when techniques change, there are "natural" tendencies toward the alteration of market structure—toward greater con-centration if optimal scales become larger, toward less concentration if optimal scales become smaller.

The basic technological characteristics of various industries thus tend to give us, to a first approximation, an explanation of existing market struc-tures. There are some industries, at least, where techniques are such that every firm can grow large enough to exploit every advantage of large-scale or mass production, and each firm can still be small enough, relative to the total demand for industry output, so that no concern controls more than 1 or 2 percent of the market. These tend, other things being equal, to evolve toward atomistic and possibly purely competitive structure. There are others in which the growth of firms to a size requisite for the attainment of all economies of mass production will mean that one or a few firms can supply the whole market, and these tend, *ceteris paribus,* toward monopolistic or oligopolistic structures. At the present time it is probably fair to say that in the bulk of manufacturing industry, in much of the distributive trades, in transportation and public-utility industries, and in part of mining and of the construction industries, technology is basically inimical to the preserva-tion of truly atomistic market structures, and it explains in considerable part why we do not have this structure in most industries. On the other hand, technological considerations alone may suggest quite various degrees of concentration of sellers—once true atomism is discarded—in different in-dustries.

Similarly, changes in technology give rise to basic or underlying tend-encies toward changes in market structure. In such areas as railroad trans-portation or electrical utilities technology has from the outset required high concentration or monopoly. In the areas of manufacture and distribution, however, and to a lesser extent elsewhere, there was for a time, at least in recent history, a trend of technological development which gave rise to in-creased economies of increasingly large-scale firms in many lines. A late phase of the so-called industrial revolution, from the end of the Civil War and continuing for at least four or five decades thereafter, involved changes in technique which favored large firms and a concentration sufficient to eliminate atomistic structure in much of manufacture and distribution. This development helps explain the prevailingly concentrated, or nonatomistic, structure of much of the American economy at present. Pure or otherwise, atomistic competition is simply not technologically tenable in a large portion of the American economy. On the other hand, there is a good deal of dis-agreement among authorities as to just how high a degree of concentra-tion is required to attain all economies of scale in our industries and as to whether or not we have not exceeded the minimum requisite degree of concentration in many areas.

This leads us back to a consideration of other explanations of the de-velopment and "equilibrium determination" of market structures. Whatever fundamental tendencies are implicit in technology, the basic drive of enter-prise to escape the bounds of pure competition cannot be left out of account. The actual pattern of structural developments will follow not only a cost-saving rationale related to economies of large-scale production, but also a profit-increasing rationale based on the limitation or alteration of the char-acter of competition. Let us consider the extent to which actual market structures, and the rarity of pure competition, are explained by the drive of enterprise to eliminate or alter competition.

First, there is always open an attractive avenue for the restriction of competition by the merger or combination of existing firms to the point where the remaining number is small or concentration is high. There is little question but that existing concentration in many industries arose in part through combinations which had competition-limiting motives (as well as others) and that the degree of concentration obtained could not be fully justified on the grounds of economies of large-scale production. On the other hand, this competition-limiting motive ordinarily operated *along with others,* frequently complementing or reinforcing technological motiva-tions, and perhaps resulting in higher concentration than would otherwise have been attained. Conversely, it seems unlikely on theoretical grounds that combination simply to limit competition tends to be successful in an industry where all technological considerations tend to favor atomistic structure. This is because large firms, resulting from combination, then have little or no long-run cost advantage over small potential entrant firms, and the pressure of the entry of the latter tends to force the industry always to revert toward atomistic structure. Thus, *stable* concentrated structures are unlikely to arise from combinations based simply on limitation of competition, although dynamic instability of market structure may result. We conclude that whereas competition-limiting combination very probably results in modification of market structures which for technological reasons would in any event tend to become oligopolistic, it is unlikely to constitute a *sufficient* explanation of the abandonment of pure competition.

The same sort of logic applies to limitation of competition within purely competitive structures by private collusive agreements to fix prices and outputs. Since the tendency of sellers to "get together" and agree to limit output and raise price in order to enjoy larger joint profits is counterbalanced by a tendency of each seller to violate the agreement to his own advantage, consummation and observance of an effective collusive agreement are never certain. In a purely competitive industry the agreement-destroying tendency is likely to be dominant since each seller is so small that he alone can fail to restrict his output in conformity to agreement without inducing retaliation or upsetting the market price. Thus, as a general rule, collusive elimination of competition is a feasible alternative in already concentrated market structures. It is not likely to be workable in an industry of atomistic structure or to be a feasible means of altering basic pricing tendencies in pure competition.

There is at least one basic tendency toward removing the conditions of pure competition, however, which may operate quite generally and without especial regard to technological considerations favoring large-scale production. This is the tendency of *homogeneity* of competing sellers' outputs to be destroyed by the differentiation of their products. To be sure there are some industries, including several in agriculture, where the opportunities for product differentiation are quite slight, and others where the pressure of informed buyers forces some sort of standardization. But in the production of most consumers' goods, there is a clear tendency for sellers to differentiate their products from those of their rivals and thus seek some control over price or sales volume and some advantage in amount or security of profits. They tend to do this just as surely as they tend to equate marginal cost to price or to seek more efficient scales of plant, and they have done it in the great majority of cases. As long as we are talking about free enterprise, therefore, it is probably illegitimate to assume the general possibility of product uniformity among rival sellers, either voluntary or enforced. Market structures involving product differentiation seem to develop naturally within a capitalist economy as a corollary of the profit-seeking motive. As a result, many markets which might otherwise have the structural characteristics of pure competition have developed those of monopolistic competition. And instead of pure oligopoly we very frequently find differentiated oligopoly. Moreover, as product differentiation emerges, selling or sales-promotion expenses are incurred by all sellers, and the economies of large-scale sales promotion—logically distinct from the economies of large-scale production—may foster concentration where it would not be favored under conditions of product homogeneity. Thus, it is evident that the tendency toward product differentiation may have accounted both for the alteration of product relations within atomistic markets and for tendencies toward concentration based on a different category of economies of large-scale production.

In general, it would appear that the most basic factors accounting for the rarity of pure competition per se are (1) production technologies giving rise to production-cost economies for large-scale firms and (2) the natural development of product differentiation in many markets, together with some indirect consequences of this development. Tendencies to combine or form collusive agreements to eliminate competition have reinforced these basic tendencies toward concentration, and they have resulted in modifications of market structure which would in any event become concentrated. They do not alone, however, account for the continued tendency away from pure competition.

Under the influence of such a complex of forces congeries of market structures have developed within our economy in which pure competition is relatively rare. (This is not to suggest that it was ever very common.) Within these congeries single-firm monopoly is uncommon, oligopolies of various degrees of concentration are the most common type, and industries in monopolistic competition (shading into differentiated oligopolies of low concentration) are of considerable importance. This is not to imply that industries in each of these categories behave in a way drastically different from those in pure competition—we leave this as an open question to be investigated. Nor is it to imply that there is any progressive trend through time in structural developments as, for example, toward ever increasing concentration. We refer to the status quo and why we have it. (Prediction of future developments requires a complicated type of crystal gazing in which we shall not engage here.)

Although pure competition is relatively rare at this time, it is true, nevertheless, that there is a significant sector of industries—in agriculture, some mining, and a little manufacture—which have structural characteristics approximating those of pure competition and where technological and other considerations have evidently been so far unfavorable to the escape from pure competition. Combination, collusion, and product differentiation have not been feasible alternatives to sellers in such areas. Thus, in the absence of governmental interference, they have behavior tendencies closely approximate to those predictable by the theory of purely competitive price. Yet the proviso, "in the absence of governmental interference," suggests the final avenue for the destruction of pure competition, when all else fails. There has been in the principal remaining areas of pure competition a concerted and largely successful drive by sellers to induce governmental authority to intervene and through legal devices encourage or require quasi-monopolistic restriction of output and setting of price. The drive is ordinarily justified on the ground of prolonged distress conditions (as discussed above) or on the ground of "evening up" the positions of sellers in competitive industries with those of sellers in concentrated industries.

Thus, where we have purely competitive market structure, we may still not have purely competitive pricing but rather government-regulated price and output or price and output fixed by a government-sponsored cartel. Some of the tendencies of such cartel pricing are suggested in the analysis of monopoly pricing, although logically we discover an additional form of price-making mechanism. It is, moreover, one the operation of which—depending as it does on political decision making as well as on the profit-maximizing calculus of sellers—is much less predictable than a market mechanism and deserves detailed scientific study which it has not yet received.

CONCLUSION

The immediately preceding discussion suggests that pure competition, and especially unregulated pure competition, is a rather rare market situation in the modern economy. It may thus be well to reiterate, in conclusion, the substantial reasons which favor our having discussed this hypothetical sort of price-formation process at length and before ever turning to pricing under more typical conditions. These reasons are quite clear. First, although it is oversimplified and otherwise removed from reality, the purely competitive economy gives us a simple model within which the general function of a free price system may be observed. Oversimplification and artificiality are thus virtues if they assist us in learning the elements of a complicated process. Second, the actual economy, with many different market structures, may perform enough like a purely competitive economy that this simple model may allow us to make some very rough general predictions about the working of the actual economy. Third, a purely competitive world (or one not significantly different from it) seems to have been the implicit reference of most of those political economists who, from Adam Smith on, have argued for a *laissez-faire* (that is, hands off) governmental policy toward the economy. They justified nonregulation by referring to how a purely competitive economy regulated itself. It may be useful to recognize the nature of this mythical economy to which they referred and also to see how it differs from the real economy of then or now. Fourth, although pure competition may not be a feasible alternative in the real economy, a study of its hypothetical properties assists us in developing *norms* of desirable performance applicable to any industry, regardless of structure. Some of these norms are fulfilled under pure competition, and others are not, but a study of purely competitive pricing provides a good initial device for defining and developing norms. And, in certain respects at least, the performance of a hypothetical purely competitive industry or economy is a source of norms of performance (though not necessarily of structure) for any industry or economy.

Normative issues aside, analysis of the purely competitive economy has had the further advantage of establishing, on the abstract level, a definite law of behavior for prices and outputs which an economy would obey under the guidance of free and unrestricted competition. This pattern will at least serve as a measuring rod for other behavior we may encounter. It clearly poses an important question: To the extent that this is not the pattern of behavior imposed by the price system we have, what *is* that pattern of behavior and toward what goals does the enterprise system automatically govern itself?

To this point we have examined the process of price determination and the regulatory function of price in industries in pure competition and for a hypothetical economy in pure competition. We are now ready to turn to pricing in more complex situations.

SUPPLEMENTARY READINGS

EDWARD H. CHAMBERLIN, *The Theory of Monopolistic Competition*, Chap. II.

J. E. MEADE AND C. J. HITCH, *Economic Analysis and Public Policy*, New York: Oxford University Press, 1938, Part II, Chaps. 1-3.

ABBA P. LERNER, *The Economics of Control*, New York: The Macmillan Company, 1944, Chaps. 1-18.

GEORGE J. STIGLER, *The Theory of Price*, Chap. 9.

ARTHUR R. BURNS, *The Decline of Competition*, New York: McGraw-Hill Book Company, 1936, Chap. 1.

5 PRICING IN MONOPOLIZED
MARKETS

The preceding discussion of how an economy would work if all the markets for all commodities were in pure competition clearly poses some questions about the actual economy of the United States. Granted that our economy is not generally atomistic in structure, and granted that its behavior is probably not that ascribed to a purely competitive system of markets, how does it behave? Is there a law of behavior which the economy we have does obey? These queries can be satisfied if we can determine, for the types of industries which we have in fact: (1) how firms determine their prices and outputs; (2) how industry prices are made for groups of rival firms and to what ends; and (3) how the resulting system of prices for all industry operates to accomplish its regulatory functions.

Any investigation of pricing in the real world, of course, is guided by the fact that a number of market types are important, including monopoly, monopolistic competition, and several sorts of oligopoly. Each significant market category must be investigated separately. There is some advantage to beginning this investigation by considering simple or single-firm monopoly—the industry in which one firm controls all the supply of a good and is not troubled by the competition of any very close substitutes. Such monopoly is, to be sure, not the most common thing in our economy, although there are important instances of substantial monopolization of entire industries. But the sort of pricing which occurs in single-firm monopoly represents in simplified and extreme form a tendency of pricing in the oligopolistic industries which are so important in our economy. For in these industries there is an element or "degree" of monopoly, which may tend to be exploited in somewhat the same way as a simple monopolist exploits his position. We can, therefore, learn most rapidly about some significant tendencies in real pricing by considering first the determination of price and output by a single-firm monopolist. Thereafter, both the similarities and differences between monopolistic and oligopolistic pricing may be considered in detail.

A. THE MEANING OF MONOPOLY: ITS BASES AND ITS TYPES

DIFFERENCES BETWEEN PURELY COMPETITIVE AND OTHER PRICING

Monopolistic pricing, like pricing in oligopoly or monopolistic competition, turns out to be different and more complicated than purely competitive pricing. The reasons for this are fairly evident. In the first place, the underlying market structures in monopoly and oligopoly are significantly different from that of pure competition. Instead of many competing sellers in a market there are ordinarily a few, often a very few, and in the case of simple monopoly only one. Where there are several rival sellers in a market, moreover, their products are very often differentiated and susceptible to further dynamic differentiation or product variation. Both concentration of numbers and product differentiation tend to give the individual seller a degree of control over his own price, or *price jurisdiction,* which he does not possess in pure competition. His exercise of this jurisdiction may affect price behavior considerably.

A second difference between most actual pricing and the variety attributed to pure competition is that the scope of closely interrelated "price" decisions which a firm must make is much greater. If we suppose the firm to have a given and unchanging product and one which is identical to that of many rival sellers, then we may reasonably suppose that his principal concern is the simple one of adjusting production costs (there being no selling cost) to the going market price for the product in a single (the present) time period. But in monopolistic and oligopolistic markets and in markets in monopolistic competition the decisions which the firm must make include (1) the adjustment of current output in the light not only of production cost variations but also of connected price variations, (2) variations of its product according to the effect of these variations on present and future demand and on cost, (3) variations of selling costs according to their effect on demand, and (4) adjustment of present price and cost in the light of their effects on future price. In a word, the firm in practice has to devise instead of a limited output decision a complicated price and market policy embracing price, output, product, production cost, and selling cost in both present and future dimensions. The function of the resulting price system, and of the competitive mechanism from which it stems, is thus quite complicated. We can now begin to cut into those complexities by considering pricing in a simple monopoly.

THE DEFINITION OF SINGLE-FIRM MONOPOLY

Single-firm monopoly occurs when one seller sells a product for which there is no close competitor or rival. This idea is, of course, not as simple as words can make it seem. Is a monopolist still a monopolist if the product to which he has sole right has close substitutes? Does a sole seller of Camel cigarettes have a monopoly if another seller has Chesterfields, or is the match monopoly in Ruritania really a monopoly if there are other sellers of mechanical cigarette lighters?

In one sense, a seller has a distinct product to monopolize whenever his output is at least slightly differentiated from every substitute so that at least some buyers consider it somewhat different from other products. Any firm with a protected design, package, or trade-mark is thus a monopoly in some degree. But it may still have competitors or rivals in the sense that other products are such close substitutes that its price changes could significantly affect their sales and that changes in the prices of these substitutes will substantially influence its demand. When a monopolist has a product which is simply one of a differentiated group of many close but imperfect substitutes, he "has competitors" and is really a participant in "monopolistic competition." When the monopolist's product has a few important substitutes close enough that he and the sellers of these substitutes take account of each other's price reactions in setting their own prices—where the prices and sales of their products are recognized to be significantly interrelated—the monopolist "has rivals" and is essentially in an oligopoly situation. These are the common settings for "monopoly" today—monopoly plus competition or plus rivalry.

But neither is "single-firm" monopoly. We reserve this category for the case where the individual seller has a product with no close substitutes—where the cross-elasticity of demand between his product and every other product in the economy is very low. This means not only that he has a product which buyers distinguish from all others, but also that he is neither in monopolistic competition with a large group of imperfect but close substitute products nor in oligopolistic rivalry with a few such products. There is no group of close substitutes for the monopolized product, concurrent changes in the price of which will substantially affect the demand for the output of the monopolist, and there is no rival product the price of which will respond significantly to the monopolist's price changes. Single-firm monopoly is thus monopoly without either effective competition or rivalry.

We should hasten to say that no firm has probably ever been *quite* a single-firm monopoly. But there are a number of instances where substitutes are distant enough and effective rivalry slight enough that conditions of single-firm monopoly are approximated. These would include aluminum-ingot production before World War II, nickel production, telephone communications, and others. Monopoly pricing is thus well worth examining for its own importance as well as for the light it casts on quasi-monopolistic situations.

THE EMERGENCE OF MONOPOLY

In a formal sense, the preceding is perhaps a sufficient general definition of single-firm monopoly. But it is by no means an explanation or definition of the conditions which make single-firm monopoly possible. A related question is "Why do monopolies develop?" or "What are the conditions necessary for a monopolist *to remain a monopolist in the long run* if he once gets to be one?" It is evident that monopoly will tend to occur systematically, or to be perpetuated in stable fashion through time, only in those industries where a single seller, once established, can produce profitably while enjoying a sufficient advantage over *potential entrant* sellers to prevent or discourage them from entering his industry by producing identical or close-substitute products. If profit maximization is assumed as a motive for all sellers, monopoly will remain through time only where a single seller can make larger long-run profits while pricing so as to discourage entry than by pricing in such a way that entry will be attracted. The single seller in effect must enjoy some advantage over sellers who might wish to enter the industry, which permits him to operate profitably without inducing them to enter—or, strictly, a sufficient advantage to permit him to operate more profitably (in the long run) while pricing to exclude entry than while pricing at a level which will attract entry. There must in effect be some *barrier to entry* in the way of potential rivals, for if there were not, there ordinarily would be rivals, and a single-firm monopoly would not remain in the long run. This necessary condition clearly distinguishes single-firm monopoly from pure competition, where there is necessarily little or no obstacle in the way of competitive entry.

What sorts of advantage might permit a single firm to operate profitably in an industry while discouraging others from entering? Several possibilities may be mentioned. First, it may be possible that the economies of the large-scale firm are such that a single firm can supply the entire market at a lower cost than two or more firms could—one firm of lowest cost or smaller scale can supply all the market will take at the lowest price consistent with covering the average cost of production. In this case unrestricted competition of firms will tend to drive out all but one, or, in any event, it will be profitable for existing firms to merge into one. If single-firm monopoly emerges in this setting, as it is likely to, then the single seller enjoys an advantage over potential entrants in that any new firm, built to supply less than the whole market, will have significantly higher costs and will also be vulnerable to the low-cost competition of the established monopolist if they try to enter the market. Then the established monopolist is likely to be able to charge a price somewhat above his own average cost without attracting entry.

This situation where economies of scale make one-firm production the most economical is one version of so-called "natural monopoly." It is probably encountered, for example, for railroad transportation along any single route. Another instance of natural monopoly is that in which supply by more than one seller is basically inconvenient and costly to consumers, as in the case of telephone service. Here also monopoly tends to develop more or less naturally, and there exists a protective barrier against entry into the monopolist's field. In cases of the natural-monopoly type it has been the tendency of public authority to help nature along by granting an exclusive franchise to a single firm in any market and arbitrarily excluding entry, and thereafter to regulate the monopolized industry as a public utility.

The barrier to entry which permits establishment and continuance of monopoly may just as easily be institutional or legal in character. The principal sorts of legal barriers to entry are patents and trade-marks. Under the law of the United States a patent grant of monopoly for a period of 17 years may be allowed to the inventor of any new article, device, or process. If one firm gains patent control of a strategic process for manufacturing a good, it can exclude others from its use for the 17-year period, and it may thus enjoy a substantial and possibly overwhelming advantage in cost over potential competitors who could produce only with an inferior process. It can thus possibly produce and sell at a price which is profitable to it but at which any other seller, using inferior technique, could not make a requisite profit. Similarly, a firm may gain patent control over a new product—such as, for example, television tubes—and enjoy an absolute monopoly in its production by excluding others, except so far as close-substitute products which do not "infringe" the monopolist's patent rights can be developed. Needless to say, by no means every patent is sufficient in importance to assure its holder of single-firm monopolistic control of an industry, but some have this effect.

Trade-marks, or brand names attached to the product to identify it, are also protected by law against imitation by rival sellers.[1] As far as the established seller is able, by advertising and by the general development of his reputation, to establish a clear preference in the minds of consumers for the product bearing his trade-mark, he may enjoy an advantage over rivals or potential rivals which would permit him to dominate the market at a profitable price while others could sell only at lower and possibly unprofitable prices. Athough the leverage of a trade-mark is probably seldom great enough to permit profitable establishment of a single-firm monopoly, it is not impossible that it could be.

[1] Copyrights covering books, music, and so forth, afford similar protection.

A further type of barrier to entry may be imposed when a single firm manages to acquire control of all or most of a strategic raw material source required for the production of a product. This may permit it to exclude all competitors absolutely at will or, if not, to enjoy an advantage equal to difference in cost which potential competitors must incur in order to use an inferior source of materials. In either case monopoly of the raw material source may permit the owner to establish a monopoly in the industry processing the material and to earn a satisfactory profit while charging a price which will not attract entry. This sort of barrier to entry is essentially made possible by a law of property permitting unrestricted private ownership of natural resources.

It is worth noting in connection with the analysis of the conditions which may make monopoly possible that a single-firm monopoly in the theoretical sense does not need to be world-wide; it exists whenever a seller is the sole supplier of a group of buyers who have no access to close substitutes for his output. A single seller may be a monopolist in a given market or geographical region even though potential close substitutes are available in other regions, provided that transportation costs or other barriers, such as tariffs, preclude these potential substitutes from entering his market. Here his strategic barrier to entry, in addition to those which enable him to monopolize his regional market, are essentially transport costs and other barriers to the free movement of goods among areas. It is also evident that such regional monopoly inheres in the fact not that "foreign" products are poor potential substitutes for "domestic" ones, but that they would be high-priced articles when delivered in the domestic area at a price sufficient to cover production cost plus shipping cost (and possibly plus tariffs). That is, at their possible prices they are poor substitutes for the product of the monopolist if he charges a lower price; more exactly, the buyers will not take them as long as the local monopolist chooses to sell for less. (At different delivered prices, the cross-elasticity of demand between domestic and imported products is low or zero, and the domestic can dominate the market.) Thus, it is quite clear that the regional monopolist is a monopolist "within limits"—up to a price sufficient to attract imports—and that his monopoly may be sustained by the fact that he can charge a price high enough to be profitable but low enough to exclude entry of substitute products from other areas. Single-firm monopoly thus need not imply the ability of a seller to charge every conceivable price without attracting entry. It implies merely the ability to charge a profitable price without doing so or, strictly, the ability to make greater long-run profits at a price which will exclude entry than at a higher one which will attract it.

TWO CATEGORIES OF MONOPOLY

It appears, therefore, that some barrier to entry—or advantage over potential entrants—is a necessary condition of the stable maintenance of monopoly through time. Since the height of the barrier to entry may vary from case to case, it should be useful to subclassify single-firm monopolies according to the condition of entry affecting them. Two categories may be recognized. First, we may identify the single-firm monopolist who may without attracting entry charge any price which is to the advantage of industry profits—he may set price to maximize the profit of the industry and have it all for himself without attracting entry. Since he could desire no price higher than this, he has essentially absolute monopoly. We may refer to it as monopoly with blockaded entry or without effective threat of entry. Second, we may identify the monopolist who cannot set a price to maximize industry profit without attracting entry but who may set a lower, yet still profitable, price at which entry will not be attracted. This sort of monopoly— that with effective threat of entry—will tend to remain monopoly through time as long as the monopolist finds it more profitable (or otherwise desirable in the long run) to exclude entry by holding price below that which would maximize industry profits than to charge a higher price, attract entry, and share industry profits with others. In our analysis of monopoly pricing below we shall refer first to the simple case of monopoly without threat of entry and later to the more complex case of monopoly subject to threat of entry.

The preceding discussion of the conditions of entry necessary to establish and perpetuate monopoly refers explicitly to the case of single-firm monopoly. But it may apply as well, as we shall discover in Chapter 6, as a description of conditions necessary for establishment and preservation of a given limited group of sellers in oligopoly. Similarly, oligopolistic industries may be subclassified according to the height of the barriers to entry protecting established sellers.

In conclusion, it may be noted that although we have identified a range of alternative conditions sufficient to permit establishment and maintenance of single-firm monopoly in an industry, we have developed no unique theory of just when single-firm monopoly must and will emerge.

The bases of monopoly in any given market are seen to be primarily either technological or legal-institutional. Where technology favors monopoly through economies of the very large-scale firm, there is a tendency toward monopoly, and it may emerge. But it is at least possible that the resulting drive toward monopoly will be checked at some point and that a concentrated oligopoly of a few large firms will become stabilized, even though one firm alone could be more efficient. To know whether and when this may happen, we would have to delve at length into the considerations theoretically affecting the dealings among a few large and perhaps equally powerful firms. An antitrust law which threatens single-firm monopoly in any field may act as a deterrent. Conversely, it is not impossible that in an industry where the most economical production could be had with two or three or a few firms, as well as with just one, merger might lead to monopoly and that the very large size at which an additional firm would have to enter to be efficient might act as an effective deterrent to entry. Again, we would require an adequate theory of the dealings among a few firms to predict when monopoly will and will not emerge. Lacking this, given technological conditions favoring high concentration within an industry suggest simply the possibility of the emergence of monopoly, but concentrated oligopoly is generally an equally probable alternative.

So far as monopoly may rest upon institutional grounds—such as patent control, resource control, trade-mark, or government franchise—it is impossible to predict in any general fashion just how often a single firm will gain a sufficient advantage over all others to create and maintain a single-firm monopoly. Perhaps the probabilities are against this development, except where the government decides to find an industry a public utility and grant a monopoly franchise. This is primarily because, if oligopoly develops first, several firms may gain counterbalancing advantages (if advantages are to be gained) and no one may get enough advantage to support monopoly control. The principal way for monopoly to be brought about is then through their merger, but, as we have already indicated, it is difficult to predict when this will occur.

Thus, the most we can do is to suggest that there are certain circumstances affecting entry which may come into being and may favor control of an industry by at the most a few firms. In this case single-firm monopoly may emerge, but we are not sure when it will. Experience suggests its emergence is rare. We thus take monopoly as we find it and analyze its pricing tendencies when or if it does emerge.

B. PRICE DETERMINATION AND MARKET PERFORMANCE BY THE MONOPOLIST

PRICE AND OUTPUT DETERMINATION WITHOUT THREAT OF ENTRY

Let us first analyze the determination of price and output by a single-firm monopolist in the situation where he is subject to no effective threat of entry —where he may set a price to maximize industry profit without inducing any other seller to enter the industry. A monopolist with this ultimate in strength can arrive at a price and output policy not only without concern for the reactions of any other prices but also without fear of making potential competition real. He has a market all to himself to exploit more or less as he will. How will he determine his price and output?

As we have indicated, the monopolist must make a wider range of decisions than we have considered heretofore. But he must at any rate make one common to all markets—how much to produce of a given good and what to charge for it at any given time. We will first consider how this principal decision is likely to be made in single-firm monopoly, taking as given for the moment his decisions relative to product design, selling cost, and so forth.

For any seller the simple price-output decision for a period can be conceived as resting on (1) the seller's demand curve for that period and (2) his cost curves appropriate to that period. The single-firm monopolist's choice of a price and a rate of output, in either short or long run, follows the same logic as that developed for a seller in pure competition. That is, the monopolist will try to select that rate of output which maximizes his profit, and this will presumably be the output for which his marginal cost is equal to his marginal receipts from sales.

The monopolist's position in this matter is unique only in the relationship which exists between the volume of his sales and the price he can receive for them. The seller in pure competition views his sales volume as having no effect on selling price. He can offer as much or as little as he will without influencing the market price for his good because he controls only a minute proportion of the total industry supply. The monopolist, on the other hand, controls the entire supply of a good, and he will find that variations in his sales volume produce definite associated variations in price. In short, the more he produces, the lower the price per unit will be. In diagrammatic terms the seller in pure competition faces a demand curve for his output which is simply a horizontal line at the going price. The demand curve of the monopolist facing no effective threat of entry is in effect simply a negatively sloped industry demand curve, and shows a clear inverse relation of sales volume and price, as in Figure 25.

The single-firm monopolist not threatened by entry, moreover, will view the position of this demand curve for his output as impervious to any price-output decisions he himself may make. Since there are no close substitutes for or direct rivals of his product, he can select any price on this demand curve without inducing any rivalrous reactions of other prices. Further, no price adjustments he may make will induce competitors to enter his field and thus to "take away" a share of the industry demand curve from him. Finally, the position of his demand curve is not sensitive to the prices of any limited group of substitutes—but only to other prices in the economy as a whole. All of this is summarized by saying that the monopolist is the sole seller in a theoretical industry and that the demand curve for his output, short- or long-run, is the theoretical industry demand curve in every sense. Thus, he can maximize industry profits without regard to competition, rivalry, or potential entry.

Knowing or estimating the demand for his product, the monopolist can select the most profitable output by balancing the variation of selling price

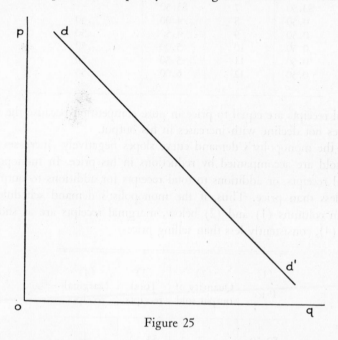

Figure 25

in response to variation in output against the corresponding variation in production cost. In effect, he will set his marginal cost curve (let us say for the short run) against his demand curve, and will maximize industry profits at the output where marginal cost is equal to his marginal receipts—where the addition to total cost incurred in producing the last unit of output equals the addition to total receipts earned by selling it.

The marginal receipts from sales—the additions to total receipts for additions to output sold—follow a different course in monopoly than they do in pure competition. Since the purely competitive seller can extend his sales with no reduction in price (his demand curve is a horizontal line), any addition to output sold adds as much to his total receipts as the selling price of that output. A sector of a seller's demand curve in pure competition might follow the pattern shown in columns (1) and (2) on the next page. Then the marginal receipts should be equal to price, as shown in column (4).

(1) Price	(2) Quantity of output sold	(3) Total receipts (1) × (2)	(4) Marginal receipts (Addition to total receipts per addition to quantity)
$0.50	7	$3.50	—
0.50	8	4.00	.50
0.50	9	4.50	.50
0.50	10	5.00	.50
0.50	11	5.50	.50
0.50	12	6.00	.50

Marginal receipts are equal to price in pure competition because the seller's price does not decline with increases in his output.

But the monopolist's demand curve slopes negatively—increases in his output sold are accompanied by reductions in his price. In monopoly the marginal receipts, or additions to total receipts for additions to output, are always less than price. Thus, if the monopolist's demand schedule is as shown in columns (1) and (2) below, marginal receipts are as shown in column (4), consistently less than selling price.

(1) Price	(2) Quantity of output sold	(3) Total receipts	(4) Marginal receipts
$0.50	7	$3.50	—
0.49	8	3.92	.42
0.48	9	4.32	.40
0.47	10	4.70	.38
0.46	11	5.06	.36
0.45	12	5.40	.34

When a monopolist extends his output—let us say by one unit—the price he receives for all units falls. The additional benefit or receipts the monopolist gets from one more unit are, therefore, not as much as its price, but less than that price by the receipts lost through falling price on the other units.[2]

[2] Thus, in the preceding table, an eighth unit of output can be sold at a price of 49 cents. But it does not add 49 cents to the receipts of the firm, since in order to sell an eighth unit, the price of all units must decline from 50 to 49 cents. This entails a virtual loss of 1 cent per unit on the preceding seven units, or a loss of total receipts of

In considering extension of his output, the monopolist is obviously concerned mainly with the marginal receipts from that extension, not with the
price. The fact that in monopoly the marginal receipts of an additional output are always less than its price simply reflects a very essential aspect of
monopoly pricing—because an increased output means a lowered price, there
is always a virtual drag on or deterrent to extending output.

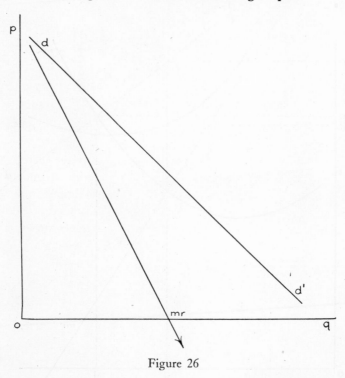

Figure 26

The marginal receipts resulting from any monopoly (or other) demand
curve can be plotted as a curve derived from this demand. Where p is price
and q quantity of output, the marginal receipts may be defined as $d(pq)/dq$;
that is, as the rate of change of total receipts corresponding to change in
output. Thus, the demand curve dd' in Figure 26 has corresponding to it
the marginal receipts curve mr. The curve mr shows the rate of increase
of total receipts in response to increasing output sold. It will be clear that
*the position of the marginal receipts curve depends on the elasticity of the
demand curve from which it is derived*—the more elastic the demand, the
closer to price will marginal receipts be. If demand is more elastic than
unity, marginal receipts are positive; if demand is unit elastic, marginal re-

7 cents. Setting this loss against the added 49 cents for the eighth unit, we get marginal
receipts of 42 cents.

ceipts are zero; and if demand is less elastic than unity, marginal receipts are negative. The student should consider the preceding propositions until their logic becomes obvious to him.

Profits are maximized by the monopolist by choosing that output for which marginal cost of production equals marginal receipts from sales. His

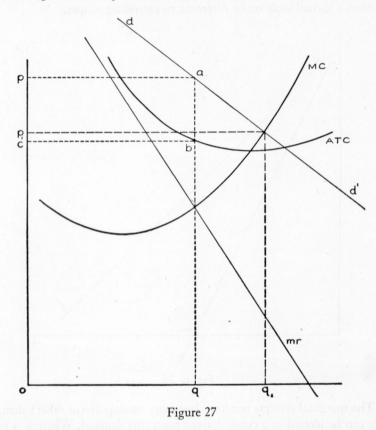

Figure 27

decision as to how much to produce and what to charge in a short period is charted in Figure 27, which brings together the monopolist's demand and marginal receipts curve and his short-run cost curves. Here *dd'* is his demand curve, *mr* the marginal receipts drawn therefrom, *ATC* the average total cost of production, and *MC* the marginal cost. (Average variable cost and average fixed cost curves are omitted for the sake of simplicity.) Assuming that the monopolist's motive is to maximize his profit for the short period, he will extend his output just so long as the added aggregate cost of additions to output is less than the added aggregate receipts they bring in sales. This will bring him into equilibrium at the output *oq*, charging the price *op*, where marginal cost equals marginal receipts. This output evidently makes the aggregate profit, measured by the rectangle *abcp*, the largest obtainable with this cost and demand. (The student should momentarily disregard the price p_1 and the quantity q_1.)

In this way the monopolist should decide, for a short period, (1) the price he will charge, (2) the output he will produce, and (3) the rate at which he will utilize his given fixed plant.

The monopolist's long-run adjustment of output to demand and price should follow strictly similar lines, provided we view his product as invariant and exclude selling costs. The monopolist should choose that long-run rate of output, and corresponding scale of plant, for which long-run marginal cost is equal to the marginal receipts expected over the longer period. If in Figure 27 we read all curves as applying to the long-run rather than the short-run calculations of the seller, the same solution applies without change.

Although our analysis so far is limited by certain arbitrary assumptions, it should now be possible to detect some tendencies inherent in monopoly pricing. What sort of price results tend to emerge from monopoly, and how do they differ from those of pure competition?

MONOPOLY PERFORMANCE AND PROFITS

Remembering that we are still speaking strictly of the monopolist who may maximize industry profits while disregarding any threat of entry, let us see how the price-output performance of the monopolist tends to differ from that of the purely competitive industry.

The relationship in monopoly of price to the average cost of production, and the resultant size of profits, is one important matter. For the short-run, to be sure, the general *limits* on monopolistic price-average-cost relationships are the same as those for a competitive firm. Price, that is, may be above or below or equal to average total cost, so long as it exceeds average variable cost. The single-firm monopolist may find himself in a short-run position where net losses are inevitable and may still produce, even though he fails to recover all of his fixed or sunk costs. Thus, the short-run relation of his demand to his cost does not have to be like that shown in Figure 27; the output at which marginal cost equaled marginal receipts could be one where price was less than average total cost.

This does not mean, however, that a single-firm monopoly is just as likely to incur short-run losses, and no more likely to make short-run profits, than a competitive firm. There is certainly a greater disposition toward higher profits and prices in monopoly. If there is any industry output at which market price exceeds cost and allows a profit, the monopolist is free to and presumably will choose this output. The short-run returns of a seller in pure competition, on the other hand, are at the mercy of a market price which always tends to be driven to the level of marginal cost. The monopolist can reject such a price (p_1 in Figure 27, the equivalent of short-run competitive price) [3] and can choose any higher price that allows more profit. Although the single-firm monopolist *may* sustain short-run losses, therefore, he is less likely to do so than any other sort of seller.

Long-run excess profits are also more likely to occur in single-firm monopoly. As in pure competition, the effective minimum for long-run monopoly price is at a level equal to average cost. But there is no effective price maximum as long as the monopoly is maintained. In pure competition, with free entry, profits in excess of normal return to investment tend in the long run to be eliminated. In single-firm monopoly, with completely impeded entry, long-run excess profits can be as large as the relation of costs to demand allows. The monopolist is free to choose the price which maximizes industry profit, and, therefore, he will tend to arrive at a price greater than average cost if there is such a price. Monopoly thus has a clear predisposition toward long-run excess profits.

It has sometimes been the fashion to refer to the excess profit of the monopolist (the area *abcp* in Figure 27) as a return to whatever it is he possesses which impedes competitors from entering his market and thus eliminating his profit. The excess profit might, for example, be called the earning power of his patent on a process, his public franchise to monopolize a field, or his trade-mark. Such a terminological venture is useful in calling attention to the institutional source of most monopoly earnings. When we proceed along this line, however, to the extent of calling this return a cost (since it is the necessary return on the investment that would be made in the patent or franchise if the monopolist had had to pay all it was worth to him in excess profits), we are obliterating a valid distinction between costs and excess profits and simply confusing the issue. We cannot whistle away the idea of excess profits. Explaining the source of excessive earnings does not keep them from being excessive.[4]

There is, in sum, a tendency in monopoly toward profits in excess of the necessary rewards to capital invested in producing resources and to management. Such profits are the earnings of artificial scarcity, maintained by a monopolist with the aid of some barrier to competitive entry which protects him. Against this must be set the fact that it is always possible to find an unfortunate monopolist who, even through the fullest exploitation of his monopoly power, is barely able to make ends meet. In an instance of this sort, private production could not be had without monopoly.

The argument so far is that in specific monopolized fields there will

[3] That is, it is the price equal to marginal cost.

[4] At the same time it is necessary to distinguish between costs and excess profits by defining the monopolist's costs very carefully—generally as the market value of all factors, like labor and capital goods, employed, but excluding the market value of special barriers to the entry of other sellers. In practice this poses a complex problem.

tend to be a relation of the monopolist's demand curve to his cost curve such that the monopolist can and will earn a long-run excess profit. This implies in turn that, relative to any given level of factor prices which determines the level of his cost curve, the individual monopolist should be able to command a demand curve which lies above his average cost curve for some outputs. If it does, the pursuit of a rational policy of monopolistic output restriction can then yield an excess profit. What are the fundamental conditions for such a relation of factor prices to the level of the demand curve of the monopolist? They would seem to reside in the fact that the monopolist is protected from the development of the competition of substitutes in each of two senses. First, others cannot enter to produce close substitutes in his field, thus forcing him to accept smaller shares of the industry demand curve until he can do no better than break even at going costs. This is implied in the definition of single-firm monopoly. Second, there is not a tendency for the development of numerous distant substitutes (other products making up other industries) in such a fashion as to reduce the demand for each monopolized industry, relative to factor prices, in such a way as to make excess profits impossible. This may be attributed to the fact that buyer preference patterns and inventive ingenuity are simply not such as to permit this or that the institutional protections enjoyed by monopolists might discourage such a development. The monopolist is protected in his individual field by the fact that there is not the possibility, given buyer preference patterns, of an indefinite multiplication of new distant-substitute products and industries such as will tend to eliminate the profitability of his established position. Given this condition, long-run excess profits tend to emerge in monopoly.

MONOPOLY PERFORMANCE—OUTPUT RESTRICTION

A second aspect of monopoly pricing is that output tends to be set at a level where the marginal cost of the monopolistic firm is less than price. That is, the additional cost to the monopolist of producing the last unit added to output is smaller than the price buyers are willing to pay for that unit. This is the natural result of setting output so that marginal cost equals marginal receipts (see Figure 27). The excess of price over marginal cost will be found in either the short run or the long run.

To compare this pricing performance with that of industries in pure competition, we must be careful to specify the definition of marginal cost to be employed and also the time period in question. Let us first make the comparison between monopolized and purely competitive industries in the long-run equilibrium. The strategic relation in pure competition, as discussed on pages 165 to 168 above, is that the money value of marginal real cost to the industry is equated to price. The long-run industry average cost curve measures this marginal cost, and when long-run price is set to equal industry average cost, the indicated equality to money value of marginal real cost to the industry is attained. The fact that the firm's marginal cost in pure competition also equals price is of only incidental importance, since industry output is varied by varying the number of firms.

What is the relation to price of money value of marginal real cost to the industry in monopoly? In single-firm monopoly the firm's marginal cost curve is an industry marginal cost curve, since industry output is necessarily varied only by varying the output of the firm. But does it measure the money value of marginal real cost to the industry, or does it provide some other measure of industry marginal cost? In general, it measures any increment to the money costs of the firm and industry due to an increase in output. Such increments in cost will necessarily be due in part at least to increments in real cost—in the physical quantity of productive factors employed to extend output. They may, in addition, be due to induced increases in factor prices paid by the monopolist, if such price increases are in fact induced. Now if the monopolist's output variations have no effect on the factor prices he pays—if the prices of all factors are given to him—then the only source of cost increment to him is real cost increment, and his marginal cost curve will necessarily reflect the money value of marginal real cost to him and his industry. If, on the other hand, his output increases induce factor-price increases, the rise in the prices paid to all factors as a result of output extension will be reflected in his marginal cost, and it will thus represent a marginal money cost to the industry which is higher than money value of marginal real cost (cf. pages 165 to 166 above). Should industry output variation induce factor-price variations, the monopolist, as the single administrative unit for the whole industry, will take account of these in calculating his marginal cost, whereas the individual seller in a competitive industry would disregard them in calculating his marginal cost as not being caused by his own small output variations. In comparing monopoly and competitive output in this chapter, we shall provisionally assume that factor prices are given to the monopolist and not influenced by his output variations— thus neglecting the cases where this is not true. (The cases where there is an induced factor-price variation will be considered in Chapter 8 as a variety of monopsony.) Upon this assumption, the monopolist's long-run marginal cost curve measures the money value of marginal real cost to the industry, and it has the same significance as the long-run industry average cost curve in pure competition.

The comparison between long-run relations of price to marginal cost in pure competition and in monopoly is now clear. In pure competition the long-run equilibrium output is such that the money value of marginal real cost to the industry equals price; in monopoly output is virtually restricted so that the money value of marginal real cost to the industry is less than price.

This discrepancy between marginal cost and price (assuming that marginal cost measures money value of marginal real cost to the industry) is a first and primary source of divergence between the performance of the monopolized and the purely competitive industry—or of monopolistic output restriction. A second may be found in the fact that in monopoly the aggregate costs of producing successive outputs, from which aggregate costs the marginal cost is calculated, may not be the minimum attainable. Where a purely competitive market structure can survive with many firms giving as low a cost as any other market structure could, we have seen that, with all firms producing at lowest-cost scales, the aggregate cost of producing every industry output in the long run is necessarily minimized, and the industry marginal cost refers to changes in such aggregate costs. In monopoly it may also be minimized as long as, because of economies of large-scale firms, one firm can produce the output required more efficiently than two or more firms could. But it is possible for monopoly to be established behind some institutional barricade to entry and for the single firm then to attain uneconomically large size so that it produces the required output at a higher aggregate (and average) cost than that attainable if two or more smaller firms were supplying the same output. In this event its marginal cost is derived from an aggregate cost curve which is higher than the minimum attainable for successive outputs in the relevant range. Then there are two sources of discrepancy from the output performance attributable to pure competition: (1) output is set so that marginal cost equals marginal revenue and is less than price, and (2) the marginal cost is not the "most desirable" marginal cost, being derived from an other than optimal aggregate cost curve, and may be higher than the most desirable marginal cost. To this may be added any restriction due to the reflection of induced factor-price increases in the monopolist's marginal cost curve, to be discussed in Chapter 8 below.

To simplify the problem, however, let us provisionally disregard the last two potential sources of output restriction and center upon the one which tends always to be present—the tendency to set output so that marginal cost is less than price. In the long run monopolistic output is so determined, and thus output is smaller than it would be if the money value of marginal real cost were equated to price. It is thus a smaller output than would obtain if the monopolistic industry behaved like a competitive industry. Monopoly output is oq in Figure 27, whereas the output where money value of marginal real cost equals price is oq_1.

The same conclusions apply to short-run monopoly output. Given invariant factor prices, the short-run marginal cost curve of the monopolist (or of the competitive industry) will represent the money value of marginal real cost to the industry in the short period. The monopolist sets his output so that the short-run marginal cost is less than the price; the competitive industry sets its output so that the short-run marginal cost (see pages 136 to 139 above) is equal to price.

COMPARISON OF MONOPOLISTIC AND COMPETITIVE OUTPUT

The conclusion of the preceding section is that the monopolist sets his output so that the money value of the marginal real cost to the industry is less than the price, whereas the competitive industry extends output until the money value of the marginal real cost is equal to the price. It appears then that in some sense the competitive industry tends to produce a larger output than the monopolized industry.

The sense in which this is necessarily true is *not* that many firms in pure competition in a given industry would produce a larger output than a monopolist would *in the same industry*. It is not necessarily true, for example, if we were to find a monopolist following rational output-restriction policies in supplying steel in some market, that a government edict which required steel output to be supplied by 500 firms of equal and legally limited size—and thus instituted atomistic competition—would result in a larger steel output. The fact that firms in pure competition would extend output to the point where money value of marginal real cost was equal to price, whereas the monopolist would hold output short of this point, would necessarily mean that a competitive structure would give larger output in a given industry only if it were clear that, under monopoly, marginal costs would not be lower relative to demand. To conclude that the virtually restrictive effects of monopoly pricing meant an equivalent actual output reduction, we would have to know that, regardless of whether there were competitive or monopolistic structure, (1) the industry demand curve would occupy the same position, (2) factor prices entering into costs would be the same, (3) techniques of production would be the same, and (4) the efficiency in the scale of the firm would be the same. If these conditions were fulfilled, then the money value of the industry marginal real cost could be the same under either structure, and monopoly would necessarily produce less. But if, for example, with a given demand, a monopoly would secure lower costs through lower money factor prices, more efficient technique, or scale of greater efficiency, this cost saving might counterbalance or outweigh the virtually restrictive effects of monopoly price policy, and monopoly might give us an output as great as or greater than competition would.

To indicae that this is possible is by no means to conclude that it would be the case in most or all industries. But it is clearly possible. First, it is possible that monopolies might pay lower factor prices relative to demand than competitive industries. This is not likely in the case of a few isolated monopolies, but in a world of monopolies (considered as an alternative to a competitive world) it would be quite possible. So far as it held, the depression of factor prices relative to commodity prices could lower money costs so as to counterbalance monopolistic output restriction in part or entirely. We shall return to this matter when we discuss the problem of a world of monopolies. So far as we are dealing with the individual or isolated monopolistic industry, which would presumably get factors no cheaper than competitors in the same industry would, however, this possible offset to monopolistic output restriction may be neglected.

Second, it is not impossible that a monopoly might tend on the average through time to develop more efficient techniques and thus enjoy lower costs than a competitive industry would. This possibility will be discussed in a succeeding section. So far as this were true, monopolistic output restriction might be offset wholly or in part.

Most important perhaps is the possibility that in given industries the economies of the large-scale firm are so great that a monopolist can attain much lower average and aggregate cost of all relevant industry outputs than a large number of smaller firms could. In this case pure competition would not be a "natural" market structure, and the forces of competition themselves would tend to bring about concentrated oligopoly or monopoly. But if pure competition were forced upon the industry—as by a legal edict limiting the size of every firm—the industry average and marginal cost might be so high that even though it was equated to price, competitive output would be smaller than monopoly output. In short, the virtually restrictive effects of monopolistic price policy might be outweighed by monopoly's greater efficiency in scale in a given industry.

Thus it is clear that we cannot say with any surety that within each specific industry a competitive market structure will give us a larger output than a monopolistic structure. It would, other things being equal, but this condition may not be fulfilled. Monopoly may have counterbalancing output-increasing tendencies where there are great economies of large-scale production, or if monopoly secures better techniques, or for other reasons. There are many industries where these "advantages" of monopoly are absent or small and where, therefore, monopoly would tend in the net to restrict output. But there are others where the reverse is true.

Consequently, is there any truth to the generalizations that monopoly always leads to output restriction or that monopoly outputs tend always to be smaller than competitive outputs? There is the following truth in them. First, in any situation where industry costs and demands would be the same regardless of whether the market structure was purely competitive or monopolistic, the monopoly will tend to produce absolutely less output than the competitive industry would. Second, *monopolies always tend toward a virtual restriction of output,* according to the standard set by competitive industries, in that they extend output only to where marginal cost equals marginal receipts rather than extending it to where marginal cost equals price. Therefore, they do not meet the same output standard which is met by industries in pure competition.

It follows from the preceding analysis that, so far as the output-restrictive tendencies of monopoly are considered undesirable, the indicated remedy is not necessarily to insist upon a purely competitive structure, since this structure might give a smaller output and lower efficiency. The indicated remedy may be to induce or force the monopolist to extend his output to where price is equal to marginal cost.

The preceding analysis is pursued largely on the plausible supposition that for the industry the level of demand and the level of factor prices would not be affected by the choice between competition and monopoly. Extended to the economy made up entirely of monopolies, this would become an assumption that the relation of factor prices to total money purchasing power would likewise be unaffectedly the choice between a monopolistic and a competitive economy. This latter supposition is not so plausible. We shall consider this problem in a later section in this chapter, and also consider how employment and output in the economy as a whole may be affected by monopoly.

MONOPOLY PERFORMANCE—EFFICIENCY IN SCALE AND UTILIZATION

What is the tendency of monopoly in the long run with respect to efficiency in scale and utilization of firm? It has been seen that in the long-run equilibrium in pure competition every firm is forced to operate at the scale and rate of utilization of plant which gives the lowest attainable cost per unit of output (pages 142 to 148 above). In monopoly this is evidently not the case. A single firm supplies the entire industry output, and the scale at which it will operate will be determined as that supplying the output at which its long-run marginal cost curve intersects its marginal receipts curve. It would be a sheer coincidence if this intersection were found at just that scale at which the monopolist would get lowest costs per unit of output—unless, of course, there were a wide range of scales all with the same lowest unit cost. The profit-maximizing output and scale of firm may thus be either larger or smaller than the scale which would give lowest costs per unit of output, and it is much more likely to be one of these than to be the same as the lowest-cost scale. So far as the chosen scale diverges from the lowest-cost scale, so will the rate of utilization of the plant diverge from the lowest-cost rate of utilization (see pages 117 to 120 above). The relation of the profit-maximizing scale to the lowest-cost scale for the monopolistic firm will depend on the size of the market (position of the industry demand curve) and the extent of the economies of large-scale firm. Monopoly is especially favored, as we have seen, if scale economies are so great that the monopolist will maximize profits while still operating short of the lowest-cost scale. But it can obviously exist also where the monopolist is operating beyond the lowest-cost scale. In sum, the monopolist is likely to find long-run equilibrium at a scale of operations either smaller or larger than that giving lowest costs per unit of output.

This does not mean, however, that monopoly is necessarily less efficient than pure competition. The reason for this is that the criterion of optimal efficiency is *not* in general operation at just the industry output which would give the firm or firms their lowest costs per unit. Where lowest costs are attainable at only one industry output rate, this would imply an essentially arbitrary choice of output rate, without regard to the size of demand, or to the relation of marginal cost to price. In general, it may be said that the desirable rate of industry output from a social standpoint is determined by the relation of industry marginal cost to price—to a first approximation as that output where money value of marginal real cost to the industry is equal to price. This may not be the output at which the firm's costs per unit are minimized. The only valid general criterion of efficiency is that the desirable industry output—*or any output*—should be produced at the lowest attainable aggregate cost of producing *that output*. We want a certain industry output x_1 at the lowest aggregate (and average) cost per unit which is attainable; we do not want some other industry output x_2 just because it could be produced at a lower cost per unit of output than x_1. Whatever output we get, optimal efficiency merely requires that the aggregate cost of producing it be the lowest attainable.

This condition is fulfilled in purely competitive long-run equilibrium (if we accept going techniques as given). Any output is produced by a multiplicity of firms, each with a lowest-cost scale or long-run rate of output much smaller than the total industry supply. Where this is the case, any industry output is most efficiently produced by procuring just such a number of firms that all of them may produce at lowest-cost scale, and output is most efficiently varied by varying the number of firms. This is in fact what takes place in pure competition in the long run, and efficiency in scale is thus optimal. The fact, however, that this optimal efficiency in producing any output—including the socially most desirable output—is attained consistently with having each firm produce at lowest-cost scale, is an incident of the fact that the corresponding output of the firm is a very small fraction of industry output, so that any of a conceivable range of outputs can be had by varying the number of firms of lowest-cost scale.

Where, on the other hand, a single firm of lowest-cost scale is approximately large enough (or too large) to supply the entire market, the lowest unit cost of producing successive outputs cannot be had by continuously varying the number of firms. Over a considerable range of outputs, the lowest aggregate and unit cost of obtaining various outputs is to be had by varying the scale of a single firm. Thus, there will be a considerable range of outputs which can be had at the lowest attainable aggregate costs of these outputs while operating a single firm at other than its own lowest-cost scale. Provided that the single firm can produce the outputs in question at a lower cost than two or more firms of smaller scale could, it gives us optimal efficiency at those outputs, even though it might get lower average costs at different outputs. Where the lowest-cost scale of the firm is large relative to the size of the market, therefore, optimal efficiency in the sense of obtaining the lowest aggregate cost of producing any output is not generally to be had coincidentally with operating the firm or firms at lowest-unit-cost scales.

It follows that the mere fact that a monopolist is unlikely to operate at his lowest-cost scale is not proof of any true inefficiency. The only efficiency question is whether he is producing his going output at a lower cost than two or more firms could. The answer to this question can conceivably be either positive or negative. If the monopolist enjoys such economies of scale that he is producing on the declining phase of his long-run average cost curve, he is certainly more efficient at the going output than two or more firms would be. He may even have an output which takes him a certain limited distance up the rising phase of his long-run cost curve and still produce more efficiently than two firms could. It is, however, possible that the monopolist will reach "excessive size"—attaining a scale and rate of output for which unit costs are higher than could be had by two or more smaller firms. In this case he may be inefficient in scale and utilization of plant.

It should be noted that so far as the scale curve of the firm has a long flat bottom—showing minimized unit costs over a wide range of outputs—it is quite probable that the monopolist will give optimal efficiency, but it is also quite probable that equivalent efficiency could be had just as well with two or more firms.

We thus conclude that the monopolist may or may not give optimal efficiency in scale and utilization of plant at the output which he produces. However this may be, he has a clear tendency to produce a smaller output than that which would be socially desirable, since he does not extend output to the point where the money value of marginal real cost would be equal to price. This point has been discussed in the preceding section.

In this and the immediately preceding sections we have analyzed the character of the market performance of the monopolistic industry in long-run equilibrium with respect to profits, output restriction, and efficiency in scale and utilization of plant. Several other aspects of monopoly performance remain to be evaluated. Before proceeding to this evaluation, we must remember that our explicit reference so far has been to the performance of a single-firm monopoly which is faced with no effective threat of entry and which can thus maximize industry profits while disregarding the threat of entry. But there is another category of monopoly to be considered—that where an effective threat of entry makes it impossible for the monopolist to price so as to maximize industry profit and still remain a monopolist. It should be useful to note to what extent price-output determination in this category may differ from that previously discussed and how, if at all, conclusions with respect to profits, efficiency, and output restriction may differ in this case.

MONOPOLY PRICING SUBJECT TO A THREAT OF ENTRY

The preceding analysis—both of monopoly price-output determination and of the long-run performance of monopoly—refers explicitly to the monopolist faced by no effective threat of entry. This is the monopolist who can view the industry demand curve as unequivocally the demand curve for his own output and can maximize industry profits (to be received solely by himself) without attracting other sellers to enter the industry. Thus, his marginal receipts curve for the purposes of price calculation is simply the marginal receipts curve drawn from the industry demand curve. The intersection of his marginal cost curve with this marginal receipts curve determines the price and output which will maximize the industry profit, which is exclusively his own profit.

Monopoly thus protected from effective threat of entry may indeed exist. There is, however, a second category of monopoly wherein the seller is not so protected. This category may be defined to include all cases in which the monopolist (initially the sole supplier in an industry) cannot set a price high enough to maximize industry profits without attracting entry but can set a somewhat lower price and exclude entry. That is, if the monopolist in the long run sets price and output where his marginal cost equals industry marginal receipts, other sellers will enter, and he will not receive all the industry profits. If, however, he sets price somewhat lower—thus not maximizing industry profits—others will be deterred from entering, and he may have this smaller industry profit all for himself. Here it is not always true that the established monopolist will set price so as to maximize industry profits—to be shared in the long run with others. He may instead charge a lower price and earn a smaller industry profit, all for himself. Rationally he should do this if the total industry profit he will receive under the lower-price policy is larger than the share of the bigger industry profit he will receive if he maximizes industry profit but must eventually share it with others. The case of monopoly subject to a threat of entry, since it opens up this alternative possibility, obviously requires separate analysis.

The possibility of this kind of monopoly is suggested by the fact that the barrier to entry—or advantage which the monopolist enjoys over potential entrant firms—may be high enough that the monopolist can set a price sufficient to earn some supernormal profits without inducing other firms to enter, but low enough that if he were to set a higher price, sufficient to maximize industry profits, other firms would enter and share the market with him. When we recognize that much monopoly may be based on patent or resource control which confers a significant, but not indefinitely large, cost advantage on the monopolist, or may be based on a limited transport-cost advantage, as in the case of regional monopoly, we see that this sort of situation is quite conceivable. A monopoly might be protected by such a limited barrier to entry from the outset. Or it might arrive in this situation, after previously enjoying a complete barricade of entry, because of technological developments or other changes which reduced the effectiveness of its barriers to entry.

Whenever such a situation does exist, it is marked by the fact that there is presumably some maximum price—lower than the price that would maximize the industry profit—above which the monopolist cannot go without attracting a further firm or firms to enter the industry. This may be designated as a "limit price" for the monopolist *qua* monopolist. Corresponding to it, with any given industry demand curve, is a "limit output"—the amount buyers will take at the limit price and less than which the monopolist cannot produce without attracting entry (since, if he did, the market price would tend to be bid above the limit price). The monopolist may charge the limit price or less and produce the limit output or more, and still remain a monopolist in the long run. But higher price or smaller output will induce entry.

At just what level this limit price will be found in a given institutional and technological situation affecting entry is not easy to predict in unique fashion. This is because the tendency of new firms to enter a monopolized industry is influenced not only by the level of their prospective costs as compared to those now incurred by the monopolist and by the going level of price, but also by their conjectures as to how the monopolist will react to their entry if it takes place. In short, potential entrants may not view the going price of the monopolist as that which he will charge after entry. They may feel that the postentry price would be lower, if the monopolist would open market warfare on a new competitor, or higher, in the event that existing price is set low as a "bluff" to discourage entry. The limit price is thus not necessarily the price just above which an entrant could make a profit with the market share he could command—it may be lower or higher than that. So far as the going price of the monopolist is "read" by potential entrants as stating the monopolist's intentions as to future price policy, however, the limit price may tend to approximate that above which entrants could begin to make a profit.

In any event, assuming that potential entrants are in some way significantly influenced by the going price policy of the monopolist—because they view it as predicting the neighborhood of future price, perhaps, or for other reasons—there will probably exist some limit price at or below which entry will be discouraged, but above which entry may take place. The monopolist himself will presumably estimate this price and consider the relative desirability of not going above it. If this limit price is lower than that which would maximize industry profits, the monopolist has a twofold

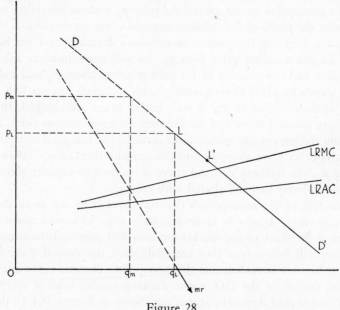

Figure 28

choice—(1) to stay at the limit price, discourage entry, and have a certain industry profit for himself, or (2) to charge the price which will maximize industry profits, attract entry, and thereafter share industry profits (maximized or otherwise) with another firm or firms.

The general character of the monopolist's price-calculation problem when faced with a threat of entry is illustrated in Figure 28. The long-run industry demand curve may be supposed to appear as DD' in this figure; the corresponding marginal receipts to the industry as output is extended is shown by mr. The monopolist's long-run average and marginal costs are shown by $LRAC$ and $LRMC$. In this case industry profits would be maximized (so long as industry costs are this monopolist's costs) at the output q_m and the price p_m, where the monopolist's marginal cost is equal to industry marginal receipts. In fact, this is the adjustment the monopolist would seek if faced by no threat of entry, and is precisely the same sort of adjustment previously shown by the output q and the price p in Figure 27.

If there is an effective threat of entry, however, there is by definition a price lower than p_m, above which the monopolist cannot set his price without inducing other sellers to enter the industry. Correspondingly there is a larger output than q_m, below which the monopolist cannot set his output without attracting entry. These are found at the price p_L and the corresponding quantity q_L in Figure 28, and may be designated respectively as the limit price and limit quantity (*maximum* limit price and *minimum* limit quantity) set by the threat of entry.

If the monopolist cannot exceed the price p_L without attracting entry, it follows that the range of the industry demand curve above point L thereon is *not* in the long run the present monopolist's demand curve for his own sales. If he sets a higher price than p_L, he will share industry sales with other sellers, and the quantity of his sales at prices above p_L will not be as large as shown by DD'. Correspondingly, his marginal receipts will not be as large as those shown by mr if such higher prices are charged. In short, the industry demand curve and the industry marginal receipts curve are not in the long run the present monopolist's demand and marginal receipts curve if he essays to set price above p_L and the quantity short of q_L. At or below the price p_L, the industry demand curve is his own to exploit; above p_L it will be an industry demand shared with others.

What will be the monopolist's demand curve if he sets price above p_L and attracts entry? It may be quite uncertain, since he cannot make certain estimates of the share of the market entrants will gain and the competitive policy they will follow once they are established. But even if these matters can be predicted, it is evident that the monopolist's demand curve after entry will lie to the left of the DD' curve, showing smaller sales at every price. (Such a conjectured demand curve is not shown in Figure 28.) In the long run the monopolist will thus make at any price above p_L a smaller profit than the total industry profit and a smaller profit than that shown by the relation of DD' to the monopolist's $LRAC$ curve. In particular, if he were to try to maximize industry profit at the price p_m, he would not receive the maximized industry profit indicated by the relation of $LRAC$ to DD' at the output q_m.

It follows from this that the long-run profit which the present monopolist will receive by maximizing or attempting to maximize industry profits at p_m will not necessarily be the largest profit he can receive, since this maximum industry profit, even if attained, will be shared. This is also true of any other price above p_L; the corresponding industry profit will be shared. How might the monopolist make a larger long-run profit than by charging p_m?

Two alternatives are apparent. First, he might charge a price lower than p_m but higher than p_L on the ground that he would attract *less* entry than at p_m, and thus possibly get a larger long-run profit for himself. Second, he might charge the price p_L (supplying the quantity q_L), exclude all entry, and have the somewhat smaller industry profit all to himself. In general, then he might, depending on the relations of industry demand to cost and the level of the limit price, find his own maximum long-run profit by charging either the price p_m, or a price between p_m and p_L, or the price p_L. He should presumably choose that price which will maximize his own long-run profit, and only in one of the three possible situations will this amount to pricing so as to maximize industry profit. One clear possibility is that he may find it most profitable to charge the price p_L and produce the quantity q_L, thus excluding all entry. All of a smaller profit "pie" may be more pie to the monopolist than a share of a larger profit pie.

If the monopolist finds it more profitable to charge a price above p_L and attract entry than to charge p_L and exclude it, we have a case which in the long run is not single-firm monopoly. Dynamic instability of the market structure is indicated. The only true monopoly case with threat of entry is, therefore, that in which the monopolist prefers to charge the limit price p_L and produce the limit quantity q_L, and thus exclude entry. He will tend to do this wherever the long-run profit he can gain at this price and quantity is larger than that which he could gain by sharing a larger industry profit with others. A limit price, which is lower than that which would maximize industry profit, will thus be charged in monopoly wherever (1) there is an effective threat of entry and (2) the monopolist anticipates larger long-run profits by pricing to forestall entry than by pricing to attract it. In this case stable monopoly at a less than industry-profit-maximizing price is possible, provided only that the monopolist does not overestimate the limit price and inadvertently attract entry.

It is thus quite possible in the case illustrated in Figure 28 that the monopolist will find long-run equilibrium by charging the price p_L and producing the quantity q_L. This conclusion cannot be drawn from this diagram alone, since the present monopolist's anticipated demand conditions were entry attracted are not shown. But the aggregate profit received at q_L could easily exceed any profit share the monopolist might get by charging a higher price and attracting entry. The limit price p_L shown in Figure 28 is high enough to allow a liberal excess profit. Theoretically, it could be considerably lower (such as at L' or lower) and still possibly allow the largest long-run profit available to the monopolist. The closer it falls to the monopolist's *LRAC*, however, the smaller the chance, *ceteris paribus,* that the monopolist will find it advantageous to adhere to the limit price.

Where the monopolist subject to a threat of entry chooses to charge a limit price and exclude entry, to what extent are our preceding conclusions concerning monopolistic pricing, as developed for the no-entry case, revised? The limit price is by definition a lower price, and the limit quantity a larger quantity, than those which would maximize industry profits. Thus, under a threat of entry which is forestalled by limit pricing, the following alterations in our previous conclusions are required:

1. Monopolistic excess profits will still remain but will be smaller than in the no-entry case.
2. Monopolistic output, with given industry demand and cost curves, will be larger than in the no-entry case. Marginal cost may still be less than price, but if so, it will tend to be closer to price. It is not impossible that marginal cost may even exceed price at the limit output so long as average cost is less than price at this output and profits here are more attractive than those promised after attracting entry.[5]
3. The general conclusions concerning efficiency in scale are not altered —except so far as a low limit price may imply the destruction of monopoly where the monopolist has inefficiently large scale.

With a threat of entry which is forestalled, therefore, monopolistic tendencies toward output restriction and excess profits are reduced although probably not obliterated. Where threatened entry is not forestalled, the long-run pricing problem becomes one of oligopoly, to be considered in the next chapter. So far the limit price has been viewed as set by the threat of entry of other firms. Such a limit price may also be set in effect by the threat of governmental interference, which the monopolist may view as probable should his going price appear to be exploitative or excessive.

The sort of impact of threatened entry or interference on monopoly (or oligopoly) pricing which is illustrated here may be quite important in the real economy. Some practical limit on monopoly price is simply a reflection of the fact that no capitalist monopoly is absolute or impregnable, whatever legal or institutional protections it depends on. Any barrier against entry is only so high. Any monopolist's pricing power has a corresponding limit, and it may be a limit which precludes maximization of industry profits. In exploiting his monopoly, the monopolist has a problem similar to that faced by the government in taxing beverage spirits. If the per-gallon tax becomes sufficiently high, a substitute supply of bootleg spirits will appear in spite of the law and the revenuers.[6]

MONOPOLISTIC POLICY AS TO PRODUCT, SELLING COST, AND
PRODUCTION TECHNIQUE

The preceding analysis has dealt solely with the price and output policy of the monopolist for a single short or long period in a given situation of de-

[5] This is possible because where marginal cost exceeded limit price at the limit output, restriction of output to where marginal cost would equal limit price would raise price and attract entry.

[6] For a more detailed analysis of limit-price problems, see J. S. Bain, "Pricing in Monopoly and Oligopoly," *American Economic Review,* March 1949, pp. 448-464.

mand and cost. The supposition that the monopolist's demand and cost conditions are given implies in turn that we view as given the values of variables which affect the level of demand and cost—the product, the level of selling costs, and the technique of production. Essentially, then, we have inquired how the monopolist will set his output and price, once he has made a given choice with respect to (or takes as given): (1) the precise character and design of his product, (2) the level or rate of his selling or sales promotion costs, and (3) his technique of production. Yet the character of his product and his production technique and the size of his selling costs are not in general arbitrarily imposed upon or given to the monopolistic or other seller. He has some range of choice in these matters, and a part of his policy will involve making choices in these regards in such a way as to enhance or maximize his profit. It is thus apparent that we have so far really analyzed only one major aspect of the monopolist's market policy—his choice of price and output—and must also give some attention to his *concurrent* choices with respect to product, selling cost, and production technique.

The monopolist's policy in these regards may be considered in both its static and its dynamic aspect. We may consider first how the monopolist will choose among any given range of alternatives with respect to product or amount of selling cost or techniques. But we may also consider how he will respond through time to continually developing or changing alternatives in these regards and further the manner in which he himself may attempt to develop new alternatives which will enhance his profit. Let us first consider the character of the monopolist's adjustment to a given range of available alternatives in the areas mentioned.

At any given time the monopolist may be viewed as having in general a range of alternatives with respect to product. His position as a monopolist will ordinarily be confined to a product of some given general sort, as defined in terms of function and design—such as electric light bulbs or fountain pens. But "within" the product limits of his monopoly there may ordinarily be a considerable range of choice with respect to the exact design, quality, raw material components, and other characteristics of the product. Thus, he might produce light bulbs which were fat or slim, with tungsten or with carbon filaments, longer or shorter lived, frosted or plain, and so forth. One aspect of his policy must be a product policy by which he selects the precise product which he will offer for sale. Can any generalizations be offered concerning the monopolist's product policy in this respect?

As a general rule it may be observed that for each variant product which the monopolist might produce, there exists potentially (1) a different industry demand curve, (2) a different cost curve, (3) a possibly different condition of entry, and, finally, (4) a different "maximum" profit. The monopolist may thus calculate for each product alternative available to him the corresponding demand, cost, and entry conditions and the corresponding largest attainable profit for that product—found where marginal cost for that product will equal marginal receipts from the demand for it or alternatively at the effective limit price for that product. If now the monopolist follows a policy of profit maximization in all regards, and if he is limited to the selection of a *single* product design and quality, he will presumably select the product which promises the largest long-run profit. Among the various provisional "maximum" profits attainable with various products, he should select the largest, or the *maximum maximorum* (maximum of maxima) profit. If he is not limited (as he in general will not be) to a single product design, he will select that variety of product designs which offers the largest over-all profit. This most profitable variety might turn out to be a single product design. But he might, for example, gain greater profit through producing high-, medium-, and low-quality lines of his product and offering them at some price differentials.

The general logic of the monopolist's product policy—to find the product design or variety of designs which will maximize his profits—is presumably no different than that of sellers in other market situations. The monopolist's product policy, however, is formulated in a situation where there are no established rivals or competitors, whose customers might be attracted in large numbers by distinctive characteristics of the monopolist's product, or who might react to his product changes with changes of their own. The only competition is that of "goods in general," from whom a small fraction of buyer purchasing power may be attracted by "better" product design. Similarly, there are no entrants (provided the monopolist does not go above limit price) to introduce new product designs in the industry which might attract some of the monopolist's customers. One firm is selecting product design for the whole industry, and in so doing it is influenced only by the effect of this design on the demand for this industry output as compared with the demands for other industry outputs (and possibly on the limit price). The producer is not influenced by the potential effect on one seller's demand of attracting customers *within the industry* from one seller to another, since there are no rival sellers. It is apparent that the monopolist's product policy is oriented essentially to maximizing *industry* profits, subject to any limits on price imposed by a threat of entry. He aims toward that product design or variety of designs which will give either the greatest industry profit or the greatest industry profit which, through pricing, he can maintain for himself.

In the light of the preceding analysis, are there any generalizations which may be drawn relative to the probable differences between monopoly product policy and product policy in other market structures? Comparisons with pure competition alone will not be especially fruitful since in that case product variety is supposed to be absent and presumably, therefore, unable to survive. Pure competition might even be viewed as applying only to instances where the product is irrevocably given to all sellers. It is thus more meaningful to compare monopoly with other situations in general, where there may be extensive differentiation of product as among sellers as well as rivalry or competition, and possibly easy entry. The major potential differences between monopolistic and other product policy should arise from the consequences of competition or rivalry and of entry. Where there are several or many sellers, it is possible, if not probable, that each will compete with others by designing his product so as to secure for himself the most profitable share of the market, at the same time disregarding or taking less than full account of the reactions of his rivals in their product policies or of the consequences for him of nonretaliatory and independent parallel actions by his competitors. This orientation toward attracting buyers from within the industry, competitors' retaliatory or parallel policies being disregarded or viewed as outside his control, will imply that the seller envisages a different relation between his product design and his demand than a monopolist would, and thus he will be induced to follow a somewhat different product policy. Moreover, the over-all industry product policy will be the result of several individual firm policies rather than that of just one.

The exact differences between monopolized and other industries in the design or variety of designs of industry product which will emerge are difficult to predict without detailed specification of the character of available product alternatives, the character of buyers' choice patterns among them, and the precise character of rivalry or competition among sellers in the industry. Further analysis will suggest, however, that in the case of competitive or rivalrous supply, there are several possible tendencies of divergence from monopolistic product patterns, one or more of which may be followed in particular circumstances. These include (1) a tendency toward greater product variety (under conditions of unrestricted rivalry in both product and price), and (2) a tendency toward higher quality or more elaborate design of product (at least under conditions of price collusion and product rivalry). These possible differences will be discussed in succeeding chapters on oligopoly and monopolistic competition.

A third potential difference between monopolistic and other product policy concerns the choice of product designs which will reduce industry profit. The monopolist, if he can control his field and exclude others, will generally reject any product alternative which would reduce industry profit, *even though buyers would prefer this product* and though it might drive higher-profit products from the market under competitive conditions. Thus, a monopolist in rubber tires might find it unprofitable to build very durable tires, even though they cost no more to make, if the increased durability meant smaller average demand and smaller profit over time. Under competitive conditions, however, the individual seller may be led to produce any product which will increase his profit at the expense of others; similarly, the entrant seller under easy entry should follow the same tendency. In this event, any product which may be profitably produced, for part or all of the market, may be brought into production, and the arbitrary exclusion of products potentially more desirable or cheaper to the buyer may not take place. Any of these tendencies of competitive product policy, of course, may be limited or fully checked if several sellers in an industry act collusively on product and price and can exclude entry—and thus act like a monopolist—but the potential divergences of competitive product policy are clear.

Related to the monopolist's product policy will be a policy with respect to sales promotion and selling cost. Wherever a seller supplies all or part of a product which is distinguishable from others and he supplies enough of this product himself that his sales price will vary perceptibly with the volume of his sales, he may find it to his advantage to attempt to influence buyer preferences by advertising or other sales promotion, and thus to "shift his demand curve to the right"—in order to secure a higher price for given sales volume or a larger sales volume at a given price. These conditions are not fulfilled in pure competition, which comprehends cases where the individual seller's product is identical to and will not be differentiated from that of many competitors, and where the share of the industry output he supplies is so small that he can sell any output he is able to produce at a going market price. Here sales promotion by the individual firm has no basis or advantage—promotion of individual firm demand is impossible; promotion of industry demand is pointless. The monopolist finds himself in a much different position, supplying all of an industry output. Although he has no competitors or rivals within the industry whose customers he might capture through sales promotion, his output is in general competition for the buyer's dollar with those of all other industries, and the demand for his output varies with the price he charges. He may thus find it attractive to turn buyer preferences toward his and from other industry outputs by sales promotion, thus shifting his demand curve to the right.

Taking his product for the moment as given, the monopolist's selling cost problem has the same sort of solution as his product problem. For each possible amount of selling cost (expended to the best advantage) there should correspond a particular position of his industry demand curve. In general, up to some limit, demand should be increased by increased selling costs, although not necessarily in steady ratio to selling costs as those are increased. For each possible amount of selling costs the monopolist should now calculate the corresponding position of his industry demand curve and the maximum profit—after deducting selling costs—which he can earn with that demand curve. He should choose that amount of selling costs which will give him a *maximum maximorum* profit—the largest of all the provisional maximum profits attainable. This means, in general, that he will increase selling cost so long as the increment to selling cost is less than the corresponding increment to profit as calculated before selling cost, and up to the point where these increments become equal. It should be noted, moreover, that the monopolist presumably varies his selling costs without eliciting any significant reaction in the prices of or the sales promotion outlays on the outputs of other industries—these he takes as given in arriving at both price and sales promotion policies. Moreover, he is not affected by the possibility of attracting buyers from other sellers *within his industry,* since there are no sellers of this sort, but is only concerned to influence buyer preferences as between his output and a range of distant substitute outputs produced by other industries.[7]

One other basis for monopolistic selling outlays may be noted. So far as the seller's monopoly position and protection from entry rest on the reputation of an established trade-mark or brand name, he may be able to heighten the barrier to the entry of others by increasing his selling costs and thus be able to secure higher prices without attracting entry. This may make it profitable for him to incur larger selling costs than he would if the threat of entry were not a problem.

Given these considerations, what generalizations can be drawn concerning the size of monopoly selling costs? Quantitative estimates are impossible without further knowledge of the shape of the functional relationship of selling cost to demand—which we lack—and of the impact of selling cost on the condition of entry. We can say that it is possible or probable that the monopolist will incur some selling costs, and perhaps more if he is subject to an effective threat of entry than if he is not. In addition, it is probable that he may incur less selling cost than would competitive or rivalrous sellers within the same industry, if each had a differentiated product to promote. This would be true so far as within a group of sellers of close-substitute products each would find a very large apparent response of his demand to selling cost, resulting from attracting buyers of close substitute products— an opportunity not offered to the monopolist. The detailed possibilities here are numerous, however, and will be discussed further in succeeding chapters.

A third area within which the monopolist should make choices is that of production techniques. Given the choice of product, a range of production techniques is ordinarily available, and with each the cost of production or the shape and position of the seller's cost curves may be different. The monopolist's profit-maximizing policy should evidently have the same long-run tendency as that of sellers in any other market structure who could at least temporarily enhance profits by lowering costs. That is, he should presumably seek the lowest-cost technique available for any output, or, more

[7] Technically, the monopolist's equilibrium is determined as follows: Let p be price, q quantity, c aggregate production cost, and s aggregate selling cost. Then $c = c(q)$, $p = f(q, s)$, and the monopolist solves for a maximum of $q.p - c - s$.

generally, the technique associated with the long-run cost curve permitting the largest aggregate profit. There is certainly no reason why he should deliberately select inferior or excessively expensive techniques if he is in business for a profit.

The apparent potential sources of difference between the monopolist's and others' long-run choice from a given range of available techniques are the following. First, the monopolist would deliberately choose the most efficient technique; he would not be forced to do so by the pressure of established competitors or new entrants. Thus, if the monopolist is led by error, undue conservatism, or any other cause to fail to adopt the most efficient techniques, he is, nevertheless, likely to be protected from losses, and competition will not force him to pursue a more efficient policy in order to survive. As a result an inferior technological policy *might* result. Second, monopoly profits might furnish an adequate source for financing the introduction of the most efficient techniques—if large initial investments were required—whereas low-profit competitive sellers might lack funds for such financing. This condition, however, would rest fundamentally on some rationing of credit to enterprise, which made it necessary for enterprise to turn to internal financing or distorted the relation of cost to technique for externally financed enterprise. Third, the monopolist's "most efficient" technique will not necessarily be the most efficient for the industry in those cases where two or more firms can operate more cheaply than one. Fourth, the riskiness of a given technological innovation, as reflected in the distribution of the relative probabilities of profiting or losing from its introduction, may be smaller to the monopolist than to the seller under competitive conditions. (The same may apply to product innovation.) This may induce the monopolist to adopt a desirable technique which a competitive seller would not adopt. Since the phenomenon of risk arises mainly under conditions of dynamic change in technical opportunities, we shall defer discussion of this influence on monopoly policy to the next section.

Arraying these conflicting possibilities, we do not find it possible to predict at all safely either greater or less long-run technological efficiency for monopoly, so far as efficiency rests on the long-run selection from a given group of technological alternatives. Further analysis will be necessary, however, as we consider the problems of dynamic response to continually changing alternatives, and of the development of alternatives by enterprise through time.

Before turning to the dynamic problem, some brief recapitulation of the monopolist's policy problem under given conditions of buyer tastes and of availability of techniques and products may be in order. It was first observed that with a given product, selling cost, and production technique, the monopolist would seek a profit-maximizing price-output adjustment. Further, he would vary product (given selling cost), selling cost (given product), and production technique (given both)—while simultaneously varying price and output to best advantage—in order to secure from each variation a *maximum maximorum* profit position. Considering his problem as a whole, it is clear that he must consider simultaneous adjustment of price, output, product, selling cost, and production technique in order to secure just that combination of values of these five variables which will maximize his profit.

Our treatment of this problem, by successive approximations dealing with the adjustment of two to three variables at a time, reveals certain strategic tendencies in the over-all adjustment of the monopolist. An advanced mathematical treatment would be required to treat the monopolist's entire policy-making problem at once. Lacking this, we have been able by a method of successive approximations to determine that there are inherent in monopoly (1) certain output-restrictive and price-raising tendencies, (2) certain tendencies in product policy and selling-cost policy divergent from those of competitive markets, and (3) some possibility of divergent tendencies with respect to efficiency of technique.

These are tendencies so far as the monopolist properly calculates the functional relationships governing his profit opportunities and expertly arrives at a true profit-maximizing solution. So far as he falters as an appraiser of market conditions or a wizard at policy making, his behavior tendencies may waver from those predicted and miss the predicted mark. The very complexity of the policy-calculating process just analyzed suggests that, because of human fallibility, actual monopoly behavior may represent only a very crude approximation to that predicted by theory, and very precise policy solutions may not even be attempted. This possibility is enhanced if there is considerable uncertainty surrounding the estimation by the monopolist of certain strategic functional relationships. Nevertheless, the theory developed above should validly predict certain tendencies or directions of adjustment affecting real monopoly.

C. THE DYNAMICS OF MONOPOLY POLICY

SELECTION OF PRODUCT AND TECHNIQUE

Let us now consider two further aspects of monopoly behavior. The first of these concerns its process of adjustment to changing data—such as changing buyer preferences, changing range of available techniques, changing money purchasing power, etc.—presuming that such changes are given to the firm and beyond its influence. The second concerns its activity in *initiating* changes in the controlling data to which it adjusts—particularly in developing new products and new techniques of production which increase the range of alternative products and techniques from which it may choose. Both of these aspects of monopoly behavior deserve analysis.

We may first consider the behavior of monopoly through time with respect to changes in product and in production technique. The character of the monopolist's response to changing or developing opportunities in product design and productive technique is largely suggested by the preceding analysis of his selection among any given set of alternatives. So far as given additional alternatives are presented to him from time to time, the monopolist should pursue the same rationale of selection among the progressively revised range of alternatives as has been described for any given range of alternatives. He should pursue a policy of product change which maximizes his profits, and this may be a different policy from that of a competitive industry. There may be a different rate or pattern of "progressiveness" in product with monopoly so far as unprofitable alternatives which might be exploited under competition are rejected and so far as product variety may be continually restricted. The monopolist's policy in reacting to evolving technological opportunities may be the same as or different from that under competition, depending upon the relative importance of certain opposed tendencies which may cause monopoly behavior to diverge in one direction or the other from the competitive. We thus cannot say with any surety that a monopolistic industry will be more or less progressive in responding to given developments of technological opportunity.

Two qualifications, however, may be offered to the preceding comments. First, the establishment of a seller in a monopolistic position which is surrounded by some barrier to entry may increase the attractiveness to him of successive "risky" innovations of product or technique. Either product innovations or technological innovations will presumably be made by a seller because they are likely to increase profits—by increasing his demand relative to cost or by lowering his costs relative to demand. In either case the seller will have an incentive to make such potentially profit-increasing change *only provided* that after he makes his innovation there is at least some time period during which he enjoys a profit advantage from increased demand or reduced cost before imitation or entry by others drives him to a profit position no better than that he enjoyed before. If a full competitive adjustment to his innovation took place an hour after he made it, he would have no profit incentive ever to make a product or technological innovation.

Under competitive conditions the existence at least of lags in the adjustment of the industry to innovations is a necessary condition to elicit innovations from any seller. Monopoly, which precludes entry and competitive adjustment, tends to offer larger profit rewards to any potentially profit-increasing innovation. This in itself is not conclusive since a smaller positive advantage may suffice as an inducement. Suppose, however, that there is considerable uncertainty as to whether a product or technical innovation will increase demand or reduce costs—which might be expressed as there being a two-out-of-three chance that costs will be reduced 10 percent at any output, and a one-out-of-three chance that they will rise by 5 percent. Now a monopolist, protected from entry, is in a position to reap the maximum potential benefit to profits from a risky innovation of this sort, as well as being exposed fully to the possibility of loss. If the innovation "succeeds," he may add the reduction in costs to his long-run profits; if it "fails," he suffers a loss equivalent to the cost increase from experimenting with a bad technique. A competitive seller, on the other hand, while being equally exposed to the risk of loss from a bad choice, may not anticipate equal gains from a good choice. The process of imitation and competitive entry may allow him extra profits from successful innovation over only a relatively short interval, after which prices are again driven to the same relation to cost as obtained before the innovation. Successful innovation does not add to the profits of the industry or the seller by so much or for so long under the pressure of competition and entry as in monopoly, whereas unsuccessful innovation is just as damaging.

If this is the case, the disposition to make investments for "risky" innovations is reduced in competition, since the "effective odds" on any such innovation become less favorable. It is thus possible that monopoly may have a tendency toward a more rapid rate—and perhaps a more desirable rate—of product and technological development than competition. This tendency must be considered in conjunction with complementary and opposing tendencies previously discussed.

The second qualification to previous comments on progressiveness in monopoly concerns the timing of innovations. Presuming that an innovation will eventually prove attractive to sellers in either sort of industry, it is likely that, *ceteris paribus,* the innovation will be made earlier in a competitive industry. Let us consider the case, for example, of a cost-reducing and profit-increasing technical innovation in the production of a given product. Given the cost-reducing opportunity, the monopolist will make the innovation only when he reaches the point where, output being given for future periods, the average total cost of production with the new technique is less than the average variable cost with the existing plant, the fixed cost of which is sunk. A single seller already invested in a going technique, in other words, will not scrap his existing plant until this will save him money over all, and this may involve his "using it out" a good deal before making a change. In competition, on the other hand, although established sellers will tend to behave the same way, new entrants will tend to introduce new techniques as soon as the average total cost with them is less than the expected market price, since the entrant has no old investment to play against the new. The timing of given innovations, thus, may be advanced in competition, although the social advantage or disadvantage of this fact is not immediately clear. In any event, this timing tendency is only one of several, and it must be considered in conjunction with other tendencies affecting the disposition to make certain innovations at all.

DEVELOPMENT OF PRODUCT AND TECHNIQUE

The preceding analysis refers explicitly to the manner in which monopoly tends to respond to developing opportunities for technological and product innovation. For purposes of argument we have supposed that such opportunities—including new ones from time to time—simply appear or are given to the monopolist, without any effort on his part, so that all he has to do is decide whether or not to exploit them. We argue as if product alternatives and technological alternatives "grew on bushes" and as if a new crop emerged each year to be picked or passed by at the monopolist's discretion. Argument on this level is meaningful since one strategic question is what the monopolist does with an opportunity once it is at hand. The implicit supposition that new opportunities for innovation just appear automatically, however, is erroneous.

These opportunities are invented or developed through human efforts devoted to research and experiment. They are not necessarily developed at any automatic rate through time, moreover; the rate of development may vary, and, in particular, it may vary in response to the incentives to invention or to the relation of the prospective rewards of invention to the costs of undertaking it. To be sure, the desire to invent may exist to some extent apart from the prospective financial rewards of invention. But inventive activity is costly in effort to the individual inventor or in money to the firm that hires him. And the disposition to incur the costs of experiment and research will certainly be importantly affected by the size of prospective rewards. Such rewards generally are provided by an enterprise system; the development and introduction of a superior product or technique promises the enterprise extra profits—for a certain time until imitation and entry eliminate them under competition or for a longer period under monopoly. Enterprise profit from successful invention which creates the basis for innovation in industry, by providing a source of rewards to invention, provides an incentive to the inventor who can get some of the reward or to the enterprise itself to undertake or sponsor inventive activity by sponsoring organized research. This is clearly suggested by the systematic outlays which many firms make for organized research departments. Now it is further possible (1) that the prospective rewards to enterprise of successful invention will be greater under some market structures than others so that the incentive payment to invention will be greater and (2) that, as a consequence, there will tend to be more inventive activity, more useful invention, and thus more rapid technological progress in industries where the rewards are high than in those where they are low. The extent to which this is true, and the extent to which the relative progressiveness of monopoly is correspondingly influenced, requires examination.

So far as inventive activity is undertaken or directly financed by enterprise, a necessary condition for undertaking it (if we suppose a profit-maximizing policy) is that the prospective reward from the results of inventive activity will exceed its cost. Profits from operations must be increased by enough to exceed research costs for any given increment to research activity. To be sure, there is no precise relation between research cost input and the potential profitability of the output of discoveries or inventions, so that exact calculation of the best amount of research expenditure or of the results of any given amount of this expenditure is impossible. Nevertheless, it seems likely that some rough sort of relation will hold over time—more research, more cost, more results—and that firms will take into account the relative probabilities of finding a profitable invention from alternative amounts of research effort and expenditure and balance the net prospects of gain against the costs of alternative research programs. Such a net prospect of gain will emerge from a consideration of (1) the probability of success in bringing forth a profitable invention, and (2) the size of the extra profit it will create. Thus if there were, from a research program costing $1 million, a one-in-five chance of obtaining an invention which would bring an extra profit of $10 million, the net prospect of gain might be counted as $2 million, to be balanced against the $1 million research cost. If this sort of calculation influences research endeavor, it follows that the larger the profit that enterprise in an industry can gain from any given potentially profitable invention, the more likely it is to undertake research. Thus, in the preceding example, if the successful invention resulting (once out of five) from a research outlay of $1 million would yield the firm only $4 million in profit, its net prospect of gain ($800,000) would not induce it to undertake research on this scale. Higher profit prospects from successful research will tend to favor research effort, and on the average they should result in more research effort. And, so far as the rate of inventive progress is related to the volume of research effort, it should also favor more rapid technological progress.

If this is true, it would appear that monopoly should in this respect be more favorable than competition to inventive progress. The monopolist, being protected from entry, is enabled to reap the maximum potential reward from a successful invention, since for as long as his monopoly is sustained he can add the resulting increase in the difference between price and cost to his industry profit. The competitor, on the other hand, can enjoy extra profits from successful invention only for a limited interval—until imitation by competitors and entry have driven price again to the level of cost. The competitor stands to gain less by successful invention, but to lose just as much (that is, the cost sunk in unfruitful research) by unsuccessful inventive effort. In this case there may be many research programs which the monopolist would find it attractive to undertake but which the competitor would reject. It then appears that monopoly may have a tendency to favor more frequent or more extensive research activity than competition and thus more rapid progress in the discovery of products and techniques.

The tendency so identified, of course, is only one among several, and to evaluate the net tendency of monopoly as regards progressiveness we need to consider together several tendencies, some complementary and some conflicting. To summarize our preceding arguments briefly, monopoly behavior tends to diverge from competitive industry behavior in the respects listed below.

1. Since profits to the firm from any given successful invention or innovation tend to be larger with monopoly than with competition, risky innovations will be made more frequently, provided that the successful innovation would promise increased profit in either case. Similarly, more intensive research to develop new products or techniques as candidates for innovation will be favored.

2. In addition, monopoly profits will provide sources of internal financing for research or innovation, whereas, with some rationing of externally supplied credit, competitive firms may be unable to finance as much desirable innovation and inventive research.

3. On the other hand, many product innovations which would appear profitable to the competitive firms may appear unprofitable to the monopolist. This fact tends to dampen or even outweigh the tendencies just described toward more rapid innovation and invention so far as product development is concerned.

4. No similar counter tendency is found in the case of technological innovations tending to reduce the cost of producing given goods, although the *timing* of innovations may be virtually delayed in monopoly, other things being equal.

5. Undue conservatism or overestimation of risk may retard progress in monopoly without correction by competitive forces.

Taking these considerations together and lacking quantitative evaluation of conflicting tendencies, we find it difficult to decide whether monopoly will in the net be more or less progressive than the competitive industry. The preponderance of a priori considerations, however, point to greater technological progressiveness in monopoly; progressiveness in product is much more difficult to assess. Moreover, it is impossible on the basis of qualitative arguments like the preceding to estimate the *degree* of advantage in progressiveness to either market structure; it might be large or insignificantly small.

The preceding, of course, compares single-firm monopoly with the competitive industry, the latter being defined as subject to easy entry and sufficiently atomistic that individual sellers pursue independent policies and do not act in collusion as a single monopolist would. This is a comparison of extremes. It must be recognized, therefore, that between the monopolistic and competitive extremes there may be other market structures, largely of the oligopolistic variety, where behavior tendencies diverge in some ways from each of the extremes. The group of sellers within the industry may enjoy some protection from entry even where single-firm monopoly is not established—thus increasing incentives to research and innovation—even though imitative rivalry among established sellers may take place. With the protection of the patent law the innovating seller may enjoy a limited defense for a period of time against imitation and entry, though not as great a protection as the single-firm monopolist. Thus, the quasi-monopolistic market structures found in oligopolies or resulting from patent protections within these or other industries may give rise to further variants in progressiveness. The analysis of the progressive tendencies of single-firm monopoly are useful in identifying the general relation of monopolistic or exclusionary power to progressiveness as it is found in other industries. Nevertheless, additional considerations arise in such industries, and they will require examination in the succeeding chapters.

RESPONSE TO CHANGING DEMAND AND COST

So much for the dynamics of monopoly policy with respect to product and production technique. A further question concerns the behavior through time of the monopolist in adjusting to changing demand and cost, whether fluctuating with the business cycle or growing or declining secularly. Salient characteristics of purely competitive market behavior in the face of changes of this sort have been observed to include: (1) considerable price flexibility with cyclical fluctuations of demand and cost—which result largely from cyclical changes in money purchasing power and factor prices—as output is continually adjusted so that short-run marginal cost equals price; (2) corresponding cyclical instability of enterprise profits; (3) occasional or frequent prolonged periods of adjustment to declining demands, with prolonged losses to enterprise; (4) continued pursuit of long-run equilibrium adjustments to evolving demand and cost conditions wherein price will be driven to the level of long-run average and marginal costs. To what extent may monopoly behavior in response to changing conditions differ from that just described?

It is evident that in monopoly response to fluctuating demand and cost conditions should, provided each short-run period is considered separately, involve adjustment of output to make short-run marginal cost equal to marginal receipts. If this is true, it is possible that the cyclical flexibility of price in monopoly will be just as great as that in pure competition, given certain fluctuations in demand and cost. Thus a downward shift in demand induces a corresponding downward shift in marginal receipts, a lower intersection of the latter with an up-sloping marginal cost, and, if the relation of marginal receipts to price is unchanged, a lower price. Three qualifications must be attached to this generalization, however.

First, if the elasticity of industry demand changes as the demand shifts, this will influence the relation of marginal receipts to price, and a short-period equilibrium with lower (or higher) marginal receipts equated to marginal cost may not mean a correspondingly lower (or higher) price. For example, if the elasticity of industry demand decreased as demand shifted backward in the cycle, the decreased elasticity, which favors a higher profit-maximizing price for the monopolist, might counteract any tendency toward price reduction. In pure competition, on the other hand, cyclical variations of the elasticity of industry demand, of which individual sellers take no account, would not similarly influence price flexibility. Monopoly could thus give rise to greater cyclical price rigidity (or, under opposite relations of demand elasticity to cyclical shifts in demand, greater price flexibility) than pure competition.

Second, if the monopolist adjusts price cyclically, he does so deliberately as a matter of choice; price is not automatically flexible as in pure competition. Therefore, if he is sufficiently uncertain of the elasticity of industry demand that he does not know whether or not a price change would increase his profits, he is free to pursue an arbitrary rigid price policy (or other arbitrary cyclical price policy). In competition the seller has no such discretion; cyclical price flexibility is imposed upon him. Third, the imposition of a long-run limit price on the monopolist may narrow the range of feasible short-run price variations and give rise to reduced price flexibility. It is thus at least possible that under monopoly less cyclical flexibility of price—and consequently greater cyclical flexibility of output—may be found.

Does this imply that the monopolist's earnings will tend to be more stable in the face of cyclical fluctuations? Not necessarily. If demand should become less elastic in a depression—increasing the profit opportunities from high prices—or if the threat of entry becomes less severe so that the limit price is higher relative to cost, then the impact of reduced demand on earnings might be lessened and cyclical income instability reduced. In the absence of such special circumstances, however, the monopolist who maximizes short-run profits in both prosperity and depression should experience a fluctuation of income of a severity comparable to that found in pure competition. The major difference is that since the monopolist tends on the average to make an excess profit, a situation of reduced demand in depression is much less likely to lead to net losses. If there is an industry output in a depression at which a profit can be made, he will make it (unless limit-price considerations deter him), whereas the competitive industry will find the position of lower profit or larger loss where short-run marginal cost equals price. In brief, the monopolist tends to do better profit-wise at all times than the competitive seller, and thus he is likely to have larger profits or smaller losses in a depression period.

The same sort of observation applies to the impact on the monopolistic industry of a secular decline in demand. Suppose that the monopolist has approximated a long-run equilibrium adjustment to a given demand situation, and now the demand begins to decline steadily over time. Like a competitive industry in a similar situation, he will pursue new long-run equilibrium adjustments to progressively reduced demands by reducing the scale of his investment, but meanwhile he will be faced with a short-run excess of capacity relative to that which would be most profitable. This will mean lower profits than those received in a long-run equilibrium until capacity is finally adjusted to reduced demand. So far the analysis is exactly parallel to that of a competitive industry in the same situation. The difference in the monopoly case is twofold. First, the monopolist at all times is able (except as limited by the threat of entry) to make the largest attainable short-run industry profit with the given excess capacity, or the smallest attainable loss, whereas the competitive sellers are driven to the lower profit position where short-run marginal cost equals price. Therefore, their losses with any given amount of capacity are greater, and these could be lessened if they united to follow a monopolistic pricing policy. Second, the monopolist in the long-run equilibrium will probably have enjoyed some excess profit, and his output and producing capacity will have been restricted to permit this. When demand declines, therefore, he will tend to make smaller profits than before but not necessarily tend to incur net losses. The initial cushion of his monopoly profit position protects him. The purely competitive industry, on the other hand, starting from an equilibrium position involving zero excess profits, immediately suffers net losses as demand declines and may continue to do so until a new long-run balance is established. It is thus more likely to become "distressed" under conditions of declining demand.

INTERTEMPORAL PRICE AND COST RELATIONS

One further remark may be added concerning the dynamics of the monopolist's price-output adjustments through time. We have argued above that the monopolist tends in either the short or long run to seek an adjustment in which marginal cost equals industry marginal receipts, or alternatively a limit price. This would imply that in any short period, whatever long-run adjustment he has reached or is pursuing, the monopolist attempts to maximize the profit of that short period and so for each time interval in turn. This action is quite consistent with maximization of all profits through time as long as it may be supposed that the profit of any future period is unaffected by the price charged and cost incurred in a preceding period. But it is evidently quite possible that there may be intertemporal relationships between industry prices and costs in one period and industry profits in another. And when the seller is a monopolist who can set industry price, incurs all industry costs, receives all industry profits, and is, therefore, in a position to influence future profits by varying present prices and costs (a position quite different from that of the seller in pure competition), he will presumably be influenced by these intertemporal relationships in determining his price policy from period to period.

The principal potential intertemporal relationships which may influence him are:

1. A relation between price charged for his product in earlier periods and the level of demand for it in later periods. (Demand in some period 2 might shift in response to variations of price in period 1.)
2. A relation between the selling cost of earlier periods and the demand of later periods. (Demand in some period 2 might be increased by an increase of selling costs in period 1.)

Given such intertemporal relationships, the monopolist will presumably wish to follow that pattern of price and selling-cost policies over a succession of time periods which will maximize his aggregate of separate period profits through time (future profits perhaps being discounted by an appropriate interest rate). This will imply that he will not necessarily set price so as to maximize each successive short-period profit in turn, since he should be willing to set price at another level in any present period if this resulted in an addition to future-period profits greater than the resulting subtraction from present-period profits. Similarly, he may incur present selling costs which will increase profit only in some future period.

Thus, it is apparent that the monopolist may not be led to set price at any one time so as to exploit fully the current market. Two principal examples of this sort of behavior are frequently cited. First, over long periods reduction of price below current profit-maximizing prices may stimulate demand in future periods (shift the demand curves of those periods to the right) enough to increase aggregate profit through time—perhaps by stimulating buyer interest in the product through wider distribution. It has been suggested that the aluminum monopoly from 1910 to 1930 followed a relatively low-price policy (lower than would maximize current profits) in order to make aluminum more widely known and so to expand the demand for it more rapidly. Second, with fluctuating demands reduction of price in times of depressed demands may conceivably result in reduced demand at high prices (or increased elasticity of demand at high prices) in succeeding periods of prosperity. In this case the monopolist may not cut depression prices as far as current profit maximization would suggest because he fears that a low price would "spoil the market" in later periods. So far as this consideration is operative, cyclical price rigidity may result.

The preceding discussion of the dynamics of monopoly policy reveals the possibility of numerous deviations from the behavior predicted for long-run monopoly equilibrium, and it suggests considerable elaborations of this prediction. Such modifications of our previous predictions, of course, must be taken into account in evaluating the effect of monopoly on social welfare. It should be emphasized, nevertheless, that these deviations from and complications of the long-run tendencies of monopoly adjustment do not deprive the simple long-run equilibrium model of major predictive value. In spite of numerous complications and qualifications, it is evident that monopoly will continually pursue a long-run equilibrium adjustment to changing data and that its performance, in general, will tend toward or roughly approximate those predicted by the equilibrium model. Thus, the predicted tendencies toward excess profits and virtual output restriction and certain equilibrium tendencies regarding product, selling cost, and technique are likely, at least in some rough fashion, to be actual tendencies of monopoly performance. Let us now turn to the evaluation of monopoly behavior from the standpoint of social welfare.

D. MONOPOLY AND ECONOMIC WELFARE

INCOME DISTRIBUTION AND EFFICIENCY

The market performance of any type of industry may be evaluated from the standpoint of its contribution to aggregate economic welfare by inquiring into the impact on welfare of the response which the industry makes to the effective demand for its output. We may inquire in turn how the response of a given type of industry to effective demand affects, in the economy as a whole, aggregate output and employment, efficiency, income distribution, the allocation of resources among uses, progressiveness in technique and product, and stability. In the preceding chapter we evaluated in this manner the performance attributed by theory to industries in pure competition. Here we shall similarly evaluate the performance attributed to the single-firm monopoly, both in general and as compared to that of pure competition. Again, it is necessary to consider the effects of monopoly on welfare both in the situation where a single monopoly or a few monopolies exist in an economy composed largely of industries with competitive or other structures and in the case where industries are dominantly monopolistic—at the extreme in a world of monopolies.

The most easily evaluated impacts of monopoly are on income distribution and on efficiency of production. As argued above (pages 203 to 205), the monopolistic industry has a general tendency in the long run to earn some amount of excess profits—larger if there is no threat of entry, smaller if there is one, but in general some excess profit. If this is true, the income from the sales revenue of any monopolized industry tends to be distributed differently between hired factors (including labor, loan capital, and land) on the one hand and enterprise owners on the other than it would be in pure competition. The former receive a smaller and the latter a larger share of industry income. Since the profit recipients tend to have larger personal incomes on the average than hired factors or those receiving their incomes, monopoly tends to increase the inequality of personal income distribution. It does so, moreover, essentially by rewarding contrived scarcity rather than the performance of a useful economic function. Consequently, if one views more unequal income distribution as socially undesirable, monopoly has undesirable income distribution effects. This judgment may be tempered, however, to the extent that monopolistic profits provide an incentive to invention and innovation.

Monopoly in only one or a few industries, of course, would not have very great effects on economy-wide income distribution. It would not necessarily be true, moreover, that hired factors employed in the monopolized industries would receive lower wage rates or other factor prices than those in other industries. So far as these factors were freely mobile to other industries, factor prices would tend to be equalized as among monopolistic and other industries, and the impact of monopoly excess profits would be spread thinly over all other income recipients in the economy. The income distribution effect would be present, but it would not redistribute an important fraction of the total income of society. A few monopolists would be richer; everyone else would be very slightly poorer. If monopoly becomes widespread, however, so that sellers in all or most industries receive monopolistic excess profits, then income distribution may differ greatly from that of a purely competitive economy. The general level of hired factor prices will be substantially depressed relative to the level of commodity prices, and the resulting difference will be received as excess profits by monopolistic enterprisers. All of the preceding, of course, refers to the *sharing* of whatever money and real income is produced by the economy. It does not refer to any positive or negative effect which monopoly may have on the size of real income at any given time or through time.

The effects of monopoly on efficiency in production cost are quite clear up to a certain point. In the first place, given the techniques of production, the extent of economies of large-scale production will determine whether or not monopoly in a given industry in the long run will give lower real and money costs of producing required outputs than pure competition. It may or it may not, but it is quite possible that it may. In cases of "natural monopoly" it certainly would. In the second place, even where monopoly is more efficient in scale than firms in a purely competitive structure could be, it may or may not in the long run be as efficient in scale as two or more firms (some sort of oligopoly) would be. Monopoly is possible in either case (see pages 210 to 213 above). Thirdly, given the techniques of production, monopoly, therefore, may or may not produce its output at the lowest aggregate cost of production at which it could be obtained. On the other hand, the purely competitive industry, where economies of scale are slight enough to permit its natural survival, does obtain the lowest attainable cost with given techniques. In other words, pure competition, in its natural setting, gives long-run maximal efficiency in scale. Monopoly, which has many possible settings, may or may not give long-run maximal efficiency in scale.

In any event, monopoly within a given industry may frequently give greater efficiency than a purely competitive structure would. Some brief elaboration on the possible sources of its advantages in scale may be in order, however. Economies of large-scale production which give the monopolist lower costs than competitive sellers may be either (1) *real economies,* resulting from a saving in the quantity of real factors used per unit of output—and in a corresponding saving in money costs—or (2) *strictly pecuniary economies,* resulting only from the ability to buy factors at lower prices because of increased bargaining power. So far as the monopolist's lower costs rest upon strictly pecuniary economies, as they may to some extent, real efficiency is not increased and no real saving to society results. The main effect is to redistribute income as among (1) the hired factors, (2) the monopolist, and—possibly—(3) the monopolist's customers. The issue here becomes one of income distribution rather than one of real efficiency. Nevertheless, lower money costs with large scale, secured for whatever reason, may make possible the establishment of monopoly.

Monopolistic efficiency cannot be fully evaluated, however, on the arbitrary assumption that techniques of production will be no different with purely competitive and monopolistic structures. As we have seen (pages 218 and 231 above), there are certain conflicting tendencies causing choice of production technique and technological progress to be different in monopoly than in pure competition. No absolutely conclusive a priori prediction can be made as to whether monopoly will on the average through time have more or less efficient techniques. There is a net indication, however, that monopoly may give rise to more rapid technological progress than pure competition. This more rapid rate would also appear to be more desirable or to lead to lower aggregate real costs through time. The monopolist has as an inducement to innovation, in the form of added profit, a larger share of the resultant cost saving than the competitive seller. It is thus possible, and even probable, that monopoly has an efficiency advantage from superior technique over pure competition, which should be weighed with other potential advantages and disadvantages already described.

The preceding comparison is strictly between the two extremes of single-firm monopoly and pure competition. In this comparison it appears a strong possibility that monopoly may frequently give greater efficiency than pure competition could in the same industry, and also that monopolized industries perform better relative to ideal standards of efficiency than purely competitive industries do in their own best setting. No comparison, however, is so far suggested with oligopoly, an intermediate market structure. This comparison will be made in the following chapter.

The foregoing comparison also has been largely in terms of the performance of the individual industry, whether monopolistic or purely competitive. The comparison between a purely competitive economy and a world of monopolies might lead to similar conclusions. However, it would seem probable that in a world of monopolies there would be a high proportion of industries in which monopoly was an artificial contrivance and gave rise to no economies or to diseconomies of scale as compared to less concentrated market structures.

OUTPUT AND EMPLOYMENT—A FEW MONOPOLISTS

The next issue concerns the effect of monopoly on output and employment —when monopoly is found in one or a few industries and when it is found throughout the economy.

The effects of monopoly on output in the single industry were analyzed on pages 205 to 210 above. The conclusions were as follows: (1) With given industry demand and with the monopolist's marginal cost function the same as the competitive industry's supply curve, the monopolist will produce a smaller long-run output than the competitive industry. (2) If the monopolist has different costs because of differences in firm scale, techniques, or factor prices, monopoly may produce either a larger or a smaller output than a competitive industry would in the same situation. (3) Nevertheless, monopoly generally tends to produce less than a "competitive-type" output, where price would equal average cost or the money value of marginal real cost or both. That is, even if it has an absolute superiority over competition in a certain industry, it fails to meet the "ideal standard" of an output at which cost is in a certain relation to price. It certainly does not tend generally to produce the largest output at which it could break even —that where price equals average cost.

The preceding refers to the size of monopoly output. What of the size of monopoly employment? Where demand and cost (both real and monetary) would be the same with monopoly or competition, the monopolistic output restriction would obviously carry with it a corresponding restriction of employment of productive factors. Wherever it produces a smaller output than a competitive industry would and has no higher real costs, it employs fewer factors. Suppose, however, that it produces as great or greater an output, because of lowered real costs through increased real efficiency in scale or in technique. If output is the same, employment will again be less since real costs are lower. Employment will also be less even though output is greater up to some limit. Up to this limit, output extension would not counterbalance real-cost-saving effects on employment. Beyond some limit, however—that is, if output increases due to monopoly are great enough—it could also employ more factors. This might be the case if the real cost savings of monopoly accrued in an industry with a rather elastic demand for its output. Whatever the case as regards absolute effects on employment, however, it would tend to employ fewer factors than if it reached an "ideal" output.

The argument is not the same if a monopolist is led to produce an output as great as or greater than that of a competitive industry because of lower money factor prices with no real cost savings. Here output and employment are directly correlated. If the monopolist, with the same real costs, produces as much as a competitive industry would because of lower factor prices, his employment is the same: if more, more; if less, less. In general, it is clear that the monopolist may have a larger or smaller output than a competitive industry in the same situation; that he will have a smaller than "ideal" output in any case; that he may have a smaller or larger employment, although in cases of increased real efficiency due to monopoly, he may have an equal or larger output but a smaller employment.

What is the significance of this from the viewpoint of over-all output and employment in the economy? Let us consider the question first for the economy in which there are only a few monopolistic industries in an otherwise competitive or quasi-competitive economy. It is at least possible that monopoly (as compared to a competitive alternative) will restrict both output and employment (and raise the price) in an industry. The prices of monopolized goods are raised relatively to those of competitive goods; buyers substitute the competitive goods for the monopoly goods in some degree; fewer monopoly goods are produced and purchased and fewer factors employed in producing them. Although there may be a restriction of the output of monopoly goods, however, there is not necessarily a restriction of the aggregate output of the economy. If the resources excluded from employment in monopolized industries move freely to other industries and if in those other industries money factor prices adjust downward relatively to industry demand curves so as to permit absorption of the otherwise disemployed factors, aggregate employment will not be impaired. The only necessary general condition for this is that the general level of money purchasing power and the general level of money factor prices coadjust to permit full employment. The primary impact of a few monopolies, restricting their own output and employment may thus be entirely on the allocation of resources among the production of various products and on the distribution of income (through excess profits). If it falls on aggregate employment, this will be (1) because unused resources are available for employment in the monopolized industry and are immobile so that they do not shift to other industries when unemployed, or (2) because factor prices will not adjust relatively to over-all demand or money purchasing power in other industries sufficiently to permit absorption of additional factors. It is possible that the redistribution of income resulting from excess profits, by dampening the tendency to spend from income, may worsen the prospect of such an adjustment. This analysis of this and related matters will be discussed below. In general, however, it is not strictly necessary that monopolistic restriction of output and employment in a few industries should result in any reduction of over-all employment and output for the economy as a whole. An *allocation* and an *income distribution* effect will tend to result but, under favorable circumstances of factor mobility and adjustability of factor prices to money purchasing power, an employment effect may not result.

The same argument applies to cases where, as a result of monopoly, employment is restricted but output is not. The disemployed factors may be absorbed elsewhere. In this case, we shall discover below, there may still be an adverse allocation effect so far as monopoly output is not extended to the level where the money value of marginal real cost equals price. Where both output and employment are greater with monopoly than with competition, it does not follow that over-all employment in the economy is increased. This would be so if the monopoly drew on otherwise unemployed resources for extra factors without reducing employment elsewhere. But it is quite possible, consistent with our preceding arguments, that monopolistic output extension would simply result in the shift of factors from other industries to the monopolized industry, with no net employment change, provided that the over-all relation of money purchasing power to money factor prices did not become more favorable to aggregate employment. Even where monopoly employs more factors and produces greater output than competition would, moreover, it may still be responsible for adverse allocation results so far as its output is such that the money value of marginal real cost is less than price. We shall reconsider this matter below.

OUTPUT AND EMPLOYMENT—A WORLD OF MONOPOLISTS

Let us now consider the effect upon aggregate employment and output of a world of monopolists—the results of having each industry in the economy controlled by a single-firm monopolist. As in the preceding case, it will appear that monopoly may have, under different conditions, a favorable, adverse, or neutral effect on either output or employment. The simplest

assumptions under which this may be demonstrated are that in each industry the monopolist will have the same real costs as the competitive industry
would and that, if he pays the same factor prices, he will have a marginal
cost curve the same as the competitive industry's supply curve. There is thus
no difference between competition and monopoly with respect to the price-
determining cost curve, except so far as its level may differ if there are differences in money factor prices. In this situation will output and employment (which, with given real costs, are directly linked) be restricted by
monopoly?

The answer to this will depend upon the manner in which the relation
of the aggregate money demand for all goods (or total money purchasing
power) to the level of money factor prices is affected by the introduction of
monopoly. If (1) the total flow of money purchasing power, which determines the general level of money demands for goods, and (2) the level of
all money factor prices, which determines the positions of all cost curves, are
both given and fixed, *then* the imposition of monopolies will result in smaller
output and employment, higher commodity prices, and larger profits than
if all industries were competitive. Each monopolist, with a marginal cost
curve no different in shape and level than the supply curve of a competitive
industry and with the same demand curve, will set output where marginal
cost equals marginal receipts instead of where it equals price, thus restricting
output and employment throughout and raising money prices. The given
flow of money purchasing power will buy fewer goods at higher prices, and
employ fewer factors at given prices since a share of each dollar goes to excess
profits. In this case (with given purchasing power and factor prices) if competitive pricing would just result in full employment, for example, monopolistic pricing would result in less than full employment.

The reason that this conclusion need not hold in all instances is that we
cannot necessarily carry over to the whole economy the assumptions which
may be appropriate to a single industry—namely, that the relation of total
money demand to money factor prices is given. For the economy as a whole
it is quite possible that an aggregative adjustment of money factor prices
relative to total money demand will occur that will eliminate any unemployment which general monopolization tends to create, although at the expense
of increased excess profits or other compensating effect. We have seen that
with identical cost conditions, and with unchanged aggregate demand and
money factor prices, a world of monopolists will tend to produce less output
and employ fewer factors than a competitive economy would, thus possibly
creating unemployment. This is because the intersection of the monopolists'
marginal cost curves with the various marginal receipts curves will occur at
smaller outputs than the intersections of the same curves with the industry
demand curves. If, however, upon the introduction of over-all monopoly,
money factor prices will be caused to fall relative to aggregate money de-

mand (if, for example, money factor prices will fall while the flow of money purchasing power remains constant), then the virtual output-restrictive effect of monopoly may be reduced, and perhaps wholly offset.

If money factor prices fall (given the money demand for all goods), each monopolist's cost curve shifts downward relative to his demand curve, thus inducing him to increase his output or to reduce the output restriction which results from equating marginal cost to marginal receipts instead of to price. If money factor prices will fall far enough relative to money demand, monopolists as a group may not really reduce output at all. The outputs at which marginal costs equal marginal receipts with the lowered factor prices may on the average be the same outputs as those for which marginal costs equaled price (under competition) with higher factor prices. It follows that a free adjustability of money factor prices downward relative to aggregate money demand will be a sufficient condition for monopoly to have no adverse effect on over-all output and employment. Given this adjustability, the impact of monopoly would be entirely on income distribution and on allocation, not on employment. Excess profits would generally emerge so that the share of income paid to hired factors would decrease, and the proportions in which various goods were produced might be altered, but not employment. Downward adjustments of the money prices of hired factors relative to money demand would avoid possible employment impacts of monopoly by absorbing them instead in increased income distribution effects.

The same general line of argument applies to world-of-monopoly cases wherein the monopolists would have lower real costs than competitive industries. It is quite possible, even if money factor prices and aggregate money demand remain unchanged, that a world of monopolists with lower real costs would produce larger outputs than competitive industries. Their cost curves might, because of lower real costs, permit this. It is not possible, however, with given money purchasing power and factor prices, that they would employ as many factors. A single monopolistic industry with a rather elastic demand might. An economy of monopolies, with constant purchasing power (or unit elastic demand over all) could not, since with some share of this constant purchasing power going to excess profits, the remainder would not employ as many factors at constant prices. With excess profits resulting from over-all monopoly it will necessarily restrict employment if total money demand and money factor prices are given even though it may extend output. Output cannot be extended far enough by increased real efficiency—given money purchasing power and factor prices—to sustain employment. On the other hand, a free adjustability of money factor prices relative to money purchasing power may reduce money costs relative to demand enough to permit maintenance of employment at the competitive level. In this respect, the argument is exactly the same as that for the simpler case described in the preceding paragraph. The general conclusions are (1) that a world of monopolies will tend to restrict employment, though not necessarily output, if the relation of total money purchasing power to money factor prices in monopoly will be no different from that in competition and (2) that a free adjustability of money factor prices downward relative to money purchasing power, which will give any desired lower ratio of money factor prices to purchasing power in monopoly, will avoid any employment-restrictive effects of monopoly. A third obvious conclusion is that some downward adjustment of factor prices, but a limited one only, might mitigate the potential employment-reducing effects of monopoly but not entirely avoid them.

The preceding defines the logical possibilities with respect to the effect of over-all monopoly on employment. But which of these possible effects is most likely to emerge? This will obviously depend upon the tendencies which govern the relationships of the flow of total money spending in the economy to (1) commodity prices and (2) factor prices and which may cause these relationships to vary as the level of real income and employment vary.

The introduction of monopoly opens up an excess-profit gap between hired factor prices and commodity prices. Then, instead of all money purchasing power going to purchase hired factors, as in pure competition, only a fraction (although probably a large fraction) of money purchasing power is available to purchase hired factors. It follows that a higher ratio of money purchasing power to hired factor prices is required to maintain a given level of employment than in pure competition. For example, if total money purchasing power were $20 billion per month and wages were $200 per month per man, expenditure of the $20 billion under pure competition, if labor were the only factor, would result in the employment of 100 million laborers. All the $20 billion would go to hired factors. But if under monopoly 25 percent of all purchasing power, or $5 billion, always went to excess-profit incomes, leaving only $15 billion for wages, wages would have to decline to $150 per month, total purchasing power remaining the same, in order to permit the same level of employment. The ratio of money purchasing power to monthly money wages must rise from 100 million to 1 and become 133⅓ million to 1 in order to sustain the same level of employment.

One possibility is that under the impact of monopoly factor prices will in fact adjust relative to money purchasing power sufficiently to sustain full employment. This would happen if (1) money factor prices would adjust downward freely while at the same time (2) total purchasing power was sustained at an unchanged level by the fact that recipients of excess profits, as these emerged, spent their increased incomes as rapidly as the hired factors from which they were taken away would have spent the same money. In other words, the redistribution of income away from hired factors and in the direction of excess profits would not reduce the rate at which total income, resulting from an initial expenditure of money purchasing power, was respent, and thus a decline of hired factor prices would not induce a corresponding decline of total spending or purchasing power in the next period. For example, suppose the rate of spending per month has been $20 billion under pure competition with labor receiving it all and spending it all in each successive month. Suppose further that with the introduction of monopoly wages fall (sufficiently to maintain employment for the time being) and labor now receives $15 billion and excess-profit recipients $5 billion. For money spending to remain unchanged in the next month, the profit recipients must spend their $5 billion just as labor spends its $15 billion, or, in general, the total spending of the two groups must remain at $20 billion. This would permit period-to-period maintenance of the same level of employment under monopoly. If, on the other hand, for example, labor continued just to spend its reduced income, whereas excess-profit recipients spent only half of theirs and hoarded the rest (at least until employment fell), each cut in wages would induce a corresponding decline in money purchasing power, and no cut in money wages would be sufficient to restore the employment level of pure competition. We shall return to this point below.

The possibility that money factor prices will adjust downward freely relative to money purchasing power, thus permitting monopoly to have no effect on employment, is generally identified with the condition that a change in income distribution in the direction of excess profits, or of greater inequality, will have no net effect on the rate of spending from money income. If this is true, it may in addition be true (although this will not be discussed here) that an initial reduction of employment (as would occur with rigid money factor prices under monopoly) will lead to an increased rate of money spending relative to factor prices until the original level of employment is restored. That is, money purchasing power might adjust upward relative to factor prices, just as well as factor prices adjusting downward relative to money income, sufficiently to maintain the same rate of employment. This would mean that money income would seek a relation to commodity prices sufficient to maintain a given level of employment regardless of income distribution.

This, then, is one of the possible effects of monopoly on employment—exactly no effect, at least as long as the quantity of factors willing to work is the same with the reduced real wages paid them in monopoly. Since any initial tendency of over-all monopolistic restriction to disemploy factors of production should tend to cause their prices to fall—as unemployed factors bid against others in seeking employment—it is a quite conceivable effect, provided money purchasing power will be sustained as factor prices are bid down. Even if money factor prices are rigid, it is not impossible that the reduction of real output initially consequent on monopolistic restriction will lead to an expansion of money spending until employment is restored. In these cases the entire impact of monopoly would be upon income distribution and allocation and not upon employment.

There is at least some question, however, whether indeed the flow of money spending from a given income is insensitive to changes in income distribution, or more generally whether, with changes in income distribution from excess profits, money income and factor and commodity prices will tend to adjust relatively to each other so as to maintain a given level of employment. This is primarily because analysis and observation suggest that, as income distribution becomes more unequal with excess profits, there may be some systematic alteration in the rate of spending from the money income which corresponds to (or is necessary to sustain) a given level of employment. In brief, if we classify all spending as either *consumption* spending (on consumer goods) or *investment* spending (on capital goods), it is suggested that the proportion of income spent on consumption with a given level of employment will decline as income distribution becomes more unequal, whereas the amont of investment spending may not increase just so as to maintain total spending at a constant level. Investment spending might remain constant or decline; it might also increase less than enough, just enough, or more than enough to maintain spending constant. This range of possibilities with respect to investment spending will not be analyzed here; suffice it to say that there are conceivable circumstances in which any of these alternative effects on investment spending might be felt.

If the altered income distribution resulting from monopoly leads to a reduction of total spending from the money income which corresponds to a given level of employment, then over-all monopoly will indeed tend to restrict employment. Suppose, for example, that with over-all competition the flow of money purchasing power is $20 billion per month and that all of this, when received as income, is repeatedly respent at the rate of $20 billion per month. Then money purchasing power will remain stable at $20 billion per month through time, and it will result in the steady employment of a certain quantity of factors at the going level of money factor prices. Suppose now that over-all monopoly is imposed and factor prices fall enough to permit maintenance of the previous level of employment, provided that money spending stays at $20 billion per month. (This fall in factor prices might result, for example, in a payment to hired factors of $15 billion—instead of $20 billion—and a payment to excess-profit recipients of $5 billion per month.) Now suppose also that, with income thus redistributed, people will tend to spend each month less than their full money incomes as long as employment remains at the same level but perhaps will spend as much as their full money incomes when employment has fallen by some amount—say by 15 percent. Then, following the initial factor-price cut, spending out of income, and therefore income itself in successive periods, will tend to decline progressively, perhaps becoming stabilized when it is reduced enough that employment is cut by 15 percent. Therefore, the initial factor-price cut, which would have been sufficient to keep employment unchanged if money income had remained at $20 billion, will, in fact, not be sufficient, and employment will fall as money income responds downward to factor-price reductions. If people in effect refuse to spend a sufficient amount out of income to maintain the previous (competitive) employment level—no matter how far money incomes and prices fall—then no factor-price cut, however great, can permanently restore the previous level of employment. In effect, money income may tend to "follow" factor-price changes induced by monopoly in such a way that a new ratio of factor prices to money income which would permit maintenance of employment cannot be attained.

Generalizing the argument, it is possible that under pure competition the tendency of people to spend various amounts relative to their money incomes (all, or greater or less than all) at various levels of employment may result in the establishment of a given ratio of money income and purchasing power to factor prices, which in turn fixes a given level of employment. If now monopoly is generally introduced, a certain higher ratio of money income to factor prices will be required to maintain the same level of employment, as an excess-profit share of any money income is now not available for hiring factors. But the propensity to spend out of all income at various employment levels may be so reduced by the resulting income redistribution that the new ratio of money income to factor prices which tends to emerge—though perhaps higher than before—is not high enough to maintain the same level of employment. More unequal income distribution, by reducing the propensity to spend, leads to a ratio of money income to factor prices which sustains a lower level of employment. If this is the case, about the same results should ensue regardless of whether adjustment to monopoly takes place by factor prices falling relative to money income or by money income adjusting upward relative to rigid factor prices. Rigidity of factor prices is significant only so far as money income is also rigid, in which case they would result in a prima-facie restriction of employment through monopoly.

Just as monopoly could restrict the tendency to spend sufficiently to reduce employment in spite of factor-price movements, it might of course also increase the tendency to spend sufficiently to increase employment. This would presumably be the case if investment spending were so increased because of monopoly profits as to outweigh any decline in consumption spending, and thus to create so high a ratio of money income to factor prices that employment was increased. The probability of such a development can be assessed only in terms of a full analysis of all the determinants of the rate of investment spending.

In general, then, we can arrive at no unique conclusion concerning the impact of over-all monopoly on the general level of employment. It may tend to restrict it, augment it, or leave it unchanged. Further prediction of the relative probabilities of these various results can be derived only from a detailed analysis of all the determinants of the rate of spending and its relation to money factor prices, to which we shall refer in a later chapter. In summary, it may be recalled that even though restricting employment, monopoly *may* tend to increase total output because of increased efficiency. Finally, if it should be demonstrable that in certain circumstances the income-distribution effects of monopoly were in the net favorable to employment, this would temper the previous adverse judgment of monopoly as fostering greater inequality per se.

A NOTE ON FACTOR MONOPOLY

In concluding this analysis of the effect of monopoly on output and employment, it should be re-emphasized that we have been speaking through-out of *enterprise monopoly*—that is, of monopoly by firms engaged in the production and sale of commodities—and that we have not referred to *factor monopoly* or monopolistic sale of a basic factor of production like labor or land. In general, we have assumed that the basic factor prices are either competitively determined or are arbitrarily given at certain levels, while at the same time enterprises engaged in buying factor services and selling commodities made from them pursue monopolistic price-output policies. Our conclusions thus apply to the effects of enterprise monopoly per se, unalloyed with factor monopoly. They do not apply in general to the consequences of enterprise monopoly and factor monopoly operating to-gether, nor do they apply to the consequences of factor monopoly alone as it might operate in a situation where there was pure competition among enterprises. In effect, the possible consequences of factor monopoly, whatever the competitive situation among enterprises, have been neglected, and will receive separate treatment in Chapter 12 of the second part.

The reasons that our conclusions with respect to enterprise monopoly cannot be applied without change to factor monopoly deserve brief mention at this point. Two essential aspects of the operation of enterprises as identi-fied here are (1) that they operate by buying factors or factor services and selling commodities produced with them and (2) that they design their price-output policies so as to maximize their profit or, in effect, the difference between the buying price of the factors they purchase and the selling price of the commodities they sell. To this end, monopolistic enterprises tend virtually to restrict output and employment, but, as we have seen, this end *may* be realized through the depression of factor prices relative to commodity prices rather than through the actual restriction of output and employment. Enterprise monopolists may be able in effect to maximize their profits by taking some income away from the factors which they purchase rather than by actually restricting the supply of the goods they produce. This is essentially because they are buyers as well as sellers and because the suppliers from whom they buy *may* be "exploited" sufficiently that no net output restriction is necessarily a part of a profit-maximizing policy.

On the other hand, the sellers of factors—whether competitive or monopolistic—are in a significantly different position. First, they typically do not buy and sell: they simply sell services which belong to them. For example, the labor union is a bargaining agent for workers selling their own services, or land owners sell the services of their land. As a consequence, there is no supplier who may be forced to absorb the impact of income-increasing policies of factor sellers. They can only try to sell for more; they cannot "buy for less." As a result, *actual* restriction of supply—not offset by a decline in buying prices—will be the only avenue by which a factor monopoly can increase its income where restriction tends to increase income. Second, factor sellers will not attempt to maximize a profit or difference between buying and selling price. There is no general agreement as to what labor unions, for example, will try to maximize—whether aggregate wages per year, unit wages per hour or week, or something else—but whatever they attempt to maximize, it is certainly not a difference between purchase outlay and sales revenue.

Because of the uncertainty concerning the motivation of factor sellers—and especially labor unions—it is difficult to develop a simple theory of the character and consequences of factor monopoly. But it is evident that *if* monopolistic factor sellers, in attempting to maximize some measure of revenue, are led to adopt restrictive policies which involve withholding some of the factor supply from the market, then continued pursuance of such policies will tend per se to reduce employment of factors, since it is only by such restriction of employment that the factor sellers can increase their incomes. This is because there is no supplier who through lower buying prices can absorb the impact of the restriction. Thus the impact on output and employment of factor monopoly pursuing a restrictive rationale may be necessarily and distinctly different from that of enterprise monopoly operating in an economy with competitive factor markets.

It follows that where enterprise monopoly and factor monopoly operate together, or where factor monopoly operates alone, the possibility of maintaining full employment—at least with certain assumed motivations of the factor monopolists—may be much smaller. For example, any tendency for money purchasing power to adjust relative to factor prices in such a way as to permit full employment may be countered by an administered rise of factor prices which restricts it, etc. ad infinitum. Stagnant underemployment or various dynamic movements of money purchasing power (including inflationary spirals) may ensue. These possibilities will be explored below. For the moment, we may re-emphasize that the analysis of the impact of enterprise monopoly on aggregate employment is not transferable without substantial modification to the effects of factor monopoly on aggregate employment.

ALLOCATION OF RESOURCES

Monopoly, whether it exists in only a few industries of an economy or throughout, has predictable effects on the distribution of income, but its effects on employment are, a priori, rather uncertain. There is no similar uncertainty with respect to its effects on the allocation of resources among uses, or, to put it differently, on the composition of the aggregate output of commodities. Both where there are some monopolies in an otherwise competitive or quasi-competitive economy and where every industry in the economy is monopolized, the allocation of resources among uses will tend to diverge distinctly from that attributable to a purely competitive economy, and, in general, it will tend to be less desirable. This may be demonstrated readily by considering in conjunction (1) our previous discussion of the conditions of ideal allocation and of how they are approximated with universal pure competition (pages 163 to 170), and (2) our discussion of the principles of monopolistic output restriction (pages 205 to 208).

In the analysis of the conditions of ideal allocation, it was shown that, with any given level of employment and distribution of income, the best possible allocation would occur when in each industry the final unit of any given factor employed resulted in an increment in output which provided the same additional satisfaction to buyers. For example, the final hour of labor employed in each industry should add goods of identical importance to buyers. Subject to the assumptions that all industries pay the same money price for units of any factor used in common and further subject to the convention of measuring buyers' satisfaction and comparing the satisfactions of different buyers according to the money prices they pay for goods, it was shown this sort of allocation would be attained if in every industry simultaneously output was such that the money value of marginal real cost to the industry was equal to price. Then the last dollar's worth of factors (and the last unit of any given factor) employed in each industry would produce an output of the same dollar value and, according to the convention of measurement adopted, of the same satisfaction-providing power. It was furthermore shown that in the long-run equilibrium an economy in pure competition would tend, subject to certain possible exceptions, to propagate such a set of relationships of marginal costs to prices and thus to reach an approximately ideal allocation. If all industries were purely competitive, the composition of aggregate output would approximate that there the money value of marginal industry real cost equaled price in every industry, and this would represent a tentative ideal in allocation.

Suppose now that instead of an economy in which every industry is purely competitive, we have an economy in which some industries are purely competitive (or behave about like purely competitive industries) and some are single-firm monopolies, and suppose further that such an economy reaches or approaches a general long-run equilibrium. In the purely competitive industries output will be so adjusted that the money value of marginal real cost to the industry equals price (pages 163 to 170 above). In the monopolized industries, however, output will in general be restricted so that the money value of marginal real cost is in general less than price (see pages 205 to 208 above [8]). In this circumstance, and retaining the assumption that all industries are paying the same price for any given factor, allocation is demonstrably other than ideal. For in this case the last dollar's worth (and last unit) of any factor employed in any monopolistic industry is bringing forth an output of higher money value—and satisfaction-providing power—than the last dollar's worth (and unit) of this factor employed in any competitive industry, and a shift of resources from competitive to monopolistic industries could increase total satisfaction.

Suppose that two industries, one competitive and one monopolized, are both employing but a single factor—labor—at the same wage rate of, let us say, $1 per hour. In industry A, the competitive one, suppose that the money value of marginal real cost to the industry is $1. Then the price, to which this marginal cost is equated, is also $1. This means that in the competitive industry the last dollar's worth—and the last hour—of labor added to employment in the industry is adding an output of goods worth $1 to buyers. If in the monopolized industry, B, we find a money value of marginal real cost of $2, price will necessarily be somewhat higher than marginal cost—let us say $2.50, since the monopolist restricts output so that marginal cost is less than price. Then the last dollar's worth—and the last hour of labor—in industry B is adding an output worth $1.25 to buyers. If this is the case, allocation is demonstrably not ideal, since satisfaction, as measured by dollar value of output, could be increased by a shift of resources from A to B. If, departing from this initial equilibrium, we were to induce or force the shift of an hour of labor from A to B, what would happen? An hour less of labor employed in A would mean approximately one less unit of good A (the marginal real cost of a unit of A at this point is one labor hour) and a loss of goods worth $1 to buyers, or perhaps slightly more than $1, since the marginal satisfaction of goods increases as their supply is reduced. An hour more of labor employed in B would mean about one-half additional unit of good B (presuming the marginal real cost of a unit of B does not vary abruptly from its current level of two labor hours) and the addition of goods

[8] Subject to the *possible* exception of the monopolist who is open to a threat of entry, for whom the limit price is the most profitable one, and for whom the limit output at this price is such that marginal cost exceeds price—see pp. 217-218.

worth $1.25 to buyers, or a little less than $1.25, since the marginal satisfaction from a good declines as its supply is increased. The shift of an hour of labor from A to B would thus result in an increase in total buyers' satisfaction as measured by the dollar values they assign to goods. So would the shift of successive additional hours of labor from A to B, with diminishing marginal satisfaction and price for B and increasing marginal satisfaction and price for A, *until the point was reached where the ratio of price to the money value of marginal real cost was the same in industries A and B.* Suppose, for example, that after the shift of 1,000 units of labor from the competitive industry A to the monopolized industry B—increasing the output of the latter and diminishing that of the former—a point was reached where the price of A was $1.15 with a marginal cost of $1 and the price of B was $2.30 with a marginal cost of $2. Then no further shift of resources between the two industries could increase total satisfaction, and allocation would be demonstrably ideal. But until this point was reached, allocation could be improved. It is, therefore, obvious that the initial allocation, which naturally emerged from the juxtaposition of competitive and monopolistic equilibria, was not ideal.

The general rule, of course, is that ideal allocation (under the assumptions made) requires that in every industry the ratio of price to money value of marginal real cost be the same. Otherwise, some other allocation, involving a shift of resources from industries where the ratio is lower to one where it is higher, will add to total satisfaction by adding goods of higher value and subtracting goods of lower value. It follows that in any economy which includes both competitive and monopolistic industries, the allocation arrived at in the long-run equilibrium is not ideal, since satisfaction could be increased by shifting resources from the competitive to the monopolized industries—reducing the outputs of the former in order to extend the outputs of the latter. This is true also so far as the industries in an economy, though not strictly in pure competition or in single-firm monopoly, follow the diverse pricing tendencies identified with purely competitive and monopolistic industries.

If a combination of monopolized and competitive industries will not give ideal allocation, what of a world of monopolies? Under conditions wherein every industry was a monopoly, the money value of marginal real cost would in each industry be less than price. Would allocation then be ideal? Not in general. For although the monopolist in each industry set output so that his marginal cost was equal to marginal receipts (and less than price), the discrepancy between price and marginal receipts—at the point where it equaled marginal cost—might differ between industries.

In general, the relation of marginal receipts to price depends on the elasticity of the demand curve from which the marginal receipts are derived. With high elasticity of demand marginal receipts are close to price; with lower elasticity marginal receipts lie further below price. Therefore, if two monopolized industries have demand curves of different elasticity, marginal receipts will be closer to price in the industry with the more elastic demand curve for its output.

It follows that if in each of these two industries the seller sets output so that his marginal cost equals marginal receipts, in one case the resulting ratio of price to marginal cost will be higher than in the other. The ratio of marginal cost to price, where in every case marginal cost equals marginal receipts, will depend on the elasticity of demand at the point where the equality is found. Thus, in one monopolized industry, X, with a less elastic demand, a marginal cost of 1\$ might equal marginal receipts when price was \$1.50, and in another monopolized industry, Y, marginal cost of \$1 might equal marginal receipts when price was \$1.20. If, with different elasticities of demand among industries, the ratio of marginal cost to price is thus different in different monopolized industries, then allocation is obviously not ideal. In the preceding example a shift of resources from industry Y to industry X would increase satisfaction, since, on the margin, a dollar's worth of resources so shifted would add about one-and-a-half dollar's worth of satisfaction in X and take away only about one-and-a-fifth dollar's worth of satisfaction in Y. Whenever the ratio of price to the money value of marginal real cost is different in different industries, allocation is not ideal since a shift of resources from industries where the ratio is low to those where it is high could improve allocation.

So far, therefore, as we may in general expect that different monopolized industries would have demands for their outputs of different elasticities, allocation would not tend to be ideal as among monopolies, or within a world of monopolies.

The preceding argument proceeds from the premise that whenever the ratio of price to the money value of marginal real cost is not the same in all industries, allocation can be improved by shifting resources among industries until it is. This is certainly true under the assumptions that all industries pay the same price for units of any factor and that money prices paid by buyers are an acceptable index of satisfaction. There remains unanswered, however, an implicit question. Would the attainment throughout industries of the same *ratio* of price to marginal cost secure actually ideal allocation, or is it in addition necessary that the money value of marginal real cost should *equal* price, so that the ratio in question would everywhere be one to one?

Certainly when the ratio of price to the money value of marginal real cost is the same in all industries, even though not unity, the allocation of *employed* resources is ideal in the sense that no shift of these resources among industries could then improve satisfaction. It has been argued, however, that unless price is in addition everywhere equal to money value of marginal real cost, the allocation will not be ideal as between *employed* and *unem-*

ployed resources or between *work* and *leisure*. A consistent discrepancy between money value of marginal real cost and price, it is argued, which implies that the payment to the marginal unit of any resource will be smaller than the value of the output which it adds, will pay the resource less as a reward for foregoing leisure than it adds to total satisfaction through added output. Therefore, in the case of labor, at least, the inducement to forego leisure will not be as great as the addition to total satisfaction which results from foregoing leisure (since labor does not then receive the entire product it adds at the margin), and labor will not be induced to offer itself for employment up to the ideal margin where the value of leisure foregone is exactly equal to the value of addition to output. The validity of this point, however, rests largely on the supposition that in any event total money purchasing power tends to adjust to wages and other factor prices so as to permit the employment of all labor that wishes to work at the going wage level—so that in no case is labor involuntarily idle. If this were true, then a more desirable level of employment would be attained with marginal costs equal to price instead of less than price. But if in either event involuntary leisure would be involved—as must generally be assumed possible—and if the amount of involuntary leisure might be affected in either direction by moving from one situation to the other (through resulting influences on the ratio of money purchasing power to factor prices), then adverse employment effects do not *necessarily* follow from having prices proportional to rather than equal to marginal costs. We may in any event accept the condition of price being everywhere in the same ratio to marginal cost as a criterion of ideal allocation *as of a given level of employment*. A world of monopolies will not tend to fulfill this condition; a purely competitive economy will fulfill it and also that of price-marginal-cost equality.[9]

The preceding treatment has dealt with the effects of monopoly by segregating them into effects on employment, on efficiency, on income distribution, and on allocation of resources among uses. Thus, we have said that monopoly may have certain effects on employment and total output and that at the same time it may result in a certain pattern in the distribution of the real income which is created when it is present. Then, given the employment, output, and income distribution which emerges, we have evaluated the character of allocation of this output, inquiring whether or not it will be ideal. The meaning of ideal allocation according to this definition is a restricted one—it refers to the best allocation *so long as we have the employment, output, and income distribution to which monopoly gives rise*. It does not refer to the allocation which would be ideal, for example, if income were differently distributed, as it might be in pure competition, and if as a result

[9] Cf. Abba P. Lerner, *The Economics of Control* (New York: The Macmillan Company, 1944), Chap. 9.

aggregate consumer demands were differently apportioned among different goods. The relatively unequal distribution to which monopoly gives rise, for instance, may result in more intense demands for luxuries as compared to necessities than we would get with purely competitive income distribution. For the purpose of appraising monopolistic allocation we have inquired how well it adjust outputs to this structure of demand found when monopoly is present, and not how well it adjust outputs relative to the demands which would be found under some more satisfactory sort of income distribution. In essence, we have made an analytical separation of the income distribution effects and the allocation effects of monopoly, and we have not considered them together.

If we do consider them together, it is apparent that the allocation which emerges in monopoly might be compared with the ideal allocation subject to some different pattern of income distribution—for example, the purely competitive—rather than to ideal allocation subject to monopolistic income distribution. If this were done formally, it would probably appear that monopolistic allocation diverges from the former standard more seriously than from the latter. It has also been argued that the income distribution effects of monopoly are in themselves satisfaction reducing, in that persons with larger incomes, which are increased by monopoly, receive less satisfaction per dollar of income spent on goods than do persons of lower incomes, which are decreased by monopoly. This point has not been accepted in the preceding analyses of ideal allocation—if it were, evaluation of ideal allocation under any system of income distribution becomes very complicated.

Similarly, it is clear that the allocation effects of monopoly may be considered in conjunction with its over-all employment and output effects. If monopoly diverges somewhat from the allocation which would be ideal with the output and income distribution it creates, it is evident that any adverse effects on total output augment its over-all satisfaction-reducing effect and any favorable effects on total output reduce it. In addition, the implicit income distribution effects of any changes in employment it induces should be taken into account in the final reckoning.

Our analysis of the effects of monopoly could thus be made more elaborate by considering formally in conjunction all of its separate effects which may affect the aggregate satisfaction the population gets from material goods. Our bit-by-bit analysis, however, should suffice as a means of identifying general tendencies. On this level, the comparison of competition to monopoly as developed to this point may be summarized.

A purely competitive economy would not necessarily give full employment, but it should tend, in given circumstances, to give some determinate level of employment either full or otherwise and a corresponding level of total output. It would not necessarily give ideal income distribution—however that is defined—but it would give an income distribution which included no excess profits. It would tend to give an allocation of resources among uses which was ideal as long as the going level of employment and output and the going pattern of income distribution held. Suppose that instead of a purely competitive economy we have one in which some industries are purely competitive and some monopolized. Compared to the purely competitive economy, this economy may give either a higher or a lower or the same level of employment. It may also give either higher or lower or the same aggregate output—although its output effects here will tend to be more favorable (relative to a given employment effect) when in the monopolized industries there are great economies to large-scale firms. The partly monopolized economy will tend to give a more unequal distribution of income—by creating excess profits in monopolized sectors—except so far as possible employment-increasing effects counterbalance these tendencies. The allocation of resources among uses—relative to that which would be ideal with the given employment and income distribution—will be less satisfactory than in pure competition. The outputs of monopolized industries will be too small relative to those of competitive industries and also probably not in the best relation to each other. If a world of monopolies is compared with a purely competitive economy, similar conclusions follow with respect to output and employment·and with respect to income distribution, except that income distribution effects of excess profits will be greater. Again, allocation will tend to diverge from the ideal since outputs will be set so that marginal costs bear different relations to prices in different industries.

Thus the true impacts of monopoly on the economy are made clear. Monopoly—in some industries or in all—does not necessarily result in less aggregate output and employment, although it may (a matter which will require further analysis). It has a virtual restrictive impact on output and employment, but if the movements of the relation of money purchasing power to factor prices which follow from monopoly are of a certain order, no over-all restriction may occur. The impacts of monopolistic restriction, however, will fall on income distribution and on allocation. Excess profits will tend to emerge and allocation will tend to be distorted from the ideal, too small a proportion of employed resources being used by the monopolized industries as compared to the competitive and in the more restrictive as compared to the less restrictive monopolies. All of the restrictive effects of monopoly *may* be spent in these directions without adverse effect on over-all employment or output.

This comparison of monopoly and competition so far neglects possible differences in progressiveness and in effects on over-all stability; it also neglects the significance of monopolistic selling costs. We turn now to these matters.

PROGRESSIVENESS, STABILITY, AND SELLING COST

It is much more difficult to assess the relative desirability from the standpoint of aggregate welfare of the performance of monopoly with respect to progressiveness, to the incursion of selling costs, and to the impact of monopolistic pricing on over-all economic stability. This is because (1) the a priori predictions of monopolistic performance in these respects, and of its differences from competitive performance, are somewhat indefinite and ambiguous, and because (2) economic theorists have as yet failed to develop entirely adequate and unambiguous working standards of ideal behavior in the respects mentioned, in terms of which a given performance may be assessed. Consequently, it is appropriate that we limit ourselves here largely to posing questions concerning the character and relative desirability of the stated aspects of monopoly performance.

Some conflicting tendencies in monopolistic behavior with respect to product choice and progressiveness in product were discussed on pages 218 to 231 above. First, monopoly would probably tend to select, from a given range of product alternatives with known demands and costs for each, a smaller variety of products to produce than an industry of competitive sellers would. Second, it would tend to reject as unprofitable certain opportunities for product improvement which would be exploited in the course of competitive rivalry for a market. Third, it would certainly tend to avoid product choices which would reduce industry profit, even though such choices were demonstrably preferred by buyers. On the other hand, it is likely to be less deterred by the riskiness of any potential product choice—the demand for which is uncertain—because it will gain more from successful choices and lose no more from unsuccessful ones, and for the same reason it is likely to invest more in the development of new product alternatives. Any net tendency in its product performance as compared to that of a competitive industry is thus difficult to identify.

Even if we could identify it precisely, the operational standards by which it could be judged are not very adequately developed. We can say definitely that we wish an adjustment and rate of development of product in any line which give the greatest satisfaction to buyers relative to the real cost of production and that this will also ordinarily involve some optimal variety of products in any industry so as to cater to diverse buyer tastes. We do not have, however, fully developed criteria of the relations of costs to demands under which product optima would be attained, and it is thus not feasible to give a conclusive judgment any particular predicted complex of product behavior.

Two aspects of monopoly performance, however, may be tentatively evaluated. First, the tendency of monopoly to avoid products which would yield lower industry profits, even though buyers would be as well or better satisfied while making smaller outlays and with reduced costs, is a presumptive deviation from any conceivable version of optimal product behavior. Second, restriction on variety of products will tend to reduce total satisfaction where there is great diversity in buyer tastes. Third, the tendency of monopoly to avoid those competitive improvements of the quality of products which would reduce industry profits in competitive industries probably results in avoidance of excessive product improvements (that do not add enough to buyer satisfaction to justify added cost) which might occur under competition. Fourth, any tendency to proceed more rapidly with product development and introduction because of reduced risk and better financing is probably to the net advantage of the consumers. A net evaluation of monopolistic product as compared to competitive product performance is thus difficult on any basis. We shall return to the issue in the succeeding chapter on oligopolistic markets.

As regards progressiveness in production technique, we have seen (pages 218 to 231 above) that there is an a priori probability that monopoly will be more progressive than pure competition in development and adoption of cost-reducing techniques, although this is not entirely certain and although a similar probable superiority over oligopolistic structures of various sorts is by no means evident. Taking this probability of more rapid technological change as a premise for the moment, is it more desirable socially? Again, full operational standards for judging this matter have not been worked out. Since it would appear, however, (1) that monopoly will not in any event tend to change techniques at a rate so rapid as to raise aggregate costs of a given output through time, but will only approach or reach the lowest-cost policy, risks being taken into account, and (2) that pure competition would probably progress more slowly, then monopoly would appear to give better welfare results.

The finding of pages 222 to 223 above is that monopolies will probably incur some selling costs, although how much we cannot predict without further knowledge of the relation, product by product, between buyers' demands and the amount of selling cost. Moreover, we lack a clear operational standard of how much selling cost is consistent with maximizing overall welfare. It may be argued that a certain amount is desirable in order to inform buyers of alternatives available to them and permit them to make optimal adjustments to these alternatives, but we have no clear criterion of how much this is. Beyond that desirable level further selling costs, devoted simply to a tussle for the buyer's favor, are a priori of doubtful desirability, but again we do not have ready means of measuring where an excess sets in. It is thus difficult to reach a clear indication of the level of selling costs monopoly will attain or of the desirability of alternative levels. The fact, however, that monopoly may tend to incur smaller selling costs than a competitive industry with differentiated products would mean that it is less likely to incur excesses of selling cost. This tendency will be considered further on pages 307 to 320 in the succeeding chapter.

The impact of monopoly on over-all economic stability will presumably be primarily via the impact of its price-output adjustment to given levels of cost and demand or of its readjustment to changing cost and demand. Again we face a dual difficulty. First, the differences in the character of responses between monopoly and competition are not entirely clear. A general adjustment permitting some average excess profit over time is, to be sure, predicted for the monopoly case. But different price flexibility as the result of readjustment to changing data by no means necessarily follows, although it is a possibility under certain circumstances. Second, whatever specific differences might be predicted between competitive and monopoly adjustments, the differential effects on over-all stability are not evident. Extended analysis will give no conclusive answer to this question. Monopoly may have some effect on stability, however, via its impact on income distribution. So far as monopolies create excess profits, they make income distribution less equal, and they divert more of the total income of the economy into the hands of relatively few wealthy individuals. The spending of such large incomes is only in part for ordinary consumption; a large portion is spent on investments. Investment spending is much less stable over time than consumption spending, and it is much more susceptible to fluctuation. It may thus be argued that high-profit monopolies indirectly dispose the economy toward spending habits more susceptible to disruption by periodic boom and decline than would obtain if income were more equally distributed. That is, fluctuations in aggregate spending or demand may be accentuated because of monopoly.

The normative evaluation of monopoly as compared to competition, however, is in general not conclusive with respect to progressiveness, selling cost, and contribution to over-all stability. Some probable aberrations from ideal product behavior in monopoly are indicated, but not necessarily a product behavior inferior to that of other market structures. Some probability (not certainty) of a more desirable rate of technological progressiveness in monopoly than in competition is indicated, but not necessarily an ideal one. The evaluation of selling cost behavior and of impact on stability is not entirely conclusive. For the most part, therefore, our comparative evaluation of monopoly must rest on the consequences of its almost inevitable effects on income distribution and allocation and of its possible effects on efficiency, output, and employment, as reviewed above.

It is also well to underline the fact that our analysis and evaluation to date refer explicitly to single-firm monopoly behavior. It will be important to determine the extent to which monopolistic tendencies so identified are and are not registered in the oligopolistic industries, which are often popularly thought of as "monopolies."

E. CONCLUDING REMARKS

SIMPLE MONOPOLY VERSUS DISCRIMINATING MONOPOLY

The foregoing chapter has treated in turn the definition of single-firm monopoly, the analysis of monopolistic determination of price, output, product, technique, and so forth, and the evaluation of predicted monopoly performance from the standpoint of its impact on aggregate welfare. It should now be appropriate to point out that the analysis of monopolistic price-output determination, from which several crucial predictions are developed, has rested on some explicit and implicit assumptions concerning the character of the monopolist's market, subject to which the monopolist's price-output policy can be of only a very simple sort. These assumptions are probably fairly descriptive of actual conditions in many monopolistic and quasi-monopolistic industries, so that the resulting analysis should have direct applicability to much actual monopoly pricing. Moreover, so far as alternative market conditions are encountered in monopoly, which require basing an analysis on somewhat revised assumptions, it will appear that the simple monopoly analysis already developed has revealed, nevertheless, the most important tendencies in price-output determination found in monopolies facing most other types of markets. However, it is true that under market characteristics alternative to those assumed in the preceding analysis, monopoly price-output determination may be somewhat more complicated in character, and it may reveal *added* tendencies—in addition to those already revealed in the simple monopoly analysis. It is thus desirable that at this point we should specify the limiting assumptions on which the preceding analysis rests and should indicate the character of alternative assumptions which may be more appropriate to some actual monopoly situations.

A first assumption on which the preceding analysis has explicitly rested is that the monopolist is facing a market in which there are many small buyers, each of whom buys so little of the total industry output that by varying his purchases he can have no perceptible influence on total industry sales or on the industry price at which a given output will sell. Each buyer is thus so unimportant that he is in no position to induce the monopolist to make him any concession in price. He thus takes any of a range of alternative prices quoted by the monopolist as given, and—if permitted to do so by the monopolist—he freely adjusts his purchases to that price, presumably so as to bring the marginal satisfaction or benefit from the final unit purchased into balance with that price. In this case each buyer puts forth a conventional demand scheduled for the product, and the monopolist faces a genuine market demand schedule for his output, showing alternative amounts buyers will take at alternative prices he sets. The whole of the preceding analysis rests on this many-buyer assumption and on its implications concerning the existence of a market demand curve. If, alternatively, the monopolist should face a market with one or a few buyers, one or more of whom bought a significant share of industry output, the analysis would have to be revised, for in this case an individual buyer or a few buyers would probably be able to influence the selling price by bargaining with the monopolist and would do this instead of essentially holding forth a demand schedule of offers to buy at alternative prices. Then monopolistic price determination might be quite different than in the many-buyer case. Although fewness of buyers is evidently not the typical case (at least in commodity markets), this variant of monopoly pricing is sufficiently important to require separate treatment. We will discuss it in Chapters 8 and 9 below, under the heading of *bilateral monopoly* (one seller versus one buyer—the archetype of this situation).

The assumption of many buyers and of the existence of a given market demand schedule is fundamental to the preceding analysis. Given this, the monopolist may proceed to choose among prices on the supposition that a determinate amount of purchases corresponds to each, a fact which gives rise to a determinate marginal receipts curve which shows the effects on total receipts of setting various alternative prices. But this is not the only assumption; two implicit assumptions have also been made.

First, it has been implicitly supposed that the monopolist is effectively limited in dealing with buyers simply to setting a market price for his output and supplying each buyer with what he chooses to buy at this price, or, what is the same thing, to offering a given market supply to buyers in general and permitting their competition to determine the market price at which it will be bought. In either case he is thus limited to the schedule of price-quantity alternatives shown on the market demand curve. This presupposes that each buyer is free to adjust to any going market price by buying as much as he wants at that price. The monopolist can thus set price p, and let buyers take the quantity q they want at this price, or he can instead set the lower price p', and let buyers take the larger amount q' they desire, etc.

Now if this is the case, the monopolist is obviously not getting every dollar he could from buyers for various quantities he sells. This is because any buyer, left free to adjust to a market price, will presumably extend purchases to where the added satisfaction derived from the last unit purchased is equal to the added satisfaction available from goods which could be bought with the same money (the price of the good). But the *total satisfaction* from all units the buyer purchases should then exceed the satisfaction obtainable elsewhere from the *total outlay* made on the good (price times quantity bought) since the satisfaction from units prior to the last one bought should be (according to the principle of diminishing marginal satisfaction) greater than that of the last. If this is so, then the monopolist, in charging the same market price for all units, is not exacting all the buyer would be willing to pay—he should hypothetically be able to exact a greater outlay than the going price times the quantity bought. Thus, suppose the monopolist sets a price of $1 and the buyer freely elects to buy ten units at this price, for a total outlay of $10. The satisfaction of the last unit of the ten to him is presumably one dollar's worth—that is, the added satisfaction one dollar would bring elsewhere. But the satisfaction of the ninth unit of the ten may be 1⅛ dollars' worth, of the eighth 1¼ dollars' worth, etc., so that the total satisfaction from the ten units may be, let us say, 17 dollars' worth—in the sense that it would take $17 to acquire elsewhere the satisfaction which would be lost if he were deprived of the good altogether. Then, the monopolist, if he could drive this buyer to a corner and make him an "all-or-nothing" bargain, should be able to exact up to $17 for ten units, or an average price of $1.70.

The ability of the monopolist to do this to each buyer in turn, which is frequently referred to as an ability to practice *first-degree price discrimination,* would result in a substantial increase in his average price and his profits. It would also result in a substantial alteration of the output which he would finally produce, since implicitly he would now be able to sell added units to any buyer without reducing the price he could receive for previous units, and his marginal receipts curve would not fall below the demand curve as it does with simple monopolistic price determination.

It follows that our preceding analysis, based on the assumption that the monopolist just sets a price and lets buyers adjust (and does try to exact the maximum attainable total outlay for any quantity bought) is not accurately descriptive of monopoly price-output determination where first-degree price discrimination can be practiced. How serious a limitation is this on the applicability of the "simple-monopoly" price analysis we have developed? For the many-buyer markets to which it refers the limitation is probably not serious. With many buyers for a commodity, establishment of the degree of direct contact with each buyer necessary for the driving of an all-or-nothing bargain may be quite impractical or unduly expensive to carry out. The same may apply to indirect devices for approximating first-degree discrimination, such as "stair-step" pricing, which would permit a buyer a few units at a high price, a few more at a slightly lower price, a few more at a lower price still, etc. (In this case, unless an absolute quantity limit were placed on every buyer, resale of units by buyers could also make such discrimination unworkable.) Finally, the antitrust law would generally frown on such practices and discourage sellers from attempting them. The simple-monopoly analysis thus probably does not lose applicability very much because of the actual or potential existence of cases of first-degree discrimination in many-buyer markets. Nevertheless, there may be certain market conditions especially favorable to the practice of this sort of discrimination, and when we shift to markets with one or a few buyers, the feasibility is greatly enhanced. It will thus be necessary, in Chapter 9 below, to consider this case of discriminating monopoly further.

A second implicit assumption of the preceding analysis supposes a further restriction on the alternatives open to the monopolist. That is, not only is he limited to setting a market price and permitting buyers to adjust to it, but he is able to set only a *single* market price available to all buyers. It is supposed that he cannot separate his buyers into submarkets and set different prices for different groups of buyers. The seller can set, among alternative prices p, p_1, and p_2, only one of these prices, permitting all buyers to adjust to it; he cannot set, for example, the price p_1 for some of his buyers, while at the same time he sets the price p_2 for the rest of them. An obvious alternative situation is one in which the monopolist could by some device separate his buyers into two or more submarkets and charge different prices in them. If the elasticities of the demand curves in the different submarkets had a certain difference, the monopolist could then increase his profit by setting different prices, and, therefore, he presumably would engage in this sort of price discrimination. If he did so, he would engage in what has been called *third-degree price discrimination*—the setting of different prices in different submarkets for the same good or closely related goods.

To what extent is our preceding analysis oversimplified by omitting consideration of this pattern of price discrimination? It should be noted first that third-degree price discrimination is feasible under some but not all conditions. To succeed in setting different prices for a single good in two different submarkets, the monopolist must have a means of separating groups of buyers systematically, and also he must possess a good which cannot readily be resold by one group of buyers to the other, since if it were, buyers in the low-price market would tend to supply those in the high-price market and obliterate any intended price difference. Physical characteristics of the good which preclude retransfer after initial delivery—such as immediate perishability (found in the case of electric power), high shipping costs to the other market, or supervision by the seller throughout the period of use—are generally necessary if resale is to be forestalled and effective discrimination permitted. Since these conditions are absent more frequently than not, discriminatory pricing of a single good is probably not the most usual case. An equivalent of this sort of discrimination, however, may be possible even where transfer is easy. The monopolist may, with no need of segregating buyers, find separate submarkets for different varities or qualities of a given type of good—inherent in differences among buyers' preference patterns—and find it possible to sell to these different market segments with differences in price substantially greater than the differences in the costs of the goods with which they are supplied. At the same time retransfer may not be a problem because of established preference patterns. If this version of third-degree price discrimination is taken into account, discrimination in monopolistic markets may tend to occur more frequently. Thus, it may be concluded that although discriminatory pricing will probably not tend to be universal in monopoly, it may tend to emerge in a significant share of cases. If this is so, our analysis of simple-monopoly pricing, with one price only, is not fully adequate to all actual or possible monopoly cases, although it may be to a good many of them. An analysis should evidently be developed of third-degree price discrimination by monopoly, and this will be done in Chapter 9 below.

It may be indicated, however, that subsequent analysis will show that the basic tendencies of monopolistic pricing with third-degree discrimination are not essentially different from those of simple monopoly. Price differences among groups of buyers tend to emerge—some paying more and some less than under simple monopoly in most cases—and profits are thereby enhanced. Since in each separate submarket, however, the monopolist is still restricted to setting a price to which buyers may adjust (thus necessarily lowering the price of all units to extend sales), the same output-restrictive tendencies remain as in simple monopoly. The analysis of third-degree price discrimination by monopoly will thus reveal elaborations of, but few basic changes in, the predictions of the simple-monopoly analysis. This is not so true of the analysis of first-degree discrimination alluded to above, which will also be discussed in Chapter 9 below.

In sum, our analysis of simple-monopoly pricing provides a good first approximation to an adequate and comprehensive theory of monopoly price-output determination. Elaborations and exceptions may be treated later.

EMPIRICAL EVIDENCE OF MONOPOLY BEHAVIOR

In preceding sections we have appraised the general significance of monopoly behavior for the welfare of the economy, at least so far as it can be determined by exploring the logic of monopolist's price and output policies. The conclusions we have arrived at concerning how monopolies act, of course, have an abstract basis. They are reached by describing the relevant market conditions faced by the monopolist in a series of assumptions and then by deducing the course of monopoly action directed at maximizing profits. It is interesting to inquire whether these conclusions are supported by evidence of actual behavior by monopolists.

One of the more complete studies of a single-firm monopoly concerns the aluminum industry, where from before 1900 and until the time of World War II the Aluminum Company of America (Alcoa) had a substantial single-firm monopoly in the production of virgin aluminum ingots for the

United States market.[10] This monopoly was at first secured by a patent on the basic extraction process, which expired in 1909. Thereafter, monopoly was maintained largely by Alcoa's substantial control of the necessary ore reserves and by an alert policy in dealing with potential new entrants to the industry. Foreign competition was excluded up to a certain margin by tariff and otherwise (it has been alleged) by international agreements among aluminum producers. In any event, the monopoly continued secure until the outbreak of World War II, when the government undertook a major expansion of aluminum-producing facilities to meet military needs.

The price policy followed by Alcoa over a long period of years seems to have been roughly consistent with what theory would lead us to expect from a monopoly. Aluminum-ingot prices were on the average high enough to yield excessive profits over a long period. On the other hand, they were not always high enough to exploit Alcoa's current position fully; during the 1920's Alcoa apparently lowered price and sacrificed immediate profits in order to promote the growth of the demand for aluminum, and thus to enhance future profits.

The scale and rate of utilization of Alcoa's plants seemed, in general, to be consistent with maximum efficiency. The company was by 1930 considerably larger than the minimum size necessary to realize all the economies of large scale, but that it had become large enough to encounter serious diseconomies of large-scale management was not evident. Aluminum output was virtually restricted so far as price was presumably higher than long-run marginal cost.

Alcoa's monopoly was, of course, not complete. As any monopoly must, it had its limits. For aluminum ingot, it faced the growing competition of aluminum scrap metal, which is suitable for some but not all of the uses to which aluminum is put. Some of the products made from aluminum, moreover, which Alcoa produced in integrated operations, faced effective competition by substitutes, whereas others did not. Aluminum electric cable for a time competed with copper cable (until the price ratio became such that copper was excluded), but aluminum alloys for aircraft had no effective substitutes. This led Alcoa to pursue a pricing policy common to monopoly and also theoretically predictable—namely, discrimination among the prices charged to different classes of buyers.

The tendency of monopolies to strive to protect their positions from the intrusion of substitutes is seen in Alcoa's policy toward magnesium, an effective substitute for aluminum in many uses. Together with a foreign company, Alcoa is said to have long had indirect control of patents covering the processes whereby magnesium is extracted, alloyed, and made into a structural metal. These patents were licensed exclusively to a single com-

[10] See Donald H. Wallace, *Market Control in the Aluminum Industry* (Cambridge: Harvard University Press, 1937).

pany for its sole use. The price policy was such that the magnesium price was sufficiently above the aluminum price that magnesium offered no serious competition to aluminum in its major uses. Magnesium production remained insignificant. This situation was altered somewhat when the government undertook to stimulate magnesium production during the war emergency.

There is thus much in the recent history of market behavior in the aluminum industry which is consistent with the general theoretical predictions developed above. It is true, however, that available data do not permit any detailed, precise, or conclusive verification of these predictions.

SINGLE-FIRM MONOPOLY IN THE PUBLIC UTILITY FIELD

In the aluminum industry we find a fairly good example of the behavior of an unregulated single-firm monopoly. Most such monopoly industries in our economy, however, are not free to pursue unregulated price policies but are subjected to public price regulation. These are principally firms in the electric utility, gas utility, water supply, and local transportation fields, which enjoy local monopolies in most areas, and in telephone and telegraph communications. In these industries it has generally been accepted that competitive supply results in a less satisfactory service to consumers or that competition is self-destructive and unstable to no good end. Since the supply of basic consumer necessities is also involved, public authorities (usually state or local governments) have declared such industries to be "natural monopolies" and have helped nature along by granting monopoly franchises to firms in the various localities. In turn, the rates of such utilities have been subjected to regulation by public commissions in order to insure consumers of reasonable prices for the utility services. Type and quality of service are also regulated. Rate regulation generally includes establishment of a "fair" general level of rates, and also fixing the pattern of price discrimination among various classes of users.

Monopoly behavior under regulation may thus be substantially different from that ascribed to unregulated monopoly. Precisely the sort of behavior which is obtained, however, depends strongly upon the attitudes and abilities of regulatory bodies, upon the restrictions placed upon regulation by the courts in protecting the regulated monopolies from "confiscation of property without due process of law," and upon the effect on normal incentives to efficiency and progress of a close limitation of profits. Characterization of the behavior of price and output in regulated monopolies would require much special study. It seems fair to say, however, that not all of the tendencies inherent in monopoly are overcome by regulation as it exists and that purely competitive behavior certainly does not result.

The study of price regulation, however, lies outside the field of this volume. Therefore, we turn next to the problem of the behavior of groups of monopolists.

SUPPLEMENTARY READINGS

KENNETH E. BOULDING, *Economic Analysis*, 2d ed., Chap. 25.

R. F. KAHN, "Some Notes on Ideal Output," *Economic Journal*, vol. 45, pp. 1-35.

JOE S. BAIN, "The Normative Problem in Industrial Regulation," *American Economic Review*, Supplement, March 1943.

CLAIR WILCOX, *Competition and Monopoly in American Industry*, Temporary National Economic Committee, Monograph No. 21, Washington, 1941.

JOSEPH A. SCHUMPETER, *Capitalism, Socialism, and Democracy*, New York: Harper & Brothers, 1942, Part II.

6 PRICING AND PRICE POLICY IN OLIGOPOLISTIC MARKETS

The single-firm monopoly is important in the public utility sphere in the United States, but it has had minor significance in mining, manufacture, or elsewhere. Likewise, purely competitive market structures are relatively uncommon, at least outside of the field of agriculture. The typical industry in the United States—especially in the areas of processing or manufacture, contract construction, and the distributive and service trades—falls somewhere between the poles of single-firm monopoly and pure competition. It departs from the conditions of pure competition either in that the sellers are not many and small or in that their products are not perfect substitutes —or in both—but it does not reach the situation of a single seller controlling the entire industry output. The usual structural condition in these areas is that there are a number of sellers in the industry, each of whom sells a product which is a close but not a perfect substitute for that of other sellers and which he can protect from exact or very close imitation. Thus, each seller has what might be called a "degree of monopoly" in his own product. In addition, it is very frequently true that not every seller is so small as to supply an insignificant share of the aggregate industry output; instead, one or more sellers may supply a substantial fraction of the output, and a few sellers may supply much or most of the output. This is extremely common in manufacturing industries and also in some of the distributive trades. Finally, it is not uncommon that an established group of a few sellers may "share a monopoly position," in the sense that there are barriers protecting them as a group from the entry of outsiders to their industry.

The large number of industries which lie between the extremes of pure competition and single-firm monopoly may be subdivided into a number of categories. In Chapter 2 above we have placed them in three such categories.

1. *Monopolistic competition.* This is found in the industry where there is a large number of small sellers, selling differentiated but close-substitute products. Since each seller supplies a small fraction of the market, any feasible output, and corresponding price, variation by any of them will presumably have no perceptible effect on the price or sales of his competitors and will elicit no response from any of his competitors. Thus, there is no

direct interfirm interdependence or rivalry. However, concurrent output-price variations by many or most of such sellers will affect the sales or prices of remaining sellers, so that they are in effect bound together by competition.

2. *Pure oligopoly*. This is found in its simplest form when a few sellers, producing identical products, supply the entire output of an industry and where each supplies a significant fraction thereof. The output-price variations of each, thus, will distinctly affect the sales or prices of the others and will tend to induce responses so that there will be a recognized rivalry among all sellers. Unless further subcategories are established, the category must also include all homogeneous-product markets wherein one or more sellers (ordinarily a few) control significant shares of the industry output, the remaining sellers being either large or small. In general, the category is charatcerized by the existence of one or more sellers controlling enough of industry output to cause it (them) to react if others alter their outputs and prices.

3. *Differentiated oligopoly*. This is similar to pure oligopoly in that some or all sellers control significant fractions of the market but different in that the products of the several sellers are close but not perfect substitutes. Consequently, there is recognized rivalry among some or all sellers, but, in addition, each enjoys the individual degree of monopoly imparted by product differentiation. In general, differentiated oligopoly may be considered a general category of which pure oligopoly is a limiting subcase. This view is reasonable in light of the fact that in nearly all oligopolistic markets there is at least some slight degree of product differentiation among rival sellers.

In the present chapter we shall consider the determination of price, output, and related matters in oligopolistic markets of both types. (The case of monopolistic competition will be discussed in Chapter 7.) The major analytical problem in the case of oligopoly is to discover the tendency of price-output determination in a market where sellers supplying some or all of the industry output have a recognized interdependence and rivalry. Before turning to this analysis, however, we should first consider (1) the several possible distinct subcategories of oligopoly and (2) the bases, or reasons for emergence, of oligopoly in many industries.

A. TYPES OF OLIGOPOLY; REASONS FOR ITS EMERGENCE

SUBCATEGORIES OF OLIGOPOLY

As previously indicated, oligopoly has been implicitly used in our system of market classification to refer to all industries in which there is neither (1) a large number of very small sellers or (2) a single monopolistic seller. Thus, though to a first approximation it may be thought of as referring to industries "with a few sellers," it more generally comprehends every case in which one or more sellers control significant shares of industry output. It is, therefore, evident that the oligopoly category must potentially include a large variety of situations which differ among themselves with respect to the *degree of seller concentration,* or number-and-size-distribution of sellers. There may be signicant differences among oligopolies with respect to the total number of sellers in the market, to their relative size, and to whether or not there are some sellers which individually control insignificant shares of the market. Although there are manifold possible subcategories of oligopoly as distinguished on the basis of seller concentration, it may suffice to identify only a few principal types most commonly found in American industry. These may be designated as:

1. Industries with a very few sellers only (and no small sellers), with each seller controlling a significant share of the market. For example, five sellers control the entire market in equal or varying proportions.
2. Industries where a very few sellers control the great bulk of industry output—and a small number of small sellers divide the remainder.
3. Industries with a moderately few sellers only. For example, ten to twenty sellers supply the total industry output, and each a significant share of it.
4. Industries where a very few or a moderately few sellers control the bulk of the industry output and where a substantial number of small sellers share the remainder. For example, seven large sellers supply 85 percent of the industry output and 35 small sellers divide the remainder; or, four large sellers supply 60 percent of industry output, and 200 small sellers share the remainder.
5. Industries where one seller supplies a large share of the industry output, the remainder being shared by a large number of small firms (a limiting case).

Oligopoly, whether of the pure or the differentiated variety, may include all of these subcases as well as intermediate and adjacent subcases not specified. And it seems quite probable that there may be distinct differences in price-output behavior as among these subcases. It is correspondingly difficult to develop any single simple theory of oligopoly pricing which will apply equally to all of these subcategories as distinguished on the basis of seller concentration. It is true, however, that all oligopoly cases (excepting the limiting case 5 above, which is rare in fact) have one thing in common— the domination of price-output determination by the recognized interdependence and rivalry of a few large firms, whose policies as determined in the light of this interdependence will tend to "set the pace" for the industry. Thus, it is possible to ascertain certain central tendencies of pricing in oligopolistic markets by analyzing price making in simple few-seller cases of the variety of (1) or (3). Thereafter, it is necessary to consider the alterations in this analysis which are required if a competitive fringe of a few or many small sellers is present in the market. We shall follow this procedure in the present chapter.

So far we have suggested that oligopolistic industries may be divided into (I) pure oligopolies and (II) differentiated oligopolies. Further, either (I) or (II) may be divided into oligopolies of (A) high concentration among a few sellers and (B) moderate concentration among a few sellers; and (A) and (B) may in each case be subdivided into oligopolies (1) without competitive fringes and (2) with competitive fringes. There is at least one further characteristic of oligopolistic industries upon the basis of which they may be meaningfully subdivided; this has already been suggested by the preceding analysis of single-firm monopoly. This characteristic is the *condition of entry* to the industry or, in effect, the height of the barrier which established firms can place in the way of potential entrants wishing to enter the industry. Although numerous entry conditions can be imagined and do exist, we may provisionally draw a simple distinction between (a) oligopolies of "blockaded entry," where established sellers can jointly charge a price which will maximize industry profits without attracting entry, and (b) oligopolies subject to a threat of entry, where pursuance of such a price policy would result in the attraction of additional firms to the industry. As in the case of single-firm monopoly, the analysis of pricing must recognize this significant potential difference among oligopolies, along with the others already mentioned.

REASONS FOR THE EMERGENCE OF OLIGOPOLY

The term oligopoly, as we have found, refers typically to an industry in which a few sellers supply all or much of the total industry output and where each of several sellers supplies a significant fraction of this output. The oligopolistic industry is thus clearly distinguished from the *atomistic* industry—found in pure or monopolistic competition—in which there are many sellers and none of them supplies much of the total industry output. A question may, therefore, be raised as to *why* many industries become and remain oligopolistic, whereas others remain atomistic in structure.

For oligopoly to emerge and remain in an industry it is obviously necessary either (1) that a few firms secure a dominant position in the industry from the date of its origin and protect this position against the inroads of established or potential competitors, or (2) if the industry has been initially atomistic in structure, that a few firms later secure and retain control of a dominant share of the market. The latter may in turn be accomplished either by the *growth* of a few firms at the expense of their many competitors, securing a larger and larger share of the market by various competitive devices, or by the *merger* or consolidation of numbers of smaller firms into large firms. In the history of the American economy we find the emergence of oligopoly in all three ways—initially with the inception of the industry, by the growth to dominant size of a few firms, and by merger.

This explains *how* oligopoly emerges but not *why*. It would appear that there are a number of contributing reasons for the emergence of oligopoly and that one or several of them may have operated in various individual industries. One important factor is the economy of large-scale production. In many industries a relatively small number of firms may be able to supply the entire market at a lower cost than more firms could attain—the output of one optimal-scale firm representing a substantial fraction of total industry demand. In these instances there is a competitive advantage in cost to the firm or firms which can grow to dominant size, or to merger, which by pooling the resources of a number of small firms can attain the economies of large scale. Where such economies have been important, therefore, it is not surprising that a few large firms have been dominant from the outset, or alternatively that competition has driven out all but a few large firms, which survived by attaining the lower costs of large scale, or that mergers have created a few dominant firms. It seems unlikely, however, that economies of scale furnish the only explanation of the emergence of oligopoly. Three other explanations may be mentioned as of independent or contributing importance.

First, existing firms in an industry may find it to their advantage to merge or consolidate in order to eliminate competition among themselves and to bring about a sufficiently concentrated structure within the industry that competition among remaining sellers may be more easily suppressed. In short, the profits of restricted competition may serve as an incentive to the accomplishment of oligopoly by mergers. Second, a few firms in some cases obtain a dominant advantage of product differentiation, such that buyers prefer their products to other varieties of the same good sufficiently that they are able to secure a major share of the market against all competitors. Third, a few firms may secure strategic absolute advantage in cost over all others which permits them to operate profitably at a price at which the others cannot survive. Then they may appropriate the whole market while remaining competitors are eliminated. Absolute advantages of this sort may be obtained by securing patents on the most economical techniques of production, by acquiring complete control of strategic raw material supplies, or by other legal or institutional devices.

Any of these three explanations of the emergence of oligopoly, or that of the economies of large-scale production, may have applied in individual cases where oligopoly has developed. Frequently, two or more such considerations have operated simultaneously. In view of the variety of contributing causes and the difference in their relative importance in different cases, it is difficult to predict in advance just what pattern of seller concentration will be found when oligopoly does develop. Further, there is no particular reason to believe that the degree of concentration attained will be just that required for greatest efficiency in production. Mergers to restrict competition, or secular growth of concerns, may result in the emergence of firms much larger than required for the lowest-cost production, and growth of firms because of various legal advantages may have little relationship to efficiency. Finally, the degree of concentration within oligopolies may change through time as the result of differential rates of growth of established firms, new entry, new mergers, etc. For purposes of a priori analysis it is convenient to do no more than to recognize the current existence of many oligopolies and to analyze the character of their present behavior and probable future development starting from this point.

Nevertheless, it is true that historically the structure of many of our oligopolistic industries has remained relatively stable over considerable periods of time and that this stability of structure requires explanation. Relatively stable oligopolistic structure seems necessarily to result from the existence of certain barriers to entry which protect a group of established firms, permitting them to operate profitably without inducing many new firms to enter the industry and share the market. These barriers to entry are in general correlative in character to the considerations which account for the emergence of oligopoly, and include:

1. Absolute cost advantages of established over potential entrant firms. These result from legal and institutional barriers to entry in the form of patents on strategic techniques, control of strategic material supplies, etc.
2. Product differentiation advantages of established firms. These are found when the brand names, sales outlets, and past advertising campaigns of established firms permit them to maintain a lion's share of the market against all potential competition without disadvantage in cost, or places potential entrants at a cost disadvantage if they are to secure equivalent market shares.
3. Advantages to established firms resulting from economies of scale. Where scale economies are very important, a new firm of efficient size would be quite large, and its entry might saddle the industry with overcapacity and possibly engender destructive competition. Hence, the large investment required for entry may not be risked.

One or more of these barriers to entry will ordinarily be present when oligopoly survives in stable fashion through time, although, as we have already seen, such barriers may be of varying height,[1] and the height of the barrier may be an important determinant of the price policies of established oligopolists.

From the preceding account of the causes of emergence of oligopoly and of the barriers to entry which permit its maintenance, it is clear that economies of large-scale production may vary widely in importance from case to case as a basis for oligopoly. It has become fashionable recently to divide all oligopolies into two main classes according to the importance of such economies—that is, into (1) oligopolies in which the economies of scale are so important that a substantially larger number of firms could not supply the industry demand without incurring significantly higher average costs and (2) oligopolies in which scale economies are unimportant, so that an atomistic or much less concentrated structure could be had without significantly higher costs. Although this dichotomous classification drastically oversimplifies the real situation and omits many intermediate cases, we shall bear in mind the broad distinction it emphasizes when we consider the public-policy problems raised by oligopolistic price behavior.

B. PRICE AND OUTPUT DETERMINATION IN DIFFERENTIATED OLIGOPOLY

FUNDAMENTAL CONSIDERATIONS

Let us now turn to the analysis of price-output determination in oligopoly. For purposes of simplification we shall refer to a simple archetype of oligopoly (among the numerous possible variants) in which a very few firms—for example, five firms—of equal size supply the entire market. (We shall remark later on any modifications in the analysis required for different patterns of oligopolistic concentration). We shall also deal initially with the general case of differentiated oligopoly—where the product of each seller is a close but not perfect substitute for those of the others—referring later to the special case of pure oligopoly. In the course of the analysis we shall consider both cases where the oligopolists enjoy an effective blockade of entry and where they are subject to an effective threat of entry.

A large number of the markets for manufactured and processed goods fall in the *differentiated oligopoly* category. The following is a partial list of familiar industries with this sort of structure: automobiles, rubber tires, gasoline and allied products, electric refrigerators, radio sets, electric razors, vacuum cleaners, soap and soap chips, cigarettes, fountain pens, prepared

---

[1] If an oligopoly is found where there is literally no barrier to the entry of new sellers, it is likely to evolve toward atomistic structure through time. This is a possibility if the only rationale of the original oligopoly was a merger to restrict competition among existing firms.

breakfast food, aircraft, farm machinery, distilled beverage liquors. The problem before us is what sort of price and output policies characterize industries of this kind.

We may begin our analysis along the usual lines by inquiring into the character of the demand curve for the output of each individual oligopolist. The following general propositions seem obvious at the outset.

First, the single oligopolist with a differentiated product—for example, the seller of a brand of electric razors with a distinctive and protected design and other substantial or ephemeral distinguishing qualities—will evidently

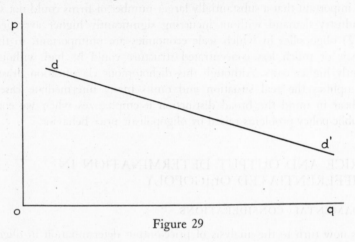

Figure 29

have a definite *ceteris paribus* demand curve for his own output, showing that there would be a definite relation of his price to his volume of sales *if the prices of his rivals were given and unchanging*. Such a *ceteris paribus* demand curve might appear as in Figure 29. Although this demand curve seems to resemble that of a single-firm monopolist, in reality it differs decidedly. If the prices of all other products, and especially of close-substitute products, were given, the oligopolist's demand curve would be generally much more elastic than the single-firm monopolist's. The oligopolist's product has close substitutes and the single-firm monopolist's product does not. If the oligopolist lowers his price *and if other prices are unchanged,* he will gain sales rapidly as buyers shift from other products to his. Conversely, if he raises price independently and other prices are unchanged, his sales will fall off markedly as his customers shift to rival sellers. The demand for the oligopolist's product would thus be very sensitive to his *independent and unmatched* price changes.

Second, this *ceteris paribus* demand curve for the oligopolist's output will, however, not represent the actual response of his sales to his price changes or be of much relevance to his pricing decisions, because he cannot assume in general that other sellers' prices will remain practically unchanged in the face of price changes by himself. Any significant gain in sales he makes by reducing prices will be at the expense of a recognized and significant loss in sales by some rival or rivals, for if each of a few sellers supplies a significant share of a common market, none of them can expand his market share greatly without noticeably reducing the sales of the others. The oligopolist, therefore, in general must assume that any price change he makes will set in course retaliatory or compensatory price changes by his rivals and that these reactions will affect the demand for his own product quite sub-stantially. The actual demand curve for the oligopolist's output—which shows the net effect of his price changes on his sales volume—will be one which registers the effects on his sales both of his own price changes and of the reactions in his rivals' prices which his own price changes induce. It is not a *ceteris paribus* demand curve, as shown in Figure 29, showing the response of one sales quantity to one price, but a *mutatis mutandis* demand curve, showing the response of one sales quantity to simultaneous changes in several prices—one leading and the rest induced.

Third, this actual demand curve for the oligopolist's output—reflecting the effects of induced price changes by rivals—can be viewed as definite, cer-tain, or uniquely determinate *only if* the character of rivals' reactions to the individual oligopolist's price changes can be definitely predicted or known. If the reactions of his rivals are determinate or definitely predictable, the oligopolist has a definite demand curve for his output. If they are inde-terminate or not definitely predictable, the oligopolist does not have a uniquely determined demand curve for his output; rather he has a range of uncertainty regarding his demand curve, or a series of alternative con-jectures concerning the probable reactions of rivals to his own price changes.

The preceding outlines the general problem concerning the firm's demand in oligopoly. The primary questions to be answered are (1) does the firm in general have a determinate demand curve or an uncertain demand curve for its output; (2) if it is a determinate demand curve, what pattern of rivals' reactions to price changes does it reflect; and (3) in either case what sort of price-output determination results from oligopolists' adjustments to their demands as they conceive of them? Analysis of these questions re-quires some consideration of the fundamental logic of oligopoly pricing.

In appraising the character of the demand curve for each oligopolist's output, a first consideration to be kept in mind is that the prices and sales volumes of the several oligopolists in an industry are directly interdependent and that this fact will evidently be mutually recognized by all of them. Every oligopolist, when he changes his price, will do so in anticipation of price reactions by his rivals, and he will decide whether or not to change his price in terms of the reactions he expects. Likewise, each of his rivals will presumably know that this oligopolist has calculated in this fashion and will view any initial price change by him as tentative, conditioned upon some expected reaction, and subject to withdrawal if this reaction is not forthcoming. In a sense, any price change by a single oligopolist may be viewed by his rivals as an invitation to make certain acceptable reactions in price or to concur tacitly in a certain acceptable course of mutual action. Thus, no oligopolist can really make prices independently; each is bound to the others in a web of interdependence.[2]

In this circumstance independent or "lone-wolf" tactics tend to be discouraged. No seller can engage in price cutting, for example, without the practical certainty of some retaliation by rivals; any seller who raises his price may be implicitly inviting his rivals to do likewise. Therefore, it is not impossible that a group of oligopolists, each recognizing his interdependence with the others, will strike upon some determinate and mutually satisfactory pattern of reactions to each other's price changes and that determinate demand curves for each will correspondingly emerge. But it is by no means certain that they will do so. To determine the likelihood that some systematic pattern of reactions—and, therefore, of price-determining behavior—will emerge, we must examine the basic motivations of sellers in an oligopolistic market (and in markets generally) and inquire how these motivations will influence their pricing behavior.

CONFLICTING ATTITUDES OF SELLERS

In oligopoly, as in fact in any market, two opposing attitudes of sellers would seem continually to be in operation. First, the several sellers in the oligopoly have an obvious common interest in maximizing the *joint profit* which together they receive from the industry. The greater the combined profit that the five sellers in our hypothetical oligopoly can make, the larger the profit "pie" that they have to divide among them. Thus, they have a definite incentive to act together, jointly or collusively, "as a single-firm monopolist would," to reap the largest possible joint profit from their combined operations. This motivation is presumably just as present among the many sellers in an atomistic industry as among the few in an oligopolistic industry, but its relevance in an oligopolistic market is much more evident. In an atomistic industry the firms are so numerous that effective collusion for joint monopoly action is next to impossible to organize, and concurrent movement toward monopoly price by all firms is discouraged by the fact that each in turn can undercut such a price to his advantage and without the danger of inducing retaliation by others. But in oligopoly the small number of firms favors collusive efforts, and each firm controls enough of the market that it is effectively unable to depart from a joint monopoly price without attracting notice and retaliation. When every firm knows this, all may be

[2] Cf. William Fellner, *Competition Among the Few* (New York: Alfred A. Knopf, 1949), Chap. I.

willing to participate in a joint monopoly program, since each is able to "police" the others in their observance of the program. Thus, in oligopoly the desire of all sellers for joint profit maximization is strategic, since such a policy is feasible as well as desirable.

If this desire were dominant and unalloyed with others, then a determinate pattern of reactions to rivals' price changes, and a determinate pattern of price behavior, could be expected in oligopoly. That is, any seller could increase his price toward the monopoly or joint-profit-maximizing level with assurance that all of his rivals would follow him, or, alternatively, all sellers would enter into a collusive agreement for joint exploitation of the industry demand curve for maximum joint profits. In either case we might say alternatively (1) that the individual sellers' demand curves had become irrelevant, and that there was simply monopolistic exploitation of the industry demand curve, or (2) that each seller's demand curve had become in a sense implicitly *a fraction or share of the industry demand curve*,[3] showing the amounts he would sell at various alternative prices on the supposition that all of his rivals always exactly matched his prices and he theirs.

If joint profit maximization were the only relevant motive of oligopolists, therefore, there would in effect be a determinate demand curve for every seller (or for all sellers acting together), and also a simple system of price-output determination, corresponding closely to that attributed to single-firm monopoly. There is, however, a second general attitude of oligopolistic sellers which greatly complicates any such simple tendency. This is essentially an attitude of fundamental antagonism with respect to the shares of the combined industry profit which each seller is to receive. Although the several sellers have an incentive to act like one firm for joint profit maximization, they are not one firm. They represent diverse and fundamentally antagonistic ownership interests, each of which would presumably like to have all of the industry profit for itself, or at any rate as much as possible. This fundamental antagonism of the diverse ownership interests has important consequences for oligopolistic behavior.

First, if there is some tendency to approach a joint-profit-maximizing policy, there is no automatic or easy way of arriving at an express or tacit agreement as to the sharing of this profit or of the sales volume from which it is derived. Irreconcilable conflict on this point *may* preclude the consummation of any agreement or forestall a course of action tantamount to it. Alternatively, it may preclude the consummation of the *most profitable* agreement or course of joint action, as some or all of the oligopolists are unwilling to commit themselves to the mercies of fundamentally antagonistic rivals (whom they therefore distrust) to the extent necessary for maximiza-

---

[3] That is, each seller would have some determinate fraction of the total industry sales volume at any of a range of alternate prices which he and his rivals concurrently charged.

tion of joint profits. Second, if the fundamental antagonism and resulting distrust are sufficient that no movement toward joint profit maximization eventuates, a stalemate, with each seller unwilling or afraid of cooperation with the others, or alternatively aggressive price rivalry in which one or more attempts to eliminate the others, is quite possible. Third, even if some express or tacit agreement is reached (perhaps with reservations which lessen its profitability), deviation from its terms, or "chiseling" by one or more of the several sellers, may periodically disrupt it as they try to gain an edge on the others by clandestine price cutting or similar tactics.

There is a definite parallel between the relations of several oligopolists contemplating an agreement or course of joint action on price and output and the relations of several nations contemplating a treaty for mutual government of certain of their activities. All the nations may stand to increase their welfare by a treaty with certain provisions. But disagreement over division of the resulting advantages may forestall the writing of any treaty, or if not may result in weakening its provisions. The reluctance of each nation to yield much of its sovereignty to a joint government it distrusts may have a similar effect. Any treaty when written may be denounced without notice or violated without notification. And war may even be declared. If this parallel is clearly understood, the fundamental complications in predicting a course of behavior for rival oligopolists may be more clearly appreciated.

Given the combination of (1) the desire by all for joint profit maximization, and (2) the fundamental antagonism among rival firms concerning division of the spoils and the control of the market, and resultant mutual distrust, it is clearly not possible to predict any unique pattern of pricing behavior, or of rivals' reactions to each other's price changes, in oligopoly. We cannot simply say that there will be concurrent pricing for monopoly results and determinate demand curves for each seller. There is a fundamental uncertainty concerning the course of oligopolistic behavior which inheres in an uncertainty concerning where the balance between the two conflicting forces outlined will be struck. Unless, or until, we can specify their relative importance and what determines it, we cannot say more in theory of oligopoly behavior and of oligopolists' demand conditions than that they may assume a range of alternative forms depending on the balance of these conflicting forces.

It follows that the succeeding analysis of oligopoly price-output determination must consist mainly of the specification of some typical alternative patterns of behavior possible in oligopolistic markets, together with comments on forms of behavior that seem to be common in fact. The principal patterns to be considered range from complete uncertainty and possibly chaotic rivalry at one extreme to effective and closely observed collusion at the other. In each case some different assumption concerning the character of the individual oligopolist's demand curve is appropriate.

UNCERTAINTY AND STALEMATE

One general possibility for oligopoly behavior is that the forces of antagonism and distrust among rivals are so strong that no collusive agreement among sellers is possible and that no regular pattern of reactions to rivals' price changes becomes established. Then every seller must price independently, and further he must remain in a state of genuine uncertainty concerning the reactions in his rivals' prices which his own price changes will elicit. This situation might persist indefinitely in an industry, but it is thought to be more typical of new industries in which the rival sellers have not had sufficient time to reconcile their differences or learn each other's habits.

If such a situation of uncertainty prevails, the individual seller obviously has no determinate demand curve for his output; rather he has a series of alternative conjectures as to the possible reactions of his rivals to either price cuts or price increases which he may make, and correspondingly as to how his own price changes will ultimately affect his sales. Under these circumstances no certain pattern of price-output determination can be attributed to oligopolistic markets—the level of price and the size of output are in general logically indeterminate within a considerable range. A stagnant price at some indeterminate level and chaotic price instability are both clear possibilities, depending on the character of the conjectures various sellers make about their rivals' reactions and on the accuracy of these conjectures.

It has been suggested that some light might be thrown on pricing in such a situation by applying to it a mathematical theory of the strategy of games like poker or chess, where each player seeks to avoid the possibility of considerable loss yet gain as much as possible consistent with safety. But it is yet to be shown that useful predictions of oligopoly behavior can be developed in this manner.[4]

One relevant hypothesis which has been advanced relative to situations of uncertainty of the type just described is that firms will attempt to minimize uncertainty by refusing to change price once a reasonably satisfactory level of price is reached—they will not "rock the boat" unnecessarily. If everyone has been charging some going price and comes to know his sales volume there, he may prefer to adhere to it instead of experimenting with his rivals' (and his customers') reactions to new prices. It has thus been suggested that oligopolistic uncertainty is strongly conducive to policies of *price rigidity*. Any price position at which independently acting oligopolists arrive

[4] See J. von Neumann and O. Morgenstern, *Theory of Games and Economic Behavior* (Princeton: Princeton University Press, 1944).

which is relatively satisfactory to profits tends to be perpetuated in the face of minor and even major changes in cost and demand.

This tendency toward stalemate at a going price (or one instance of it) has been described diagrammatically in Figure 30. At any moment the independent oligopolist with a differentiated product sells some quantity q at some unexplained price p. If he raises his price above p, he may assume that his rivals *will not* change their prices and that his sales will fall off rapidly along the elastic line dd'. If he reduces his price below p, he may assume that

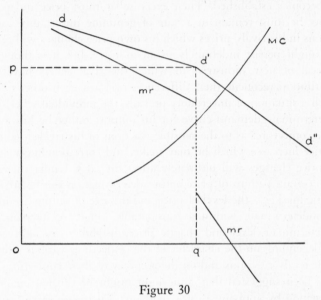

Figure 30

his rivals will match his reduction (or worse), in which case his sales will increase slowly along the less elastic line $d'd''$ (which has the same general elasticity as the "market demand" for the whole industry). Hence, the seller's demand curve is a bent line which bends at the going price p. Correspondingly, his marginal receipts are discontinuous—that is, they are positive and high at prices above p, and they are low or negative at prices below p. Now it *may be* that the seller's MC is less than mr if price is above p and greater than mr if price is below p. If so, the firm will "maximize its profit" by retaining the arbitrary price p, provided that at this price the relation of price to average cost allows what is regarded as a "fair" or satisfactory profit.[5] In this event the prices maintained by the several oligopolists are not such as to maximize their combined profits, which would be increased if they concurrently raised their prices until their marginal costs were equal to a marginal receipts on a curve drawn throughout from the industry demand curve.

[5] See Paul M. Sweezy, "Demand Under Conditions of Oligopoly," *Journal of Political Economy*, vol. 147, pp. 568 ff.

It can be demonstrated, although we shall not do so here, that if this is the pattern of price calculation followed, the rigid price may fall indeterminately anywhere between a joint-profit-maximizing, or monopoly, limit and a competitive limit, but it may not fall outside these limits. Between these limits it will be rigid at any point.

Too much importance, however, could be attributed to this elegant diagram, which rests on one very special set of assumptions concerning each oligopolist's conjectures concerning his rivals' reactions to his price changes. Perhaps, we would do as well simply to say that price rigidity at some indeterminate point within a wide range is a possibility with oligopoly pricing subject to general uncertainty concerning rivals' reactions.

EXPRESS AND TACIT COLLUSION

There is little question but that the effects on pricing and on profits of the situation of uncertainty described above tend to be unsatisfactory to the businessmen affected and that they, therefore, tend to try to overcome the antagonisms and suspicions which give rise to it sufficiently to permit arrival at mutually more satisfactory price policies. This does not argue they must in logic always succeed in doing so, but observation of many industries suggests that they do succeed, at least in a degree, in many instances. Thus, the joint-profit-maximizing motives may dominate the pricing picture, or at least play a strong enough role that uncertainty is eliminated or greatly reduced and that some quasi-monopolistic pricing pattern emerges. Consequently, it is extremely pertinent to examine a second main variant of oligopoly pricing—that of either concurrent or collusive action by all oligopolists for joint exploitation of the industry demand curve.

The technique adopted or developed to secure concurrent or collusive pricing action may vary from the formal agreement to the extremely informal understanding or convention or simply to the development by custom of a pattern of cooperative responses to rivals' price changes which come to be expected as a matter of course. Some of the principal alternatives found in practice are the following:

1. The "cartel," or formal agreement, whereby the rival sellers contract among themselves to set uniform or related prices and often to set output quotas for each seller, together possibly with exclusive market territories, limitations on capacity, etc. At the extreme, a division of profits not based on assigned output volumes may be provided for. Cartels are in a sense a logical solution for oligopolies, and in many countries they are common. They are generally illegal under the American antitrust laws, however; those we have in the United States (except for a few set up under patent licensing privileges) must operate in secrecy and are, of course, not enforceable at

law. As a consequence, American firms in concentrated industries more frequently develop alternative means of securing concurrent pricing action.

2. The *subrosa* collusive agreement covering selling price and possibly division of the market but leaving open competition on matters not covered; for example, a price agreement leaving open rivalry for sales volume via product development, advertising, etc. These are also illegal in the United States, but in a good many industries they have operated from time to time.

3. The convention or custom of *price leadership,* whereby the various sellers in an oligopoly recognize one seller (often the largest) as a "price leader" and follow his price changes closely. Rivalry of a nonprice nature, whereby the individual seller seeks to enhance his share of the market, may be left open. This type of convention has generally been legal in the United States so long as no collusive agreement can be found. It is one of the most common types of pricing convention in all sorts of oligopolies in American industry. When it is well established and long observed, it appears that a sort of *tacit agreement* or unspoken understanding may exist among the participating sellers.

4. The mutual adoption of certain common formulas for computing price, which when used by all sellers will result in identical or closely similar prices. The most familiar formula involves the addition of a customary markup percentage to the average total or average variable cost per unit of output as computed according to certain rules or conventions. Where the several sellers have also adopted a uniform cost-accounting system, this type of action can result in identical prices. Such activity is legal in the United States if no collusion is demonstrable.

5. Finally, some concurrence in price action may be secured if the rival oligopolists simply all follow conservative price policies (each having ascertained by past experience that he may expect his rivals to follow the same convention)—if they change their prices only occasionally and in response to major shifts in costs and follow the habit of just matching their rivals' price changes.[6]

Some of these devices for securing concurrent action in pricing and for introducing relative certainty as to how one price will respond to another involve actual consultation and agreement, oral or written, among the rival sellers. Others represent simply the development of certain patterns of action which all habitually follow because each sees the advantages of concurrent

---

[6] In logic and from observation it is evident that the loose concurrence secured through "mutual respect" works well only where the differentiation of the various sellers' products is substantial enough that the various sellers need not have identical prices in order to maintain some balance in the proportions of the market they hold. Thus various automobiles differ sufficiently (and in a sufficiently unmeasurable fashion) in design, size, and quality, that constant identity of Ford, Chevrolet, and Plymouth prices is not necessary to market stability. Nor is there any necessary steady differential between the Pontiac (General Motors low-medium price class) price and the Chrysler

and cooperative action and comes to believe that his rivals also see it and will act accordingly. The dividing line between devices which involve actual consultation of rivals and those which do not is indeed hazy, since in an oligopolistic market any independent price change by a single oligopolist tends to be read as an "offer" by his rivals, and an acceptable reaction to the price change may be interpreted as an acceptance of the offer by the first firm. Thus, negotiation can perhaps take place through a series of public announcements rather than through meetings of persons, and the meaning of true consensual action becomes vague.

Regardless of whether consensus is involved, however, it is evident that the various devices listed for securing concurrent action may be of widely varying effectiveness as means for attaining maximization of joint profits. Their varying form reflects in part the varying degrees to which the conflict between the cooperative and antagonistic motives of rival oligopolists permits consummation of the most profitable sort of express or tacit agreement. As a consequence, it is impossible to ascribe any single unique sort of result to "collusive" oligopoly pricing in general since it takes so many different forms. Under the general heading of collusive pricing we run the range from "extensive and perfect" collusion (reached or approached under (1) in the list above) to extremely imperfect collusion or concurrence of action of much narrower scope and lesser effectiveness.

The various possibilities of collusive and related forms of behavior in oligopoly are perhaps best described by examining first extreme forms of perfect collusion and then considering the relation of various related forms of behavior which lie between this extreme and that of completely non-collusive uncertainty referred to in the preceding section.

PERFECT COLLUSION AND THE PERFECT CARTEL

The general tendency of oligopolistic price-output determination when there is perfect collusion among the rival sellers is fairly clear. Oligopoly price and output tend to approximate those of a single-firm monopoly, so that the joint profit of the several sellers is maximized. As in the case of single-firm monopoly, however, the character of the profit-maximizing price may vary, depending upon whether or not the established oligopolists are subject to an effective threat of entry. Moreover, the precise meaning of perfect collu-

(Chrysler Corporation high-medium price class) price. In such a situation, loose concurrence in pricing is all that is required to avoid chronic instability. Where the product differentiation is slight, however, constant identity of rival sellers' prices is a condition of market stability. In the gasoline market, for example, a half-cent-per-gallon differential between any two major brands would seriously weaken any "brand monopoly" of the higher-priced seller. In such cases either price leadership or collusion will frequently be resorted to.

sion needs to be specified, and there are at least two variant meanings which deserve separate mention.

The first and most extreme version of perfect collusion is found in what may be designated as the *perfect cartel*. In such a cartel the price and output of the industry, and of each of the separate member firms, are determined solely by a central administrative agency in just such a way as to maximize the joint profit of the member firms. This aggregate profit is then divided among the participating members in some agreed fashion, but not necessarily in the proportions which would result from each selling his own output quota and incurring his own costs. Since the ultimate profit shares do not "follow" the output quotas assigned, these quotas can be determined without regard to their influence on individual firms' revenues but solely in such a way as (1) to minimize the aggregate cost of any industry output produced and (2) to produce just that industry output which maximizes the joint profit of the member firms. In effect, the central cartel office is able to determine the several outputs of the member firms and the price they will charge much as a single-firm monopolist operating several disparate plants would do.

The general principles which will be followed to attain these ultimate profit-maximizing ends are as follows: First, the cartel will learn or estimate the industry demand curve, showing the aggregate quantity which the several oligopolists may sell at each of the alternative prices which they may jointly adopt. (For sake of simplicity, we shall assume a situation where it is most profitable for the several sellers in a differentiated oligopoly always to charge an identical price.) From this industry demand curve may be calculated a marginal receipts curve, showing the additions to industry aggregate receipts for successive additions to industry output. These curves may appear as *DD'* and *MR* in Figure 31.

To maximize the joint profits of the cartel members the cartel administration should calculate that allocation of each successive possible industry output among member firms which will give the lowest possible aggregate cost of producing that output. It will thus identify a minimized industry aggregate cost curve for each output from zero outward and a certain set of quotas for the separate firms at each such output. It should then derive an industry marginal cost curve (drawn from this minimized aggregate cost curve) showing the corresponding addition to cost for each addition to industry output.

Attainment of the lowest aggregate cost for each industry output may imply the shutdown or nonoperation (and eventual dissolution and assimilation by merger by remaining firms) of certain firms, if their costs are too high or if the number of firms is excessive; only that number of firms will remain in operation which is consistent with minimized costs in the relevant output range.

For the firms remaining in operation it is evident that the cost of producing any industry output will be minimized when the output is divided among the firms just so that their individual marginal costs are equal; since if they were not, the last unit could be produced more cheaply by the firm with a lower marginal cost than by that with a higher. Thus, each *successive* industry output will be apportioned in quotas among the operating firms just so that they have equal marginal costs.

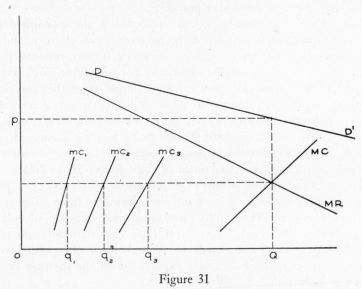

Figure 31

It follows that the combined or industry marginal cost of producing each successive industry output—implicitly marginal to a minimized industry aggregate cost curve—is simply obtained by horizontally adding the several marginal cost curves of the operating firms. Thus, in Figure 31, with three firms supposedly operating for lowest costs, the separate marginal cost curves of the firms are respectively mc_1, mc_2, and mc_3. The industry marginal cost curve is obtained by "adding" these curves together—that is, by taking the sum of the quantity readings on the three at each successive marginal cost level on the vertical scale. This summation is represented in the curve MC, which thus shows the marginal cost to the industry of obtaining each successive addition to industry output from the three firms combined, subject to the condition that the aggregate cost be a minimum for each successive industry output.

To maximize industry profit the cartel will now choose that output at which this minimized industry marginal cost, MC, is equal to industry marginal receipts, MR. This is the output OQ (sold at the price OP) in Figure 31, which will be produced by the three firms producing the quotas

oq_1, oq_2, and oq_3 (which necessarily total to OQ). This will necessarily result in the largest attainable industry profit, which will now be divided among member firms (possibly including firms shut down for cost-saving reasons) according to some agreed plan. There is no particular reason, it should be noted, for believing that the operating firms will be permitted to (or willing to) retain just the profits resulting from the sale of their quotas, which are determined on cost grounds alone. Relative bargaining strength will presumably determine the division of profits.[7]

The preceding solution is strictly applicable if the established firms which form the cartel are subject to no effective threat of entry, and thus can maximize industry profit without attracting further entrants. If they are subject to an effective threat of entry, so that new firms would enter at the price OP, but can exclude entry at a lower "limit" price, they may do this if the long-run profits promised to them by the latter policy are greater. Otherwise entry may be attracted, and the membership of the oligopoly may be enlarged, possibly with resulting overcapacity and inefficiency. Here the reasoning is precisely parallel to that developed for the case of single-firm monopoly subject to an effective threat of entry (pages 213 to 218).

If a cartel can operate with this effectiveness, it will evidently obtain price-output results which are substantially identical to those attained by a single-firm monopoly. The perfect cartel thus gives us a sort of polar extreme possibility for collusive oligopoly. If there is a perfect cartel, the notion of a demand curve for the output of the individual oligopolist becomes superfluous: there is simply conjoint exploitation of the industry demand curve by a single administrative unit.

It is not suggested, however, that any, or at any rate many, actual cartels have ever been this perfect, even where the cartel device is quite legal. It has been commonly observed that "perfect rationalization"—that is, a quota system which really minimizes costs—has seldom been obtained in actual cartels, and that frequently profits are not redivided but that each firm depends on its assigned quota for whatever profit it is to receive. If this latter is true, of course, then quota determination is very unlikely to follow cost-minimizing principles. The reasons for the failure of cartels to develop "perfection" of the sort outlined is unquestionably traceable in part to the mutual distrust among the members and to their unwillingness to surrender too much of their sovereignty to a central cartel administration.

Therefore, a second version of "perfect collusion in oligopoly" exists which probably approximates actual behavior more closely than the perfect cartel model just presented. This is found where, whether for the sort of reasons just outlined or because of the illegality of cartels, the several sellers

[7] Cf. Don Patinkin, "Multiple-Plant Firms, Cartels, and Imperfect Competition," *Quarterly Journal of Economics,* February 1947; and W. Leontief, "Comment," *ibid.,* August 1947.

in a differentiated oligopoly simply agree collusively on, or concurrently charge, a joint-profit-maximizing price which all observe. They then share the market either in agreed proportions or in proportions determined by buyer preferences among their products, and each receives those profits he can make on his own sales. Such a collusive arrangement might arise from express agreement or simply from the tacit agreement implied by a consistently observed system of price leadership.

If this is the pattern of behavior—that is, market sharing with effective collusion on price alone—then the analysis must be modified as follows: If each seller receives a given fraction of the industry demand, regardless of price, but enters into agreement to charge some price identical to that of his rivals, then he has obtained, in effect, as a demand curve for his own output (subject to joint choice of a price by him and his rivals), *a fraction of the industry demand curve*—that is, some specified proportion of industry sales at each possible alternative price. This seller's demand curve might appear as *dd'* in Figure 32. Each of the several oligopolists may envisage such a curve. The several curves will be identical if there are equal market shares, or different if there are different market shares, but each will have the same general elasticity as the industry demand curve.

To this demand curve thus derived each seller may draw a marginal receipts curve, such as *mr* in Figure 32. Now for the purposes of price agreement, and neglecting any threat of entry, each seller will wish to have his rivals agree with him on that price at which his own marginal cost equals his marginal receipts—that is, the price *OP* in Figure 32. If all sellers charge this price, this seller will make the largest profit possible from his designated market share (any threat of entry being neglected).

Each seller will make this calculation in turn, determining the joint price which will be most profitable to him. But if the average and marginal costs of the sellers are different or if their market shares are different, the several prices *OP* which will be profit-maximizing from their several standpoints need not and, in general, will not be identical. There will be a range of alternative maximizing prices (all probably in the same general neighborhood) among which the sellers must choose. Price agreement will require some compromise on a price not too far from the optimal price of any one. Each firm will thus produce *near* but not necessarily *at* the price *OP* and the quantity *oq*, determined by his own *dd'* and *MC* curves.

Since the price arrived at is determined approximately by the equality of each seller's marginal cost with a marginal receipts curve drawn from a fraction of the industry demand curve, it will evidently *approximate* a single-firm monopoly price. The results determined, nevertheless, may deviate in three ways from those of a single-firm monopoly or perfect cartel. First, since market shares are not determined so as to minimize costs, the cost of producing the attained output is likely to be higher than in a perfect cartel. Every firm is likely to get a quota, even if fewer firms could produce the chosen output more cheaply, and among producing firms the allocation of output will not generally be cost minimizing. Thus, simple collusion on price may tend to lead to higher costs than a perfect cartel would obtain.

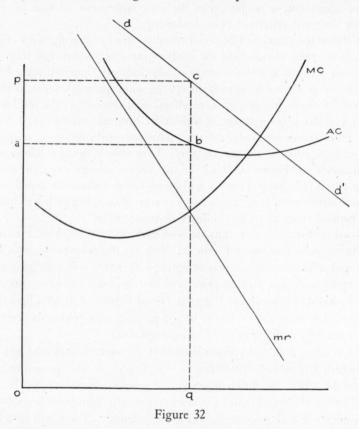

Figure 32

Second, the price and output arrived at will generally not be exactly the perfect cartel price and output. In fact, the range of alternative maximizing prices among which the firms choose may not include the perfect cartel price, since the different costs employed in calculation with price collusion alone may change the maximizing price perceptibly. Thus, the price and output may be somewhat different than under perfect cartelization or single-firm monopoly. Third, the joint profit realized by the oligopolists will be somewhat smaller than the monopoly or perfect cartel profit.

With these qualifications, however, it may be said that perfect collusion on price leads approximately to the sort of price-output results identified with single-firm monopoly.

POSSIBILITIES WITH RESPECT TO ENTRY

The precise character of the results of collusive oligopoly with respect to price, output, and efficiency of production, however, will obviously depend, as suggested above, upon the condition of entry to the industry. In general, we have distinguished two broad possibilities with respect to the condition of entry—that entry will be effectively blockaded so that the established firms can maximize industry profits without attracting entry and that there will be an effective threat of entry so that an industry profit-maximizing price will attract entry (although a somewhat lower price may not).

If there is effectively blockaded entry, then the oligopoly with perfect collusion on price should attain results approximate to those predicted for a single-firm monopoly subject to no effective threat of entry. That is, with marginal cost at least approximately equated to industry marginal receipts, there will be substantial monopolistic output restriction. An excess profit, such as *abcp* in Figure 32, will be earned in general if any such profit is available. And the efficiency of production may vary widely depending upon whether the number of oligopolists is such as to be consistent with the best realization of economies of scale, or too small or too large.

If, on the other hand, there is an effective threat of entry, such that new firms will enter if established firms charge a price as high as *OP* in Figure 32, then two further possibilities are available. Given the fact that an industry-profit-maximizing price will induce entry, the strategic question in this case is whether entry, nevertheless, can be excluded if the established firms charge a somewhat lower price and whether they will find it more profitable in the long run to charge this entry-excluding price than to charge a higher price and attract additional firms to the industry.

One possibility is that the established sellers in an oligopoly will find that a price which would exclude entry would be less profitable in the long run than a higher price which would attract it. Or, alternatively, they might conceivably overlook the threat of entry and attract it inadvertently. In either event, they may then exploit the immediate possibilities of their industry demand curve, making no alteration in their price policy because of the threat of entry. Where they do this, and thus set prices high enough to attract new sellers into the industry, entry may so reduce the demands of individual sellers that most or all of them can make only normal profits even at the most profitable price. In this instance an initially high price plus ease of entry may eventually result in excess capacity and uneconomically small-scale firms in the industry.

Suppose, for example, that each of five rival oligopolists finds himself in the position shown in Figure 32, where *dd'* represents each seller's *share* of the industry demand on the assumption of uniform collusive pricing. By virtue of a price agreement each seller might currently exploit his position at approximately the price *op*, where he would make the excess profit *abcp*. But this excess profit might induce several more sellers to enter the industry, thus dividing the total industry demand into more and smaller individual shares. Each seller's share of the market demand (*dd'*) would shift leftward. This adjustment *could* bring each seller to the position shown in Figure 33,

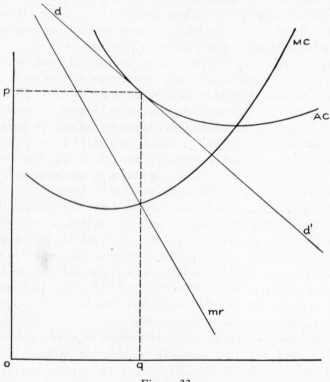

Figure 33

where price is still at a high monopoly level but now equals the high average cost associated with small-scale operations by each firm. Excess capacity and small scale have driven average costs up to the level of an industry-profit-maximizing price. Identical results for all sellers, of course, are improbable, and the whole process would depend on the original oligopolists' failure or indisposition to discourage excessive entry through a lower price policy. But this general sort of adjustment is a clear possibility if a collusive oligopoly, able to charge an industry-profit-maximizing price, overlooks the threatened entry which this price will attract.

A second possibility, already thoroughly reviewed in the case of single-firm monopoly (pages 213 to 218), is that there is an effective threat of entry and that the established sellers may find it possible and more profitable than otherwise to forestall further entry by charging a price somewhat lower than the industry-profit-maximizing price. The long-run profits of established sellers may be greater if they adhere to some such "limit" price and forestall entry than if they receive higher prices and profits immediately but share the industry demand with further firms later on. In this case the long-run

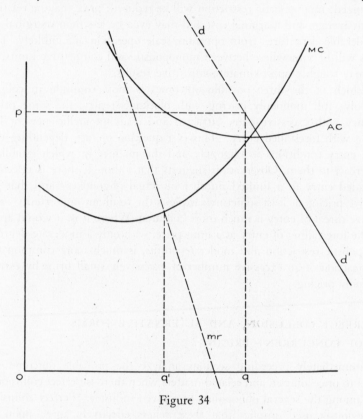

Figure 34

demand curve for the individual oligopolist who is a member of a collusive agreement is appropriately represented as truncated at a limit price *op*, as in Figure 34, reflecting the fact that he cannot go above this price and in the long run have the sales volume indicated by the dotted-line portion of the *dd'* curve, but must share it with new entrants (compare Figure 28, page 215). If we presume that limit pricing with forestalled entry offers the oligopolists the greatest profit, then each will forsake any attempt to exploit his share of the industry demand curve above the price *op* in Figure 34, and each will not wish to produce the output *oq'* at which his marginal cost equals the marginal receipts drawn from the industry demand curve. (The output *oq'* in Figure 34 is equivalent to the output *oq* in Figure 32.) Instead, each will charge the limit price *op* and produce the corresponding quantity *oq*—the several sellers will agree upon this price—and the currently established sellers will thus perpetuate their exclusive control of the market.

The results of such limit pricing by a collusive oligopoly are generally similar to those of limit pricing by a single-firm monopolist. That is, some excess profit will probably be made, although industry profits will not be maximized; monopolistic restriction will be reduced; price may be relatively close to average and marginal cost and may even be less than marginal cost. Considerable departures from optimum-scale operation are unlikely. Thus, results will lie somewhere between monopolistic and competitive limits, and they may roughly approximate competitive results.

Which of the three possible outcomes is most common in collusive oligopoly—full monopoly pricing with blockaded entry, the same pricing tendency with excessive entry attracted and resultant inefficiency, or limit pricing with forestalled entry? This is a question of fact, depending upon actual entry conditions to oligopoly and the manner in which established firms react to them. Observation suggests that although there is effectively blockaded entry to a limited number of actual oligopolies—and that here collusive pricing at least sometimes exploits the resultant opportunity—some effective threat of entry is much more common. Where it is, it would appear that the forestalling of entry at a limit price, with only a moderate degree of monopolistic restriction and moderate profits, is much more common than the attraction of an excessive number of excessively small firms by extreme monopoly pricing.

IMPERFECT COLLUSION, AND ALTERNATIVE FORMS
OF CONCURRENT PRICING

The immediately preceding sections analyze the probable outcome with respect to price, output, and related matters when there is perfect collusion on price among the several oligopolists in a given industry. "Perfect collusion," as previously used, implies that these sellers effectively agree upon and mutually adhere to a price which maximizes their long-run joint profits—exactly in the case of a perfect cartel or approximately in the case of price collusion with market sharing. In either case they attain or approximate a true monopoly price (conditions of entry being allowed for), and presumably they change prices together to maintain such a monopoly price whenever the level of the monopoly price changes because of changes in the level of the industry demand curve or in the level of the sellers' costs.

Is this simplified picture of collusive behavior a good representation of actual behavior within oligopolistic industries? Although there are probably a few oligopolies which in practice come rather close to perfectly collusive behavior as described, it is evidently much more common for actual behavior only to approximate this model behavior, and with widely varying margins of error. Thus, the behavior represented in the model for perfect collusion is better viewed as an extreme attained in a few cases and only approached as a tendency in many others, in which the conflict of antagonistic with joint-profit-maximizing tendencies precludes the attainment of perfect collusion.

To develop a more accurate theory of actual oligopolistic behavior, therefore, we need at least to indicate the nature and extent of typical deviations from perfectly collusive behavior which characterize oligopolies in which there is a tendency toward collusion but in which perfect collusion is not attained. The sources of these deviations, in general, may be thought of as twofold. First, although there is adopted within the oligopoly a fairly effective device or convention for securing concurrent pricing action, this device or convention may function imperfectly. Second, the device or convention adopted for securing concurrent pricing action may itself be rather crude or intrinsically of limited effectiveness as a means for securing a close approximation to monopoly results. We shall deal with the deviations from perfectly collusive behavior stemming from these two sources in turn.

Of the devices for securing collusion listed on pages 281 and 282, the first three are potentially rather effective means for securing concurrence on a monopoly price—that is either a cartel, or a *subrosa* price agreement, or a closely observed convention of price leadership may readily permit a close approximation to perfect collusion on price. Yet, the actual price results attained through these devices or conventions may deviate from the perfectly collusive for a number of reasons. First, we have already alluded to the fact that where there is perfect collusion on price with market sharing, each of the several oligopolists may find a somewhat different collusive price to be most profitable to him, if there are differences among firms with respect to market shares and marginal costs. As a result the actual price arrived at will tend to be a compromise among several variant versions of the "monopoly" price. This would be true even if each oligopolist had precisely the same notion of the shape and position of the industry demand being shared. *In addition,* it is quite possible that the several oligopolists will have significantly different opinions as to the character of the industry demand curve. Such demands are never perfectly known but only estimated (and differently by different persons). Besides, the combined demand for several differentiated products is a slippery notion. If there are significantly different estimates of the industry demand to be shared, then there may be a rather wide range of alternative "monopoly" prices among which the oligopolists must choose in arriving at a common price and a possibly quite significant deviation of the price chosen from the true single-firm monopoly price.

Second, the collusive oligopoly price is in fact likely to be adjusted less frequently than a single-firm monopoly price in response to shifting demand and cost. As demand and cost curves shift back and forth with cyclical business fluctuations, an oligopoly is less likely to make short-run adjustments to the changing situation than is a single-firm monopoly and much less likely to do so than a purely competitive industry. This is in part because when price is controlled by agreement or price leadership, every change in price places some strain on the controlling mechanism and increases the probability of defections from the agreement. By maintaining a relatively rigid price, the oligopolists lessen the possibility that open price rivalry or price cutting will emerge. Oligopolists may therefore try to set a price which will be workable for a wide range of demand conditions. When prices are set on this basis, any very close matching of short-run marginal costs and marginal receipts is obviously not attempted.

The tendency of oligopolistic firms to pursue relatively inflexible price policies is enhanced if their short-run average variable and marginal costs of production are relatively constant over wide ranges of output. Extension of output with given wage rates and raw material prices will thus be possible without much rise in out-of-pocket cost, and with declining average total cost, up to rather high levels of output. If rising wage rates do not cause costs to shift upward too rapidly the firms may find a rigid price consistent with long-run and not too inconsistent with month-to-month profit maximization. But the long-run price may also vary in a significant range around that at which long-run marginal costs would equal the marginal receipts from the long-run average demand.

Third, it is quite possible (and commonly observed) that although a group of oligopolists tend toward a monopoly or perfectly collusive price, this price is either sporadically or continually undercut by various sellers so that the attained selling price averages somewhat lower than the monopoly price. Since open price cutting would ordinarily attract immediate retaliation, price reductions of the sort mentioned are frequently made "secretly" to individual customers or without public announcement, in the form of special concessions, discounts, or rebates. The result is a difference between the announced or "quoted" price, which may be uniform among all sellers, and the actual or net price paid by buyers. A complicated pattern of discrimination in price among buyers may also result. In some industries this deviation of actual from quoted prices may be customary; in others it may emerge only sporadically with rapid declines in industry demand or with generally depressed business conditions. At the extreme such price cutting may completely break down collusion on quoted price and result in price warfare. In any event, this sort of deviation from perfectly collusive pricing reflects the effects of unsuppressed rivalry and antagonism among the several oligopolists in the industry.

Fourth, the fact that such secret price cutting takes place may cause the quoted price—set by a price leader or by agreement—to follow the actual price toward some lower level, where price cutting is less likely to occur, or it may preclude any attempt at the outset to agree on so high a price that price cutting will be encouraged. Thus, the threat of defections from agreement on a high monopoly price may lead to agreement only on lower prices which are more likely to be actually observed by all the oligopolists.

The effects of the first two sorts of deviation from a perfectly collusive price are generally to make price more rigid and to cause it to vary in either direction from the single-firm monopoly price. The second two types of deviation are generally downward in direction, leading to a lower than monopoly price and to smaller degrees of monopolistic output restriction. These second two sorts of deviation are likely to be less important if the oligopolists are in any event led to adhere to a fairly low limit price in order to exclude entry.

So far we have been speaking of probable oligopoly behavior where there is a cartel, or a collusive agreement on price, or an effective convention of price leadership, whereby the sellers choose jointly or by a trusted representative some "most profitable" price. For even this relatively simple case, it is clear that the price or prices which oligopolists may actually set may be in very loose approximation to any uniquely predictable monopoly price. Differences in the various sellers' estimates of industry demand may establish a wide range of alternative "monopoly" prices; the mechanics of collusion may lead to a rather rigid price; defections from price agreements or the tendency thereto may lead to a lower than monopoly price. The approximation to a monopoly price may also be poor because the means of securing concurrent pricing is crude and loose—as where sellers in an industry adhere to a formula for price making by adding a customary markup percentage to average total costs of production. It is not uncommon for sellers in oligopolistic industries—especially in those not highly enough concentrated to allow very close collaboration—to make prices by computing the "normal" or "long-run" average cost per unit of product and adding 8, 10, 15, or some other percent considered usual or proper in the industry in order to arrive at price. The "normal" cost is ordinarily computed with fixed cost allocated in such a way that average fixed cost is not much influenced by short-run variations in output, and corresponding variations in average variable cost may similarly be subdued. In effect, price may be based on a sort of long-run average cost for long-run average output and may be influenced strongly only by variations in wages and other factor prices.[8] A similar pricing pro-

[8] See R. L. Hall and C. J. Hitch, *Price Theory and Business Behavior,* Oxford Economic Papers No. 2 (Oxford: Oxford University Press, 1939).

cedure is found where merchants make price by adding a customary percentage to the direct cost of the goods on the shelves.

It will be noted that this sort of pricing policy is potentially quite consistent with one of (1) avoiding frequent price changes and adhering to an all-purpose rigid price for considerable periods and (2) making price at some limit level designed to forestall additional entry. It is thus quite possible that in setting prices by such seemingly arbitrary markup formulas, sellers are moving directly to the rational profit-maximizing goal—the most profitable price which can be had without bringing in too many competitors. At the same time, the relation of price to marginal cost is not always predictable in this instance, and the approximation to "ideal" monopoly pricing may not be very close either on the average or at any one time.

Many sellers in concentrated industries follow such a pricing policy and by so doing succeed in making roughly concurrent pricing decisions and in avoiding price rivalry. They evidently do so because collusion is difficult to arrange, legally hazardous, or unwelcome to some sellers; because their estimates of demand conditions would be so highly uncertain that they prefer a quasi-arbitrary formula to a hazardous calculation of marginal receipts; or because their thinking is dominated by the threat of additional entry. As long as the basic average costs are calculated so as to neglect short-run variations in average fixed cost—so that prices are in effect based on short-run average variable and perhaps [9] on marginal costs—and as long as the markup percentage is rationally adjusted to the elasticity of industry demand or to the threat of entry, there may be some meaningful approximation to monopolistic price and output policy. But there is room for significant discrepancies from, and much greater rigidity than, the single-firm monopoly price.

Where the sellers in an oligopolistic industry simply follow conservative price policies—adding ample but perhaps variable markups to the average cost of output and taking some pains to match each other's prices if their several calculations lead to different results—the price and output result may well be of the same general order as that already described. Price may not be made directly by independent marginal calculations, but, as there is "more than one way to skin a cat," the outcome may be a meaningful approximation—subject to a significant range of error—to monopolistic pricing. In this connection monopolistic pricing must, of course, be taken to include "limit pricing" which holds current price down to forestall future entry. It should be added that the results of pricing by a common markup formula, or by a rough system of price matching, may be modified by secret or other price cutting just as may the results of more elaborate collusive devices.

[9] If average variable costs are constant.

As we consider together the numerous possibilities for imperfection of collusion among oligopolists, it is apparent that we should not be surprised if many, and perhaps most, oligopoly prices deviated significantly from a single-firm monopoly level even though there was ample superficial evidence of concurrence or collusion on price. Two general kinds of deviation are in fact identified. First, the oligopoly price may be more rigid than the monopoly price, and it may tend to fall on either side of it. This tendency is attributable to the rigidifying effects of collusive agreements and of formula pricing, to divergences of individual oligopolists' notions of the profit-maximizing price from the monopoly price, and to the quasi-arbitrary character of most markup formulas. Second, the oligopoly price, as a result of unsuppressed rivalry, may tend to fall below the monopoly level, or indeterminately between the monopoly and competitive levels. This tendency, of course, is reinforced if there is an effective threat of entry which the established firms endeavor to block. Prices affected by these tendencies would seem to be at least as common in oligopoly as prices conforming more closely to the model of perfect collusion.

C. OLIGOPOLISTIC MARKET STRUCTURE AND PERFORMANCE

CONCENTRATION AND MARKET BEHAVIOR

We have discussed a variety of possible pricing patterns, or patterns of market behavior, which may emerge in oligopolistic industries. These range from perfect cartelization or collusion at one extreme to independent pricing subject to genuine uncertainty at the other, and include between these extremes various forms of imperfect collusion. All of these alternative forms of market behavior have been held to be at least logically possible within the simple archetype of oligopoly which we chose first to discuss—that is, within an industry with a very few large sellers only (for example, five sellers) each of whom controls a significant share of the market. And they indeed all must be logically possible in any situation where all sellers have a recognized interdependence with others and where there is the natural conflict between cooperative and antagonistic tendencies inherent in the rivalry of separate ownership interests for a single market.

This statement concerning alternative logical possibilities, however, is rather unsatisfactory in that it leaves us with no very definite predictions of oligopolistic behavior, either for the simple category of oligopoly specifically discussed or for oligopoly in general. It is, therefore, pertinent to seek answers to some additional questions concerning oligopolistic market behavior, which probe into the areas of uncertainty which remain from the foregoing analysis. These questions, or variants of one major question, might be stated as follows. First, in the simple case discussed, of a highly concentrated oligopoly with no small sellers, are all of the logically *possible* patterns of market behavior equally *probable?* Second, for each of the other categories of oligopoly mentioned on pages 268 and 269—including oligopolies with lower concentration and also with competitive fringes of small sellers—are all of the patterns of market behavior outlined logical possibilities? Third, is there any tendency toward systematic association between the pattern of market behavior and the degree of seller concentration within oligopoly such that there is at least a certain more probable pattern associated with each concentration category?

We may best dispose of the second question first—are all of the variant patterns of market behavior logical possibilities for every concentration category of oligopoly? The typical categories given on page 269, it will be recalled, included industries (1) with a very few large sellers only (for example, five sellers), (2) with moderately few—"quite a few"—large sellers only (say ten to twenty sellers), (3) with a very few large sellers and a few small sellers, and (4) with a few large sellers and many small sellers. ("Small sellers" are those supplying insignificant fractions of the total market; "large sellers" are those supplying significant fractions.) Is it logically possible that either perfect collusion, or independent pricing with uncertainty, or any form of imperfect collusion may emerge in each of these categories?

When no competitive fringe of small sellers exists (as in cases 1 and 2), the answer is certainly yes. Where every seller is large enough to be bound by recognized interdependence with others, a collusive pattern observed by all sellers is quite possible; imperfect collusion, as a consequence, is possible; independent pricing with uncertainty is also conceivable if forces of rivalry and antagonism are dominant. The main question is really whether these possibilities are all also open when the oligopoly includes not only a few sellers each of whom is large enough to have a recognized interdependence with others, but also a few or many small sellers each of whom supplies so small a share of the market that he will not affect other sellers' sales perceptibly through moderate variations in his own sales or through the price changes necessary to effect them.

The situation presented here is that there is an oligopolistic core of sellers with the same interdependence, the same individual demand conditions, and the same alternative propensities toward collusion or rivalry as noted for the simple case of a few sellers only. But there is also a number of small sellers, each of whom potentially faces a fairly elastic *ceteris paribus* demand curve for his own output, showing the response of his sales to his price changes on the potentially legitimate assumption that no other seller (large or small) will react to these price changes, since no other seller will lose sales perceptibly in consequence. We would usually expect the large sellers, recognizing their interdependence, to act like oligopolists as previously described. But the small sellers *might* be expected to act like competitors in an atomistic market, each adjusting to his *ceteris paribus* demand curve on the assumption that his own price changes will induce no reactions from rivals. Individually, they might not be restrained by a recognized interdependence, might be motivated to eschew collusion in favor of independent pricing, and might find it profitable to violate any collusive agreement flagrantly by price cuts on the ground that they could gain thereby and not induce retaliation. If this is the possible case, is it still logically possible that effective collusion may develop in the oligopolistic industry with a competitive fringe and that imperfect collusion and independent pricing with uncertainty are also logical possibilities?

It would appear that effective collusion is at least still possible in one of two forms. First, there may be effective collusion among all sellers, including the small ones, if the large sellers who desire it induce or coerce the small sellers to enter into a collusive arrangement and to observe its provisions. This is quite possible, since although the major sellers actually do not lose sales perceptibly because of the independent pricing tactics of any one small seller, they may lose because of the combined effects of such tactics by a number of small sellers (or would tend to lose in the long run if any one small seller grew spectacularly), and, as a consequence, they may make it their business to "police" the pricing of each small seller and to threaten or undertake retaliation in pricing if he does not concur in and observe a collusive price. Thus, the small seller may be forced to recognize an interdependence which his mere size does not immediately suggest. If he is so forced, effective collusion by all sellers can result.

Second, there may be effective collusion among the large sellers only, with the small sellers left to price independently as they will, provided that there are conditions of demand and cost which effectively limit the small sellers to a minor and nonexpanding share of the market in spite of their nonadherence to the collusion of the major firms. If, for example, the pattern of product differentiation is such that each small seller can receive only a tiny share of the market when charging prices close to those of large firms and has a *ceteris paribus* demand curve for his output which is not very elastic below this price, then the small firms may be unable to capture much of the market profitably by independent pricing even though the large firms are concurring on a collusive monopoly price. Or, the small firms may be at an absolute disadvantage in cost, which prevents their cutting price effectively, or may lack funds for expansion to serve a large market. In these and similar instances effective collusion, either by the large sellers alone or by all sellers, is possible in spite of the existence of a competitive fringe. When it occurs, industry output is monopolistically restricted, and most of it will sell at monopolistic prices.

As a consequence, imperfect collusion is likewise possible. It may result, as before, from rivalry or antagonism among large firms. Its probability is evidently enhanced, however, so far as small firms, periodically concurring on a collusive price, are especially liable to engage in price cutting and perhaps thus to drag the general industry price toward the competitive level. Finally, independent pricing with uncertainty is a clear possibility, particularly with the presence of a strong competitive fringe of small firms not easily policed or coerced into concurrence on a collusive price set by the large firms. Thus, in general, we conclude that all of the variant patterns of market behavior are logically possible in oligopolies with competitive fringes as well as in others—or in oligopolies in every concentration category.

Let us now analyze the third question mentioned (which subsumes the first question)—is there any association, as a matter of *probability*, between the pattern of market behavior and the degree of seller concentration within an oligopoly? This question essentially involves the effects first of the number of large sellers (whether very few or quite a few) and second of the existence and size of a competitive fringe of small sellers on the probability that one pattern of market behavior rather than another will emerge in an industry.

A first proposition which may be advanced is that a higher degree of concentration among large sellers—for example, the control of the market (or most of it) by a very few sellers rather than by a moderately few— makes close approaches to perfect collusion more probable and other patterns of market behavior less probable. Thus, we should judge the emergence of perfect collusion to be much more probable where four large firms supplied the entire market than where ten firms of approximately equal size supplied the entire market.

The reasons for this judgment are in brief as follows: First, where seller concentration is high, the force of recognized interdependence is strong because a moderate variation in sales by one seller at the expense of others affects the others very strongly; if seller concentration is low, the same percentage variation in sales by one affects the others much less. For example, if four sellers share a market equally and one doubles his sales at the expense of the others, each of the others loses one third of his previous sales; if ten sellers share a market equally and one doubles his sales at the expense of the others, each of the others loses only one ninth of his previous sales. With the strong recognized interdependence associated with high concentration, independent pricing is definitely and strongly discouraged since its effects on rivals are more definite and unmistakable. Likewise, defections from collusive agreements are especially discouraged as being certain to attract retaliation. Similarly, collusion is especially favored. By the same token, the probability of independent pricing, or of imperfect collusion, is enhanced with lower concentration. Second, collusion is probably easier to arrange, as a simple matter of mechanics, with a very few than with more sellers. Third, the antagonisms of a very few large sellers are probably more easily reconciled for purposes of agreement than those of more numerous sellers.

If we take these considerations jointly into account, it appears that close approximations to perfect collusion are most likely to be reached in industries with very high seller concentration, and that imperfect collusion and independent pricing with uncertainty are more probable where oligopolistic concentration is low. As between oligopolies with a very few large sellers only and those with a moderately few large sellers only, therefore, we should expect perfect collusion to be relatively more probable in the former case and other forms of market behavior to be relatively more probable in the latter. The precise degree of probability, however, is very difficult to assess.

The effects of the existence of competitive fringes of small firms around oligopolistic cores remain to be considered. In general, the existence of a fringe of small firms lessens the probability of stable perfect collusion, increasing the probability of imperfect collusion or independent pricing, and this tendency becomes stronger as the number of firms in the competitive fringe and the share of the market they jointly supply increase. This is because the small firms have either to be policed or to be restrained by disadvantages of cost or product differentiation to make effective collusion possible—and if they are not, at least imperfect collusion will result. Furthermore, the probability that the small sellers will be retrained or successfully coerced into collusion would seem to decline as their number and combined market share increase. If we take these considerations into account, it would appear that (1) oligopolies with a very few large firms and only a few small firms are not unlikely to achieve effective collusion, although less likely perhaps than if the few small firms were not present; and (2) that oligopolies with a large number of small firms as a competitive fringe are much less likely to achieve effective collusion—especially if the large sellers are not very few or do not supply a very high proportion of the market—and are more likely to have continually or sporadically imperfect collusion, or independent pricing, as a pattern of market behavior.

In brief summary, high seller concentration predisposes the industry toward effective and perhaps perfect collusion; low seller concentration favors imperfect collusion or independent pricing with uncertainty. Other things being equal, therefore, extreme monopolistic results are to be expected more frequently wtih high concentration, and approaches to competitive results more frequently with lower concentration. The approximate range of concentration dividing industries of "high" and "low" concentration, however, is difficult to identify precisely.

MARKET STRUCTURE AND PRICE-OUTPUT PERFORMANCE

The preceding sections have dealt with the conditions of demand in differentiated oligopoly and with the performance of oligopolistic industries with respect to the determination of price and output. Before turning to certain related matters—namely, the determination of market shares in differentiated oligopoly, nonprice competition, and performance with respect to selling cost and product quality—it may be well to summarize certain of our tentative conclusions with respect to oligopolistic price-output performance and its relationship to the structure of the oligopolistic industry.

It has been suggested previously that differentiated oligopolies may be subdivided according to two main characteristics of market structure—the condition of entry to the industry and the degree of seller concentration within the industry. Certain judgments have been advanced concerning the probable effects of each of these characteristics on industry performance. To summarize these conclusions, let us first set forth an outline classification of differentiated oligopolies subdivided by condition of entry and degree of seller concentration. This would include:

    I. Oligopolies with blockaded entry. (An industry profit-maximizing price may be charged without inducing further entry.)
        A. With high seller concentration.
           1. A very few large firms only in the industry.
           2. A very few large firms and a few small firms.
        B. With moderate seller concentration.
           1. A moderately few large firms only.
           2. A few large firms and a large number of small firms.
    II. Oligopolies with an effective threat of entry. (An industry profit-maximizing price will attract further entry; a lower price may not.)
        A. With high seller concentration.
           1. A very few large firms only.
           2. A very few large and a few small firms.
        B. With moderate seller concentration.
           1. A moderately few large firms only.
           2. A few large firms and a large number of small firms.

What general predictions have we advanced concerning these categories and subcategories? In all of the cases under I (blockaded entry) there is the clear potentiality of a close approximation to extreme monopolistic price and output tendencies—that is, industry profits approximately maximized and probably including substantial excess profits and output restricted so that price is well above marginal cost. These tendencies should be realized if there is effective or approximately perfect collusion, and are, therefore, most likely to occur in the two cases under I-A, where such collusion is especially favored by the high seller concentration. In the cases under I-B, where seller concentration is low, extreme monopolistic tendencies are also possible, but it seems more probable that imperfection of collusion (or the complete absence thereof) may lead to somewhat larger outputs and lower prices, lying somewhere between monopolistic and competitive levels.

In all of the cases under II the fact that an industry profit-maximizing price will attract further entry *may induce* the established sellers, even though they establish effective collusion, to charge a somewhat lower price than the industry-profit-maximizing price (and produce a larger output) in order to exclude entry. If this is the case, the highest probable price will be below the monopoly level, and it may even come fairly close to a competitive level. This would be true, for example, under II-A, where effective collusion is most likely. In the cases under II-B, with a stronger probability of imperfect collusion, prices should be as low or lower than under II-A.

It is possible in the cases under II, however, that the established firms will not find it attractive to forestall entry by a low limit price and will instead wish (if effectively collusive) to charge an industry-profit-maximizing price and attract further entry. If this is the case—perhaps because the entry-forestalling price would offer scant profits or because induced entry would occur only after a long lag—then effective collusion will lead to further entry up to some point, and the present market structure is unstable. Then in the cases under II-A, where effective collusion is most easily attained, we might expect high monopoly prices at the outset followed by further entry. If the diseconomies of smaller scale firms put a stop to this progression of entry early, the result may be remaining high concentration, extreme monopoly price, and an excessive number of uneconomically small firms with high average costs at or near the monopoly price. If small firms are equally economical, reduced concentration (placing the industry in category II-B-1 or II-B-2) may result, with perhaps a resultant lowering of price because of the breakdown of collusion. If, however, the industry falls initially in the II-B category, the latent desire of established firms to raise price and thus attract further entry is less likely to be realized, and imperfect collusion or independent pricing may in any event keep price below the entry-inducing level.

Taking the cases together, it appears that extreme monopolistic price-output tendencies are most probable and perhaps in the net likely in oligopolies in the categories I-A (blockaded entry and high seller concentration). They are a clear possibility in oligopolies under II-A *if* an entry-forestalling limit price is not attractive to established sellers and if the entry induced as a result does not significantly lower industry concentration. Price-output results between monopolistic and competitive levels, and perhaps approximating the competitive, are likely in all cases under II *if* an entry forestalling price is profitable to established sellers, and they are also perhaps in the net probable in cases I-B and II-B (with moderate seller concentration) because of the relative improbability of effective collusion. *There is a maximum of factors favoring an approach to competitive results in the cases under II-B.*

The preceding appraisal of results refers primarily to the size of the industry output and the height of price, as judged in both cases by the relation of price to the marginal cost of the supplying firms. It is more difficult to offer predictions relative to the efficiency of production as determined by how closely the established firms approach minimum-cost or optimal scales (the low points on their long-run average cost curves). This is because the number of firms in a given oligopoly and the scales of operation may be indeterminate over a considerable range. It would appear, however, that where the threat of entry results in a low limit price (as is always possible under II) or where imperfect collusion or independent pricing keep price down (as is not unlikely under I-B or II-B) operation at reasonably efficient scales is likely to be forced by the actual or threatened competition. Efficient operation under other cases, such as I-A, is by no means unlikely, moreover, particularly so far as established firms may merge to attain efficient scales if necessary. Chronic inefficiency is a persistent tendency only if established firms subject to a threat of entry charge a high price and induce entry and if there are substantial diseconomies of reduced scale as added firms enter. This is possible under II (and especially II-A) but not necessarily probable. In sum, although the efficiency with respect to scale of oligopolistic firms is not precisely determinate or necessarily optimal, there are few systematic deterrents to, and some forces favoring, reasonable efficiency in scale.

D. NONPRICE COMPETITION AND NONPRICE COLLUSION

MARKET SHARES AND PRICE DIFFERENTIALS

The preceding gives us certain alternative conclusions, overlooking selling costs and determination of product, concerning the general level of an oligopoly price and output. It does not, however, indicate how the various oligopolists may share the market which exists at the prices they establish. This is an important consideration, for even with a general agreement on price there may be a rivalry for sales volume.

The aggregate amount sold by the several oligopolists (and the aggregate profits they earn) will depend on the general level of price at which they arrive by concurrent action or otherwise. This price may be at a monopoly level, which fully exploits the aggregate market demand for the goods in question, or it may be at any lower level. Its level depends upon how much unanimity of opinion on price policy the oligopolists can secure, or how effective a collusion they can maintain, what the threat of additional entry may be, and how they react to this threat.

Regardless of the general level of price secured, however, the oligopolists must still share the total market volume. Suppose that major cigarette manufacturers have arrived at a general concord on a retail price for their main brands of 16 cents per package. What, in the absence of an agreement on market shares, determines the relative shares of the market secured by Camel, Chesterfield, Lucky Strike, Philip Morris, and Old Gold? And also, what determines the share secured by several other cigarette manufacturers who are in the market with, let us say, Zeros, Ropos, Hempos, and other brands?

The strategic consideration in this regard is that the several substitute products are differentiated—are viewed by consumers, correctly or incorrectly, as somewhat different products. If the products were absolutely undistinguished and undistinguishable, their prices would have to be identical. Any seller with a higher price than others would sell nothing; at identical prices market shares would be indeterminate, or they would have to be fixed by agreement. Since the products are differentiated, however, their prices can be somewhat different, especially if there are real or supposed differences in quality. And at identical prices the relative market shares will be determined by the pattern of buyers' preferences among the several brands. The relative proportions of the market secured by various sellers will thus be determined by (1) buyer preferences and (2) price differences. In the cigarette market the shares secured at 16 cents per package by Camel, Chesterfield, Lucky Strike, Philip Morris, and Old Gold are determined at any moment by the state of buyer preferences among them, prices being equal, and by the relative preferences of buyers between these 16-cent cigarettes and others of different quality sold at 20 cents, 18 cents, 14 cents, and other prices. Assuming that the oligopolists have arrived at some concord on the general level of prices, then, their relative shares will be determined both by the price differentials (if any) which they establish and by the success they have had in designing and advertising their products to secure buyer preferences.

Establishment of stable price differences which are generally announced and known is not always possible, since differentials may be the source of recurrent instability in the general level of price. When rival oligopolists have announced price differences, these are generally based on the supposition by buyers that there are corresponding differences in quality of product, since otherwise the higher-priced sellers could not allow the price differences to remain. If such price differences become a regular part of the industry pattern, there must be struck, by luck or by experiment, a nice balance between price differential and quality differential as evaluated by buyers. Ordinarily the higher-priced sellers must have been able to build up a considerable product differentiation in their favor. When they have been able to do so, a complex pattern of price and quality differentials may prove relatively tenable, may not be conducive to general price instability or war- • fare, and may be quite consistent with effective collusion on the general level of price.

There is always the chance, however, that a price differential may degenerate into a price cut, being set so that lower-priced sellers begin to "take business away" from higher-priced sellers. In a number of industries where product differentiation is not too great, this potential difficulty has become fact with the result that retaliatory price-cutting rivalry has tended to emerge periodically.

The gasoline market of the petroleum industry furnishes a good example of this. Small sellers of lesser-known brands of gasoline stay in the market by charging one or two cents less per gallon than the larger sellers of well-known brands. But the discovery of a satisfactory differential at which all sellers can maintain over time a fairly stable share of the market have proved very difficult. As a result, the large sellers have periodically begun price-cutting wars to regain their market positions. We may, therefore, add to our catalogue of generalities about differentiated oligopoly pricing that the difficulties of finding appropriate price differentials may in some cases make concords on the general level of price inherently unstable. The level of price may then be intermittently reduced as the result of price warfare. A concomitant of this tendency is that sellers in such markets tend to seek collusive agreements which stabilize interseller price differentials, even though such agreements are generally contrary to law.

The price differences which assist in determining various sellers' shares of the market can be established with less chance of stirring up discord by special, secret or unannounced price reductions. Where the market is such that flexible price concessions can be readily made, individual sellers can ordinarily adjust their net prices so as to maintain a given position in the market without at the same time setting in course retaliatory price cutting. Secret and special price concessions are frequently possible in markets for producers' goods. They can be made by allowing discounts from the announced price, on the basis of quantity of purchase or type of buyer, or simply by negotiating special terms for big orders.

One consumer good which is ordinarily priced at retail on a flexible basis is the automobile, which is sold "to meet local competition" at varying net retail prices by varying the allowance on the used-car trade-in. Where several oligopolists follow the policy of announcing given prices for their goods, but of allowing price concessions of various sorts, they aim at maintaining a favorable general level of price and at solving the apportionment of the market among them through flexible deviations from this price. Certain industries have been quite successful in pursuing this policy. But in times of declining income, when the total market is being severely reduced, individual price concessions have often degenerated into general price cuts and price wars have resulted. Reacting to this threat, a good many oligopolistic industries attempt to limit or standardize discounts and concessions by agreement or by trade-association activity, thereby enhancing the prospect for a stable price.

In sum, the general oligopoly tendency to concur on a favorable price level is tempered by the tendency, especially in bad times, of interseller price differences to lead to the breakdown of the concord and to price warring. This tendency is in turn often countered by agreements among the oligopolists regulating price differentials, discount policies, and even shares of the market, but those agreements are made uncertain by the fact that they are ordinarily contrary to the antitrust laws. What happens in the net in any oligopoly is affected strongly by chance or by a good many small considerations which have never been thoroughly investigated. Observation suggests, however, that many differentiated oligopolies manage to maintain relatively high and stable prices most of the time and suffer from price instability and price wars only in times of temporarily depressed demand or of rapid secular contraction of demand.

PRODUCT POLICY, SALES PROMOTION, AND NONPRICE COMPETITION

Our attention until now in the analysis of differentiated oligopoly has centered on the determination by the oligopolistic industry of its selling price and quantity of production. This analysis has been carried out under certain tacit simplifying assumptions—namely, that (1) the shape and position of the industry demand curve is given and not influenced by the sellers, (2) the share of the industry demand of each of the sellers at any common price or given set of prices is either given by agreement or is fixed by a given pattern of product differentiation, and not influenced by the sellers, (3) the product of each seller is of given design and quality, and (4) either the only costs incurred by each seller are costs of production of his given product, so that he incurs no costs of sales promotion, or, alternatively, his sales-promotion outlays are fixed in quantity. Thus, we have been able to concentrate on the analysis of price and output determination alone under artificially simplified conditions. At the same time, we have deliberately neglected two further related aspects of the behavior of sellers in differentiated oligopoly—the determination by each of the design and quality of product he will produce and of the quantity and disposition of his outlays on advertising and other sales promotion. Therefore, it is necessary at this point to consider how oligopolistic behavior is complicated by the introduction of product and sales-promotion policies by the rival sellers and how desirable the performance with respect to product quality and to the allocation of resources may be as a result.

The character of the product and sales-promotion policies developed in oligopolistic markets may be more easily understood if we first identify certain strategic relationships which influence the profit prospects of the industry and its individual sellers. So far we have recognized only the following: (1) an industry demand curve, showing the relation of industry sales volume to price with *given* products and sales promotion outlays; (2) provisional individual sellers' demand curves, showing for each seller the relation of price to quantity of sales if other prices are given, or alternatively the seller's share of industry demand with concurrent pricing by rivals—but in either case with given products and sales promotion outlays for each seller; and (3) individual sellers' cost curves, showing the relation of each seller's cost of production to his output, with a given product, but with sales-promotion costs either absent or fixed in quantity. The analysis has supposed adjustment by sellers to these relationships only.

In addition, we must now recognize the following further relationships. First, the industry demand will be related to the complex of designs and qualities of products produced by the several sellers. The industry demand curve will shift rightward (increase in quantity at every price) as products are "improved" or made more attractive to buyers and shift leftward (decrease in quantity at every price) as products are "deteriorated." Or, in other terms, the quantity of industry sales at any chosen price will increase or decrease with variation in the several products of the sellers. Second, the industry demand curve will similarly shift right or left (the quantity of sales will increase or decrease at any chosen price) as total sales-promotion outlays by the industry are increased or decreased with corresponding effects on buyers' preferences for the output of this industry. Third, the share of the industry demand secured by any one seller—that is, the position of his fraction of the industry demand curve (shown in Figure 32), as defined when all rivals charge the same price and change prices together, or his share of industry sales at any going industry price—will increase as he improves his product, if others do not simultaneously improve theirs, and correspondingly decrease if he deteriorates his product. Thus, any one seller may take customers away from his rivals via independent and unmatched product improvement, prices being given (and in addition bring some new buyers to the industry, as suggested immediately above). Fourth, product improvement, however, will tend to increase the seller's costs of production so that the product-cost relation must be considered along with the product-demand relation. Fifth, the share of the industry demand curve secured by any seller will similarly tend to increase as he increases his sales-promotion outlays if other sellers' sales-promotion outlays remain unchanged. (Industry demand will also increase somewhat, as suggested above.)

Sixth, if any seller in a differentiated oligopoly significantly increases his demand by sales promotion outlays or by product improvement, this will tend to induce retaliations by his rivals either in sales promotion or product, or perhaps in price. When the effects of these induced reactions are taken into account, the net effect of an individual seller's increase in sales-promotion outlay or product improvement will be much different than if no reaction had taken place. *There is thus a recognized interdependence of products and of sales-promotion outlays in oligopoly, just as there is of prices. Sellers, therefore, will not necessarily pursue independent product and sales-promotion policies, overlooking induced reactions. The determination of their products and sales-promotion outlays is subject to the same general set of considerations as the determination of their prices and outputs.*

Given the existence of these relationships in a differentiated oligopoly, what can we conclude concerning the probable course of product development and the probable amount of selling outlays? With respect to the industry as a whole, certain things are evident. Even if the several firms in the oligopoly act in perfect collusion in all respects—on product and selling costs as well as on price and output—so as just to maximize their joint profit in every way, it will generally be to their joint advantage to incur some selling costs in order to attract buyer expenditure from other industries; similarly, it will be to their advantage to improve their products up to a certain point, cost of production being taken into account. If industry demand is kept at a higher level by successive improvements of or variations in the product through time, it will also be to their joint advantage systematically to improve, vary, or restyle products through time. The extent of jointly profitable product-improvement and selling outlays, of course, will depend on the shape of the relation of the resulting added costs to the induced increments in industry demand (and it is difficult to generalize about this relationship), but, in general, even a monopolistic administration of the industry would incur some such costs. The level of selling costs and the level and pattern of improvement of products which such a monopolistic administration would achieve may be referred to as monopolistic, and *noncompetitive,* level of selling cost and product. It should be noted that a monopolistic policy in these regards may involve very substantial, *and apparently competitive,* outlays for selling and product improvement because of the resultant advantages to industry demand.

With respect now to the product and sales-promotion policies of several individual oligopolists, the following may be considered. In general, their product and selling policies may pursue any of the alternatives already suggested for their price policies—from perfect collusion to independence with uncertainty or even with unbridled warfare. At one extreme they may approximate perfect collusion on product policy and sales-promotion outlays, achieved by agreement or by a leader-follower pattern in which one firm sets what is regarded as a desirable pace for the industry and the others follow. This would yield approximately monopolistic results in the crucial respects. They may achieve some form of imperfect collusion on product and selling outlays. The same formula may be employed by all, allocating a conventional percentage of sales revenues to selling and product improvement, for example. Or there may be some movement toward a perfectly collusive policy, subject to defections as individual sellers boost their selling outlays or attempt to "steal a march" with a drastic independent product improvement. They may reach a position of stalemate, where each is pursuing a given selling and product policy and hesitates to change for fear of adverse retaliation. Finally, they may engage in active warfare from time to time, successively increasing product and selling outlays in true competitive fashion. The one tactic which appears quite unlikely is that individual oligopolists will increase product and selling outlays with genuine disregard of the probable reactions of rivals and thus *unwittingly* expend much more in these ways than is profitable from the standpoint of the whole industry.

The probable results of these alternative policies would seem to be roughly as follows: With perfect collusion on product and selling cost in a given industry we find a certain base level of selling cost and product design and cost which is consistent with maximum joint profits (though not necessarily with maximum social welfare). If there is imperfect collusion in these respects, there is a tendency toward a higher level of selling and product costs, though by an indeterminate amount, and the same may be said where product and selling policies are made independently subject to uncertainty. With market warfare, which is less likely, such costs could become very large.

Which of these policies is most common in fact? This is almost impossible to determine, since we have no good way of finding in a given industry how much selling cost and product outlay would be incurred with perfect collusion. Many observers have leaped to the conclusion that because there are substantial selling and product-improvement outlays in an oligopoly, there must be real competition or rivalry in these respects. This conclusion is potentially unwarranted, since even under perfect collusion or approximations thereto such outlays might be large. When the relative market shares of several oligopolists remain quite stable over a long period of years, the conclusion is perhaps especially suspect. As a matter of a priori probability, it would appear that the same structural conditions which favor effective price collusion also favor effective collusion (express or tacit) or product and selling policies. That is, high concentration favors effective collusion and selling and product outlays restricted to a jointly profitable level; lower concentration favors somewhat larger outlays. Similarly, the threat of entry may encourage established sellers to *increase* selling outlays in order to forestall entry. This tactic is a substitute for, but hardly equivalent to, price reductions to forestall entry.

It is, nevertheless, commonly stated today that in differentiated oligopolies it is usual that there will be (a) effective collusion on price together with (b) some rivalry in sales promotion and product policy designed to influence market shares and resulting in selling or product outlays presumably higher than the monopoly or perfectly collusive level. That is, price collusion will be combined with *nonprice competition*. If we change this to read that reasonably effective price collusion may be combined with imperfect collusion (or with independence subject to uncertainty) on selling and product policy, this is not impossible, although casual observation of existing behavior really does not verify it.

A reason that some rivalry, or imperfection of collusion, may be more likely to emerge on the nonprice than on the price level is that nonprice rivalry seems less likely to degenerate into unbridled warfare than does price rivalry. Though rival oligopolists may run up competitive selling outlays, they probably find it easier to keep this sort of rivalry within profitable bounds. This may be because of the greater institutional frictions encountered in extending selling cost or because a rival's selling or product policy may be matched by ingenuity as well as by gross money outlay. At the extreme there may be a certain rivalry purely on the level of ingenuity, with the actual expenditure on sales promotion or product not exceeding the monopoly level.

Most sellers also probably feel that a given amount spent on skillful product variation or sales promotion is a 'better gamble" to gain sales volume than an *equivalent* concession in the price of the product. Thus, a cigarette manufacturer selling 500 million packages of cigarettes per year is likely to prefer initiating an expenditure in addition of one-half cent per package, or $2.5 million, on popular radio programs and periodical advertising, to initiating a one-half-cent reduction in the price of his cigarettes, assuming that either move may be matched by his rivals. Similarly, an automobile manufacturer going into a new year is very likely to continue to charge $1,000 for his lowest-priced model rather than $950 and to put the $50 difference per car into the adoption of new body designs or mechanical features. To be sure, advertising or product variation will be matched by rivals as surely as price cuts, but less easily, less quickly, and less exactly, thus giving the individual seller a better chance to gain an edge through his own ingenuity. Preference for nonprice competition may also stem from the belief that the buyers of consumer's goods (the usual output of differentiated oligopoly) are more product conscious and advertising conscious than they are price conscious.

In any event, the fact is that sellers in differentiated oligopolies do undertake substantial outlays for product improvement and for sales promotion and that these are not only large absolutely (running frequently from 5 to 20 percent of total costs), but also probably often exceed by a significant margin the monopolistic or perfectly collusive level. It appears that the extent of this excess is factually indeterminate and also that the probable amount of the excess is indeterminate a priori, although it is unlikely, in general, to proceed to the point where excess profits are entirely eliminated.

We have now implicitly raised two questions for consideration. First, what significant alterations in the results predicted for differentiated oligopoly are introduced when various alternative sales-promotion and product policies are taken into account? Second, what is the effect of these altered results on the general welfare of consumers? These questions may be considered separately in turn with respect to sales-promotion outlays and to determination of product character and cost.

OLIGOPOLISTIC SALES-PROMOTION OUTLAYS

At the outset it is useful for purposes of analysis to draw a rough general distinction between two kinds of activities undertaken or policies pursued by firms in the endeavor to influence the demands for their products. On the one hand, we may identify *sales promotion* as the activity which is designed simply either to inform buyers of the existence, character, and price of a seller's product or to influence buyers to purchase it, but which does not involve any alteration of the product itself. The amounts expended to undertake this activity may be designated as sales-promotion outlays or *selling costs*. They are distinguished by the fact that they influence demand without resulting in any change in the product, and they are independent of production volume and clearly distinguishable from, and additional to, costs of production. Sales promotion is thus typified by advertising of all sorts, although it may also be found in the employment of direct sales representatives who perform a sales-promotion function. The essential character of sales promotion is that it is designed to influence buyers' knowledge of and preference for sellers' products without altering the products themselves. The essential character of selling costs is that they result in no change in the product and are clearly independent of, and additional to, production costs.

On the other hand, we may identify the activity of *product determination* as the selection of a design and quality of product by the seller from a few or many available alternatives. This selection will have a resultant effect on the demand for the product, since buyers will have different preferences for varied designs and qualities of products. Corresponding to each alternative product choice, moreover, will be a potentially different cost of production to the seller, which the seller will presumabaly weigh against the demand for the product in deciding the most profitable choice of product. In this setting there is the possibility of comparing (1) the qualities of various alternative products, as measured by their utility or satisfaction-providing-power to buyers, and (2) the production costs of the various alternative products. Correspondingly, we may provisionally speak of a magnitude designated as "product-improvement cost," measured as the difference between the production cost per unit for a given product and that for an "inferior" product which provides a smaller buyer satisfaction or attracts a smaller demand. If all alternative products are placed on a scale in order of demand-attracting power, there is a potential product-improvement cost difference between each pair, or a net product-improvement cost for each when compared with a given minimum cost base product. The essential character of product determination policy is that it involves an attempt to influence demand for the firm's output by selecting one product rather than another—by moving along a scale of alternative products to a certain most profitable point. The essential character of product-improvement cost is that it represents the incursion of an addition to production cost per unit of output, above some basic level, with a resultant "improvement" of product and an increase in demand for the product.

The general distinction between policies of sales promotion and of product improvement, and similarly between selling cost and product-improvement cost, is thus clear. It turns on whether or not the activity and the resulting increment to cost involves an alteration of product as well as an effect on demand for the product. In practice, to be sure, the two sorts of policy and expenditure may be difficult to distinguish. Extremely ephemeral product improvements may be employed to affect buyers' preferences and stimulate sales, and a single program of expenditure may combine both sales promotion and product improvement. For example, the building of large elaborate service stations on prominent street intersections by gasoline producers may constitute at once an improvement of product—via improved service and convenience to buyers—and a means of advertising the manufacturers' brands. Moreover, a given policy of product improvement is almost invariably accompanied by a program of sales promotion—the seller does not undertake one without the other. Nevertheless, we may draw a convenient logical distinction between sales promotion and product improvement for purposes of analysis.

Let us then turn first to sales-promotion activities and expenditures in oligopolistic markets. Such activities and expenditures will generally be found in differentiated oligopolies. When they are, how will results differ from those already predicted (with sales-promotion activities neglected) and how will buyer welfare be affected?

The volume of selling costs incurred will evidently depend in part upon the extent to which the recognized interdependence of the oligopolists influences their sales-promotion policies—upon whether their sales-promotion policies are in essence perfectly collusive, imperfectly collusive, established at some stalemate level in a situation of uncertainty, or actively rivalrous. If there is perfect collusion on sales promotion, the oligopolists will jointly approximate that combined volume of selling outlays which a single-firm monopolist would—or just that volume which permits a maximization of their joint profits. This is to say that they will add to industry selling costs so long as the increment to selling cost is smaller than the resulting addition to industry net revenue before selling cost or addition to the excess of industry sales receipts over production costs. In other words, they will seek just that level of industry selling cost which permits a maximum industry profit after covering all costs of production and selling. Their sales policy will thus turn entirely on the effect of increased industry selling outlays on the position of the industry demand curve (on their joint sales). It will not turn in the case of any seller on the increase of his sales which might be accomplished by taking customers from a rival in the same industry through an increase in selling costs, since this sort of sales increase will not add to industry profits.

If perfect collusion on sales promotion is pursued, there will be some determinate level of selling costs in any industry, its height depending on the responsiveness of industry demand to industry sales promotion outlays. It may be absolutely small or large, but it will not be large enough to reduce industry profits below maximum levels. If we presume that there is also collusion on price, the adjustment of the individual oligopolist may appear very much as in Figures 32, 33, or 34, above, depending upon the condition of entry and the reaction of sellers to it. There will, however, be one important change. The total costs of the firm will include not only production costs, previously registered in the various cost curves, but also a certain amount of selling costs. If we regard the AC curves in the three figures mentioned as measuring at the chosen output production plus selling costs per unit of output, these will be higher than if selling costs were not incurred. The total cost per unit of output will be increased by selling outlays, although presumably only to such an amount as permits a maximum aggregate industry profit. The same tendencies toward excess profit and output restriction as previously identified (affected by the condition of entry) will presumably remain.

It is logically conceivable, naturally, that collusion on sales promotion could be combined with a noncollusive pattern of pricing, in which case a variety of other patterns could emerge. Since this sort of development seems distinctly improbable, however, we shall not discuss it here.

It is quite possible, however, that each of several sellers in an oligopoly will act in an imperfectly collusive fashion in sales promotion, or will otherwise, in a situation of rivalry and uncertainty, incur selling costs in excess of the joint-profit-maximizing or monopolistic level. In any of these cases their behavior will tend to be of the following order. (1) Each seller undertakes some sales-promotion outlays which will augment his own sales—*at the expense of his rivals' sales*—sufficiently to increase his own profits *provided that* his rivals do not increase (or maintain) their sales-promotion outlays in consequence. (2) All sellers in fact do undertake their sales outlays in this fashion together, with the result that none of them gets additions to his sales as large as would occur if his rivals were passive, since the various sales promotion outlays "cancel out" or counteract each other in their effects on buyers' preferences. (3) Therefore, the sellers jointly undertake a larger volume of combined selling outlay than is consistent with maximizing joint profits; costs raised above the monopoly level and profits are smaller than monopoly profits. In essence, the several sellers in an industry undertake certain rivalrous selling outlays which simply counteract each other in their effects on individual sellers' sales and add nothing to industry demand.

This general pattern may emerge if there is imperfect collusion on sales promotion, so that selling costs are raised by some indeterminate amount above the monopolistic level as sellers depart from the collusive level in violation of the express or tacit collusion. It may emerge if there is wide-open rivalry in sales promotion or simply if all sellers have come to pursue some customary (and excessive) rate of selling expenditures and are deterred from either decreasing or increasing them because of uncertainty or adverse expectations as to rivals' reactions. In any event, total average costs may thus be increased to some degree above the previously defined monopolistic level. Industry profit may be smaller than would be attained with perfect collusion on sales promotion. The level of AC will then be higher, and aggregate profits will be lower. If there is perfect collusion on price but not on sales promotion, the net result might be as illustrated in Figures 32, 33, or 34 but with higher costs than with monopolistic sales promotion (potentially approaching zero profits). In addition, if imperfect collusion or rivalry in price exists, a variety of other patterns with lower prices but higher average total costs may emerge. The character of these patterns is readily suggested by adding to the predictions developed for imperfect collusion and rivalry in price (see pages 292 to 297) that of a tendency toward substantial selling costs and a resultant reduction of profits.

The preceding outlines the general possibilities with respect to the volume of selling costs incurred by an oligopolistic industry as measured in relation to the industry-profit-maximizing level of such costs. What can be said of the effect of the incursion of such costs on the welfare of buyers or on the aggregate satisfaction in goods and services provided by the economy? This issue has already been raised briefly in the discussion of selling costs under single-firm monopoly (pages 222 to 223), and we may now consider it at greater length in the present context.

EFFECTS OF SALES-PROMOTION OUTLAYS ON BUYER WELFARE

It is quite apparent that if selling costs in any amount are incurred, the total cost of providing goods and services is, *ceteris paribus,* raised. It costs more money at a given level of factor prices and productive efficiency to supply goods when advertising and similar outlays are added to production costs. Correspondingly, prices are likely to be higher to buyers, although this is not strictly necessary in every case. What is of basic importance, however, is that the expenditure of money on sales promotion results in the use of a corresponding amount of *real resources*—labor, capital, etc.—in sales promotion, and in the diversion of such resources from alternative pursuits. Thus, if in the economy as a whole 5 percent of the total cost of producing all goods were for sales promotion, we could say roughly that on the average 5 percent of the labor force and other resources of the economy was being employed in writing advertising copy, reading radio commercials, painting billboards, ringing doorbells, etc., instead of being employed where it would be if there were no sales promotion—perhaps in producing more steel or shoes or popcorn, or perhaps in leisure. Selling costs result necessarily in the diversion of real resources toward sales-promotion pursuits and away from other potentially productive pursuits.

It follows that the effect on the aggregate welfare of selling costs and of the resulting expenditure of resources on sales promotion depends essentially on (1) whether anything is added to aggregate buyer satisfaction by sales-promotion activities and (2) if so, whether this addition is smaller, larger, or the same as the satisfaction lost by diverting the resources thus used from alternative pursuits. If 100,000 man-hours are used per month in promoting soft-drink sales, does this add anything to buyer satisfaction; also, if these man hours were not so used, would they be used instead in producing more automobiles, for example, and if so would buyers be better off with the added automobiles and without exposure to the praise of soft drinks?

The answer to the general question posed is not so obvious as may first appear. A first essential issue is whether some or all of the resources employed in sales promotion would in fact find other productive employment if sales promotion were reduced or abandoned. A prediction on this point can be developed only by an extensive excursion into the theory of employment (which we are not prepared to undertake at this point) and even then would be of the most tentative character. In general, it appears possible that the adjustment of the total flow of money purchasing power to money factor prices might be such with sales promotion reduced or eliminated that either: (1) total employment would be the same (or even greater) so that resources previously employed in sales promotion would instead find employment in producing various goods and services; or (2) total employment would be reduced so that some or all of the resources released from sales-promotion activities would be unemployed, and possibly also some resources previously employed in direct production. What will happen must be contingent upon how readily the economy adjusts to full employment under any circumstances and upon the importance of sales promotion in stimulating the rate of consumer spending relative to a given level of factor prices. Some observers have suggested that sales promotion is essential to the creation of high employment levels, since its stimulus is needed to induce people to spend their incomes at the high rate requisite for such employment. But this opinion is an unsubstantiated guess, and all we can do at this point is to indicate the alternative possibilities.

If indeed the determinants of employment are such that sales promotion "pays its way" by creating added employment, at least for the resources it uses itself and possibly for others, then it is probably at worst neutral and possibly beneficial to the total welfare of the economy. The more difficult question arises if sales promotion does not increase employment but actually causes the diversion of resources away from producing goods, and thus results in a smaller output of their goods than would be obtained if it were curtailed or eliminated. In this case we must squarely face the question of whether the economy gains as much from sales-promotion activities as it loses in the output of goods foregone. What benefits can sales promotion supply to the buying public in general to compensate for the reduction of total output which it potentially causes?

The function and effect of sales promotion are generally (1) to *inform* the buyer of the existence of a product, its characteristics, its price, where it may be purchased, etc. and (2) to influence his preferences in favor of it as compared with other products, either of the same general sort or of a quite different sort. Thus, local newspaper advertising of weekly sales by grocery stores serves primarily to inform the housewife of currently available merchandise and current prices at different stores—its function is primarily informational. On the other hand, the usual national radio and television advertising of products such as cigarettes, soap, breakfast food, and automobiles serves no important informational function. It is designed primarily to alter the choice pattern of consumers in favor of the product advertised—to influence them to spend their money for one brand of cigarettes rather than another or, perhaps, for refrigerators rather than new sets of tires. Advertising thus addressed primarily to altering choice patterns of consumers generally consists of extolling the merits of a particular product or type of product, and also appeals for goodwill by providing free entertainment, but it frequently provides little or no concrete factual basis for the comparison of the advertised with competing products.

A first question is whether or to what extent the satisfaction received by buyers is increased by an alteration of their choice patterns through sales promotion? If a buyer is led to prefer a Buick to a Chrysler (or vice versa) by advertising appeals—or a new automobile to a summer vacation—is he, therefore, any better satisfied with what he gets for his money when he spends it than if he had never been influenced by sales promotion? This is a difficult psychological and philosophical issue which we shall not endeavor to resolve here.

It is certainly conceivable that the psychic satisfaction of a buyer might actually be increased by convincing him of the merit of, or the prestige attached to using, a given product in preference to others. On the other hand, with competing products generally advertised, it seems quite possible that the claims and counterclaims of the makers of various products tend largely to cancel each other out in their effects not only on the sales of different products, but also on the preferences of buyers for them and on the satisfaction they receive from them. Thus, it is hazardous to attribute any important increase to buyer satisfaction to the alteration in consumers' choice patterns which result from sales promotion.

The primary compensations for production potentially foregone because of sales promotion must, therefore, be sought in other directions. And there are indeed evidences of such compensations. First, the provision of information to buyers—a primary function of some and a secondary function of other advertising—may certainly add to their aggregate welfare by enabling them to know the market and thus to make the most advantageous choices in terms of price or quality. It may also stimulate competition in price and quality to some extent, with corresponding benefits for the working of the market system. Provision of information may have a special importance in educating the public concerning the existence and characteristics of new products as they are developed and introduced. Second, the use of advertising as a means of promoting the reputation of a given brand or trade-mark, which is invariably involved, leads naturally to endeavors by sellers to improve and standardize the qualities of their distinctive products, and it may thus be linked with a generally better product performance in the economy.

A third justification frequently advanced for advertising expenditures is that they "enable" firms to grow to large scale by securing a large market, thus securing the economies of large-scale production. In this event, it is argued, the economies or savings of large-scale production offset the expense of advertising so that there can be no net social loss. It is quite true that this *could* be the case. But it should be noted that if it were, it would be necessary (1) that *without* large-scale advertising, firms would be kept unduly small by the fact that there were too many of them and that each could secure only a small share of the market and (2) that when large-scale advertising was undertaken, some firms would be substantially more successful with it than others and thus grow at their expense so that the promotional effort would not be self-canceling. It is not too clear that *both* of these conditions would be found in many cases, so that sales promotion would assist the growth of firms to efficient scale. Such cases, however, are at least possible.

Fourth, there are some advantages to the economy from advertising in its support of radio and television entertainment and in its sharing of the costs of publishing periodicals. Although the quality of the entertainment which results is often justly criticized and although the effect of advertising subsidies on journals of opinion may not be wholly desirable, expenditures on advertising find some justification in the indirect or secondary benefits of paying the cost of entertainment or education.

It is thus evident that to the extent that sales promotion results in shifting resources from other employment and reducing total output, there may, nevertheless, be offsetting advantages. The problem in general, or with reference to oligopolistic markets in particular, is whether in the light of the volume and type of sales-promotion expenditures, buyers are at least fully compensated for the potential loss of output, or whether the volume of expenditure is carried to the point, or the type of sales promotion is such, that buyers are inadequately compensated for potential output losses.

Unfortunately, it is effectively impossible to measure either the benefits or the losses involved and very difficult to construct a theory predicting their relative magnitude. On the theoretical level, the following appears to be true.

First, it is not necessary that the level and type of sales promotion outlay associated with any particular pattern of seller behavior should be just such as to maximize aggregate welfare or as to assure buyers of full compensation for the output foregone either for the selling cost as a whole or for some marginal increment thereto. For example, the monopolistic level of selling costs—such as would be incurred with perfect collusion on sales promotion in oligopoly—is not necessarily consistent with maximization of social welfare just because it maximizes industry profits. Sellers in the industry may add to their joint profits with selling-cost increments which do not add to buyer satisfaction, especially if these outlays are primarily for preference-influencing purposes and if the sales-promotion campaigns of different industries more or less counteract each other and leave buyers with relatively unchanged budget patterns and unchanged satisfaction from their purchases. (This phenomenon would incidentally reflect the fact that the failure of sellers in different industries to recognize their interdependence leads them to incur more selling costs than are consistent with *economy-wide* profits.) Thus, a first conclusion is that selling costs even at the perfectly collusive or joint-profit-maximizing level *may be* excessive, although they are not necessarily so.

Second, so far as in oligopolies there is not perfect collusion on sales promotion, and selling costs exceed the monopolistic level, there is an increased probability that there will be excessive sales-promotion outlays. As sellers engage in rival and self-canceling sales-promotion campaigns within the industry, there seems to be a very strong chance that costs will be incurred which add little to the satisfaction of consumers but which potentially represent the diversion of resources from productive pursuits which would increase their welfare. Goods may then become more expensive without being necessarily better or more enjoyable. Thus, the jazz band aired by one cigarette manufacturer offsets the quiz program presented by another, and both simply maintain their relative positions in the market. The magazine claims of another company that its product is "less" irritating counter those of another that its product is "better" tasting, all at the expense of a good deal of paper, ink, and advertising-agency time. But the buyers of cigarettes probably do not obtain much more enjoyment from smoking because of this advertising, any more than the housewife's "washes" are whiter because of the plethora of "soap operas." The real cost of the good is ordinarily increased, but the buyer is not necessarily better satisfied.

This is not to say that selling costs in oligopoly are entirely wasteful from a social standpoint or that they are necessarily wasted at all. We have already indicated numerous direct benefits from them and the *potentiality* that they are fully justified by the added employment they create. There is the clear possibility, however, that selling costs may be incurred in such type and amount that the total output of the economy is somewhat reduced without compensating benefits, and this possibility seems strongest where oligopolists engage in active rivalry in sales promotion. As far as they do, it is possible that oligopolistic performance with respect to sales-promotion outlays may be less desirable than that attributed to single-firm monopoly. The comparative performance in this regard under monopolistic competition —with many small sellers of differentiated products—will be considered in the following chapter.

OLIGOPOLISTIC PRODUCT POLICY

Let us now consider product behavior in oligopoly—the determination of the quality and design of products and the resultant effects on consumer satisfaction and on costs. As suggested above, each seller in an oligopoly, or the oligopolistic industry as a whole, is generally able at a given time to choose to produce any of a range of alternative product designs or qualities, each of which has potentially a different satisfaction-providing power to buyers, a different effect on the demand for the output of the industry or the seller, and a different cost of production. Sellers presumably make their selections in such a way so as to maximize their profits, but the particular character of the choice will depend upon whether they act collusively to maximize joint profits or more or less independently to maximize their individual profits. The differences in the rationale of product selection which will characterize perfect collusion on product policy, imperfect collusion, active rivalry, etc. require some further scrutiny.

Moreover, we need also to consider how consumer welfare will be affected by the various patterns of product selection which will emerge. Two issues can in fact be distinguished on this point. First, overlooking the possibility of *variety* among the several products selected—that is, supposing that there is a single general level of design and quality for all products within an industry, with only slight differences among them—is the general level of quality attained likely to be consistent with the maximization of buyer welfare? Or, conversely, is the level of product quality likely to be too high so that the addition to buyer satisfaction for marginal increments to quality does not compensate buyers for resultant cost increases, or too low so that further improvement would more than compensate for added cost through additions to satisfaction? Second, if we recognize that substantial variety in design or quality may emerge among the several products supplied in an industry, is this variety likely to be optimal from the standpoint of consumer satisfaction?

The preceding issues refer to the process of selection from a given range of alternative products and its consequences for welfare. It is also necessary to inquire in the case of oligopoly, as we did in the case of monopoly, into the probable behavior of sellers in responding to a dynamically changing set of product alternatives through time and in developing new products for introduction.

Oligopolistic behavior in all of these regards will depend strongly on the pattern of competitive behavior among sellers—in particular on whether perfect collusion on product policy is attained or approximated or whether there is a significant departure in the direction of imperfect collusion, oligopolistic uncertainty, or open rivalry.

The pattern of behavior which will emerge if there is perfect collusion on product policy should be much the same as that already considered briefly in analyzing product performance under single-firm monopoly. (See pages 218 to 231.) Perfectly collusive oligopolists should presumably observe the following principles in selecting products from a given range of alternatives. First, as in single-firm monopoly, the oligopolists should jointly move to that level and variety of products which will just result in maximized industry profits. We may conceive of sellers as deciding on (1) the most profitable number of products and (2) the most profitable variety among them, and as then undertaking successive quality increments or improvements in each so long as the resultant addition to the joint demand for the products is sufficient to add more to revenue than is added to cost by the product improvement, prices being set at profit-maximizing levels throughout. (Effects of changes in each product on the demand for the others, of course, must be taken into account.) There should thus be a determinate number and variety of products and a determinate quality and design for each, all chosen so as to maximize joint profits. Second, each seller will avoid any individual adjustments of product—in the direction either of improvement or lessening of quality or otherwise—which would increase his demand at the expense of others enough to be profitable to him but which would not increase industry demand enough to increase joint profits. There will thus be no rivalry for shares of the market via product changes which will reduce the joint profits of the several sellers.

If this sort of behavior is pursued—as is by no means inconceivable—a certain monopolistic pattern of product variety and quality will emerge with production costs at corresponding determinate levels. Excess profits will presumably be present if entry conditions permit, as will monopolistic output restriction. What may be said of the relation of the attained level and variety of products to that which would maximize consumer welfare?

The general level of product quality is a first issue. If we discount for the moment the possibility of variety in quality, will there be a tendency to increase the general level of the quality of the products just to the point where the resulting increment to consumer satisfaction ceases to compensate for the added cost of production? Or will the attained quality of product be too low or too high from this standpoint? For example, suppose that the three "low-priced" automobiles are being built to current quality standards. They cost $1,500 each to produce, and they are being supplied at the rate of one million units per year. Is the product adjustment the best from consumers' viewpoint? Would they be better off if autos were built more simply or with lower quality, costing only $1,200 apiece, so that $300 million worth of resources could be used to supply a greater quantity of autos or of other goods? Or would they be better off if their autos were increased in quality or elaborateness to where they cost $1,700 apiece, thus requiring either fewer autos to be produced or a restriction of the output of other goods? This is the general character of the question posed.

The essential problem it implies is whether the *revenue increases* which the industry receives because of given increments of product quality, and which it balances against corresponding cost increases, are accurate registers of the increased satisfaction which will accrue to consumers. If by a given increase in product quality the industry can add $4 million to revenue and only $3 million to production cost (in which case it will adopt the higher quality product), is this an indication that consumer satisfaction is increased by more than enough to compensate for the increased cost and consequent reduction of the quantity of this or other outputs? Or if the revenue increase were only $2 million, could we be sure that consumers would not benefit enough to justify a $3 million added cost? In the case of monopoly or perfectly collusive oligopoly, the following observations seem pertinent.

First, the sellers under perfect collusion will not be led to make product improvements which would increase their sales at the expense of rivals in the industry and which thus might lead to individual revenue increases (disregarding rivals' reactions in product adjustment) that would exaggerate the benefit to consumers. Such competitive product improvements—to be discussed further below—may take place in the absence of perfect collusion. So far as collusive oligopoly avoids them, it avoids certain excessive product improvements—for which increases to consumer satisfaction do not compensate for increases in cost—and behaves better than non-collusive oligopoly afflicted with this sort of product competition. The same may be said of monopoly.

Second, it is, nevertheless, possible that the perfectly collusive industry may be led to some excess of product improvement. If each of a number of separate industries makes its monopolistic product adjustment by balancing added revenue against added cost but disregards or takes as given and beyond control the parallel actions of other industries, it is possible that each industry will anticipate a revenue increase which exaggerates the benefit to consumers of increased product quality. For example, suppose the automobile industry is one of forty industries supplying different goods to consumers, and is selling 1 million units annually at a unit price of $1,700 per unit, a unit cost of $1,500 and a unit profit of $200. Its aggregate profit is thus $200 million. It is possible that the industry might, *with unchanged price,* anticipate a sales volume of 1.5 million units if it improved its product at an added cost of $50 per unit, the price and product policies of other industries being taken as given and beyond control. With a unit profit of $150 on 1.5 million units, total profit would then be $225 million, and the industry would presumably make the improvement. It is quite possible, however, that aggregate consumer satisfaction will not have been increased by as much as the cost of supplying goods has been increased, since buyers have not been asked to pay an addition to the price equal to the addition in the cost. (In this case the price has not been raised at all.) Although it costs $50 more per unit to supply each of the previous million automobile buyers—and thus other goods with a value of $50 million cannot be produced—these buyers may be better off, for example, only to the extent of $20 per unit, or 20 million dollars' worth of goods in total. The additional half million buyers of cars may also not receive enough added satisfaction to offset the increased use of resources and reduction of other outputs available to them; they may also be superficially $20 apiece better off for the expenditure of their $1,700 apiece on autos instead of elsewhere, but the added cost of supplying this added satisfaction may be greater. If the goods each previously purchased with $1,700 had cost $1,500 to produce also, for example, it now costs $1,550 to give them a good worth only $20 more in satisfaction. This result is quite possible if any industry is in a position to attract profitable sales volume from others through quality improvements. Profit can be increased after product improvement with unit price increases which are smaller than the resultant unit cost increases, and consumers may thus be led to demand products of high quality in large numbers, although in fact the large cost increases mean that the supply of all other goods is restricted indirectly by more than enough to offset any apparent increment to satisfaction.

It should further be noted that if many industries (each taking the policies of others as given or beyond control) undertake simultaneously a product improvement, of the sort described, none of them may actually reap the anticipated benefits in revenue and profits, since consumers will not shift much toward a single product improvement when all products improve at once. Yet, having reached the excessive level of quality, each industry may find it unprofitable to adjust to lower product quality *independently*. It would lose profits to other industries by so doing unless they would also reduce quality simultaneously. A simultaneous or collusive policy by all the industries would be required to effectuate a return to more profitable product levels.

It is thus suggested that even perfectly collusive or monopolized industries may as a group be led to produce products of excessive quality or elaborateness, provided that several such industries engage in a sort of quality competition for the consumer's dollar. Their tendency toward excessive quality, however, may be less than that of industries within which the rival sellers also compete on the basis of quality.

So much for the general level of product quality in collusive oligopoly. What may be said of the influences on the variety of different designs or qualities which such an industry will find it profitable to produce? Certain tendencies which may emerge here have already been suggested in the discussion of single-firm monopoly (see pages 220 to 221). First, the collusive sellers will presumably select that variety of products—with different qualities, different prices, etc.—which is most profitable from the standpoint of their joint profits. If there are significant differences among various groups of buyers with respect to tastes and incomes, as there almost certainly will be, this is likely to mean that some variety will be in the interest of maximum profits. However, the maximum variety consistent with economical production, or a variety sufficient to satisfy best each fraction or stratum of the buying population, will not necessarily be the most profitable. Thus, it is possible that a 10-percent fraction of the buying market might be satisfied best with a low-quality, low-cost, low-price product but that more profit could be extracted from it with a product of higher quality and higher price. In general, it may be argued then that an optimal variety of products (suited to satisfying the diverse elements in the buying market) will not emerge under monopolistic or perfectly collusive oligopolistic product policy. Specifically, the sellers in such a situation will avoid introduction of any product which though increasing satisfaction would reduce profits generally. The example of the product of greatly increased durability, which would substantially lower costs of use but also reduce demand greatly, was cited in the discussion of monopoly (see pages 221 to 222). Such a product would also presumably be avoided by a collusive oligopoly, provided the threat of entry did not force its adoption.

A remaining issue concerns the progressiveness of collusive oligopoly in adjusting to new product opportunities and in developing products for introduction. The same tendencies in general should be found here as in single-firm monopoly (see pages 225 to 231) with the reduction of risks and better financing in the net favoring a more rapid development and introduction of new products than would occur in competition—subject, of course, to offsetting tendencies already noted. It is possible, however, that collusive rather than single-firm control may introduce more rigidity into the decision-making mechanism and lead to some retardation of progressiveness in collusive oligopoly as compared to single-firm monopoly.

EFFECTS OF RIVALRY IN PRODUCT

Let us now turn to product behavior in oligopoly where collusion is imperfect, or where there is independent product determination subject to uncertainty, or active product rivalry. The general pattern in these cases is that individual sellers make some independent adjustments of product which are designed to enhance their own sales at the expense of rivals in the same industry and which are inconsistent with the maximization of joint profits. These adjustments may occur in the form of deviations from a perfectly collusive product tendency (imperfect collusion), or may emerge from independent product policy in a situation of uncertainty about rivals' reactions, or may result from active product rivalry. It should be noted, moreover, that such deviations may take place when there is perfect collusion on price as well as when price is determined according to some other pattern.

When oligopolistic sellers depart from a perfectly collusive policy on product, the effects on their profits is clear. The joint profits of the several sellers will be reduced by some generally indeterminate amount, and in the case of very active rivalry they might even be eliminated. Competitive improvement of products to the point where production costs everywhere equaled price, for example, could bring about the latter in result. Previously identified tendencies toward monopolistic output restriction may remain, affected of course by the condition of entry and the system of determining price.

What of the difference in the character of the product adjustment from that of perfectly collusive oligopoly and the resultant effect on consumer welfare? The nature of the difference, and its effects, seems to depend strongly on the sort of product rivalry (subdued or active) which develops. For purposes of simplification, only two general patterns of product rivalry will be identified. First, each of the several sellers may attempt to increase his share of the market by the same policy of improving product—increasing its quality or elaborateness or size—so that in a general way the several products imitate each other rather closely and all are moved in the direction of higher quality and higher cost. Second, it is possible that different sellers will find it profitable to pursue quite different product policies—some moving in the direction of simple or low-quality products (with low price), others toward high-quality, high-price products, others toward middle ranges of price and quality. Individual sellers may in effect aim to capture particular sectors of a diverse buying market at the expense of their rivals, instead of all of them trying for more of the same market. The tendency in this case will be toward increased variety of product, cost, and price.

Which of these patterns is more likely to emerge? This would seem to depend strongly upon two factors. First, the character of the price-determining process would seem to be very important. If there is perfect collusion on price (or any close approximation thereto), which imposes approximate price uniformity on all sellers and deters them from making independent reductions of price, then the development of diverse product qualities is deterred. Since the competitive advantage of a quality reduction to a seller is likely to depend on some corresponding price reduction, he is unlikely to move lower on the quality scale if he finds observance of an effective price collusion to his advantage. Thus, product competition is forced by price collusion to proceed in only one direction—upward, or in the direction of quality improvement—and sellers will compete in product only by improvements. If sellers are not parties to an effective price collusion, however, and find no overwhelming disadvantage in independent price reductions as products are changed, then they are more likely to adjust products "downward" as well as "upward," and greater product variety may develop. A second determinant of probable product policy is the composition of the buying market—actual, or as envisaged by the sellers. In effect, the greater the differences in taste and income within the buying market, and the more equal the size of the different buyer groups, the more likely sellers are to find it profitable to develop product variety. The relative size of different buying groups is perhaps especially important. Suppose that there are five equal-sized sellers in an oligopoly and that the potential customers are divided so that 80 percent prefer product variety A, and four groups of 5 percent each prefer product varieties B, C, D, and E, respectively. No seller may find it to his advantage to cater to any group but A, provided that there would be substantial diseconomies to producing two lines at once. On the other hand, if each of the five seller groups (desiring products A through E, respectively) represented 20 percent of the total market, then each seller would probably find it advantageous to cater primarily to a different group. From the preceding it is also apparent that, *ceteris paribus,* lower seller concentration in oligopoly is conducive to greater variety of product.[10]

If conditions are conducive to uniformity of product policy and to product competition mainly by improvement of product, the following tendency is apparent. So far as each seller is led to undertake product improvements which will increase his profits by increasing his sales at the expense of his rivals—their reactions being disregarded—he may thereby add to his revenue an amount which overstates the resultant increase of satisfaction to buyers, and may correspondingly incur an added cost which is not fully compensated by an increase in buyer satisfaction. This has already been argued as a possible result of product competition between industries (pages 322 to 324), and the possibility is definitely enhanced by intra-industry product rivalry. Thus, suppose that each of ten sellers of fountain pens is initially selling 10,000 units per month at a unit price of $10, a unit cost of $9, and a unit profit of $1—with an aggregate profit of $10,000. Now any one of them might be able to undertake a product improvement which added $1.50 to unit cost, and at a price of, let us say, $11, increase his sales to 30,000 units at the expense of his rivals. (Any resultant additions to industry demand may be neglected.) In this case he could increase his sales to $330,000 and his profits to $15,000. (Unit cost is now $10.50, unit price $11, and unit profit on 30,000 units $0.50.) Yet, the buyers of his pens, who are demonstrably willing to pay only $1 per unit more for the improvement, are actually buying a pen which costs $1.50 more per unit to produce, and it is quite possible that the increment to their satisfaction is not sufficient to offset the diversion of $45,000 worth of extra resources ($1.50 each on 30,000 pens) to this improvement.

It is thus quite possible that each of the oligopolists, disregarding reactions of rivals, may undertake an excessive product improvement. Or, having made it at some time, they may be deterred from reversing the decision because they doubt that their rivals will undertake desirable reactions. Product competition in oligopoly may thus lead to, and perpetuate, excessive product quality, and to a greater degree than is found in monopoly or collusive oligopoly. It should be noted, moreover, that if all oligopolists pursue the same policy of improvement (simultaneously or in reaction to an initial improvement), none of them will reap the rewards outlined, as the shift of buyers is forestalled when all improve their products. Yet, a mutually more profitable return to products of lower quality can be made certain only by product collusion. It should further be noted that quality-increasing product competition of the sort described tends to lead to a reduction of

[10] See Peter O. Steiner, "Program Patterns and Preferences and the Workability of Competition in Radio Broadcasting," *Quarterly Journal of Economics* (May 1952), for an original development of this theory.

product variety and a tendency to imitative uniformity and that if there are diverse elements in the buying market, this means that buyers' aggregate or average satisfaction from the goods supplied will tend to be smaller than if there were diverse adaptations of the qualities and prices of the various goods to their diverse tastes and incomes.

A second possibility is that the sellers in oligopoly will engage in product competition of a sort which leads to variety in quality, design, and price, rather than to imitative uniformity at a high-quality level. Where this occurs, the result from the standpoint of consumer welfare is likely to be much better. The increased variety will tend, *ceteris paribus,* to lead to a better satisfaction of diverse consumers of diverse tastes and incomes. At the same time the pressure toward excessive product improvement is reduced (and perhaps at the extreme eliminated) so that fewer resources will tend to be "wasted" in this direction. It would thus appear that oligopolistic product rivalry which leads to distinct diversity of product—and is most likely to be found in the absence of price collusion—is more desirable than either monopoly-collusive oligopoly product policy or one-directional quality competition among oligopolists.

The foregoing is particularly evident in view of the following. First, in the situation outlined, product variety will not be restricted, as under monopolistic policy, to product variants which will enhance the joint profits of the several oligopolists. Joint-profit-reducing but satisfaction-increasing variants are likely to be adopted by individual sellers acting independently to increase their own profits. Second, the perverse product which adds to satisfaction but leads to lower industry demand and to lower joint profits— such as the good of greatly increased durability which costs little more—is much more likely to be introduced with this sort of product rivalry, since a single firm may anticipate a gain from its introduction though the industry ultimately loses. (Its introduction with quality-increasing competition is also possible, but it is perhaps more likely here.) This is not to say that product behavior will be ideal under this sort of oligopolistic policy, but it will probably be more desirable than under monopoly or under oligopolistic policies previously described.

With respect to progressiveness in developing and adopting new products in the sort of oligopolistic market being considered, there are evidently conflicting tendencies. Comparing an oligopolistic industry with some product rivalry to a monopolized industry, the following may be suggested. First, the emergence of product competition in some degree may provide an especially strong incentive for the competing firms to develop new products, and to adopt them as they become available. If this tendency is taken in conjunction with the fact that they will be disposed to adopt products which a monopolist would not, we find a virtual tendency toward more rapid product development than under monopoly. On the other hand, the individual oligopolist subject to product rivalry from other firms in the industry may find the adoption of new products, and the expenditure on developing them, more risky or potentially less profitable than a monopolist would, since successful innovations may be quickly imitated by rivals. This riskiness may serve as a brake on the tendency toward high progressiveness, and a net tendency as compared to monopoly is hard to identify.

In the preceding discussions of oligopolistic product behavior of all sorts, we have spoken principally of the choice of product design and quality by sellers from a given set of alternatives or in a given situation, and we have implied that some given and stable choice will be made in any such situation, to be altered only as new alternatives emerge. Although this may provide some reasonable approximation to actual facts, it should be noted that in some markets there may be a further tendency for sellers systematically to *vary* their products through time as a means of stimulating demand. Policies of *product variation* or *style change*—periodic change in product design regardless of whether new alternatives have been discovered—seem to be especially attractive to sellers of *durable goods,* like automobiles, refrigerators, fountain pens, ladies' dresses, or television sets. When products are potentially quite durable in use, the demand for them, which ultimately becomes largely for replacement of old units, will be quite variable, depending on how soon owners of old units can be induced to replace their old units with new ones. In this setting periodic variation in product may serve to hasten replacements and stimulate demand through time, as "new models" make the previous ones unstylish or obsolescent. Where there is systematic product variation— and it may evidently emerge in oligopolies or elsewhere—product costs are likely to be increased thereby, and without necessary compensating advantages to the satisfaction of consumers.

PRODUCT PERFORMANCE—SUMMARY

In summary, let us consider oligopolistic markets in general from the standpoint of product performance. Several aspects of product performance have been seen to be important to aggregate consumer welfare—whether product quality is increased enough, too little, or too much to balance corresponding cost increases; whether variety is consonant with maximum welfare; whether satisfaction-increasing products may be rejected because of unfavorable effects on joint profits; and how progressive the industry tends to be in developing and adopting new products. It should be desirable to make a comparison on each of these points between differentiated oligopolies and monopolies and between differentiated oligopolies and markets in monopolistic competition. The latter will be considered in detail in the following chapter, but the general comparisons to monopoly can be summarized at this time.

No single pattern of product behavior can be attributed to differentiated oligopoly as a whole, since this pattern may differ decidedly depending upon whether there is collusion on product policy or some measure of product competition within the oligopolistic industry. The following diverse tendencies seem probable in oligopolies with different sorts of product policy. First, oligopolies with perfect collusion on product policy, or a very close approximation thereto, should exhibit a product performance very similar to that of single-firm monopoly. The salient characteristics of this type of performance are (1) a lesser tendency toward excessive product quality than is likely to be found under oligopoly with product competition or under monopolistic competition, (2) probable reduction of the variety of products below the welfare-maximizing level, (3) avoidance of certain product opportunities which would reduce joint profits but increase consumer welfare, and (4) probably maximum progressiveness in developing and introducing new products, subject to the restrictions mentioned under the three preceding points.

Second, oligopolies which depart from perfect collusion on product in the direction of imperfect collusion, independent policies subject to uncertainty, or active rivalry tend to exhibit a product performance which deviates from the monopolistic "in a competitive direction," although the tendencies to deviation observed may be more extreme in monopolistic competition (with many small sellers of differentiated products). The nature of the deviation in oligopoly, however, seems to depend on further considerations, such as the composition of the buying market (as regards differences in tastes and incomes) and whether or not effective price collusion develops. One direcion of deviation, likely if there is effective price collusion or a rather homogeneous buying market, is toward (1) excesses of product quality greater than found in monopoly (though conceivably exceeded in monopolistic competition) and (2) restricted product variety, with a resulting disadvantage to consumers.

Another direction of deviation, more likely in the absence of price collusion or with a distinctly heterogeneous buying market, is toward (1) reduced excesses of product quality, clearly desirable from the standpoint of buyer welfare, (2) increased product variety, likewise desirable, (3) adoption of joint-profit-reducing but satisfaction-increasing products, also desirable, and (4) potentially but not necessarily restricted progressiveness in development and adoption of new products.

It is difficult to say a priori which of these patterns is most likely to emerge in differentiated oligopoly, although it would appear in general that the collusive pattern is most likely to emerge with high seller concentration and difficult entry and that the second noncollusive pattern (with accentuated variety, etc.) is most probable with low oligopolistic concentration and easier entry. The logic underlying these predictions is parallel to that developed relative to the probability of price collusion. Predictions of this sort, however, are almost impossible to check, and it is similarly difficult to make an objective appraisal of the product behavior found in any actual industry. The essential character of any product behavior pattern depends on the effect on consumer satisfaction of the selection by sellers of one rather than another product alternative. Unfortunately, differences in consumer satisfaction from different products are substantially impossible to measure with available techniques, the nature of product alternatives has not generally been well known to investigators, and information on cost differences is similarly scarce. Superficial observation of the apparent variety, quality, and rate of progressiveness in an industry is substantially useless if the preceding information is lacking. Thus, we remain with a range of tentative predictions concerning possible alternative product tendencies which cover a very wide range of behavior.

Nevertheless, it is tempting to make some sort of "external" appraisal of product behavior, which turns not on any measurement of relative consumer satisfactions and relative product costs, but on the appraisal by an individual (or by a "product research" agency) of whether an observed selection of alternative products "is good for" consumers, in terms of caloric intake, floor-space hours of housing, passenger miles of transportation, or ink-writing mileage. Such appraisals have their place, but it should be clearly noted that when they are made, the standard of judging product behavior shifts from that of the psychic satisfaction of consumers (however misguided its basis) to that of the judgment of another person (expert or otherwise) as to what is "good for" the consumer. Thus, a product-appraisal agency may hold that behavior in the shaving lotion industry is undesirable, what with the high cost and price of elaborately perfumed lotion, and that the consumer would be better off if he were supplied with bay rum or witch hazel by the gallon with negligible cost and price. But it discounts the possibility that many shavers may actually derive a considerable psychic satisfaction from using a fancy lotion with the lingering odor of saddle leather and tobacco. It should, therefore, be emphasized that we introduce entirely different criteria of welfare when we shift to such "external" standards. Moreover, the use of external standards implies an abandonment of the fundamental notion of the "sovereign consumer" (whose tastes and reasons for satisfaction are never questioned) and an adoption of "choice by experts" as the appropriate standard. This raises serious questions concerning the philosophic basis for evaluating economic behavior.

Casual observation does suggest, however, that whatever the gross rate of product development in various industries has been, the character of the product improvements undertaken in the past and now incorporated in existing products seems more likely in some industries than in others to compensate buyers for resulting cost increases. This reflects the fact that any product may be improved or varied in many ways and that the type of improvement or variation selected by sellers may have some influence on the ultimate increases in buyers' satisfaction. In some industries, for example, the product has been improved in a substantial and tangible fashion, in either design or quality, so that there are evident tangible compensations to consumers for the additions to cost and price. At least part of the product changes in the automobile industry from 1900 to date seem to fall in this category. Better and more efficient design has been progressively developed to the very substantial advantage of automobile users. In other industries the product has been improved in quality, changed in design, or sold with an accompaniment of auxiliary service in a manner which is attractive to buyers but which seems less likely to give them products enough better or more useful to compensate them (according to their own standards) for the added cost. Many minor variations or model changes in the automobile industry seem to have fallen in this category. Parallels may be found in other industries producing durable consumers' goods. In still other industries the product has been subjected simply to nonprogressive or slightly progressive variation or change, on the order of periodic style changes, in order to stimulate buyer interest. Periodic variations in the design of fountain pens, in the length of cigarettes, or in the "streamlining" of immobile household appliances are frequently representative of this tendency, and their contribution to buyer satisfaction often seems doubtful.

Judgments of the preceding sort, however, cannot be classed as very reliable, and a great deal of investigation would be required to permit trustworthy evaluation of alternative product policies.

E. PURE OLIGOPOLY

DIFFERENCES FROM DIFFERENTIATED OLIGOPOLY

The analysis of oligopolistic industries has thus far concerned markets in which the rival sellers have products which are significantly differentiated. It is appropriate that we should have considered the category of differentiated oligopoly first because it is in logic the general category of which pure oligopoly is a special and limited subcategory [11] and because at least some product differentiation is characteristic of the great bulk of oligopolies in the real economy. It is true, however, that there is a large group of oligopolistic industries in the economy in which product differentiation is comparatively slight and which represent approximations to the oligopolistic markets with homogeneous products which are analyzed in the theory of

[11] In the sense that, where sellers in the market are few, the *perfect* substitutability of rival products which characterizes pure oligopoly is an extreme and special case of the *close* substitutability of products which characterizes any industry.

pure oligopoly. Consequently, it is appropriate that we should now consider the predictions of this theory.

The dividing line between distinctly differentiated oligopolies and approximately pure oligopolies is roughly (and subject to some exceptions) the line between oligopolies supplying *consumers' goods* and *producers' goods*. Consumer buyers are generally rather poorly informed about the technical properties of the goods they buy, and their tastes are more diverse or susceptible to influence in the direction of diversity by the distinctive appearance or quality of the product, the reputation of the maker, and the assertions and emotional appeals put forward in sales promotion. Producer buyers have more or less technically fixed needs and generally adequate knowledge of how well various products fulfill these needs; they frequently buy according to specification, and they are relatively insensitive to sales-promotion appeals. All of this is conducive to uniformity or homogeneity of product among rival sellers supplying them.

Thus, we find that in industries like those producing steel, copper, lead, zinc, aluminum, cement, industrial alcohol, rayon, explosives, and prepared building materials, there is approximate homogeneity of product and an approximation to pure oligopoly. It should be emphasized, however, that there is only an approximation. Although within such industries the products of the rival sellers are commonly either very similar or identical so far as their physical properties are concerned, some differentiation or basis for a buyer's preference of one seller's product to another's is frequently introduced. Differences in promised delivery dates of needed materials or in auxiliary services provided by the seller, favor based on the seller's reputation or on friendship or esteem resulting from kindness to purchasing agents, and similar considerations may actually create some product differentiation in markets of the sort mentioned. Nevertheless, many of them have so little product differentiation that their behavior may be fairly predicted by the theory of pure oligopoly.

The setting for price-output determination in pure oligopoly resembles that for differentiated oligopoly in that each of several sellers in the industry supplies a significant share of the market, so that their price-output decisions become directly interdependent. In the steel industry, for example, which approximates conditions of pure oligopoly, the largest firm (U. S. Steel Corp.) controls about 40 percent of the producing capacity, the largest five firms control about 75 percent, and the largest ten about 90 percent. (In addition, there is a competitive fringe made up of a good many small sellers.) If any of the first five firms were to announce a price cut of $5 per ton below the going level on any major steel product supplied by the industry, buyers would turn to it at once and place orders to the limit of its capacity. This would reduce the orders of some rival sellers by a large enough amount to cause them to retaliate to regain the volume, and price cuts would soon become general. None of the larger sellers, therefore, can make an *independent* price cut without inducing a chain of retaliation, nor can any such firm make an independent price increase and hope to maintain its sales volume unless it can induce its rivals to increase their prices also.

Any one smaller seller would be unable to sell above the price of his major rivals. He might be able to make a price cut without engendering retaliation because he could not supply enough at the lower price to reduce the sales of any rival greatly. But concurrent cuts by several or many of the smaller sellers would induce retaliation from major firms, so the smaller sellers as a group are in the position of any larger seller with respect to independent price changes.

On the postulate of strictly independent action and no developed convention of concurrence on price changes, no large seller can be certain how his rivals will react to his price cuts or increases, and thus on this assumption no such seller has a determinate demand schedule for his own output. Price changes undertaken independently may have unpredictable results on sales. Any smaller seller's demand at prices below the general industry level might be quasi-determinate, but as a group the smaller sellers have a demand which is likewise indeterminate. In these ways the steel market (approximating pure oligopoly) resembles the automobile market (differentiated oligopoly).

The lack of significant product differentiation in pure oligopoly endows this market category with distinct attributes. First, it makes the interdependence of rival product prices much closer. In the substantial absence of differentiation all rival prices tend almost inevitably to become identical, and no generally announced price differentials are likely to be sustained. Thus, if the going price for cold-rolled sheet steel were $70 per ton, no seller of steel could maintain his market for this product if he charged perceptibly more. If any important seller cut perceptibly below $70, he would take enough business away from others to bring them with him. This is because cold-rolled sheet is made to specification, and a buyer would as soon take the product from one seller as another. In pure oligopoly, or approximations to it, therefore, the rival sellers must be able to keep their several prices close to identical if the price is to be stable and unaffected by retaliatory price adjustments. Where freight is an important portion of price, sellers must be able to maintain identical delivered prices at principal destinations if market stability is to be maintained. In pure oligopoly generally there is little or no "slack" for individual price variations.

A concomitant of this is that in approximately pure oligopoly the seller has relatively little opportunity to employ adjustments of product quality and selling costs to expand or protect his share of the market. (If the products of rivals were perfectly homogeneous, of course, there could by definition be no product rivalry, and there would be no point to advertising or sales promotion. In practice there is a slight differentiation of product and a limited opportunity for sales promotion.) In the steel market, for example, sales promotion through entertaining prospective large buyers and otherwise building "good will" may play a part. But changes in the "style" of cold-rolled sheet or advertising in trade journals that Old Glory Steel is naturally the finer, tougher, more elastic type of steel would avail little. This is because its buyers are industrial buyers: they buy to measure and to specification and are relatively unaffected by emotional appeals. In effect, because the buyers are price conscious and also buy to specification, product differentiation and sales promotion cannot become important. The results of this are that the scope of rivalry among sellers in pure oligopoly is narrowed and centered on price and that effective agreements to eliminate price cutting, therefore, become much more important than in differentiated oligopoly.

Another result of the relative absence of product differentiation, together with the restricted importance of sales promotion, is that the shares of the market secured by the various rival sellers are potentially quite unstable. In the extreme of pure oligopoly, with absolutely no product differentiation, the shares of the several rivals would be quite indeterminate even though their prices were identical. Anyone could sell the whole market if he built enough capacity and if cost conditions made it attractive for him to do so. The shares actually obtained, therefore, would be determined by price warfare, by inertia, by chance, or by agreement. In practice with slight product differentiation and some sales promotion the rival sellers have some means of controlling given shares of the market, but these shares are still potentially very unstable and subject to uncontrolled fluctuation if price rivalry among the sellers emerges.

PRICE-OUTPUT DETERMINATION

The principal behavior tendencies inherent in industries of the sort mentioned are predicted by a theory of pure oligopoly, which refers strictly to an industry with a few sellers in which there is complete homogeneity of product. Since this theory is in many respects closely similar to that of differentiated oligopoly, it will be unnecessary to develop it in detail; we may simply indicate the manner in which its analysis and predictions differ from those of the theory already discussed.

The demand situation of the individual seller in pure oligopoly is similar to that of the seller in differentiated oligopoly in major respects. That is, a *ceteris paribus* price-quantity relation, showing what would happen to his sales if he changed his price while his rivals made no change, will not be the demand curve for his output, since his own price (or output) adjustments will inevitably induce responses from his rivals which in turn influence his sales. The character of these responses, moreover, is intrinsically uncertain, so that the seller's demand curve will be potentially indeterminate unless the uncertainty has been removed by collusive agreement or by tacit collusion established by long experience by rivals with each other's policies. If there is uncertainty, many possible conjectures are possible concerning the individual seller's demand curve, including that of a kinked demand curve. (See Figure 30.) If there is express or tacit collusion, the seller's demand curve may effectively become a share or fraction of the industry demand curve. (See Figure 32.)

The major differences in the seller's demand situation in pure oligopoly are the following. First, a *ceteris paribus* demand schedule which shows the response of his sales to the price he charges, assuming his rivals' *prices* to be unchanged, will be more elastic than a similar schedule in differentiated oligopoly (shown in Figure 29). Strictly, it will approximate perfect elasticity (be approximately horizontal) on both sides of his going output, indicating a tendency to lose all sales to others if he raises his price perceptibly and an appropriation of all the customers of others if he lowers his price perceptibly. Its horizontality may not continue indefinitely toward zero or larger outputs, however. At the larger quantity point where after a very slight price reduction he took all of the customers away from his rivals, his demand curve would become the industry demand curve and turn downward. At any smaller quantity point where after a slight price increase by him his rivals were unable to supply his former customers, his demand curve would turn upward again. But his *ceteris paribus* demand curve will be generally horizontal in the neighborhood of his going output, instead of sloping, as in Figure 29.

Second, if he envisages a kinked demand curve for his output, postulating no price change by his rivals if he raises his price but a matching of his price by rivals if he lowers it, this kinked demand curve will be horizontal to the left of the kink (instead of elastic but sloping as in Figure 30), although it will have the elasticity of the industry demand curve to the right of the kink. Third, if he envisages his demand curve as a share of the industry demand curve, as under collusion, this will be potentially indeterminate and unstable in the absence of product differentiation, although this difficulty may be resolved by a market-sharing agreement. Fourth, the position of his demand curve (his share of the market) will not be subject to influence by sales promotion or by change in product quality since these are rendered respectively fruitless and impossible by the assumed absence of all product differentiation.

These differences in the seller's demand situation, however, are of minor importance to the probable character and outcome of market behavior except in one respect. This one exception concerns phenomena of product adjustment and sales promotion. Interfirm rivalry by either of these courses is evidently ruled out by the assumed conditions of pure oligopoly, although it is not inconceivable that the collusive industry might act as a unit to adjust its product and promote its sales in competition with other industries in a fashion similar to that attributed to differentiated oligopolies with collusive nonprice policies.

Otherwise—that is, as regards the determination of price and output—the possibilities are substantially the same in pure oligopoly as in differentiated oligopoly. We find the same conflict between joint-profit-maximizing and antagonistic motivation and, correspondingly, the same general range

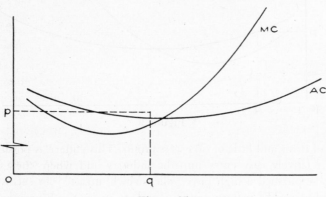

Figure 35

of alternatives in pricing behavior—including perfect collusion of several varieties, imperfect collusion, independent pricing with uncertainty, and active price rivalry. The price-output results attributable to these various pricing patterns, moreover, are substantially the same as those predicted for corresponding cases of differentiated oligopoly. (See pages 283 to 297 and Figures 31 to 34.) The relative probability that various pricing patterns will emerge would seem to depend, as before, on the degree of seller concentration, and the results will be similarly affected by the condition of entry and the manner in which firms respond to it.

As a result, a variety of patterns of price-output results may emerge from pure oligopoly, of which there are perhaps three principal types. First, there may be a typically monopolistic pattern, in which price is raised above marginal cost, output is correspondingly restricted, excess profits are earned, but production may be reasonably efficient. This result, which places the individual seller in a position like that illustrated in Figure 35, is most likely to occur where (1) a high degree of seller concentration is favorable to effective collusion on price, and (2) new entry is difficult or blockaded—as by patent controls or resource monopolization—so that high prices can be charged without inducing entry. In addition, it may be added, a stable or expanding industry demand will be favorable to effective collusion and high profits.

Second, a pattern may be reached like that illustrated in Figure 36 with monopolistic output restriction (price in excess of marginal cost) but with inefficiencies of small-scale production due to the entry of an excessive

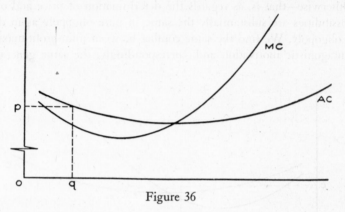

Figure 36

number of firms and little or no excess profits. This pattern is possible where there is relatively easy entry into the industry and where the established sellers have pursued a high price policy which attracted an excess of firms to the industry. The pattern may also emerge, at least as a prolonged short-run phenomenon, in an industry faced with a secularly shrinking demand.

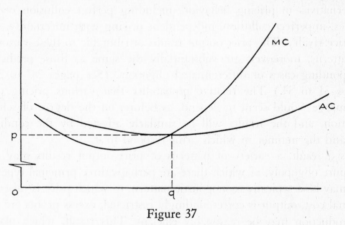

Figure 37

Third, the pattern may *approach* that illustrated in Figure 37, a competitive pattern, with price close to marginal cost and minimum average cost, little or no excess profits, and approximately optimal efficiency. This result is possible if entry is relatively easy, and is anticipated and forestalled by a low price policy. It is also possible if considerable price rivalry—which is perhaps especially probable with low oligopolistic concentration or with substantial competitive fringes—drives price toward the competitive level. Such a result, or something between it and that illustrated in Figure 35, may also emerge if there is substantially imperfect collusion.

The range of possibilities with respect to price-output adjustments are thus essentially the same as those discovered under differentiated oligopoly. The major differences are that sales-promotion costs should be largely eliminated, and phenomena of competitive product adjustment of an intra-industry variety are not encountered. It should be reiterated, however, that interindustry competition may give rise to phenomena similar to those discussed in connection with collusive product and sales promotion policies in differentiated oligopoly. (See pages 314 to 315 and 321 to 325.)

To what extent are these predictions—developed strictly for oligopoly with *no* product differentiation—applicable to those actual industries which approximate pure oligopoly but, nevertheless, do evince some differentiation of product? They would seem to give at least a notion of what is to be expected in such industries, and more accurately perhaps than a theory of differentiated oligopoly, so far as in these industries sales promotion and product competition are likely to be unimportant. Actually, however, behavior in the so-called or approximately pure oligopolies may ordinarily involve sufficient phenomena attributable to product differentiation that the theory of differentiated oligopoly, properly interpreted, would cover all oligopoly cases.

F. OLIGOPOLY AND GENERAL WELFARE

INCOME DISTRIBUTION AND EFFICIENCY

The preceding pages of this chapter have analyzed the character of competitive behavior and price results likely to be found in oligopolistic markets. Let us now turn to an evaluation of the impact of oligopolistic behavior on aggregate welfare in the economy, looking first, as we did in the cases of pure competition and of monopoly, at its effects on income distribution and efficiency.

This inquiry is of especial importance because of the importance of oligopolistic markets in the American economy. The majority of our manufacturing and processing industries are of oligopolistic structure, and oligopoly is of substantial importance in other sectors of the economy. What does this type of market organization imply for the performance of the price system in ordering economic activity? Before attempting to answer this question, it may be noted that no single clear, simple, and definite prediction can be made of market performance in oligopolistic markets. It is subject to a considerable range of uncertainty, which arises out of the relatively indeterminate behavior of individual firms in oligopoly conditions. Within this range the deliberated price policies of individual businessmen may play a large part in determining the behavior of price, output, and product. Production and price in oligopoly are only distantly governed by the "invisible hand of the market." They are directly governed, and within a considerable free range determined, by the executives of principal business firms. Depending partly on strategic aspects of market structure and partly on the judgment of the responsible businessmen, price may be higher or lower and output smaller or larger within a considerable range.

Abstract theory in its present state does not tell us exactly what patterns of price policies will emerge in oligopoly. To learn this, a detailed study of such price policies and of associated behavior is necessary. Theory plus general observation can suggest, however, certain tentative generalities about the price system under oligopoly, and it is these that we now examine.

The appraisal of the impact of oligopolistic behavior on welfare may be brief since we are in a position to proceed by comparing it to behavior under pure competition and single-firm monopoly, discussed in the two preceding chapters, and to draw on the analysis developed there of the impact of alternative patterns of price behavior. This is particularly true as far as the tendencies observed in oligopoly may in many cases be characterized as being of the sort found either in single-firm monopoly or in pure competition, or as lying somewhere between these extremes.

The effect of oligopolistic pricing on the distribution of income as between profit recipients and hired factors of production will evidently be contingent on the extent to which collusion permits the oligopolists to attain monopolistic results and on the condition of entry. It is distinctly possible, at least in highly concentrated oligopolies with difficult entry conditions, that effective collusion on price, output, product, and sales promotion will permit a close approximation to the results attributed to monopoly with difficult entry. There will then tend to be substantial excess profits and a corresponding effect on income distribution in the direction of greater inequality.

It seems on balance probable, however, with only moderate barriers to entry evident in many oligopolies, and with moderate to low oligopolistic concentration common, that excess profits will more frequently tend to be lower than full monopolistic profits and often quite moderate or small, although perhaps not so low as the zero level attributed to pure competition. This predicted lowering of profits may be attributable to limit pricing designed to forestall entry (and perhaps on occasion to the attraction of excessive entry) and to imperfection of collusion, independent policies, or rivalry with respect both to price and to product and sales promotion. Such departures from effective collusion may not ordinarily eliminate excess profits entirely, but they will reduce them both by lowering prices and by increasing costs.

In a substantial fraction of oligopolistic industries, therefore, excess profits may tend to be significantly lower than they would be under single-firm monopoly, although larger than under pure competition.

A second issue concerns the performance of oligopolistic industries with respect to efficiency. At this point we may temporarily disregard the effects on costs of sales promotion and product adjustment and center our attention only on the following question. Given the choice of products by firms in oligopolistic industries, will the number and scale of firms be such that the costs of producing the output supplied are at an attainable minimum or will costs be higher because firms are either inefficiently small or inefficiently large in scale? Will the size and number of firms be consistent with maximum attainable efficiency in production?

It is evident from earlier analysis that there is no pervasive automatic tendency in oligopolies toward attainment of such efficiency. Oligopolies are ordinarily found, or tend to continue in existence, only where there is at least some barrier to entry—some departure from the condition where a succession of very small firms could enter the industry with optimum-scale average costs no higher than any firms which may have become established. Thus, the pressure of entry does not tend to force price automatically to the level of minimum average costs, force all surviving firms to optimal scale in order to avoid losses, or force the number of firms to just that level consistent with minimum attainable costs.

A barrier to entry of some height instead typically permits established firms to raise price above the minimum cost level without inducing an automatic correction through entry and potentially to raise it high enough to permit them to operate profitably with unit costs which are not the lowest attainable for the going industry output. In this case it is possible that an industry might operate persistently either with too many firms of inefficiently small scale or too few firms of inefficiently large scale. For example, where five firms of a given uniform scale could supply industry output most efficiently, eight firms of smaller scale and with perceptibly higher costs might, nevertheless, operate profitably at a price which would not attract entry. It is equally possible that two firms so large as also to have significantly higher costs might do the same. Further, it is possible that some firms too large and some too small for best efficiency might operate in the same industry at a profitable price which would not attract further entry. As we have seen, it is, moreover, true that even where established firms disregard a threat of entry and raise prices high enough to attract entry, the result—where there are significant diseconomies of smaller scale—may be a potentially stable situation in which an excessive number of inefficiently small firms operate at a monopolistically high price with negligible profits, since the fact that the entry of a larger-scale and lower-cost firm would add greatly to industry output deters potentially corrective entry.

In sum, the barriers to entry which ordinarily are essential to the establishment of oligopoly permit a considerable potential deviation in efficiency away from the best attainable, through either excessive or insufficient scale (which correspond roughly to insufficiency and excess in the number of firms). The greater the barriers to entry, the greater the potential deviation which could be sustained in the long run. This is not to say, however, that because persistent substantial deviations from a maximum efficiency are possible, they, therefore, will necessarily occur or are more likely to occur than not.

First, the possible extent of deviation from the best attainable efficiency will depend directly on the condition of entry to the industry—the height of the barrier to the entry of successive additional firms after some are established. If this barrier is relatively low (that is, established firms cannot raise price much above minimum attainable costs without attracting entry) *and would remain low in spite of further increments of entry,* then substantial deviations from reasonable efficiency will be eliminated by its pressure. Only relatively efficient established firms will be able to forestall entry profitably, and if established firms are inefficient, they will be forced to alter their scale in pursuit of greater efficiency or be replaced by others. Since the barriers to entry appear to be of only moderate height in many oligopolistic industries, either entry or the threat of entry, therefore, seems likely to force reasonably efficient scale in a great many cases.

Second, even though the pressure of entry may not force reasonably efficient scale in some or many cases, it is to the natural advantage of established firms which have inefficient scales to reorganize their industry structure in order to lower costs and increase profits. This is not easy if the trouble is too few firms of inefficiently large size. But if there is inefficiency because too many firms are present of inefficiently small size, merger or combination of existing firms is an obvious remedy and is attractive to the firms involved. Although antagonisms among such firms may forestall such merger, the elimination of inefficiency due to small scale is certainly possible and perhaps probable in oligopoly.

Third, inefficiencies due to excessively large scale of firms can emerge only if the growth of firms to very large size actually does bring about higher cost. There is considerable doubt concerning the existence or importance of such diseconomies.

In sum, there is the possibility of substantial deviations from the most efficient scales in oligopoly, but it is not evident that these deviations are on balance probable. Reasonable efficiency in scale appears more likely to be found than not. On the other hand, at least some deviations from ideal efficiency are to be expected. The forces favoring reasonable efficiency are at best rough pressures rather than exact mechanisms, so that at the best only approximations to ideal efficiency could be expected. Moreover, the sharing of the market by several oligopolists, though they be of reasonably efficient size, is unlikely, as we have seen, to be such as precisely to minimize the cost of supplying a given output.

Two observations may be added to the preceding. First, oligopolistic firms, like any others, will be interested in the reduction of their monetary costs regardless of whether these reductions are the result of *real economies* or *strictly pecuniary economies* (see pages 236 to 237). Even though they attain reasonably low money costs, therefore, it is not strictly necessary that *real costs* be similarly low. This is a difficulty potentially encountered under any market system where firms are able to secure hired factors at lower money prices when producing and buying factors in large quantities. Second, where sales promotion becomes a regular—and, from the standpoint of the firm, necessary—part of market activity, and selling costs are regularly incurred, the potential *economies of large-scale sales promotion* may influence the development of the scale of firm. It is possible, moreover, that a firm of a size such as to give an approximation to the lowest costs of production plus selling might be substantially larger than one which would give the lowest costs of production only, and it might even be somewhat less efficient from the standpoint of production costs. Whether this sort of development is favorable to general welfare obviously depends upon the contribution to welfare made by selling costs generally.

Is oligopoly, found so frequently in our markets, in the net likely to provide the most efficient form of organization in those industries where it is found? This question is not so simple as it was in the case of single-firm monopoly or of pure competition. Each of those market structures involves an extreme and clearly defined condition with respect to the number and size of sellers, whereas oligopoly can exist in any industry with a considerable number of alternative sizes and numbers of firms. However, the following seems evident. First, there are unquestionably many industries in which *some* oligopolistic structure can be more efficient than either monopoly or atomistic competition. A few firms of certain size can produce more efficiently than either one or many. In these cases, which probably cover the bulk of our oligopolies, the particular oligopolistic structure actually found is probably more likely than not to be reasonably efficient, but it is certainly possible that it is not—that another oligopolistic structure with a different number and size distribution of firms would be more efficient. At the same time, the existing oligopolistic structure, nevertheless, may be more efficient than either a monopolistic or a competitive structure would be. Second, it is also possible that in some cases oligopoly may exist where either single-firm monopoly or atomistic competition would be more efficient—where either one firm or many firms would give the lowest attainable costs. Oligopoly may persist where monopoly would be more efficient, if market warfare is subdued or eliminated and if at the same time there are sufficient impediments to the merger of existing firms. It may persist where atomistic structure would be more efficient if there are no great diseconomies of large scale or are high barriers to entry. Finally, oligopoly may exist where it is just as efficient, but no more so, than either monopoly or atomistic competition—where production costs would not be much affected by making firms much larger or much smaller. In these cases the merits of oligopoly may be judged entirely on other aspects of performance than efficiency. In view of the wide range of possibilities with respect to oligopolistic efficiency, it is clear that detailed empirical investigation is essential to learning how efficient our concentrated industries actually are.

EMPLOYMENT AND ALLOCATION

The presumptive effects of oligopolistic behavior on the level of employment within the economy need not be treated in detail since they may be projected readily from the foregoing analyses of pure competition and single-firm monopoly. (See pages 161 to 163 and pages 238 to 247.) It has been indicated that the purely competitive industry tends to produce in a sense a maximal output and employment under given conditions of demand and cost and that there is a virtual reduction of output and employment under monopoly, possibly offset in part where monopoly is more efficient than competition. It has also been seen that in the economy as a whole pure competition does not assure full employment unless factor prices automatically adjust relative to money income to assure it; that if they do not so adjust, monopoly tends to reduce employment; that if they do, monopoly will also give full employment. It has been seen further that the strategic determinant of the effect of monopoly on employment is its effect on the relation of total spending to the level of factor and commodity prices and that this latter effect is not easily predicted.

The presumptive impact of oligopolistic behavior on output and employment follows from the fact that its performance with respect to determination of price, output, and profit tends either to approximate that of monopoly or to lie somewhere between the monopolistic and competitive extremes. It may accomplish approximately a full monopolistic restriction of output (under given demand and cost conditions) or only some smaller restriction, possibly approaching a competitive output. If the oligopolistic industry behaves like a single-firm monopoly, through collusion, our preceding conclusions with respect to the effect of monopoly on employment apply without significant modification. The virtually restrictive effects are present, but no actual restriction of employment may result when economy-wide adjustments of prices and money spending are taken into account. If oligopoly is in a sense quasi-competitive, so that, with given demand and cost, output is less restricted and price is lower, the virtual tendency to restrict employment is lessened. The net effect on employment (economy-wide adjustments being taken into account) will depend largely on how the somewhat lower profits that result affect the relation of investment plus consumer spending to the level of factor prices, and this is not easily predicted. If a more competitive income distribution favors employment, then employment should be larger than if the oligopolistic industries were monopolized. We are left with our general conclusion that the effects of market structure on the level of employment are in essence indeterminate a priori.

The effects of oligopolistic price-output policies on the allocation of resources among uses are readily evident from the foregoing analyses of allocation under pure competition and under monopoly. (See pages 249 to 255.) As we have seen, the allocation of resources among the production of various products—if we take the products as given and neglect selling costs —would tend toward the ideal under universal pure competition. If monopolistic and purely competitive industries exist side by side in the economy, there will tend to be a misallocation of resources. Monopolistic outputs will tend to be relatively too small, as they are restricted so that marginal costs are less than prices, whereas competitive outputs will be relatively too large. Within a group of monopolistic industries, allocation will deviate from the ideal so far as there are different degrees of monopolistic restriction (price-marginal cost discrepancies) in the different industries.

These central principles are readily applied in analyzing the effects of oligopolistic price policies on allocation. In such industries there may be an output restriction approximate to that of single-firm monopoly, as under perfect collusion. Or there may be a lesser degree of restriction, involving a smaller price-marginal-cost discrepancy (and perhaps a negligible one), where there is imperfect collusion, price rivalry, etc. It follows that where oligopolistic industries are found side by side with competitive industries, there will tend to be some misallocation of resources (oligopoly outputs too small, competitive outputs too large), which is large or small depending on the degree of monopolistic output restriction. Among the many oligopolistic industries there will also tend to be a misallocation of resources as between the more monopolistic and the more competitive of the oligopolies. In short, oligopoly has roughly the same effects on allocation as monopoly with the added complication that there may be much wider differences in the degree of output restriction among oligopolies than among monopolies.

The preceding takes products as given and disregards selling costs. It is evident from the earlier analysis of product and sales promotion policy (pages 307 to 332) that in oligopoly it is also possible that, from the standpoint of buyer welfare, too many resources will be allocated in the direction of sales promotion and improvement in product quality. This will be considered further in the succeeding section.

PRODUCT BEHAVIOR, SELLING COST, PROGRESSIVENESS, AND STABILITY

The performance of oligopoly in the dimensions of product determination and sales promotion has been covered in detail on pages 307 to 332, and it needs only to be briefly summarized here. As has been indicated there, there is a clear possibility that deviations from oligopolistic collusion may lead in differentiated oligopoly to the expenditure of larger amounts on sales promotion and on product improvement than would be spent by single-firm monopolies and that this increased expenditure may be to the net disadvantage of general buyer welfare, so far as buyers would benefit more if part of the money spent in these ways were spent instead in producing a larger volume of less-advertised or lower-quality product. If this occurs, oligopolistic performance is in this respect inferior to monopolistic performance and also to the performance of purely competitive markets. The latter, however, are because of their characteristics more or less immune to difficulties of this order, and the more meaningful oligopoly-competition comparison is to monopolistic competition. As we shall discover in the following chapter, the comparative performance of differentiated oligopoly and monopolistic competition may conceivably favor either.

So far as there is an excess of sales promotion and product improvement in oligopoly, it is clear that the allocation of resources among uses is distorted from the ideal—too many resources going to selling or to improving the quality of products and too little to increasing the quantity of output. This disadvantage may be offset, however, to the extent that either sales promotion or product improvement has a favorable impact on over-all employment, an offset the extent of which is very difficult to predict a priori. A further offset may be found in an improved variety of products under oligopoly (in the absence of perfect collusion), and it is conceivable that in certain settings the excesses already referred to will be avoided, variety will approach the optimal, and performance in selling cost and product will be clearly superior to monopolistic performance.

Progressiveness in the development and introduction of new products is likely to be substantial in oligopoly, but whether it will be greater or less than in single-firm monopoly is difficult to predict. The two settings for activities of development and innovation are similar in that some barriers to entry offer a degree of protection and a promise of extra profits to established sellers from successful innovations, thus decrease the riskiness of investment in research or in the introduction of new products, and provide a net stimulus to development and innovation. Likewise, in both cases intra-industry imitation and subsequent price rivalry are probably either absent or tempered sufficiently that the prospective gains of successful innovation are substantial. And in both cases excess profits are likely to be present to finance research and development activity. There are three primary differences between monopoly and oligopoly in this regard. In the first place, oligopoly, on the average, is likely to have somewhat smaller excess profits to invest in these pursuits. Second, the individual firm is exposed to a greater chance of reduced profits from innovations because of early imitation by entrants or established firms (although patent and similar protection may afford a measure of protection); and as a result, the risk of development and innovation expenditure tends to be somewhat greater than in monopoly. These tendencies favor a reduced rate of progressiveness. In the third place, rivalry in oligopoly (attempts to secure added sales at the expense of rivals) may tend to encourage more development and innovation and lead to more rapid progress. An evaluation of the relative progressiveness of oligopoly and monopoly is thus difficult. The relative progressiveness of oligopoly and monopolistic competition will be considered in the next chapter.

It was concluded in the preceding chapter (pages 223 to 225) that progressiveness in productive technique in monopoly would probably tend to be as great as or greater than in competition. Following the same logic, it would appear that oligopoly will tend to lie between monopolistic and competitive extremes in this regard.

The impact of oligopolistic behavior on stability in the economy is not easily evaluated. The general tendencies of oligopolistic adjustment to changing demand within the economy may be said to be in the direction of the monopolistic adjustment (described on pages 231 to 233). The same or modified income-distribution effects may be noted; responsiveness to shifting costs and demands may be somewhat lessened as compared to competition, etc. One added tendency may be noted in that under other than really perfect collusion oligopoly prices may tend to be more rigid or less responsive to changes in demand and cost than monopoly prices. This tendency may follow from the fact that loose collusive agreements may be kept more stable if prices are changed infrequently, or it may be a result of uncertainty or pessimistic expectations by individual oligopolists concerning the consequences of independent price changes.

So far as an oligopoly price is in fact more rigid than a monopoly price would be, profits through time are probably lessened, as profitable short-term price adjustments are less frequently made. At the same time, greater price rigidity is likely to mean, *ceteris paribus,* greater output flexibility as demands and costs shift through time. If price is not cut in response to a given cyclical decline in demand, output will tend to decline more in consequence; if it is not raised when demand revives by a given amount, output will tend to increase by more. It would thus appear that oligopolistic price rigidity would lead to greater fluctuations in output and employment in response to *given* fluctuations in money purchasing power and money factor prices. The reason that this conclusion may not mean much is that we can be by no means sure that in an economy with many rigid prices the fluctuation of purchasing power and factor prices are in fact given, or would be the same if prices were flexible instead of rigid. It is quite possible, for example, that increased flexibility of prices would lead to accentuated fluctuation of purchasing power and factor prices and that in fact, therefore, output would in the net fluctuate just as much (or more) with flexible as with rigid prices. Until we have an adequate analysis of the relation of price flexibility to general income flexibility, therefore, we cannot predict with certainty whether oligopolistic price rigidity in the net favors stability or instability of employment and output.

OLIGOPOLY AND PRICE DISCRIMINATION

Since oligopoly may frequently through collusion attain or approach a monopolistic pricing policy, it is evident that we may also expect in oligopoly monopolistic price discrimination of the kind previously discussed in connection with monopoly. That is, we may find third-degree discrimination, in which several classes of buyers are charged different prices for the same product, and we might even find first-degree discrimination, where individual buyers are dealt with separately for maximum exploitation. Active price competition, however, naturally tends to break down or eliminate price discrimination (as one seller invades the higher-priced market of another) so that departures from perfect collusion or active rivalry in oligopoly will tend to diminish or even eliminate the tendency toward price discrimination. We shall return to this matter in Chapter 9.

In oligopoly, however, there is an added sort of price discrimination which may frequently emerge. This may be designated as *personal* or *chaotic* price discrimination, referring to the fact that it is discrimination by a seller among different individual buyers and that price differences are made somewhat unsystematically and not necessarily in such a fashion as to maximize the joint profits of the several oligopolists. Personal price discrimination tends to emerge rather naturally as a by-product of imperfect collusion, when individual sellers, though nominally adhering to a common posted price, make secret price concessions on individual orders or to individual buyers in order to enhance their own sales volumes. When this occurs, some buyers from a given seller will pay lower prices than others, and there is a discrimination in price. Although such discrimination may follow some reasonably logical pattern—for example, buyers with more elastic demands may be chosen for price concessions—the resulting pricing pattern is indeed likely to be somewhat chaotic, shifting over time, and not necessarily very similar to the pattern of discrimination through which a monopolist would maximize his profits. An anomalous aspect of such price discrimination is that although it at least superficially resembles true monopolistic discrimination and may have some of the same undesirable results, it is actually a vehicle for a type of price competition which tends to improve the performance of oligopolistic industries.

SUPPLEMENTARY READINGS

EDWARD H. CHAMBERLIN, *The Theory of Monopolistic Competition,* Chap. 3.

H. S. DENNISON AND J. K. GALBRAITH, *Modern Competition and Business Policy,* New York: Oxford University Press, 1938.

WILLIAM FELLNER, *Competition Among the Few,* New York: Alfred A. Knopf, 1949.

WALTON HAMILTON, *Price and Price Policies,* New York: McGraw-Hill Book Company, 1938.

E. G. NOURSE AND H. B. DRURY, *Industrial Price Policies and Economic Progress,* Washington: The Brookings Institution, 1938.

CHAPTER 7

MARKETS IN MONOPOLISTIC COMPETITION

We have been concerned to this point with markets in pure competition, with single-firm monopolies, and with oligopolistic markets. The first two sorts of markets are not the most important in the American economy, but a detailed investigation of them is in any event justified because they illustrate certain characteristics of the pricing system in an extreme and simple form. The theory of oligopoly pricing is very closely related to the real economy since the majority of markets in manufactured goods and in mining have one sort or another of oligopolistic structure, and oligopoly is of substantial importance in other spheres. One further type of market remains to be discussed—the market in *monopolistic competition*. This designation is used narrowly here to refer to markets where there are many small sellers, and where their products are differentiated. In effect, it refers to competition within large groups of close- but not perfect-substitute products.

Monopolistic competition in a strict formal sense is probably not as important a market type as oligopoly in the American economy. Highly concentrated market structures are extremely common, and in many areas where concentration is relatively low, there will be nonetheless sufficient concentration to introduce at least some degree of oligopolistic interdependence among sellers. But a large number of industries provide close approximations to theoretical monopolistic competition. Some are manufacturing industries, and the type is quite common in the distributive trades (especially in retailing) and in the so-called service trades. In the manufacturing field a close approximation to monopolistic competition is found in the ladies' dress industry, in shoes, in millinery, and in similar consumers' goods industries where small-scale operations have proved to be economical. In the distributive field, clothing stores, drug stores, electric appliance stores, and the like in any locality constitute industries giving a reasonable approximation to monopolistic competition. In the service trades monopolistic competition is found in such markets as those populated by beauty parlors or barbers, shoe repair shops, dry cleaners, etc.

Moreover, there are a good many industries that might technically be classified as oligopolies—on the ground that there are some sellers who are big enough to have at least a weak interdependence with some rivals—in which the number of sellers is large enough and the degree of concentration low enough that they come fairly close to atomistic structure, and with respect to which the predictions of a theory of monopolistic competition may be more accurate than those of a theory of oligopoly. The leather dress glove industry, in which there are 246 firms, with 20 percent of the output supplied by the first four firms, 35 percent by the first eight, 56 percent by the first twenty, and 77 percent by the first fifty, exemplifies this large group of borderline cases. If these are considered to approximate roughly the conditions of monopolistic competition, the category is of very substantial importance in the American economy.

A. CONTROLLING CONDITIONS

MARKET STRUCTURE IN MONOPOLISTIC COMPETITION

An industry in monopolistic competition strictly occurs when a "large" number of sellers produce close-substitute but not identical products. The number of sellers should be great enough and the largest seller of the group small enough that no one controls a significant proportion of the group market. Each must control little enough that by substantially extending or restricting his own sales he does not perceptibly affect the sales of any other individual seller. There is thus no *recognized* interdependence of the related sellers' prices or price policies. Any seller may raise or lower his price enough to reduce or extend his sales volume substantially without eliciting a rivalrous reaction from any other seller in the group. The situation is like that of differentiated oligopoly except that the number of sellers is large enough that there is no recognized interdependence of price policies, and that each seller will presumably pursue an independent course.

This is the exact theoretical category of monopolistic competition. Many of the industries which we have characterized as roughly falling therein do not fulfill its conditions precisely. Although in certain industries there are many sellers of close-substitute but differentiated products, there is ordinarily some slight degree of recognized interdependence among them, or within certain subgroups of them. But this interdependence is sufficiently unimportant that they approximate markets in monopolistic competition, and an examination of the strict theoretical type may reveal a good deal about them.

The exact theoretical case would occur, for example, if in a metropolitan area there were perhaps 100 small independent grocery stores, selling similar lines of groceries but with their products differentiated by service and location, where each was *equally* in competition with every one of his 99 rivals. Any price cuts which one grocer would be likely to make would take business from his rivals, but in roughly equal proportions, so that any competitor, feeling only about $1/99$ th of the blow of the price cut, would suffer so little as not to notice it and therefore would not react. In the actual case some of the 100 groceries would be large enough that they would feel the effect of each other's price changes and have some recognized interdependence. Also, closely neighboring stores, in the same shopping center or only a block or two apart, would have a degree of recognized interdependence. Monopolistic competition would thus be alloyed with a bit of oligopoly. But the recognized interdependence would be small enough that we may emphasize the other aspect of the matter.

THE SELLER'S DEMAND CURVE IN MONOPOLISTIC COMPETITION

Price-output determination in monopolistic competition is relatively simple if we for the moment rule out both product variation and selling costs. We shall consider this simple case first. Here we have a large number of sellers producing close-substitute but differentiated products. The pattern of differentiation is frozen so that the various sellers are not changing their products over time. Two additional conditions are implicit in the existence of a large number of small sellers: (1) entry to the market is evidently easy—entry, that is, of additional close substitutes, although not of identical duplicates of existing products; and (2) collusive action by so many sellers is practically impossible. Thus, we might imagine an industry of 80 small manufacturers of cigarette lighters, differentiated by design and branding, but with all products for the moment assumed "static." No express or tacit collusion is feasible, and it is very easy for additional firms to enter the field with different brands or designs.

In this event each small seller has at any given time a demand curve for his product, showing the amounts of his product he can sell at each possible price, *provided his competitors' prices remain unchanged at their current levels.* What is the shape of this demand curve?

This matter was discussed at some length on pages 65 to 70. Evidently, the seller's demand curve will tend to be quite elastic, the elasticity depending on the value of the cross-elasticity of demand between the seller and each of his competitors—upon what percentage of each competitor's customers he can attract by a small price reduction and what percentage of his own customers he will lose to each competitor by a small price rise.

If cross-elasticity of demand is moderately high with each competitor for both price cuts and price increases by the seller, then the seller's demand curve will be very close to perfectly elastic. For example, suppose that there was a cross-elasticity of 10 between seller A and each of his competitors, so that he would take 10 percent of each competitor's customers by a 1-percent price cut, or add 1 percent to each competitor's customers by a $\frac{1}{10}$ of 1-percent price increase. Suppose further that there are 101 sellers in the industry, so that each has 100 competitors, and that all initially have the same number of customers. Then seller A would increase his customers by 1,000 percent by a 1-percent price cut, and lose all of his customers by a $\frac{1}{10}$ of 1-percent price increase. The elasticity of his own demand curve would be 1,000, or very close to perfectly elastic.

If the value of cross-elasticity of demand between pairs of sellers is typically low—for example, 0.5 or 1—then a perceptible departure from perfect elasticity is possible in the individual seller's demand curve. Either a very close approximation to perfect elasticity, or a high elasticity perceptibly less than perfect, is conceivable. The determinants of the elasticity of the individual seller's demand curve generally will be, first, the value of cross-elasticity of demand among pairs of sellers and, second, the number of sellers in the industry or the share of the total industry demand supplied by each.

It is possible that this seller's demand curve will have a continuous slope on both sides of the going price of the seller—that is, the same elasticity in response to small price increases as to small price decreases by the seller. It seems equally possible that under typical price relationships among sellers it will be kinked at the going price (or at a certain price, given the prices of other sellers), reflecting a discontinuously or suddenly higher elasticity for price cuts than for price rises. Thus, with 101 sellers it is quite conceivable that a single seller might by a 1-percent price cut gain 10 percent of the customers of each competitor (increasing his sales by 1,000 percent), whereas with a 1-percent price increase, he would lose only 10 percent of his own customers (or on the average only one tenth of a customer to each rival). Then his demand curve would be kinked at his going price, with an elasticity of 10 above the going price and of 1,000 below the going price. This possibility essentially emerges from the fact that a single seller supplying a very small fraction of the total market has many customers to gain with a price cut and few to lose with a price rise. Whether or not the seller's demand curve will be so kinked will evidently depend on the pattern of all buyers' preferences among competing goods, and either a continuous or a kinked demand curve is conceivable.[1]

The individual seller's demand curve, drawn on the supposition that his competitors will not change their prices in response to his own price changes, may appear, therefore, either as in Figure 38 or as in Figure 39. In Figure 38 we represent a continuous demand curve of high elasticity (the departure of which from perfect elasticity is perhaps exaggerated) and an associated marginal receipts curve of the conventional sort. This reflects the fact that by a small percentage price cut or increase the seller will gain or lose a large percentage of his sales volume. It is quite conceivable that this

[1] Cf. Alfred Nicols, "The Rehabilitation of Pure Competition," *Quarterly Journal of Economics,* November 1947, pp. 31-63.

demand curve may be very close indeed to horizontal (almost perfectly elastic) and that the difference between price and marginal receipts consequently will be very slight or negligible. In Figure 39 we represent a kinked

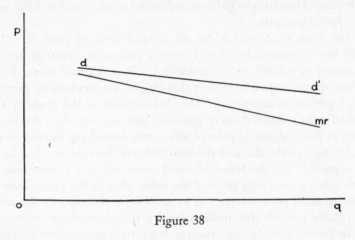

Figure 38

demand curve with distinctly higher elasticity for price cuts than for price rises at a certain price. This reflects a large percentage gain in sales for a small

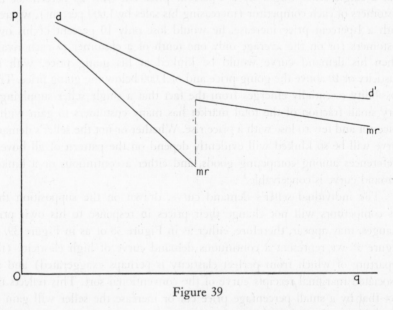

Figure 39

cut below a certain price, and a distinctly smaller percentage loss in sales for a similar small increase above the same price. The marginal receipts curve, showing additions to aggregate receipts for unit additions to output, is as a consequence discontinuous, lying higher to the right of the kink than to the left.

Pricing in monopolistic competition may be analyzed on the supposition of either sort of seller demand curve. Since the analysis of pricing is considerably more complex with a kinked demand curve and since the broad tendencies of pricing are in any event revealed by the analysis based on a simple continuous curve, we shall confine ourselves here to a consideration of pricing when the seller's demand curve is as represented in Figure 38. It should be noted, however, that a kinked demand pattern may be responsible for unique price phenomena—particularly dynamic oscillation of price around some central average.

The demand curve of the individual seller in monopolistic competition, then, may be viewed to a first approximation as a smooth continuous line of high elasticity, showing a large proportionate response of sales volume to either price cuts or price increases so long as competitors' prices remain unchanged. Two questions may now be raised about this demand curve. First, is the assumption on which it is drawn—that competitors' prices will not change in response to price changes by the individual seller—a legitimate assumption, so that in fact this *ceteris paribus* demand curve shows the net response of the seller's quantity of sales to his price? Second, in what significant respects does this seller's demand curve differ from that which characterizes markets in pure competition?

RELATIONSHIPS BETWEEN DIFFERENT SELLERS' DEMANDS

The *ceteris paribus* demand curve for the individual seller's output—based on the supposition that competitors' prices will not change in response to the seller's own price changes—evidently is the true demand curve for the seller's output in monopolistic competition for output adjustments anywhere in the neighborhood of the seller's going output. Monopolistic competition requires that each seller supply a very small fraction of industry output. If this is so, he can raise his price sufficiently to lose all of his customers without adding perceptibly to the sales of any one competitor, since the customers he loses will be divided among many small competitors. If he lowers his price enough to increase his sales substantially—for example, to double them— he will be able to do so by taking imperceptibly from the sales of each of a large number of competitors. Therefore, price changes sufficient to induce substantial increases or decreases in a seller's sales volume will affect any competitor so little that there will presumably be no reaction in competitive prices, and those prices may be taken as given. Thus, in the neighborhood of his going sales volume, the seller's demand curve is in effect the *ceteris paribus* demand curve described.

If, of course, the seller cut his price enough to extend his sales volume very greatly—for example, to increase it fiftyfold in a market with a hundred small sellers—then reactions would be induced and an assumption of no induced change in other prices would be illegitimate. Beyond some much larger output then his present one, his demand curve would take on a different character at the same time that this one seller became big enough that conditions of monopolistic competition no longer were fulfilled. It follows that maintenance of a situation of monopolistic competition in essence requires that the seller's cost curve be so shaped that he will be discouraged from producing a large share of the market, and this will ordinarily mean that he for some reason encounters some diseconomies of large-scale production when he is still supplying a small fraction of the market. If this condition is fulfilled, then the only section of his potential demand curve on which a seller will wish to operate will be a *ceteris paribus* demand curve of the sort described. Otherwise, for example, if there are significant economies of very large-scale production, an evolution toward oligopoly will be favored. It also is true that if buyers' preferences are so distributed that by cutting his price one seller takes very substantially from the customers of one rival and little or none from others, an element of oligopolistic interdependence will be introduced, the character of the demand curve will be altered, and monopolistic competition in the simple sense will no longer exist.

In monopolistic competition proper, in sum, the relevant range of the individual seller's demand curve will be very elastic and drawn on the legitimate assumption that other prices will not respond to his own price changes.

It should be noted, however, that the *position* of his demand curve—the level at which it lies—will be strongly dependent on the prices of his competitors at the moment, which will in turn depend on the quantity of their aggregate output in relation to the demand for industry output. For example, if the individual seller's 100 competitors are together currently supplying 1 million units of output, and are able to charge about $10 per unit, his demand schedule might look as follows:

Price	Quantity sold
$10.15	0
10.10	2,000
10.05	6,000
10.00	10,000
9.95	14,000
9.90	18,000

But if his competitors were producing 1.5 million units of output, and thus were able to charge about $6 per unit, his demand schedule might look about as follows:

Price	Quantity
$10.00	0
6.15	0
6.10	7,000
6.05	11,000
6.00	15,000
5.95	19,000
5.90	23,000

The position of his demand curve has shifted downward—indicating lower prices for all possible sales volumes—as industry output increased and the prices of all close substitutes, therefore, necessarily become lower. With any given set of outputs and prices, he may vary his own price enough to lose all his sales or extend them substantially without inducing price reactions from any competitor. But if the outputs and prices of all competitors change independently, his own demand curve shifts in response.

This phenomenon is evidently a slight variant of that found in pure competition, where the individual seller's horizontal demand curve moves automatically to the level of the market price received by all sellers whenever the market output changes. We may, therefore, inquire what substantial difference there is between sellers' demand curves in pure competition and in monopolistic competition or between the two market structures in general. Two differences are possible, and one of these is bound to be present. First, the seller's demand curve may have a significant departure from perfect elasticity or horizontality—a significant negative slope. This is to say roughly that he must lower his price perceptibly below its going level to attract a substantial increment of customers, and he can raise his price perceptibly above this level without losing all of his own customers. He has then a significant degree of independent price discretion, and he may depart significantly from a given uniform level of market price. However, it is by no means necessary that this will be so in monopolistic competition. The cross-elasticity of demand between pairs of sellers may be high enough that individual demand curves do not depart significantly from perfect elasticity, and then in this respect the demand situation in monopolistic competition is the same as in pure competition.

There is, however, a second difference from pure competition that will persist even if the seller has a substantially horizontal demand curve. This is that, with product differentiation, the individual sellers' demand curves need not all be at precisely the same level at the same time—they are not necessarily faced with a single uniform market price for all their outputs at any given time in the market. In pure competition every seller's demand curve is in essence a horizontal line at the same level of the going market price since the products are perfect substitutes and no buyer will pay more for one than another. In monopolistic competition, on the other hand, the products are imperfect substitutes to buyers—regarded at least as somewhat different. It is thus quite possible—even though every seller's demand curve is very close to horizontal—that different curves may simultaneously lie at somewhat different levels. Sellers number one through eighty may each be charging a price of $10 per unit, be able to extend sales substantially without significantly cutting price, and be exposed to a total loss of customers by a 1-percent price increase. At the same time, given those prices, seller number eighty-one may be able to sell at no higher a price than $9.50 and may be able to gain all the buyers he can supply at this price, whereas seller number eighty-two in effect has an approximately horizontal demand curve at the price of $11. Thus, in monopolistic competition—even with horizontal demand curves —we find that the several sellers' curves may simultaneously lie at different levels, and instead of the single market price of pure competition we have potentially a related variety of different prices, reflecting buyers' different evaluations of various products. In addition, of course, each seller's demand curve *may* also slope significantly so that each has a narrow range of alternative prices from which to choose in a given situation rather than a single price.

Related to this difference is another. Since products are differentiated, they may also be presumed to be *variable* and also subject to sales promotion. As a result, any seller is potentially able to shift the relative position of the demand curve for his output either by varying its design or quality or by changing the amount of his selling costs. This facet of the problem we shall neglect for the moment, however, as we turn to simple price-output determination with given products and given selling costs.

If we momentarily disregard the shiftability of sellers' demand curves via product variation and sales promotion, however, it is clear that the similarities of monopolistic to pure competition are more impressive than the differences. The sellers are many and small in both cases, so small that any one may undertake independent price or output adjustments without inducing responses from competitors in the industry. In both cases the seller's demand curve—reflecting the preceding fact—is horizontal or approximately so, reflecting his ability to sell only at or approximately at a given market price level. In both cases this demand curve moves up and down with market output and the general level of market price so that the seller must always take this level (determined by market-wide adjustments) as given or approximately given. In both cases he is either exactly or approximately at the mercy of an impersonal market price. The differences—that in monopolistic competition the seller may in a given situation have a narrow range of choice over price and that the several sellers' prices may differ somewhat with differences in quality or buyer esteem—seem substantially less important than the similarities. This will appear as we analyze the process of price determination in monopolistic competition.

B. PRICE AND OUTPUT DETERMINATION IN MONOPOLISTIC COMPETITION

ADJUSTMENT BY THE SINGLE SELLER

The process of price-output determination in monopolistic competition may be analyzed by considering, first, the adjustment of the individual seller to a given situation of demand for his product, and, second, the industry-wide

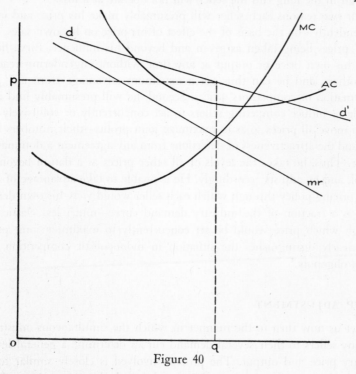

Figure 40

or market adjustments of all prices and outputs which occurs when all sellers make their separate adjustments.

The adjustment of the individual seller is extremely simple. At any time, with given prices and outputs for all competing sellers, we conceive of the individual seller facing an elastic demand curve for his own output. This demand curve lies at a level determined by the prices of all competing products, which are in turn determined by the relation of total industry supply to industry demand. It may be perceptibly sloping, like that in Figure 40, or approximately horizontal, like that in Figure 17 (page 132).

In either case the seller will independently try to maximize his profits by choosing that price and output at which his marginal cost is equal to his marginal receipts, as drawn from the demand curve. This will involve the choice of an output such as oq and a price such as op in Figure 40. If the demand curve slopes perceptibly, there will be a perceptible, but not large, discrepancy between price and marginal cost, as shown there. If not, marginal cost will approximately equal price, as in the adjustment in pure competition (see Figure 17).

In the absence of knowledge concerning the level of other prices, it is impossible to say whether this adjustment will permit an excess profit or not, although in the long run the seller will not operate at a loss.

For two reasons each seller will presumably make his price and output independently—on the basis of the effect of his price on his own sales, other sellers' prices being taken as given and beyond his influence. First, he can adjust his own price or output at any time without engendering reactions from others, and he can thus get a maximum advantage from any given conformation of competitors' prices. Second, he will presumably find it impossible to induce competing sellers to act concurrently or collusively with him to move all prices so as to maximize joint profits—their numbers being great and the attractiveness of defections from any agreement a dominant influence. Thus, he takes the levels of all other prices as a datum beyond his control, and he adjusts accordingly. He is unable to take advantage of a collusive pricing policy through which each seller would view his own demand curve as a fraction of the industry demand curve—much less elastic—and through which price would be set concurrently to maximize joint profits. This clearly distinguishes the situation in monopolistic competition from that in oligopoly.

GROUP ADJUSTMENT

Let us now turn to the manner in which the simultaneous adustments of many sellers to their several demand curves determine a general level of industry price and output. The process involved is closely similar to that found in the case of pure competition, and described on pages 136 to 145. In pure competition, as we have seen, the seller's demand curve is a horizontal straight line at the level of the going market price for the single homogeneous good. The level of this demand curve (the market price) is determined at any time by the relation of the total industry output to the industry demand curve for the product. Given any level of their demand curves, sellers will independently but simultaneously adjust their outputs to them so that for each marginal cost equals price. If the total output thus forthcoming is equal to the total amount buyers will take at the initial price, the industry is in provisional equilibrium. If, however, the sum of seller outputs thus determined is greater than buyers will take at the price, price will fall and sellers' demand curves shift downward, causing a readjustment of sellers' outputs. (If outputs are smaller than buyers will take at the price, price will rise.) Price (and seller demand curves) will thus move to a provisional equilibrium level such that the sum of the outputs which sellers wish to supply (with marginal cost equal to price) is identical to the total amount buyers will take. This has been defined as the price-output combination at which the sum of marginal cost curves of all sellers intersects the industry demand curve. If in the provisional equilibrium there are excess profits or net losses, price will be further adjusted in the long run through entry or exit.

In the case of monopolistic competition, the argument is closely similar. Each seller has a demand curve for his output which is either approximately horizontal or very elastic. The level of this demand curve—that is, the price or narrow range of prices at or within which it lies—is determined by the general level of his competitors' prices, which in turn is determined by the relation of the total of their outputs to the industry demand curve for them. Given any initial level of their demand curves, sellers will independently but simultaneously move to adjust their outputs and prices to them so that for each marginal cost equals marginal receipts (as in Figure 40 or Figure 17). If the total output thus forthcoming is equal to the total amount buyers will take at the prices anticipated, the industry is in provisional equilibrium. If, however, the sum of seller outputs thus determined is greater than buyers will take at the intended prices, prices will tend to fall below those indicated by the dd' curves. The sellers' demand curves will thus shift downward— showing their independent price alternatives at the new level of price—and they will readjust their outputs and prices to their dd' curves in their new positions. This process will continue until a provisional equilibrium is reached in which prices and the levels of sellers' demand curves have become such that the amounts which they produce with marginal cost equal to marginal receipts is just equal to the amounts buyers will take at the prices set. If excess profits or net losses are now encountered, entry or exit may lead to further adjustment of price.

Thus, we see the close parallel of the adjustment processes in pure and monopolistic competition. In both a general level of industry price and output is determined by the interaction of the industry demand and the total industry supply as determined by all the firms' marginal costs. The sellers' demand curves are elastic and shifting lines, the shifts in which reflect the responses of price to shifting industry supply, and which eventually reach a level such that they induce sellers to supply just the quantities of output which buyers will take at the equilibrium price. The major difference is that the seller's demand curve may be slightly sloping in monopolistic competition so that sellers may have a slight choice over price and may set outputs so that marginal costs are slightly below price rather than equal to it. Correspondingly, the industry equilibrium may be found at an output just short of that at which the summation of the marginal cost curves of all sellers intersects the industry demand curve, rather than right at this intersection.

The process of market adjustment may thus be viewed as one of the successive adjustments of each of many sellers to a dd' curve (showing the relation of *independent* price to output changes) which shifts in response to the simultaneous price or output adjustments of all sellers, and continues shifting until all dd' curves have reached positions such that each seller can produce an output at which mc equals mr and actually sell this output at the price shown by his dd'. At this point the aggregate output which sellers, according to independent profit-maximizing calculations, wish to supply, is equal to aggregate demand at the corresponding prices. And at this point there will be at least an approximate equality of marginal cost to price for all sellers, as in pure competition.

It may be emphasized that when every seller adjusts output and price in this fashion—so as to equate his marginal cost to marginal receipts drawn from his *ceteris paribus* demand curve—he not only assumes (correctly) that his competitors will not react to his adjustments, but also he overlooks or is not influenced by what will happen to his price when all his competitors extend their outputs simultaneously (though independently) with his, or to his sales when they simultaneously cut their prices with his. The shifts in his demand curve which ensue from simultaneous adjustments by all competitors do not deter him from trying to exploit this demand curve independently in each new position, taking each shift as a datum outside his control. He is led, through the high elasticity of his *ceteris paribus* demand curve, to produce larger outputs and ultimately to accept lower prices than if he had viewed his demand curve as a fraction of the industry demand curve on the postulate that each of his competitors would simply match his own price or output changes. The reason he does not take the latter view is that this postulate would presumably be incorrect—his competitors would pursue independent courses unless assured that others would not, and would cut prices even if he did not. Thus, because effective collusion is presumably impossible to arrange with large numbers and no recognized interdependence restrains individual sellers' policies, price decisions are not oriented to the elasticity of the industry demand curve or share thereof, as in collusive oligopoly, but to the deceptively high elasticities of the various sellers' *ceteris paribus* demand curves, with the ultimate result that joint profits are not maximized and that prices are lower and outputs larger than if they were. Here we see the major distinctions between pricing in monopolistic competition and in collusive oligopoly.

When a provisional industry equilibrium is attained in monopolistic competition, each seller will be producing with his marginal cost equal to the marginal receipts drawn from his *ceteris paribus* demand curve, as in Figure 40, this demand curve having shifted in the process of group adjustment to where buyers will take his output *oq* at the price *op* and a similar *oq* output at a similar *op* price from each seller in the industry. Such an equilibrium will tend to be reached with any given number of sellers in the industry.

So long as we take the number of sellers as arbitrarily given, it is impossible to say whether this equilibrium will permit excess profits to sellers, as in Figure 40, zero profits, as in Figure 41, or net losses. The results in this regard, given the level of industry demand, will depend on the number of sellers and the level and shape of their marginal and average cost curves, which together fix the provisional industry equilibrium level of sellers' demand curves and prices, and the relation of price to average cost. In the short run a provisional equilibrium of any of the three sorts may be maintained. In the long run, however, a provisional equilibrium which involves net losses to some or all sellers will lead to exit, and one which involves excess profits may lead to entry.

GROUP EQUILIBRIUM

The long-run adjustment involving entry and exit is extremely simple if we suppose a situation in which all firms are always identical with respect to the level and shape of their cost curves and of their separate demand curves, so that their profit or loss positions will always be identical in any situation, and if additional entrants will always have cost and demand curves identical to those of established firms. In this simplified situation it is apparent that if the provisional equilibrium places all firms in a net loss position (the *dd'* curve of each lying completely below his *AC* curve), some firms will leave the industry. As they do, the industry supply will be restricted, the price will rise, and correlatively the *dd'* curves of remaining sellers will shift upward. Long-run equilibrium will be reached when enough exit takes place that the *dd'* curve of each seller rises to tangency with his average cost curve, as in Figure 41, at which point he will charge the price at which he can break even, *op* in Figure 41, and produce the quantity *oq*.

Conversely, if the provisional equilibrium places all sellers in an excess-profit position like that shown in Figure 40 and there is easy entry, additional firms will be attracted to enter the industry, industry supply will be expanded, price will fall, and correlatively the *dd'* curves of all sellers will shift downward. Equilibrium will again be reached when the demand curve of each becomes tangent to his average cost curve, at the price *op* and quantity *oq* in Figure 41.

With free exit and entry and identical cost and demand positions for all firms, therefore, the industry in monopolistic competition tends in the long run to reach a no-excess-profit or normal-profit equilibrium. In this equilibrium each firm is producing with price equal to average cost. If its demand curve slopes perceptibly, price will be slightly above the firm's marginal cost; if it is approximately horizontal, price will equal marginal cost also. The

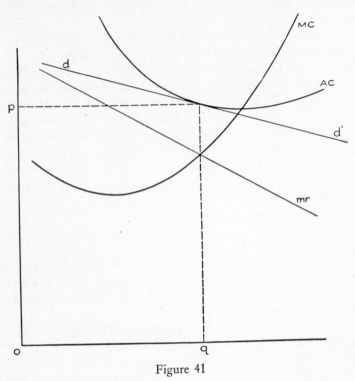

Figure 41

close similarity of this equilibrium result to that attributed to pure competition is evident.

The major differences from purely competitive equilibrium arise if there is a significant slope to the demand curve of the individual seller. In this case the equilibrium will theoretically be reached for each firm where his sloping demand curve is tangent to his average cost curve (see Figure 41), and this will be at an output slightly smaller than his minimum cost output and a price slightly higher than this minimum cost. At the same time price will slightly exceed rather than equal marginal cost. The reason, in common-sense terms, that equilibrium is reached at this point rather than where price equals minimal average cost is that with a slightly sloping demand curve each seller tries to enhance his own profit by a corresponding slight restriction of output and raising of price at all times until profits are eliminated by the entry of a sufficient number of firms to force all to produce at uneconomically low rates.

However, the deviation from a purely competitive equilibrium is likely to be relatively slight. Excess profits are absent in both instances. In monopolistic competition there may be a slight deviation from optimal average cost and, since price is equated to this slightly higher cost rather than to optimal cost, a slightly smaller industry output. But with the probability of very elastic seller demand curves in monopolistic competition, the deviation from purely competitive equilibrium results are not likely to be important.

The properties of the preceding equilibrium, however, rest in part upon the existence of identical demand and cost situations for all sellers—or some equally peculiar symmetry in the relations of their demands to their costs—and upon easy entry. Neither of these conditions will of necessity be exactly fulfilled in fact. Some firms will ordinarily enjoy more advantageous relations of demand to cost than others, and potential entrants may be at some disadvantage relative to established firms. In this case any industry equilibrium would be likely to find some sellers in the normal-profit position, and others, with especially popular products or "strong" trade-marks, still earning excess profits. In effect, the "monopoly" positions of some of the sellers would ultimately be rendered valueless by the pressure of entry, whereas other such positions would retain some value. Tentative stability would be reached, then, when no potential entrant felt he could make normal or better profits by entering the industry. Very large excess profits for any seller, however, are made improbable if there are no important artificial barriers to entry.[2]

Should product variation and selling costs be ruled out (as we have done by assumption so far), it is not clear that monopolistic competition would yield *significantly* different results than pure competition. The former would resemble the latter in that long-run excess profits would be absent or small. It would differ in that there might be a slight price-marginal-cost discrepancy and a slight departure from optimum scale whenever equilibrium was reached, reflecting an equivalent departure from minimum attainable cost of industry output. And there would be a variety of brands rather than a single homogeneous product.[3] But if we do not correct for the rotation of the earth in a snowball fight, perhaps these differences in a dynamic economy can be neglected.

[2] For the original (and more detailed) development of this theory, see Edward H. Chamberlin, *The Theory of Monopolistic Competition,* 5th ed. (Cambridge: Harvard University Press, 1946), Chap. 5.

[3] It may be argued that the advantage of variety to consumers compensates at least in part for the departure from minimum aggregate cost.

C. SALES PROMOTION AND PRODUCT ADJUSTMENT

NONPRICE COMPETITION AMONG MANY SELLERS

The behavior of sellers in monopolistic competition also involves product policies and sales-promotion policies; an appraisal of performance in monopolistically competitive industries thus must take account of the performance of firms with respect to the determination of product and the level of selling costs.

Like the single-firm monopolist or the seller in differentiated oligopoly, the seller in monopolistic competition has the opportunity to influence the demand for his output by altering the design or quality of his product or by sales-promotion activities. Also like sellers in either of these other market categories, he will presumably tend to adjust his product to that level permitting him a maximum profit and to follow the same course with respect to selling costs.

The rationale of his policy in these respects, however, will potentially differ from that affecting sellers' policies in differentiated oligopoly. In that case we have seen that the policies of one seller designed to improve the relation of the demand for his product to his costs by changing his product, or to increase demand by increasing selling costs, will be designed in the light of his knowledge that his competitors, or rivals, will react to his alterations in product and selling cost so far as their own sales are perceptibly affected thereby. In consequence he will tend to be deterred, partly or wholly, from product or selling cost adjustments which enhance his sales at the expense of rivals, and which are not consistent with a maximization of the joint profits of all oligopolists in the industry. In monopolistic competition, on the other hand, the individual seller supplies—and because of cost conditions is able to supply—so small a fraction of the market that his product and selling cost adjustments (like his price adjustments) will presumably have a negligible effect on the sales of any one competitor. (However, the addition of many such small effects may enable him to enhance his sales very significantly at the expense of his competitors as a group.) He will, therefore, be led to pursue product and selling cost policies which are made in disregard of potential reactions in competitive policies of similar sort, which are gainful to him largely because they levy a loss on the sales of other sellers in general, and which are inconsistent with the maximization of the joint profits of all sellers in the industry.

When each of many such sellers pursues such a policy independently but simultaneously with the others, it is possible that their several product and selling cost adjustments will tend to cancel out each others' intended effects on individual firms' sales and that all will lose potential joint profits in consequence of their essentially competitive policies. In this respect the behavior of the group of sellers in monopolistic competition is similar to that of a group of single-firm monopolists, each of whom pursues an independent policy in the regards mentioned, taking the product and sales-promotion policies of monopolists in other industries as given or beyond his control. The major difference in an industry in monopolistic competition is that since the various sellers' products are rather close substitutes (whereas the outputs of several single-firm monopolists are by definition distant substitutes), there will be an increased opportunity for the individual seller to enhance his sales at the expense of others by sales promotion or product variation. Thus, excessive selling costs and excessive product improvement become very distinct possibilities within industries in monopolistic competition.

What results are likely to emerge from sales-promotion and product-determination policies in an industry in monopolistic competition?

SALES PROMOTION AND SELLING COSTS

Let us first examine probable behavior with respect to sales promotion and selling costs, the nature of which has been discussed on pages 312 to 313. Taking each seller's product for the moment as given, any seller is presumably in a position to enhance his profits by an independent increase in his sales-promotion activities and selling costs. The formal argument here is as follows: Any single seller in a given situation will regard his competitors' products, prices, and sales-promotion outlays as given, beyond his control, and nonresponsive to his own selling cost adjustments. He will thus reason that by an independent increase in his selling costs he may attract customers away from his competitors (only a few from each competitor, but many in the aggregate), or, in effect, he may cause the *ceteris paribus* demand curve for his product (*dd'* in Figure 40 or 41) to shift upward or to the right. Each seller in turn will tend to increase his selling costs so long as the added revenue made possible by the shift in his demand curve (through either larger output or higher prices) exceeds the addition to selling cost plus any addition to production cost if output is extended.

Each seller in turn will reason and act in the same general way and thus will have a tendency to increase his selling costs up to some most profitable point. However, when all sellers pursue such independent policies simultaneously, none of them actually reaps the extra reward in revenue which he expects from his independent adjustment, since the various sales-promotion campaigns cancel each other out in large part and none of them causes much of a shift in buyers from one seller to another. Thus, the individual seller demand curves actually do not shift upward as anticipated by each seller in turn, and aggregate selling costs are increased beyond the level consistent with maximum joint profits. Instead costs become higher and with them equilibrium prices.

If we pursue this argument on the supposition that each seller sees his way to increased profits in exactly the same way—that is, higher demand and generally higher price through higher selling costs—we are led to the following conclusions. First, selling costs will tend to be high—higher than in monopoly or differentiated oligopoly in general—since sales-promotion policies are not restrained by recognized interdependence and since the existence of many close substitutes may make the individual seller's demand very responsive to increases in his selling costs. Second, since all firms will incur selling costs, the average cost per unit of output will tend to be raised thereby, and in long-run equilibrium (after adjustment by entry or exit) the industry price will tend to be higher and the industry output smaller than in the absence of selling costs. In general also, the number of firms consistent with a profitless equilibrium will be smaller.

This is the outcome emphasized by Chamberlin in his *Theory of Monopolistic Competition,* where this problem was first explored. It is a possible outcome, but it should be noted that its fundamental premise—that each firm in turn will see its way to independent profit increases via the same route of increased selling costs and ultimately increased prices—implicitly rests on some rather special suppositions concerning the structure of buyer preferences and the responsiveness of buyers to sales promotion appeals. One supposition consistent with the foregoing prediction is that all or most buyers are at least somewhat responsive to selling costs and that all or most of them have a similar degree of responsiveness, so that all sellers, in order to maintain or increase their markets, will be led in the same direction of increased sales-promotion expenditures up to a given common level.

It should be noted, on the other hand, that if there is a very considerable *diversity* in the responsiveness of various buyers to sales-promotion appeals and a substantial number of buyers in each of two or more categories of responsiveness, then all sellers may not be led in the same path of sales-promotion activity. Suppose, for example, that half the buyers in the market are quite susceptible to sales-promotion appeals and prefer a heavily advertised good at higher prices to a nonadvertised good at lower prices, and that the other half of the buyers are not advertising-conscious but instead quite price-conscious, preferring a nonadvertised good at a given price to an advertised good at any higher price. Then it is by no means evident that all sellers will find it advantageous to pursue similar sales-promotion policies. If some or many of them go after increased sales by intensive sales promotion and build up costs and prices thereby (each seller pursuing essentially the sales volume available from advertising-conscious buyers), this tendency immediately creates an opportunity for other sellers to corner the price-conscious sector of the buying market by offering their products without advertising. The nonadvertisers then enjoy a demand or price which, though below that of aggressive advertisers, is sufficiently high, with their lower costs, to yield them extra profits. If we generalize this argument, it appears that a substantial diversity among buyers with respect to responsiveness to sales promotion and to price may lead to corresponding diversities in the sales-promotion policies of sellers in monopolistic competition and in the levels of their costs and prices. If there is easy entry to the industry, it is still quite possible that excess profits will be generally eliminated in the long-run equilibrium, with each subgroup of sellers (divided on the basis of sales-promotion policies) crowded to the point where demand curves are tangent to average cost curves.

The probability of the development of diversity of this type seems substantially greater in monopolistic competition than in differentiated oligopoly. First, with the much larger number and smaller size of sellers there is more likelihood that an individual seller will find it advantageous to cater to the preferences of a relatively small fraction of the buying market. Second, individual sellers' adjustments of sales-promotion policies are unrestrained by recognized interdependence. And third, the absence of price collusion, and of other deterrents to downward price adjustments, makes it much more probable that a seller will seek advantage through the combined policy of lower pricing and restricted sales promotion.

The effects on the general welfare of performance in monopolistic competition with respect to sales promotion obviously depend upon whether the behavior pattern is in the direction of uniform policies among sellers, with all promoting sales competitively in about the same way, or in the direction of diversity. We have already referred, on pages 316 to 320, to the difficulties of determining to what extent sales-promotion outlays ultimately add to the satisfaction of buyers. Whatever may be decided in this regard, the following is apparent with respect to monopolistic competition. First, if a pattern of uniformity among sellers in competition via sales promotion develops, selling costs tend to be relatively large, to be incurred sufficiently to reduce the joint profits of the sellers, and thus to be more probably excessive from the standpoint of buyer welfare than in other market structures. Second, if a pattern of diversity develops, selling costs for some fraction of sellers may still be quite large. However, the fact that buyers will be offered a choice between the heavily promoted good and the lightly promoted one, at a corresponding difference in prices, will permit each buyer to select an alternative relatively close to his own first preference, and this should lead to a better adjustment of selling cost to resultant buyer satisfaction than is found in other market structures.

Casual observation of many industries which approximate monopolistic competition suggests that the pattern of diversity may be quite common and that performance as to sales promotion may be quite satisfactory from a social standpoint in this sector.

PRODUCT BEHAVIOR

The analysis of product behavior in monopolistic competition follows much the same lines as that of sales promotion. The fundamental considerations are (1) that each seller is able to select from a range of alternative products; (2) that as he shifts from one product to another, the level of his demand curve—his competitors' products remaining unchanged—shifts, and his production costs also change; (3) that his product adjustments will not elicit reactions from his rivals and he will then pursue an independent product policy, based on the premise that competitive products are either given or outside his influence; and (4) that the seller will presumably select that product alternative which in view of the combined demand and cost effects allows him the largest profit.

Each of the many small sellers will pursue such a policy independently. Since each disregards the effects of rivalrous or parallel action by others, taking their products as given, he will count as gains from a given product change the added customers which his independent adjustment will tend to attract away from his many competitors. But when many sellers make independent product adjustments simultaneously, none may gain as much demand as anticipated, since each of the several product adjustments cancel the other's effect, in part at least, and the shift of buyers between sellers is restricted. Then the aggregate of product adjustments may be such as to reduce the joint profit of the sellers, or possibly to eliminate all profit—although, in general, we may view the elimination of profits as jointly accomplished by product adjustments, selling cost adjustments, and entry or exit. The tendency to carry product adjustments to a mutually unprofitable level is presumably much stronger in monopolistic competition than in differentiated oligopoly, since in monopolistic competition neither recognized interdependence nor product collusion will place any restraint on competitive product adjustments.

The outcome of this product competition, like that of competitive sales promotion, may be of divergent sorts. The composition of the buying market may be such that all sellers are led to compete via similar policies of product improvement, each in effect attempting to shift his demand curve upward, largely by attracting customers from his competitors, through improving the design or quality of his product and raising his costs. In this case—applying the argument developed for product rivalry in oligopoly, on pages 325 to 329 —the following is evident. First, since the parallel independent policies of the many competitors tend to cancel each other out and to forestall the shift of customers which each seller anticipates from each successive product improvement, no seller gains in demand as much as he expects from product improvements, and the added costs of improved products turn out to be greater than the added revenues. The increases in *industry* demand and revenue are insufficient to compensate for the increases in cost from product improvements; a collusive group of sellers would forego many unprofitable increments to product quality which the competitive industry undertakes. Second, the level of product quality will tend to be generally raised to such an extent that the added satisfaction to buyers will not fully compensate for the resultant additions to cost. This is reflected in the fact that the individual seller can, in his *ceteris paribus* reasoning, attract added customers away from his competitors by a quality improvement which adds more to unit cost than he needs to add to price in order to increase his profits.

This pattern of product development is generally similar to one already described for differentiated oligopoly with product rivalry, which as we have seen may also lead to a reduction of joint profits and an excessive level of product quality. In a given situation of consumer preferences this tendency probably is more severe in monopolistic competition, however, since with atomistic market structure the individual seller's attempt to improve his own profits by competitive quality increases is not at all restrained by recognized interdependence. In addition, the small seller, with only a small fraction of the market himself and nearly all of it to attract away from others, may tend to envisage a larger proportional response of his own demand to a given product improvement. If the composition of the buying market is such as to favor parallel policies of competitive product improvement by all sellers, therefore, there seems to be a probability of a larger excess of product improvement in monopolistic competition than in any alternative market structure.

A different situation is encountered when the composition of the buying market is such that the various sellers are led to pursue quite divergent product policies. For example, the market may be made up in part of buyers who are strongly quality-conscious and not especially price-conscious—being willing to pay substantially more for higher quality—and in part of buyers who are more price-conscious, or willing to accept substantially lower quality in order to get a somewhat lower price. In this case some sellers may see increased profits in policies of product improvement and relatively high price, whereas the very fact that they pursue such policies tends to make it more profitable for others to emphasize lower quality, cost, and price. Market equilibrium with respect to products may then tend to be characterized by a substantial variety of qualities, costs, and prices. To be sure product competition may exist among a number of sellers at each quality level, so that the product adjustment will not necessarily be ideal from the standpoint of buyers, and joint profits will definitely not tend to be maximized. However, it is clear that since a maximum attainable product variety tends to develop,

with buyers able to choose among a wide range of alternative product qualities, costs, and prices, there will tend to be a much better balance of the cost
of product improvement against the resulting increment to buyer satisfaction
than where uniform product improvement policies are pursued. In fact, the
pattern of product selection should be better from the buyer's standpoint in
this variant of monopolistic competition than in any other market situation.

The probability of such a diversity of product policy developing, moreover, is greater in monopolistic competition than in differentiated oligopoly.
Relatively small sellers may find it profitable to cater to the special desires of
small sectors of the buying market, and the absence of recognized interdependence or collusion on price removes potential restraints on independent
product-price adjustments.

The preceding refers to the selection by sellers of product design or
quality from a more-or-less given range of alternatives. A related question
concerns the performance of sellers in monopolistic competition in developing and introducing new products. As is usual on the issue of progressiveness
in product, it is difficult to make any general predictions. On the one hand,
active product competition evidently provides something like a maximum
incentive to develop and introduce new products, and the individual seller
will not be at all restrained from making innovations because they tend to
reduce industry profits. In this respect faster progressiveness than in monopoly or oligopoly is favored. On the other hand, the threat of quick imitation
of innovations by established competitors or new entrants, plus the lack of
large excess profits to finance research, tend to discourage invention and
innovation. Thus the net relation of progressiveness in monopolistic competition to that in monopoly or oligopoly is difficult to appraise on a priori
grounds.

D. MONOPOLISTIC COMPETITION AND GENERAL WELFARE

THE COMPARATIVE MARKET PERFORMANCE
OF MONOPOLISTIC COMPETITION

In the preceding two sections we have considered the impact on social welfare
of the behavior of industries in monopolistic competition with respect to
product determination and sales promotion. These are indeed the only
respects in which industries in monopolistic competition require special evaluation, since in other respects their behavior closely approximates that of pure
competition, already evaluated. As we have seen, excess profits tend to be
eliminated in monopolistic competition, so that the impact on income distribution and on employment should be about the same as in pure compe-

tition. In the long run equilibrium operations should be at approximately optimal scale, so that the performance with respect to efficiency is also similar. Although there may be slight marginal-cost-price discrepancies in monopolistic competition, they seem likely to be negligible, so that allocation should be closely similar to that in pure competition except for the allocation of added resources to sales promotion and product improvement. Other distortions of allocation seem likely to be negligible in comparison to that produced by monopoly or collusive oligopoly. The effects of behavior in monopolistic competition on progressiveness in techniques and on stability likewise promise to be similar to those of purely competitive behavior. In brief, we can characterize the merits and shortcomings of monopolistic competition in all essential respects as roughly the same as those of pure competition, except for the added complications of product behavior and sales promotion. It is also true of monopolistic competition that it is a tenable market structure only where there are no substantial economies of very large-scale production to favor the development of oligopoly or monopoly. The similarities noted obviously follow from the fact that in pure and monopolistic competition we encounter the two main variants of *atomistic competition*—competition among many small sellers, ordinarily accompanied by easy entry.

MONOPOLISTIC COMPETITION VERSUS OTHER MARKET FORMS

More broadly, it may be interesting at this point to compare the institution of monopolistic competition with all other types of market organization we have considered. For markets in general three fundamental factors condition the emergent price behavior: (1) whether or not the individual seller has rivals or competitors producing an identical product; (2) whether the number of rivals producing an identical or close-substitute product is none, few, or many; and (3) whether additional entry to the market is easy, difficult, or impossible. These three conditions may be labeled briefly as degree of product differentiation, degree of concentration of sellers in an industry, and condition of entry.

Of these conditions, two seem to be of dominant importance from any standpoint—the number of sellers and the degree of the ease of entry of more sellers. Where the number of sellers is large and entry is easy (the second condition almost always accompanies the first), we generally find little net restriction of industry output below a practical maximum, little or no excess profits, reasonably low costs, and a rather flexible price over time. This is true of both pure competition and monopolistic competition, which are dominantly similar in these respects. To be sure, they have one significant difference with respect to product differentiation. In monopolistic competition this difference may give rise to a slightly greater number of sellers relative to a given demand, to production at slightly less than optimum scale, to some selling costs, and to a variety of products in an industry rather than a single standardized product. But the differences are probably not as significant as the similarities.

Where the number of sellers is few and entry is correspondingly more difficult, a basically different system of behavior is introduced. Price results, stemming from the intrinsically interdependent decisions of a few large sellers, are no longer automatically or quasi-automatically determined by impersonal market forces, but emerge from deliberate price policies. They therefore become much more difficult to predict except by investigating a large number of considerations which condition the formation of such policies. The most significant of such considerations are the degree of ease of new entry to the industry and the degree of oligopolistic concentration. From oligopolistic industry, therefore, we get a number of significant sub-patterns, depending on these and other considerations. The dominant single motif, however, is some restriction of aggregate output and some tendency toward excess profit (these tendencies being stronger as new entry is more difficult).

These are of course not the only significant potential differences in performance between atomistic and concentrated industries. In particular, relative performance with respect to efficiency and progressiveness, and relative effects on income security, as discussed above, must also be taken into account.

EMPIRICAL EVIDENCE OF INDUSTRY BEHAVIOR
IN MONOPOLISTIC COMPETITION

Observation of business behavior in industries which approximate conditions of monopolistic competition lends some support to the theoretical predictions just developed. In the manufacturing field the ladies' dress industry is a fair example.[4] There are many small dress manufacturers, located in New York, Los Angeles, and other metropolitan centers. Large scale offers negligible advantages in cost, since the basic technical units, after designing and pattern drafting, are the cutting shears and the sewing machine. Competition is extremely active in both price and nonprice phases. Each seller differentiates and varies his line of dresses through annual or seasonal style changes and engages in a modicum of sales promotion through hired sales representatives, entertainment of buyers from retail stores, and so forth. Prices are ostensibly fixed in conventional "price lines"—for example, cotton dresses may be priced wholesale at $1.87, $2.87, $3.87, and so on, and rayon dresses at $8.75, $10.75, etc. Each seller produces in certain price lines. Com-

[4] See Nelson and Keim, *op. cit.,* Chap. 3.

petition takes place continually by variation of the quality, as measured in style, fabric, and workmanship, of the products offered in given price lines and, alternatively, by shifting products of given quality from one price line to another. Nonprice and price competition are inseparably blended.

The average result of this sort of competition over time is for most sellers to drive price to the level of cost, allowing barely normal profits. Selling costs are quite small. It has not been ascertained whether a price-marginal-cost discrepancy occurs or whether firms operate at less than the optimum scale. But the general effects of independent price and product policies by a large number of sellers and of unrestricted and easy entry to the industry are evident.

The same general phenomenon is observed in groups or "industries" of retail sellers in given localities—for example, in men's haberdashery and clothing stores in any metropolis. There will be a large number of such stores, including the men's clothing departments of department stores. Non-price competition occurs partly in terms of basic product—the quality of the clothing bought and sold—partly in terms of service, location of store, beauty and "snob-appeal" of the store, partly in terms of credit facilities offered, and partly in terms of newspaper and radio advertising. Price competition takes place through varying the regular margin or markup earned on clothing and through cut-price "sales." The two sorts of competition combine in most cases to drive costs upward a bit toward price and to drive price downward toward cost. The net results are similar to those attributed to the ladies' dress industry. Sales-promotion costs, as distinct from the costs of performing the basic function of assembling, storing, displaying, and delivering the goods, can hardly be characterized as an excessive or large proportion of total costs. A considerable variety of product quality—especially as represented in convenience of store location, amount of personal service, character of credit facilities, etc.—is notable.

A number of our retail distributive industries fall in the pattern just described, and more of them would if it were not for certain special phenomena. Retailing, after all, is especially suited to small-scale operations by many sellers. A first such phenomenon is the integration of retailing and manufacturing in certain industries, where the manufacturer has reached forward to acquire his own retail outlets. This has occurred in the petroleum industry in certain regions and in the optical supply business. Here the oligopolistic pattern of the manufacturing industry is imposed on retailing, even though each oligopolist may operate many retail outlets. Another factor is the growth of horizontal combinations or "chains" in drug stores, groceries, auto supplies, and the like. This may introduce enough concentration into retailing to make the market structure dominantly oligopolistic. Finally, independent retailers in the drug, grocery, liquor, appliance, and other fields have in most states secured legal interference with price competition among them, through so-called "fair trade" laws passed by the various states. (The consistency of these laws with basic federal law is under attack at the moment.) These have tended to lessen price competition, to accentuate non-price competition, and to attract excessive entry into the affected fields. Any detailed evaluation of competition in the distributive trades must take account of these and other complicating factors.

SUPPLEMENTARY READINGS

EDWARD H. CHAMBERLIN, *The Theory of Monopolistic Competition*, Chaps. 5-7.
J. E. MEADE AND C. J. HITCH, *Economic Analysis and Public Policy*, Part II, Chaps. 4-6.

CHAPTER 8

THE EFFECTS OF CONCENTRATED BUYING

To this point all of our discussions of price determination have rested on one important implicit assumption—that wherever goods are sold, there are *many buyers,* none of whom buys a significant proportion of the total output of an industry. In effect, we have assumed that whatever the degree of concentration among sellers, the structure of the buying market is atomistic.

For the great bulk of markets this is a fair and reasonable assumption. Practically all consumers' goods are sold to a multitude of small buyers, since in the nature of things consumers are many and their individual purchases are small. A considerable part of producers' goods are also sold to many buyers, none of whom buys enough to influence the market price seriously, and for those also our assumption is correct. But for certain producers' goods the buying market is concentrated or, in other words, dominated by a few large buyers. (This is also true of buying in factor markets, like those for labor, but we shall consider this problem later on.) Observation and common sense suggest that when this market situation is found, the determination of price may follow a course somewhat different than that heretofore described. We must, therefore, pause to consider the peculiarities of pricing in industries with concentrated buying markets.

A. THE RATIONALE OF BUYER BEHAVIOR

WHEN BUYERS ARE MANY

Where a good is sold to very many small buyers, no one of them buys enough that he can hope to influence the market price of the good. Each buyer necessarily accepts the going price as given and at this price buys whatever his financial means and his preferences dictate, since he cannot perceptibly influence a going price even by refusing to buy altogether. The student will readily recognize himself to be just in this position in buying any consumer's good. A small buyer is in a position with respect to buying price similar to that of the individual seller in pure competition with respect to selling price. To the small buyer the supply curve of a good is from his standpoint perfectly elastic or horizontal at the going market price, regardless of the shape of the *industry supply curve,* just as the demand curve for the output of a purely competitive seller is also perfectly elastic at going price, regardless of the elasticity of the industry demand curve.

When all of many buyers in an industry regard each alternative market price for a good which may emerge as given and beyond influence and determine their purchases at any price as if it were given, the conventional market or industry demand curve for the good emerges. Each buyer will stand ready to purchase a certain determinate quantity of the good at each possible alternative price, and he will do this quite regardless of the shape of the industry supply curve which shows the alternative amounts sellers are willing to supply to buyers as a group at various prices offered. The amount the buyer will take at each price will be found at that point where the money value of the marginal benefit (whether direct consumer satisfaction or enterprise revenue) of the final unit he purchases is equal to the addition to his outlay to acquire this good. Since he regards the supply curve of the good *to him* as horizontal at any going price, this marginal outlay will be simply the price of the good; therefore, he will stand ready to purchase at any price such a quantity that the money value of the marginal benefit from the last unit purchased is equal to the price of the good. (More generally, we may say that he will purchase various goods in such proportions that their marginal benefits stand in the same proportion as their prices; see pages 33 to 37.) The schedule of alternative amounts which a buyer will thus purchase at alternative prices is a true demand schedule (by one buyer) in that it really implies the passive acceptance of any alternative price, a willingness to buy some determinate quantity at each of many prices regardless of industry supply conditions, and an absence of any effort by the buyer to set the price or to influence it by bargaining with sellers or otherwise. This pattern of buyer behavior is definitely implied by any analysis of market pricing in which sellers are held to face together an industry demand curve.

When in a market with many buyers we "add up" the individual demand schedules of all the small buyers (taking at each alternative price a sum of the quantities they will purchase), we get the market or industry demand schedule, graphically represented in the market or industry demand curve to which we have so frequently referred in preceding chapters. This is like its component individual buyer schedules or curves in that it implies passive acceptance by buyers of each price, no attempt by them to influence price, and a given relationship of the aggregate quantity purchased to the price charged which is independent of the shape or slope of the industry supply curve.

The suppositions just outlined underlie the postulate that in the typical industry there is a genuine market demand curve. Such assumptions seem perfectly appropriate as applied to practically all consumers' goods industries and to a majority of producers' goods industries. Similarly, we have constructed the cost curves—that is, the relation of cost to output—for any seller on the supposition that he buys labor, equipment, materials, etc., also under competitive conditions, where he is such a small buyer that he cannot perceptibly influence the prices of what he buys by varying his purchases. Thus, we have assumed that costs are calculated by sellers who in buying take the prices of productive factors as given. This is also quite proper for the majority of cases.

When there is such a market demand curve, reflecting a given schedule of the alternative aggregate amounts buyers will purchase at alternative prices, price-output determination should pursue the course predicted by the analysis of preceding chapters. If there are many small sellers, who likewise have no significant control over price, industry price and output will be more or less automatically determined by the interaction of buyers' alternative bids, as represented in the market demand curve, and sellers' alternative offers, as represented in the industry supply curve. (See pages 136 to 139 and 142 to 148.) If there is a monopolistic seller, he is in a position to select that price-output combination shown on the market demand curve which is most profitable to him. Let us now consider how these conclusions are altered when buyers are few.

WHEN BUYERS ARE FEW

To what extent is our earlier analysis of demand altered when the number of buyers in the market is small, or, at the extreme, only one? When there are only a few buyers the supposition that they will simply make certain alternative purchases at alternative prices, taking any going price as if given, disregarding the shape of the industry supply curve, and not attempting to bargain for a low price, is no longer necessarily valid. A large buyer, instead of accepting the market price of something he buys as outside his control, will ordinarily be able either to set the price at which he buys or negotiate for a favorable price. In so doing he will look to the shape of the industry supply curve, which shows the prices sellers are willing to take for various amounts supplied. He can either set or bargain on price because he buys enough that by restricting his purchases, or threatening to do so, he can affect the sales volume of sellers enough to force them to accept a lower price or to bargain. Thus, he faces a supply curve of the good he purchases which is not perfectly elastic to him.

The general effect of fewness of buyers on price is evident to anyone. First, it will tend to result in lower buying prices. Second, the sellers supplying a market of a few buyers will not have a given market demand for their output but will rather be faced with specific prices set or bargaining offers made by the buyers of their outputs. Third, in the course of setting or bargaining for prices buyers will be led, if the industry supply curve is other than perfectly elastic, to choose the quantities they purchase so that these quantities are different than those which would be purchased if buyers were many. Fourth, large buyers purchasing labor and materials with which to produce will recognize it if the prices of these things will vary as they buy more in order to extend their outputs, and they will take account of this influence on the relation of costs to outputs. We shall therefore wish to analyze both the effect of concentrated buying on the price and output of the good bought and its effect on the cost curves of the producer buyers.

The following more precise comparison of the rationale of buying when buyers are few with that when buyers are many may be made. First, the large buyer of a given good (large enough to influence or bargain for its price) presumably has, like the small buyer, a schedule of marginal benefits from successive additional units he may purchase of the good, expressible in money values—for example, the benefit added by a fifth unit of good A acquired per month is valued at \$1, that of the sixth unit at \$0.80, etc. This marginal benefit may be direct satisfaction to a consumer (valued at the price of goods of equal satisfaction-providing power foregone in order to acquire satisfaction from the instant good), or it may be the amount added to the revenue of a producer-buyer by using the further unit of the instant good in production. In any event, we may conceive the large buyer of a given good as essentially having a schedule relating the quantity he buys of the good to the money value of the marginal benefit received from successive added units bought. This schedule is precisely of the same sort as that we have attributed to the small buyer, so that to this point the analysis is unchanged.

Second, the large buyer will almost by definition have some power to influence price. He will ordinarily be able to influence price by varying the amount he will purchase, since he purchases all or a substantial fraction of the total supply. If he purchases from many small sellers, this will be reflected in the fact that the supply curve of the good to him will be other than perfectly elastic, sloping either up or down as quantity purchased increases. If, for example, it slopes upward to the right, this will reflect the fact that sellers are willing to take various prices the buyer may set, but they will supply successively more of the good to him as he successively increases the buying price. It should be noted that if a large buyer faced a perfectly elastic supply curve for the good he purchased, his position would be like that of a small buyer and the analysis of his action would be no different than that already developed for a small buyer. But ordinarily he will face a sloping supply curve for the good in the market for which he is a large buyer.

It follows that, given a sloping supply curve to the buyer, which registers willingness of sellers to supply alternative amounts at alternative prices, the large buyer is in a position *to set price,* or to choose to pay one of a certain range of alternative buying prices. But, the amount he can secure of the good will be dependent on his selection of price. This distinguishes the large buyer very clearly from the small one, who may only accept a going price as given and decide how much to buy at that price. The larger buyer has at least some control over his buying price.

Third, in deciding how much to buy and at what price, the large buyer should presumably decide on that quantity (and corresponding price) at which the money value of the marginal benefit from the last unit purchased is equal to the marginal outlay, or addition to aggregate outlay, made to acquire that unit. This is true with small buyers, also, but for them the marginal outlay is the same as the buying price of the good so that the money value of the marginal benefit is equated also to this price. If the supply curve to the large buyer slopes, however, reflecting varying price of all units with varying quantity bought, the marginal outlay will differ from the buying price, and the buyer's quantity of purchases will not be such that the money value of the marginal benefit is equated to this price. Thus, the large buyer tends to buy a different quantity than would small buyers with the same marginal benefit schedule and facing the same industry supply conditions. This will be explained further with diagrams in the succeeding section.

In sum, there are several strategic differences in the behavior of the large buyer. First, although he has presumably a schedule of marginal benefits from successive increments to his purchases of the good affected, this is not expressed in a genuine demand schedule of alternative offers to purchase alternative amounts at alternative prices. Rather, guided by this marginal benefit schedule and by the sloping supply curve of the good to him, the large buyer determines a price (out of a range of alternatives) and makes it the effective price at which he buys. The demand schedule gives way to a determination of price by the buyer, just as in selling monopoly the supply schedule gives way to a determination of price by the seller. Second, the price he determines and the quantity he buys will be such that the money value of his marginal benefit from the last unit of the good purchased equals the marginal outlay made to get it, and generally does not equal price. Thus, his buying price and quantity of purchases will usually be different than that which would be arrived at with many small buyers in the same situation.

The preceding statement of the character of price-output determination rests on two important assumptions. First, in supposing that the large buyer faces a determinate supply schedule for the good he buys, we have assumed that there are many small sellers of the good, since if there were not there would not necessarily be a genuine supply schedule. Where not only buyers but also sellers are few, it is still true that price will be set by bargaining to which the buyers are party, but price-output determination will follow no simple pattern. We shall consider this special case under the headings of bilateral monopoly and bilateral oligopoly. Second, we have overlooked the possible consequences of oligopsonistic rivalry among a few large buyers, which may throw off the fine calculus of advantage which a single large buyer might pursue. This difficulty will be considered subsequently. The preceding analysis of the rationale of concentrated buying refers primarily to the situation of one or a few large buyers, unaffected by inter-buyer rivalry, buying from many small sellers. We shall now consider this case further, returning later to the special characteristics of alternative concentrated buying situations.

B. CHARACTER AND CONSEQUENCES OF MONOPSONY

PRICING UNDER SIMPLE MONOPSONY

Some further insight into the character of concentrated buying may be gained by considering the extreme case of a single buyer of the entire output offered in a market, or *monopsony*, where the *monopsonist* is supplied by many small sellers. Suppose that in a given colony of an imperial nation a trading company is given a government monopoly (and monopsony) on all commerce, and therefore is the sole possible buyer for the tobacco crop of the colony, which is produced by several hundred small independent farmers. How will it regulate its purchases?

In general, it will try to act in such a way as to maximize its profit from buying and selling tobacco, taking account not only of what the tobacco is worth to it for resale, *but also of the varying supply price of the tobacco from the farmers*. The character of its calculation may be made clear by Figure 42. Here *dd'* represents at successive points the money value of the marginal benefit to the firm of the last unit of tobacco purchased when it purchases various alternative quantities—presumably the addition to the sales revenue of the firm attributable to reselling any final unit of tobacco acquired. (The curve *dd'* is thus presumably derived from the demand for tobacco by those to whom the trading company resells.)

This curve would be the demand curve of the buyer for tobacco *if he had no control over price* or were faced by a perfectly elastic supply curve for tobacco at any going market price. Because this is not so, it is not a genuine demand curve, since the supply is not perfectly elastic and since, therefore, the firm will set a buying price rather than offer to buy various alternative amounts at various alternative prices. Each of the prices shown on dd' simply represents the net value to the monopsonist of an increment to his purchases of tobacco at the corresponding quantity point.

Against this curve dd' he will place the supply curve for tobacco from the colony, SS' in Figure 42. (In a short period this would be the summed marginal cost curves of the many tobacco farmers.) This is a conventional supply curve for an industry of sellers in pure competition, and it shows unequivocally the amounts sellers stand ready to supply at various prices.

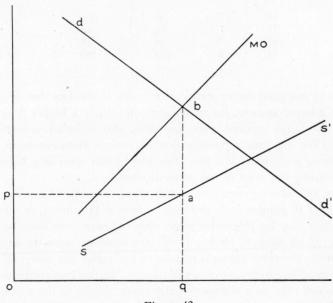

Figure 42

Now if the curve dd' were the aggregate demand curve of many small buyers, or alternatively if the monopsonist took no account of the varying cost of supply, price and quantity for raw tobacco from the farm would be determined at the intersection of SS' and dd'. (See pages 136 to 139.) This intersection determines what is, on the alternative assumptions stated, the competitive price and quantity.

But the monopsonist, as sole buyer, will naturally take account of the minimum prices, shown on SS', at which various alternative quantities of tobacco can be bought and also of how these minimum prices increase as he extends his purchases of tobacco. If the supply curve slopes upward to the right so that supply prices increase with output, the monopsonist will find that by increasing his purchases he raises the total necessary outlay for tobacco very steeply.

Thus, if the supply curve shows the price-quantity relation indicated in columns (1) and (2) of the following table, the additional or *marginal outlay* on tobacco by the buyer rises as shown in column (4).

(1) Price, in guineas	(2) Tons supplied	(3) Total outlay, in guineas	(4) Marginal outlay of the buyer, in guineas
10	5	50	—
11	6	66	16
12	7	84	18
13	8	104	20

This rise of marginal outlay above price is due to the fact that in order to purchase a larger amount, the monopsonist must pay a higher price for all units in the larger amount, including those also included in any smaller amount. (We are thus supposing that he cannot *discriminate* in buying price, buying some units at a low price and further units at a higher price without raising the price of the previous units.)

Thus, the tobacco monopsonist will say to himself, "I can buy 5 tons of tobacco at 10 guineas each, or instead 6 tons at 11 guineas, *in which case the sixth ton costs me 16 guineas more, since in getting one more ton I raise the price of all tobacco.* Hence, I will not consider hereafter simply the supply price of various amounts of tobacco but rather the *marginal outlays* incurred in adding to my purchases of tobacco." In this case the monopsonist evidently will refer to a *marginal outlay curve,* drawn to the supply curve, which shows the rate of increase of his total outlay with increase in his purchases (always assuming he buys every unit of any amount at the same minimum supply price). This is the curve *MO* in Figure 42 (a prototype of column (4) in the preceding table).

To maximize his return on tobacco operations, the monopsonist will evidently purchase such a quantity that his marginal outlay (for the last unit purchased) just equals the added money value to him of the last unit purchased. In the example in Figure 42, this will be the quantity *oq* of tobacco, for which the monopsonist will pay the unit price *op*.[1] These results in terms of price and output are distinct from those of competitive buying, since many buyers, having the aggregate demand curve for the good *dd'* and facing the same industry supply curve, would arive at a price and quantity determined by the intersection of *dd'* and *SS'*.

[1] See Joan Robinson, *The Economics of Imperfect Competition* (London: Macmillan & Co., Ltd., 1933), Chap. 18.

RESULTS OF MONOPSONISTIC POLICIES

The basic conclusion drawn from this example is general. With competitive buying from many sellers price and output will tend to fall where the money value of marginal benefit to buyers equals the supply price of sellers. With monopsony price and output tend to be set where the money value of marginal benefit equals the monopsonist's marginal outlay, and these will not be such that the money value of marginal benefit equals supply price unless the supply curve to the monopsonist is horizontal.

Are further conclusions apparent concerning the effects of monopsony on price and output? Several possible effects of monopsony must be considered, including its effects on the quantity purchased from sellers, on the price paid to sellers, and, if the monopsonist is a producer who sells an output made with what he purchases, on the quantity and the selling price of his output and on his profits.

If we assume that the monopsonist has a schedule of value of marginal benefits from his purchases identical to the market demand curve of a group of many buyers whom he virtually replaces, certain conclusions are apparent. First, when the industry supply curve faced by the monopsonist is up-sloping so that the supply price of the good he buys rises as he increases his purchases, monopsony results in a restriction of quantity purchased below the competitive level. This is because the monopsonist's marginal outlay then rises above the supply curve and because this induces him to set his purchases short of the quantity where the value of marginal benefit equals supply price. (Competitive buyers, on the other hand, would disregard that effect of increases in their aggregate purchases which is shown in the monopsonist's marginal outlay curve, and they would arrive at the larger output where value of marginal benefit equaled supply price.)

Second, again with an up-sloping supply curve, the monopsonist will pay a lower price to sellers than would competitive buyers with the same demand curve. His restriction of purchases is in fact oriented toward obtaining the lower buying prices corresponding to smaller quantities on the industry supply curve he faces. Suppliers thus receive smaller prices and incomes than they would with competitive buying.

Third, if he is a producer buyer, he will tend to produce a smaller output, since he purchases fewer raw materials, and his output will tend to sell at a higher price if it constitutes a significant fraction of the supply in his selling market. The tendency to restriction of his output may be offset in part if other raw materials can be substituted for the monopsonized good in production, but it will hardly be offset entirely. In the example illustrated in Figure 42 his output would be restricted proportionally to his purchases, since the monopsonized good is his only production input.

Fourth, the monopsonist-producer will tend to make a larger profit by virtue of his monopsony than would competitive buyers having the same demand curve and facing the same supply curve for a given good. This is obvious, since by restricting his purchases the monopsonist foregoes the purchase of quantities (between the intersection of dd' and SS' and that of dd' and MO in Figure 42) for which marginal outlay by the monopsonist or by the group of competitive buyers exceeds the value of the marginal benefit. If competitive buyers had been able to break even by purchasing the competitive quantity at the competitive price, therefore, the monopsonist would make some excess profit attributable to his monopsonistic policy.

It does not follow that every monopsonist will necessarily make a monopsonistic excess profit. The size of the monopsonist's excess profit per unit is given by the gap between the average cost or supply price of purchases by the monopsonist and the value of the *average* benefit (net of other costs) from the monopsonized goods. An excess of this value of average benefit over average cost does not follow necessarily because the value of marginal benefit exceeds the supply price. In effect, it is conceivable that the value of the average benefit may lie below the value of the marginal benefit from purchases at some points, if the monopsonized good is combined in production with others with first increasing and then decreasing returns—and sufficiently below that the monopsonist can only break even while exploiting his monopsony to the full. (This is parallel to the proposition that a monopolist's average costs may exceed his marginal cost and equal his selling price even though marginal cost is below price.) Such a profitless monopsony could occur either (1) where competitive buying would yield losses and monopsony was necessary to break even or (2) where the monopsonist sold his output in competition with other monopsonists (enjoying alternative favored buying positions), a sufficient number of whom could enter his selling market to drive selling price down to the level of monopsonistically lowered average costs. (In the latter case the curves showing the values of the average and marginal benefits of each monopsonist would in effect lie lower than those of the aggregate of competitive buyers he replaced. This would account for the elimination of profits, while monopsonistic restriction of total purchases and output would be in part offset by the entry of added monopsonists.) Subject to these exceptions, however, the tendency of monopsonistic buying is to create an excess-profit margin, just as the tendency of monopolistic selling is to create a similar margin. In Figure 42 where the monotonically declining marginal benefit curve implies a higher average benefit curve throughout, an excess profit per unit (larger than ab) is clearly implied.

In general, we may expect monopsonistic buying positions to be protected by sufficient barriers to entry to alternative monopsony positions that monopsonistic excess profits will be earned and monopsonistic restriction of purchases will not be much offset because of entry. In either event, monopsonistic lowering of purchase prices will tend to remain. Where monopsonistic excess profits are earned by virtue of the restriction of purchases, it is obvious that the reduction in buying price obtained by the monopsonist will not be fully passed on to customers for the monopsonist's output, but will be retained at least in part to furnish the monopsonistic excess profits.

In the appraisal of excess profits of monopsony two observations should be added. First, the position of the single large buyer may differ from that of a group of many small buyers not only in that he possesses monopsony power in his buying market but also in that he possesess monopoly power in his selling market. If this is the case, he has a double incentive to restrict output below the competitive level—since the value of the marginal benefit from his purchases declines more steeply than that of competitive sellers because of the recognized slope of the demand curve in his selling market. Correspondingly, he has a double source of potential excess profit. We shall return to this matter on pages 390 to 393. Second, the monopsonist who is subject to a threat of entry—either of other monopsonists to compete in his selling market or of other buyers to compete in his buying market—may be led to forestall such entry by tempering his monopsonistic policy and buying more, at a higher price, than he otherwise would. The phenomenon here is strictly parallel to that of lowered selling price by the monopolist who would forestall entry.

It should be noted in conclusion that the effects of monopsony on the quantity purchased just described should be found only where the competitive supply curve for the good purchased by the monopsonist evidences increasing cost with increasing supply. Where the competitive supply curve is horizontal (constant costs), no change from the competitive buying price will result from monopsony, provided the supply curve lies at the level it would with competitive buying, since the marginal outlay curve of the monopsonist coincides with the supply curve. (SS' and MO are the same.) If the supply curve slopes downward to the right, evidencing declining supply price with increasing output, as is perhaps conceivable, the effect of monopsony will be to extend the output beyond the competitive level as well as to lower the price. Thus, if dd' and SS' are as shown in Figure 43, MO will be below SS' and the monopsonistic price and output will be at op and oq, whereas competitive price and output would be op_1 and oq_1. Monopsony thus *can* result in a volume of production the same as or greater than that associated with competitive buying. But it will evidently never tend to result in a higher than competitive buying price.

Where the monopsonist buys from a competitive industry or group of sellers, however, it is almost certain that the short-run supply curve will show increasing cost, and it is very probable that the long-run supply curve will also slope upward to the right. This is generally true of agricultural industries, from which concentrated buying is most common.

Thus, the probable tendency in monopsonistic buying from competitive suppliers is for restricted output, increased price to consumers, lowered price to the basic suppliers, and excess buying profits to the monopsonist.

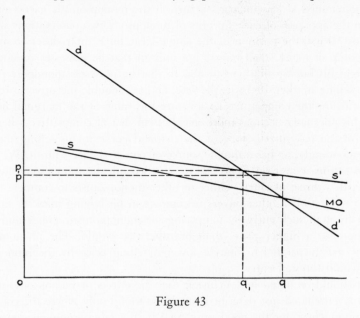

Figure 43

GENERAL IMPACTS OF MONOPSONY ON WELFARE

The preceding section argues in effect that monopsonistic buying from a competitive industry will in general result in a lower buying price and smaller purchases from the supplying industry than would competitive buying, and probably in monopsonistic excess profits. Overlooking exceptions to and qualifications of this rule, what effect would such monopsonistic restriction of the outputs of one or a few supplying industries have on the economy as a whole? To ascertain this, we must carefully investigate the broader implications of a given up-sloping supply curve for the output of a monopsonized supplying industry.

This supply curve suggests that if the price for the output of the supplying industry is cut below the competitive level, the industry will continue to produce but will produce necessarily less at successively lower prices. Such behavior in turn implies that at lower prices the industry will employ fewer resources, reducing its employment of labor, land, and capital, that the resources released, therefore, will either become idle or will find employment in other industries, and that at least some of the resources still employed will receive reduced incomes. The effect of the monopsony on the economy as a whole will evidently depend upon how elastic the supply of the monopsonized industry is and also on whether the resources released as industry output declines become idle or find alternative employment.

At one extreme all the resources might be perfectly mobile, in the sense that they would move freely to other industries if their rates of pay in the monopsonized industry were cut at all below the prevailing competitive rates for the economy as a whole. But in this event, the industry would have a perfectly elastic long-run supply curve (costs could not be driven down at all), and the monopsonist would have no monopsony power whatever (MO would be identical with SS').

The up-sloping supply curve evidently supposes that at least one resource employed by the supplying industry is immobile (cannot be employed elsewhere) or imperfectly mobile (will accept lower than the prevailing economy-wide price before leaving this industry) so that some or all of it will accept lower prices as the industry demand for it is reduced, and thus give the industry lower costs at smaller outputs. It also supposes that one or more factors used by the industry either is mobile, so that some units of it will leave employment in the industry rather than accept successively lower prices, or will prefer idleness to employment at lower prices. (If all factors were entirely immobile and shunned idleness, the industry supply curve would be perfectly inelastic and the monopsonist would employ them all at a zero price.) The typical up-sloping supply curve which gives the monopsonist his advantage thus rests on the *imperfect or partial mobility* of factors away from employment in the monopsonized industry. It is accompanied either by potential mobility to other industries or by mobility to idleness of some of the resources of the industry uses.

From this it follows that the impact of a monopsony on the economy as a whole *may* be entirely upon allocation and income distribution, as it will if the monopsonistic restriction takes advantage of imperfectly mobile resources to pay them lower prices, but if all disemployed resources move to other industries. Here, the output in the supplying industry is restricted, incomes of factors still employed there are reduced, and monopsonistic profits probably created. But the shortage of output in this industry is compensated by an increase in that of other industries. The principal effect on total output is on its composition—on the allocation of resources among uses.

It is also possible that the impact of monopsony may be entirely on total output and income distribution. That is, the monopsonistic restriction may make idle resources which refuse lower rates of pay, but no resources may move to other industries. Then the loss of output in the monopsonized industry is not counterbalanced by increases in output elsewhere, and the aggregate output of the economy is lessened.

More probably, monopsony will have an admixture of these two effects. By lowering price and output in the monopsonized supplying industry, the monopsonistic buyer will drive some resources to other industries, where they increase other outputs, and will drive some to idleness. Thus, monopsony will affect both aggregate employment and output and the allocation of resources among uses. It may be worth while noting that very immobile resources under monopsony will mean very inelastic industry supplies, so that monopsony can drive buying price very low with little restriction of output.

It may also be pertinent to reflect upon the potentialities of a world of monopsonies—of having very many industries of an economy each subject to monopsony buying. Here the possibility of mobility of resources among industries is greatly reduced if not eliminated. The combination of many individual monopsony restrictions, therefore, does not necessarily mean an aggregate restriction of output equal to the sum of the individual output restriction if the various monopsonies were found only one at a time in an economy. Under general monopsony pressure, the prices of all employed factors may be forced downward relative to commodity prices, so that all costs and supply curves shift to lower levels.

If this adjustment can take place relative to a given aggregate money purchasing power, aggregate output will not be much restricted, and the entire burden of monopsony may fall upon income distribution (a shift from wages and rents to excess profits and a lowering of the relative prices of the less mobile factors), except so far as employable resources prefer idleness to low rates of pay. This model may be appropriate to colonial economies subject to monopsonistic employment of the bulk of the labor force. It should be noted, however, that such a slight effect upon employment rests upon the possibility of money factor prices being forced down while purchasing power is sustained, and this may not be accepted as a foregone conclusion.

THE MONOPSONISTIC BUYER AS A MONOPOLISTIC SELLER

The previous analysis of monopsonistic pricing employed the convenient device of a curve showing the money value to the monopsonist of the marginal benefits of successive increments to his purchases. The meaning of this schedule may be made clearer by using a more general analysis in which we refer to the demand *for what the monopsonist sells* (and from which this schedule of marginal benefits from what he buys is evidently derived) and to his costs of production. In this way also we may recognize explicitly the effect of monopsony on the cost curves of producing firms with monopsony power.

Let us refer again to our monopsonistic buyer of the tobacco crop of a colony. The schedule of money value of marginal benefits referred to for any such buyer is evidently not an expression of the monetary value of consumer satisfaction from tobacco but rather a measure of the additions to the revenue of a producer or merchant attributable to the acquisition of further units of a raw material, supposing resale in either modified or original form. As such, it is derived from the demand which the merchant or producer will meet when he resells the product in either unaltered or altered form.

The monopsonistic tobacco buyer intends to resell the tobacco, either before or after processing it or using it in production of cigarettes and cut plug;

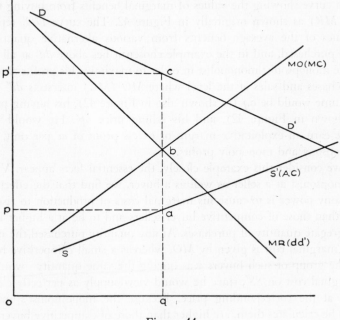

Figure 44

the amount he is willing to pay for it depends upon the demand curve for tobacco in his selling market. It follows that we can trace his policy as a buyer and a seller together by placing his costs, including the cost of leaf tobacco, against the demand for his offering as a seller.

There are numerous possible variant situations which could be illustrated: here we shall choose a very simple model. Let us suppose that the monopsonistic buyer of tobacco is also a single-firm monopolistic seller of tobacco with a given demand curve for his output—*DD'* in Figure 44. Let us also suppose that he is simply a trader or merchant, so that he just buys and sells tobacco, with no additional production costs.

The supply curve for tobacco as he buys it is *SS'*, the same as in Figure 42, and the marginal outlay drawn thereto is similarly *MO*. Now the supply price of tobacco to the monopsonist represents his entire average cost of production, and it is, therefore, evident that SS', showing the buying price per unit for various amounts, is the monopsonist's *average cost curve* $(AC = SS')$ and that the marginal outlay curve is his marginal cost curve $(MC = MO)$. In effect, his marginal cost of production rises more steeply than a competitive buyer's would because the unit price of materials to him rises as he buys more.

The curve MR represents the marginal receipts corresponding to the demand curve (DD') in his selling market, and it is thus equivalent to his own curve showing the values of marginal benefits from buying tobacco $(dd' = MR)$ as shown originally in Figure 42. The curve DD' represents the values of the average benefits from various alternative quantities of tobacco purchased, and in the example chosen it lies above dd' at all points.

The monopsonist-monopolist in order to maximize his profits should set his purchases and sales at the level where MO (MC) intersects dd' (MR). His volume would be oq (as shown also in Figure 42), his buying price op (also shown in Figure 42), and his selling price op'. He would in this example earn an exploitative margin or excess profit of ac per unit, a sum of monopsony and monopoly profits.

If we consider this example closely, the essential facts appear. Viewing the monopsonist as a seller as well as a buyer, we find that the effect of his monopsony power is to cause his marginal costs of production to rise more steeply than those of competitive buyer-sellers and to lie at a higher level at any aggregate quantity of purchases. At any quantity purchased the monopsonist's marginal cost is given by MO, whereas a small competitive buyer—when the group of such buyers was buying the same quantity—would find his marginal cost on SS', since he would view supply as perfectly elastic to himself at the corresponding price. Because the monopsonist's marginal costs, as he calculates them, are higher than those of competitive buyer-sellers would be, he finds that his marginal cost equals any given marginal receipts curve at a smaller output and quantity of purchase than would be found by competitive firms and at a lower buying price. In addition, the monopsonist may be a monopolist, as in the present example, in which case his marginal receipts curve (dd') lies lower than those of competitive sellers would at any given output. (Competitive sellers, having no individual influence on selling price, would find their marginal receipts equal to the price shown on DD' with any given group output.) In this case there is a double tendency for output restriction with monopsony (MR is lower and MC higher), and a greater tendency to lower buying price and raise selling price.

In the example given competitive price and output (with many small buyer-sellers of tobacco) would evidently be found at the intersection of DD' and SS' since the slope of neither curve would be taken into account by firms with no influence on either buying or selling price, and output would be extended until average cost was equal to price. The monopolistic output (with monopsonistic restriction absent) would be found at the intersection of SS' and MR, and the monopsonistic output (with monopolistic restriction absent) at the intersection of MO and DD'. The monopolist-monopsonist, as indicated, influenced both by the accentuated rise of his marginal costs because of monopsony power and the accentuated decline of his marginal receipts (or value of marginal benefit) because of his monopoly power, arrives at the smaller output oq, with corresponding buying and selling prices.

It may be emphasized that in this highly simplified example, wherein the value of the average benefit to the monopsonist of his purchases (DD') always lies above the value of his marginal benefit (MR), monopsonistic restriction is necessarily accompanied by the earning of an excess profit, part of which is appropriately regarded as a monopsonistic profit. This would also result if the value of the average benefit should be the same as the value of the marginal benefit. If the value of the average benefit should lie below MR over some range, however (see page 386), excess profits could be absent although the monopolist chose to purchase the profit-maximizing quantity determined by the intersection of MO and MR. Such a profitless outcome should occur only in extreme and rare cases.

C. OLIGOPSONY AND BILATERAL MONOPOLY

A FEW BUYERS SUPPLIED BY MANY SELLERS

What is the significance of this analysis for pricing in actual business practice? Needless to say, there are virtually no actual cases of absolute monopsony in commodities; the preceding analysis cannot often be applied directly to commodity markets. Behavior similar to that just described may be found, however, where there are very *few* buyers of a competitively sold raw material, and where they exercise collusion to concur on a monopsony buying policy. Such concurrence may be obtained either by agreement or by buying price leadership, whereby one of the buyers sets a low buying price which others follow.

This is essentially the case of a collusive *oligopsony* (few buyers) buying in a competitive raw material market. The principal opportunities for such buying are found where a few large processors buy a raw material from farmers or other small producers. Monopsonistic buying practices have been alleged to occur in the raw tobacco market, where a few large cigarette makers buy most of the tobacco; in the central cattle market, dominated by a few large meat packers; and in the midcontinent crude oil market, where a few large oil companies buy most of the crude petroleum. We cannot investigate the validity of these allegations here, but such behavior is theoretically quite feasible.

Where a collusive oligopsony operates effectively in buying competitively supplied raw materials, the effects will, of course, depend on the character of market supply. In the agricultural sphere, at least, supply prices probably increase with output. Collusive oligopsony would then tend to restrict supply, lower the income of the farmer, and raise consumer prices. The accomplishment of these effects, however, depends on further effective collusion among the processors in keeping up their selling prices. Perhaps because of the threat of new entry or for other reasons, it is quite possible that such firms would actually purchase and produce more, sell at lower prices, and necessarily pay more per unit for the increased volume of purchases than would perfectly collusive oligopolists subject to no threat of entry. The outcome here is quite uncertain and could best be ascertained by detailed investigation. Where the oligopsony is successfully selfish, however, restriction of output and an enhancement of the oligopsonists' share of income at the expense of both consumers and suppliers tend to result.

To the extent that some rivalry develops within the oligopsony with respect to buying price, as one large buyer bids price above the monopsony level in order to secure added supplies at the expense of his rivals, the results will tend away from the monopsonistic and toward the competitive. Buying prices will tend to be higher than in simple monopsony, and with a rising supply curve to the buyers, the quantity bought will tend to be larger. The possibilities here are parallel to those already discussed for the setting of oligopolistic selling price.[2]

BILATERAL MONOPOLY AND BILATERAL OLIGOPOLY

An equally important case of concentrated buying is found where a few buyers acquire a good from an oligopoly of a few sellers. This situation occurs, for example, in the selling market of the rubber tire industry, where a fairly concentrated oligopoly of tire manufacturers sells much of its output to the three major automobile companies and to a few mass distributors such as Sears Roebuck, Montgomery Ward, and several auto supply and service station chains. It plays a significant role in the sale of important steel products, where an oligopoly of steel mills sells sheet and other steel to a few automobile firms, and tin plate to a few can manufacturers. There are several other important cases of this sort.

Where a few sellers supply a few buyers we have oligopoly plus oligopsony, or appropriately *bilateral oligopoly*. This evidently issues us into the environment of negotiation, bargaining, power maneuver, and economic warfare, where price may fall anywhere within rather wide limits. Formally

[2] For an extended discussion of oligopsony, see William H. Nicholls, *Imperfect Competition within Agricultural Industries* (Ames: Iowa State College Press, 1941), Chaps. 4-9.

in this case there is neither a true market demand curve nor a true market supply curve. Rather the buyers, guided by the marginal benefits from added purchases, and the sellers, guided by their marginal costs of added production, will determine price and output by bargaining, and so-called impersonal market forces are totally absent.

The simple theoretical prototype of this confused situation is that of bilateral monopoly—one seller selling to one buyer. Analysis of this situation, if we neglect the possibility of the use of discriminatory pricing principles in bargaining, reveals the following: (1) The monopsonist wants a restricted monopsony output and a low price. (2) The monopolist wants a restricted (but potentially different) output and a high monopoly price. (3) The result may fall at either limit if one party has dominant bargaining strength or it may fall uncertainly between the price limits indicated, with corresponding effects on quantity. Adequate formal treatment of behavior in bilateral monopoly, however, really requires reference to the theory of first-degree price discrimination by either buyer or seller, and this leads to somewhat altered conclusions. We shall postpone detailed analysis of this problem until the succeeding chapter.

Much the same range of alternatives holds good for bilateral oligopoly as for bilateral monopoly. In this case, however, the scales may be fairly strongly tipped in favor of the buyers, since each of them can act independently to drive a hard bargain as he seeks supply, whereas to resist this pressure the sellers must have effective collusion on price and maintain it under duress. Thus, large buyers from the rubber tire industry during the 1930's continually kept their buying prices at very low levels, allowing subnormal profits to tire makers, through vigorous but apparently not collusive use of their bargaining power. In general, however, seller dominance, buyer dominance, or balanced power are all possible, so that the determination of price and output within bilateral oligopoly is genuinely uncertain over a considerable range.

The significance of bilateral oligopoly market situations in our economy is largely to compound the uncertainty concerning the way in which resources will be allocated, goods priced, and incomes distributed. The student may already have observed that bilateral oligopoly or bilateral monopoly situations may frequently occur in the labor market. This will be discussed in Chapter 12 of the second part of this work.

We have spoken in Chapters 5 and 6 of the behavior of prices and outputs in an economy which is a world of monopolies or of oligopolies—where in most selling markets sellers possess a degree of monopoly power and attain some approximation to a monopolistic relation of marginal and average costs to price. The corresponding effects upon income distribution (in the direction of excess profits), upon aggregate output, and upon the allocation of resources among uses have been discussed. To appraise the behavior of the real economy, we must compound with the effects of monopoly and oligopoly in selling markets those of monopsony, oligopsony, and bilateral monopoly and bilateral oligopoly in buying markets.

The additional effects of simple monopsony and oligopsony are fairly clear. They add to the distortion in the allocation of resources, further tend to create excess profits, and thus reduce other distributive shares. But they have an effect on aggregate output mainly so far as there is immobility of resources from industry to industry or so far as the effects upon income distribution affect employment. (Lower real prices of hired resources may result in fewer resources seeking employment, or the ratio of money purchasing power to prices may be adversely affected.)

Where there is bilateral monopoly or oligopoly in buying markets, however, the final outcome of the relation of prices to costs—and with it allocation, income distribution, and perhaps total employment—is made logically uncertain over a significant range, and an observation of actual behavior is the only reliable guide. With the markets for labor increasingly assuming bilateral-monopoly characteristics, and with a good deal of bilateral oligopoly in the markets for producer's goods, it is hazardous to draw logical deductions concerning price-output behavior in the economy unless we allow a substantial margin for error. Further investigation of the bilateral-monopoly problem in the succeeding chapter may shed further light on this issue.

D. MONOPSONY AND ALLOCATION

We may here refer again, for the benefit of those interested in a further discussion of allocation, to our treatment of the effect of monopolistic pricing on the output of an industry and the allocation of resources among uses. In Chapter 5 (pages 205 to 210) it was assumed that the monopolistic seller bought factors of production (or raw materials) under competitive conditions, so that the prices he paid for factors did not vary in response to variations in his output. His marginal cost curve was thus drawn on the assumption of given factor prices, and it thus reflected at each point only the money value of the marginal real cost—of the real factors added to produce another unit of output.

Even on this assumption, the monopolist restricts output, since he sets output where marginal cost so defined equals marginal receipts rather than extending output until such marginal cost equals price, as a competitive industry would.

But now if the monopolistic seller is also a monopsonistic buyer, for whom the prices of purchased factors rise with his output, his marginal cost curve no longer is drawn on the assumption of given factor prices, and it no longer represents simply the money value of the marginal real cost. It represents this *plus the increment to money outlay on all* ("inframarginal") *factors employed prior to the instant increment in real cost.* (That is, the *marginal money cost* to the monopolist and his industry—explained on pages 165 to 166—exceeds the money value of marginal real cost.) The marginal cost curve of the monopolist-monopsonist thus lies above the curve which would show the money value of marginal real cost and rises more steeply. When the seller sets output so as to equate this marginal cost to marginal receipts, therefore, he chooses an even lower output and higher price than he would have if he had equated the money value of marginal real cost to marginal receipts. There is thus a *double* restriction of output—monopolistic restriction *and* monopsonistic restriction.

The cost curves shown in Figure 44 are not strictly comparable to those represented for the monopolist in Chapter 5, since the latter reflected a rising marginal real cost within the firm due to diminishing returns against some fixed factor (and no rise in factor prices), whereas those in Figure 44 presuppose no such tendency within the firm (but rather constant marginal real costs to the firm—it always costs the firm one unit of tobacco bought to have one unit to sell). The only reason for the rise in money costs in Figure 44 is thus the rise in the buying price of tobacco.

If we recognize this, the following general comparison may be drawn. The curve AC (SS') in Figure 44 represents the money value of marginal real cost for the monopolist. (In this respect it is comparable with the MC curves drawn in Chapter 5, but not otherwise.) The MO (MC) curve represents the marginal money cost for the monopolist including the effect of induced factor-price increases for all units of factors used (the money value of marginal real costs plus the money cost of inframarginal factor-price increases).

If the monopolist-monopsonist were to set output so that AC was equal to MR (which he would not), he would restrict output somewhat below the level where AC intersects DD' (the competitive level). He would in this way set the money value of marginal real cost equal to marginal receipts. This much restriction was attributed to monopoly in Chapter 5, where the marginal cost curve was drawn on the assumption that factor prices were invariant and thus reflected only the money value of marginal real cost.

But the monopolist in Figure 44 in fact sets output where MC equals MR, since he is concerned mainly with the total rise in his money costs, and he thus restricts output below the level where AC equals MR and further raises price. The first output restriction (from ($AC = DD'$) to ($AC = MR$)) may be referred to as *monopolistic* output restriction, and the second (from ($AC = MR$) to ($MC = MR$)) as *monopsonistic* restriction. Where the monopolist is also a monopsonist facing increasing factor prices with increasing output, the two restrictions are added and the total restriction increased.

Since the criterion for competitive output is that output be set so that AC intersects DD' and equals price (thus putting the money value of marginal real cost equal to price), it is evident that the departure from competitive output is greater when the monopolist has monopsony power of the sort mentioned than when he does not. (The preceding does not exhaust all the possible variant cases of monopsony effects—for example, where the monopsonist's factor prices decline with increasing output—but may serve to indicate the general character of monopsony effects in the typical case where the supply curve to the large buyer rises with increasing purchases.)

Let us apply the preceding findings to the analysis of allocation of resources among uses. Ideal allocation requires in general that the output in each industry be such that the money value of marginal real cost be equal to price or, at the least everywhere in the same proportion to price, when all of the various industries are paying the same price for any factor of production used in common. As we have seen, this condition will be satisfied with universal pure competition. It will not be satisfied with some industries monopolized (but without monopsony) and others in pure competition, because in the monopolized industries output will be set so that the money value of marginal real cost equals marginal receipts and is less than price. Monopoly outputs will tend to be relatively too small.

If monopsony existed without monopoly—so that the firm equated marginal cost to selling price but this marginal cost was higher than the money value of marginal real cost—then there would again be an excess of price over the money value of marginal real cost, because of monopsony alone in this case. And allocation would be distorted as between the monopsonized and competitive industries so far as they were paying the same price for factors used in common or so far as the monopsonized industry *would* pay the same factor prices as competitive industries if it did not follow monopsonistic policies. In either of these cases the monopsonized industry, when it did not extend output to where the money value of marginal real cost equaled price (with the same factor prices as competitive industries at this point), would create a situation in which the last unit of any factor employed in the monopsonized industry yielded a product of greater value than a similar unit employed in a competitive industry, so that allocation could be improved by shifting resources from the competitive to the monopsonized industry.

When monopoly and monopsony are compounded (the monopolistic seller is also a monopsonistic buyer), the two effects on allocation are compounded. In the monopoly-monopsony industry the firm's marginal cost is equal to marginal receipts and less than price, and the money value of marginal real cost is less than the firm's marginal cost. Now if the factor prices paid by competitive and monopoly-monopsony industries are the same, or would be the same if monopsony power were not exercised, the restriction of output in the monopoly-monopsony sector is greater than it would be with monopoly alone, where the money value of marginal real cost would equal marginal receipts. The value of the increment to output produced by the last unit of a factor employed in the monopoly-monopsony industry is even higher relative to the value of the corresponding output increment in competitive industries, and a greater shift of resources from the competitive to the monopoly sector would be required to restore ideal allocation.

SUPPLEMENTARY READING

JOAN ROBINSON, *The Economics of Imperfect Competition,* London: Macmillan & Co., Ltd., 1933, Chap. 18.

J. R. HICKS, "Annual Survey of Economic Theory: The Theory of Monopoly," *Econometrica,* vol. 3, pp. 215 ff.

WILLIAM H. NICHOLLS, *Imperfect Competition within Agricultural Industries,* Ames: Iowa State College Press, 1941.

WILLIAM FELLNER, "Prices and Wages under Bilateral Monopoly," *Quarterly Journal of Economics,* August 1947.

9 PRICE DISCRIMINATION

We must now consider some more complicated phases of the determination of price and output which we have to this point neglected, and which arise out of the practice of *price discrimination*.

A. GENERAL CHARACTER AND TYPES OF PRICE DISCRIMINATION

THE MEANING OF PRICE DISCRIMINATION

Price discrimination refers strictly to the practice by a seller of simultaneously charging different prices to different buyers for the same good. If at approximately the same time a steel manufacturer sold one buyer ten tons of hot rolled strip at $80 a ton and another buyer ten tons of the same hot rolled strip at $70 a ton (all conditions of sale and delivery being the same in the two cases), he would be discriminating in price between the two buyers.

The concept of price discrimination may be reasonably extended to include, however, a seller's practice of charging different prices to different buyers for different varieties of the same good if the price differences are not the same as or proportional to the differences in the costs of producing the several varieties of the good. For example, if an automobile manufacturer produced his "low-priced" car at a cost of $1,200 per unit and his "medium-priced" car at a cost of $1,300 per unit and sold his low-priced car at $1,500 and his medium-priced car at $2,000, he might be said to be practicing price discrimination. Further, when two different goods are yielded from the same basic production process, with a considerable share of their costs identical but with certain separate added costs for each, their sale at a difference in price which is not proportional to their difference in cost may also be designated as price discrimination. For example, suppose an aluminum producer produces basic ingot at a cost of 15 cents a pound, part of which he turns into roofing at an added cost of 2 cents a pound and part of which he makes into an alloy sheet for aircraft bodies at an added cost of 4 cents a pound. If now he sells roofing at 18 cents a pound and aircraft sheet at 25 cents a pound, he is essentially practicing price discrimination.

Price discrimination may thus be encountered in various guises. Although for purposes of analysis we shall speak only of the simplest version of price discrimination—the changing of different prices for the same good —the conclusions arrived at are readily applicable to the more complicated versions.

Monopolistic price discrimination, as this term is used in economic theory, refers to the establishment by a monopolistic seller (or by collusive oligopolists) of a pattern of discriminatory prices which, subject to specified limitations on his ability to discriminate, is such as to permit him to maximize his profit—to the adoption of the most profitable of available alternative patterns of price discrimination. The formal theory of price discrimination generally refers to such monopolistic discrimination. We may also recognize, however, various types of price discrimination which are not oriented to the maximization of the sellers' profits, such as, for example, the *chaotic price discrimination* which may emerge from secret price cutting or price warfare in oligopoly or from sellers' adoption of an arbitrary discriminatory pricing formula as an incident of imperfect collusion. Such price discrimination, generally identified with other than perfectly collusive oligopoly, is not such as to lead to the maximization of the joint profits of the sellers in the industry; it yields lower profits than would a pattern of monopolistic discrimination. In the following pages the discussion will be centered primarily on monopolistic price discrimination, with some comments on chaotic price discrimination. It may be emphasized that in general the predictions of the theory of monopolistic price discrimination are applicable both to single-firm monopoly and to collusive oligopoly, and possibly to other situations.

TWO TYPES OF MONOPOLISTIC PRICE DISCRIMINATION

As was indicated in Chapter 5 on monopoly (pages 259 to 263), the simplified theory of monopoly pricing developed there avoids a consideration of price discrimination by supposing that there are certain restrictions on the action of the monopolist in dealing with his customers. The theory of *simple monopoly* (so called to distinguish it from discriminating monopoly) rests on the assumption that there are many small buyers in the monopolist's market, and in addition assumes:

1. That the monopolist, in effect, can deal with his buyers only by setting a market price for his product and then permitting each buyer to take what quantity he will at that price. Or—which is the same thing—he can determine a market output or supply, offer it to all buyers, and let their bidding determine a market price, at which price each buyer will purchase the amount he desires. The monopolist sup-

posedly cannot deal with individual buyers separately to the end of driving all-or-nothing bargains in which the quantity each buyer is to take and the price to be paid by that buyer are jointly established so as to allow the monopolist a maximum gain from each buyer.

2. That, being limited in effect to setting a market price, the monopolist cannot establish more than *one* market price, and that this single price will be accessible to all buyers alike. The monopolist supposedly cannot set one price for his product to one group of buyers, simultaneously set a higher price for the same good to another group of buyers, and then prevent the latter buyers from being supplied at the lower price.

These suppositions underlie the theory of simple monopoly pricing, and also the conventional theory of collusive oligopoly pricing, which have been developed in Chapters 5 and 6. These theories are generally satisfactory for predicting behavior in a majority of cases, since the limitations on sellers which they assume are in fact present in most markets. A seller can effectively set two or more prices for the same good simultaneously only if a barrier to the retransfer of purchases among buyers is naturally present or can be artificially erected, and such barriers are in most cases not found and cannot be built. (If buyers are able to resell to one another freely, all original sales to buyers will tend to move through the lowest price market, and a single market price will tend to develop.) Similarly, the ability of the seller to drive all-or-nothing bargains with individual buyers (or to accomplish the equivalent) rests on impediments to retransfer and on other special conditions which are not commonly found. The theory of simple monopoly (or of collusive oligopoly) pricing thus has major predictive value in its elementary form.

Nevertheless, we must definitely recognize the existence of a range of cases where at least one of the two assumed restrictions just mentioned is not present and where discriminatory pricing of some sort is thus possible. In those cases where the monopolist, although restricted to setting market prices, can make effective two or more different market prices for the same good at the same time—and can enhance his profits thereby—he is said to be able to engage in *third-degree price discrimination*.[1] In those cases where the monopolist is able to deal individually with each buyer to drive an all-or-nothing bargain, he is said to be able to engage in *first-degree price discrimination*.[2] (So-called second-degree discrimination refers to an improbable in-between case which will not be examined here.) Both third-

---

[1] See A. C. Pigou, *Economics of Welfare,* 4th ed. (London: Macmillan & Co. Ltd., 1932) Part 2, Chap. 17.

[2] *Ibid.*

degree and first-degree price discrimination appear to have some importance in fact.

In this chapter, therefore, the rationale and the general effects of these two variations of monopolistic price discrimination will be investigated, by considering in each case how profit-maximizing sellers would arrive at discriminating prices, how the price-output results will differ from those expected under simple monopoly, and what will be the resultant effects on general welfare. First the relatively simple case of third-degree discrimination will be analyzed, and then first-degree discrimination. We shall also consider briefly the phenomenon of chaotic discrimination and its differences from monopolistic discrimination of both sorts. Finally, we shall comment on the application of the theory of first-degree price discrimination to the prediction of price-output determination in situations of bilateral monopoly.

In the preceding outline of problems of discrimination we have spoken uniformly of discrimination in selling price by a monopolistic seller (or by a collusive oligopoly). As we shall indicate in the succeeding discussion, there is a strictly parallel range of price-discrimination phenomena which are potentially present in monopsony (or collusive oligopsony), affecting buying rather than selling prices. Our analysis of monopolistic discrimination of either the first or third degree may thus be directly adapted to deal with monopsonistic discrimination of the first and third degrees. This will become apparent in the succeeding sections.

B. THIRD-DEGREE PRICE DISCRIMINATION

THE DISCRIMINATING MONOPOLIST'S PROBLEM

The commoner type of monopolistic price discrimination found in practice is third-degree discrimination, in the exercise of which the seller sets two or more different market prices to two or more separate groups of buyers of the same good. (For purposes of simplified analysis we may confine our attention to the case of only two prices and only two buyer groups.) A common instance of such discrimination is found in the practice of some domestic manufacturers of selling at a relatively high price in the home market and "dumping" at a lower price in the export market; another instance is found in the sale of electric power by power and light companies at one price to householders and at a lower price to industrial power users.

The essential conditions for the practice of third-degree discrimination are (1) the ability of the seller to segregate buyers into groups or submarkets in a meaningful fashion so that he can enhance his profits by charging different prices in the two submarkets, and (2) his ability to prevent—or the existence of natural circumstances which prevent—the retransfer of goods from the lower- to the higher-priced submarket. Both conditions are necessary. The first is probably found rather frequently, the second less frequently. However, in the case of a good such as electric power, which the initial buyer cannot readily redeliver to another, or in the case of a good sold to both domestic and export markets, where transportation costs would generally forestall the reshipment of exported goods back to the domestic market, and in many related cases, the second condition is also fulfilled.

The general rationale of third-degree price discrimination is the segregation of buyers into separate submarkets with separate submarket demand curves of different price elasticity, and the increase of profit (above the simple monopoly level) by charging a relatively high price in the submarket in which demand is less elastic and a lower price in the submarket in which demand is more elastic. In common-sense terms, if a seller can find in his market one group of buyers who are willing to pay a rather high price without restricting their purchases very much and another group of buyers who will purchase very little at so high a price but who will extend their purchases rapidly as price falls below a somewhat lower level, he may be able to make more profit by setting a separate price for each group (higher for the former, lower for the latter) than if he limited himself to choosing the most profitable *single* price at which he could sell to the two groups combined. As we shall see, the potentiality of increasing profits by charging different prices to different submarkets in which the elasticities of demand for the good are different inheres in the fact that the relations of marginal receipts to price will correspondingly be different and that thus a more profitable relation of marginal cost to marginal receipts can be accomplished with discriminatory pricing.

Precisely how will the monopolist proceed to maximize his profits when third-degree discrimination is open to him? Actually, he faces two distinguishable problems. First, taking any division of his total market into submarkets as given, how will he arrive at the most profitable combination of prices and outputs in those submarkets? Second, if there are available to him alternative ways of dividing his buyers into submarkets, so that he may set up more or fewer submarkets or apportion buyers among them in different ways, how will he arrive at the most profitable of available congeries of submarkets? Let us confine our attention to the first question only for the time being—how the seller will arrive at separate prices and outputs for two or more given submarkets, with a given buyer population in each submarket.

The character of profit-maximizing discriminatory policy in this case may be most easily understood first by considering an arithmetical example. Let us suppose that there is a monopolist who faces in his *total market* a market demand schedule for his output like that shown by the first two columns of the following table.

(1) Price (P)	(2) Quantity (Q)	(3) Marginal receipts (MR)
$65	46	
		$41
64	48	
		39
63	50	
		37
62	52	
		35
61	54	
		33
60	56	
		31
59	58	
		29
58	60	
		27
57	62	
		25
56	64	
		23
55	66	
		21
54	68	
		19
53	70	
		17
52	72	
		15
51	74	

The marginal receipts drawn from this demand schedule are shown in the third column; they show the addition to total receipts for each *unit* addition to output. (Since, in this example, output can be increased only by steps of two units, marginal receipts are calculated for each step as the change in the total receipts divided by two, thus reducing the measure to one of change in total receipts per unit increase in output. Thus, if output is increased from 48 to 50 units, total receipts increase from $3,072 [48 × 64] to $3,150 [50 × $63], an increase of $78 in total receipts. This amounts to an increase of $39 to total receipts for each of the two units added.) This marginal receipts schedule shows addition to total receipts for additions to output *under simple monopoly pricing*: if all units are sold to all buyers at a single price, which price may be set at any of the alternative levels shown.

Now let us suppose for purposes of simplification that the seller has a marginal cost schedule which reveals a constant marginal cost of $25 per unit at every relevant output. To maximize his profits through simple monopoly pricing (being limited to the choice of a single market price), he will evidently seek that price-output combination where marginal cost equals the marginal receipts drawn from the total market demand curve. In the preceding table we see that this point is found (where marginal receipts equal 25) at a price of $56 and with an output of 64. This profit-maximizing solution is precisely of the same order as that previously explained in Chapter 5 (pages 197 to 203)—the simple monopoly or nondiscriminating solution.

Suppose, however, that the total market is actually divisible into two sectors or groups of buyers, the separate demand schedules of which are of different elasticity and which can be charged different prices. In the following table we represent in the first two columns the total market demand schedule shown just above, and in the third and fourth columns the separate quantities which may be sold at each price in each of two separable submarkets.

(1) Price (P)	(2) Quantity (Q) in total market	(3) Quantity (Q₁) in first submarket	(4) Quantity (Q₂) in second submarket
$65	46	15	31
64	48	16	32
63	50	17	33
62	52	18	34
61	54	19	35
60	56	20	36
59	58	21	37
58	60	22	38
57	62	23	39
56	64	24	40
55	66	25	41
54	68	26	42
53	70	27	43
52	72	28	44
51	74	29	45

It will be noted that, with the total market demand curve previously shown represented again in columns (1) and (2), the items in columns (3) and (4) in each horizontal row show the component parts of the total quantity in column (2) which can be sold respectively in the first and second submarkets. Thus, we see that at a price of $65, 46 units can be sold in all, of which 15 units will be taken in the first submarket and 31 units in the second submarket. At each price in turn the item in column (2) is the sum of the items in columns (3) and (4).

It should also be noted that if we take column (1)—(price)—and column (3)—(quantity in the first submarket)—together, we have a separate demand schedule for the first submarket. Similarly, columns (1) and (4) together comprise a separate market demand schedule for the second submarket. It is the horizontal sum of (quantities in) these two schedules that has produced the total market demand schedule.

Under simple monopoly pricing the seller would have decided to produce an output of 64, which would sell at a price of $56, since at this point his marginal cost of $25 equals marginal receipts drawn from the total demand curve. This would mean that he would sell 24 units in the first submarket and 40 units in the second submarket, all at a price of $56. We now present him with the alternative, however, of setting two different prices in the two markets and of apportioning any output he produces between the markets in a different way than if he charged a single price. Can he increase his profits thereby?

THE PROFIT-MAXIMIZING POLICY

It appears that he can definitely do so. To demonstrate why this is so, and precisely what price changes he should make to maximize his profit from price discrimination, we must analyze the two separate demand schedules for the first and second submarkets, in particular calculating the marginal receipts schedule from each of these separate demand schedules. In the following table, we show in the first two columns the demand schedule in the first submarket—columns (1) and (2) correspond to columns (1) and (3) in the preceding table—and in the third column the marginal receipts schedule drawn from this demand schedule. In the next two columns, (4) and (5), corresponding to columns (1) and (4) in the preceding table, we show the demand schedule in the second submarket, and in the last column the marginal receipts schedule drawn from that demand schedule.

Comparing these two schedules, a significant difference is apparent. At any common price the demand schedule for the first submarket is substantially more elastic than the demand schedule for the second submarket. For example, at the simple monopoly price of $56 the elasticity of demand in the first submarket is approximated at −2.3, whereas, at the same price, elasticity of demand in the second submarket is approximated at −1.4. Correspondingly, marginal receipts lie higher at any common price in the first submarket.

(1) Price (P)	(2) Quantity in first sub-market (Q_1)	(3) Marginal receipts in first sub-market (MR_1)	(4) Price (P)	(5) Quantity in second sub-market (Q_2)	(6) Marginal receipts in second sub-market (MR_2)
$65	15		$65	31	
		$49			$33
64	16		64	32	
		47			31
63	17		63	33	
		45			29
62	18		62	34	
		43			27
61	19		61	35	
		41			25
60	20		60	36	
		39			23
59	21		59	37	
		37			21
58	22		58	38	
		35			19
57	23		57	39	
		33			17
56	24		56	40	
		31			15
55	25		55	41	
		29			13
54	26		54	42	
		27			11
53	27		53	43	
		25			9
52	28		52	44	
		23			7
51	29		51	45	

If both submarkets are being sold at $56, the last unit added to sales in the first submarket (the 24th in that market) has brought marginal receipts of $33, whereas the last unit added in the second submarket (the 40th in that market) has brought marginal receipts of only $17.

Now this last bit of information requires careful evaluation. It says that the seller by selling 24 units at $56 instead of 23 units at $57 in submarket one actually thereby added $33 to his total receipts. It states also that by selling 40 units at $56 instead of 39 units at $57 in submarket two he thereby added only $17 to his total receipts. When one reads up and down the two marginal receipts schedules, it is similarly apparent that if the seller, starting at the simple monopoly price of $56, were to sell one less unit in submarket two (at $57) he would thus lose only $17 of the total receipts, and if he were to sell this unit instead in submarket one (thus cutting price there to $55), he would add $31 to his total receipts. Since the $31 gain exceeds the $17 loss, he could increase his revenue and profit from selling 64 units by raising the price and selling less in submarket two and lowering the price and selling more in submarket one.

How much output should he shift from the second to the first submarket and what corresponding price difference should he establish in order to maximize his profits? Starting with a given total output and common price (64 units and $56 in this example), he should shift units from the market with the less elastic demand to that with the more elastic demand until the respective prices and outputs are such that the marginal receipts in two markets are equal. Thus, if we suppose the seller to be producing 64 units for sale and initially selling in both markets at $56, he can increase his profit by lowering price in the first submarket and raising his price in the second, and correspondingly shifting sales from two to one, until he is selling 28 units at a price of $52 in submarket one and 36 units at a price of $60 in submarket two. At this point the marginal receipts in both markets stand at $25, and no further shift of output or change in prices would be advantageous.

That his profit has been increased by this shift is easily demonstrated. Selling 64 units (divided 24 and 40 between submarkets one and two) at $56, his total receipts were:

$$64 \times \$56 = \$3,584$$

If he sells instead 28 units at $52 in the first submarket and 36 units at $60 in the second, his total receipts are:

$$28 \times \$52 = \$1,456$$
$$36 \times \$60 = \quad 2,160$$

$$\text{Total} \quad \$3,616$$

Since the cost of producing 64 units is the same in either case, profit is larger with the indicated price discrimination. By similar calculations for all alternative sets of prices and quantities by which 64 units can be disposed of, we can easily prove that it is just that combination such that marginal receipts are equalized in the two markets which will give the greatest receipts and profit for the given output.

More generally, of course, it can be said that in disposing of any given output (not only the simple monopoly output) in two or more separable submarkets, the monopolist can maximize his profits by dividing the output between the markets so that their marginal receipts are equal and that this will lead to different prices in the markets except when the relation of marginal receipts to price is the same in all—or, in other words, except when the elasticity of demand is the same in all at relevant common prices. (If the elasticity of demand is the same in all, the monopolist has no discriminatory power or incentive to discriminate.)

We thus arrive at the first rule of price discrimination—any given output will be allotted between two (or more) submarkets so as to equate the marginal receipts from the two markets, and this will give rise to a determinate price difference between the two markets unless the elasticity of demand is the same in both. Except in this limiting case, third-degree discrimination will permit larger receipts from any output, and thus a larger profit, than a single price, such as is associated with simple monopoly pricing, possibly could. With a given output discrimination will result in raising price and decreasing sales in the market of less elastic demand and lowering price and increasing sales in the market of more elastic demand, as compared to what prices and sales would be if all units were sold at a single uniform price.

The preceding answers some of our questions: price discrimination can increase profits, and a profit-maximizing pattern of discrimination for any given output can be defined if we can identify the separate marginal receipts schedules in the separate markets. We have a further question to answer, however. If output is not given, but is also a variable to be determined by the discriminating monopolist, how does he codetermine his output, its division among submarkets, and their several prices for a maximization of profits?

The answer to this question is found by combining an old principle with a new one. The old principle is that to maximize profits the monopolist should set output so that his marginal cost equals marginal receipts. The new principle is that, where discrimination is possible, any alternative output should be apportioned among submarkets so that their marginal receipts are equated. If we combine these principles, it appears that the monopolist should choose the output at which his marginal cost is equated to a marginal receipts schedule which shows the relation of marginal receipts in his several submarkets to their combined output, when every such output is divided among them to equalize marginal receipts. Given this output, he will divide it among them as indicated, at corresponding prices.

To calculate the output thus described, we need first to derive a horizontal summation of the marginal receipts schedules of the several markets. In our example of two markets we may do this by adding, *at each level of marginal receipts,* the quantities sold in the two markets; thus, we derive an aggregate marginal receipts schedule which shows the relation of total output to marginal receipts if every output is sold subject to optimal discrimination. Since we have shown only a segment of each of two demand schedules, this is not possible from the figures shown except where the two segments of marginal receipts schedules shown overlap, as they do from the marginal receipts value of $33 to $23.

In this range, we may develop the following information from the table on page 408. In column (1) we show the values of marginal receipts from 33 to 23; in column (2) the outputs in the first submarket at which these alternative values are reached; in column (3) the same output information for the second submarket. *Column (4) shows the total quantity saleable in the combined markets at each level of marginal receipts.*

(1) Marginal receipts (MR)	(2) Corresponding quantity in first sub-market (Q_1)	(3) Corresponding quantity in second sub-market (Q_2)	(4) Total quantity ($Q_1 + Q_2$) saleable at indicated level of marginal receipts
$33	24	32	56
31	25	33	58
29	26	34	60
27	27	35	62
25	28	36	64
23	29	37	66

(With information on added segments of the two demand curves, we could extend this table to cover all attainable levels of marginal receipts.) What does this table tell us? For the scheduled range of values of marginal receipts, columns (1) and (4)—or the aggregated marginal receipts schedule—show us the relation of the seller's aggregate output to his marginal receipts from this output, subject to the condition that any output be divided between the submarkets according to principles of optimal discrimination so that marginal receipts are equalized, or as shown in columns (2) and (3).

The manner in which the monopolist will set output to maximize profit is now easily seen. He will choose that output where his marginal cost schedule intersects the aggregated marginal receipts schedule, and he will then apportion this output between the submarkets as indicated. Thus, suppose as before that his marginal cost is constant at $25 per unit at any relevant output. Then he will produce 64 units (at which the aggregated marginal receipts schedule reaches $25), and he will apportion 28 units to the first submarket at a price of $52 and 36 units to the second submarket at a price of $60. (These prices are found in the table on page 408.)

If instead, his marginal cost were constant at a level of $31 per unit, he would produce 58 units, apportion 25 to the first submarket at a price of

$55 and 33 to the second submarket at a price of $63. The profit-maximizing solution is evidently arrived at by simultaneously (1) choosing output so that marginal cost equals marginal receipts from the combined submarkets and (2) allocating output among the several submarkets so as to equate their marginal receipts and establishing corresponding price differences.

It will be noted in the preceding example that with marginal cost at the same level in both cases (for example, $25) the profit-maximizing simple

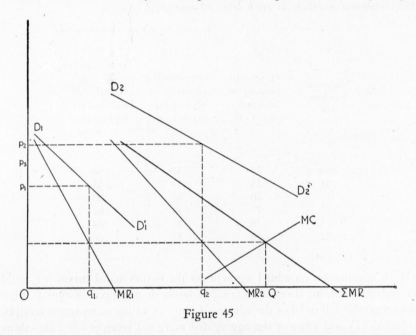

Figure 45

monopoly output is the same as the profit-maximizing aggregate output under discriminating monopoly—64 in both cases—although with discrimination, of course, the prices and quantities sold in the individual submarkets are different. From this it should not be concluded that discriminating monopoly output is always the same as simple monopoly output: this will be true in general only with linear demand schedules (and then with some exceptions).

The preceding argument may be summarized by restating it in terms of demand and cost curve analysis. Let us suppose that the monopolist faces two separate submarkets for the same good and that the market demand curve in the first is represented by D_1D_1' in Figure 45, whereas the market demand curve in the second is represented by D_2D_2'. Marginal receipts at various outputs in the first submarket are shown by the line MR_1, and in the second submarket by the line MR_2. To determine the profit-maximizing combined output the monopolist should in essence first make a horizontal summation of the MR_1 and MR_2 schedules, adding the two quantities at each marginal receipts level. This summation is shown in the ΣMR schedule, which in effect represents the relation of combined output in the two markets to marginal receipts, provided any combined output is allocated between the two markets so as to equalize their marginal receipts. The monopolist's marginal cost for his total output (from which both markets will be supplied) is shown by the line MC.

The monopolist will now obviously maximize his profit by producing the output at which his marginal cost equals marginal receipts—the output OQ at which MC intersects ΣMR—and will allocate this output between the two markets so that their marginal receipts are equalized, selling oq_1 in the first submarket and oq_2 in the second submarket. (The sum of oq_1 and oq_2 is necessarily OQ.) This will mean that he sells at the price op_1 in the first submarket (the price corresponding to the output oq_1 in that market) and at the price op_2 in the second submarket. Price discrimination is thus in evidence. If the monopolist had pursued simple-monopoly pricing principles, charging the most profitable single price to the two markets, his price would lie at op_s, the calculation of which is not shown in Figure 45. In this case he would have sold less in submarket one and more in submarket two, and he would have made less profit since MR_2 would be below MR_1 when the price was the same in both markets.

The preceding argument is developed explicitly for two submarkets. It will follow precisely the same lines in the case of three or more submarkets.

THE EFFECTS OF THIRD-DEGREE PRICE DISCRIMINATION

What are the general effects of discriminatory pricing of the third degree? This question may be most easily answered by comparing the results of such discriminatory pricing with those of simple monopoly pricing. In the first place it is obvious that with third-degree discrimination buyers will be charged two or more prices instead of a single price, and any individual buyer will not have the opportunity to buy at an existing lower price than that set to him by the discriminating monopolist. Second, the profit of the discriminating monopolist will be higher than if he were limited to fixing the most profitable single price for all submarkets, since only by discrimination can he equalize marginal receipts in various submarkets. Third, the total output supplied to the combined markets may be the same as or more or less than that supplied under simple monopoly. The effect will depend, in general, on the shapes of the several submarket demand curves and also on whether or not discrimination leads to supplying a submarket not supplied at all under simple monopoly pricing.[3]

[3] For further treatment of this subject see Joan Robinson, *Economics of Imperfect Competition* (London: Macmillan & Co., Ltd., 1933), Chaps. 15 and 16.

Fourth, the usual order of price effects is that under discrimination prices will tend to be higher in submarkets where demand is less elastic (at common prices) and lower in submarkets where demand is more elastic than if there were simple monopoly pricing. It is possible, however, that where discrimination leads to an output extension *with decreasing average and marginal costs,* all markets may have lower prices and be supplied with larger outputs than if there were simple monopoly pricing. This is not demonstrated here, but ready references are available.[4]

Fifth, the price-raising and output-restrictive effects of any monopoly remain, with the same general effects on allocation: price tends significantly to exceed marginal cost. Sixth, allocation is further affected in that under discrimination the relation of price to marginal cost will vary in different submarkets. Thus, whatever the general restrictive impact on industry output as a whole, there is a further tendency toward allocating too much of output to submarkets with more elastic demand and too little to submarkets with less elastic demand from the standpoint of aggregate welfare. Finally, it is probably the view of most people that the practice of charging a high price to John Smith and a lower one to Peter Jones for the same good is unethical or unjust; to borrow the words of Merriam-Webster, such a price difference is viewed as "an unfair or injurious" distinction in treatment. Since those making policies in the market place must ultimately answer to public opinion, this value judgment must be seriously considered.

THE SEGREGATION OF BUYERS BY THE DISCRIMINATING MONOPOLIST

Until now we have considered only the manner in which the monopolist will discriminate in price between two or more given submarkets, given the composition of each of these submarkets. That is, as a beginning point in analysis, we have supposed either that both the number of submarkets and the identity of the buyers in each submarket are given to the monopolist and beyond his control or that he has already determined these matters himself.

In some circumstances the number and composition of submarkets may be more or less irrevocably given to the discriminating monopolist. For example, the monopolist faced with a practically indivisible domestic market and a similarly indivisible export market may be in this position. In these cases the foregoing analysis covers the only problems presented for solution. In other cases, however, the monopolist may be able to exercise some discretionary control over the number and composition of the submarkets to which . he sells. He may, for example, be able to divide his buyers alternatively into

[4] Joan Robinson, *Economics of Imperfect Competition,* Chaps. 15 and 16.

two, three, or four submarkets, each to be charged a different price, and he may be able to classify buyers as to submarkets in various alternative ways. If he has discretionary control over the number and the composition of his submarkets, according to what principles will he establish them and classify buyers as among them?

The general principles which govern profit-maximizing action in this regard are as follows: As among alternative allocations of buyers among submarkets, some will be more profitable than others when exploited by third-degree price discrimination. The relative profitability of alternative allocations will depend basically on the degree to which individual buyer demand schedules of different price elasticity are segregated into different submarkets. The most profitable attainable allocation of buyers among submarkets will be that which gives the greatest differences between demand elasticities of different submarkets and consistent with this creates the maximum number of different submarkets with different demand elasticities. On the other hand there may be extra costs to the monopolist of administering more complicated submarket divisions, so that these costs must be offset against the virtual advantages of more complicated submarket structures. In general, therefore, the monopolist may be expected to choose among alternative submarket alignments available to him the one which permits the greatest and most precise distinctions among buyers on the basis of the price elasticities of their demand curves, so long as the extra costs of administration do not outweigh the virtual gains from more precise discrimination.

MONOPSONISTIC DISCRIMINATION OF THE THIRD DEGREE

The discussion of third-degree discrimination has so far referred to the monopolistic seller who is able to divide his buyers into two or more submarkets with demand schedules of different elasticity and who is able to charge different prices in the different markets. It is evident that a similar possibility of discrimination may be presented to the monopsonistic buyer. In brief, the monopsonist—defined in general as one who faces a sloping supply curve for a good he purchases—may be able to subdivide his suppliers into two or more markets with supply schedules of different elasticity and to discriminate in buying price in such a manner as to increase his profits.

The condition for effective monopsonistic discrimination is in effect that the monopsonistic buyer be able to segregate buyers into submarkets in which the supply curves have different elasticities at common prices. If he can do so, it will be to his advantage to allocate any given amount he purchases among submarkets in such a way that the *marginal outlay* in each submarket is the same. (This is the equivalent of the condition of equal marginal receipts in all submarkets for the discriminating monopolist.) In general, he will (1) purchase any given amount in such proportions from several submarkets that the marginal outlays are the same in all (with different buying prices as elasticities of supply differ) and (2) purchase a total amount such that the marginal benefit from the last unit purchased is equal to the marginal outlay in both markets. Diagrammatically, this output would be found where the marginal benefit schedule or curve intersected the combined or aggregate marginal outlay schedule, which schedule shows the relation of marginal outlay to amount purchased subject to the condition that for any amount the marginal outlays in the several submarkets are always equated.

The general effect of third-degree monopsonistic price discrimination will obviously be that a higher buying price will be paid in submarkets with more elastic supply schedules and a lower price in those with less elastic supply schedules. Such discrimination will permit the monopsonistic buyer larger profits than simple monopsonistic pricing would, and it will also have adverse allocation effects parallel to those encountered in third-degree monopolistic price discrimination.

C. FIRST-DEGREE OR "PERFECT" PRICE DISCRIMINATION

THE BASIS OF FIRST-DEGREE DISCRIMINATION

A less common type of monopolistic price discrimination is found in so-called first-degree discrimination. This sort of price discrimination, when it is fully accomplished or practiced in the most effective attainable fashion, is marked by the fact that the seller makes a potentially different bargain with each of his buyers instead of setting just two or a few market prices, each of which is available to a number of buyers. It is also marked by the fact that the seller in essence makes an all-or-nothing bargain with each buyer, specifying both the quantity the buyer can receive of the good and the total amount of money he must pay to get it, rather than simply establishing a unit price at which the buyer may purchase and allowing him to buy as much as he wishes at that price. The amount of money required of the buyer for the quantity of the good supplied to him is moreover the maximum amount the buyer will be willing to pay rather than do without the good altogether.

The essential difference of first-degree monopolistic discrimination from both simple monopoly pricing and third-degree discriminatory pricing is that the seller does not set a market price to each buyer—either the same price to all buyers or several different prices to several groups of buyers—and then allow him to purchase all the units he will at the price or prices set. *Instead the seller implicitly charges each buyer the highest price he will pay for each unit of the good he receives, and a different price for each such unit,* or, what is the same thing, he makes the buyer pay all that he will, under threat of being denied the good altogether, for any total quantity which the seller decides to supply to him. This is definitely different from letting the buyer take as much as he will at a specified market price. At the same time the seller determines the quantity of the good to be supplied to each buyer which, when priced in this way, is the most profitable to the seller. Thus, first-degree price discrimination is sometimes referred to as *perfect discrimination* since it obviously involves the maximum possible exploitation of each buyer in the interest of the seller's profit and a greater exploitation than is possible under third-degree discrimination.

The character of first-degree or perfect price discrimination may be made clear by considering the demand schedule for a good by an individual buyer and the possibilities for exploitation which it offers. Let us imagine the demand schedule of an individual buyer for a certain good to read as follows:

Price	Quantity
$10	1
9	2
8	3
7	4
6	5
5	6
4	7
3	8
2	9
1	10

This demand schedule shows the alternative quantities which the buyer will take at alternative prices per some period of time, like a month. For example, it says in effect that if the price were $10, the buyer would take one unit per month; if instead it were $9, he would take two units per month, etc. The market demand schedule—either for the entire market or for each of two or more subdivisions under third-degree discrimination—is the sum of a number of such individual buyer demand schedules.

If the seller follows either simple monopoly pricing or third-degree discriminatory pricing, he will set in the market in which the individual buyer purchases, some market price, determined by the relation of his marginal cost to the marginal receipts drawn from the market demand schedule in that market. Let us suppose that, in the market in which the buyer mentioned purchases, the monopolist finds it most profitable to set a market price of $7. Then the individual buyer whose demand schedule is represented will purchase four units of the product per month, and all other buyers will adjust to the price set in comparable fashion. This will mean that the buyer in question pays $28 for four units.

So long as the seller is limited to setting a market price in one or more markets, each buyer is in a similar position: he can acquire as many units as he wants at the price set, and the total revenue extracted from him will be equal to the market price times the quantity he takes. In particular, he is able to acquire all units he purchases—four units in the case presented—at the same unit price he is willing to pay for the last unit—in this case at the $7 he is willing to pay when his purchases move from three to four units.

The question now arises whether at a price of $7 per unit for four units, or at any other market price, the seller is obtaining from the buyer as much as he would be willing to pay rather than be denied access to the good altogether. Would he be willing to pay, for example, more than $28 for four units, or more than $30 for five units, rather than be denied access to the good altogether? If he would, then the setting of a market price, either by simple monopoly pricing or by third-degree discriminatory pricing, will not yield the monopolist the maximum profit he might extract at any given quantity of production.

It would seem to follow from our analysis of consumer choice (pages 33 to 37) that the buyer will be willing to pay more for a given quantity of a good if forced by the threat of being shut off from it altogether than he will have to pay if allowed simply to adjust his quantity of purchases to a stated market price. As a first approximation, the following might seem to be true of a buyer like the one whose demand schedule has been given. Not only will he be willing to buy one unit at $10 or two units if the price is instead $9, and three units if it is $8 or four units if it is $7. But it may also be true that he can be forced to pay $10 for a first unit, *plus $9 for a second,* plus $8 for a third, plus $7 for a fourth, etc. so that the monopolist could extract $19 for two units, or $27 for three units, or $34 for four units, etc. In this case forcing him to pay the maximum attainable amount for any quantity will in general bring larger receipts than if the seller simply sets a price and lets him adjust to it. Thus, if the price is set at $7, the buyer would take four units and pay $28. But the monopolist may be able to make him pay $34 for four units ($10 plus $9 plus $8 plus $7) if he offers him "four units or nothing" as alternatives.

Why should this be so? The theory of consumer preference suggests that, given any market price for a good, the consumer extends his purchases to the point where the money value of the marginal benefit to him of the last unit added to his purchases (for example, the fourth unit at $7) is equal to the market price. But the marginal benefit from added units of any good declines as more are added, so that presumably the benefit from each of the units other than the last one added—*of the inframarginal units*—is greater than that of the last unit. Therefore, the buyer should be willing to pay for a given number of units an amount greater than the price which induces him to purchase the last unit times the number of units. If in the preceding example, one unit would be worth $10 to him, a second unit worth $9, a third unit $8, a fourth unit $7, then he should be willing to pay more than $28 for four units *if forced*. If the monopolist sets a market price of $7 and allows him to purchase four units, the buyer is enjoying "surplus" of the total value of the benefit from all units of the good over the amount he is paying, and the monopolist can charge him more than $28 if he can threaten him with the alternative of getting none of the good.

How much more can the monopolist get in general? We have already suggested that one possibility is that he can in effect receive for the separate units of any aggregate quantity the succession of separate prices shown on the buyer's demand schedule above that quantity, when that schedule is constructed to show changes of price with successive quantity increments of one unit. Thus, in the demand schedule above we can get total receipts obtainable at any aggregate quantity by adding up the prices at successive quantity points down to that quantity—two units will bring $10 plus $9, or $19; three units will bring $10 plus $9 plus $8, or $27, etc. (It should be noted in this case that the *average price* per unit will exceed the price obtainable by market pricing; for example, four units will bring $34, or an $8.50 per unit average price, as against $7 with market pricing.) *If this is the case, it is clear that with perfect discrimination, the demand schedule of the buyer effectively becomes a marginal receipts schedule of the seller, showing the added receipts obtainable for each addition to quantity supplied; it may also be called a perfect discrimination schedule.* Similarly, the buyer's demand curve represents the seller's marginal receipts curve, and it is also the perfect discrimination curve.

For exactly this relationship to exist, it is necessary that the extraction of a larger amount of money from the buyer by perfect discrimination does not make enough incursion on his total purchasing power to cause him to reduce his purchases of all goods, including the one sold subject to perfect discrimination. Thus, if the buyer would purchase one unit if the price were $10, two units if the price were $9, and three units if the price were $8, he will also presumably be willing to pay $27 for three units ($10 plus $9 plus $8) only if this added expenditure—the excess of $27 over $24—is a small part of his total purchasing power and does not cause him to restrict purchases of this and other goods because his real income has been significantly reduced. In general, we may say that the perfect discrimination schedule, showing added prices obtainable for added units down to any quantity point, will be approximately the same as the buyer's demand schedule so long as his expenditure on the good in question is a small fraction of his total expenditure. This is the case we have supposed in the preceding illustration.

If, on the other hand, the good commands a significant portion of his total expenditure, the perfect discrimination schedule will lie somewhat below the demand schedule, showing lower added prices for added units than if the buyer were charged a single market price for all units at any quantity level. Thus, in the preceding example, although the buyer might take one unit at $10, two units if the price were $9, and three units if the price were $8, he might be willing to pay only $8.90 for a second unit if he were charged $10 for a first—or $18.90 for two units—and only $7.85 for a third if he had been charged $18.90 for two units—or $26.75 for three units. The schedule or curve showing the possibilities of perfect discrimination, and the seller's marginal receipts thereunder, may thus lie slightly below the conventional demand schedule or curve if the good commands a significant share of the buyer's income.

For purposes of simplification let us concentrate on the the case where the buyer's demand schedule is the same as the schedule showing the possibilities of perfect discrimination. In this case (as in the other) the seller can obviously get a larger revenue for any given quantity sold, and thus a larger profit, by perfect discrimination rather than by setting a market price and allowing the buyer to adjust his purchases. Precisely how will he maximize his profits with perfect discrimination?

PERFECTLY DISCRIMINATORY PRICE-OUTPUT POLICY

Let us reconsider a single buyer with whom the seller is dealing, with the demand schedule previously mentioned, that is:

(1) Price	(2) Quantity	(3) Marginal receipts with market pricing	(4) Marginal receipts with first-degree discrimination
$10	1		
		$8	$9
9	2		
		6	8
8	3		
		4	7
7	4		
		2	6
6	5		
		0	5
5	6		
		−2	4
4	7		
		−4	3
3	8		
		−6	2
2	9		
		−8	1
1	10		

Column (1) in this table shows alternative market prices, and column (2) the alternative amounts the buyer will take at these alternative prices. Column (3) shows the conventional marginal receipts from added sales *under market pricing*. That is, if two units are sold at $9 instead of one unit at $10, marginal receipts are $8; if three units are sold at $8 instead of two units at $9, marginal receipts (from the third unit) are $6. This is the conventional marginal receipts schedule with which we are acquainted.

Now if the seller were dealing with this buyer alone through market pricing, he would wish to select that price-quantity combination at which his marginal cost equaled marginal receipts. For example, if his marginal cost were constant at $4, he would set a price of $7, at which the buyer would take four units and where marginal receipts equal $4. This would give him the largest possible profit from market pricing.

If he can subject the buyer to perfect discrimination, however, his policy will change. Under first-degree discrimination, he can exact the maximum revenue for any quantity by threatening to withhold supply altogether. If he can do so, he can get $10 for a first unit plus $9 for a second, plus $8 for a third, etc. Then his marginal receipts obtainable from added amounts sold, shown in column (4), will be the same as the price schedule in column (1). *Because he need not, under perfect discrimination, lower the price of inframarginal units in order to extend his sales,* his marginal receipts schedule is higher at all points than under market pricing. Now if his marginal cost is constant at $4 he will maximize profits by selling the buyer the output of seven, at which marginal receipts (a la perfect discrimination) reach $4. He will sell him seven units in essence in the following fashion: $10 for the first unit, $9 for the second, $8 for the third, and so forth down to $4 for the seventh—a total of $49 for seven units. All he need do to accomplish this is to offer the buyer seven units for $49 on an all-or-nothing basis—the buyer must take seven units for $49 or get nothing at all. The *average price* obtained will be $49 divided by seven, or $7 per unit.

It is apparent that although the same general principle of profit maximization applies under perfect discrimination as elsewhere—that is, marginal cost is equated to marginal receipts—the outcome in pricing and output is distinctly different from that of simple monopoly. First, because under perfect discrimination the marginal receipts schedule lies higher than under market pricing (in many cases coinciding with the demand schedule), the output at which marginal cost equals marginal receipts will be larger (in many cases such that marginal cost equals the price the last unit purchased would bring under simple market pricing) *so that a "competitive" output is attained.* Second, the average price for the quantity sold will be higher than could be obtained for that quantity under market pricing by simple monopoly. Third, the profits of the monopolist will be the highest attainable—higher than under market pricing of either the simple or third-degree discriminatory type. We thus get an essential elimination of monopolistic output restriction, but we have a retention of monopolistic high prices and excess profits.

So far we have dealt only with a single buyer subjected to perfect discrimination. The more general case is that in which the monopolist deals separately with each of many buyers.

The extension of the preceding analysis to this case may be developed as follows: Let us suppose that every buyer spends so little of his income on

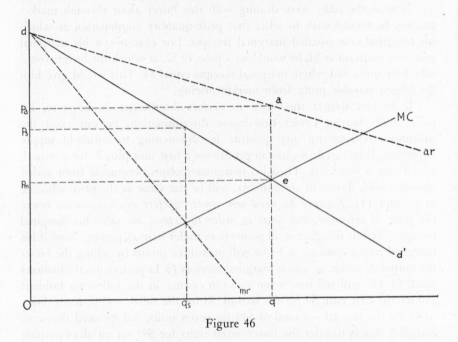

Figure 46

the good in question that his individual demand schedule for the good indicates the marginal receipts obtainable from selling him various amounts under perfect discrimination (his perfect discrimination schedule is the same as his demand schedule). Then the *market* demand schedule faced by the monopolist—which is defined as the horizontal summation of the individual demand schedules of all the buyers he faces (showing the sum of the quantities taken at each alternative price)—is also the aggregate perfect discrimination schedule for the monopolist. That is, the market demand schedule also shows the monopolist the successive prices or receipts he can receive from successive additions to sales under perfect discrimination, or it represents his marginal receipts schedule under such discrimination. Diagrammatically, the market demand curve is then a perfect discrimination curve or curve showing marginal receipts to the perfectly discriminating monopolist. This curve is represented by *dd'* in Figure 46.

To maximize his profits the monopolist will choose to produce that output at which his marginal cost is equal to the added receipts obtainable from the last unit sold. If he were limited to simple market pricing in dealing with his buyers—being able only to set a price and allow buyers to take what quantities they would—the curve dd' would be his market demand curve in the usual sense, showing the average price for or average receipts from sales of various alternative quantities. His marginal receipts curve with such simple market pricing would be below dd', at mr. He would thus choose to produce the output oq_s, at which his marginal cost equals marginal receipts as calculated for simple market pricing, and to sell all units of this quantity at the uniform price op_s.

If, on the other hand, the monopolist is able to practice perfect discrimination, the curve dd' becomes his marginal receipts curve, as indicated above, since he is now able to sell successive added units at the successive prices shown on dd' without in effect lowering the prices of preceding units to that of the marginal unit. He will thus maximize his profits by producing the output oq in Figure 46, where MC intersects dd'. Although oq is his profit-maximizing output, however, op_m is not the average price of that output, but it is merely the price of, or marginal receipts from, the last unit produced. The quantity oq will be sold to many buyers, each being charged by terms of an all-or-nothing bargain the maximum amount obtainable for the quantity represented by his share of the market demand curve down to the marginal price chosen.

The average price of or average receipts from output (the relationship of which price to output under perfect discrimination is shown by ar and not by dd') will be substantially higher than op_m, at op_a. Diagrammatically, the monopolist's total receipts will be represented by the area $d\,e\,q\,o$ (or $p_a\,a\,q\,o$). The resultant profit will necessarily be larger than that obtained with simple monopoly pricing, since average receipts are larger at any chosen output.

In effect, where the good commands little of the income of the buyers, the market demand curve becomes the marginal receipts curve of the perfectly discriminating monopolist, showing at every point the additions to revenue obtainable under perfect discrimination. The maximization of profits implies the choice of a total output such that marginal cost equals marginal receipts thus defined, although the average price of all units is clearly higher than the marginal receipts from the last unit because of the application of perfect discrimination to each buyer in selling him his determined share of the total output. This same analysis applies where the good absorbs a sufficient share of buyer income that the perfect discrimination curve lies below the market demand curve, except that in that case the output chosen will be somewhat smaller.

EFFECTS OF PERFECT DISCRIMINATION

The effects of perfectly discriminating monopoly on price and output are thus in the general case the same as those previously described. First, output tends to be the same as that attributed to pure competition in the sense that it is set where the marginal cost equals the price of the last unit sold. Simple monopolistic output restriction is thereby eliminated; the output is clearly larger than with simple monopoly. This holds except to the extent that the perfect discrimination curve lies below the market demand curve. Second, the average price of the good to buyers is higher than under competition, and monopolistic profits are at the maximum attainable level. The adverse allocation effects of simple monopoly thus tend to be eliminated by perfect discrimination, but the adverse income-distribution effects remain or are accentuated.

One very important point in logical analysis emerges from the preceding consideration of perfect discrimination. If we compare simple monopoly or monopolistic third-degree discrimination—both of which involve the setting of market prices—with perfectly discriminating monopoly, it appears that the significant difference is the following: Whereas with market pricing (all units sold at the same price and the buyer allowed to purchase what he will at a market price) the monopolist must in essence accept a lower price for all units in order to sell more units, with perfect discrimination he need not do so. He can extend his sales by selling further units at a lower price, while still, in essence, receiving an unaltered price for preceding units produced. In effect, the market-pricing monopolist suffers from the downward slope of the market demand curve much more acutely than the perfectly discriminating monopolist, as the price of all units must drop with the price of added units, and thus with any given demand curve his marginal receipts drop off much more rapidly with added output and are lower at any given output. It is because of this implication of market pricing as a technique of dealing with buyers that the phenomenon of monopolistic output restriction as we have previously described it emerges. Marginal receipts lie below the price of the final unit so long as the demand curve slopes, and a profit-maximizing adjustment such that marginal cost equals marginal receipts thus means a virtually restricted output or a smaller output than if marginal cost were equated to the price of the last unit sold. If, however, the monopolist can employ perfect discrimination, and need not accept a lower price for all units in order to extend sales, the downward slope of his demand curve affects his receipts much less since his marginal receipts curve tends to coincide with the demand curve. Now, equating marginal cost to marginal receipts tends to be the same as equating marginal cost to the price of the last unit, and what we have identified as monopolistic output restriction tends to be eliminated. The perfectly discriminating monopolist is thus led to choose an output such that marginal cost equals the price of the last unit sold, just as the purely competitive seller, whose market price is unaffected by his own output, does. Market pricing is thus a necessary basis for monopolistic output restriction as generally understood; perfectly discriminatory pricing offers an escape from such restriction (although not from monopolistic income distribution effects).

What is the practical importance of first-degree or perfect monopolistic discrimination in the real economy? Is it a common alternative to market pricing? As we have emphasized previously, the necessary conditions for perfect discrimination are monopoly (ability of the seller or collusive sellers to exploit the buyer without having him shift to a substitute source of supply), feasibility of establishing contact with the buyers to determine all-or-nothing bargains or something approximate thereto, and ability to prevent retransfer of purchases among buyers. This combination of conditions is obviously not encountered with great frequency in practice.

It is readily apparent that, given the initial condition of monopoly, the second and third conditions are much more likely to be fulfilled if the number of buyers to which the monopolist sells is one or a few rather than many. There is essentially a natural setting for perfect discrimination if there is one buyer only, and the setting is approximated with a few buyers. If there are many small buyers, first-degree discrimination is much less likely to be practicable.

On the other hand, where one or a few sellers face one or a few buyers, the situation is complicated by the opposition of monopolistic and monopsonistic tendencies, so that the outcome may not be the same as attributed to the perfectly discriminating monopoly in which the seller is dominant in exploiting buyers. Discriminatory phenomena may remain but in the special setting of *bilateral monopoly,* which will require special treatment. We shall postpone consideration of perfect discrimination in bilateral monopoly cases until later in this chapter.

The simple operation of perfect discrimination as analyzed will be found only where the monopolistic seller is dominant in establishing terms to buyers, and this will tend to be the case only if buyers are many and if at the same time the necessary conditions outlined happen to be fulfilled. As suggested, such cases are few in practice. It may, nevertheless, be possible that some *approximations* to perfectly discriminatory pricing do emerge in fact where there are many buyers. It has been suggested that professional men, like physicians, may be able to achieve some approximation to perfect discrimination in pricing their services separately to each client. It has also been suggested that there may be some approach to perfect discrimination when a service is sold to buyers at a high price for the first few units per period of time, a lower price for a few more, etc., through a "step-rate" of the sort often established in selling electric power to householders.[5] But the application of the principles of perfect discrimination is likely to be confined largely to cases where buyers are few, and here the preceding analysis must be modified to some extent (see pages 432 to 436).

MONOPSONISTIC DISCRIMINATION OF THE FIRST DEGREE

Just as third-degree monopolistic discrimination has a logical counterpart in third-degree monopsonistic discrimination, so there may be perfect monopsonistic as well as perfect monopolistic discrimination. First-degree or perfect monopsonistic discrimination implies that the monopsonistic buyer, faced with an up-sloping supply curve for the good he purchases, can purchase successive units of the good at separate supply prices and will not need to bid up the prices of all units of the good in order to acquire more of the good. Suppose for example that a monopsonistic buyer is faced with the following supply schedule for a good:

(1) Price	(2) Quantity supplied	(3) Marginal outlay under market pricing	(4) Marginal outlay under perfect discrimination
$1	1		$2
		$3	
2	2		3
		5	
3	3		4
		7	
4	4		5
		9	
5	5		6
		11	
6	6		7
		13	
7	7		

If limited to setting a single market price and accepting all units supplied at that price—that is, if in order to get a given supply, he had to pay for all units the price necessary to bring forth the last increment to supply— the monopsonist could in effect either buy one unit at $1, or 2 units at $2 each, or 3 units at $3 each, etc. In this case his marginal outlay schedule

[5] See Kenneth E. Boulding, *Economic Analysis,* 2d ed. (New York: Harper and Brothers, 1948), pp. 539-543.

rises above the supply schedule—marginal outlay exceeds price at every quantity (column 3)—and he will be led to restrict his purchases on this account. His average outlay or average cost schedule for acquiring the good is in effect the supply schedule of the good, since the prices of all units must be the same as the supply price of the marginal unit purchased. If, on the other hand, the monopsonist can discriminate perfectly in purchasing, he should be able to pay $1 a unit for one unit plus $2 for a second unit, plus $3 for a third unit, etc. Then two units will cost him $3 instead of $4, three units will cost him $6 instead of $9, etc. In this case his marginal outlay schedule (column 4) is the same as the price-schedule in column (1), and he is not led to restrict purchases as a simple monopsonist would. His average outlay or average cost schedule thus lies at a lower level (showing smaller average prices at each output) than the supply schedule for the good.

The monopsonist should maximize his profits by buying that quantity at which the value of his marginal benefit from the last unit acquired equals his marginal outlay for that unit. Suppose that the monopsonist has a marginal benefit schedule for the good in question as follows:

Quantity purchased	Value of marginal benefit of last unit
1	$13
2	11
3	9
4	7
5	5

He will wish to select that output at which the value of the marginal benefit of the final unit is equal to the marginal outlay necessary to acquire it.

If the buyer is limited to simple monopsony pricing—to setting a market price for all units and accepting what is offered at the price—his marginal outlay for successive units will be given by the third column of the table on page 426. He will, therefore, presumably purchase four units of output, since the marginal outlay for the fourth unit ($7) is equal to the value of his marginal benefit from the fourth unit. He will pay the price of $4 for each of these four units purchased.

If, on the other hand, he is able to practice perfect discrimination in buying, his marginal outlay for successive units will be given by the fourth column of the table on page 426. He will then presumably purchase five units, since the marginal outlay for the fifth unit ($5) equals the value of the marginal benefit from the fifth unit. In purchasing these five units he will in essence pay $1 for the first, $2 for the second, and so forth up to $5 for the fifth unit. His total outlay will be $15 for five units, so that his average outlay for or average cost of five units will be $3. The fact that the price of inframarginal units is not altered by purchasing added units makes his marginal outlay schedule coincide with the supply schedule, whereas his average outlay schedule lies correspondingly below the supply schedule. The tendency to monopsonistic output restriction is thereby removed, although monopsonistic reduction of average buying price and monopsonistic profit tendencies remain.

Diagrammatically, the argument may be presented as follows. In Figure 47, suppose that SS' is the supply curve faced by the monopsonist, MO

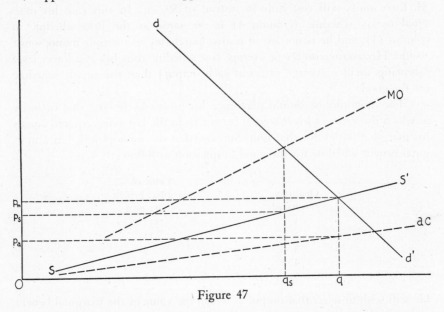

Figure 47

the conventional marginal outlay curve, ac the average price at which various quantities can be obtained under perfect discrimination, and dd' the curve showing the value of the marginal benefit of added purchases to the monopsonist. Under simple monopsony, with market pricing, the monopsonist would purchase the quantity oq_s, where marginal benefit dd' equals conventional marginal outlay MO, and pay the uniform price of op_s per unit. His average outlay or average cost curve would be SS'. Under perfect discrimination, his marginal outlay curve becomes SS', and ac replaces SS' as his average outlay or average cost curve for the good. He will then purchase the quantity oq, paying the price op_m for the last unit acquired, lower prices as shown on SS' for all preceding units, and an average price of op_a. Monopsonistic profits are necessarily higher, average price is still lowered, but the quantity purchased is "competitive" in the sense that it is found where the value of marginal benefit equals the supply price of the last unit purchased. Thus, we note in perfectly discriminating monopsony tendencies strictly parallel to those found in perfectly discriminating monopoly.

Similar remarks may also be made about the practical importance of perfectly discriminating monopsony. It is likely to be rare, if present at all, where the monopsonist faces many small sellers. But it may be important if he faces only one or a few sellers. Here, however, there is a natural op· position of perfectly discriminating monopoly and perfectly discriminating monopsony, to which we shall turn.

D. CHAOTIC PRICE DISCRIMINATION

THE SETTING FOR CHAOTIC DISCRIMINATION

Before we turn to the problem of bilateral monopoly, let us consider for a moment some other forms of price discrimination which are common in any economy.

Both third-degree and first-degree monopolistic price discrimination are characterized by the fact that the price differences among buyers which are established are such—subject to the limitations to which the seller (or sellers) is subject—as to maximize the profits of the monopolist (or the joint profit of the collusive oligopolists). With third-degree discrimination, given the most favorable division of buyers into submarkets that the monopolist can establish, the price differentials between markets will be the most profitable ones attainable under market pricing. With first-degree discrimination the price differentials among buyers implicit in making different all-or-nothing bargains with different buyers are the most profitable ones conceivable to the monopolist.

It should not be concluded, however, that all the sorts of price differences likely to develop in markets are consistent with maximization of the profits of the monopolist or the joint profits of a group of oligopolists. So long as there is single-firm monopoly, and thus no possibility of intra-industry rivalry, there is no compelling reason that any price discrimination which is adopted should not be of the profit-maximizing variety. Except so far as the single firm monopolist is poorly informed of demand conditions in his market, or too dull to figure out a profit-maximizing discrimination, or not interested in maximizing profits, he should tend toward monopolistic discrimination as previously described. The same should apply to oligopolists with substantially perfect price collusion. But where oligopoly is found, there is no certainty or central probability that there will be both perfect collusion on price and a substantial absence of price rivalry among sellers. As we have seen, it is quite possible that oligopolistic collusion may be somewhat imperfect, so that the price policies established are not such as to maximize the joint profits of the sellers, and it is also possible that there will be some price rivalry. Both the imperfection of collusive arrangements and the phenomenon of price rivalry in oligopoly may be sources of patterns of price discrimination which are not consistent with joint-profit maximization for the oligopolistic sellers, and which may be seriously inconsistent with it. Such price discrimination, which does not conform to joint-profit-maximizing standards, may be generally labeled as "chaotic" discrimination, the term "chaotic" not necessarily implying complete disorganization, but rather some systematic departure from a joint-profit-maximizing pattern.

TYPES OF CHAOTIC DISCRIMINATION

Two principal sorts of chaotic discrimination may be mentioned. First, it is observed that some forms of imperfectly collusive agreement (express or tacit) on pricing by oligopolists establish quasi-arbitrary patterns of price discrimination by each seller. A principal version of such an imperfectly collusive agreement is found in so-called basing-point delivered pricing of an industrial good with high shipping costs by several disparately located producers. In order to secure effective collusion when the sellers are differently located relative to potential buyers and shipping costs from the seller's factory to the buyer's plant are high, there must be collusion on the *delivered price*—that is, on the price at the buyer's plant inclusive of shipping costs thereto. A common basing-point formula for securing such collusion in delivered price involves every seller quoting a delivered price at any delivery point equal to a base price at the factory of the seller nearest to the buyer, plus freight charges from that factory to the delivery point. Thus, if sellers were located at New York and Chicago, buyers in the vicinity of Chicago would be quoted a delivered price equal to a Chicago base factory price (before freight) plus freight from Chicago, and they would have this same price quoted to them by both the Chicago and the New York seller, regardless of whether the goods were shipped at low cost from Chicago or at high cost from New York. Similarly, buyers in the vicinity of New York would be quoted a price equal to an identical or similar New York base factory price plus freight from New York, regardless of whether the goods originated in and were shipped from New York or Chicago.

When each of two or more sellers quotes delivered prices on this basis, a discrimination in price among his buyers may emerge. Thus, if the New York seller sells to buyers close to Chicago, at a price which thus is calculated to include almost no freight, but incurs heavy shipping costs in sending his goods to Chicago, he receives a *net price* (delivered price less freight costs he incurs) which is smaller than the net price he receives on sales near his own New York factory, where the shipping costs he incurs are small. To sell in an area where the delivered price is not calculated to include his actual shipping costs (but only those from a factory nearer to the buyer), he must take a smaller net price than he gets by selling close to home, and he thus discriminates in net price between buyers close to him and close to a rival seller. The same argument applies to the Chicago seller if he sells both in his own vicinity and in that of New York, receiving in delivered prices less than full freight costs incurred if he sells to a buyer who is located closer to a rival seller. Thus, under collusive delivered-pricing formulae of the basing-point variety, a sort of geographical price discrimination by each seller among his buyers emerges as a by-product of the effort to maintain effective collusion on delivered price.

Now, it should be noted that the pattern of price discrimination which thus emerges is rather arbitrary (it is not sought as an end in itself, but it is an incident of the pursuit of other ends), and there is no reason to suppose that it will be consistent with the maximization of the joint profits of the several oligopolists. *Given a basing-point agreement,* any one seller may add to his profit in certain circumstances by selling at a discriminatorily low net price to distant buyers located near other sellers, but it is extremely improbable that the total pattern of discrimination by all sellers will even distantly approximate that which a single-firm monopolist practicing third-degree discrimination from several disparately located plants would establish as among buyers at different locations. Thus, an arbitrary and nonprofit-maximizing pattern of discrimination emerges as an incident of imperfect collusion on price, presumably because a jointly more profitable sort of price agreement would be so complicated as to be difficult to administer or so obvious as to be vulnerable to antitrust law.

A second sort of chaotic discrimination may emerge if there is price rivalry in oligopoly which takes the form of secret and special price cuts to individual buyers by one or more of the sellers, with the result that some buyers pay an officially quoted price and other buyers variously lower prices. This type of discrimination is evidently quite common in oligopolistic markets, and it results essentially from the fact that destructive price rivalry is more easily avoided by sellers if they make special and secret price concessions to particular buyers rather than openly announced price cuts available to all buyers. When price discrimination emerges in this fashion, it is again extremely unlikely that it will conform to a pattern of joint-profit-maximizing discrimination, and it is quite possible that the pattern will be less profitable than one of simple uniform pricing to all buyers.

What is the impact on welfare of these types of chaotic price discrimination? Like any other sort of discrimination, they are open to attack as unjust or inequitable in that different buyers are treated unequally by a seller. Like other sorts of discrimination, they have adverse allocation effects. Unlike monopolistic discrimination, they may not enhance the joint profits of the oligopolistic sellers, and they may actually reduce them. And they may not be entirely inimical to the interests of buyers. To be sure, arbitrary price discrimination associated with geographical pricing formulae in general is a part of a collusive effort to maintain prices, and it may actually lead to higher total freight costs and higher prices than more effective collusion and discrimination would. But chaotic discrimination emergent from secret price cutting in oligopoly is frequently a vehicle for lowering prices and profits, and perhaps the only workable vehicle in the absence of direct governmental control. Its unfavorable aspects, thus, may be counterbalanced in part or full, or overbalanced, by its favorable effects.

E. BILATERAL MONOPOLY AND THE PRINCIPLE OF DISCRIMINATION

A principal use of the analysis of first-degree or perfect price discrimination is in the understanding of tendencies inherent in markets in which both the number of sellers and the number of buyers are small—*bilateral oligopoly*—or (at the extreme) in which, with only one buyer and one seller, there is *bilateral monopoly*. In these cases, which are found in some commodity markets and in many labor markets, the market price mechanism is evidently not operative in the usual sense. On one hand, there is one buyer (or a few potentially collusive buyers) who wishes to set monopsonistic terms for the price and supply of the good being sold—presumably, if possible, perfectly discriminatory monopsonistic terms. On the other hand, there is a monopolistic seller (or a few potentially collusive monopolistic sellers) who presumably wishes to set perfectly discriminatory monopolistic terms for the price and supply of the good. The buyer and seller interests are opposed and in conflict.

In this situation there will obviously be no automatic determination of a market price at the intersection of a demand and a supply curve (there is no genuine demand curve or supply curve in this case), nor can we say that there will be necessarily either a monopolistic or a monopsonistic outcome. Rather there will be a bargaining process between seller and buyer in which a quantity of output and a total payment of buyer to seller will be determined. Although ordinary market price analysis supplies no valid prediction of the outcome of this bargaining process, the theories of perfectly discriminating monopoly and monopsony, considered together, do. The essence of the situation is the opposition of a buyer who would like to be a perfectly discriminating monopsonist and a seller who would like to be a perfectly discriminating monopolist.

The tendencies of bilateral oligopoly generally are suggested in simple form by the analysis of the extreme case of bilateral monopoly, with one buyer and one seller. This setting for perfect discrimination is obviously ideal, and the tendencies would appear to be as follows: The monopsonistic buyer may be supposed to have a schedule of the value of the marginal benefit to him of added quantities of the good he buys, constituting in a sense his tentative demand schedule for the good. If he is a producer buyer, who resells what he buys in unchanged or altered form, this schedule may

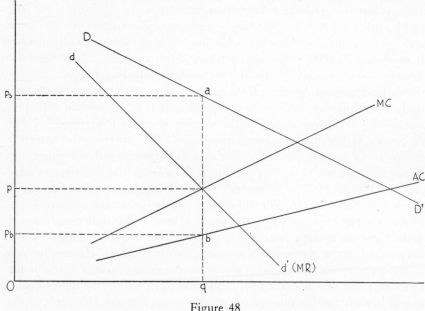

Figure 48

be viewed as derived from the additions to his sales receipts resulting from added quantities purchased and as a sort of *marginal receipts* curve derived from the demand for the product he himself sells.

The demand curve for what he sells measures the average receipts from his sales, some or all of which are attributable to the good purchased. For example, suppose we refer again to our monopsonistic tobacco trader, who buys tobacco and resells it in unaltered form and with no costs other than that of tobacco purchased. In Figure 48, *DD'* represents the demand curve for tobacco in his selling market—where we shall suppose that he must sell through simple monopoly pricing—and thus the average receipts or average price obtained by reselling various amounts of tobacco purchased. (These average receipts are all attributable to tobacco purchased as he has no other costs. If he did, we would wish to substitute for *DD'* a schedule showing the *share* of the average receipts attributable to tobacco purchased at each quantity point.) To the curve DD' is drawn the curve dd' (MR) which represents the marginal receipts the monopsonistic trader obtains as a seller from successive increments to tobacco purchased and resold, and thus the value of the marginal benefit to him of successive increments to tobacco purchases.

On the other hand, we have to consider the cost functions of the basic monopolist who sells to the monopsonist—in this case the monopolistic tobacco grower who sells tobacco to the trader. Let us suppose that his own average costs of production for various quantities are represented by AC, and his marginal costs by MC. Given these demand conditions of the buyer and cost conditions of the seller, what price-quantity solution will emerge? It is evident that the buyer will wish to drive a perfectly discriminatory monopsonistic bargain. To do this he will wish to buy that quantity at which his marginal benefit (MR) equals his marginal outlay. With perfectly discriminatory buying his marginal outlay at any output will presumably be the marginal cost to the supplier of the last increment to that of output. Hence, the supplying monopolist's MC curve is the marginal outlay curve to the perfectly discriminating buyer, and the supplying monopolist's AC curve is correspondingly the average cost or average outlay curve to this buyer. The buyer will then wish to buy the quantity oq, at which MR intersetcs MC. He will wish to pay op for the last unit but lower prices as indicated on MC for all preceding units. This will mean he will wish to pay an average price for all units of op_b, or just enough to cover the average cost of the supplier and keep him in business. He will be able to resell this quantity at op_s (as found on the demand curve DD' for his own sales) and thus reap the total profit (abp_bp_s) from the combined operation of himself and his supplier. (It may be noted that the MC curve of the supplier, which with perfectly discriminatory buying is the marginal outlay curve to the monopsonist, corresponds to the average outlay or average cost he would face if limited to the *simple* monopsony policy of setting a buying price for all units purchased. This MC curve in Figure 48 thus corresponds to the SS' curves of Figures 47 and 44, which show the average outlay or cost to the simple monopsonist. The marginal outlay to the simple monopsonist—MO in those figures—would be above MC in Figure 48, whereas the average cost or outlay to the buyer would lie at MC instead of at AC.)

The seller, on the other hand, will wish a perfectly discriminatory monopolistic bargain. This will be found at a quantity where his marginal cost (MC) is equal to his marginal receipts from the last unit sold. With perfectly discriminatory selling, his marginal receipts at any output will presumably be the value of the marginal benefit to the buyer of the last increment to that output. Hence, the monopsonist's dd' (MR) curve, showing his (the monopsonist's) marginal receipts from reselling goods bought, will also be the marginal receipts curve to the perfectly discriminating seller. The seller will then wish to sell the quantity oq, at which MC intersects MR, the same quantity desired by the monopsonist. He will wish to sell oq by selling the last unit at op and all preceding units at higher prices as indicated on MR. This will mean that he will receive an average selling price of op_s for the quantity oq, appropriating the total available revenue of the buyer for himself, so that when the good is resold at op_s he will reap the total profit (abp_bp_s) from the combined operations. (It may be noted that the dd' of the buyer, which with perfectly discriminating selling is the marginal receipts curve of the seller, would be the average receipts or demand curve to the *simple* monopolist, whose own marginal receipts curve would be below dd'. The curve dd' in Figure 48 thus corresponds to dd' in Figures 27 and 46 and not to *mr* in those figures.)

This is the setting for bargaining. Both seller and buyer have an interest in the same quantity of output, which is such as to maximize their joint profits. But they have a fundamental disagreement over the average price at which tobacco will pass from seller to buyer. This average price cannot go above op_s or below op_b, but it is theoretically indeterminate between these limits, which define a "bargaining range." Depending upon the relative bargaining strength of seller and buyer, the price may fall anywhere between op_b and op_s. In any case, quantity should approximate oq, and the final price for tobacco resold by the monopsonist to outsiders should be op_s, but the price as between the bilateral monopolists is indeterminate within the indicated limits.

It will be noted that the tendency of bilateral monopoly (between a monopolistic seller and a monopsonistic buyer who is in turn a monopolistic reseller) is to arrive at a price-quantity solution for the final market—to which the monopsonist resells—the same as would be reached if the monopolist and the monopsonist were members of a single firm with a monopoly in the final market. There are no *added* output restrictions because of the passage of the good first through a bilateral monopoly market on its way to the final market.[6] That is, the determination of output at the point where the marginal cost curve intersects what is in effect the counterpart of the demand curve *within the bilateral monopoly market* achieves a "competitive" output level for this market, although any monopolistic output restriction in a final market (where the buyer resells) will remain.

How accurate a prediction of bilateral monopoly behavior is likely to be provided by the preceding theory? For actual or hypothetical cases where (1) there is actually only one seller and one buyer (or alternatively per-

---

[6] This absence of added restriction is essentially due to the clear tendency toward perfectly discriminatory tactics by both seller and buyer. If either should attempt to operate through market pricing to his opponent, additional restriction would necessarily result, for then the marginal receipts curve to the seller would lie lower than dd' and the marginal outlay curve to the buyer would lie higher than MC.

fectly collusive oligopsonistic buying versus perfectly collusive oligopolistic selling) and (2) the good or service involved in the market is the output of a firm with determinate money costs and with a determinate motivation, like profit maximization, the prediction should be as good as can be developed by conventional theoretical methods. However, cases of the preceding type are evidently found very rarely in fact.

If either of the aforementioned conditions is not fulfilled, the applicability of the analysis is less certain. Situations which have the general characteristics of bilateral monopoly in the sphere of commodity markets (where the seller has determinate costs and a presumed profit-maximizing motive) are in general actually bilateral oligopoly situations—a few buyers facing a few sellers—and perfect collusion on either side may not necessarily be assumed. If there is imperfect collusion or rivalry on either side of such a market, the tendencies attributed to true bilateral monopoly may not be entirely fulfilled, particularly as regards the determination of a level of output and the application of principles of perfect discrimination in determining output and price. A sort of bargaining range for price still evidently remains, but both price and output results might deviate considerably from those previously predicted.

A second difficulty in applying the bilateral monopoly analysis is that many markets of the bilateral monopoly type are in effect markets for labor services in which the seller is a trade union. In these cases a "cost of production" is hard to identify, as is any equivalent source of a supply curve for the service being sold. Moreover, the motivation of the seller is difficult to identify. Profit maximization is evidently not a meaningful goal for a trade union, and what it is that such a seller tries to maximize is difficult to ascertain or to generalize about. In such cases, therefore, the bilateral monopoly analysis is not very helpful for purposes of prediction unless we can attribute some supply curve and some specific motivation to the monopolistic seller of labor services. The existence of a bargaining range for price is still likely, but we cannot say for certain that there is a determinate tendency for "output" or quantity of labor purchased. We shall refer to this matter again in Chapter 12 in the second part.

SUPPLEMENTARY READINGS

JOAN ROBINSON, *The Economics of Imperfect Competition,* Chaps. 15 and 16.
A. C. PIGOU, *Economics of Welfare,* 4th ed., Part 2, Chap. 17.
WILLIAM FELLNER, "Price and Wages under Bilateral Monopoly," *Quarterly Journal of Economics,* August 1947.

10 THE PRICE SYSTEM FOR COMMODITIES

In the preceding six chapters we have considered how business enterprises producing and selling commodities are likely to behave in determining prices, outputs, and related matters under various competitive conditions, and the probable character of their resultant market performance as measured by such things as the size of profits, the size of selling costs, productive efficiency, and the relation of actual output to the most desirable output.

We have considered the operation of enterprises within five principal types of selling market structure—those designated by the terms pure competition, monopolistic competition, pure and differentiated oligopoly, and single-firm monopoly. The analysis of such selling markets has been conducted mainly on the supposition that industries of each type sell to many buyers and that the underlying markets where these sellers purchase their supplies and incur their costs also have many buyers. It also has been conducted on the supposition that a seller in an industry is generally limited to setting or accepting a single market price which is effective for all buyers. In addition, we have considered the effects of monopsonistic or concentrated buying and the practice of discriminatory pricing in monopolistic or monopsonistic settings.

A. THE SCOPE OF THE GENERAL CONCLUSIONS OF PRICE ANALYSIS

What conclusions, or rather what a priori logical deductions, can we draw from this analysis? First, we have been able to arrive at predictions of the price-output and related decisions of the individual firm in various market situations. The analysis giving rise to these predictions proceeded by assuming a given individual seller demand curve (or, in the case of oligopoly, a complex participation in an industry demand) appropriate to the market structure, a given set of money factor prices, and, correspondingly, some given cost curve for the firm. For other than purely competitive situations, some demand-selling-cost and other relations were also assumed. Given these assumptions, the subsequent analysis predicted how a firm operating in various types of industry structure will adjust cost to demand to determine price and output, and how also it will determine product, selling cost, etc. The analysis has been modified to accommodate situations where, in place of unvarying money prices for productive factors, the firm faces a certain sloping supply curve for factors which endows it with monopsony power. As a result, we have some prediction of the "equilibrium of the firm" in pure competition, single-firm monopoly, oligopoly, and monopolistic competition both without and with concentrated buying and with both simple and discriminatory pricing. Such equilibria are not logically determinate in all respects within oligopoly, oligopsony, or bilateral monopoly or oligopoly, although regular behavior may occur in such instances.

Second, we have analyzed the interactions of the decisions of firms within various types of industry market structures to ascertain the probable outcome with respect to price, output, and related matters for an interrelated group of firms, or industry—in effect, the industry equilibrium in various situations. This analysis has been made on the assumption of a given industry demand curve, to which the member firms jointly adjust and from which their interrelated individual demands are derived, and generally also on the assumption of either given factor prices which enter into the costs of the several firms or given supply curves for factors. From this analysis we have gained an idea of the determination in various market structures of the price, output, selling cost, product, profits, and so forth—where the member firms are adjusting with given cost curves to a given industry demand. Certain significant differences in the probable equilibria of monopolistic, competitive, oligopolistic, and other types of industries have thus been predicted. The virtual impact of various individual industry equilibria upon the general economic welfare has also been the subject of comment.

Although the response of the single industry to a given demand and cost situation has been our primary emphasis to this point, we have also discussed at two points the interrelated behavior of a whole economy of industries in the simplified situations alternatively of universal pure competition and universal monopoly. For these hypothetical cases we have analyzed the tendency, for the economy as a whole, of employment, of the distribution of income as between profits and other income shares, of the allocation of resources among uses, of selling costs, of productive efficiency, and of progressiveness and stability. This analysis has been conducted generally on the assumption that there is a given constant flow of total money purchasing power (or aggregate demand for all products) and an adjustable general level of money factor prices. In effect, aggregate demand has been supposed to be constant, whereas the general average level of prices for hired factors of production has been supposed to be freely adjustable relative to the aggregate demand.

At this juncture it may be useful to extend the last sort of analysis, at least briefly, to comprehend situations for the economy as a whole of a more realistic sort. Our analysis of the interaction of the whole system of commodity prices and outputs has so far referred primarily either to the hypothetical case in which every industry in the economy has a purely competitive structure or to the equally hypothetical case in which every industry is a single-firm monopoly. (Some attention has been given to the case where some industries are purely competitive and the rest are single-firm monopolies.) Examination of these hypothetical cases is useful as a means of ascertaining in a general way the implications for economic performance in an enterprise system of competitive as opposed to monopolistic tendencies in market structure and behavior. But it is not entirely adequate for the purpose of predicting performance in the very complex economy that we actually have. In the actual economy it is apparent from general observation that there are some industries which might at least roughly be designated as purely competitive and a few that would qualify in a general way as single-firm monopolies. In addition, however, and comprehending the majority of cases, we find many oligopolistic industries and many which have the approximate characteristics of monopolistic competition. In effect, the real enterprise economy is an admixture of industries with all of the sorts of market structure reviewed in the preceding chapters, with some added complications of price discrimination, bilateral monopoly, and monopsonistic buying. A remaining task of analysis is to inquire what are the over-all performance tendencies of an enterprise economy of such a complex and variegated character.

Full analysis of these matters is an almost overwhelming task in view of the very great complexities of actual market structure. Not only do we have industries with almost every conceivable variation of market structure, but also the complex structure of modern production is such that a given final good, ready for use by the consumer, is made up of components which have passed through a succession of different markets, each with a potentially different structure. Thus, steel may be sold to a manufacturer of tin cans in a market where bilateral oligopoly rules, and tin cans to food packers in an oligopolistic market. Agricultural products may be sold to packers in a market of purely competitive character. The packers may sell canned goods to wholesalers, wholesalers may sell them to retailers, and retailers sell them to consumers in a succession of markets which are either differentiated oligopolies or in monopolistic competition. The same complexity is encountered with almost any good as it or its components move through a succession of industries and markets.

It is thus not feasible in an elementary treatment to take account of every actual complexity in analyzing over-all economic performance. We may, however, attempt to arrive at certain tentative generalizations concerning performance in an economy in which some of the actual complexities are encountered.

In the succeeding pages we shall suggest certain tendencies which are apparently to be expected in the performance of an actual economy composed of a variety of industrial markets of variegated structure and with various interrelationships, considering in turn predictable tendencies with respect to employment, allocation, efficiency, income distribution, selling cost, product behavior, progressiveness, and stability.

B. SUMMARY AND SYNTHESIS OF SPECIFIC PREDICTIONS

AGGREGATE EMPLOYMENT

Under the assumption which we have chosen and which seems most appropriate for an analysis of economic behavior in the sphere of commodity markets alone—that is, that there is a given constant flow of money purchasing power to which the level of money factor prices readily adjusts—it is possible to develop valid predictions of actual tendencies in over-all economic performance in many respects. But it is probably true that an analysis resting on these assumptions can cast little light upon the determination of the aggregate level of output and employment. The co-existence of stable money purchasing power and flexible money factor prices (arbitrarily assumed) effectively begs the question of the determination of the level of employment, for if money demands for commodities, and indirectly for factors, will remain steady while factor prices seek such a level as will employ all of them, there must be full employment in the sense that all factors wishing to work will be employed. We have been at pains to point out that in competitive, monopolistic, oligopolistic, and monopsonistic economies any tendency to output restriction by individual industries will not result in less than full employment *if* purchasing power is constant and factor prices freely adjustable. Under these circumstances the impact of monopolistic or other restriction necessarily falls upon allocation, selling costs, stability, progressiveness, income distribution, etc., but not primarily on employment. This is true regardless of what complex assortment of market structures is encountered in fact.

The explanation of the level of employment, and of the effect on it of various sorts of pricing, is to be found in the things which determine the ratio of the general level of factor and commodity prices to the rate of flow of money purchasing power. There is reason to believe that factor prices do not always adjust relative to money purchasing power in such a way as to permit full employment, and that this is so regardless of whether pricing is monopolistic or competitive. Until the manner in which this ratio is determined and what influences it are established, we are unable to assess the effects of various sorts of price-cost behavior on the level of employment. When it has been established, we may be able to see how employment is influenced by price behavior in commodity markets.

Anticipating a later discussion of these matters, however, it may be pertinent to emphasize the various ways in which general monopolistic, oligopolistic, and monopsonistic restriction *may* lessen aggregate employment and output and result in unemployment of resources. First, if both money purchasing power and money factor prices are given and rigid, or if their ratio will not adjust in response to a change in price-cost margins due to monopolistic restriction, then a noncompetitive system will tend to employ fewer resources than a competitive system. This is because with restriction, and with given costs, commodity prices will be higher than the competitive level and a given money purchasing power will buy fewer goods. If, then, an unrestricted or competitive system would just give full employment, a restricted or monopolized system will give less than this. A first setting in which restrictive output policies may reduce employment is, therefore, where there is a specific rigidity in the ratio of money factor prices to money purchasing power, and where employment would be barely adequate in the absence of restriction.

A second possible influence of monopolistic pricing on the level of employment may be via its effect on the rate of flow of money purchasing power or on the ratio of this flow to money factor prices, *provided this ratio is subject to influence*. It may do so by affecting the distribution of income as between profit receivers and hired factors of production. At any given level of factor prices an increase in the degree of monopolistic restriction will ordinarily mean that prices exceed average costs by larger amounts, reducing the share of all income going to wages, interest, and rents, and increasing the share going to profits.

This in turn may influence the tendency to spend and thus to create new income in two ways. First, it may influence the volume of expenditure on consumption goods. Ordinarily we should expect that an increase in the size of profits relative to wages, etc. would tend to restrict aggregate consumption spending, since it would make income distribution more unequal and would thus increase the disposition toward saving from large incomes. On the other hand, larger profits may increase the *incentive* to business investment, thus leading to more investment spending, which may partly replace, fully compensate for, or outweigh the loss of consumption spending. The net effect on money purchasing power of excess profits resulting from monopolistic restriction of output will thus depend (1) on the relative propensities toward consumption spending of profit receivers and of the recipients of other distributive shares and (2) on the relation between size of profits (above the practical minimum) and the volume of investment spending. Since these magnitudes cannot be known a priori and have not been satisfactorily measured, we cannot appraise here the effect of the existing degree of monopoly restriction on the flow of money income. It may be positive, negative, or neutral. But a definite positive or negative effect on spending (relative to the level of hired factor prices) will have a corresponding influence on total employment.

It should be noted, however, that if monopoly restriction is to have a favorable net effect on production and employment, it must have a sufficient *stimulus* on money income to outweigh its virtually restrictive effect on production at any given level of income and factor prices. That is, it must improve the ratio of money purchasing power to hired factor prices by more than enough to outweigh the increase in commodity prices relative to factor prices. Supposing that factor prices do not *automatically* adjust to secure full employment, but that their ratio to money purchasing power may be influenced by forces favorable to spending, then monopolistic restriction may affect employment either way.

In sum, the effect of general monopolistic and monopsonistic restriction on total employment will depend on the character of the fundamental relationship of money purchasing power to factor prices, which may be of three principal sorts:

1. The ratio of money purchasing power (Y) to money factor prices (W) may be freely adjustable because money factor prices can and will fall relative to purchasing power so as always to secure full employment. Here the restrictions mentioned will not influence employment at all except in so far as fewer resources choose to work with an altered income distribution.

2. The ratio of Y to W is fixed and rigid, either because both are absolutely fixed or because they must change together. Here the imposition of monopoly restriction is bound to lessen employment and output by raising the ratio of commodity prices to income and to factor prices.

3. The ratio of Y to W is not freely adjustable to secure full employment, but it may be influenced in either direction by forces affecting the propensity of income recipients to spend. Here monopolistic restriction may either increase or decrease total employment, although it has to influence the ratio of spending to factor prices quite favorably to cause employment to increase.

This is as much as we can say on the matter on the basis of our discussion to this point, and the conclusion holds regardless of the particular variety of market structures which is encountered in the actual economy. We shall investigate the matter further in the chapters in the second part.

RESOURCE ALLOCATION

The preceding analyses of economic behavior in the area of commodity markets, however, do permit us to form some tentative predictions concerning numerous other aspects of the over-all performance of the economy, among them performance with respect to the allocation of resources among uses. The crucial question here concerns the relative quantities in which various goods are produced. What is the ratio of beef output to auto output to the output of aluminum coffeepots, and is it the best ratio from the standpoint of buyer satisfaction?

The analysis of this question is most easily conducted on the simple assumptions (previously adopted) that a certain aggregate volume of resources is employed in all uses, that there are a certain number of goods to produce, and that all the price system does is to fix the ratio in which the various goods are produced. We assume that there is a given level of employment of resources and that the problem is simply how these resources shall be allocated among a predetermined range of uses or lines of production.

When the problem is thus simplified, it can be shown that buyers will get the most satisfaction from a given amount of employed resources if those resources are so allocated that a certain uniform balance is struck between price and cost in every line of production. Specifically, their satisfaction will be greatest if the goods are produced in just such proportions that for every good the ratio of price to the money value of marginal real cost is the same.[1] If this condition is met, the last unit of real cost in every line nets an equal amount of satisfaction to buyers (as measured by price), and no shift in allocation could then enhance total satisfaction.[2]

As we have seen, the system of commodity prices in any enterprise economy acts as a guide to or governor of the allocation of resources among uses. Given the levels of purchasing power and of factor prices (as finally determined by the forces which influence the strategic ratio of these two levels), the relative quantities in which all of the available goods are produced are determined by the prices of the goods, which are in turn determined by the complex of relative buyer demands for various goods and by their relative costs of production.

[1] The aggregate cost of production being minimized for the quantity produced of each good and all industries paying the same price for any given factor. See pp. 163-170.

[2] This argument postulates a certain intercommensurability of different buyers' satisfactions—that is, supposes that if Brown pays $1 for a necktie, it represents the same satisfaction that Smith gets from a penknife bought for $1. Some such assumption is essential to any concept of aggregate satisfaction.

At any time the buyers of goods express a complex of interrelated demands for all available goods—a willingness to pay a given pattern of prices for given quantities offered of all goods or alternatively to purchase given quantities of all goods when there is a given set of prices for them. The relationship of price charged to quantity taken for any one good necessarily depends on the prices, or quantities offered, of all others. Correspondingly, there is for each good in turn a willingness by buyers to purchase certain alternative quantities at given alternative prices, given the prices of other goods—in effect a demand schedule for each good—although the position of each such demand schedule depends on the prices of other goods and shifts as those prices change.

Enterprises in any line of production, seeking profit, tend to extend their production whenever the marginal costs of production (as determined by money factor prices and the relation of cost to output) are short of their marginal receipts as ultimately derived from the demands for their goods. When all enterprises in an economy pursue such a course simultaneously, readjusting as various separate demands for goods shift, outputs and prices for all goods are mutually determined such that in the final balance or general equilibrium: (1) the prices of all goods stand very roughly in the same relation to their average and marginal costs of production, but potentially in various different specific relations, depending on market structures, and (2) the relative outputs of goods are those which buyers are willing to take given the pattern of relative prices thus established.

The crucial question is whether, in the general equilibrium thus established, the composition of total output (or the ratio of the quantity of each output to that of each other one) is to the maximum advantage of consumers. This in turn depends on the structures of the various markets for goods, which determines in each the final balance which will be struck between price and the money value of marginal real cost at the output selected.

We have previously shown (see pages 163 to 170) that if all of the given range of goods were produced under conditions of pure competition, the composition of aggregate output would be such that every price would tend toward equality with the money value of marginal real cost, and that allocation would then be demonstrably ideal. We have also indicated that if certain goods were monopolized, so that output was so restricted that marginal cost was short of price, whereas others were produced so that marginal cost equaled price, allocation would not be ideal, since a balanced ratio between price and marginal cost would not result and could be effected only by shifting resources toward the production of the monopolized goods and away from the other lines. Nonideal allocation results when relative outputs are such that the ratio of price to marginal cost is different for different industries.

With those general guides, what can be said of allocation at a given level of employment in the economy we have? In this economy certain markets are purely competitive, with prices tending to equal marginal cost; some are in monopolistic competition, with presumably slight price-marginal-cost discrepancies; a few are single-firm monopolies with larger discrepancies of this sort, except where public regulation intervenes; many are oligopolistic, and in these the relations of price to marginal cost are various and not definitely predictable. Monopsonistic elements introduce further discrepancies, as does discriminatory pricing of the third degree. If one good came directly to the consumers from each market, it would be extremely improbable that any close approximation to ideal allocation would result. With each final good passing through and affected by a vertical sequence of markets, from raw materials to retail distribution, and with different markets in the sequence having different structures and giving rise to different price-cost relationships, the allocation picture is confused.

In fact, it is quite impossible to say a priori just what sort of allocation our system gives us, or how far it departs from the ideal, except to note that very close approximation to the ideal is highly improbable. It is quite possible that in a significant degree we get relatively too few of certain goods and too many of others. At the same time, it must be pointed out that in a free-enterprise system, where any restrictive monopoly is subject to the interference of competition or of public authority if it is restrictive beyond a certain point, there are definite limits to the distortion of allocation. The discrepancies from the ideal at any time are not likely to be huge.

PRODUCTIVE EFFICIENCY

We have also been able to develop certain tentative predictions concerning tendencies in efficiency by enterprises producing commodities, and these may be briefly summarized here. Before summarizing them, however, it should be emphasized that these predictions, in effect, bear on only one aspect of productive efficiency in general. The analysis of enterprise behavior in commodity production is limited in its scope to a consideration of how effectively business concerns organize given the available productive resources or factors for the production of given commodities. It does not inquire into the intrinsic efficiency of the resources available—for example, the degree of skillfulness or strength or ingenuity of labor—or into what determines these things, and it is thus unable to offer predictions on these matters. This is not to say that the matters thus neglected are unimportant —for the contrary is evidently true—but merely to emphasize that they are not treated by price theory or by conventional economic theory in general.

Moreover, the price theory we have considered actually does not analyze all phases of the efficiency of use of given resources by business enterprises.

What it neglects along this line is the matter of the internal efficiency of the business organization—the questions of whether or not the enterprise chooses the most efficient technique of production within the framework of which to use resources and of whether or not the management of the enterprise is skillful or astute enough in directing the use of resources to get the lowest attainable production costs. These questions conventional price theory avoids by assuming in general that the enterprise tends to select always the lowest-cost technique of those available and that it exploits this technique effectively. The theory presented thus does not really analyze the technical alternatives open to business management; and it does not analyze the determinants of the specific efficiency of actual management performance relative to the ideal. It considers what happens given the choice of techniques and given the level of internal management efficiency. From this it follows that conventional theory casts little light on such questions as the comparative efficiency of resources and the comparative efficiency with which they are likely to be organized in, for example, enterprise economics and socialized economics. Yet, these questions are of the greatest practical importance.

The aspect of efficiency in production which has been principally emphasized by the theory considered concerns the extent to which the scale of operations of the business firm is likely to conform to the most efficient scale. This is a relevant and important question so far as productive efficiency is affected by scale, both because of certain economies of large-scale production and certain possible diseconomies of still larger-scale production. Concerning such efficiency in scale, certain predictions have emerged concerning the tendency within any industry as it approaches its particular long-run equilibrium and concerning the complex of all industries as the economy approaches a general equilibrium.

As such equilibria are approached, the relative efficiency with respect to the scale of operations by firms would seem likely to depend in some degree on the structure of the industry. If the industry is purely competitive, or approximately so—in the sense that in addition to having a homogeneous product it reaches and maintains an atomistic structure in the absence of artificial interferences of any sort—we have seen that optimal efficiency in scale of firm is likely to be approached in the long run, so that the industry output is supplied by a large number of small firms each having a scale consistent with the lowest attainable cost. Moreover, this adjustment is essentially forced on the participant firms by an impersonal market price, moving under the pressure of independent firm policies in output determination and of easy entry and exit. It should be emphasized, however, that such an adjustment and such a market structure will tend to be found only where the most efficient known technique of production happens to be such that the output of an optimal-scale firm constitutes a small fraction of the amount of the industry output which buyers demand, and if the free movement of market price is unhampered. If an atomistic structure is maintained artificially—as by government edict—or if there is similar interference with the working of market price as a regulator, then optimal efficiency will not be automatically attained; its attainment may on the contrary be definitely forestalled. If economies of large-scale production are such as to make production by a few large firms more efficient than production by many small ones, then in the absence of artificial interferences an atomistic structure will not be attained, and the problem becomes necessarily one of efficiency in scale with oligopoly or monopoly.

What has been said of the setting of pure competition and its tendencies in efficiency may also be said, without significant modification, of monopolistic competition, when this is construed as referring to the industry with many small sellers and with differentiated but close-substitute products. Here again the situation is naturally tenable only if economies of large-scale production do not favor fewness of sellers, and here again the market adjustment should favor approximately optimal efficiency in scale if this condition is met. There are the added complications, however, of selling costs and of the effects of product adjustment on the welfare of buyers.

When we turn to that segment of industries in which structure is not atomistic, however, we can no longer suppose that ideal efficiency in scale is more or less automatically forced on sellers by the response of market price to the output policies of independent firms and to easy entry and exit. Interdependent firm policies or collusion emerge, and entry may be far from easy, with the result that scales of producing firms may conceivably diverge significantly from those which would give the lowest attainable costs of outputs produced. We have seen that there is a wide range of possibilities here. Single-firm monopoly *can* be the most efficient from the standpoint of scale economies, but it can also be maintained when two or more firms could produce as efficiently or more efficiently than one. Oligopoly can offer optimal efficiency in scale of firms, and it may in the long run be forced to approximate it if entry is relatively easy, but it need not. Either an excessively large or an excessively small number of firms (from the standpoint of efficiency in scale) is possible with oligopoly, as is a size distribution of firms which is other than the most efficient. Without detailed empirical investigation we are thus in a state of considerable uncertainty about the probable efficiency in scale of a large sector of the actual productive organization.

Certain systematic tendencies diverging from optimal efficiency, however, have been noted. When there is *monopsony,* or monopsonistic power on the part of firms buying factors of production or producers' goods from other firms, the relation of the firm's money costs of production to output will tend to be different from the relation of its real costs of production to output, since factor and raw material prices respond to output changes along with the physical amounts of factors used. When this is the case, the firm which moves to minimize money costs may not thereby minimize real costs of production, and over-all efficiency in scale is impaired. More generally, we may say that the movements of real costs (in relation to output), which society should wish to see minimized, are not always the same as the movements of the money costs of firms in relation to output and that an enterprise system which is motivated by money profit maximization and money cost minimization may, therefore, tend to diverge somewhat from the ideal in its social performance with respect to costs.

The preceding refers to long-run tendencies with respect to the scale of the producing firm. Can anything be added with respect to the short-run capacity of the productive plant relative to demand? (It should be emphasized that capacity adjustments are essentially short-run problems, since, in general, in the long run firms will presumably not tend to provide much more than the necessary or most efficient capacity for their planned output.) It seems evident that capacity adjustments—*given the long run adjustments of scale*—should move toward reasonably efficient levels with any market structure. However, in the *process* of a long-run adjustment there may be aberrations from efficient capacity correlative to developing aberrations from efficient scale. Thus, if an oligopolistic industry is over time becoming overcrowded with too many firms of too small a scale, a prolonged transition period may witness redundant or excess capacity of plant by all or most firms, the final elimination of which may see the problem converted from one of excess capacity of efficient-sized firms to one of inefficient size of firms. Since we are uncertain about the tendencies of adjustments in scale, however, we must be similarly uncertain about tendencies toward excess capacity.

One further suggestion has been made concerning efficiency tendencies in an enterprise economy. It has been suggested that the incentive to seek for or attempt to develop more efficient techniques of production, and to introduce them once they are discovered, is potentially affected by the structure of the market, so far as this in turn affects the prospective gain to the firm from successful innovation and perhaps also the fund of accumulated profits available for research and innovation. It is thus possible that we shall find—as among atomistic, oligopolistic, and monopolized industries—different sorts of performance with respect to developing and introducing techniques. A tentative hypothesis developed in the preceding chapters is that performance in this regard in atomistic industries may diverge considerably from the ideal and that performance may be better with oligopoly or monopoly. Much further investigation, however, would be required adequately to test this hypothesis.

INCOME DISTRIBUTION

In the preceding chapters, we have also considered the impact of price-cost equilibria in various types of commodity markets on the distribution of income as between the earnings of hired factors of production (labor, land, and capital) and the profits received by enterprise. (We have yet to consider income distribution as among the several hired factors of production.) As regards the tendency for profits to command a share of income in various types of market structure, little need be said in summary of previous remarks. There is a tendency toward elimination of all excess profits in atomistic market structures with easy entry, whether in pure competition or monopolistic competition. In monopolistic, oligopolistic, and monopsonistic situations—which together have major importance in our economy —excess profits do tend to emerge and to be maintained with the aid of some barriers to entry, although in widely differing degree depending on the height of such barriers. Discriminatory pricing enhances such profits in some cases. As a result, two general tendencies may be noted for the economy as a whole. First, some share of aggregate income goes to enterprise owners in the form of excess profits, although various statistical estimates suggest that on the average over time this share falls short of 5 percent of the total net income generated by enterprise. Second, the profitability of enterprise varies widely as among industries (and also among firms within the same industry) with the result that not all enterprise fares equally well in this regard.

The difficult questions about excess profits are whether or not they perform a useful or necessary function in the economy, and what the proper standards are for judging them as a whole or in particular cases. Here we encounter the conflicting considerations that they effect a greater inequality in personal income distribution than would otherwise exist but that to some extent their occurrence seems to be an incentive to efficiency, progressiveness, and a desirable rate of investment spending. We shall consider these matters further in Chapter 15 in the second part.

SELLING COSTS

Another thing affected by the operation of business competition is the allocation of resources between the production of goods and the selling and distribution of goods. We have indicated in preceding chapters that in oligopolistic industries with differentiated products and in industries in monopolistic competition, there is a tendency to incur selling costs which are potentially a significant proportion of total costs. This tendency in varying degree affects virtually the whole range of consumers' goods in our economy as well as some producers' goods. When this tendency is found in each of many individual industries, it seems apparent that in the economy as a whole we shall find a diversion of an important fraction of our employable resources away from production and toward "selling" activities of one sort or another.

The crucial questions are, of course, whether this is in the net to the advantage of buyers as a group and whether some different rate of expenditure of resources on sales promotion would be more desirable socially. We have suggested previously that, although some selling costs are likely to be desirable as a means of disseminating information, there is at least a strong possibility that they may be incurred in such quantity—and qualitatively for certain sorts of sales promotion—that buyers are not rewarded for the loss of aggregate output which they may necessitate. Whether excessive selling costs could really be eliminated and this action be consistent with the maintenance of a free-enterprise system, however, is a crucial question.

PRODUCT BEHAVIOR

Some related questions are raised with respect to the determination of product design or quality by firms in those instances where alternatives are open to them in this respect. Since the possible patterns of product behavior in monopoly, differentiated oligopoly, and monopolistic competition have been reviewed in preceding chapters, we may make only a few summary remarks at this point. In an economy which contains many industries in these categories, it is distinctly possible that product behavior may diverge systematically from the ideal in many areas and in several different ways. Product quality which is excessive from the standpoint of the buyer in view of its ultimate cost, and undesirable limitations on the variety of qualities and designs of product offered to the buyer, may both be the result of product competition in certain settings. Yet, these tendencies are revealed only as logical possibilities by price analysis. More desirable product tendencies may instead be found, and in our present state of knowledge we cannot predict definitely the sort of product behavior to be expected.

PROGRESSIVENESS IN THE MODERN ECONOMY

An additional aspect of the performance of an economy is its progressiveness. Progressiveness, which may be measured by the rate at which an economy expands its aggregate or per-capita output over time and also by its success in continually increasing the variety and want-satisfying power of the products which make up this output, is unquestionably influenced by many factors, of which the character of commodity market structures within an enterprise system is only one. The question of whether business operations within the existing market frameworks are as conducive to progress as they would be under some other feasible alternative framework is, therefore, perhaps unduly narrow. On the record, the capitalist economy, just as it has been and is, has been extremely progressive in the introduction of new techniques and products and in resultant expansion in the quantity and quality of output. This historical progressiveness is perhaps its principal claim to eminence as a system of economic organization. Upon this background the main question raised to this point is whether the complex of market structures found in the present-day economy is reasonably favorable to continued progress.

There are a number of possible answers to this question. One would hold that the great progress achieved by capitalism was the result of free and active competition and that the increasing concentration of markets into tight oligopolies of firms, afraid to compete actively, is inimical to progress via innovation and forward-looking investment. Another answer would maintain that a highly concentrated and quasi-monopolistic business organization is best equipped to accomplish the marvels of research and engineering which are essential to continued progress, and perhaps that lagging progress is more commonly found in the "backward" sector of industries of atomistic structure. Still a third would hold that the profits of monopoly are a necessary lure to innovation, and always have been, and that a pattern of some monopolistic restriction is an intrinsic and, in the net, desirable aspect of capitalism.

From the analysis we have developed in preceding chapters, only a certain amount of light can be shed on this rather controversial issue.

1. Although it is probably true that the possibility of securing a superior earning position and protecting it in the form of a monopoly is a lure to invention and innovation, and that monopolistic profits are a source of funds to finance these activities, the continued defense of old monopoly positions may restrict progress. It may be added that when concentration proceeds to the point where one firm or closely knit group at the same time benefits from an old monopoly position *and* has the principal chance to innovate and replace the old monopoly with a new one, the probability of innovation is seemingly smaller than where the old monopolist and the potential innovator are distinctly different people. This argues that *very* highly concentrated market structures may be relatively inimical to progress.

2. Most oligopolistic market structures of the American economy, however, probably have not as yet proceeded far enough toward perfectly collusive monopoly seriously to reduce competitive innovation. In most of our oligopolies there is probably a sufficient element of nonprice competition to promote a fairly rapid rate of progress in adopting new techniques and introducing new products. Moderately concentrated oligopolies may well

turn out a more rapid rate of progress in technique and product than any other sort of market organization.

3. Further development of market structures toward single-firm monopolies might well be inimical to progress.

4. Within the general framework of modern market structures, less restrictive price and output policies would in many cases be consistent with the maintenance of strong progressive tendencies.

5. Atomistic market structures, wherein the pressure of easy entry tends to erase all excess profits and to increase the risks of innovation to the firm, may be less conducive to progress than moderately concentrated structures which enjoy moderate protections against entry.

ECONOMIC STABILITY

The effect of the system of commodity pricing on the stability of the economy or, conversely, on its susceptibility to fluctuations of income and employment has already been referred to at several junctures. As a general background for any discussion along this line we must recognize that the capitalist economy will experience fluctuations in income and employment pretty much regardless of the structure of commodity markets or of the relations of commodity prices to costs. Observation and theory both support this conclusion. We must also recognize that such fluctuations in income will generally be accompanied by connected fluctuations in wages and other factor prices and that such fluctuations in the cost of producing commodities will probably have more effect on the course of the "business cycles" than will movements in price-cost relationships. Finally, therefore, the influence of such price-cost relations on stability will be only moderate.

The responses of price-cost relationships and of commodity prices to fluctuations in income form a rather complicated pattern for our whole economy. As money income expands with upswings or movements toward prosperity, the demand curves for most products shift upward and to the right, tending to elicit both larger outputs and higher prices. At the same time factor prices (wages, interest, rents) also rise, though often lagging behind the rise in demands, causing the cost curves of firms to shift upward. This further accentuates the tendency of prices to rise, but it does temper the rise of output somewhat. As money income declines with downswings or movements toward depression, the reverse of these movements takes place: demand curves shift down to the left, tending to reduce prices and outputs, and the fall in factor prices shifts cost curves downward, accentuating the decline in price but tempering the decline in output. So much for the general mechanics of price-output adjustments in response to fluctuations in income or purchasing power under competitive or quasi-competitive conditions. Where factor-price determination occurs largely in bilateral monopoly situations, less definite predictions can be made.

It is also important to note that as income fluctuations take place, factor prices are for a variety of reasons *relatively* inflexible or sticky, so that they do not fluctuate as rapidly or as widely as income does and do not fully compensate for these fluctuations. The costs of producing commodities are, therefore, relatively inflexible, and practically regardless of how commodity prices adjust to these costs, the basic inflexibility of factor prices makes it likely that income fluctuations will cause parallel fluctuations in employment and output.

The issue with respect to commodity price movements is, therefore, how commodity prices adjust to shifting demands and shifting costs over the course of the business cycle, and what effect this adjustment has on the nature and impact of the basic income fluctuation. The salient aspect of these adjustments in the modern economy is that goods' prices may behave in various ways because of differences in market structures and price-determining situations. We have a sector of the economy in some approximation to pure competition, including a number of agricultural products and a few basic manufactures, although government interference with price and output in this sector is becoming the rule. A large sector of our extractive, processing, and manufacturing industry forms an oligopoly area in the economy, where pricing follows certain patterns peculiar to this category. Some manufacturing industries and many distributive industries are in some approximation to monopolistic competition. Finally, most public utility industries are dominated by local single-firm monopolies, whose prices, however, are determined by public regulatory bodies.

The tendency of price in unregulated pure competition is to respond very actively and quite automatically to fluctuations in demand and cost. As we saw in our analysis of purely competitive markets, a moderate shift in demand in a purely competitive industry will ordinarily produce a noticeable shift in price even if the level of costs (factor prices) is unchanged. When costs also shift in the same direction as demand, the shift in price is larger. In the purely competitive sector, therefore, we tend in the absence of regulation to get very flexible prices over a cycle of income and, correspondingly, relatively stable outputs. Price movements compensate for much of the shift in demand; therefore, output is much less affected. This movement takes place independently of the control of any sellers, who cannot influence the movement of market prices.

Such price behavior tends to minimize the fluctuation in output. But it is likely to maximize the corresponding fluctuations in the short-period profits of the sellers involved and, therefore, to make the whole situation rather unpopular with them. Further, it is possible that the very flexibility of price will accentuate the tendency of buyers to anticipate price fluctuations by buying in advance during upswings and withholding purchases during downswings, and it is possible that this may cause such upswings and downswings in income to proceed more rapidly and possibly to greater extremes. So much for the impact of unregulated purely competitive pricing in a fluctuating economy.

Within the oligopoly and unregulated-monopoly sector of the economy there are many variants in price behavior. If there is a central tendency, however, it is toward relative inflexibility of prices in the face of fluctuating income. The rationale of inflexible price policies in monopoly and oligopoly has been developed in preceding chapters. We have also emphasized the *ability* of sellers in such markets to control prices deliberately in spite of shifting demands. Statistical studies indicate that in fact prices in the industrial sector have changed less frequently and by smaller percentage amounts than prices in the purely competitive or "market-controlled" sphere.

The impact of such pricing on the economy is fairly evident. Prices respond less readily to given shifts in demand and in cost, and, therefore, output and employment fluctuate more. By the same token the short-run profits of sellers fluctuate less than they do in pure competition. The impact on output and employment of given fluctuations of income are, therefore, accentuated. At the same time the tendency of buyers' speculation on price movements to accentuate income movements may be considerably less than in pure competition.

Prices in regulated single-firm monopolies generally tend to be quite inflexible because of the rigidities implicit in such regulation, and they thus augment the tendencies of the oligopoly sector. Prices in monopolistic competition tend ordinarily to be fairly flexible over time, and they may fall in with the purely competitive sector. We thus tend to have, in a broad sense, a flexible-price sector and an inflexible-price sector in the economy, each with its own virtual impact on the course and effect of fluctuations.

When these sectors are combined and operate together, as they do, certain additional phenomena emerge. First, the flexible price sector of the economy is considerable enough that the general response of prices to income fluctuations is sufficient to set up cumulative movements in the economy —to cause buyers to speculate on price changes enough to accentuate upswings and downswings in income. The whole price system is *not rigid enough* to forestall cumulative movements in income based on speculation. Therefore, such considerable partial rigidity as there is only accentuates the response of output and employment to given income fluctuations in the rigid price sectors, without adequately dampening the basic fluctuations of income. The mixed system, therefore, is particularly unstable, and it is susceptible to maximum swings of employment and output.

A second result of the mixture of flexible and inflexible prices is that the net incomes of sellers in the flexible-price sector—and especially of farmers—tend to fluctuate much more than those of sellers in the concentrated industrial sectors. Farmers, therefore, tend to be very poor indeed in business depressions, even though they may fare exceptionally well in prosperity. Their depression plight is accentuated by the fact that although their incomes fall off steeply in depression, the manufactured goods they must buy are somewhat inflexibly priced. This situation may lead to serious social problems, to regional economic distress, to banking and mortgage difficulties, and so on. It was this special distress in the agricultural sphere which led certain economists to emphasize the price rigidity problem and to support government programs of crop control and agricultural price support as means of improving the financial welfare of farmers. As a result, we are currently tending toward artificially pegged farm prices and an entire economy of relatively inflexible prices. The merits of such a system may be debated.[3]

FURTHER ASPECTS OF ECONOMIC BEHAVIOR TO BE DISCUSSED

The preceding is a brief review of predictions of economic behavior which may be drawn from the analysis of enterprise activity in the sphere of commodity markets. Although this analysis permits us to make potentially valid predictions on a number of aspects of economic performance, it is intrinsically limited by its assumptions and so not able to offer valid predictions on two essential matters. Commodity price theory per se does not deal with the determination of the relative prices and shares of income earned by the several factors of production which enterprises employ. Land, labor, and capital are dealt with in this theory as more or less lumped together and as receiving some combined average earning "of hired factors," which is identical to the combined costs of production of all enterprises. We must, thus, turn in the succeeding part to an extension of the preceding analysis which will attempt to explain the determination of the relative prices of and distribution of income as among land, labor, and capital. A second matter which can be dealt with adequately only on more general assumptions than those so far employed is the determination of the general level of employment. We shall consider this problem also in the second part of this work.

SUPPLEMENTARY READINGS

DONALD H. WALLACE, "Industrial Markets and Public Policy," *Public Policy Yearbook*, Cambridge: Harvard Graduate School of Public Administration, 1940.

BEN W. LEWIS AND OTHERS, *Economic Standards of Government Price Control*, Temporary National Economic Committee, Monograph No. 32, Washington, 1941.

[3] For a discussion of the effects of flexible and inflexible prices, see Alvin H. Hansen, *Fiscal Policy and Business Cycles* (New York: W. W. Norton & Co., 1941), Chap. 15.

Part 2

THEORY OF DISTRIBUTION AND EMPLOYMENT

11 THE DISTRIBUTION OF INCOME
—COMPETITIVE CONDITIONS

A. THE PROBLEMS OF EMPLOYMENT AND INCOME DISTRIBUTION

CHARACTER OF THE SUCCEEDING ANALYSIS

In preceding chapters we have analyzed the determination in a free-enterprise economy of various commodity prices and outputs, of the allocation of resources among uses, and of related phenomena. The theory of commodity pricing there developed has been deduced, however, from certain limiting assumptions. First, we have assumed, whenever the entire economy as a unit was being considered, that there is for the economy as a whole a given constant flow of money purchasing power, to which both commodity and factor prices may adjust without influencing the flow itself. We have thus seen what would be the equilibrium tendency of relative commodity prices and outputs if purchasing power were given and constant and if factor prices (which make up costs) were free to adjust to such a given volume of buying power. Second, we have so far failed to distinguish among the particular prices of different factors of production—labor, land, and capital—speaking instead essentially of a certain average or composite price of such factors which adjusts to a given money purchasing power. Although we have thus observed certain things about the determination of the average money price of all productive factors in various situations, we have not as yet analyzed the determination of the relative (comparative) prices and income shares of the different factors of production.

For certain purposes, theorizing on this restricted plane is a valid and useful procedure. It allows us, while avoiding undue complexities, to examine certain tendencies present in the determination of the outputs and price-cost relationships for commodities sold in various market situations and in the allocation of productive factors among the production of various goods. It also reveals some tendencies present in the determination of the relative shares of income going to profits and to hired factors as a group as the average price of hired factors adjusts to any going level of money purchasing power.

But by the nature of the assumptions made so far we have avoided two essential problems: the determination of (1) the relative prices and income shares paid to different factors of production—that is, of the "functional" distribution of the income paid out as the cost of producing commodities— and (2) the relation between the volume of purchasing power and the average level of factor prices, which evidently helps to fix the level of employment. It is clear that we have not dealt with the first question. And we have so far begged the second by assuming purchasing power to be a constant magnitude to which factor prices are free to adjust. We must now relax our restrictive assumptions and attempt to develop first a theory of functional income distribution and second a theory of the determination of the level of employment. An ultimate aim, which economic theory has not yet fully attained, would be to combine the theories of pricing, distribution, and employment into a single, unified explanation of the simultaneous determination of commodity prices and outputs, wages, interest rates, rents, profits, and the level of employment of the several productive factors.

A first step, which we shall undertake in this and the succeeding two chapters, will be to develop a theory of the distribution of income among the several hired factors of production, while a second step, undertaken thereafter, will be to analyze the determination of the general level of income and employment. It may seem to the student at the outset a bit awkward to consider first how some given income tends to be distributed, and only later the determination of how big this income will be and how many will share in its distribution—especially if the two questions are essentially parts of a single larger one. Initial understanding of these complex questions is greatly facilitated by separating them, however, and we shall thus first consider the income distribution problem in isolation from the employment problem.

To do this we shall for the time being continue to beg the question of the level of employment by continuing to assume that full employment is automatically maintained—that is, by assuming that there is a given constant flow of purchasing power to which the *general level* of factor prices freely adjusts to permit full employment. But we shall now inquire specifically into how the relative prices and the relative income shares of the several hired factors of production are determined in such a situation.

It is apparent that what this procedure will actually give us is a theory of income distribution *under conditions of full employment.* And it should be anticipated that, although such a theory may be useful as a first approximation to a more adequate theory, it may not fully answer the question of how income is distributed if there is less than full employment. This latter question, however, has not as yet been adequately treated by economic theorists. We shall, therefore, proceed to develop our full-employment theory of income distribution at the outset, and comment later on needed modifications in the theory if it is applied to underemployment situations.

PRODUCTIVE FACTORS AND DISTRIBUTIVE SHARES

In analyzing income distribution, we may first consider certain fundamental terms and ideas useful in the succeeding analysis.

Business enterprises in general function by acquiring certain basic productive services, either from human beings or from the earth's resources, and by combining them into useful products. All production must draw entirely and exclusively on such basic services. One firm may buy goods (semi-processed basic resources) from another, but in so doing it is merely acquiring these basic services indirectly. The "factors of production" include all such services, or the sources which provide them. "Factor-price determination" refers to the pricing of such services, whereas commodity-price determination refers to the pricing of the goods made by combining them.

Basic productive services may be conveniently subdivided on the basis of origin. A common and useful subdivision recognizes two productive factors—"labor" and "land." "Labor" in this sense is used to refer to human beings in general, or to whatever productive services they provide. "Land" is used to refer to natural resources in general, or the services they provide, and would thus include agricultural land, factory sites, urban residential and commercial land, forest land, coal mines, oil wells, deposits of uranium ore, etc.

Each of these "factors" may be subdivided into as many grades or types as may be convenient for analysis—labor into various geographical and occupational groups, and land into such subcategories as those just indicated. The payments to or prices of labor are generally referred to as *wages,* those of land as *rents*. These terms are thus given somewhat broader definitions than is common in nontechnical discussion.

Are labor and land thus defined the only factors of production? A third candidate for inclusion is often suggested, namely, *"capital";* this is also often held to be a "factor of production." The sense in which capital may be so regarded, however, requires careful definition. Capital in the sense of capital goods—factory buildings, machinery, inventories, or any good to be used in further production—evidently represents a special class of commodities, produced for use in the production of further commodities or services. In an ultimate sense, capital goods may thus be classed with other commodities, as the output or embodiment of the basic services of land and labor. As such, they would not claim status as an additional factor of production.

At any given time in a developed industrial community, however, there is on hand a large body of previously produced capital goods, which on the average are quite durable and will contribute for some time to further production. From any current standpoint, this existing stock of capital goods represents a body of fixed factors, akin to land, upon the services of which production may draw.

Any short-run analysis will recognize existing capital goods as a third factor of production, earning (potentially) *quasi-rents*. As we contemplate longer periods for analysis, however, it must be recognized that existing capital goods will wear out and will have to be replaced, and that new or additional capital goods may be added. For such longer periods, capital goods revert to the status of produced commodities, or, in effect, of the output or embodiment of the services of land and of labor. Capital goods thus do not qualify in the long run as a third factor of production.

But the initial acquisition and the retention (by replacement) of capital goods does require the use of funds or money, to be "invested in" such goods—that is, paid for them without the immediate yield of consumption satisfaction to those who make the payment. The productive services which go into making capital goods must be paid for, and in advance of the time when the capital goods provide services in further production; purchasing power must be "tied up" in them for an interval during which those who supplied the purchasing power receive no direct benefit in consumers' goods. It may thus be argued that "money capital," or investable funds, constitutes a third productive factor, which is used in conjunction with other factors in the process of production to facilitate the production and use of capital goods.

Whatever we call them, it is evident that investable funds are required, and also that the supply of such funds is a source of earnings to their suppliers, in the form of *interest* payments. These arise as the suppliers of funds pay less for capital goods than the goods are expected to earn over time as they are used, or, in effect, as they pay the cost of producing capital goods and receive an income stream the gross sum of which exceeds this cost.

Within a capitalist system, the interest paid for invested money is thus a third distributive share, in addition to wages and rents. It is paid for the services of invested money, *and it is "earned"* (as a part of quasi rents) *by the capital goods in which the funds are invested*. The basic additional factor may thus be regarded as investable funds, and the basic service that of investing these funds to finance acquisition and retention of capital goods. The provision of this service is in turn reflected, however, in the continued production (initially or for replacement) and use of actual capital goods, which in use provide direct productive services which are rewarded sufficiently to pay not only their cost of production but also the interest on the funds the investment of which made their acquisition possible. The use of investable funds, to which interest payments are made, is associated with the production and existence of a special class of commodities—capital goods—which are produced for use in production in conjunction with labor and land, and which directly earn the income from which interest is paid.

It may be noted, however, that investable funds are advanced not only for investment in capital goods, but also for such things as consumer loans, or for the purchase of any asset, including land, which may yield a future income stream. Such funds will also earn interest in these pursuits, so far as less will be paid for any future income stream than the gross sum of all payments in this stream. Thus the use of investable funds and the earning of interest arise not only in connection with the use of produced capital goods, but generally in connection with the purchase of the right to any future or nonimmediate series of incomes. Interest is mentioned primarily in connection with capital goods because they are the principal source of such series of delayed or future returns. But interest also is earned if a future series of rents is bought,[1] and, if labor power could be sold, could be earned in buying the rights to the future wages of labor.

It will be noted that in addition to wages, rent, and interest, there is apparently a fourth distributive share—namely, the *profits* going to enterprise. Correspondingly, it has sometimes been the fashion to suggest that we should recognize a fourth productive factor, called *enterprise* or *entrepreneurship*. Most of the functions performed by the ownership-management group in the modern enterprise, however, consist in the supply of the other productive factors—particularly the *labor* of management and administration and the money *capital* for investment in the concern.

To explain the earnings of such labor and capital it is unnecessary to recognize a separate factor of production; it is only logically consistent to attribute such earnings to their true sources. After deduction of the costs of labor and capital supplied by the enterprise group, nevertheless, a residual may remain which also goes to the owner-manager group. This share may be meaningfully referred to as true *profits,* a fourth distributive share. But it is pointless for most purposes to refer to a fourth productive factor corresponding to profits. We may say, in effect, that enterprises use labor, land, and capital, disbursing distributive shares of wages, rent, and interest; that they sell the resultant product for a revenue; and that any residual difference between the sales revenue and the total of the payments mentioned goes as a true profit to enterprise.

Profits are thus logically defined as *net of* or *in addition to* all wages (including wages of management), all interest (including interest on owners' investment), and all rents attributable to natural resources employed.

---

[1] Land, or any other nonwasting or irreplaceable asset, has no "cost of production" above which it can be said to earn an interest return. But it will tend to have a market price which is sufficiently below the undiscounted sum of its future returns that an interest return is allowed on the funds paid by its purchaser.

Under general equilibrium conditions, they would represent mainly a return to artificial or noncompetitive restriction of output, and no "productive" function would be rendered in return for them. Under conditions of dynamic change, however, the profit residual may be enhanced by enterprise activities which might be viewed as a special productive function corresponding to the reward. This will be discussed in Chapter 15.

In sum, the system of business enterprises which operate in selling commodities also operate by buying the services of productive factors, which may be classified as labor, land, and capital. Enterprises make money payments for these services, which, as wages, rent, and interest, constitute (together with residual profits) the flow of money income upon which people depend for a living.

One reason for distinguishing among the incomes paid for various sorts of productive services is found in differences in their character. Labor yields human services, land the services of inanimate natural resources, and capital the services of invested money. Another reason is found in the difference in the relation of the human recipient of the income to the service for which it is paid. Wages are ordinarily payments to the individual for his own labor —for expended effort of some sort. Rents, as received for the services of natural resources, are not paid as rewards for effort expended by the recipient but accrue by virtue of the *ownership* of the resources in question. The institution of rent payments as incomes to individuals thus emerges from the character of *property* in natural resources. Interest similarly is a payment not for human service (unless for the "abstinence" of the supplier when he is an individual supplying his savings) but for the release of money funds which the individual or institution in question has the power to release. It is thus again a payment to ownership or to institutional position. Profits, as a possible (but not inevitable) residual left to the enterprise or to those who own or control it, also evidently have a source in ownership or property. It is in part because of the important distinction between human effort on the one hand, and property or institutional position on the other, as sources of income, that it is important to trace the determination of the relative shares of income going to labor and to land, capital, and enterprise.

A GENERAL VIEW OF THE PROBLEMS OF PRICING,
DISTRIBUTION, AND EMPLOYMENT

The immediate question to be answered is how the prices and the relative income shares of labor, land, and capital, thus defined, and the residual income share to profits, are determined. Before proceeding to this task, it may be well for a moment to consider in more detail how this analytical question is related to the ones previously posed concerning commodity pricing, and to those still deferred concerning the determination of the level of income and employment.

Economic activity in a market economy may be conceived of as proceeding through time in a circular flow, or more precisely, in two reciprocating circular flows—one of real productive services which are converted into goods and flow in this form to buyers, and the other of money payments, which flow to enterprises as purchasing power seeking goods, through en-

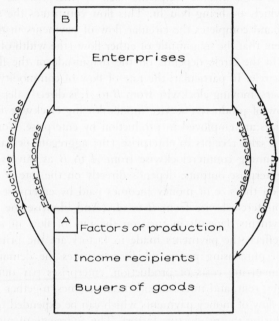

Figure 49

terprises to productive factors as wage, interest, rent, and profit payments, and from these factors around again as purchasing power seeking goods from enterprises. This circular flow proceeds, in reciprocating fashion, simultaneously in two directions.

In Figure 49, we may conceive of the principal "way stations" in this perpetual flow as (1) enterprises, (2) recipients of income from enterprises (which in general supply enterprises with the services of factors of production), including profit receivers, and (3) buyers of the outputs of enterprises. Categories 2 and 3, however, are actually identical, since income recipients are the buyers of outputs.

Within this model, we may view a flow of real services and goods as proceeding in a clockwise direction. The services of factors of production flow from A to B, as labor, land, and capital are employed. At B they are combined and emerge in the form of outputs of goods and services, and thence flow back to buyers of these outputs (who are also the suppliers of productive services), thus completing the circle.

Reciprocating with this real flow and proceeding in the opposite direction is a flow of money payments. Thus counterclockwise from B to A runs a flow of wage, interest, and rent payments, constituting remuneration for hired productive services, and of profits, which are the residual rewards (if any) left to enterprise. From A counterclockwise to B the flow of money continues from these income recipients back to enterprises as payment for the outputs which are being bought. This flow constitutes the sales receipts of enterprises and completes the circular flow of payments in the economy.

It is evident that the magnitude of either flow (the width of the stream) at any point in the circle depends on the magnitude of the flow at other points in the circle. In particular, the rate of flow of commodity outputs delivered to buyers, moving clockwise from B to A, is directly dependent upon the rate of flow of productive-service inputs flowing clockwise from A to B as factor services are employed in production by enterprise. Conversely, the rate of flow of sales receipts to enterprise (the aggregate demand price for all output), running counterclockwise from A to B as buyers spend their incomes for enterprise outputs, depends directly on the rate of flow of factor incomes—on the size of money incomes paid by enterprise to factors—proceeding counterclockwise from B to A. (And likewise the rate of flow of income payments depends in turn on the rate of flow of spending for outputs.) In effect, the payments made to factors are the principal source of the flow of purchasing power which constitutes the demand for commodities. In incurring costs of production, enterprises pay out money incomes in wages, rent, and interest, and these incomes, together with profits, constitute the flow of money payments which can be expended for the goods produced by hiring the productive factors. The aggregate of money income payments, or costs, flows through the economy to become the primary source of the aggregate of money demands for the outputs produced. In turn, these aggregate money demands are the primary source of income payments. Thus, in the circular flow of money payments, there is a sort of circular interdependence of the money demand for goods and the money income payments to factors of production.

Certain properties of these reciprocating circular flows of real services and goods and of money payments should now be emphasized. First, neither need necessarily proceed at a constant rate through time. It is obviously possible for the rate of use of productive services to be increased or decreased, with a resultant variation in the flow of commodity outputs. It is also possible for the flow of money payments to vary—for the aggregate of purchasing power expended for goods to exceed or fall short of preceding income payments. This is because income recipients as a group—including profit receivers or enterprises themselves—may decide to spend less than they receive by "hoarding" money or increasing their liquid balances, or they may decide to spend more than they receive by "dishoarding" money or reducing their liquid balances. This variation in the rates of flow of both money payments and real output is possible and in fact does occur.

Second, in a highly specialized economy dependent on money exchange and where enterprises operate for a money profit, the flow of money payments may be viewed as essentially eliciting or bringing forth the flows of productive services and commodity outputs. Thus, it is the offer of money purchasing power for their outputs which induces enterprises to produce and supply outputs, and the offer of income payments by enterprises which induces productive factors to offer their services for employment. The flows of commodity outputs and productive services *respond to* flow of money payments.

Third, the rate of flow of productive services (that is, the rate of employment) and the rate of flow of commodity outputs (that is, aggregate output) which will be attained with any given rate of money flow depend directly on the *prices* of commodities and on the prices of productive services which determine the costs of these commodities, since these prices determine how much real services and goods can be bought with a given amount of money. More generally, the ratio of the *money price level* (average money price of goods and services) to the rate of money flow will determine the level of output and employment. Now this ratio *may* more or less automatically adjust (that is, prices may adjust relative to money income or money income relative to prices) so as to secure full employment of all factor services—as we have assumed in the analysis of commodity pricing for the economy as a whole. But it may not, and the reasons it may not require investigation—or, more generally, we need to investigate at some point the determinants of the ratio of the price level to the flow of money income.

Fourth, the adjustment of factor and commodity prices relative to a given flow of money income may in turn affect the flow of money income itself—for example, a downward movement of factor and commodity prices may result in a responding downward movement of the money flow, or an upward movement of prices in an upward movement of the money flow. When we assume that the money flow remains constant while prices adjust, we arbitrarily rule out this possibility. But the possibility is in fact definitely present, and it is thus ultimately necessary to analyze the interaction between movements in money payments and movements in the price level in order to determine when, respectively, stability and instability in income and prices will be found. It is also necessary to consider how the interaction of prices and money income will affect the ratio, which is maintained through time or in any final equilibrium which may be reached, between money income and prices, and will thus affect the level of employment.

Given the preceding outline of the general function of a market economy, what are the primary questions to be answered concerning its function as a unit and how do various separate analyses contribute to answering them? We have broken up these questions into three main groups, of which we have already dealt with one, are about to deal with another, and will later deal with a third.

The first concerns the determination of *the composition of the aggregate output of commodities* (the allocation of factor services to the production of various goods), of the relative prices of various goods, and of the relation of these prices to costs of production. This is the broad question we have attacked in the preceding ten chapters. To simplify the analysis of this issue, we have asked in effect how the preceding things will be determined with any *given* flow of money purchasing power (aggregate demand for goods) when the average level of factor prices adjusts freely relative to the purchasing power, no distinctions being drawn among the several productive factors which enter into costs. Precisely, we have assumed a constant and self-sustaining flow of money purchasing power at any given level, which remains invariant in spite of upward or downward movements in money factor prices. In terms of our circular flow diagram, we have taken as given at a constant width the flow of sales receipts or aggregate demand entering enterprises from the right at B, and have analyzed how the economy-wide complex of enterprises will adjust to this flow when the money prices paid to factors as a group (through the income stream moving down from B to A) move freely to a level consistent with full employment. (In these circumstances, the size of the factor income stream, including profits, necessarily becomes the same as that of the stream of sales receipts, although the division of the income stream among various factors has not been investigated.) Given these assumptions, we have been able to predict certain tendencies in allocation, relative commodity prices, price-cost relationships, and so forth, for a situation which more or less automatically reaches full employment. But we have, as previously noted, simply assumed that the money income to average factor price relation is such as to produce full employment. And we have not investigated the determination of the relative prices of the several factors or of the relative shares of the income stream which they will receive.

The second question, to which we turn at this point, concerns the determination of such relative factor prices and income shares. That is, we shall try to extend our analysis to include an explanation of the ratio of wages to rents to interest, and the consequent sharing of the factor income stream among labor, land, and capital as this stream flows to recipients of income payments made by enterprises. As indicated, we shall conduct this analysis on the assumption that the flow of money purchasing power entering enterprises from the right at B is constant at a given rate and that the average level of factor prices adjusts freely to permit full employment. But we shall extend the analysis to explain how the factor income stream (which in this situation should also be constant at the same level as the aggregate demand stream) is shared among the several hired factors and with profit receivers.

The third question, to which we do not turn as yet, concerns the determination of (1) the size of the money income stream, (2) whether it will be stable or changing through time, and (3) the ratio of the flow of money income to the average level of prices, which in turn determines employment. To answer this question, we shall have to drop the simplifying assumption on which preceding questions were approached—namely, that the circular flow of money payments proceeds at a constant rate regardless of adjustments in factor and commodity prices—and analyze in detail what determines the level of the money flow (from B to A to B to A, etc.) with any given level of prices, or more generally, what determines the ratio of the money flow to the level of prices. For the time being, however, we are begging this and related questions by assuming a constant flow of money purchasing power and the automatic attainment of a ratio of money prices to this flow which permits full employment.

B. COMPETITIVE FACTOR-PRICE DETERMINATION

INITIAL ASSUMPTIONS—PURE COMPETITION AND "SYMBOLIC" FACTORS OF PRODUCTION

The analysis of the determination of relative factor prices and income shares (even on the simplifying full-employment assumptions adopted) is not as uncomplicated as the preceding brief account of the problem might seem to suggest. At first glance, it might appear that the analytical problem is simply one of analyzing the interaction, according to patterns already established, of several related demands for the several factors—derived from commodity demands—with given supply conditions for these factors. The reasons that a really satisfactory explanation of factor prices and income distribution is not so easily derived are threefold.

First, the supply conditions for the several factors of production tend to be different in each case and very difficult to appraise. None of the basic factors is in any evident sense a produced good with a given cost of production which determines what will be supplied at a price. Labor consists of human services supplied by independent human beings, and the relation of its supply to the price offered for it can be explained only in terms of human psychology—individual psychology in an atomistic labor market or group and leadership psychology where labor sells its services through unions. Land is an inanimate good, present in nature without cost of production to human beings, but ordinarily owned in an enterprise system by individuals whose own psychologies in turn influence the relation of its supply to price. Capital, in the sense of investable funds, is a supply of money available for use in obtaining deferred benefits from the use of capital goods, and it may be supplied jointly by individuals who save some of their incomes, and by credit institutions effectively empowered to create new money under certain conditions. Explanation of the supply of capital requires reference both to individual psychology governing saving and the holding of money and to the policies of credit institutions or of the governments which control them. Thus, an adequate theory of income distribution can be developed only after an extended consideration of the special conditions of supply for the several different factors of production.

Second, the determination of the share of income going as interest to capital—even if the character of supply of investable funds is firmly established—involves the joint determination of the extent to which capital goods will be used by enterprises in producing their outputs. It is thus impossible to develop a theory of distribution which explains the share of income going to interest without at the same time developing a theory explaining the conversion of basic productive factors into capital goods, the reasons for the use of capital goods, and the determinants of the volume in which they will be used relative to any given volume of final consumer output. Since this "capital theory" can be complex indeed, an adequate theory of income distribution is correspondingly complicated.

Third, the determination of relative factor prices is obviously influenced by the structure of the markets in which both factor services and commodities are sold, and these structures may be widely various and complex. There are three levels on which market structure is in fact a strategic influence on income distribution—that of the selling markets for commodities, that of the buying markets for factors, and that of the selling markets for factors. There may be competition, oligopoly, or monopoly in the selling markets for commodities produced with factors; competition, oligopsony, or monopsony on the buyers' side in the markets where factors are sold; and competition, oligopoly, or monopoly in the selling of factors to these buyers. In each possible combination of successive market structures the forces bearing on the determination of income distribution are somewhat different. An adequate theory must take account of all alternative situations which are likely to be found in fact, and it is thus extremely complex.

When developing a theory of income distribution, there is thus some merit in the procedure of establishing its most basic elements in a simplified manner, initially putting aside the many complexities outlined above. This may be done by adopting certain arbitrary simplifying assumptions concerning the character of factors and the structures of markets, and determining in the assumed simple situation the fundamental tendencies in factor-price and income-share determination. Subsequently, we may elaborate this analysis by adopting more realistic and detailed assumptions concerning the nature of factors and the structures of markets.

Therefore, we shall pursue the following course in developing a theory of income distribution. As previously indicated, the analysis will rest, in general, on the assumption of a given constant flow of money purchasing power to which the average level of money factor prices freely adjusts. In addition, we shall assume for the time being—in this and in the following chapter—that there are no complexities in the supply characteristics of factors or no complexities arising from the character of capital goods. We shall assume, in effect, that there are several (for example, three) productive factors, and that each factor is equivalent to some basic inanimate commodity, a given limited quantity of which is available for use in the economy in each successive time period. Each factor is available without being produced and without cost of production, and the supply of each factor is quite independent of that of every other. Thus, in each successive interval of time there is a certain stock available of factor A, on which the economy may draw for production, a similar independent stock of factor B, and a similar stock of factor C. Production of commodities is carried on by combining these factors in a productive process. We shall further assume that there are given supply conditions for each factor—either that each has a perfectly inelastic supply, so that all the quantity available will be offered for use at any price by its owners, or that there is for each factor a given supply curve which indicates that certain alternative quantities will be supplied at alternative prices.

A further assumption, adopted in this chapter only, will be that all relevant market structures are purely competitive. We shall assume (1) that every firm purchasing productive factors in turn sells its output in a purely competitive market, (2) that every firm buying factors does so in a market where there are many small buyers, or purely competitive buying, and (3) that in every market for factors there is purely competitive selling—that is, there are many small sellers of each factor and no differentiation among different units of any factor. No enterprise, that is, has any degree of monopoly power in selling its output or any degree of monopsony power in buying factors; in addition, no seller of a productive factor has any degree of monopoly. Pure competition is universal at every possible level. In the following chapter, while retaining the supposition that each factor is a basic inanimate commodity with given and independent supply conditions, we shall modify our assumptions concerning market structure and consider the effect on factor pricing of monopoly and monopsony at various levels.

Finally, we shall assume in this chapter that for each factor there is only a single homogeneous market in which all units of the factor are sold and to which all buyers have equal access. The possibility of subdivision of any factor supply among disparate submarkets is thus neglected for the moment. In the following chapter, however, we shall consider this possibility.

In this highly simplified situation, our task is to determine the principles which govern the determination of the relative prices of several factors and their relative income shares. We may do this by considering the determination of factor prices or quantities of factors used in turn for the individual firm, for the industry of such firms, and for the economy as a whole. In so doing, we shall center attention only on the long-run adjustments of firm, industry, and economy—on adjustments over periods of time sufficient for the quantities of all hired factors used to be freely varied by the firm. We thus neglect any special analysis of short-period adjustments, although these may easily be worked out.

PURCHASE OF FACTORS BY THE FIRM UNDER PURELY
COMPETITIVE CONDITIONS—FIXED RATIOS OF FACTORS

In the competitive situation just described, let us first investigate the activities in the long run of the individual firm buying factors. These will stem from the firm's demand for such factors and from the conditions of supply for each of them. The firm's demand for factors is essentially derived from the demand for its output. For the firm with a purely competitive selling market, the latter is a perfectly elastic horizontal line at the going market price for the output. This market price serves as the beginning point for the firm's calculation of its demand for factors.

If the factor markets are also purely competitive, the supply of each factor to the firm is also perfectly elastic at some going price. Since the price of labor, for example, is beyond influence by any seller or buyer thereof, the supply curve which represents the amounts of labor any firm can buy at various prices is simply a horizontal line at the going wage rate, as in Figure 50. The firm in effect can take as little or as much labor as it wishes at the going wage rate, but it cannot lower and would not wish to raise this wage. The same is true of each factor market; in each, the firm is faced with a given fixed price.

Suppose now that the firm is buying three factors—land, labor, and capital, or, let us say, factors A, B, and C, each with a money price which is given to the firm. It is also faced in its selling market with a given money price for its output. The only decision it need make with respect to the factor markets, then, is how much of each factor to buy. How is this decision made?

The complexity of the choice will depend upon whether the proportions of the various factors are fixed or variable—upon whether or not the firm may acquire the factors in proportions which vary with variations in their relative prices. Therefore, we shall successively consider (1) purchase of fac-

tors in predetermined fixed proportions and (2) purchase of factors in potentially varying proportions.

In the first situation, the firm must observe certain technologically fixed
ratios or coefficients among the several factors; for example, for each 5 units
of factor A, it must employ 3 units of B, and 1 unit of C. (This might correspond to 50 laborers, $30,000 invested in plant, and 1 city lot of land.) In-
creases in output can be accomplished only by equal percentage increases in
the amounts of all factors employed. In effect, the firm cannot substitute

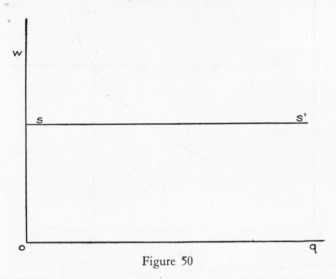

Figure 50

one factor for another in any degree, and as a result the various factors do
not compete with each other. Output must be increased by fixed "doses" of
combined factors—in the example in question, always in a 5-3-1 ratio.

In addition, the price of each factor is given to the firm, let us say at
$5 per unit for A, $8 for B, and $10 for C. Each additional dose of factors
would thus cost the firm a constant amount—in this case ($25 + $24 +
$10) = $59. These payments constitute the costs of production of the firm.
The average cost per unit of output for the firm at any output will simply
equal the sum of factor payments made to secure that output, divided by
the output; the marginal cost of production will be the addition to factor
payments for a unit addition to output.

This marginal cost will tend to increase beyond a certain output if "the
firm" is in effect an imperfectly divisible unit against which the proportions
of hired factors vary. That is, average and marginal costs of output will rise
as output is extended beyond a certain point (even in the long run), because of the declining efficiency of management beyond a certain scale of
firm. Rigidly mixed identical doses of the three factors (A, B, and C in the

5-3-1 proportion) will produce successively less output as diminishing returns are encountered.

With this progressive rise in marginal cost, the competitive firm will set output at the point where marginal cost is equal to the price of its product, as in Figure 51. At this output of goods, it will employ a *corresponding* amount of factors, necessarily in fixed ratio; for example, it may employ

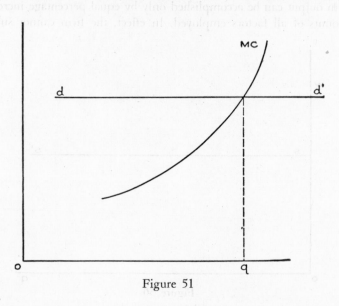

Figure 51

500 units of *A*, 300 of *B*, and 100 of *C*. By determining its output, it thus also exactly determines its demand for each factor, given the price of its output and the set of prices for the three factors. The *relative* quantities of the various factors employed is set by the fixed technical ratios which rule. *The absolute quantities employed depend upon the relation of the total money price of a composite dose of factors to the money price of the good produced, upon the productivity per dose of factors, and upon the rate at which this diminishes at the margin with increasing output.* The individual firm determines only the quantity of factors to employ, and it cannot affect their market prices. It will produce only if price covers average costs, but if we view one firm alone, a short-run excess of price over average costs is quite possible.

PURCHASE OF FACTORS BY THE FIRM—
VARIABLE RATIOS OF FACTORS

We may now drop the somewhat artificial assumption of fixed technical ratios among factors, and consider a second situation where it is recognized that the firm may vary the proportions in which factors are employed in order to obtain any chosen output. In actuality, various factors are substitutes for each other; labor, for example, may be substituted for capital, or capital for labor. Instead of using factors *A*, *B*, and *C* always in a 5-3-1 ratio, the firm may experiment with other ratios, such as 6-2-2, 4-4-1, and so forth. At each level of output it is free to choose a specific proportion among the factors. *It will presumably make its choice in such a way as to minimize the cost of the output.*

The proportions in which the factors are employed will thus obviously depend upon their relative prices. The choice is also necessarily conditioned, however, by the nature of the substitutability of one factor for another. Such substitution relationships observe certain regularities under substantially all conditions of production. In general, the proportions of any two factors may be varied (increasing the amount employed of one, decreasing that of the other) to produce a given constant output. But starting from any initial combination, successive *unit decreases* in the amount of any one factor will require successively *larger increases* in that of the other in order to maintain a constant output.

This fact is sometimes expressed by saying that the *marginal rate of substitution* of any factor *A* for any other factor *B* must increase as *A* is progressively substituted for *B*. Such a typical relationship is illustrated in the following table, which shows the various alternative combinations of two factors, *A* and *B*, that may be employed to obtain a given output of 1,000 units of a certain product:

COMBINATIONS OF FACTORS *A* AND *B* FOR (Q = 1,000)

Units of factor *A*	Units of factor *B*
40	61
45	55
50	50
55	46
60	43
65	41

This table says that the firm can produce 1,000 units of output by employing 40 of *A* and 61 of *B*, *or* by employing 45 of *A* and 55 of *B*, and so forth. The firm can use less of *A* and more of *B*, or vice versa. If either factor is successively decreased in quantity at a uniform rate, however, the quantity of the other factor must be increased at an increasing rate in order to maintain the same output.

Thus, a decline in the use of *A* by 5 from 65 to 60 can be compensated by an increase in *B* of 2, but a further decline in *A* of 5, from 60 to 55, requires an increase of 3 in *B* if output is to remain unchanged. *The mar-*

ginal rate of substitution of B *for* A *rises from* 2-5 *and* 3-5. This tendency is, of course, an effective check against a firm using any one factor entirely and to the exclusion of others.

The sort of relation shown in the preceding table is charted in Figure 52. The curve labeled "$Q = 1,000$" shows the various proportions of A

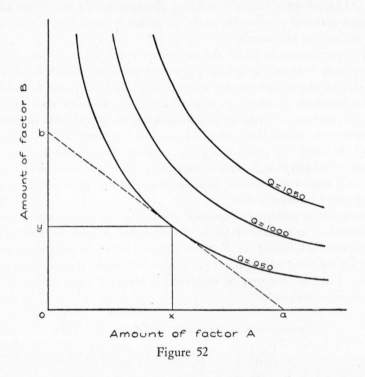

Figure 52

and B which may be employed to produce 1,000 units of output. A similar curve, of similar shape, may be drawn for every other alternative level of output—thus the curves labeled "$Q = 950$" and "$Q = 1,050$." Each such curve is an *isoquant*, or curve showing combined factor quantities necessary to produce a constant quantity of output.[2] With factor B on the vertical axis, the slope of the isoquant, which increases as B is increased, measures the marginal rate of substitution of B for A, whereas the reciprocal of this slope measures the reciprocal marginal rate of substitution of A for B. At any level of output, the general principle of the increasing marginal rate of substitution of one factor for another holds, and it is quite as applicable to the covariation of three or more as to that of two factors.

[2] We neglect here, and thus leave for more advanced treatments, the effect of the indivisibilities of hired factors (encountered short of optimum-scale outputs) and of the existence of diminishing returns of the composite of hired factors against a fixed "firm" (if any) on the substitution conditions among factors. See Boulding, *op. cit.*, Chap. 23.

It may be noted that the stated tendency—toward an increasing marginal rate of substitution of one factor for another as the one is substituted progressively for the other always just sufficiently to hold a constant output —is in effect a corollary of the previously stated law of diminishing returns (discussed on pages 99 to 104). In its traditional form, this law refers to the response of output to an increase in the quantity used of one factor when the quantity of another factor is held fixed or constant. It states (on the basis of empirical evidence) that as the quantity of a variable factor is increased against a constant quantity of a fixed factor (thus increasing the proportion of the variable to the fixed factor for purposes of production), the additions to output obtained by successive unit additions of the variable factor will, after a point, progressively diminish. In effect, the *marginal products* of added units of the variable factor will progressively decline as more and more of it is used in combination with a fixed amount of another factor.

This is a useful thing to know, but the knowledge is directly applicable only to cases in which the quantity of some factor is actually fixed and invariant in quantity—for the firm, largely in the short run. In the long run no factor (possibly excepting management) is actualy fixed in quantity to the firm; each of several hired factors is freely variable in quantity. How may the law of diminishing returns be applied to the productivity relationships of several such freely variable factors?

One thing which is apparent is that each factor in turn would exhibit "diminishing-return" tendencies if it were increased in quantity while the others were held constant in quantity—there would be diminishing marginal products from increments to any one factor in this situation. Thus, if a firm is producing 1,000 units of output with 55 units of factor A and 46 units of factor B, it would be true: (1) that if the quantity of A were held at 55 units while the quantity of B was increased to 47, 48, 49, and 50, the additions to output due to successive unit increments in B would become progressively smaller; and (2) that if the quantity of B were held constant at 46 units while the quantity of A was increased to 56, 57, 58, and 59 units, the additions to output due to successive unit increments in A would become progressively smaller.

Each factor in turn would yield diminishing marginal returns if it were increased in quantity while the others were held constant in quantity. (This is true unless so little of any factor were being used that it at first yielded increasing marginal returns, but no firm would actually operate with such a proportion of factors—our remarks thus refer to the diminishing-return tendencies which are found within the range of economically conceivable proportions of factors.)

Now if this is true—that output would increase at a diminishing rate as either factor was increased against a constant quantity of the other—it follows as a corollary that if either factor is increased and the other decreased (instead of being held constant) just so as to maintain a constant output, then there will be an increasing marginal rate of substitution of that factor for the other as it is progressively increased. The tendency toward such an increasing marginal rate of substitution is thus a reflection of the fact that each factor is in a state of diminishing returns against the other if its quantity is increased.

It should also be noted that the marginal rate of substitution of one factor for another, at any point on an isoquant, is the same as the reciprocal of the ratio of the marginal productivities of the two factors at that point. That is, if with 45 units of A and 50 units of B used to produce 1,000 units, the marginal rate of substitution of B for A is 6:5, it is also true that the ratio of the marginal productivity of B (if it were increased with A held constant at 45 units) to the marginal productivity of A (if it were increased with B held constant at 50 units) is necessarily 5:6.

So much for the relation of the law of increasing marginal rate of substitution to the law of diminishing returns. Because of the operation of the same set of physical laws, we observe a relation between the quantities of any two factors employed and the quantity of output obtained like that represented by the family of isoquants in Figure 52.

Of what importance is this relationship to the firm buying factors? It is principally the following: If the firm wishes to maximize profits, it must not only adjust its output so that marginal cost will equal the price of its output, but it must also choose that proportion among the factors which keeps the cost of every output at a minimum. And this minimization of cost—a selection of the *cheapest* combination of factors at each output—is reached by balancing the relative prices of various factors against their marginal rates of substitution one for another. *To minimize costs for any output, the firm will necessarily choose such a combination of any pair of factors that the marginal rate of substitution of* A *for* B *is equal to the ratio of the price of* B *to that of* A.

This principle may be illustrated simply from the table on page 475, which gives certain substitution ratios for increments in either of two factors.

Suppose that A costs the firm $3 per unit and B costs $5 per unit. With 50 units of A and 50 units of B, the total cost of 1,000 units of product would be ($150 + $250) = $400. Consider now substituting one factor for another in either direction. The firm will not substitute 5 units of B for 5 of A (moving upward in table) since this would increase costs by $10. But it will substitute 5 units of A for 4 of B, thus reducing costs by $5, and it is willing to substitute 5 *more* of A for 3 of B, moving to the combination 60-43, and leaving costs unchanged at $395. It will *not* substitute another 5 of A for 2 of B (moving to the 65-41 combination), however, since costs would rise to $400 again.

The firm therefore finds the optimum proportion for producing 1,000 units of output at 55-46 or 60-43, or in the range between these points, where the *marginal rate of substitution* of A for B is 5 to 3. It will be noted that this rate is the inverse of the A-B price ratio of 3:5.

At *every* output, the firm will make this sort of adjustment in the proportion of factors employed. It will minimize the cost of securing any output by employing factors in such proportions that the marginal rate of substitution of any factor A for any other factor B is equated to the ratio of the price of B to the price of A.

This solution may be represented diagrammatically in Figure 52, where each of several isoquants shows the varying factor combinations required to produce a given output. The varying slope of any isoquant shows the varying marginal rate of substitution of B for A as the proportions are varied. The dotted line *ab* is drawn to represent the inverse of the B:A price ratio—that is, the ratio of the price of A to that of B, when both of their prices are given to the firm. (The distance *ob* represents the amount of B which can be bought with a given amount of money; the distance *oa* the amount of A which the same amount of money will purchase. Then the line *ab* represents all combinations of A and B which can be bought with the given amount of money, and its slope represents the ratio of the price of A to that of B.)

Where such a line *ab* is tangent to a given isoquant, then the marginal rate of substitution of B for A is equal to the inverse of their price ratio, and at this point the firm finds the minimum-cost combination of factors for producing that output—thus in Figure 52, *ox* of A and *oy* of B to produce 950 units.[3] (That this is a cost-minimizing solution is verified by the fact that at the point of tangency we find the largest output which can be produced with the outlay to which *ab* refers, or the smallest outlay [as represented by successive lines like *ab*] with which the output in question can be produced.)

At any output which the firm chooses to produce, it will presumably minimize the cost of that output by employing available factors in such proportions that their marginal rates of substitution stand in the indicated relation to their price ratios. When this cost-minimizing combination is calculated for each of any relevant series of successive alternative outputs, the firm arrives at its cost curves for output, showing the minimized average and marginal costs for successive outputs. The level of these cost curves depends on the level of productivity of the combined factors (in terms of output obtained) and on the given prices of the factors. Given these cost curves, the firm chooses to produce that output for which marginal cost is equal to

[3] See J. R. Hicks, *Value and Capital*, Chaps. 6 and 7; and Boulding, *op. cit.*, Chap. 23, for a more detailed treatment.

price. It thus arrives not only at a determinate output, but at a determinate quantity of each factor to be purchased and used.

The amount it purchases of any factor then obviously depends on a complex of considerations—the price of the output it produces, the prices of the factors it buys, the general level of productivity of the factors, and the substitution relations among them. Given all these determinants, the quantity of any factor the firm purchases is its *demand* for that factor at its going price.

In addition, is it meaningful to speak of a firm's "demand curve" for any one factor, which would show the amount of the factor it would purchase at each of a range of factor prices? Assuming to be given the price for the firm's output and the prices of all other factors, we can trace the effect of the changes in the price of some one factor upon the quantity of it which a firm will buy. Thus, under the assumptions noted, we might plot a firm's demand curve for labor. As the price of labor is reduced, other factor prices remaining constant, the firm should simultaneously (1) substitute labor for other factors, to the end of minimizing cost of output, and (2) vary (that is, extend) output to *keep* marginal cost equal to price. Thus a reduction in the price of labor should increase the quantity a firm will purchase. The line showing the resulting relation of quantity purchased by a firm to price could be labeled the firm's demand curve for labor.

Thus, there might be a firm's "demand curve" for labor, for capital, or for land. In a sense each firm, in maximizing profits, is continually hiring each factor at the point where this "demand curve" intersects the supply curve for the factor.

PURCHASE OF FACTORS BY THE PURELY COMPETITIVE INDUSTRY

Let us now shift from a single firm in pure competition to an industry of such firms and inquire how the combination of their actions affects the determination of factor prices and employment. We have indicated that, where there are uniformly competitive conditions in factor markets, the supply of each factor to the firm will be perfectly elastic. Each factor price is given regardless of the amount taken, because any firm is too small a buyer to affect the price of any factor.

If we assume that there is one homogenous, economy-wide market for each factor, the same should be true of the small industry. That is, the total purchases of any factor by the industry would be so small that the industry cannot influence its price—the price of each factor is given to the industry. This may at any rate be assumed for purposes of illustrative argument.

The only new matter to be discussed for the industry, therefore, is the interaction of competing firms' demands for factors, in determining the quantities of several factors purchased at given prices. This interaction is linked with the familiar process of determination of long-run price and output for a competitive industry.

First, the process by which any *given* number of firms select outputs for which marginal cost is equal to price results in the determination of an industry price and output at which this is simultaneously possible for all firms. At such a provisional equilibrium point, all firms would be employing the various factors in determinate amounts and proportions—that is, such that for each firm marginal cost was equal to price, and that for each the several factors were employed in such proportion that their marginal rates of substitution were in balance with the ratio of their prices.

Second, the existence at this point of any excess profit or net loss induces entry or exit, until each firm is driven to the point of producing also at minimum average cost and to selling at a price equal to this cost. As this long-run equilibrium point was approached, each firm would correspondingly adjust its purchases of each factor according to the principles previously noted, and a given aggregate industry purchase of each factor would result. In this equilibrium the price of the industry's output under the pressure of free entry equals minimum average cost. There are no true profits, and the total payments to factors necessarily equal the total sales receipts of the industry. For an industry of competitive firms purchasing factors, the pressure of competitive price-output adjustments tends to force the industry purchases of hired factors (given their prices) to such a determinate long-run point.[4]

Can we now meaningfully speak of an industry's long-run "demand curve" for any factor—for example, labor. If we assume the prices of other factors to be given, we can trace the effect of a change in the price of one factor on the amount of it the industry buys. In this case, a reduction in the price of a factor will (1) induce its substitution for other factors to some extent, and (2) lower the minimum average unit costs of production of every firm, allowing (with a given demand for the industry's output) a larger total output. The addition to output will be supplied by the entry of new firms. The combined adjustments of substitution and entry should result in a determinate extension of the purchases of the factor by the industry.

The response of industry demand for the factor to change in its price

---

[4] The number of firms in such an equilibrium is determinate and finite provided the firm reaches minimum average costs at some finite output, on either side of which its average costs would be higher. The firm's U-shaped long-run average cost curve in turn results from the fact that the "firm" is not perfectly divisible or variable in size, and possibly from the indivisibilities of hired factors at very small firm outputs. We have neglected here, however, the effect of both sorts of indivisibility on substitution conditions. Recognition of these effects will not significantly modify our conclusions concerning industry equilibria.

will evidently depend strongly upon (1) the elasticity of demand for the product of the industry, (2) the degree or rate of substitutability of the factor in question for others (that is, how rapidly its marginal rate of substitution for other factors increases as its use is increased relative to that of other factors), and (3) whether added firms will be as efficient, or less or more so, than those preceding them. Reflecting all these conditions, a line can be drawn showing the relation of an industry's purchases of a factor to its price, and this might be called an industry's demand curve for a factor—for example, labor. It should be strongly emphasized, however, that such a curve is *not* simply an addition of individual firms' demand curves for a factor, since several industry-wide adjustments not taken into account in defining the firm's curve do enter into the definition of an industry demand curve.

PURCHASE OF FACTORS BY A COMPETITIVE ECONOMY

In investigating in turn the firm and the industry in pure competition as purchasers of factors, we have been able to elicit certain principles governing the quantity of factors such a firm or industry will take at given prices. But because the prices of factors may be assumed given to any one firm or industry, we have not yet come to grips with *the determination of factor prices* and with numerous important related matters.

We may now carry our analysis a step further by considering the purchase of factors *by a competitive economy*—that is, by an economy made up of a large number of industries in pure competition, all buying factors in purely competitive factor markets. We thus broaden our viewpoint to consider the interactions of the decisions of all buyers of all factors in a completely competitive situation.

Although the assumption of pure competition in all markets is unrealistic, the simultaneous consideration of the whole economy brings us much closer to fundamental issues than any analysis of individual industries ever could. The pricing of any productive factor is essentially an economy-wide phenomenon and cannot be fully understood by a particular analysis of individual industries. By considering the whole economy we bring into focus an essential consideration which must condition the outcome of income distribution and employment: the supplies of the various factors cannot be regarded as perfectly elastic to the economy—all factors are scarce and relatively inelastic in supply, and their prices thus remain to be determined. An added consideration is, of course, that the payments made to factors for the economy as a whole are the incomes from which demands for goods are forthcoming, and that the relations of total factor payments to total demand for goods must thus be made a part of the explanation of factor pricing and employment. This problem, however, we temporarily avoid by assuming a given flow of money purchasing power which remains constant in spite of factor-price adjustment. On this assumption, let us consider the problems of factor-price determination for the economy as a whole.

We suppose then that there is an economy of purely competitive industries which buy all factors in purely competitive factor markets, and that there is a given constant flow of money purchasing power or aggregate demand price for all outputs, regardless of the prices or rate of money payments to factors. These industries must thus buy a group of factors each of which is in relatively inelastic supply to the economy.

To simplify the problem further at first, let us suppose that for the economy each factor is in perfectly inelastic supply. That is, each factor is available in a fixed quantity per unit of time, and all of it can be bought at any price the market offers.

In these circumstances, the money price of each factor will necessarily move to such a level that the total demand for it by all industries in the economy will just equal its fixed supply—that is, to the level consistent with full employment. More generally, the family of money factor prices will arrive at such mutually consistent levels that this will be true simultaneously for all of them.

Let us trace the process which is implied. To any given *arbitrary* set of money prices for factors, all industries would tend to adapt themselves until each industry was in a purely competitive, long-run equilibrium (the interrelated prices for various industry products having reached a stable mutual adjustment). At this level there would tend to be a determinate aggregate economy-wide demand for each factor. But at these arbitrary money prices, the aggregate demand for any factor might either exceed or fall short of its fixed supply. That is, as firms in each industry strove to extend output to where the selling price of output was equal to the minimal average costs of production, as determined by the arbitrarily given level of factor prices, it might turn out either that not all the factor units required to accomplish this with going factor prices were available, or that not all available factor units were required. If the demand exceeded the supply for any factor, the money factor price would tend to be bid up until, with a tendency toward substitution against the factor and restriction of output due to higher costs, demand for it was equated with supply. If demand fell short of supply, competition among sellers in the factor market would drive the money factor price down, until with substitution in favor of the factor and extension of output, due to lower costs, demand was equated with supply.

Such an adjustment would proceed simultaneously for all factors until a mutually consistent set of money prices for them, such that for each in turn the demand of firms for it would just equal the total supply, was established. For the whole economy there would be a covariation of factor prices, factor proportions, commodity outputs, and commodity prices until a position was reached where there was full employment of every factor and where simultaneously every industry was in purely competitive long-run equilibrium with respect to cost-price relations and factor proportions. In this case (which, it must be emphasized, supposes universal pure competition, a given *constant* rate of flow of money purchasing power, and perfectly inelastic supplies of all factors) the end result would be full employment of all factors, price-average-cost equality for all industries and firms, and a total of money payments to factors which was just equal to the total flow of money sales receipts to firms. No true profits (in excess of total wages, rents, and interest) would be earned.

Two aspects of the resulting equilibrium of prices for the economy may be emphasized. First, the economy reaches an equilibrium *money factor-price level*—or average money price of factors—such that with the given flow of money payments all factors are fully employed and the total flow of money payments is spent in purchasing them. This equilibrium level of average money prices will depend upon the relation between size of the flow of money payments and the size of the aggregate supply of factors—there must be such a price level for factors that their total supply can just be bought with the total flow of money payments.

Second, for each of several factors to be just fully employed simultaneously, a certain relation of their relative prices must necessarily be reached. Competitive firms will employ factors in such proportions that their marginal rates of substitution equal the reciprocals of their price ratios. With some arbitrarily given ratio as between the prices of two factors, firms as a whole in the economy would employ some quantity, x_a, of factor A, and some quantity, x_b, of factor B, the ratios of the two quantities being such that the marginal rate of substitution of A for B equals the ratio of the price of B to the price of A in every firm. But unless their price ratio is initially "just right," this will not result in the full employment of both A and B at once. That is, supposing that the quantity firms wish to employ of A, x_a, is just equal to the total supply of A, the quantity they wish to employ of B, x_b, may be greater or less than the supply of B available. This is because when the factors are employed in just such proportion that their marginal rate of substitution equals the inverse of an arbitrary ratio of their prices, the resultant demands for them need not in both cases at once equal the total supplies of them.

As a result, equilibrium requires an adjustment of their relative prices to a certain point—an adjustment which will in fact automatically ensue as the price of an underemployed factor is bid down by excess supply or the price of an "overemployed" factor (one for which demand exceeds supply) is bid up by excess demand. *This equilibrium price ratio will necessarily be equal to the inverse of the marginal rate of substitution which will prevail between the factors throughout the economy when both are just fully employed.* That is, the price ratio will move up or down sufficiently to induce firms (which will employ factors only so that marginal rates of substitution are equal to the inverse of factor price ratios) to offer exactly full employment to both factors simultaneously.

As given quantities of any two factors move into use, they will necessarily be distributed among competitive firms in such proportions that in each firm the marginal rate of substitution between them is the same. This is so because every firm at any time faces the same pair of prices in the same pair of homogenous markets for the factors. If both factors are to move into use in just such amount to use the entire supply of each, the ratio of their prices must move to where its reciprocal is equal to the marginal rate of substitution between the factors which will be found simultaneously in all firms when the total supply of both factors is in use.

The equilibrium price ratio will thus depend (1) upon the substitution conditions between the factors, as described by the production isoquants in all of the lines of production and as defined by the going techniques of production, and (2) upon the relative quantities of the two factors which are supplied when both are fully employed. Since an increase in the quantity of one factor used relative to that of another leads generally to an increase in the marginal rate of substitution of the first factor for the second, it is therefore evident that an increased supply of any one factor would result in a lowering of its price relative to that of other factors if all were to be fully employed at once.

The preceding may be illustrated diagrammatically as follows. Suppose that we view a single firm, and its isoquant map showing substitution conditions between a pair of factors in producing its output, as representative of all firms in the economy and their respective isoquant maps in their several lines of production. Suppose further that this firm employs all of the factors in the economy, but according to competitive principles—that is, it takes factor prices as given, employs factors in such proportion that their marginal rate of substitution equals the inverse of the ratio of their prices, and is forced to operate where selling price equals average and marginal cost. The isoquant map of such a firm, showing alternative proportions of two factors needed to produce alternative outputs, is shown in Figure 53. This isoquant map simply says, with the curves Q_1 through Q_4, that the firm, given its technique, can produce an output Q_1 with any of the combinations of factors A and B shown on the Q_1 curve, an output Q_2 with any of the combinations of factors A and B shown on the Q_2 curve, and so forth.

Now let us suppose that the firm is to be induced to absorb in production the quantity oa of factor A and the quantity ob of factor B. What price ratio between the factors will induce it to employ the two factors in just this proportion? To ascertain this, we must determine the marginal rate of substitution between factors A and B when employed in this proportion. This marginal rate of substitution is evidently given by the slope of the isoquant Q_3 at point x, which slope gives the marginal rate of substitution of B for A when they are combined in the quantities ob and oa. The

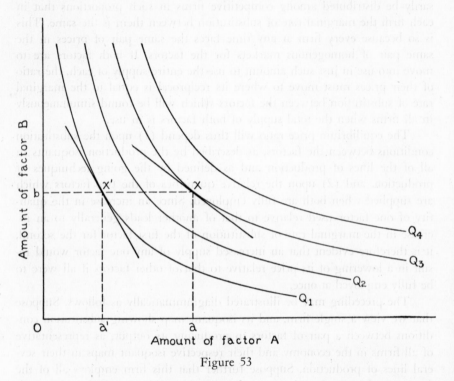

Figure 53

firm will experience this marginal rate of substitution, which we will estimate visually at $3:5$, if it employs all of both factors. (That is, 3 units of B will replace 5 units of A on the margin.) It follows that it can be induced to employ the factors in the given proportions only if the ratio of their prices is the inverse of this substitution ratio—that is, if the ratio of the price of B to the price of A is $5:3$—for example, \$10 to \$6. This price ratio, shown by the reciprocal of slope of a line tangent to Q_3 at x, must be attained to induce the simultaneous employment of the factors in the indicated quantities. If it were otherwise, the firm would employ them in other proportions.

Precisely the same principle applies to the economy of competitive firms —under full employment the equilibrium ratio of the prices of any pair of factors must equal the inverse of their marginal rate of substitution throughout the economy when both are fully employed. And this ratio will, if there is a constant flow of purchasing power, emerge automatically through a competitive adjustment of relative factor prices such as to assure full employment of both factors.

Suppose now that while the quantity of B remained constant at ob, the quantity of A available were instead oa'. Now the marginal rate of substitution of B for A would be given by the slope of Q_1 at the point x', and this marginal rate of substitution is higher since the proportion of B to A has increased. We may now visually estimate the marginal rate of substitution of B for A at $6:5$—it will take 6 units of B to replace 5 units of A at the margin. Now the price ratio required to induce the firm to employ the factors in the indicated proportion (ob of B to oa' of A will be $5:6$—the ratio of the price of B to the price of A must move to 5-to-6 (indicated by the reciprocal of the slope of a line tangent to Q_1 at x') if the firm is to be willing to employ the factors in this proportion. Thus, if the price of A were \$6, the price of B would have to be \$5 now instead of \$10. This illustrates the fact that an increase in quantity of one factor relative to another (of B relative to A in this case) leads to an increase in the marginal rate of substitution of the now more abundant for the now scarcer factor, and requires a decrease in the relative price of the augmented factor if the supplies of both it and the other are to be fully employed. Conversely, of course, a decrease in the supply of a factor used in production should lead to an increase in its relative price.

This principle is also directly applicable to an economy of competitive firms. An increase in the supply of any factor relative to that of others, given the techniques of production, will require a decline in its relative price if all factors are to remain fully employed, and competitive factor-price adjustments will tend to force this decline in relative price. Thus, an increase in the supply of labor, relative to a given supply of land and capital goods and with given techniques, will tend to bring about a decline in the competitive wage of labor as the added labor finds employment.

The condition for an equilibrium of relative factor prices under full employment has so far been stated in this form—that the inverse of the ratio of the prices of every pair of factors shall be equal to their marginal rate of substitution throughout the economy when both are fully employed. The ratio of the price of A to the price of B will equal the marginal rate of substitution of B for A. This principle may also be stated in an alternative form. As we have pointed out, the marginal rate of substitution between any pair of factors (for example, of B for A) is with any given combination equal to the inverse of the ratio of their marginal productivities (for example, the ratio of the marginal product of A to the marginal product of B). It follows that our equilibrium condition is also that the ratio of the prices of any two factors must under competitive conditions be the same as the ratio of their marginal products. If the combination of factors is such that both are fully employed, their prices must stand in the same ratio as their marginal products do in this situation. The tendency of the relative price of any factor to decline as its supply is increased relative to those of other factors is thus understood as reflecting the resultant decline in the marginal product of that factor in accordance with the law of diminishing returns.

Supposing variations in the quantity available of any one factor, can an economy-wide "demand curve" for the factor be constructed? It could be on the supposition that other factor supplies remained unchanged. The response of the price of such a factor to changes in the quantity offered for use would reflect an economy-wide composite of adjustments to such changes, including substitution between this and other factors and the changes in all costs, prices, and outputs, resulting from an increased or decreased supply of this factor, as the economy moved from some initial general equilibrium position to a second.

The preceding refers largely to the determination of the relative prices of productive factors, and shows that this turns, under full employment conditions, largely on the relative abundance of the factors and on the conditions of substitution among them (their relative marginal productivity) at the point where they are fully employed. What of the relative shares of income which each of several factors will receive? It is obvious, of course, that the income share of each factor in competitive equilibrium will be equal to its equilibrium price per unit times the number of units employed, and that income shares will follow from this relationship. In addition, it appears that if one factor is so abundant relative to others that its marginal rate of substitution for others is very high (its marginal productivity relatively very low), then the income share of that factor will be inclined to be small, and that of the *relatively* scarce factors very high, provided a relatively large absolute quantity, nevertheless, is employed. Thus, in an undeveloped frontier country of rich resources, land may be so abundant relative to labor that its competitive price is negligible and its competitive income share small, while labor receives almost the entire income. But in an old overpopulated country, labor may be so abundant relative to land that the substitution relationship is reversed, land prices are high, and landowners will receive a large share of income as determined through competitive markets.

How will an increase or decrease in the supply of one factor relative to that of others affect its income share? This will obviously depend on the elasticity of the economy-wide demand for the factor, which will in turn depend primarily on the substitutability between this and other factors. Thus, if the marginal rate of substitution of land for labor will increase rap-

COMPETITIVE FACTOR-PRICE DETERMINATION

idly if labor supply is slightly restricted, and decrease rapidly if the supply of labor is slightly increased, then a slight reduction in labor supply should lead to a considerable rise in its competitive price and an increase in its share of its total income, while a slight increase in labor supply should greatly reduce its competitive price and lessen its income share. Conversely, if a change in the supply of a factor leads to only a slight change in its marginal rate of substitution for other factors, the demand for it will be elastic; given supply changes will induce small price changes; and supply reduction will decrease and supply increases augment its income share.

Although these and similar principles are developed from an analysis resting on extremely simplified assumptions, they may have wide application to the world of practical affairs.

ECONOMY-WIDE DETERMINATION OF FACTOR PRICES
WITH ELASTIC FACTOR SUPPLIES

So far, we have assumed that the supply of each factor is perfectly inelastic to the economy—every unit of a given supply will accept any price offered rather than forego employment. It is obvious, however, that this may not be the case for at least some factors. An alternative is that such factors will not be offered for use unless a certain minimum price is paid, and that different units of a given factor supply may have different "reservation" prices, so that in effect some of the supply may be obtained at a low price, and successive additional amounts at successively higher prices. In this case, there will be a positively sloping supply curve for the factor, indicating the alternative amounts which will be supplied at successive alternative prices, and, potentially, the entire withdrawal of supply if price falls below some minimal level.

The relation of the supply of a factor to the price offered for it may potentially be of two sorts. First, there may be a given relation of the supply of the factor to the money price offered for the factor—a relation which holds inflexibly between supply and the dollars-and-cents price *regardless* of the buying power of the dollars involved (that is, regardless of the level of commodity prices in terms of money). Such a supply relationship would seem illogical (since the suppliers of factors should presumably be more interested in the real purchasing power of the incomes paid them than in the absolute number of dollars received), but it is not impossible to conceive. Second, there may be a given relation between the supply of the factor and the *real price* offered for the factor—that is, the quantity of commodities which the money paid to the factor will purchase at the going level of commodity prices. In this case, the supply of the factor offered will bear no fixed relation to its money price (unless commodity prices are arbitrarily given), but it will bear a definite relation to the real purchasing power of the money price paid the factor. In this case, the supply curve relating the money price of the factor to its supply will shift with every change in commodity prices which may occur in a process of adjustment.

Let us first consider the case in which the factors do not have perfectly inelastic supplies, but instead have given money price supply curves, showing a fixed relation between factor supply and money price of factors re-

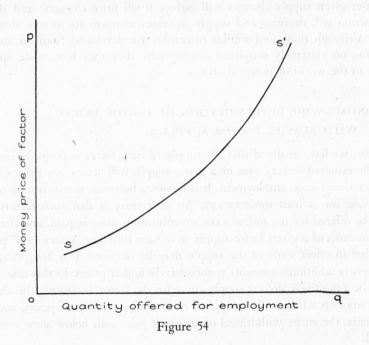

Figure 54

gardless of the level of commodity prices. Such a supply curve is shown in Figure 54. In this case, to what extent is the preceding analysis of competitive factor-price determination altered?

Under the assumed conditions, the burden of the preceding analysis applies without serious revision, but it must take account of one important added circumstance. Instead of the total supply of each factor being available at any price the competitive market may finally set, factor supply is contingent on the payment of a certain money price or range of prices, and the supply will presumably be larger as the price is higher and smaller as the price is lower. To secure employment of the total supply of any factor, the money price set in the market must be as great as that necessary to attract the units of the supply having the highest supply price; if it is lower, then some units of the supply will refuse employment and remain unemployed. For example, the supply schedule for a given factor A might read as follows:

Price	Amount supplied
$5	50,000
4	45,000
3	40,000
2	35,000
1	30,000

This schedule says that if $1 is set as the price for the factor, 30,000 units of the factor will be supplied; if instead $2 is set as the price, 35,000 units will be supplied, etc. If this is the case, supposing the total supply of the factor to be 50,000 units, a market price of $5 will be necessary to induce the total supply to be offered for employment; if it is lower, some units of the supply will refuse employment, and there will thus be unemployed factors.

Such a supply curve may tentatively be supposed to exist for each of the several productive factors. If now an economy-wide complex of competitive firms bids for these factors, and a competitive equilibrium is approached, the processes of adjustment earlier described are complicated to the following extent. Firms will still take the prices of factors as given to them. They will adjust their employment of factors so that the marginal rate of substitution between any pair of factors equals the inverse of their price ratio, and so that simultaneously, in the long run, marginal and average costs equal the selling price of output. If the resultant demands for factors at any initial set of factor prices do not equal the supplies of those factors which are forthcoming at those prices, then factor prices will tend to be bid up or down in response to an excess of demand or of supply.

As prices adjust, however, factor supplies now respond to the price changes, so that price adjustments induce not only changes in the proportions and amounts in which firms use factors, but also the supplies of factors available for use. Evidently, the equilibrium price situation which will be approached requires (1) that the *price level* (average price) of factors be such that all of the factors offered for employment at those prices can be employed by full expenditure of the given flow of money purchasing power, (2) that the demand for each factor be just equal to its supply at that price, and (3) that therefore the ratio of the prices of each pair of factors be equal to the inverse of their marginal rate of substitution when the amounts of the factors supplied at these prices are employed in combination throughout the economy. In effect, instead of determining just relative factor prices and a general money level of such prices when the supply of each factor to be employed is absolutely given—as it does with perfectly inelastic factor supplies—the competitive price system now also determines simultaneously the quantities of each factor which will be attracted into employment. The money supply curves for factors interact with the substitution conditions among factors in all lines of production and with the total flow of money purchasing power to determine the level of employment and the relative and absolute prices of all factors.

How may the results now differ from those which would be obtained if the supply of each factor were perfectly inelastic, so that all of it would inevitably be employed? Principally, it is evident that full employment is by no means assured for all or any factors. General unemployment is quite possible. If the flow of money purchasing power is constant at a given level, and if the money price necessary to induce full employment of each factor is quite high, then there may simply be too small a flow of money to hire all units of all factors simultaneously. Suppose that there is a total supply of factor A of 100,000 units per year, which will require a price of $5 to induce all of it to be offered for employment, and a total supply of 50,000 units of B, which will require a price of $10 to attract all of it. Then a total expenditure of $1 million is obviously necessary to induce full employment of A and B. If the total flow of money purchasing power is limited to $750,000 per year, there will not be full employment of both factors unless the units of their supplies which require the highest prices are willing to accept less. There may be less than full employment of *both* A and B, unless their relative prices stipulated in their supply curves are such relative to their substitution relationships as to induce firms to employ all of one (at the maximum or a higher price) while employing less than all of the other. In the latter case, the burden of unemployment would fall entirely on one factor, and this would reflect the fact that the relative price required to induce it to be supplied proportionally to the other factor was higher than the relative price which would induce competitive firms to employ it proportionally.

In general, the employment of any factor may be restricted by the fact that some or all of its units have relatively high money supply prices. We might observe much less than full employment of one factor, many units of which would accept only rather high prices, side by side with full employment or close to full employment of other factors, all or most units of which would accept lower prices. In effect, there is still some ratio of the factor prices which a competitive economy will pay where all units of all factors are employed, and this is equal in the case of any pair to the inverse of their marginal rate of substitution when both are fully used. But the ratio of the money prices which will just induce all units of all factors to be supplied may differ from this ratio. In this case simultaneous full employment will not be attained except where the flow of money purchasing power is great enough to bid all factor prices to or above the levels necessary to attract the total supply.

If underemployment of one or more factors should ensue for the reason mentioned, this much is evident. The unemployment would be "voluntary" in the sense that it would result from the unwillingness of unemployed factors to accept as low a money price as a competitive market would offer. An equilibrium with some amount of unemployment would be quite tenable, however, provided there were a given flow of purchasing power and inflexibly stipulated money factor prices. At this equilibrium, as before, the total of factor payments would equal the total receipts of enterprise, with no true profits for competitive industry. But net unemployment could result, and if it did, it would be the result of arbitrary money factor prices.

It is also evident that such unemployment would in a sense be arbitrary because of the arbitrarily given flow of money purchasing power. If the factors in fact simply stipulated for given money prices along certain supply curves, any unemployment could be eradicated by simply increasing the flow of money purchasing power, and bidding up to the level of money factor (and commodity) prices sufficiently to attract all factor supplies into employment. The suppositions on which the preceding model rests—that both the flow of money purchasing power and the money supply prices of factors are inflexibly given—is, in fact, somewhat unrealistic if adjustments over any considerable period of time are considered. For short-run adjustments, however, such inflexibilities may occur, and in these cases the preceding analysis may have some predictive value.

A second and perhaps more realistic case is that in which each factor of production has a given supply curve which relates the supply offered of the factor not to its money price but to its real price—that is, to the purchasing power in terms of commodities of the money price paid to it. This is equivalent to saying that there is a given relation between the supply of the factor and its money price *as adjusted for changes in the commodity price level*. If this were the case, then the economy-wide supply curves for factors of production would intrinsically be expressed in "real" terms—that is, each one would express the relation between the amount of real goods implicitly offered in payment to a factor and the quantity of the factor which would be offered for employment. Actually, of course, enterprises would pay money prices and factors would hold out for money prices. But if the decisions of factors or their owners turned on "real income" considerations, we would find that the money price supply curves of factors were not arbitrarily given, but shifted progressively in response to shifting commodity prices until a final equilibrium was reached.

In this equilibrium it would, of course, be true that the money price of each factor had reached a level where all units of the factor offered for employment at this money price were employed, thus determining a level of employment for each, and that the prices of any pair of factors stood in a ratio equal to the inverse of their marginal rate of substitution with the indicated amounts combined in employment. But it would also be true that all units of any factor willing to work for the real income which its money price could purchase were employed, since if they were not their supply would not be in balance with demand and they would bid down their money price until this condition was fulfilled.

There would still presumably be unemployment, but it would be truly "voluntary" in the sense that the only unemployed units would be those which refused to work for the real income which the market in equilibrium would pay. Such a complete elimination of "involuntary" unemployment, with progressive adaptation of the money prices of factors until the "real" prices paid them were equal to the real withholding prices of the marginal unemployed units, is quite possible so long as the flow of money payments is unaffected by the process of factor-price adaptation.

If this were true, and if in addition all suppliers of factors thought ultimately in "real" terms, considering the prices required to induce them to work in relation to the commodity prices on which they spent their incomes, the specific level of the flow of money payments would be of no consequence. The same real equilibrium of employment, output, and *relative* prices of commodities and of factors would be struck at any level of money income. The only thing influenced by the size of the money flow would be the absolute level of money prices for commodities and factors.

A world where the flow of money payments was in effect self-perpetuating and where factor supplies were determined only by the real prices they would receive, would obviously be a very simple economic world. The level of employment of all factors, the level of output, the relative prices of commodities, and the relative shares of total income received by various factors could work themselves out to a long-run equilibrium without setting up any cumulative or frustrating disturbances in the flow of money payments. The flow of payments would be a neutral consideration in the economy, and it would not be surprising if people came to calculate alternatives primarily in real terms, viewing money strictly as a "veil."

A remarkable sort of balance would then tend to be struck by a purely competitive economy. Perhaps the most significant aspect of this equilibrium is that there would be for each factor, regardless of the size of money payments, a determinate level of employment involving no involuntary unemployment. The relative shares of income going to the various factors would depend upon their relative productivity under prevailing techniques, upon their relative scarcity, and upon the relationships between the quantities of them which would be supplied and the real prices offered for them.

Otherwise we cannot say a priori how large the wage bill, for example, would be relative to the total of interest or rent payments. But we can say that in the situation noted (self-perpetuating flow of payments, universal pure competition, and calculation of economic alternatives primarily in real terms) the result would be quite automatic, free from any deliberate control by individuals, and definitely determined at a unique competitive equilibrium level.

ECONOMY-WIDE DETERMINATION OF FACTOR PRICES
UNDER PURE COMPETITION—SUMMARY

In the preceding pages, we have analyzed the determination of factor prices in an economy where all factor and commodity markets are purely competitive under three successive assumptions concerning the supply conditions of the factors. In every case the analysis has rested on certain basic simplifying assumptions: (1) that there is a given constant flow of money purchasing power, which is unaffected by adjustments of factor and commodity prices, (2) that each factor is a basic inanimate commodity available in given and limited supply in each time period, and with a given relation of the quantity supplied to the price offered, and (3) that there is a single homogeneous market for each factor, in which all firms make their purchases. As regards specific supply conditions, however, we have successively assumed: (1) that each factor has a perfectly inelastic supply, so that the total quantity will be made available at any price offered; (2) that there is an elastic supply curve for each factor which relates the quantity of the factor supplied to the money price offered, so that in general larger proportions of any total factor supply will be made available at successively higher money prices, but that money factor prices are governing regardless of the flow of money purchasing power or the level of commodity prices; and (3) that there is an elastic supply curve for each factor which relates the quantity of the factor supplied to the real price offered for it (that is, to the quantity of commodities its money price will purchase), so that the relationship of the factor supply to the money price offered shifts in direct response to commodity price changes which occur in the process of an adjustment. Under these general assumptions and under the special alternative assumptions outlined, what conclusions have been drawn concerning competitive factor-price determination?

Some conclusions hold in general for *all* alternative factor supply situations. First, the purely competitive equilibrium will in every case involve in each industry a price-cost relation such that price is equal to marginal and to minimal average cost and that there are no excess or true profits. This follows from the fact that with easy entry and with atomistic competition in all industries both in selling output and buying factors, the firms buying factors will—whatever the quantity of factors ultimately supplied in equilibrium—bid up the prices of factors and bid down the prices of commodities to the point where average costs are everywhere equal to prices, and to where the firm can survive only at optimal scale, so that a profitless long-run equilibrium is reached.

Second, the equilibrium will never involve the unemployment of factors which are willing to work at the money prices which the competitive market offers them, since with a constant flow of purchasing power seeking their services, factor prices will always be bid down by any excess of supply over demand until they reach the level where supply equals demand—that is, where all factors which wish to work at the going money price are employed. However, this does not mean that every unit of each factor on hand will be employed, since the competitive market price may be insufficient to induce some units to be offered for use, on the ground either that the money price per se is too low or that the real price (commodities purchasable with the money price) is too low. But there can be no *involuntary* unemployment, where factors wish to work at the price offered but are not employed.

Third, the prices of the factors employed will necessarily stand in a determinate relationship—such that the ratio between the prices of any two factors will be equal to the inverse of the marginal rate of substitution between the factors (found simultaneously in every firm in the economy) when they are employed in the quantities offered in the competitive equilibrium. This is equivalent to saying that their prices must stand in the same relation as their marginal productivities in all lines with given quantities of each employed. Fourth, the absolute level of real factor prices will, of course, be determined by the absolute productivity of the factors in the going state of technique—whatever their total product, they receive it all. Fifth, their relative real prices and relative shares of real income depend on the relative quantities in which they are supplied and on the substitution conditions among them.

The preceding is true under our general assumptions regardless of the particular character of factor supply curves. Let us now review the differences in the character of a competitive equilibrium with different factor supply situations. The character of factor supply curves will potentially affect the extent to which the entire supply of any or all factors is employed under competitive equilibrium, and, so far as the relative quantities of various factors employed are affected, their relative prices.

If all factor supplies are perfectly inelastic—if every unit of any factor will be made available for use at any price offered—it follows that in competitive equilibrium there will be full employment of all factors (their prices will fall relative to money purchasing power until all are employed). It also follows that their relative prices will be unequivocally given, so that the ratio of the prices of any two factors is equal to the inverse of their marginal rate of substitution in all lines of production when the full supply of each is in use.

If factor supplies are not perfectly inelastic, but instead stand in a given elastic relation to the money prices offered for them, then it is not necessary that, with a given flow of money purchasing power, the total supply of each should be employed. Relatively high money reservation prices (below which some of the units of one or more factor supply will not be made available for use) may mean that the given flow of money purchasing power is insufficient to sustain full employment of one or all factors. Then the competitive equilibrium will simply fix a determinate level of employment for each factor, where the price offered for each brings forth a supply equal to the amount firms are willing to employ, and where the total flow of money purchasing power is spent on buying factors in general. The prices of any pair of factors will necessarily stand in a ratio which equals the inverse of the marginal rate of substitution between the factors with the determined levels of employment, but such price ratios are potentially quite different than would obtain if the total supply of each factor were employed. If in this circumstance one factor receives a higher relative price than it would with perfectly inelastic factor supplies, this is because a high reservation price for some units of this factor has led to at least some restriction in the quantity of it employed.

In this case, as we have indicated above, there may be "voluntary" unemployment of some units of one or more factors, because the competitive money price offered is insufficient to induce them to be supplied. But the maintenance of such unemployment in equilibrium would seem to be largely arbitrary or accidental—the incident either of a fixed flow of money purchasing power (which should in fact be able to be increased through credit devices) or of an arbitrary stipulation by a certain factor or factors for a money price above the level where full employment can be had. Although such arbitrary stipulations may occur in the actual world, the unemployment encountered should be easily eliminable in the assumed situation. On the one hand, it would be remedied by increasing the money flow in the economy—as, for example, by governmental creation and expenditure of new money. This would overcome any unemployment caused by simple arbitrary rigidity of the money prices of factors, provided that such money prices were not adjusted upward as the money flow increased. More generally, such unemployment would not persist (or could be altered to a more rational level) if the factors or their owners ceased holding out for arbitrary money prices, and adjusted their stipulations with an eye to the *real income,* in terms of commodities, which their money incomes would buy. If this were the case, the economy-wide "supply curves" for factors of production would intrinsically be expressed in "real" terms—that is, each one would express the relation between the amount of real goods implicitly offered in payment to a factor and the quantity of the factor which would be offered for employment. The money prices of factors would necessarily adjust to a level where no unit of any factor willing to work at the real price offered was unemployed. Any unemployment then would be rationally voluntary, and in a sense unemployment would be absent in that the value of leisure to unemployed units of any factor would exceed the value of the real goods they could obtain by working.

If indeed factor supply curves do expressly state a relation of real factor prices to quantities supplied, then the following differences in adjustment are to be noted. First, the final equilibrium will find every unit of each factor employed which is willing to work at the real price offered by the market, although there may be voluntarily unemployed units which will not be offered for use at such a price. Second, the relative prices of the factors will be determined by the marginal rates of substitution among the factors when such quantities are employed. Since in this case the money prices of factors per se are of no consequence to those supplying the factors, the same equilibrium of quantities employed and relative prices should be reached regardless of the size of the flow of money purchasing power and of the consequent level of money prices of commodities and factors.

LIMITATIONS OF THE PRECEDING ANALYSIS

In the preceding pages we have attempted to develop, by arguing from certain highly simplified assumptions, an understanding of the basic forces influencing the determination of factor prices and of income distribution in an enterprise economy. We have been enabled to see how the demand by business firms for productive factors, as determined in the aggregate by the flow of money purchasing power seeking the firms' outputs and in the case of each factor by the substitution relation between that and other factors, interacts with the supplies of the several factors to determine a set of absolute and relative factor prices at a determinate level of employment. The crucial importance has been seen of (1) the varying marginal rates of substitution among factors as their proportions are varied, (2) the character of the supply curves for factors, and whether supplies are determined by real or money prices, and (3) the size of the flow of money purchasing power in those cases where factor supplies are related to money rather than to real prices.

In addition, we have been able to advance a specific prediction of the pattern of factor prices and of income distribution which would emerge in one very simplified set of circumstances in an enterprise economy. There is attractiveness in the concise simplicity of the equilibrium tendencies thus predicted, and this appeal may explain the disposition of some economists to confuse the simple model world for which these tendencies are predicted with the one we actually have. It should therefore be re-emphasized most strongly (1) that conditions in the actual world in many respects do not conform at all closely to those so far assumed for purposes of argument, and (2) that the theory developed can only be viewed as a drastically oversimplified and rather distant first approximation to an adequate theory based on assumptions more adequately descriptive of real conditions. We have developed it first only because it is a convenient first step in the development of a more adequate theory, and because a more adequate theory is perhaps most easily developed by beginning with this simple one and modifying it progressively through the introduction of additional and more realistic assumptions.

Let us then review the crucial simplifying assumptions made above which must eventually be modified in order to arrive at a more general and adequate theory of income distribution. First, we have assumed throughout that there is in the economy a given and constant flow of money purchasing power (entering firms as sales receipts for their outputs and leaving them as income payments) which remains unchanged from period to period through time as the competition of firms in selling goods and buying factors, and of those owning factors in selling them, leads to adjustments of both commodity and factor prices. We have assumed that upward or downward movements of factor and commodity prices will induce no corresponding movement in the flow of money purchasing power to firms as sales receipts or to income recipients. This is equivalent, as we have seen, to assuming that in final equilibrium there can be no involuntary unemployment of factors—that a ratio between the flow of money payments and the level of commodity and factor prices will be struck in which every unit of any factor which is offered for employment at the going factor price will be employed. To be sure, voluntary unemployment of a rather capricious character and amount could be encountered if factors required arbitrary money prices, unrelated to real prices, in order to be induced to work, but if they do not do this, there could be voluntary unemployment only to the extent that the real price offered by a competitive market in equilibrium was insufficient to bring some units into use. The theory of income distribution developed is thus in essence a full-employment (no involuntary unemployment) theory of income distribution, since it implicitly rules out by assumption the possibility of involuntary unemployment.

This may not be very realistic. A self-sustaining flow of money income through the economy which remains constant in spite of factor-price adjustments may not be found in fact. It would be found if in effect the aggregate sales receipts of enterprises, received in any given time period and either distributed to hired factors or held or distributed as profits, were always exactly respent in the following time period, and thus created in that period an aggregate demand price for goods or aggregate of sales receipts for enterprises exactly the same as in the preceding period. Then the flow of purchasing power to and through enterprises would be at the same rate in each succeeding month or quarter or year as in the preceding one, and would be constant through time. For this to be so, income recipients as a group (including profit receivers) would have always to spend no more and no less than their current incomes—would never spend more by dishoarding cash balances and never spend less by hoarding some current income to add to cash balances. Then a supply of goods would always create its own demand, in the sense that the total of money income payments made to produce any aggregate of goods would always be spent to buy these goods, sustaining a constant money flow.

Now although such a constancy of the money flow might be found from time to time in the progress of an economy, it cannot be generally assumed. Dishoarding and hoarding do occur, and the money flow thus does wax and wane through time. More important, the money flow may respond in a systematic way to factor-price adjustments, so that, for example, a downward movement in hired factor prices will induce some corresponding downward movement in the flow of money purchasing power, and an upward movement in factor prices some corresponding increase in money purchasing power. If this is so, it is by no means assured that competitive adjustments in factor prices will bring about a ratio of these prices to money purchasing power such that involuntary unemployment is eliminated. If, for example, beginning with a set of factor prices and a money flow such that there was some involuntary employment, every downward adjustment of factor prices brought about a proportional decline in the money flow, full employment could not be attained. Automatic full employment, thus, cannot be safely assumed for all conceivable circumstances.

It remains for us to develop a theory of the determination of the level of employment, which is in essence a theory of the determination of the ratio of factor and commodity prices to the rate of flow of money purchasing power through the economy. This theory will suggest that in alternative circumstances we may find either full employment or involuntary unemployment. If this is the case, it follows that the theory of income distribution developed so far is directly applicable (even given other limiting assumptions) only to situations where full employment will be attained. It will require modification if it is to offer predictions for cases in which there is a systematic tendency toward involuntary unemployment of some units of one or more productive factors.

A second general assumption made above which oversimplifies matters drastically is that each factor is a basic inanimate commodity, with a supply which is given and independent of the supply of any other factor, and with some given supply curve relating the amount made available to the real or money price offered. Adoption of this assumption has made it possible for us to avoid consideration of the peculiarities of the supply conditions of each of the three basic factors—labor, land, and capital—and of the interrelationship of capital supply with other factor supplies. We must shortly elaborate our theory by taking at least some account in our assumptions of the peculiar supply problems and interrelationships which actually exist in order to develop predictions more directly applicable to the actual determination of factor prices and income shares.

A third assumption on which the preceding analysis has rested is that there is pure competition in all markets for commodities and for factors. That is, all firms sell their outputs in purely competitive markets, and buy factors in markets with many small buyers, many small sellers, and homogeneous factor supplies. The theory of income distribution developed is thus clearly a theory of competitive income distribution. It does not take into account the effects on income distribution of monopoly in commodity markets or of monopsony or monopoly in factor markets—or of monopolistic or monopsonistic tendencies which may emerge from oligopoly or oligopsony at the various levels. We must thus proceed to modify the competitive theory by introducing appropriate assumptions concerning the existence of other than purely competitive situations in commodity and factor markets.

Fourth, we have assumed that for each of a few basic factors there is a single homogeneous market, with all units of any factor identical, in which all firms in the economy make their purchases of that factor. This means we have neglected the possibility that the units of any basic factor may differ somewhat in quality and character, and that they may be sold not in a single market, but in a series of quasi-separate markets, each with a provisionally given fraction of all buyers and a provisionally given segment of the factor supply, between which submarkets there may be less than perfectly fluid movement of either buyers or sellers. This possibility needs clearly to be taken into account in developing a theory more adequately descriptive of the real world.

In sum, all of the four assumptions outlined which have been made in developing a theory of income distribution to this point must be relaxed or modified as we proceed in the development of this theory.

CHARACTER OF THE SUCCEEDING ANALYSIS

As a matter of procedure, we shall pursue the following order in relaxing the several assumptions reviewed above. First, in the next chapter we shall relax the last two assumptions just mentioned—that there is a single homogeneous market for each factor and that all markets are purely competitive—and will consider the determination of factor prices and income shares in a variety of disparate submarkets for factors and subject to various possible monopolistic or monopsonistic influences. For purposes of this analysis we shall continue to assume that each factor is a basic inanimate commodity (although possibly with some differentiation among units or groups of units within the total supply), and that there is a constant flow of money purchasing power in spite of price adjustments, so that absence of involuntary unemployment is assured. We shall thus attempt to determine in relative isolation the importance of monopolistic and monopsonistic tendencies on income distribution, without complicating the analysis through a simultaneous consideration of the character of actual factor supplies or the effects of underemployment.

Second, in Chapter 13 we shall take into account the peculiar characteristics of the actual supply conditions for capital, labor, and land, and thus try to develop more specific predictions concerning the relationships among the factor prices known as interest, wages, and rent under both competitive and monopolistic conditions. In this analysis we shall continue to assume the absence of involuntary unemployment.

Third, in Chapter 14 we shall relax the assumption that the behavior of the money income flow is such as to assure full employment, and will analyze in detail the determination of the level of employment, and concurrently of the level and movement of money income and of the money price level.

Finally, in Chapter 15, we shall reconsider the theory of income distribution under conditions of underemployment as well as of full employment, and under conditions of dynamic change in money income as well as of stability or equilibrium, concluding with a review of the determinants and probable behavior of enterprise profits in alternative situations.

We turn immediately, however, to the influence of monopoly and monopsony on income distribution, and to that of the existence of disparate submarkets for factors, under conditions which lead inevitably to stable equilibrium.

SUPPLEMENTARY READINGS

JOSEPH A. SCHUMPETER, *The Theory of Economic Development,* Cambridge, Mass.: Harvard University Press, 1934.

J. R. HICKS, *Value and Capital,* Part II.

OSCAR LANGE AND F. M. TAYLOR, *On the Economic Theory of Socialism,* Minneapolis: University of Minnesota Press, 1938.

JOHN MAYNARD KEYNES, *The General Theory of Employment, Interest, and Money,* New York: Harcourt, Brace and Company, 1936, Chap. 3.

J. R. HICKS AND A. G. HART, *The Social Framework of the American Economy,* New York: Oxford University Press, 1945.

THE DISTRIBUTION OF INCOME

12 —DISPARATE SUBMARKETS, MO-

NOPOLY, AND MONOPSONY

In the process of developing a more realistic theory of income distribution, two modifications may now be made in the analysis of the preceding chapters. First, we shall recognize the existence of disparate submarkets
for any basic productive factor, like labor or land, and inquire into the determination of the separate prices of the various segments of any factor
supply in its separate submarkets. Second, we shall abandon the assumption of pure competition at all relevant levels and consider the consequences
for income distribution of monopoly and monopsony. These analyses may
be most easily pursued while retaining previous assumptions that there is
a constant and self-sustaining flow of money purchasing power and that
each factor is a sort of basic inanimate commodity with a supply independent of that of other factors.

A. DISPARATE SUBMARKETS FOR PRODUCTIVE
   FACTORS

THE EXISTENCE OF SUBMARKETS

So far we have spoken for purposes of analysis as if each of two or three
basic productive factors were a single homogeneous good or service sold in
a single market to all firms in the economy. In this event, for example, every
labor hour sold would be like every other, and every hour of land service
like every other. Moreover, each would be bought from a single homogeneous market.

These conditions are obviously not found in fact. The assumption that
they are represents a considerable forced simplification of a complex reality. Therefore, it is desirable to recognize at least briefly the complications
of analysis introduced by nonhomogenity of productive factors and by the
corresponding existence of disparate submarkets for each factor.

The desirability of doing so is suggested by a consideration of some actual characteristics of the market for labor. Labor as a factor of production is not a homogeneous commodity but a series of imperfect substitute commodities differentiated by skills, quality, and location. Thus, there is common labor, carpentry labor, machinist's labor, various grades of supervisory and managerial labor, and so forth. Buyers do not demand labor in general but have an express demand for each type. Sellers of labor similarly offer some specific type of labor, at least at any one time. For each skill or special type of labor service there thus tends to be a separate submarket, with its own conditions of demand and supply and with a quasi-independent price-determining mechanism. Similarly, the submarket for any specific skill tends to be subdivided further on the basis of location. The services of specific laborers are immediately available only in areas contiguous to their residences, and thus only to buyers whose plants are located near them. There thus tends to be for each skill a series of quasi-separate local markets, with local demand and supply conditions, separated by barriers of distance and transport cost. Other subdivisions of the labor market could be recognized. In framing the general analytical problem, we may assume the presence of such segmentation in the market for any productive factor.

EFFECTS OF FACTOR IMMOBILITY AS AMONG SUBMARKETS

As long as no additional complexity is recognized and we still suppose the existence of purely competitive buying and selling conditions in each submarket for a factor, we should modify the conclusions of our previous analysis in the following fashion. First, if we suppose that in each submarket for a factor both the supply of the factor there and the circumstances determining the demand for it (that is, demand conditions for outputs it produces and availability of other factors) are provisionally given, then in each such submarket a provisional equilibrium would tend to be established, of the sort previously ascribed to any homogeneous total market for a factor. Within each submarket an equilibrium factor price would be determined, balancing demand for the factor against its supply, such that the ratio of the factor price to the prices of other factors would be determined by its marginal rate of substitution for them, and that its absolute price, together with those of other factors, would be such as to produce an equality of average total cost with the selling price of output. In effect, given the factor supply in each submarket, there would be a separate purely competitive factor-price equilibrium in each such market.

Second, unless the relative supplies of the factor in various submarkets were related in a single unique fashion to the relative demands, this would result in an economy-wide family of disparate prices for the factor in the different submarkets—various differentiated fractions of the total factor supply would receive different prices. Thus, in the case of labor, the provisional equilibrium wage might be $2 per hour for San Francisco carpenters, $1.50 per hour for Memphis carpenters, $1.75 per hour for Memphis skilled mechanics, $2.25 per hour for Boston skilled mechanics, $300 per month for New York City junior accountants. With constant total purchasing power and adjustable factor prices, full employment could obtain in every sub-market, but identity of prices for any factor as among submarkets would not in general be found.

Third, this solution would be only provisional or transitional unless units of the factor were wholly immobile from one submarket to the other. So far as there was mobility of the units of any factor between submarkets, there should be a tendency (if sellers of the factor seek the largest available return) for units of the factor to shift from low-price to high-price markets, thus readjusting relative supplies and bringing the prices of the factor in various submarkets closer together. Thus, some Memphis carpenters receiv-ing $1.50 an hour might tend to move to San Francisco, where the wage was $2 an hour, resulting in a rise in the Memphis wage and a fall in the San Francisco wage. Or carpenters might try to become skilled mechanics for higher pay, if possessing the requisite ability.

If there were absolutely free mobility of the units of any factor among submarkets, of course—such, for example, that any laborer could perform any task as well as any other laborer and was ready to move anywhere for extra compensation—then the price of any factor would become the same in every submarket and we would have the equivalent of a single homo-geneous market for the factor. If any laborer could offer an hour of brick-laying or an hour of chemical laboratory research work with equal facility, and if bricklaying paid $3 per hour as compared with $2.50 for laboratory research, workers would shift to bricklaying until the two rates were equalized. If labor were perfectly mobile and moved freely in pursuit of the highest wage regardless of where the work was offered, then the wage rate of New Orleans steamfitters would inevitably equalize with that of steam-fitters in Seattle. Supply would simply shift from market to market until the wage rates everywhere were equal.

With less than perfect mobility but nevertheless some mobility of units of the factor among submarkets—which will ordinarily be found in fact—factor-price differentials among submarkets for any factor would tend to approach a determinate pattern. This would be such that in any submarket with a higher factor price than another submarket, the favorable price dif-ferential was insufficient to attract units of the factor from the other sub-market, because either (1) factor units in the lower-priced market were ab-solutely immobile or not usable in the higher-priced market, (2) the lower efficiency of such units in the higher-paid pursuit would result in their get-ting no more than they were at present, or (3) the cost of movement of factor units to the higher-price market was such as to outweigh the price advantage. In effect, the "natural" limitations on mobility of various segments of the total supply of a factor among alternative uses or locations, together with the relative supplies of and demands for the factor in various uses and locations prior to any factor movement, would determine a competitive pattern of price differentials for any productive factor.

In this case, factor-price differentials as among submarkets would not be closely related to differences in the elasticity of demand for the factor as among submarkets. In some submarkets the demand for a factor might be quite inelastic to price change, because in the lines of production there involved the marginal rate of substitution of the factor for others would fall rapidly if its supply were restricted and because the commodities produced had inelastic demands, so that a high factor price and resultant high costs would not much restrict output or the use of the factor. In others, where other factors were readily substituted for the one in question and commodity demands were more elastic, the demand for the factor might be much more elastic to price change. In this event, a very moderate restriction in supply of the factor in the submarket of inelastic demand would result in a much higher factor price than in the other submarket. With no other than "natural" impediments to factor mobility, however, there would be no necessary relation of factor-price differences to differences in demand elasticity as between two such submarkets. With perfect factor mobility, the factor would receive the same price in both submarkets. With natural limitations on mobility, either of the submarkets might have the higher factor price, depending on the initial relative supplies and the character of barriers to movement. In the labor market, for example, occupations which might exact very high wages without losing much employment would earn no more than others unless the supply of labor for such occupations was relatively limited and mobility into those occupations was naturally restricted. The elasticity of demand for labor in specific submarkets would not be a matter of great moment.

On the other hand, the imposition of artificial barriers to the movement of a factor supply among submarkets, with resulting artificial restrictions on the supply of a factor in particular submarkets, could lead, even under conditions of competitive buying and selling in each submarket, to artificial differentials among them. In this case, moreover, the elasticity of demand for the factor in particular submarkets (as determined by interfactor substitution conditions and the elasticity of demand for the commodities produced) would have a potentially strong influence on the pattern of price differentials for the factor. If in addition to restriction on factor mobility, there is monopolistic restriction of the actual supply offered of any factor (relative to the total supply present in the submarket), the possibility of large intermarket differentials, of course, is enhanced. We shall consider such monopolistic restriction shortly.

Our theory of factor pricing under universal pure competition is thus easily modified to recognize the existence of disparate submarkets for the several productive factors. With every submarket purely competitive, the same general tendencies of ultimate balance, at full employment, between factor and commodity prices and among factor prices, remain. Thus, commodity prices would still tend everywhere to equal average and marginal costs, and the ratios between factor prices would be in balance with the marginal rates of substitution between the factors in every submarket. Instead of a single price for any factor, however, there would now be a family of prices for it, interrelated in a complex fashion through various pairs or groups of submarkets. And the balance described would tend to be struck in each submarket as well as for the economy as a whole. Detailed analysis of such a complex balance is best pursued through the use of mathematical equations permitting the use of numerous variables and dimensions. It is generally clear without such analysis, however, that in the absence of artificial restrictions or factor mobility, the pattern of prices for any factor as among submarkets would depend on the degree of mobility of units of the factor among submarkets, as determined by such natural conditions as cost of movement, extent of convertibility as among specialized uses, and relative supply in various submarkets when movement is impossible. It is also clear that artificial restrictions on factor mobility among markets may, even in an otherwise competitive setting, create arbitrary factor-price differentials which are of substantial magnitude and which are systematically related to differentials in the elasticity of demand for the factor in different submarkets.

B. THE EFFECTS OF COMMODITY MONOPOLIES ON HIRED FACTORS

GENERAL EFFECTS OF COMMODITY MONOPOLY ON HIRED FACTOR PRICES

Our analysis has thus far rested on the assumption that all factor and commodity markets are purely competitive. We must now relax this assumption and consider the effect on factor-price and income-share determination of the existence of monopolistic and monopsonistic tendencies in various markets. There are two distinct levels on which such tendencies may be encountered—in commodity markets and in the markets for factors themselves. The firms which buy factors may sell their outputs in markets which depart significantly from pure competition. And in the market or submarket for any factor there may also be departures from pure competition through monopsonistic buying or monopolistic selling of the factor. We shall analyze the impact of noncompetitive tendencies at these two levels in turn. Since we have in effect already begun our analysis of the effect of commodity monopoly on income distribution in Chapter 5 above, we shall turn first to this phase of the matter.

An outstanding aspect of the organization of the modern economy is that the selling markets for the majority of commodities are monopolistic or quasi-monopolistic. Oligopolistic structure is extremely common, and there are some single-firm monopolies. Markets in pure competition, and in monopolistic competition—which, as we have seen, closely approximates the behavior tendencies of pure competition—are in the minority. In monopolistic and oligopolistic markets there is some tendency toward the setting of output so that marginal cost is less than price and toward excess profits. Recognition of this fact requires the modification of our analysis of factor pricing, which has so far assumed that all selling markets were purely competitive. In what way are our previous conclusions regarding factor prices modified if we recognize that the purchasers of productive factors more often than not sell their outputs under monopolistic or quasi-monopolistic conditions? Assuming, that is, that they still buy factors in competitive factor markets, how does monopolistic commodity pricing affect wages and rents?

The effect of commodity monopolies on the general level of factor prices has already been discussed briefly on pages 235 to 247. Although this effect may be reviewed here, it is important to note that it has already been counted once. We should not make the unfortunate mistake of double counting by measuring this effect of commodity monopoly once in analyzing commodity pricing and once more in analyzing factor pricing.

As we relate the theory of monopolistic pricing to our general theory of income distribution, a first thing to note is that if the phenomenon in question is indeed commodity monopoly *alone*—existing in a setting where all factor markets are purely competitive on both the buying and the selling side—then the principles governing the proportions in which the firm employs factors are unchanged. Moreover, there is no necessary tendency within the economy for the *relative* prices of hired factors to be different in equilibrium than they would be under universal pure competition.

Suppose that either one, some, most, or all firms in the economy sell their outputs under conditions which depart significantly from pure competition, and that in the long run they produce outputs at which selling price significantly exceeds marginal cost and probably also average cost. Then by definition the outputs of these firms virtually differ from competitive outputs—that is, with the same demands and the same hired factor prices, equation of marginal cost and price would result in larger outputs than these firms produce. On the other hand, if these firms buy each factor in a homogenous market wherein there are many buyers and many sellers, each firm will necessarily regard the price of any factor as given, or the factor as in perfectly elastic supply, as would the firm with a purely competitive selling market. It follows that at any output which the monopolistic firm chooses to produce, it will presumably pursue the same logic as a purely competitive firm in hiring factors. That is, it will minimize the cost of any output by employing any pair of factors in such proportions that their marginal rate of substitution equals the inverse of the ratio of their prices. Thus, the determinants of the proportions in which factors are employed will be the same for monopolistic firms as for firms selling in purely competitive markets.

When monopolistic firms behave in this way, and an economy-wide equilibrium is reached, will the *relative* prices of the several hired factors of production thus tend to be any different than they would under universal pure competition? *Ceteris paribus,* they will tend to be the same, since any pair of factor prices will in equilibrium tend to assume a ratio equal to the inverse of the marginal rate of substitution between the factors in all lines of production, given the aggregate amounts supplied of each factor. An adjustment of relative factor prices such as to secure simultaneous full employment for all will take place in the same fashion as under universal pure competition. Two possible exceptions to this rule, however, may be noted.

EFFECTS ON REAL FACTOR PRICES AND ON EMPLOYMENT

The first stems indirectly from the fact that monopolistic policies tend to result in a virtual reduction of the real prices paid to hired factors of production. Where monopolistic policies are pursued, outputs are set so that marginal costs are less than prices rather than so they are equal to prices, as under pure competition. At the same time, price is generally (except in limiting cases) also in excess of average cost, so that an excess profit is earned by enterprise and emerges as a share of income not distributed to hired factors. Finally, the average cost of production (at any given level of factor prices) may be higher than the lowest attainable for the given output, if the number of firms is either too large or too small in view of the economies and diseconomies of scale that affect production in the industry.

If this is the case, the real price paid to productive factors—as influenced by the ratio of money factor prices to the prices of monopolized commodities which are purchased with factor incomes—is generally lower than they would be if a competitive price-cost adjustment were secured. A competitive adjustment would in general require first that marginal cost be equal to price, and second that the cost of any output produced be at the attainable minimum. If this were secured, instead of the monopolistic adjustment, excess profits would be reduced or eliminated as a share in income, and as a result the ratio of affected commodity prices to factor prices would be reduced (with either no profit margin or a smaller one standing between prices and costs), so that the quantity of commodities purchasable with any given factor income would be larger. Further, the cost of production of the previously monopolized goods at any level of factor prices might be reduced, with a more efficient adjustment of scales of firms or an output which permitted lower average costs, so that again the ratio of the affected commodity prices to factor prices would fall. For both reasons, a competitive adjustment would result in a higher real price to productive factors than the monopolistic adjustment.

Conversely, monopolistic restriction in this sense virtually reduces the real prices paid to hired factors.[1] If all industries were monopolized, this tendency would be everywhere observable, and every commodity price would tend to be higher relative to factor prices than it would be with a competitive adjustment. If only some industries are monopolized, the latter is true only of the commodities so affected, but the relation of the average price of all commodities to factor prices will be increased. So far as money factor prices are equalized among industries because of factor mobility, this reduction in the real prices of factors will affect all units of any factor, and not just those employed in the monopolized industries.

Monopolistic selling of commodities, therefore, tends to reduce real factor prices below a competitive or attainable higher level. As it does so, fewer units of one or more productive factors may be offered for use than if real factor prices were higher, and the full-employment (that is, no-involuntary-unemployment) equilibrium of the economy may thus involve a lower level of employment of one or more factors. Now if the elasticity of supply to the economy as a whole is different for different factors, so that a given proportionate reduction of real price causes a larger proportionate reduction in the supply of one factor than in that of another, then the ratio of the quantities which any pair of factors are supplied may be changed because of the downward pressure of monopolistic commodity pricing on their real prices. Thus, a provisional 10-percent reduction in all real factor prices might lead to more reduction in the supply of one factor than in that of another. Then the *relative* prices of the two factors will be affected by monopolistic commodity pricing. With one of them relatively scarcer, its marginal rate of substitution for the other will fall, and its relative price, in equilibrium, will rise. Thus the reduction in real factor prices forced by

[1] It may be noted that where there is single-firm monopoly with a falling long-run average cost curve over all relevant ranges of output, so that marginal cost is always less than average cost, a full competitive adjustment such that marginal cost equaled price would be untenable, since net losses would result. However, it would be feasible to increase real factor prices by carrying output at least to the point where price was equal to average cost, and whenever monopoly is operating short of this latter point, it could increase the real price of hired factors by moving to this point.

monopolistic output restriction will in effect be borne more heavily by those factors with less elastic supplies. Both the proportions in which factors are combined in production and their relative prices will be altered.

EFFECTS ON RELATIVE PRICES OF HIRED FACTORS

A second exception to the rule that relative factor prices will be unaffected by monopolistic selling of outputs may be explained as follows. In some industries factors may tend to be employed in different proportions than in others, with any given set of factor prices, and with marginal rates of substitution everywhere in balance with these factor prices. For example, in industry *A* there may be 100 units of labor employed for every 10 units of land when there is a given equilibrium ratio of their prices, and in another industry, *B*, 50 units of labor may be employed for every 10 units of land when there is the same factor-price ratio. Now if monopoly is imposed in some but not all industries, or in differing degrees in different industries, the proportions of the various industry outputs will be different than under universal pure competition; allocation of factors among uses will be shifted. As this takes place, suppose that the more monopolistic industries, whose outputs are restricted relative to others, employ some factor in a higher proportion to other factors than is average for the economy—for example, a monopolized industry which restricts its output relative to others is industry *A* above, whereas the average proportionate use of labor is found in industry *B*. Then the monopolistic output restriction in effect tends to increase the supply of one factor relative to others throughout the rest of the economy, as units of that factor disemployed in the monopolized industry seek and find employment elsewhere. As they do so, their marginal rate of substitution for other factors increases, and their relative price must tend to fall. Thus, monopolistic restriction in any industry employing a disproportionately large amount of a given factor will tend to result in a decline in the relative price of that factor, since its shift to the production of alternative outputs places it more heavily in uses in which its marginal rate of substitution for other factors is higher when it is combined with them in any given proportion. This tendency may be counteracted, of course, so far as the supply of that factor is more elastic than average in response to real price changes.

Aside from these two exceptions, however, commodity monopoly will not affect *relative* prices of hired factors, since these relative prices still tend to be determined directly by the marginal rates of substitution between factors in all lines of production, given the economy-wide supplies of the several factors. We have argued further that with complete mobility of factors from industry to industry, the price of any factor will obviously be the same in all industries, monopolistic and otherwise, as factor units will shift about until such uniformity is attained. Thus all units of a factor will bear the real-income-reducing effects of monopoly, and not just those employed in monopolized industries, as the average of factor prices is reduced relative to commodity prices by the inclusion in the average of commodity prices of the prices of monopolized outputs.

If units of a factor are less than perfectly mobile from one industry to another so that their prices to a monopolistic industry will decline relative to the prices of those employed in other industries as monopolistic restriction of output and employment takes place, then the effects of monopolistic restriction on the relation of factor to commodity prices may be more localized. With less than complete mobility of factors among submarkets, moreover, monopolistic selling of goods is likely to be associated with monopsonistic factor buying. The further effects of monopsonistic buying will be considered in a succeeding section.

SUMMARY

Commodity monopoly alone (uncomplicated by monopsony), has further effects on income distribution. First, even though the *relative* prices of the hired factors might be unchanged because of monopolistic commodity pricing, we have seen that their *absolute* real prices (in terms of commodities purchasable with money prices received) will be virtually reduced by monopolistic pricing of goods. The monopolistic firm will determine output so that its marginal cost is less than price and so that, ordinarily, its average cost is also less than price and allows the firm an excess profit. Further, it may be that its average real cost of producing the chosen output is greater than the lowest attainable, because of an excessively large number of firms or excessively small number of firms, or because smaller outputs can only be produced at higher average costs.

These tendencies together do not necessarily lead to a restriction of overall employment or output. As we have seen in Chapter 5 (pages 235-247), monopolized outputs, set where marginal cost is less than price, are smaller than outputs determined by competitive principles (with marginal cost equal to price) would be if factor prices and demands were the same in either case. However, the virtual restriction of aggregate output attributable to monopoly will not necessarily be realized if there is a constant flow of money purchasing power and if competitive factor prices adjust more or less automatically so as to eliminate any involuntary unemployment. Whether there are only a few monopolized industries, or many or all industries are monopolized, the output-restrictive tendency of monopoly (tending correspondingly to create unemployment if money factor prices remained at a level consistent with full employment under universal pure competition) will tend to be offset by a decline in money factor prices, relative to commodity prices and to a given flow of total purchasing power. This will tend to reduce money costs relative to money demands enough to eliminate involuntary unemployment. The actual level of employment should necessarily be reduced only so far as fewer units of productive factors are offered for use at the reduced real factor prices.

But monopolistic price policies do lead to a commodity price level which is higher relative to money factor prices than that which would be obtained with competitive output policies. If there are a few monopolies, the relation of the average level of commodity prices to factor prices will be influenced slightly; if all firms are monopolies, the effect will be general and much larger. As a consequence, the real prices of the hired factors of production are lowered by monopolistic restriction.

Second, there will tend to be excess profits. As noted before (see pages 203 to 205) monopolistic or quasi-monopolistic pricing will ordinarily give rise to a margin of excess profits, over and above the returns to all hired factors, which is received by the owners of enterprise. Monopolistic enterprises thus receive a share of total income which they would not if they pursued competitive output adjustments; hired factors of production are deprived of a share of total income they would otherwise receive. Depending on the frequency of monopolistic selling of goods and on the extent of monopolistic restriction where it is found, this income share might vary from small to very substantial.

Under certain simplified conditions—where all industries operated under conditions of constant average cost, so that the restrictions of some outputs or the extension of others resulted in no change in the average costs per unit of output with given factor prices—the excess-profit share earned by monopolistic sellers would be the only source of reduction in real income to hired factors which would result from monopolistic selling. Since the average real cost of production of monopolized or other goods would by and large be unaffected by changes in particular outputs resultant from monopoly, the only source of a rise in the ratio of commodity to factor prices would be the emergence of the excess profits earned where monopoly was found.

If, on the other hand, the incidence of monopoly entails an increase in the average cost of production of at least some goods (at any given level of factor prices), because of an uneconomical number of firms in monopolized industries or because costs are higher at the altered outputs, there is a further source of reduction in the real prices paid to hired factors. The higher costs reflect a reduction in the output of goods per unit of factors employed, and, even if there were no excess-profit margin, require a higher ratio of commodity to factor prices. In this case, the reduction of the real income of hired factors may exceed the amount of excess profits earned by monopolistic selling of commodities.

In summary, the effects of monopolistic commodity pricing on income distribution appear to be as follows. First, such pricing is generally associated with the earning of excess profits greater than would be received with competitive output adjustments (where marginal cost equals price), leading to the diversion to enterprises of an income share they would not otherwise receive. (The excess profit with such a competitive adjustment might be zero or some positive amount, but would in any event be smaller than with monopolistic pricing). This excess-profit share reflects a lowering of factor prices relative to the average of commodity prices, and thus a reduction of the level of the real prices of hired productive factors.

In addition, the real prices of productive factors may be further lowered because of an increase, as a consequence of monopoly, of the real costs of production to which commodity prices are related. This also tends to result in a higher ratio of commodity to factor prices. As the result of lowered real prices to factors, the quantities of them offered for employment and employed may be reduced, and the employment of some factors may be reduced in greater proportion than that of others. The last tends to result in a change in the relative prices of the hired factors. Next, the reallocation of factors among employment in various industries as a consequence of monopoly may place given factors more largely in occupations where their marginal rate of substitution for others is lowered, resulting in a further alteration of the relative prices of hired factors. These effects will be felt equally by all the units of any factor supply within the economy if the factor is completely mobile among the submarkets supplying various industries. If factors are imperfectly mobile, the effects will tend to be in part localized to particular submarkets, and correspondingly the pattern of prices for any factor as among its submarkets may be altered from that which would occur with purely competitive commodity selling.

So long as there is a constant flow of money purchasing power to which hired factor prices adjust, however, commodity monopolies will tend to reduce employment of factors only so far as the reduction in the real incomes of hired factors cause fewer factor units to be offered for employment. This phenomenon may be alternatively described as a lowering of the full-employment (that is, no-involuntary-unemployment) level of the economy.

C. MONOPSONISTIC BUYING OF FACTORS

THE INCIDENCE OF MONOPOLY AND MONOPSONY
WITHIN FACTOR MARKETS

The most significant modifications of a theory of income distribution based on the assumption of universal pure competition must come through altering the assumptions to recognize fewness of buyers and fewness of sellers of the factors of production.

Monoposony or concentrated buying is extremely common in factor markets, and especially in markets for labor. The fewness of buyers in factor markets stems generally from the high concentration of the output of many industries in the hands of few firms (from oligopolistic commodity market structures) and from the fact that both labor and land are sold in many submarkets, in any one of which only a small fraction of all the buyers and sellers of labor or land are situated. Thus, concentration in factor buying is the more or less "natural" result of industrial concentration and of the nonhomogeneity and imperfect mobility of any total factor supply. Buyer concentration may be further increased or enhanced artificially by the organization of firms for the purposes of joint or concerted bargaining in the determination of factor prices. When this occurs, for example, an "employers' council" or other such group may constitute an effective monopsony for the purchase of labor of a given sort within a given area. Local monoposony or oligopsony in the purchase of factors is effective and can remain because of barriers to the entry of competing buyers and because of the imperfect mobility of the monopsonized factors to other occupations or other areas.

The counterpart of concentrated buying in the various submarkets for factors is concentrated selling in such submarkets. In the case of land, this may easily result from the concentrated ownership of a given sort of land or natural resource in a given general area, resulting in monopoly or oligopoly in a particular submarket. The selling of labor has become concentrated largely via unionization on either craft or industry bases and by the emergence of the union leadership as the single seller of the services of a large membership. Unionization has often proceeded to the point where there is a single monopolistic seller of a given type of labor for a single local submarket. In some cases, the union becomes a single seller for a group of local submarkets when it bargains on an industry-wide basis.

Unionized monopoly or oligopoly in the selling of labor may be of at least two general types: where the union is a bargaining agent for a membership to which there is essentially free entry by any laborers who wish to join, and where entry to the union is impeded by certain barriers such as arbitrary limitation, admission fees, unusual apprenticeship requirements, and so forth. In the second situation, the significance of labor monopoly is greatly increased as the mobility of labor among occupations and areas is reduced.

Because both monopolistic and monopsonistic tendencies are frequently present in factor markets, under modern conditions it is not the most usual thing to find monopsonistic buying of a factor together with competitive selling of the factor, or monopolistic selling of the factor with competitive buying. Monopsony and monopoly, or concentrated buying and selling, are more typically combined in a bilateral monopoly situation, as, for example, where a union seller of a factor faces a single buyer or organized or collusive buying group. This is perhaps the most common setting today for factor-price determination.

The general character of modern factor markets may be explored best by considering successively the following possible cases:

1. Monopsony with competitive selling.
2. Monopolistic selling with competitive buying.
3. Bilateral monopoly, where one buyer deals with one seller.

We may pursue the analysis of these cases while retaining our simplifying assumptions concerning the constancy of the flow of money purchasing power and the identification of each factor as a basic inanimate commodity with independent supply conditions.

We shall consider first the case of monopsonistic buying from competitive sellers.

THE EFFECT OF MONOPSONISTIC BUYING
ON FACTOR PRICES

Monopsonistic buying of a productive factor is characterized by the fact that the purchaser is faced by a supply curve for the factor which is not perfectly elastic. Instead of being able, like the competitive buyer, to buy any quantity of the factor he desires at a price which is beyond his influence, the buyer with monopsony power finds that the price he must pay for the factor varies with the quantity he purchases. Typically, the monopsonistic buyer will face an upsloping supply curve for the factor—that is, the price of the factor to him increases if he purchases more and decreases as he purchases less.

We shall confine our attention to cases in which there is this sort of supply curve to the buyer, as illustrated in Figure 55. If faced with such a supply curve, the buyer may enjoy only simple monopsony power, so that the price of all units purchased must be bid up to the level shown on SS' as any quantity on SS' is purchased. In this case, the marginal outlay for added units of the factor rises above SS', along MO. (See pages 382 to 384.) The buyer may alternatively enjoy perfectly discriminatory monopsony, however, in which case successive units of the factor can be purchased at the separate prices shown along SS'. In this case, the average price for any quantity is lower than shown on SS', and SS' is the marginal outlay curve to the buyer. (See pages 426 to 429.) We shall consider here only the case of simple monopsony, as the only one likely to be found in factor markets.

Monopsonistic power may be possessed by a firm purchasing factors either when it is the sole buyer of a factor in a particular market or when it is one of a few buyers. If there is either a single buying firm or a perfectly collusive group of a few buyers—with no rivalry in purchasing a factor from a given submarket—there should be a determinate relation of factor price to factor supply for the buyer. With oligopsonistic buying in the absence of perfect collusion, the relationship of factor price to factor supply as viewed by the firm may be less definite because of uncertainty concerning rival buyers' actions, so that a definite or unique supply curve for the factor

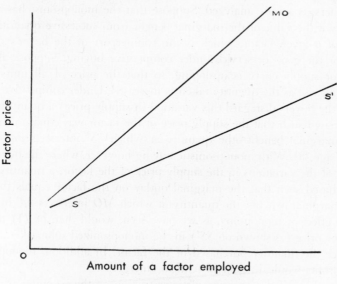

Figure 55

may not be apparent to the firm. The general tendencies of oligopsonistic buying, however, should be suggested by the analysis of simple monopsony by a single buyer.

What is the scope of the factor monopsony to be examined? In the American economy there is no general monopsony or significant degree of concentration of buying for the whole of any major productive factor—land, labor, or capital. Monopsony and concentration of buying are peculiar to the various smaller submarkets for a factor—for example, for particular labor skills or occupations in particular localities. Monopsony power in the purchase of factors is made possible (1) by the impediments to the mobility of hired factors as among various submarkets, and (2) by the impediments to the entry of added buyers of factors to specific submarkets, which keep the number of buyers at one or a few. For purposes of our argument here we shall accept the existing limitations on the entry of additional buyers to submarkets for factors as generally given, and examine how established monopsonies may exploit factor immobility. It may also be interesting, however, to consider the theoretical possibilities of a single monopsony affecting the purchase of most or all of the supply of a productive factor.

Let us first consider the effects of factor monopsony in a single submarket for a given factor of production—supposing that monopsonistic buying is encountered there in an economy in which all other factor markets are purely competitive on the buying as well as on the selling side. We have seen in Chapter 8 that the effects of monopsony on the price and output of a single good or factor, when that good or factor is considered in isolation from others, is simply analyzed. Suppose that the monopsonist has a given schedule of the value of the marginal benefit from successive quantities purchased of a given factor, which is the counterpart of the buyer's demand curve for the good or service under competitive buying. Suppose also that the factor supply curve is upsloping, so that the price of all units of the factor unit rise as the quantity taken is increased. Under competitive buying (where the buyers disregard this variation in supply price) a quantity would be purchased such that the supply price of the factor was equal to the value of the marginal benefit—the quantity at which SS' intersects dd' in Figure 42, page 383. With monopsonistic buying however, where the buyer takes account of the variations in the supply price of the factor, a quantity would be purchased such that the marginal outlay on the factor equals the value of the marginal benefit—the quantity at which MO intersects dd' in Figure 42. The effect of monopsony, as we have seen, would then be (1) to lower the factor price (as shown on SS') in the monopsonized submarket, and (2) to reduce the quantity purchased of the factor. In addition, monopsonistic excess profits would in general tend to emerge.

The effects of this monopsonistic restriction on the economy as a whole are also easily seen in this case. The existence of an upsloping supply curve for the factor in a particuar submarket is presumaby indicative of imperfect mobility of the factor units there employed to other submarkets—that is, the total factor supply will not desert this submarket if the going factor price is somewhat reduced below the prices for the factor in other submarkets, but some of the supply will either shift to other submarkets or elect to remain unemployed, thus reducing the local supply. It follows that the specific monopsonistic restriction will lead to (1) an alteration in the pattern of prices for the factor in question as among submarkets, such that the factor price in the monopsonized market is relatively lower than it would be under universally competitive buying, and (2) a shift of some units of the factor from employment in the monopsonized industry, and to either employment in other industries, or idleness, or both. The incidence of monopsony in a single submarket is thus to alter the allocation of the monopsonized factor as among industries, and to alter the pattern of prices of the factor as among submarkets, in such a way as to effect a systematic deviation from competitive allocation and factor prices. In general, units of the monopsonized factor in the specific submarkets will receive lower prices than under universal pure competition, and allocation will be less desirable than under universal pure competition. Further, the reduction in the monopsonized factor price will tend to be reflected in an addition to the excess profits of the monopsonistic buyer.

THE EFFECT ON RELATIVE EMPLOYMENT OF FACTORS

This argument may now be generalized to take account of the relationship between the use of a given monopsonized factor which a firm purchases and other factors which are substitutes for it in production. Rather than referring to a given schedule of marginal benefits for the specific factor and its supply curve, we may now more generally refer to the demand for the output of the monopsonistic buyer, the substitution conditions among factors used in producing its output, and the marginal cost (from all factors employed) of producing its output.

As we have seen, the firm buying all factors under pure competition will produce any output with such a combination of factors that the marginal rate of substitution between any pair of factors is equal to the inverse of their price ratio, and will produce an output such that marginal cost (derived on the supposition of constant factor prices) is equal to marginal receipts.

If the firm has monopsony power in the buying of one or more factors, this adjustment will be altered as follows. First, the monopsonistic purchaser of factors will now minimize the cost to him of any output not by using factors in such proportion that the marginal rate of substitution of any factor A for another factor B is equal to the ratio of the price of B to the price of A, *but by using the factors in such proportion that the marginal rate of substitution of A for B is equal to the ratio of the marginal outlay on B to the marginal outlay on A.* The latter is in fact the general rule for cost minimization—for example, when one unit of A will replace two units of B, the firm will make the substitution only if the marginal outlay on a unit of A (added) is less than twice the marginal outlay on a unit of B (subtracted), regardless of the ratio of their prices. The rule developed for competitive buying—that the marginal rate of substitution would equal the inverse of the ratio of the prices—is evidently only a corollary of this general rule applicable to cases where factor prices are invariant to the firm and marginal outlay equals price in each case.

Now, if the firm minimizes its cost of any output by balancing marginal rates of substitution against marginal outlays, it is evident that any monopsonized factor with an upsloping supply curve to the buyer will tend to be used in smaller proportion then if there were competitive buying of the factor (in which case any response of its price to the amount used would be disregarded by the purchasing firm). Suppose that a firm is producing a given output, and buying factors under competitive conditions at given market prices as determined by the interaction of aggregate demand and supply for the factors, in which case this output is produced by combining factors A and B so that the marginal rate of substitution of A for B is equal to the ratio of the price of B to the price of A. Suppose further that the firm now obtains monopsony power in purchasing factor A, so that although it can continue to acquire A in the going quantity at the same price, it can lower the price of A by buying less of it. Now, the marginal outlay on the monopsonized factor, A, will exceed its going price, whereas the marginal outlay on the nonmonopsonized factor, B, will still be the same as its price. Thus, the ratio of the marginal outlay on A to the marginal outlay on B will be greater, with given quantities purchased of each, than it was with competitive buying of both factors. It follows that the cost-minimizing combination of the two factors (such that the marginal rate of substitution of A for B equals the ratio of the marginal outlay on B to that on A) will require a lower marginal rate of substitution of A for B than was required with competitive buying of both factors. This in turn requires the use of a smaller amount of the monopsonized factor (A) and a larger quantity of B, in order to produce a given output at minimum cost, than under universally competitive buying. And with an upsloping supply curve for A, the price paid for A will be lower than under competitive buying.

The general principle involved is obviously that the imposition of monopsony in one factor, reflected in a tendency of the price of that factor to the firm to rise as it increases its use of that factor, restricts its tendency to substitute that factor for others. Thus, with any given set of factor prices being paid, monopsony in one factor will tend to reduce the proportion of that factor used in producing output, as nonmonopsonized factors tend to be substituted for it. The precise difference in the quantity of a factor used to produce a given output under monopsony, of course, will depend on what the level of the factor price to the firm would be under pure competition as compared to the level and elasticity of the sloping factor supply curve under monopsony. Provided that monopsony involves ability (1) to buy the factor in the competitive quantity at what the competitive price would be (and not at a much lower price) and (2) to depress the factor price by buying less than this quantity, then monopsony will certainly lead to an absolute reduction in the quantity of the monopsonized factor used to produce any given output, and in a corresponding lowering of its price.

If more than one factor is monopsonized by the buyer, the same general rule applies. If the buyer combines factors so that their marginal rates of substitution are in balance with their marginal outlays, there is a counterbalancing restrictive tendency (at any output) on the use of the several monopsonized factors. The proportions used would be altered from the competitive level so far as the relationship of marginal outlay to price was different for different factors—as the result of different elasticities of supply to the buyer for the different factors.

The preceding refers to the effect of monopsony on the quantity of a factor employed *in producing a given output;* it is evident that at any given output monopsony tends to reduce the use of the factor from the monopsonized submarket and to reduce its price in that submarket. A second probable effect of factor monopsony is on the output of the good produced by the monopsonist. The tendency of the monopsonized factor price to rise as the purchaser takes more of it will correspondingly tend to cause the marginal cost of production of the purchasing firm to rise more steeply than it would if the factor were in perfectly elastic supply to the firm. It will also tend to cause marginal cost to be higher at the output which would be produced with competitive factor buying, if the monopsonistic factor price attained at this output is as high as the competitive. This tendency will be offset in part by the substitution of other factors for the monopsonized factor, but not entirely. If now the marginal cost of production to the firm does rise more steeply and lies higher in the neighborhood of the competitive output, it is evident that the output at which the firm's marginal cost equals marginal receipts from its sales will be smaller. The resultant restriction of output is a second source of the reduction in the use of the monopsonized factor, and a further source of reduction in its price.

In sum, monopsonistic buying of a factor in a particular submarket within the economy tends to restrict the use of the factor in that submarket by inducing substitution of other factors for it and by restricting output of the good produced by the monopsonist. The consequent reduction in its use tends to lower its price in the submarket below the level which would be attained if there were competitive buying within the same submarket and with the same submarket supply curve for the factor. The combination of these restrictive effects is reflected in the equalization of the marginal outlay on the factor with the value of the marginal benefit from its use at a smaller quantity used of the factor, at which smaller quantity the value of its marginal benefit is higher and its price is lower. Correspondingly, a monopsonistic excess profit will tend to emerge as an income share to the monopsonistic buyer.[2]

---

[2] It is conceivable that there might be monopsony subject to something like free entry, in which case the excess profits gained by any monopsonist via reducing factor prices and restricting his output would be reduced or eliminated as additional monopsonists, drawing on additional monopsonized factor supplies, increased the aggregate output of the good in question until price equaled average cost for all. In this case, monopsonistic output restriction would be reduced or eliminated (although monopolistic output restriction could remain) and excess profits would vanish. This possibility—of free entry of added monopsonists while preserving monopsonies in general—seems fanciful, however, and we need not consider it further here.

The restriction accomplished in a single monopsonized field will have several effects on the economy as a whole. Immediately, it will tend to reduce the quantity of the factor used in the monopsonized submarket, to reduce its price in that submarket, and to create monopsonistic excess profits. The pattern of prices of that factor as among different submarkets will thus tend to be altered so that the price in the monopsonized submarket is lower than it would be with universally competitive factor buying. Further effects, however, must be noted. First, the restriction of the use of the factor in the monopsonized submarket will be accompanied by a shift of disemployed units of the factor to employment in other submarkets, where, by assumption, there is competitive buying. This will represent a misallocation of these factors, since in the monopsonized markets the marginal real cost of output will tend to stand lower relative to the value of output than it does in other markets. Second, some factor units which are disemployed because of factor-price reduction in the monopsonized market may be immobile, or may prefer unemployment to moving elsewhere. In this case, monopsony will reduce total employment, although the factor units involved are "voluntarily" unemployed. Third, although the real price of monopsonized factor units is very obviously reduced, there will also be a tendency toward the reduction of the real prices of all factors in the economy so far as the price of the good produced by the monopsonist is raised relative to the level of factor prices in general. This will reflect the fact that a certain part of the resulting monopsonistic excess profit is essentially a subtraction not from the earnings of factors in the monopsonized submarket alone but from factor earnings in general.

The preceding refers to the effects of factor monopsony in any situation —regardless of whether the monopsonist's selling market is monopolized or competitive. Ordinarily, monopsony in the firm's buying market may be matched by some degree of monopoly in its selling market. In this case, we may say in general that the effects of commodity monopoly on income distribution are compounded with those of monopsony. It should be noted, however, that the impact of such monopoly on income distribution will be felt equally by factors throughout the economy (as previously argued) only as far as factors are completely mobile from one submarket to another. As far as monopsony is a reflection of imperfect factor mobility, it is apparent that when factor monopsony is conjoined with commodity monopoly, the effects of such monopoly will tend to be borne disproportionately by the monopsonized factors, and felt somewhat less by factors in other submarkets. The greater the reduction in price which factors in the monopsonized submarket will accept under the pressure of monopoly-monopsony restriction before shifting to unemployment or to other submarkets (that is, the less elastic their supply) the greater the proportion of the effects of commodity monopoly they will bear, and the less factors in other parts of the economy will suffer.

A WORLD OF MONOPSONIES

The preceding refers explicitly to the effect of factor monopsony in one or a few of the many submarkets for a given productive factor. It is evident, however, that because of the segmentation of actual factor supplies among many submarkets, and of their imperfect mobility, factor monopsony is likely to occur simultaneously in many or most submarkets for a factor rather than in only a few. It is thus pertinent to consider the effects of such widespread monopsony on income distribution. These effects are most easily revealed by an analysis of a world of monopsonies for a factor, in which *every* submarket for the factor is subject to some degree of monopsony power by purchasers.

Let us suppose that in each of the several hundred submarkets for a given factor, the purchaser or purchasers have some monopsony power, in the sense that the factor price to the buyer will vary upward as he buys more of it. At the same time suppose there is competitive buying of all other factors. What total effect will emerge from the simultaneous exercise of monopsony power in the many submarkets for the given factor?

It is apparent that each of the monopsonistic buyers will separately tend to make the sort of adjustment already attributed to the isolated monopsonist. That is, taking the supply curve to him of the monopsonized factor in his particular submarket as showing a given relation of the money price of the factor to the quantity purchased, he will adjust his output and his use of the factor in such a way that, as compared to the results of competitive factor buying, he produces a smaller output, uses less of the factor both absolutely and in proportion to others, and correspondingly pays a somewhat lower price for the factor. He moves back or leftward on the supply curve of the factor to a point where factor quantity and price are both smaller than under competitive buying.

Now if this action were undertaken by a few monopsonists only, other submarkets for the factor having competitive buying, the units of the factor disemployed because of monopsonistic restriction would tend to shift (entirely or in part) to the nonmonopsonized submarkets, where they would be absorbed at a new (and somewhat lower) competitive price, and the end result would actually be restricted use of the factor and relatively lower price for it in the monopsonized submarkets. But if *all* submarkets are monopsonized, so that there is simultaneous restriction everywhere in use of the factor, what is the result?

Analysis of this question requires some examination of the character of the supply condition or supply curve for a factor to any single monopsonist in a single submarket. In general, it may be argued that the upsloping supply curve for a factor in any one submarket, although it shows explicitly a relation of quantity supplied to money factor price, fundamentally represents a relation of quantity supplied to *relative* factor price—of quantity supplied to the ratio of the factor price in this submarket to its prices in other submarkets. The monopsonist in effect faces no arbitrarily fixed relation of money factor price to supply. The supply curve of the factor to him lies at a level on the money price scale determined by the prices of the factor elsewhere.

If prices of the factor elsewhere are all lowered, this curve will shift downward. It will show perhaps the same elasticity (rate of increase of price with increased purchases), and the same relation of supply to the ratio of the "local" price to prices elsewhere, but will also show that a lower money factor price is necessary to acquire any given quantity of the factor. If prices of the factor are forced down in all submarkets, all submarket supply curves for the factor shift downward.

A common-sense way of putting this is to say that if a single monopsonist restricts his use of a factor, he cannot force its price down very much, since given competitive prices for the factor elsewhere stand as alternatives toward which units of the factor in his submarket will shift rather than accepting very much lower prices. If every submarket is monopsonized, however, each monopsonist can in fact force down his factor prices much more by a little restriction of factor use, since prices in all alternative submarkets are being depressed simultaneously. Thus, simultaneous monopsony policies in all submarkets bring about a substantially lower level of prices for the factor everywhere. At this lower level of factor prices, however, each monopsonist may still face a fairly elastic relation of factor price to supply, since the relation of his factor price to other such prices (all now lower) still determines his ability *individually* to affect the factor price by varying his purchases. Thus, we say that the factor supply curve in each submarket is shifted downward by simultaneous monopsony policies, while retaining roughly the same elasticity to the individual monopsonist, rather than saying that the individual monopsonist views his factor supply curve as substantially less elastic.

Now if there are only one or a few monopsonized submarkets, out of many for a given factor, as we have assumed previously, the competitive prices of the factor in alternative submarkets may be assumed to be more or less given in the face of monopsonistic adjustments, and the supply curve of the factor to any monopsonist will show a substantially given relation of money factor price to supply and will not shift as the monopsonist adjusts. Then actual restriction of factor use in monopsonized submarkets will result, as previously predicted. If, on the other hand, all submarkets are monopsonized, simultaneous restriction in all submarkets, tending to lower the factor price everywhere, will cause all submarket supply curves for the factor to shift downward, reducing the money price at which any quantity can be obtained by a monopsonist, although the supply curves will presumably retain about the same elasticity at their new levels. This downward shift of all the supply curves for the monopsonized factor will obviously tend to offset the tendency of monopsonists to employ less of the factor in question. Although the excess of marginal outlay over price for the factor leads to virtual restriction of use, the downward shift lowers both price and marginal outlay at any quantity purchased, thus lessening or entirely negating the restrictive tendency of monopsony.

This downward adjustment of supply curves for the factor might be sufficient to maintain an unchanged aggregate employment of the factor. In this case the supply curves would have to lie enough lower, relative to their competitive positions, that the marginal outlay on the factor was generally in the same relation to the prices of other factors as the price of the factor would be to other factor prices with universal competitive buying. Only in this way would the ratios of the marginal outlays on factors remain unchanged in the face of monopsony and remain in balance with the marginal rates of substitution among factors which are consistent with unchanged employment for all. The downward adjustment would tend to proceed this far, however, only if, given a constant flow of money purchasing power, all units of the factor were in general willing to accept lower real prices and continue working—if the lowered real price would not restrict the available factor supply. Otherwise, simultaneous monopsony restrictions will tend to force a downward shift of factor supply curves simply to such a point that monopsonistic buyers are willing to purchase all units of the factor offered for employment at the reduced real prices. In effect, the virtual restriction on factor use by many monopsonies will be offset by lowered "asking-price" schedules (supply curves) for the factor sufficiently to eliminate involuntary unemployment of the factor (provided, of course, that there is a given constant flow of money purchasing power). Voluntary unemployment will tend to be increased so far as the over-all reduction of the real price of the factor causes fewer units to be offered for employment.

The answer to our initial question concerning the restriction in use of a factor if each of its submarkets is monopsonized is thus as follows. The total restriction on its use will not be as large as the sum of all the individual monopsony restrictions which would occur if each monopsony existed separately in an economy of otherwise competitive factor markets. Simultaneous monopsony will force a lowering of the supply curve for the factor in every market which will offset the virtual restrictions of all the monopsonies enough to maintain a situation of no involuntary unemployment.

As this economy-wide adjustment takes place, certain tendencies of ubiquitous monopsony are apparent. First, the price of the monopsonized factor throughout the economy will be forced lower than any isolated monopsonist would force it. Although the power of any one of the many monopsonists to reduce the factor price below those in other submarkets is still small, the simultaneous exercise of this power by a world of monopsonists leads to a substantial reduction in the factor price everywhere, as the mobility of the factor among submarkets does not *actually* limit the monopsonists in their ultimate ability to reduce the factor price. With the prices of the factor in all other submarkets falling, factor units in every submarket accept successively lower prices without shifting elsewhere. Second, large monopsonistic excess profits—much larger in each case than the monopsonist in isolation could secure—will tend to emerge. Third, over-all employment of the monopsonized factor will be restricted as far as the substantially lowered real price for the factor causes fewer units to be offered for use. This will, in turn, be reflected in a somewhat reduced real price to other productive factors (now combined with the monopsonized factor at less favorable marginal rates of substitution), and to possible repercussions on their use. Fourth, as far as there are different degrees of monopsony in different monopsonized submarkets for a factor (different elasticities of supply of the factor), there will be a systematic distortion of the relative price pattern for the factor as among submarkets away from the competitive norm, and a corresponding distortion of allocation. The principal finding of the analysis of simultaneous monopsony, however, is that it may greatly alter the distribution of income as between the monopsonized factor and the excess profits of enterprise.

We have considered the case in which a single factor of production is subject to monopsony in all of its submarkets, while at the same time there is purely competitve buying of all other productive factors. To what extent are our conclusions modified if two or more factors are simultaneously subject to such monopsony pressure? The foregoing analysis clearly suggests that in this case each of the monopsonized factors will be subject to a strong downward pressure on its price, that restrictions in the employment of both may be induced by the resultant reduction of real earnings, and that monopsonistic profits will tend to be larger than if only a single factor were monopsonized.

In general, widespread monopsony affecting most or all of the submarkets for one or more factors—even though the degree of monopsony power in each submarket (as reflected in departure of the factor supply curve there from perfect elasticity)—is not large—will tend to result in a substantial lowering of the real prices of monopsonized factors and in the share of total income received by these factors, and in a corresponding shift of income to excess profits. Correspondingly, there will tend to be some employment effects and some movement of allocation away from the competitive standard.

Is the situation in anyway altered if the number of individual monopsonists purchasing a factor is small rather than large? Suppose that instead of having many small submarkets for a factor, each of which is monopsonized by a buyer taking a correspondingly small fraction of the total factor supply, we have a few submarkets for the factor, each monopsonized by a correspondingly very large buyer. Or suppose at the extreme that there is simply one large monopsonistic buyer for the total supply of the factor— one employer only—as might be found with governmental or government-sponsored monopoly of all productive activity or with a collusion in factor buying among all firms in the economy. In these cases, will the effect of monopsony on the price of the monopsonized factors be significantly different from that already described?

If there is one single monopsonist for the whole economy-wide supply of a factor, a distinct difference should be found. To such a monopsonist the supply of the factor should be much less elastic than it is to any one of many small monopsonists, since the single buyer when he cuts the factor price will not tend to lose factor supply to other markets. Intermarket mobility of units of the factor is no longer present as a source of high elasticity of factor supply to the buyer, who will find units of the factor withheld from use at lower prices only so far as some units prefer idleness at a lowered real price. With a much less elastic supply of the factor, the monopsonist will find that his marginal outlay in it is much higher relative to price, and he will thus have the incentive as well as the power to restrict his use of the factor until its price is driven to much lower levels. Even a very low price may not cause much actual restriction in the total employment of the factor, but its price will tend to be much lower than if there were a group of many small monopsonists. Correspondingly, monopsonistic excess profits will tend to be much larger with a single monopsony of the total factor supply.

The present section has dealt with the general phenomenon of ubiquitous monopsony—monopsonization of the supply of a factor in all or most of its separate submarkets. The potential effects of such monopsony are evidently a substantial reduction of the price and income share of the monopsonized factor, together with some reduction in its employment. It should be emphasized, however, that these tendencies are identified strictly for the case wherein the monopsonistic buyers of the factor purchase from *competitive sellers* of the factor. That is, in each monopsonized submarket, there are many small sellers of the factor, each having available so small a portion of the total submarket supply that he cannot perceptibly influence this total supply by varying the proportion of his own supply which he places on the market, and thus cannot bring any bargaining pressure to bear on the monopsonist to secure a favorable price.

In this case, there emerges a determinate supply curve in each submarket. Given other submarket prices and commodity prices, there is a definite schedule of amounts of the factor that will be offered at a corresponding schedule of money factor prices. The monopsonist may exploit this curve to his own advantage, choosing the price-quantity combination which suits him best. His situation is thus distinctly different from one in which a single seller or group of collusive sellers of the factor withhold supply at any price in favor either of negotiating a price with the buyer or of simply stipulating a given fixed price as the only one at which supply would be forthcoming.

The existence of competitive factor selling is thus the basis for the emergence of the effects of monopsony just analyzed. Therefore, it is important to note two things. First, since the suppliers of hired factors of production tend to suffer distinctly from monopsony as long as they continue to compete in selling, they have a very strong incentive to combine or organize in some way to eliminate competitive factor selling, and to institute instead some monopolistic or quasi-monopolistic control of the factor supply. That is, factor monopsony probably tends to *induce* factor monopoly over time. Second, if it does so, the effects of monopsonistic buying will tend to be altered or even eliminated. The erstwhile monopsonist may lose all monopsony power and face a fixed price dictated by a monopolistic factor seller (at which the supply of the factor to him is made perfectly elastic), or, more probably, bargaining within the framework of a bilateral monopoly may replace simple monopsony. It is thus important that we consider monopolistic factor selling and bilateral monopoly in factor markets, since through time these are likely to emerge in reaction to initially monopsonistic situations.

One further comment may be added relative to the phenomenon of factor monopsony. We have assumed in all preceding analysis of such monopsony that the power of monopsonists is limited to that of *simple monopsony*—that is, to an ability simply to set one of a range of alternative prices at which all units of the factor offered will be purchased, the amount offered becoming larger as the price set for the factor is raised. It is thus implied that the monopsonist cannot pay different prices to different units of the factor supply; he must pay every unit the price required to bring forth the last or marginal unit in the total supply obtained. When this is true, of course, the marginal outlay on the factor exceeds the price paid at any quantity point, and tendencies of monopsonistic restriction emerge.

If, however, the monopsonist could practice perfect discrimination in buying a factor, the tendency to restrict use of the factor or to reduce its employment, in the case either of isolated monopsony or of ubiquitous monopsony, would vanish, since the marginal outlay on the factor would now be the same at any point as the price of the last unit acquired, or the same as the marginal outlay with competitive buying. This is apparent from the analysis of perfectly discriminatory monopsony on pages 426 to 429. On the other hand, the *average* price paid to all units of the factor would be reduced as with simple monopsony, and excess profits would similarly tend to emerge. We have not emphasized this possibility because with many competitive sellers of a factor perfectly discriminating monopsony seems in fact quite unlikely to be practicable.

D. MONOPOLISTIC SELLING OF FACTORS

CHARACTERISTICS OF FACTOR MONOPOLY

Parallel to the possibility of monopsony in the purchase of productive factors is that of monopoly in their sale. A single "seller" may control the entire supply of a factor within a given submarket (or even, hypothetically, within the whole economy), or there may be concentrated control of the factor supply by a few sellers in a given submarket or in the economy as a whole. In this case, provided that the seller or sellers enjoy a sufficient protection from the entry of added factor units to the market in question to give them some influence over the factor price, monopolistic or concentrated control of the factor supply may provide the basis for monopolistic or oligopolistic factor-pricing policies which aim at establishing a factor price above the level which would be set with purely competitive selling of the factor. When this in fact occurs, we encounter factor monopoly or monopolistic factor pricing.

This is not to say that in the case of factor monopoly we can be certain that the price will always be raised above the competitive level, or, when it is raised, that the increase will be in some uniquely determined amount. In the latter respect, factor monopoly differs basically from commodity monopoly. The commodity monopolist is defined as an enterprise which has the exclusive right to make and sell some good, and which operates by buying productive factors and selling the output made from them. Assuming that it desires to maximize profit, it will presumably choose an output and price such that its marginal cost of production equals its marginal receipts from sales. The cost-quantity relation which, together with demand for what it sells, determines the monopolist's price and output— that is, his marginal cost curve—is presumably given regardless of the particular identity or number of the persons involved in the ownership and control of the monopolistic firm. This is the case because where supply is made available basically by purchasing services from others and reselling them, either a single entrepreneur or a partnership of 2,000 entrepreneurs could perform the same function and would tend to find the same relationship of cost (from purchased services) to output. Thus, the supply-determining cost curve, and the profit-maximizing price and output, are given in commodity monopoly substantially without regard to the number of participants in the control of the monopolistic enterprise, since the addition of participants to the ownership group does not tend to augment supply or to change its relationship to cost. The monopolistic price, as we have seen, will tend to be higher, and the monopolistic output smaller, than those associated with pure competition.

In what basic respects is the character of factor monopoly different? The most basic difference is that a factor monopoly is by definition not a buying-and-selling enterprise, but simply a selling individual or group which sells the services of what it already has or owns, and has the exclusive right to sell this sort of service to the buyers in a particular market. Thus, the factor monopoly might be an owner or a combine of owners of all land available in a given market, or a combination of laborers with the sole right to sell labor services in a particular market.

The importance of this difference should be carefully evaluated. The mere fact that the monopolistic supplier or suppliers sell what they own without buying from others does not mean that the supply is without cost to them. In the case of labor, for example, the laborers supplying their services may have definite "real costs," both in the aggregate and on the margin, of supplying their own services—that is, the value to the laborers of the leisure foregone in order to work. In this respect, factor monopoly is not necessarily different from commodity monopoly, although the costs (which are not reflected in payments to others) may indeed be more difficult to appraise and may not be closely calculated. Nor does it follow necessarily that a factor monopoly will not pursue or wish to pursue a "maximizing rationale"—that is, to choose a price and output such as to balance the marginal cost of supply (whatever it may be) against marginal receipts from added employment of the factor. It is quite conceivable that such a rationale, similar to that of commodity monopoly, might be pursued.

Even if these characteristics of commodity monopoly are matched, however—that is, existence of determinate costs of supply and a desire to maximize the excess of return over cost—the fact that a factor monopoly sells (as exclusive supplier to a market) some or all of that amount of a basic resource that one or more persons originally control, is the origin of one inescapable difference of factor from commodity monopoly. This is that the supply at the disposal of the factor monopoly, and the relation of cost to supply which the monopoly finds, will vary depending upon the proportion of all conceivably available factor units represented by or under the control of the factor monopoly, and conversely on the proportion of such units not represented, or excluded from access to the market in question. A factor monopoly is not a buyer-seller which can make supply available essentially by purchasing what it sells, but rather a selling agency for the owner or owners of some number of units of a total factor supply. It therefore can be said to have no definite supply available (with respect to which returns should be maximized), and no definite relation of cost of the quantity of supply, until it is known how many units of potentially available factors are represented by the monopoly, and how many excluded. And since the number of units respectively represented and excluded may vary arbitrarily and quite widely, no single cost curve and no single monopoly pricing tendency is identifiable until the number of factor units represented by the monopoly is specified.

For example, a labor union might have a protected position as a monopolistic supplier (for example, by virtue of a closed-shop contract with all employers) of the services of all glass blowers in a given market. Within this market there might be potentially 500 glass blowers available. If all of these were represented by the union, a sort of marginal cost curve, relating value of leisure foregone to added hours of glass-blowing labor might be constructed for the group of 500, and the monopolistic union might then set a wage and corresponding volume of work which was such that the addition to total wage receipts for the last hour of labor just balanced the value of leisure foregone to supply it. If, on the other hand, the union were to limit its membership to 350 glass blowers (and exclude all others from employment in this market), a curve showing the relation of added cost to added hours of labor *for the 350* would presumably lie considerably to the left of the same curve for a membership of 500—the marginal cost curve regulating supply would shift because fewer units of factor supply were represented, and because the supply of any given aggregate number of hours of work would be more onerous or costly to 350 than to 500 men. Correspondingly, the union would presumably maximize the advantage of this reduced membership by a higher wage and smaller supply of labor than if its membership were 500.

In sum, we may argue (1) a factor monopoly in a given market may represent various alternative quantities of factor units or numbers of participant factor owners; (2) the supply for which it tries to maximize advantage, or relation of cost to supply which it takes into account in so doing, will vary depending upon the number of factor units or participant owners represented; and (3) the level of its maximizing monopoly solution (for which marginal cost of supply equals marginal receipts) will thus depend on the proportion of the total available factor supply which is effectively represented by the factor monopoly. In general, supposing conventional maximizing calculations throughout, the "monopoly" factor price will be higher the fewer the factor units which are represented by the agency enjoying a monopoly in selling the factor service, and lower the greater the number of units so represented. It would appear that since progressive reduction of participation by factor owners in a factor monopoly to an extreme degree is at least conceivable, and since such restriction leads to progressively higher monopoly prices (which it does not in the case of commodity monopoly), much greater extremes of monopolistic restriction and price raising are conceivable with factor monopoly than with commodity monopoly. This is essentially because "exclusiveness" clearly tends to raise the cost of supply to the monopolistic agency in factor monopoly, but not in commodity monopoly.

Thus, we find that factor monopoly may have, given a desire to maximize the advantage of the factor units represented, a price-raising tendency similar to that of commodity monopoly, although this tendency is distinctly more variable with a factor monopoly, and depends on the quantity of factor units it represents. Given some such number of units, however, it is possible that a conventional monopoly pricing policy would be followed. That is, the factor monopoly would calculate the marginal receipts from added sales, the marginal cost (if any) of supplying successive amounts (this marginal cost representing a valuation of the real costs to factor owners), and the satisfaction-maximizing price and quantity of supply at which this marginal cost was equal to marginal receipts. Then, even if the factor monopoly represented all of the factor units which would have been supplied in a competitive market, it would tend to set a higher than competitive price, since the marginal cost of supply would now be equated to marginal receipts rather than to price. If it represented fewer factor units, it would tend to raise price even more markedly.

There are many reasons to believe, however, that this price-raising tendency of factor monopoly—predicted as an outcome of the pursuit of the sort of maximizing rationale just described—may not always be fully developed. The reasons for the moderation of this tendency are in large part parallel to those which affect commodity monopolies. First, there is the problem of the threat of entry. As any factor monopoly raises the factor price above the competitive level in its market, it makes it attractive both to owners of factor units now supplying other markets, and to owners of factor units potentially within its market but excluded from access to it by the monopoly, to attempt to become alternative or competing sellers within its market. Although the factor monopoly presumably enjoys some protection in the form of a power to exclude such entry, this may not be unlimited. In order to forestall competitive entry, therefore, it may be induced to pursue a lower price policy than would maximize the advantage of the group immediately represented, and even to admit other potentially competitive factor owners to representation, in order to secure the best long-run result for its own constituency. At the extreme this might result either in the admission of "all owners" to representation by the monopoly, or in a very close approach to competitive factor-pricing policy. Barring the latter, the factor price might be set indeterminately within a range above the competitive price.

Second, there is the problem of the imperfect cartel. The monopolistic factor seller may frequently be simply an agent for (or cartel of) a group of basic suppliers, who represents them collectively in establishing a given factor price in a particular market. In this case, pursuit of a full monopoly policy, such as would restrict employment to the point where the marginal cost of supply equaled marginal receipts from sales, requires not only that such a point be found, but also that the total receipts from sales at such a point be divided among all suppliers represented, including those that may be partially employed or unemployed in the interests of maximized total benefits to the group. In effect, such a perfect cartel policy will be agreeable to all participants only if a method for dividing the gains can be agreed upon. If it cannot—and in particular if a satisfactory method for rewarding suppliers whose factor units would be unemployed in the interest of maximum aggregate gains cannot be found—then the cartel may find it necessary to pursue a price policy which will provide some employment and direct earnings therefrom to all or most participating suppliers, and this may require a lower price and larger total employment than an ideal monopoly policy would. For example, though a union might in some sense maximize the aggregate advantage of the group by setting wages at $15 a day and securing employment for only 750 of its 1,000 members, the fact that no mutually satisfactory method can be found of rewarding the unemployed 250 from the earnings of the others might lead to a decision to gain employment for all 1,000 members at a wage of $12 a day. Where mechanisms for dividing the spoils of a monopolistic price policy cannot be developed, and the pressure to secure employment and direct earnings for all suppliers represented is strong, the tendency is obviously away from monopolistic and toward competitive factor pricing, although this tendency may be moderated if there is artificial restriction on the number of suppliers represented, or if partial employment of the factor units of all suppliers is feasible.

The preceding suggests reasons why the factor monopoly, even though attempting so far as circumstances permit to maximize the aggregate advantage of the suppliers it represents through a price at which the marginal cost of supply equals marginal receipts, might in fact arrive at a price much closer to the competitive level. A further possibility is that the factor monopoly—as an agency representing a group of suppliers—will make no attempt to calculate or arrive at a price which would maximize the aggregate advantage of the suppliers represented. The costs which would enter into such a calculation—real or subjective costs to the suppliers—may be ambiguous or scarcely known, and the concept of a maximum *aggregate* of satisfaction (maximum excess of returns over real costs) may represent an abstraction in which the suppliers represented would be uninterested. If such maximizing calculations are abandoned or never considered, we may find instead more or less arbitrary policies which set what is regarded as a high (that is, "fair") price consistent with securing what is regarded as a reasonable rate of employment for all or most suppliers represented. If policies of this sort are pursued, actual factor prices may obviously be set at or near the competitive level, or anywhere within a considerable range above this level. Restriction of the membership of suppliers in the factor monopoly will in this case also, however, tend to be associated with higher prices.

In view of these considerations, which are such that a factor monopoly might in effect attempt to raise the factor price above the level of competitive selling much, little, or even not at all, we cannot safely ascribe any unique rationale to the price policies of factor monopolies. It does appear, however, that circumstances may very frequently be such that a factor monopoly will be motivated to raise the factor price at least somewhat above the level consistent with competitive factor selling. This may be true even where there is competitive buying of factors—that is, where there is no monopsonistic depression of factor prices. It will very clearly tend to be true if the factor monopoly is faced with a monopsonistic buyer, since here the negation of monopsonistic power (for example, by establishing a perfectly elastic factor supply to the buyer at a fixed price) may permit both a higher price and a larger rate of employment. Thus, we may assume in general that factor monopolies will very frequently pursue policies of setting the factor price at least somewhat above the level which would be associated with competitive factor selling.

Factor monopolies, then, may exist and may tend to raise factor prices above the competitive-selling level. For analysis of the consequences of factor monopoly, however, we must recognize initially that it may conceivably occur in many diverse settings and patterns. A primary distinction is to be drawn between factor monopoly which faces competitive buying and that which faces monopsony, since in the first case we have the more or less simple phenomenon of the monopolist dealing with many buyers, as an alternative to dependence on a market competition on both sides, and in the second we have the situation of bilateral monopoly, introduced essentially as an alternative to monopsonistic exploitation of a competitive factor supply. As a consequence, we shall consider in turn and separately (1) factor monopoly under conditions of competitive buying and (2) factor monopoly faced by monopsonistic buyers. A further distinction may be made (especially pertinent with competitive factor buying) between the cases where the firms buying factors are competitive sellers of their own outputs and where they are monopolistic sellers. Accordingly we shall deal in turn in the three succeeding sections with (1) factor monopoly where there is both competitive buying of factors and competitive selling of commodities, (2) factor monopoly where there is competitive buying of factors but monopolistic selling of commodities, and (3) factor monopoly where there is monopsonistic buying of factors (ordinarily coupled with monopolistic commodity selling).

In addition, a distinction must be made in each of these cases among factor monopolies of various scope and frequency. Generally we may distinguish situations in which (1) there are factor monopolies in only one or a few of the many submarkets for any factor, (2) there are factor monopolies in most or all of the submarkets for one or more factors, and (3) there is a single economy-wide monopoly for one or more factors. We shall consider the indicated cases and subcases of factor monopoly in turn below.

EFFECTS OF A SINGLE FACTOR MONOPOLY
IN AN OTHERWISE COMPETITIVE ECONOMY

The general tendencies of factor monopoly are most easily revealed by an analysis of monopolistic factor selling in an economy which is in every other respect purely competitive. Let us suppose that throughout an economy (1) there is pure competition in the selling market for every commodity, so that all factor buyers sell their outputs under purely competitive conditions, and (2) there are many small buyers in every market or submarket for every factor, so that each factor buyer regards any factor as in perfectly elastic supply to him at any prevailing price. Let us further continue our supposition that there is a constant flow of money purchasing power seeking commodities and factors, which will not vary in response to price adjustments.

Now in this situation, competitive-factor selling would lead to the establishment of an equilibrium of employment and price for every factor of production, with relative factor prices everywhere such as to be in balance with the marginal rates of substitution between factors, with each factor price at such a level that all units of the factor which wished to work were employed, and with all income going to hired factors and no excess profits. With perfect factor mobility among uses there would be a single uniform price for all units of any factor; with imperfect mobility, a pattern of related prices for each factor would exist in its several submarkets. Such a competitive equilibrium of factor prices has been analyzed in Chapter 11 and on pages 503 to 507 of the present chapter. We may take the *competitive equilibrium* factor prices which would result under universal pure competition as a reference point in analyzing the effect of factor monopolies if they are introduced into or exist in an otherwise competitive situation.

How will factor prices, incomes, and employment differ if, in this otherwise purely competitive economy, one or more factors of production is monopolized on either a local or an economy-wide basis? Let us consider first the case of a single monopolistic seller of some factor *A*, who has a monopoly in one submarket for the factor, while there is competitive selling of the factor A in all other submarkets, and of all other factors in this and all other submarkets. If this local factor monopoly were not present, a certain competitive factor price, W_c, would rule for factor A in this submarket, and the buyers of the factor would be adjusted to this price by using A in such proportion to each other factor that the marginal rate of substitution of A for any factor B would equal the ratio of the price of B to the price of A, and by producing such an output that the price of the output was equal to average and marginal cost. If now a single seller gains control of the supply of A in this submarket, what will ensue?

It is at least conceivable that nothing would happen. The seller might be content (perhaps as an agent for a group of basic factor suppliers) simply to get as high a price for A in this submarket as it receives in others and to maintain employment, and the competitive price may already fulfill these requirements. Or the seller might be committed simply to secure for the quantum of factors under his control (for example, the previous competitive supply) the largest possible aggregate revenue (any costs of supply being neglected), and this would already be obtained if, with competitive full employment of available factors, the demand for factor A were in effect more elastic than unity at the going price, so that a price increase would reduce aggregate revenue. But it is also quite conceivable that the monopolistic seller would wish to raise the price of A in his submarket and obtain a supercompetitive price—in the interests perhaps of greater aggregate revenue (if the demand for the factor were less elastic than unity) or of a greater excess of reward over sacrifice.

In this case, the factor monopolist may increase the factor price, raising it above the level, W_c, which would rule with competitive selling. His ability to do so, of course, will depend upon his ability really to limit the supply of A in his submarket—to withhold or exclude units of A previously employed there and to exclude the entry of further units from other markets. Given this power to control supply and exclude entry, the monopolist can and perhaps will raise the price of the factor above the competitive level.

This price increase is a first and obvious result of such a factor monopoly. The price of A in this submarket will stand higher relative to the prices of A in other submarkets than it would with competitive selling; if A would receive the same price in all submarkets with uniformly competitive selling, it will now receive a superior price in the monopolized submarket.

Further effects of the monopolistic pricing of the factor, however, must be taken into account. First, the increase in the price of factor A in the monopolized submarket will (1) induce buyers to substitute other factors for A at any given output, and (2) raise the average and marginal costs of buyers and thus induce them to produce smaller outputs and further restrict the use of A. A net effect of the monopolistic factor price increase is thus to restrict the use of the monopolized factor, A, in the submarket in question; some restriction, in fact, is essential to raising its price above the competitive level. A related effect is to restrict the outputs of the goods produced by using monopolized units of A, and to raise their prices. Their prices, however, which in the long run will rise as much as their average costs, will increase in smaller proportion than the price of A, since their costs are composed in part of prices paid to nonmonopolized factors, which are now used relatively more than A. In a new equilibrium, excess profits of factor buyers will be unchanged at zero; since they were initially zero, production must be restricted enough to keep commodity prices equal to average costs.

Second, the real price of units of A in the monopolized submarket will be increased as well as their money price. The latter will have been increased relative to the prices of factors employed in all other submarkets, and thus relative to the prices of commodities in general, and it will also have been increased relative to the prices of commodities produced by using units of A from the monopolized submarket, since the costs of those goods—to which their prices will be equated—will rise less than the price of A.

Third, the aggregate income received by units of A employed in this submarket (that is, the factor price times the quantity employed) may either increase or decrease. This will evidently depend upon the elasticity of demand for the factor in this submarket.

As the price of any factor A is varied within a single submarket, other factor prices remaining unchanged, the quantity purchased will exhibit a corresponding variation, determined fundamentally by the substitution conditions between A and other factors and the elasticity of demand for the outputs being produced. A demand curve for any factor A in a particular submarket, such as dd' in Figure 56, thus emerges. Under competitive selling, the equilibrium factor price in this submarket is implicitly found at the intersection of this demand curve and the competitive supply curve of the factor, ss'. This establishes a competitive rate of employment, Q_c, and a competitive factor price, W_c.

Now if the demand for factor A is inelastic at the competitive price, a price increase for A would restrict its use in such small proportion that the total income paid to A would increase. This is evidently the case if the competitive factor price is initially W_c in Figure 56, since at W_c the demand for the factor is inelastic and the marginal receipts to added units (mr) are negative. An increase of factor price from W_c up to the level W_1, would increase the total income to A from this submarket. If on the other hand the competitive factor price were initially W_1, increases in it—for example, to W_2—would necessarily reduce the aggregate income to the factor in this submarket, since the demand curve is elastic above this point.

In either event, the factor units which remain employed under monopoly receive higher unit prices than they would with competitive selling, and the rate of employment is reduced within the monopolized submarket. If this is true, certain broader consequences of the monopolistic factor price must be recognized.

First, aggregate employment (throughout the economy) of the monopolized factor will be reduced unless all units disemployed in the monopolized

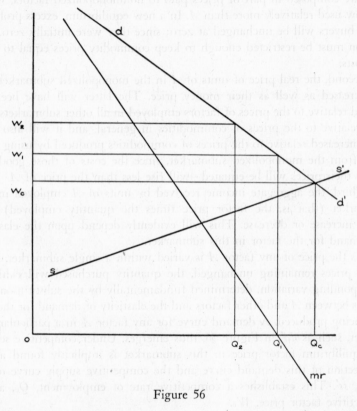

Figure 56

submarket shift to other submarkets and find employment. If some of the disemployed units are immobile, or if reduced employment is accomplished by partial utilization of each unit, aggregate employment and output tend to be reduced. Second, allocation of factors among uses is distorted from the competitive norm, since the value of the outputs produced by a unit of the factor from the monopoly submarket tends to be higher (because higher money factor prices must be covered in costs) than in other submarkets.

Third, although the units of A employed in the monopolized submarket earn more per unit and perhaps more in the aggregate than they would under competitive-factor selling, their gain is at the expense of other hired factors in the economy—smaller real incomes tend to be received by units of A employed in other submarkets, by any units of A disemployed, and by units of all other factors, as the prices of goods produced by use of units of A from the monopolized sector are raised relative to other factor prices generally. Since hired factors as a group would receive all income with universally competitive buying and selling, no one group of factor suppliers can attain a better income position than it would get through competitive selling *except by appropriating some of the income of other groups.*

Does this imply that no individual factor monopoly would be justified or desirable within a competitive economy? Not necessarily. There is nothing especially "right" or "wrong" about a strictly competitive income distribution, either as between different factors or as among units of the same factor in different submarkets—the pattern simply emerges more or less automaticaly under the specified conditions. Consequently, it is difficult to characterize aberrations from this pattern as more or less desirable. Two comments, however, are perhaps pertinent. First, labor monopolies, as far as they tend to shift aggregate income from land and capital to labor (as they may if the demand for labor in monopolized markets is inelastic), may be viewed as a device for increasing the share of labor as opposed to property incomes, and thus for lessening the inequality of income distribution (as far as property-income receivers are generally well-to-do). Second, it may be considered unfair by many that some units of a given factor, like labor, should receive higher rewards than other units of the same factor— and partly at the expense of the latter—by restricting employment in and entry to particular submarkets.

GENERAL MONOPOLIZATION OF A FACTOR SUPPLY

So much for the single isolated factor monopoly in an otherwise competitive economy. Let us now consider instead the case in which most or all submarkets for a given factor within the economy are monopolized, but where there is still competitive factor buying and commodity selling throughout. In this case, it is possible that the monopolistic seller for the factor in each submarket in turn will raise the price of the factor above the competitive level for that market. If this happens, and if at the same time the aggregate flow of money purchasing power remains unchanged and all other factors are sold competitively, what effects will be felt?

First, the factor-price increase will lead to a reduction in the use of the factor in all submarkets, and thus to a reduction in the total employment of the factor; its proportion to other factors will be reduced and total output will be cut with higher money costs (and commodity prices) in the face of given aggregate purchasing power. The factor will be able to command a higher money price by virtue of a restriction of its supply to the economy. This will also represent on the average a higher real price, since the average costs of commodities and their prices will be based in part on the prices of nonmonopolized factors, which will not rise proportionately with those of the monopolized factor. By the same token, the real prices of nonmonopolized factors must be reduced.

Second, the pattern of price differentials for the factor as among submarkets will probably differ from that associated with purely competitive selling, as far as in different submarkets different degrees of monopolistic restriction are imposed. Differences in the elasticity of demand for the factor in different submarkets will make large price increases more attractive to factor sellers in some markets than in others. It is thus possible, since commodity prices will rise generally with higher costs, that monopolized factor units in some submarkets will actually lose in the net, through factor-price increases insufficient to compensate for increased living costs, whereas others will gain considerably. Third, relative commodity prices, and the allocation of resources among various lines of production, will be correspondingly distorted from the competitive patterns. Fourth, the share of total income received by the monopolized factor may either increase or decrease, depending on the elasticity of demands for it, although on the average the real price of the monopolized factor units employed will increase. Fifth, units of the monopolized factor disemployed by virtue of the monopoly policy will lose unless there is mechanism for rewarding them from the incomes of employed factors, and *all* units of the monopolized factor can conceivably gain only if the demand for the factor is inelastic.

In this connection, it is worth re-emphasis that, if we take as a beginning point an equilibrium with universal pure competition, factor monopolies can increase the prices of their factor units (and potentially their share of total income) only by actually restricting the supply of the factor.[3] The competitive price is effectively the maximum market price which a system of enterprises can be made to pay for the competitive supply of the factor, given the supply conditions for other factors; they will react to a higher price by employing less, or, to put it another way, can be induced to pay more only if less of the factor is made available. Factor sellers can increase their earnings only by actually restricting supply.

In this respect, their situation is distinct from that of commodity monopolists, who conceivably can make monopolistic gains without actually raising prices or restricting output. In that case, as we have argued (pages 238 to 247), the tendency of such monopolists to raise price and restrict output (so that marginal cost equals marginal receipts rather than price) may be offset by a decline in costs, as the factors which firms purchase accept smaller prices rather than unemployment. The tendency toward monopolistic restriction of commodity outputs may thus be canceled out by

[3] Unless, that is, perfectly discriminatory selling should be feasible.

the suppliers of the monopolistic firms when they accept lower incomes and reduce the commodity monopolists' costs. The factor monopolists, however, have no suppliers available to absorb the impact of their restrictive policies. The factor monopolists sell but do not buy, and thus there are no "third persons" to give them lower costs and thus permit them to increase their gains without actually raising their prices or cutting their supply. Their costs, if any, are their own, and cannot be reduced. Their incomes, either gross or in the sense of the excess of their rewards over any real costs or sacrifices they may incur, can thus be increased only by actually restricting supply and actually raising price.

The conclusions just developed concerning the effects of monopolization of a factor in all or most of its many submarkets by a large group of local monopolistic sellers apply in general to the hypothetical case in which a single monopolist might control the entire supply of a factor within the economy and be in a position to determine its price. The principal difference, perhaps, is that a large single monopolist, controlling the entire supply of a factor, would not be limited by the threat of entry of factor units from other markets in the way that a small local monopolist is, and could thus raise price more steeply if he so desired. Otherwise, we may conclude similarly that such a monopolist could raise the real price of the factor above the competitive level only by restricting its supply, and that the income share of the factor might thereby be either increased or decreased depending on the elasticity of demand for the factor within the economy as a whole. It is possible that such a monopolist might fix a single uniform price for the factor throughout the economy, in which case the distortions of factor-price differentials and of allocation attributed to a group of separate monopolists might not be encountered. It is also possible, however, that the single monopolist might practice third-degree discriminatory pricing as among various buyers of the factor, in which case similar effects would ensue.

So far, we have considered only the case of monopolistic selling of a single factor, either in one or a few submarkets or in most or all submarkets. The effects of simultaneous monopolization of two or more factors, either in isolated cases or generally, are readily predictable from the preceding analysis. All factor-price raising of the monopolistic sort will tend to reduce employment of the affected factors (given the aggregate flow of money purchasing power) and to reduce output. However, the potential gains to one monopolized factor of a price increase tend to be offset by monopolistic price raising by the others, since if all money factor prices are raised simultaneously, commodity prices will tend to rise proportionally and no factor will tend on the average to secure a larger real price. Yet, sellers of any factor would tend to lose (in unit price at least) by abandonment of monopolistic pricing unless other factor sellers did the same simultaneously. The general conclusion is that gains of monopolistic factor selling in an otherwise competitive economy may be realized by a given seller only so far as the economy is supplied in part by factors sold either competitively or with a lesser degree of monopolistic price raising than the seller in question accomplishes.

In concluding this argument, it may be well to emphasize that the ability of monopolistic factor sellers to increase the real price of their factor units by raising their money prices (albeit at the expense of reduced employment) rests on the supposition that the total flow of money purchasing power remains stable, or at any rate does not respond sufficiently to upward adjustments of money factor prices to forestall any change in real price. Then, with a given money demand for factors, higher factor prices necessarily mean smaller employment, and if a single factor price is raised, there will be an improvement in its ratio to other factor prices and to commodity prices. This supposition of a constant money demand for factors is evidently appropriate if the only factor-price increase is within a single submarket wherein a small proportion of all factors is employed, since then no perceptible response of total purchasing power to the factor-price change would be expected. If there is a general increase in the money price for all units of an important factor within the economy, however, it is possible that total purchasing power will respond significantly, and perhaps even increase proportionally. Such a response, in fact, is predicted by certain theories of income and employment. It should be noted that if the aggregate level of money purchasing power should increase always in the same proportion as the money price of a given factor—so that a constant ratio of the money flow to the factor price were maintained—then monopolistic raising of the money factor price would not tend to increase the real price of the factor at all. The price level of all factors and commodities would simply tend to rise proportionately at a constant employment level, with no eventual restriction in the employment of the monopolized factor, and no gain to the monopoly except perhaps in the process of adjustment of income to the new price. In this case, only a continual restriction of supply of the monopolized factor would produce monopolistic gains, and this would lead to progressive inflation of money purchasing power and all prices, with the price of the monopolized factor held in at an advantageous ratio throughout. We shall return to this problem in Chapter 15 below.

FACTOR MONOPOLY TOGETHER WITH COMMODITY MONOPOLY

The second setting in which factor monopoly may be evaluted is that in which (1) there is purely competitive buying of all factors—that is, many small buyers of any factor in each market or submarket, but (2) some or all buyers of factors are nevertheless monopolistic sellers of their own outputs. Any firm buying factors, that is, views the price of each factor as given to him and combines factors so that the marginal rates of substitution of any one for another equals the inverted ratio of their prices. But some or all firms restrict their outputs so that their marginal costs are less than their selling prices, and ordinarily earn excess profits.

In this case, as we have seen (pages 507 to 514), purely competitive selling of factors will lead to the establishment of determinate prices and rates of employment for all factors. Although these factor prices, and probably the rates of employment, will tend to be lower than they would be in the absence of monopolistic commodity selling, they are in essence the highest prices which the market will offer at the given rates of employment as long as the commodity monopolies referred to remain in existence. Suppose now that in this situation monopolistic selling of factors is instituted. Will this modify the distribution of income significantly, and in particular will it be a device for reducing or eliminating the excess profits earned by firms through the exercise of their monopolistic power as sellers of commodities?

It is not evident that in general it will. The firm with monopoly power in selling its commodity earns an excess profit by holding output to a point where marginal cost and average cost are less than price, and by being able to exclude the entry of other firms which would drive the price of its output down. If it is a competitive buyer of factors, it also minimizes its cost of any output by striking the designated balance between marginal rates of substitution and relative prices for every pair of factors. If factors are being sold competitively, the factor prices which enter into its costs lie at a certain level, and its profit-maximizing output is at a corresponding level.

The raising of these factor prices by monopolistic factor sellers will raise the level of its average and marginal cost curves. But it does not follow that the commodity monopolist will thereafter produce the same commodity outputs at the same prices, thus yielding his previous profits directly to the factor sellers. With higher costs, he will presumably restrict output further, so as to maintain the gap between selling price and marginal and average costs—for example, to maintain an equality of marginal cost and marginal receipts. His response to a monopolistic increase in factor prices will thus be a corresponding increase in the selling price of his commodity, together with a restriction of its output. As a consequence, his excess-profit margin may very well be preserved, and the *real* prices of hired factors (fewer of which will now be employed) will not necessarily increase at the expense of his profits.

In effect, the mere raising of factor prices to a firm with monopoly power in selling its output does not deprive it of this monopoly power. It will continue to exercise it, and perhaps to reap an excess-profit reward from it, in spite of considerable factor-price increases, and thus continue to subtract from the real earnings of hired factors. Administered increases of the prices of hired factors, given a certain constant flow of total purchasing power, may succeed only in restricting employment and output of the factors, without necessarily altering the distribution of income as between profits and hired factor earnings.

The preceding provides a general answer to the question posed—that is, monopolistic factor-price increase, in general, will not tend to eliminate the excess profits of commodity monopolists, whose power to raise commodity prices relative to costs is not removed by making costs higher. This proposition may be argued in detail either for the case of the isolated monopolistic commodity seller or for that of a world of such sellers, but it is sufficiently obvious that we need not develop it here.

One general qualification to this general argument, however, may be noted. An upward shift in hired factor prices by virtue of monopolistic factor selling not only tends to raise the level of the cost curves of commodity monopolists relative to their demand curve, but also to reduce their outputs in general. If this restriction of output raises the real costs of production by forcing producers to operate at higher or less efficient points on U-shaped average cost curves, thus increasing the excess of average over marginal cost, then the equilibrium with monopolistic factor prices may result in a reduction or elimination of the commodity monopolist's excess profits, as their demand curves now reach or approach tangency with their higher average costs. In this case, however, commodity prices would still tend to have risen as much as factor prices, and the reduction in excess profits would be reflected in reduced productivity of factors in general rather than in any increase in the average of their real wages.

The general rule (further elaborations of which need not be developed here) is, therefore, that monopolistic factor-price policies by sellers in markets with competitive factor buying will not serve in general to secure for factor sellers all or part of the excess profits of commodity monopolists. These will tend either to be held (or dissipated in lower efficiency) by the commodity monopolists in spite of higher factor prices. Factor monopoly in this setting will tend to restrict the aggregate output and real income to be shared, and perhaps permit sellers of one factor to gain at the expense of others, but it will not tend to raise the real prices of hired factors as a group.

BILATERAL MONOPOLY IN FACTOR MARKETS

The effects of factor monopoly may appear in a somewhat different light if it exists in opposition to factor monopsony. We have seen that where there is competitive buying of factors, factor monopoly can in general increase the welfare of any group of factor sellers only by restricting employment, and only at the expense of other factor sellers in the economy. In effect, when there is uniformly competitive factor buying the results of competitive factor selling cannot easily be improved, from the standpoint of all hired factors as a group, by market-pricing devices. Their aggregate returns in this situation are the maximum attainable, barring discriminatory factor selling, with given commodity market structures. Where there is monopsonistic buying of factors, however, the situation is otherwise. In this case, monopsonists will take advantage of competitive factor selling to depress factor prices below the competitive level and at the same time to restrict employment, so that competitive factor sellers will not receive as much as the rewards which would result from competition in both selling and buying of factors. It follows that in this case factor monopolies *may* be able to counteract or offset monopsony buying power, and in so doing secure a higher factor price without any restriction and perhaps with an increase of employment, and without offsetting losses to other factor sellers. Looking at the issue in another way, monopsonistic buying may be used to offset monopolistic selling of factors, and so employed it may overcome the price-raising effects of factor monopoly while increasing employment.

This result is by no means automatic, however, for when monopoly is placed in juxtaposition to monopsony, we do not automatically arrive at the equivalent of competition. We arrive at bilateral monopoly, which, as we have seen, may lead to a variety of outcomes in the market. It should thus be useful to consider the principal possibilities of bilateral monopoly situations in factor markets, especially since they have become increasingly common in the modern economy.

In this connection, the theory of bilateral monopoly in commodity markets, developed on pages 432 to 436, provides a convenient starting point. It was argued there that when a single seller and a single buyer exist in a market, the desire to use market-pricing devices by either or both is unlikely. That is, the seller is unlikely to try just to set a price at which a buyer will purchase as much as he wishes; likewise the buyer will not try simply to fix a price at which the seller will supply what he wishes. Rather, each will attempt to practice the principles of perfect discrimination by establishing an all-or-nothing bargain specifying a given quantity to be sold and purchased and a lump price thereon. If this stratagem is attempted by both buyer and seller, both will find the same quantity of purchase and sale to be potentially the most profitable, so that any bargaining process between them is likely to lead to quick agreement on the amount of output to pass from seller to buyer. This will tend to be the competitive quantity, for which marginal cost of the seller equals marginal receipts of the buyer (as derived from his selling market). The lump price at which this quantity will change hands, however, is indeterminate within a wide range.

If this sort of calculation were pursued in the case of bilateral monopoly for a productive factor, the results would tend to be of the same order. In Figure 57, suppose that *SS'* represents what the supply curve for the factor units involved would be under competitive selling—that is, the quantities which would be supplied by sellers at various alternative given prices beyond the control of the sellers. As such, it also represents implicitly the marginal cost *to the factor suppliers* of making various successive amounts

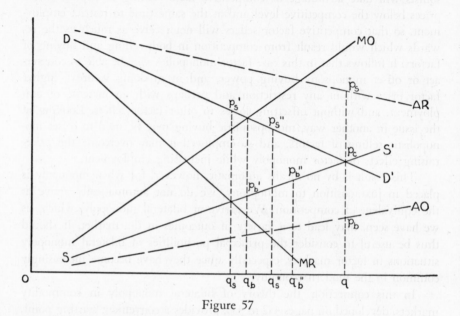

Figure 57

of their services available [4]—in the case of labor, for example, it might represent value of leisure foregone by the marginal unit supplied at successive quantities of supply. Suppose, further that *DD'* represents what buyer's demand curve would be under competitive buying—that is, the quantities that would be taken at various alternative given prices beyond the control of the buyer. As such, it also represents the value of the marginal benefit *to the buyer* of successive additions to his purchases—or his own marginal receipts from reselling what he purchases.[5]

If the principles of perfect discrimination are applied in the bargaining between buyer and seller, two further curves become relevant. If the buyer were to practice perfectly discriminating monopsony in buying the factor, he would buy successive units along *SS'* at separate prices as given on *SS'*,

[4] *SS'* in Figure 57 corresponds to *MC* in Figure 48.
[5] *DD'* in Figure 57 corresponds to *dd'* in Figure 48.

and would pay for any particular quantity an average price shown on AO (his average outlay for the factor).[6]

If the seller were to practice perfectly discriminatory monopoly in selling, he would sell successive units at separate prices as shown along DD', and would receive an average price for any quantity shown on AR (his average receipts from sales).[7]

Now if the seller could dominate the bargain with the buyer, he would wish to produce the quantity oq at which his marginal cost (SS') equaled his (the seller's) marginal receipts under perfect discrimination (DD') and to sell at the price identified by p_s on AR. The buyer, given similar domination, would find that his profit would be maximized by equating his marginal benefit from purchases (DD') to his (the buyer's) marginal cost under perfect discrimination (SS'). He would wish to purchase the quantity oq also, but at the price identified by p_b on AO. Thus, there would be a tendency for seller and buyer to arrive at an all-or-nothing bargain for the seller to supply and the buyer to use oq of the factor, but at a price which might lie anywhere between p_s and p_b, depending on relative bargaining strength and skill.

Thus, the result of bilateral monopoly in a factor market, provided the logic of perfect discrimination were applied, would tend to be a *competitive* quantity of use for the factor (the same as would be arrived at with competitive buying and selling—at the intersection of what correspond to market demand and supply curves). Aberrations in allocation attributable to either simple monopsony or simple monopoly tend to disappear. On the other hand, a competitive price for the factor—at p_c—would be arrived at only coincidentally. The price may lie between p_c and p_b, in which case the income of the factor units is reduced in favor of monopsonistic excess profits, or between p_c and p_s, in which case the buyer's income (including excess profits of any commodity monopoly) is shifted to the earnings of the factor units. It will be noted that in this case factor monopoly *can* capture the excess profits of the buyer, whereas with simple market pricing it cannot.

It will be noted also that pursuit of this logic results in a distinctly larger quantity of use of the factor than would either simple monopoly selling (where a single selling price is set without discrimination), or simple monopsony buying. With simple monopoly, the seller would face a market demand curve DD' for the factor, which would give his average receipts from sales in various quantities. He would find his own marginal receipts lower at MR. He would thus, to maximize aggregate returns over cost, sell the quantity oq_s', at the price p_s' (where his own marginal cost, SS', inter-

[6] AO in Figure 57 corresponds to AC in Figure 48.
[7] AR in Figure 57 corresponds to DD' in Figure 48.

sects MR). That is he would set the price p_s' and allow the buyer to take what he would, which would be oq_s'. With simple monopsony, the buyer would face a market supply curve SS', which would give his average outlay for various quantities purchased, and would find his marginal outlay higher at MO. He would, in order to maximize profits, wish to buy the quantity oq_b', where his own marginal benefit from purchases, DD', intersects MO, and buy at the price p_b'. That is, he would set the price p_b', and allow the seller to supply what he would, which would be oq_b'.

Thus, it is apparent that reliance on *market pricing* by either the monopolist or the monopsonist (as opposed to perfectly discriminatory all-or-nothing bargains) leads back to either monopolistic or monopsonistic restriction, if either one or the other can dominate the market and set the price. It would be only the application of the logic of first-degree discrimination to bilateral monopoly which would lead at all *automatically* to a competitive rate of use of the factor, although even here the factor price is indeterminate within a potentially wide range.

The question now arises as to whether *in fact* bilateral monopoly in factor markets will result in the employment of the logic of perfect discrimination, and whether, therefore, the introduction of a factor monopoly to oppose an established factor monopsony (or vice versa) will lead to the elimination of monopolistic (or monopsonistic) restriction of factor use in the market. We have argued previously (pages 432 to 436) that, with a single buyer and a single seller only, perfect discrimination finds its ideal setting and the perfectly discriminatory bargain should emerge. It may be pertinent, however, to contemplate other possibilities.

The monopolistic factor seller is not ordinarily a firm with complete control over an "output"—it is (in the case of a labor union, for example) frequently an agency representing a large number of individual suppliers who have banded together for purposes of dealing with buyers. As such, it may not have the power or the authorization to make all-or-nothing bargains specifying both quantity of the factor to be purchased and the average price of this quantity; it may be limited to bargaining for a factor price only, with the quantity to be purchased and the quantity to be supplied being left open to the discretion of the buyer and of the many individual suppliers. This would appear frequently to be the case when a labor union and employer arrive at a contract wage rate for a given future time period.

If the process of bargaining between seller and buyer in the factor market can produce no more than a fixed price for the factor, then the "perfect-discrimination" outcome is no longer to be expected, and we are back in the realm of market pricing and its consequences. What may these consequences be? A very considerable range of possibilities is evidently open. At one extreme, the seller might dominate the bargain and succeed in establishing the fixed price for the factor which was to his greatest advantage under market pricing—that is, p_s'. At this price, the buyer would take only oq_s', and the seller would be content to restrict supply to this level to hold up the price. In this case, bilateral monopoly would give the same results as simple factor monopoly facing competitive factor buying—restriction of employment with a monopolistic factor price. At the other extreme, the buyer might dominate the bargain, and establish a factor price p_b'. At this price sellers would supply only oq_b', and the buyer would be content to restrict his purchases to this level to hold the factor price down. Here, bilateral monopoly would give the result of simple factor monopsony faced with competitive selling—restricted employment and a monopsonistic price.

Suppose, however, that neither seller nor buyer dominates, and that there is a compromise on the factor price. It would then appear that the price could fall indeterminately between p_s' and p_b', and that a degree of restriction on factor use would tend to result, depending on the distance of this price from the competitive price, p_c. It is possible, though a priori perhaps not especially probable, that the process of bargaining between buyer and seller could establish the competitive market price, p_c, for the factor. If it did so, sellers would be willing to supply and buyers willing to take the competitive quantity oq at this price, and a genuine competitive adjustment would emerge. (It would emerge, that is, *provided* that given this compromise price sellers did not set supply short of oq in order to influence the price arrived at when bargaining on it was "reopened" at a future date, and buyers did not set purchases short of oq with the same incentive. If such stratagems are pursued, even a compromise price of p_c may not give a competitive rate of factor use.)

It is equally possible that the factor price may be established somewhere between p_s' and p_b', but not at p_c. For example, the bargain might be struck at p_b'', which is a bit above p_b' but still reflects a net advantage to the buyer, or at p_s'', which is a bit below p_s' but reflects an advantage to the seller. In any case of this variety, some monopolistic or monopsonistic restriction tends to remain. At a price p_b'' (between p_b' and p_c) sellers will presumably supply a quantity q_b'', while buyers will restrict purchases to this level to hold price down. At a price p_s'' (between p_s' and p_c) buyers will presumably take the quantity q_s'', while sellers will restrict supply to this level in order to hold price up. With the product of bargaining in bilateral monopoly being limited to establishment of a market price, therefore, the maintenance of some degree of either monopolistic or monopsonistic restriction of factor use, with corresponding effects on the factor price, seems probable. In general, unless we can predict the relative strength of seller and buyer in bargaining, the degree of restriction and the amount and direction of deviation of the factor price from the competitive level are unpredictable.

The impacts of monopolistic or monopsonistic tendencies, potentially emergent from bilateral monopoly, need not be reviewed here. In general, it seems clear that they will not necessarily be eliminated by bilateral monopoly. It seems safe to predict, however, that bilateral monopoly, involving the compromise of bargaining between buyer and seller, will lead to less restrictive effects on factor use and less distortion of income distribution than monopoly or monopsony alone. Organization of sellers to counteract monopsonistic factor buying, or of buyers to counteract monopolistic factor selling, therefore, is likely to be beneficial to the welfare of the economy as a whole.

The fact that the outcome of bilateral monopoly bargaining in factor markets is theoretically indeterminate within such wide limits (given the general assumptions we have so far been able to develop) represents a serious deficiency in modern price theory. The great bulk of labor markets today are ostensibly of a bilateral monopoly structure, and for all of these we have been able to develop no really definite predictions concerning the level of factor prices and the rate of employment. For a more adequate theory it is essential to develop generalizations concerning the determinants of the relative strength of seller and buyer in such markets, and thus of the level and character of the bargain likely to be struck.

SUMMARY

At the outset of this chapter, the analysis of competitive-factor pricing was extended to explain the determination of a pattern or family of specific prices for each basic productive factor when the units of the factor are sold in a number of disparate submarkets among which factor units are imperfectly mobile. In long-run equilibrium, the emergence of a determinate competitive price pattern for each factor was predicted, determined in effect by the extent of limitations on factor mobility. Following that analysis, we have considered the effects on income distribution of monopolistic pricing in commodity markets, of monopsonistic buying and monopolistic selling in factor markets, and of bilateral monopoly bargaining in such markets. In brief, it has appeared that commodity monopolies not only tend to shift income from hired factor earnings to excess profits, but also potentially to alter the relative income shares of different hired factors. Factor monopsony has similar tendencies, and in addition a specific tendency to restrict factor employment. Factor monopoly tends to raise the incomes of factor units in the monopolized markets by restricting their employment, and results in the reduction of factor incomes in other markets. It will not, unless perfectly discriminatory monopoly can be practiced, tend to recover for the hired factors the profits of commodity monopolies. The juxtaposition of monopsony and monopoly in factor markets results in the determination of factor prices by a bargaining process rather than by market prices or a dominant seller or buyer. The results which will emerge from such bilateral monopoly situations are theoretically indeterminate within a wide range, although it seems probable that the extreme tendencies of both monopoly and monopsony may be in part avoided.

In the discussion of other than purely competitive market forms, we have focused the analysis on the extreme cases of single seller monopoly, single buyer monopsony, and bilateral monopoly in the formal sense. It should be apparent that the tendencies of oligopoly selling, oligopsony buying, and bilateral oligopoly—not discussed explicitly—may tend to approximate those of the extreme cases to which they correspond, or to fall between those of the extreme cases and competitive tendencies.

It may be well to reiterate the fact that the preceding analysis was developed on the assumption of a given self-sustaining flow of purchasing power in the economy, permitting attainment of full employment of all factors via price adjustments. The predictions, therefore, apply explicitly to situations of this sort. We shall note, however, that most of the predictions developed apply with slight modification to situations where the rate of flow of money purchasing power responds in some pattern to adjustments in factor prices.

The analysis has also been pursued on the assumption that each productive factor is a sort of basic inanimate commodity, with a given supply or supply curve in each period of time which is independent of the supply of any other factor. Thus, we have not investigated potential supply interdependence among factors, nor the peculiar supply characteristics of actual factors of production. (The only excursion into this area has been a consideration of the real costs which determine the shape of a factor supply curve—necessary for an analysis of the policies of factor monopolies.) In the succeeding chapter we shall alter our assumptions to recognize the peculiar supply conditions of the actual productive factors, and inquire to what extent the preceding analysis must be modified to predict actual factor-price determination.

SUPPLEMENTARY READINGS

JOHN T. DUNLOP, *Wage Determination under Trade Unions*, New York: The Macmillan Company, 1944.

JOAN ROBINSON, *The Economics of Imperfect Competition*, Ch. 20-26.

GEORGE J. STIGLER, *The Theory of Price*, Ch. 15.

13 LABOR, LAND, AND CAPITAL

Two basic simplifying assumptions have underlain our analysis of factor pricing to this point. First, we have assumed that in the economy there is a constant flow of money purchasing power through time, to which factor prices may adjust. This implies in turn that involuntary unemployment cannot persist. Second, we have assumed that each of the factors of production is a sort of basic inanimate commodity, available in fixed amount in any time period, and with a supply which is independent of that of any other factor. Thus, we have argued as if there were, in each period, limited binfuls of some basic substances, A, B, and C, which were used in all production, and have analyzed how the relative prices of these substances would be determined and how they would share in the income from production.

We may now relax the second of these assumptions, and recognize for purposes of analysis the actual characteristics of the productive factors and their supply conditions. Investigation of the characteristics of actual productive factors will permit us to introduce more specific assumptions concerning their supply conditions, and thus to develop more specific predictions on their pricing. It will also reveal a certain interrelationship among them—namely, the interrelationship of the supply of capital goods with the supplies of labor and land, and with the supply of investable funds. Examination of the origins and character of "capital," in the sense both of investable funds and of specialized goods used in further production, will reveal major aspects of the character of production and of economic behavior which have heretofore been neglected. Therefore, we must consider the special characteristics and supply conditions of labor, land, and capital, and the implications of these characteristics and conditions for the determination of factor prices and income distribution.

A. LABOR AS A PRODUCTIVE FACTOR

THE CHARACTER OF LABOR, AND INSTITUTIONS
AFFECTING ITS SUPPLY

There are in essence only two basic productive factors—the services of human beings, or *labor,* and the services of natural resources, or *land.* It is impossible to say that one is more important, since each is indispensable to the other. Of the two, however, labor has, through the history of capitalism in Western countries at least, been able to command a preponderant share of the total income from production, and is in this sense at least the "more important" of the two basic factors.

To understand the conditions of supply for labor, we must understand first what it is, and second the institutional arrangements subject to which it is made available for use. Labor from the standpoint of economic analysis is the *services* of human beings—their activity, whether physical or mental or both, devoted to production. The source of these services, of course, is ultimately the individual human being, who is a sort of exhaustible reservoir of labor service with a definitely limited capacity to supply services within any given short interval of time. The human being himself could be viewed abstractly as a sort of basic productive agency, like a machine, which can perform useful services up to a certain rate through time, and over a limited total interval of time.

The control of the human being under the modern Western form of government resides with the being himself. That is, the individual is a free person who can sell and contract to sell his services to whom he wishes for such length of time as he wishes, or can refuse to sell his services and remain idle for any interval he chooses. The individual human being thus "owns himself" and has the basic control over the supply of labor service. Such an institutional arrangement is clearly distinct from that of slavery, where some categories of persons can actually be purchased and sold much like livestock, and where the purchased or slave laborer does not have much discretion over how much or where he will work. It is also distinct from a feudal arrangement, wherein the individual's freedom of choice with respect to work was subject to numerous systematic restrictions, or from an arrangement under an authoritarian state which requires the individual to work and perhaps designates the place and type of occupation. Our system of freedom of the individual and free contract for labor is, of course, subject to infringements, such as draft for military service and perhaps (as in England during the last war) draft for designated labor in times of national emergency. But, by and large, our system is essentially one of individual freedom in the sense described, and of individual free choice with respect to supplying one's own labor services. Economic necessity may induce or effectively force the individual to offer his labor services regularly for hire, but he certainly retains ultimate discretion as to where, for whom, and how much. The fact that habit and tradition may bind most individuals to a very fixed pattern of work does not erase this fundamental fact.

THE SUPPLY CONDITIONS FOR LABOR

The consequences of this basic institutional framework for the supply of labor are important. Since labor is supplied by individuals who can make their own decisions, the fundamental determinant of labor supply is the psychology of the individual. That is, his attitude toward work in general— the way he balances the advantages of working, such as the wages paid him and the enjoyment of labor, against the advantages of leisure—and toward various types and places of work will be the fundamental determinant of how much labor will be supplied at a given wage either for the whole economy or in particular occupations. There are obviously wide differences among individuals with respect to attitudes toward work, leisure, and income, and also wide differences among countries or regions within countries. We shall not analyze this matter here. Whatever the attitudes are, they will presumably give rise in the case of any individual to some individual supply schedule linking the quantity of labor service offered to any available wage rate. If there is competitive selling of labor, with each laborer reacting independently to a going wage rate, there will be for any group of individuals selling their services in a given market a market supply schedule of the same order. In any case, the primary determinant of the shape of the supply curve will be individual attitudes toward work, leisure, and income.

The shape of a typical individual's supply curve of his own services is not definitely known, but it is generally thought to slope upward to the right (positively) above some critical wage, indicating a willingness to supply somewhat more hours of work per day, week, or month if wages per hour are higher. Below a certain wage, however, the individual's supply curve of his services may slope downward to the right (negatively), reflecting the fact that below this wage he will be willing to work longer hours at lower wages "in order to eat." For some part of the potential labor supply, moreover, there may be a wage below which, or a wage interval within which, no labor services will be offered. Thus, married housewives may join the hired labor force only if the wage in outside employment exceeds a certain level, or perhaps work only if the wage is either (a) quite high or (b) so low that the family sorely needs the earnings of an added individual. All of the preceding applies to the individual faced with a wage offer from a single source (opportunities potentially represented by other offers being neglected). If a worker is faced with several alternative wage offers for his services—for example, in different occupations or different localities—his supply curve of his own services in any one submarket will presumably show no supply below a wage sufficiently low to induce him to shift his services to another submarket.

The market supply curve for labor in a given submarket under conditions of competitive selling of labor is an aggregation of the individual supply curves of a large number of individuals, reflecting the shapes of these individual curves as well as the various levels below which various individuals will refuse to supply any services. Such a market supply curve is generally thought to slope upward to the right above some critical wage level, indicating that more hours of work per week or month will be offered by individuals at higher wages, and also that added individuals will be attracted into the hired labor force at higher wages. If, in addition, workers employed in other submarkets can be attracted, there will be an added reason for increase of labor supply with higher wages in the given submarket, and supply may be quite elastic to wage increases. Below a critical wage level, the supply curve of labor may become very elastic to further wage reductions in the given submarket, if workers "desert" to other submarkets which offer higher wages. As far as workers are relatively immobile among areas and occupations, however, the supply may decrease only moderately even with steep wage reductions, and with extreme immobility from a given submarket supply may increase again with very low wages, as more workers join the labor force and workers offer to work longer hours in order to maintain a given living standard.

In general, therefore, the following would appear to be true. In a submarket for labor from which there is considerable mobility of employed labor to other submarkets, there should be a supply curve for labor which slopes upward to the right throughout, and is quite elastic to wage changes, reflecting that large proportional increases in labor offered will be induced by small proportional increases in price. This supply curve may approach perfect elasticity below a wage similar to that obtainable for similar ability or skill in other submarkets. In a submarket for labor to and from which there is restricted labor mobility, the supply curve should again be positively sloping over much of its range but less elastic, and rather than becoming very elastic below a certain wage it may remain relatively inelastic and even assume a negative slope in low-wage ranges, reflecting a greater labor supply at very low wages than at somewhat higher wages.

A competitive supply curve reflecting the reaction of the aggregate labor supply (in all submarkets together) to changes in the general level of wages should have the general characteristics of a supply curve in an isolated submarket from which there is little or no mobility. (This is because in both cases alternative wage opportunities are absent.) That is, from some critical wage level up, the supply curve should slope positively, reflecting increased aggregate labor supply at increased wage rates. Below this level, however, supply may increase also with *decreases* in the wage rate, as people offer to work longer to maintain some living standard. Too much importance could probably be attached, however, to the negatively sloping ranges of labor supply curves, whether they refer to the aggregate labor supply or to particular submarkets—at any rate for the modern American economy. Real wages seem generally to be at such a level that the reaction of labor selling in competitive markets would be to restrict supply with moderate wage decreases and increase supply with wage increases. Thus, in the relevant ranges the competitive market supply curve for labor as a whole may be regarded as positively sloped. There will be differing elasticities of labor supply in different submarkets, and presumably a moderate or low elasticity of the total labor supply in response to general wage changes.

The elasticity of the labor supply in each of many quasi-separate submarkets is a matter of significance because labor is distributed among many occupations and areas and is imperfectly mobile from one to another. There are barriers to mobility among occupations in the form of differences in individuals' abilities, differences in education and training, and differences in personal preferences as to type of work. Thus, not every plasterer is intrinsically able to qualify as a statistician (or vice versa), and relatively few people are financially able to acquire education as surgeons or lawyers. The offsprings of corporation executives, once given a college education, may prefer low-paid white-collar jobs to higher-paid employment involving manual labor. Similarly, labor is not perfectly mobile among geographical areas. The cost of moving may deter labor from shifting to take advantage of higher wages in other areas, or traditional preferences for a state or a climate may induce people to live and work where wages are not as high as elsewhere.

Given these impediments to mobility, it is typical that competitive supply curves for labor in the various submarkets will diverge significantly from perfect elasticity. This will reflect the fact that although added labor supply will be attracted from other submarkets by higher wages, the amount attracted by any small wage increase will be limited, and that labor will "desert" to other submarkets only in limited degree with any small wage reduction. The level of any submarket supply curve, of course, will depend on the general level of wages in alternative occupations, and the general level of wages (and of all submarket supply curves together) will be determined by the relation of the total demand for labor of all sorts to its aggregate supply.

TENDENCIES IN WAGE DETERMINATION

What are the implications of these characteristics of labor supply for the determination of wages? First, it may be noted that labor is indeed a basic productive factor with a supply substantially independent of that of any other factor. In this respect, its characteristics accord with those assumed for productive factors in the analysis of preceding chapters. Second, it is evidently not an inanimate commodity available in nature without effort on anyone's part, but is rather made available by human effort and potentially at some cost—in the loss of leisure or the irksomeness of working—to at least many of its suppliers. As a consequence, it will not generally be supplied *in toto* at any price offered—it will not have a supply which is perfectly inelastic to the price paid. Some minimal reward will be necessary to elicit any supply, and the amount of the supply will vary with the wage offered. As we have seen, larger supplies will probably be elicited at higher wages once some critical wage is passed. Thus, the assumption of some given elastic supply curve for labor in general seems appropriate, and that part of the preceding analysis which rests on such an assumption seems most applicable to the explanation of labor prices. In particular, a change in the demand for labor will tend to affect the volume of employment as well as the price.

Third, the fact that the total labor supply is distributed among many submarkets, and is imperfectly mobile between such submarkets, suggests that a universally competitive determination of wages would indeed result, in equilibrium, in a pattern of at least quasi-permanent wage differentials among occupations and areas. The analysis of competitive factor-price differences among disparate submarkets, developed in the preceding chapter (pages 503 to 507), seems definitely applicable here.

Fourth, the departure of the competitive labor supply curve from perfect elasticity in the typical submarket will provide a setting for the exercise of monopsony in buying labor if the number of buyers is one or a few. This will be true, of course, as long as the laborers in any given submarket (ordinarily many in number) sell competitively and do not organize for collective bargaining or wage setting. Monopsonistic wage-lowering is thus a threat to unorganized laborers selling their own services.

Fifth, with or without monopsony there is evident no reason, if there were a given self-sustaining flow of aggregate money purchasing power, that competitive wage adjustments should not secure employment for all workers who wished to work at the money wage offered by the market or markets to which they had access. We have discovered nothing peculiar about the supply of labor which would void our previous conclusion to this effect.

There is one possible characteristic of competitive labor supply, however, which might preclude the most rational competitive adjustment of the volume of employment. This is that laborers may relate the supplies they offer directly to money wage rates, and not to real wage rates (to the purchasing power in terms of commodities of money wages received). Suppose that they do this, withholding some supply of the money wage is below a certain level, regardless of the level of commodity prices. Then, if there is a given constant flow of aggregate money purchasing power, these arbitrary money-wage stipulations *may* lead to the maintenance of considerable unemployment. Such unemployment would in a sense be voluntary, in that unemployed labor refused to work at the money wage the market offered, but it might involve the unemployment of laborers who would in some sense be willing to work at the real wage offered if only they considered rationally the going relation of commodity prices to the wage rate. There is no general agreement, however, as to the extent to which laborers may take money instead of real wages as a meaningful measure of their earnings.

LABOR MONOPOLY

Applying the analysis of foregoing chapters, it is clear that with competitive selling of labor and with a given constant flow of money purchasing power, an equilibrium wage rate or family of related wage rates would tend to emerge within an economy, and at the same time an equilibrium level of labor employment. This would involve, under the assumptions stated, no involuntary unemployment. The height of the real wage of labor and its share in total income would evidently depend in every case on the quantity of labor made available relative to that of other productive factors and on the conditions of substitution between labor and other factors. Such a wage rate would tend to be highest if there were both competitive selling of commodities and competitive buying of labor. Commodity monopoly and labor monopsony would both tend to depress the real wage of labor and labor's share in income, and to create excess profits to enterprise. They would probably also tend to reduce the level of employment, as far as less labor was offered for use at reduced real wage rates.

Competitive selling of labor is no longer the mode, however. Labor is typically (although not in every case) organized into unions, and the union or its representative becomes an agent of the union members who either sets a wage for their services or negotiates with employers to determine a wage. In this case, the determination of labor supply, or its reaction to the wage rate, is no longer governed by a multitude of individual decisions of individual laborers, and does not depend in any simple and direct sense on the psychological attitudes of individuals toward work, leisure, and income. The supply of labor, or the price at which it will be supplied, is determined by collective decision of the union membership or by the representatives of the unions who attempt to promote the interests of their membership in some seemingly appropriate way. Labor supply and price thus depend in this setting much more directly on the character of group psychology or on the psychology and motivation of leadership groups within a union.

There appears to be very little in the way of systematic understanding of the motives and calculations which underlie the policies of labor unions or of union leadership groups. In setting a wage, or bargaining to establish one, do they strive for a maximum wage, a maximum total income to a given membership, an optimal balance between marginal increment to income and marginal labor effort required, a wage low enough to provide full employment to all members, or what? Do they take systematic account of individual members' preferences as regards work and leisure? No general answers to these questions have been developed. The reason that they have not may well be that there is great diversity in the motivations and policies of unions, so that no typical pattern can be identified. A good deal may depend, moreover, on the size of the union (which will affect the extent of direct participation of the membership in decision making), upon whether it can obtain a "closed-shop" contract with employers (requiring employment only of union members), and on whether the union restricts its membership rigidly or accepts all qualified applicants for membership without discrimination.

With the rather bewildering array of possibilities of various sorts which are open, about the most that can be said of a brief general nature is that the labor unions are monopolistic sellers of labor, or more generally cartels of laborers who appoint agents to represent them, and that such unions may systematically endeavor to establish wage rates at least somewhat higher than would obtain with competitive selling of labor. In short, the labor union has the general attributes previously attributed to factor monopolies in general (pages 529 to 551).

The effects of union organization on wage determination should also be similar to those attributed to factor monopolies generally. If there is competitive buying of labor, unions may be able to raise the wage rate above the competitive level by restricting the volume of employment, and, if demands for labor are inelastic, thus raise the share of income received by labor. They will not in general succeed in this case in recapturing for labor the profits derived from commodity monopolies. If there is monopsonistic buying of labor, the emergence of unionization creates bilateral monopoly situations in labor markets. (Otherwise, previously competitive buyers may organize to bargain with unions, bringing about the same situation.) In this case, labor unions may evidently increase wages to or above a competitive level while perhaps increasing employment, although at the extreme they might raise them far enough to restrict it. As we have seen, approximately competitive results can emerge from bilateral monopoly in markets for such a factor as labor, but deviations in either monopsonistic or monopolistic directions are quite possible.

One very probable effect of the selling of labor by a number of separate unions to separate submarkets is to create a pattern of wage differentials quite different from the competitive pattern. If some unions are faced with very inelastic demands for labor and pursue high-wage policies, they may secure much higher wages for a given sort of ability than is secured elsewhere, yet membership restrictions may forestall labor from other submarkets from entering the high-wage submarket and equalizing wage rates between them. Rather capricious distortions of the wage pattern may generally result, with a net loss to workers in submarkets where unions secure only moderate or low wages. Another phenomenon is that workers in nonunionized areas or occupations may receive competitive or monopsonistic wages very substantially lower than those of unionized laborers in their protected occupations, even though the unionized and nonunionized workers have very similar skills and abilities. Notoriously low wages in white-collar occupations (compared to those of organized manual laborers) have often reflected this tendency. Thus, it appears that many seeming inequities within the population of laborers as a whole may be a by-product of their forming various organizations for the collective determination of wages.

B. LAND AS A PRODUCTIVE FACTOR

STRATEGIC CHARACTERISTICS OF LAND AND ITS SUPPLY

The second of the two basic productive factors is *land,* or the services of natural resources. Economists have used the term land generally to include the services not only of the land surface of the globe, used for agriculture and building sites and so forth, but also of every physical resource which exists in nature. Thus, land includes the services of coal, oil, stone, mineral ore, the waters of seas and rivers, etc.—of all natural resources other than labor. In the interest of precise statement, we shall designate this productive factor as *land services,* to distinguish it from the natural resources which supply the services.

The fundamental characteristics of land services so considered are obvious. They are essentially the services of inanimate basic commodities which are available in nature without any cost of production in terms of human effort. Yet these services are obviously essential to production, and will be able to command a price from enterprises engaging in production if they are scarce enough (naturally or by artificial control) that their marginal rates of substitution for other factors are less than infinity. This is equivalent to saying that land services, in any quantity employed, must have a positive marginal product in order to command a price from firms bidding for them. If they did not, they would be so plentiful as to become a "free good."

Since land services flow from natural resources, it may appear that their supply is irrevocably given or fixed. This is not true in every relevant sense, although the quantity of ultimately available natural resources is augmented at a negligible rate through time. The processes of nature alter the available land surface somewhat over relatively short time intervals with river delta building, the receding of glaciers, volcanic action, and so forth, but these changes are for periods of one or a few human generations so inconsequential relative to the total land surface that they can be neglected for purposes of analysis.

What is more important perhaps, is that within historical intervals the quantity of resources known by and accessible to human beings within a given economy may change rapidly. Thus the opening of American continents to European settlement after the fifteenth century, the expansion into the interior of North America in the eighteenth and nineteenth centuries, and the discovery of petroleum in the Middle East in very recent times represent major additions to the natural resources known and available for use by the economies of Western Europe and the United States. The supply of land services from such resources has therefore in some meaningful sense frequently increased relative to the supply of the services of a more slowly changing labor force.

But land services cannot increase in quantity indefinitely as long as people confine their activities to this planet; the quantity available to a given economy increases in no regular or predictable pattern; and it cannot in any significant degree be deliberately increased by productive activity of people. Thus, as of any given time, it is fair to speak of available land services as existing in a supply which is, to a close approximation, not subject to systematic expansion.[1]

On the other hand, the quantity of natural resources available for use may definitely decrease through time, through depletion or exhaustion. Limited deposits of minerals, oil, or coal can be simply used up, and agricultural or forest land may be exhausted by use and subsequently perhaps destroyed by erosion. In some cases, men may have no way of preventing ultimate resource exhaustion other than refraining from using the resources; in others, the mode of use may determine whether or not and to what extent exhaustion occurs. In any event, at a rate depending upon the character of the resource and the type of exploitation, the supply of natural resources and of the services they render may be reduced through time, and historically they have been. Generally we must recognize land services as including the services of depletable resources which are irrevocably exhausted

---

[1] This rule is subject to one exception. So far as human beings create capital goods which are of such character that they are effectively indestructible and never require replacement once built—like fills in tidal flats to create new dry land surface, or other relatively permanent alterations of the earth's surface—a category of productive agent which has all the essential properties of natural resources is added to the supply of resources from that point on. For purposes of analysis, we may legitimately neglect this phenomenon.

in the course of use, of relatively indestructible resources which are likely to yield a more or less perpetual flow of productive services regardless of type of use, and of potentially destructible but also potentially perpetuable resources, the preservation or exhaustion of which depends on the mode of exploitation. A part of the flow of land services available for production thus tends to decline through time, although other parts may remain relatively stable almost indefinitely.

In sum, the quantity of natural resources useful for production on the globe was available originally (from the standpoint of modern civilization) in some fixed aggregate which could not be significantly increased. Although the quantity of such resources known by and accessible to a given economy may increase from time to time, any amount of already known and accessible resources tend either to remain fixed or to be exhausted. Therefore, the flow of productive services from them tends either to remain stable or to decline through time.

Given the indispensability of land services in production, enterprises will be willing to pay for them as long as they are scarce enough that they have a positive marginal productivity when combined with other factors. They will then assume a market value or price (determined by their quantity relative to that of other factors and by the substitution conditions between them and other factors); those who control them will be able to command a corresponding share of the income from production. The share of income which resource holders do or could extract from the sale of land services—that is the *rent* of their land—has also been referred to as a share of income or output which may be *imputed* to land services, as in some sense the share of income or output which they actually contribute. There is really not much meaning to this "imputation" doctrine; all factors are required for production, and it is not possible to say for what share of output any one alone is responsible. All that can be said is that with market purchase and sale of all factors, resource holders will receive such and such an income share, labor another certain income share, and so forth. It is totally meaningless to say that the shares thus received are therefore in any sense correct or just, or incorrect or unjust. Value judgments concerning how income *should* be distributed cannot logically be derived from an analysis of how a market system distributes it. It is simply the expression of an independent value judgment to say that all income "belongs" to labor because only labor represents human effort, or that a certain portion "belongs" to each factor because it can get it from a market.

THE SUPPLY CONDITIONS FOR LAND SERVICES

What are the supply conditions for land services which interact with the demand for them to determine their price? That is, in what way will the supply of land services *offered for use* (from any aggregate potentially available at a given time) respond to the price buyers are willing to pay for them? Or, what is the shape of the supply curve of land services, or of particular types of them?

Two circumstances—one natural and one institutional—affect the supply conditions for land services in the modern enterprise economy. The natural circumstance is that, since they are by definition the services of inanimate commodities or agencies of production which simply occur in nature, they have no cost of production in terms of human effort. The fact that human effort must be used in conjunction with land services to make an output does not disprove this observation. For example, the fact that coal must be mined or agricultural land plowed by human labor to secure a useful output does not erase the fact that the services of the coal or of the arable land are initially available in nature free of human effort. It is these services, free of human effort, which are land services per se. Therefore, there is no real cost which must be overcome or offset in order to induce land services to be supplied, and no increase in their real cost with an increasing rate of use of land services. (It also follows that the total of any payment made for land services is all in the nature of a net gain above costs, which are zero. The term *rent,* as applied to the earnings of land, has thus come to connote a return against which no offsetting cost is placed.)

The institutional circumstance is that, in our economy, there is a system of private property in natural resources, which means that they are generally owned outright by private individuals who have the right to use them, exclude others from their use, sell their services for whatever they will bring, and keep the resulting income. It has generally been presumed that such individuals will be interested in holding productive resources for the income they will bring and will sell or use their services so as to realize the largest gross income obtainable.

If we combine these two circumstances—that land services have no cost and that resources are held by private owners who wish to sell or use these services for the maximum gross revenue—certain conclusions follow with respect to the supply conditions for land services. If there is competitive selling of land services (as a whole or of any type used in a given submarket) so that the seller has no control over price and takes any going market price as given, then each seller will tend to offer his entire supply of land services at any *positive* price which prevails in the market. This is because at any given positive price he can obtain the greatest gross income by selling his total supply of services. He will not, however, continue to supply land services at a negative price (which would imply his paying enterprises to induce them to use these services); as price tends to fall below zero he will withdraw enough of his supply to prevent a negative price from developing. It follows that the supply curve of land services by any individual competitive supplier should be *perfectly inelastic* to price change at all prices above zero, but become perfectly elastic to the left of total quantity available as price reaches zero.

May the same be said of the market supply curve of land services as supplied by a group of competitive sellers? It may in general if all the units of the supply will command an identical price at any given time, so that it is impossible for some units to have a zero or negative price while others are commanding a positive price. This will hold if all units of the supply are homogeneous, with no differentiation in terms of location, quality, etc. Then the entire land service supply will be offered when any unit of it commands a positive price (the total supply will be perfectly inelastic at all positive prices); and when the single uniform price for land reaches zero, enough of the total supply will be withdrawn to forestall a negative price.

If, however, the various units of the land service supply are differentiated in quality or location so that some units command a higher price than others, *and so that some units will command first zero and then negative prices while others command successively lower positive prices,* then the total supply of land services will become elastic to change in their prices. As the price for "better" land services falls successively, the price for "poorer" land services will become zero and then negative, and as it becomes negative they will be withdrawn from supply. Conversely, a successive rise in the price of "better" land services will result in the price of poorer land services exceeding zero and cause them to be added to the total land supply. Suppose, for example, that in a given agricultural country there are 1 million acres of rich bottom land and 1 million acres of rocky hillside land, and that they are related in quality so that when the rent per acre on bottom land is alternatively (*a*) $10, (*b*) $7, and (*c*) $4, the rent which farmers would pay for hillside land is alternatively (*a*) $2, (*b*) −$1, and (*c*) −$4 (negative prices implying farmers would have to be paid these amounts to use the hill land rather than rent the bottom land at the corresponding rental rate). In this case it appears that if the rent of land is at level (*c*)—that is $4 for bottom land and −$4 for hill land—the total supply will be the services of 1 million acres of bottom land, no hill land being supplied. If rent is at the level (*b*)—that is $7 for bottom land and −$1 for hill land—total supply will still be the services of 1 million acres of bottom land, and land supply is perfectly inelastic to price change for movement between the rent levels (*c*) and (*b*). If, however, rent rises to level (*a*)—that is, $10 for bottom land and $2 for hill land—the services of the hill land will now be supplied and total land supply will be 2 million acres. Land supply is elastic to price change for the movement between rent levels (*b*) and (*a*). With differentiation among units of the land supply, a market supply curve for land services which is elastic to price change is quite consistent with a perfectly inelastic supply curve at positive prices by each supplier, provided that positive and negative prices for different units of the supply can exist simultaneously.

The preceding refers to the supply conditions for land services under competitive selling, where each supplier takes the going price as beyond his influence. Suppose, on the other hand, that there is monopolistic selling of land services—that is a sufficient concentration of land holding that the sellers of land services can influence their price. Then supply may be arbitrarily restricted so as to secure the largest aggregate return from the monopolized land service supply as a whole, and will presumably be set where the marginal receipts from the sale of added land services equal zero. In this case the competitive supply curve for land services is replaced by a determination of land service supply by the monopolistic landholders.

The rule that the competitive supply of land services by an individual supplier is perfectly inelastic may have more exceptions as applied to particular time intervals. These arise from the fact that the future value of land may be significantly affected by its present rate of use; land may be subject to *depletion*, in the sense either that it will simply be used up after a while, or that the potential rate of flow of services in the future will diminish as the current rate of use is increased beyond a certain point. Thus, the oil from an oil well is eventually used up, or the future crop-producing ability of agricultural land may be impaired if the current intensity of use exceeds a certain level. If this is so, and if the effects of current use on future yield are encountered soon enough to affect the calculations of the present owner, then his supply of land services may at any moment be somewhat elastic to the price offered for them. He may restrict the supply of land services offered at very low prices if this will enhance the future supply available and if he expects higher prices later on; as current prices rise relative to those expected in the future, he may increase the present supply offered at the expense of future supply available.

This tendency seems likely to be observed primarily in the case of resources subject to a distinct and fairly rapid rate of depletion, sufficient to influence owners' incomes strongly over a short enough period of time that they do not disregard the effect. Perhaps forest lands and oil deposits would be good examples of rapidly depleted resources, whereas depletion effects might be largely disregarded in the case of most farming land. In other cases, like that of "site" land (used simply as a place to put buildings), there may be no depletion problem at all. Where depletion effects are important, we find an added reason for the elasticity of the market supply of land to price change (in addition to that of differentiation among units of land supply).

LOCATIONAL AND OTHER DIFFERENTIATION
OF THE LAND SUPPLY

We must now consider two further characteristics of land supply which are of some importance for a detailed analysis of pricing. First, resources occur in various specialized forms, and the services of particular subcategories of them are suitable for certain uses but not for others. Second, resources are distributed or scattered over geographical space and either are immobile so that their services can contribute to production only at a given site, or can be made available for use in production elsewhere only at a cost for transportation.

The occurrence of land services in different specialized forms is obvious when we recall that they include for purposes of analysis the services of all natural resources. Thus, coal deposits, oil pools, copper ore deposits, iron ore deposits, arable farm land, and mountainous forest land are distinct basic commodities the services of which are in general poor substitutes. or not substitutes at all in use or production. It follows that land services as a factor of production actually include a very considerable number of substantially different productive factors, with independent supplies, each of which, however, has the general characteristics attributed to land services as a category above. The determination of land service prices actually involves the determination of each of a number of separate prices for substantially independent natural resource factors.

At the same time, the supply of any particular land service factor may include units which are imperfect substitutes for each other in particular uses. For example, farming land in general might be used for grazing, for wheat production, or for truck gardens, and various units of it will be relatively superior in some of these uses and relatively inferior in others. There is thus a further differentiation of the land service supply such that various units of a given sort of land service are differentiated in quality and are imperfect substitutes in use. This fact will obviously influence the determination of the prices of particular units of any variety of land service supply, with a tendency for price differentials to reflect differences in quality or productivity. As we have seen above, such differentiation will also tend to impart elasticity to the market supply of land services in general or for a particular use.

The fact that resources are immobile or imperfectly mobile has similar implications. Certain types of natural resources are completely immobile in the sense that any productive process to which they contribute must be carried on at the places where the resources occur. This is true, for example, of agricultural land, which can be used for farming only where it occurs, the other productive factors being brought to its location for purposes of production. When it is true, some units of land will lie farther than others from the buyers of the products grown or otherwise produced on the land, and it will therefore cost more per unit to transport their outputs to market. The land service supply is then effectively differentiated as to location, and, given the locations of markets, corresponding differences in the prices which enterprises are willing to pay for land services will tend to emerge. This is as true of the services of urban site land (for locating factories, stores, and houses) as it is of those of agricultural land.

In the case of other varieties of natural resources, there is a partial mobility. For example, mineral ores may be moved from their deposits to processing mills many miles away. Such mobility is in all cases only partial, however, in the sense that transport costs for movement must be incurred, and there are higher transport costs as the original deposits are farther from markets. Consequently, different deposits are imperfect substitutes for each other, and corresponding price differentials will tend to develop in the market. At the extreme, these may be such that the services of unfavorably located land are worthless (have a zero or negative price), while the services of favorably located land command a positive price. For example, high-grade coal deposits in the interior of the South American jungle might have no value at the present time, whereas low-grade coal deposits in the Ohio Valley might command a considerable price. Some rise in coal prices, however, would result in the distant deposits assuming a positive value and in an augmentation of the supply of coal.

In past times when such matters as the differentials among agricultural land rents were pressing issues, the locational immobility of resources was much emphasized in the analysis of land service pricing. Actually, such immobility raises no especially difficult theoretical problems, and neither does the fact that land services are actually made up of a number of substantially independent natural resource factors rather than constituting a single homogeneous factor. Our basic observation—that in general land services are available in naturally fixed quantity, are without a cost of supply, and will tend to have a supply which responds automatically to price under competitive selling conditions—all still hold in spite of the complications just reviewed. We must simply recognize, for purposes of detailed analysis, that in actuality there are several independent land service factors of this sort instead of one and that the supply of each is made up of imperfectly substitutable units which will command somewhat different competitive prices according to their specific efficiencies in production. For purposes of a non-detailed or general analysis, we shall not abstract unduly from the essential aspects of reality if we view land services as a single homogeneous productive factor of the general properties previously described.

TENDENCIES IN THE DETERMINATION OF LAND RENTS

Let us now consider the implications of the peculiar characteristics of land service supply for the determination of land prices or rents in an enterprise economy. Like labor, land service is a basic productive factor with a supply substantially independent of that of any other factor—land cannot be converted into labor or labor into land. Unlike labor, it is also the service of an inanimate commodity which is available in nature without any cost of production in terms of human effort, and in ultimately fixed quantity. This difference has two strategic implications. First, except for discovery of new resources, the quantity of land services available for use in any area or in general will not be significantly augmented through time, whereas the quantity of labor available for employment may vary greatly with population changes. The proportion of available labor to available land service may thus vary significantly (and has done so) over decades and centuries. Second, at any given time, the supply of land services offered from those ultimately available will be relatively insensitive to price, varying principally only as far as units of inferior grade come to command a positive price because of the increased relative scarcity and price of superior units. The supply of land services is thus relatively "price-inelastic." The supply of labor services from any given population, on the other hand, may have a considerable price elasticity, and this will reflect the fact that many units of labor service which could command a positive price will not be supplied at lower labor prices, although more of them will be offered as the wage rate increases.

In what way is the preceding important? First, at any given time, with a given labor population and given land resources, a competitive equilibrium in which the ratio of wages to rents equals the marginal rate of substitution of land services for labor and in which all units offered for employment of both labor and land services are employed will presumably involve employment of all of the available land services which will command a positive price but only part of the available labor supply which could do so. Some of the latter will tend to be withheld from employment because of insufficient wages. The only part of the land service supply not used will be that which if combined with labor with a zero rent charge would nevertheless give higher costs of production than result from labor plus rent charges for the services of other land—the services of land which, in effect, is sufficiently inferior in productivity or redundant in quantity that a shift of labor to it and away from intensive exploitation of superior land would reduce total output. Although both labor and land services would be fully employed in a competitive equilibrium, therefore, in the sense that all units offered for employment at the going price were employed, land services will tend to be "more fully employed" in the sense that no unit will refuse any positive price.

Given this, a competitive relation of labor price to land price, and of wages to rents as shares of income, will tend to emerge which will be determined by the relationship of the land supply to the labor supply and by the going techniques of production. Rents may constitute a minor or a major share of the income distributed by a competitive market system, depending on the values of these determinants. This leads us to a second implication of the differing characteristics of land and labor. Over considerable periods of time the human population available for employment may vary greatly, whereas the supply of natural resources is relatively inflexible. As population increases, moreover, the supply of labor at any wage rate will tend to increase similarly, or a given supply will be available at lower wage rates, if only because of the necessity for the subsistence of families. Now an increase of labor supply relative to the supply of land services will tend, *with given productive techniques,* to result in reduced wages and increased rents, as the marginal rate of substitution of labor for land services is increased. (Correspondingly, relatively inferior land will tend to be brought from idleness to use, as the increasingly intensive use of superior land lowers the marginal productivity of labor on the superior land.) Therefore, a general tendency of population increase in an enterprise economy is to reduce the wage rate and to increase the price of land. If in addition, the demand for land is inelastic, the share of total income received as land rents will increase.

This tendency, of course, may be temporarily or indefinitely forestalled (or outweighed) by the discovery of new resources or by changes in technology which either increase over-all productivity from labor and land services combined or permit production with a relatively smaller use of land services per man. Both of these counterbalancing tendencies have operated strongly in past centuries, and explain why (in spite of the gloom of early economists who discovered the principle just described) the population of Western Europe as of the beginning of the sixteenth century could expand so rapidly up to now and yet continually increase the wage rate and living standard. Yet, it is clear that population increase will tend, *ceteris paribus,* to bring about declining wages and increasing rents. The differences of wage rates in the present day as among the resource-rich United States, relatively overcrowded England, and severely overpopulated countries of the Far East are at least in part a reflection of the economic tendency just described. In a country in which resources are very abundant relative to population, competitive rents will tend to be small per unit and to constitute a small share of total income. In a badly overpopulated country, even if it had equivalent technological development, rents per unit of land would tend to be much higher, and probably would constitute a much larger share of income.

If the pressure of population upon resources becomes severe enough that land rents constitute a large share of total income in a market-regulated economy, a severe social problem may be encountered unless the ownership of land is widely distributed. If a relatively small proportion of the population owns and receives the income from land, high rents may lead to great inequalities in personal income distribution and in social unrest and opposition to the government which supports the going system of economic organization. "Land reform" movements, in short, are likely to emerge whenever land rents rise and wages fall, unless landownership is initially distributed quite widely so that rents supplement the incomes of a large share of wage earners. Opposition to the concentration of rental incomes in the hands of relatively few people is typically reinforced by the fact that rents are unearned by human effort and are simply a return to passive ownership.

Two further implications of the character of the supply of land may now be briefly noted. First, with the land supply consisting effectively of the services of a number of different and nonsubstitutable resources, and with the units of various types of land service differentiated in quality and location, different units of land service will naturally tend to receive widely different rents. Thus gold deposits and oil wells may earn much higher rents than limestone or clay deposits, fertile crop land more than relatively barren grazing land, garden land close to large cities more than distant farm land, and building-site land within cities more than site land in rural areas. And the services of some share of land, lacking the greatest extremes of population pressure, are likely to be entirely worthless. Moreover, not only will such wide differentials in land service prices tend to emerge, but also they will not tend to be lessened significantly by the movement of land among uses or among locations. Movements of population, or of the location of enterprise activity, may permit some shifting of land services among uses and some lessening of rent differentials. But whereas wage differentials among various submarkets for labor tend to be kept within relatively narrow limits by the mobility of labor among occupations and among areas, any such tendency in land-rent differentials is greatly restricted by the physical immobility of resources and by the fact that the services of various types of resources are frequently not good substitutes (or substitutes at all) for each other. Thus, a great dispersion of specific land service prices is normally to be expected. A full explanation of these, however, would require a lengthy excursion into the theory of the location of industrial activity, which we shall not attempt here.

Second, with the distinct tendency of land services toward inelastic supply, their price will tend to be quite *flexible* in response to changes in specific or over-all demand as long as they are competitively sold. With no costs of production to overcome, landowners should rationally tend to accept lower prices down to zero as the market offers less without restricting the supply offered. This will tend to be true, at any rate, except as far as long-term contracts fix the price on land services over future periods. One implication of this is that, with declines in money purchasing power, whereas a refusal of wage earners to accept lower money wages may result in considerable unemployment of labor, land rents may decline freely and result in a more stable employment of land. Correspondingly, outputs depending more heavily on the use of land may be less restricted by a general movement toward unemployment of labor than others.

MONOPOLY AND MONOPSONY IN LAND

We have spoken of the tendencies of land-rent determination under conditions of competitive selling and buying. What should be said of the possibilities of monopoly and monopsony in the markets for land?

Land services can be sold monopolistically, or can be purchased by buyers with monopsony power. As far as monopoly or monopsony is encountered, rents and the quantity of land services supplied will be affected in general in the manner described in the earlier discussion of factor monopoly and monopsony. (See pages 514 to 551.) It is unnecessary to review that analysis here, but some comments may be made on the probability that monopoly and monopsony will be encountered. Although the subject has never been much explored, it would appear that monopsonistic purchase of land services in given areas are at least as likely to develop as monopsony in labor. If there is sufficient concentration of enterprise in given areas to support monopsonistic factor-buying policies, land is certainly immobile enough, and ordinarily specialized enough as to use, to make monopsony quite feasible. If monopsony does develop, the immobility of land implies that the buyer will face a very inelastic supply curve for land services and will be able to greatly reduce rents without much restricting supply. In fact, the dominant purchaser may in effect be able to appropriate almost the entire competitive rent of land for himself, or alternatively purchase ownership of the land at a nominal figure. When landownership becomes vested in the enterprise using it, of course, any direct monopsony problem regarding land rents vanishes. However, casual observation suggests that much land service—perhaps particularly that of agricultural land and of urban site land—is sold to buyers without monopsony power.

The probability of monopoly in the selling of land services will depend largely on the degree of concentration of landownership. In the United States, at least, a wide dispersion of landownership, both generally and in particular areas, is antithetical to the effective exercise of land monopoly.

Moreover, collusive agreements of landowners would be illegal under the antitrust laws, whereas labor unions are lawful organizations. More frequently than not, therefore, we shall probably encounter dispersed ownership of land and competitive selling of land services. In the case of some natural resources, however, and in certain urban site situations, monopolistic selling of land services may be encountered, with corresponding effects of restricted land supply and increased rents. In countries where landownership is much more concentrated, the phenomenon of land monopoly may be of very considerable importance in its effects on personal income distribution. When land monopoly is encountered, a goal of revenue maximization—at a point where marginal receipts from the sale of services equal zero —seems clearly attributable to the land monopolist.

Whatever the size of the rental share in total income, and whether or not influenced by monopoly or monopsony, there has long been an ethical issue (that is, one of conflicting value judgments) concerning the desirability of private property owners receiving this share of income. The issue tends to become crucial if rents are an important share of income and landownership is concentrated in the hands of relatively few people, since then personal income distribution is seriously affected, but the issue itself arises from the fact that land incomes are unearned in the sense that human labor is not expended in order to get them. Thus, according to some value judgments, land incomes are an unearned surplus which should more properly either be distributed to labor or taxed away by the government for expenditure benefiting the entire population.

It is not our purpose to pass on such ethical issues here. Three observations, however, may be offered. First, general acceptance of the institution of private property in natural resources generally implies acceptance of the distribution of rents as an income share to private landowners. Once it is accepted, and there are numerous political reasons for doing so, it will be more consistent with other popular political ideals if landownership is very widely dispersed. Second, the objection to various individuals' receiving an "unearned" rental income from land encounters the complication that land is frequently bought and sold, so that current owners commonly have paid for the capitalized value of the rent incomes they now receive, and the true recipient of the unearned income must be traced back to previous owners who got the land "for free" or who held it while it appreciated substantially in value. To current owners, land may represent a costly investment, even though what they purchase in land is simply the right to a stream of incomes against which no real costs can be placed. It follows that any move effectively to confiscate and arbitrarily redistribute rental incomes would involve a hard-to-justify penalization of those who have bought and fully paid for the rights to their current rental incomes. Third, our contemporary tax system, which draws much governmental revenue from taxes on real property, currently appropriates a substantial share of rental income for public purposes, so that the impact of private landownership on personal income distribution in this country is considerably tempered.

C. CAPITAL AS A FACTOR OF PRODUCTION

THE MEANING AND GENERAL CHARACTER OF CAPITAL

It has been long recognized by economic theorists that labor and land are not the only factors of production, and that a third productive factor, *capital*, also in some sense contributes to production and may command a share in income. It has also been apparent that this third productive factor called capital exists in two possible senses.

First, we may potentially regard as a third productive factor *the services of capital goods*. Any observer knows that the current production of practically all commodities draws not only upon the direct services of labor and of natural resources, but also upon the services of numerous sorts of capital goods as well. In the manufacturing production of almost any item, for example, we shall find used not only the services of labor, of site land, and perhaps of some natural resources like mineral ore and mineral fuel, but also the services of buildings, machinery, tools, and further of various other previously produced goods which are raw materials from the standpoint of the given production process. Thus, shoe production draws on the services not only of labor and site land, but also on the services of capital goods such as buildings, power plants, shoe machinery, leather, thread, nails, and so forth. Parallel to labor services and land services as productive factors, we discover capital goods services, and parallel to laborers and natural resources as sources of these services, we discover capital goods. As a general category capital goods may be defined to include all previously produced goods used by enterprises in the course of further production, whether such goods are long-lived equipment like machines, or simply stocks of raw materials or semiprocessed components. In almost any specific line of production, commodities are made available by combining the services of capital goods with the services of land and labor. Moreover, production in one line will commonly depend on the use of capital goods which are the commodity outputs of other lines of production.

The use of capital goods services in production generally requires the presence of an accumulation of capital goods to provide these services. If machine services are to be used, machinery must be on hand; if leather is to be used to make shoes, some inventory of leather must, on the average, be maintained. The reason that such accumulations are required is obviously that the services of capital goods cannot in general be created or made available in very small and separate units, or, if they can, cannot be delivered in a stable continuous flow which would obviate the necessity of holding any accumulations. Thus, machine hours of service from a dynamo or a punch press cannot be made available without first making a machine, and the machine is in essence a store of a large quantity of machine services which can only be used with the passage of considerable time. Very frequently, in effect, capital goods services can be provided only by creating a durable productive instrument which will provide a flow of services by performing certain functions over some substantial time interval. In other cases, the capital goods which provide services are not necessarily durable productive instruments and are potentially divisible into small units; cement and nails as used in construction are like this, for example. But even here the fact that deliveries of such materials can hardly be made in a continuous stream synchronized with use requires the enterprise using them to hold through time some average accumulation or stock of the service-providing capital goods.

In general, therefore, an essential concomitant of the use of capital goods services is the creation and holding by enterprise of a special category of goods capable of providing a flow of services over some span of time, and thus the accumulation of a store of accumulated capital goods services significantly in advance of their use in production. It follows from this also that there will be some significant lag in time between the date of their creation of capital goods and the average date of use of their services in further production. Further time must be consumed in making the capital goods initially. Because of this, capital goods must be paid for (that is, productive services which are used to make the capital goods must be rewarded or paid incomes) some time prior to the time their services contribute to the production of salable commodities.

The preceding covers the meaning of capital in the first sense—as the services of an accumulated stock of capital goods useful in the production of further goods. Since these capital goods services are clearly distinct from and imperfectly substitutable in production for either direct labor services and direct land services, they constitute in this sense at least a third factor of production. Enterprises will presumably combine them with land and labor services according to the usual principles, thus committing themselves to the acquisition and maintenance of a corresponding amount of capital goods.

In acquiring the capital goods at whatever their cost is, they will pay or distribute an income directly to the suppliers of capital goods, and indirectly to whatever productive factors have been used in producing them. They will intend to recoup this cost, along with that of direct labor and land, from the sales revenues from their outputs. Thus, capital goods services qualify as separate productive factors also in that their suppliers are the immediate recipients of a distinct income payment.

The second meaning of capital—either alternative or complementary to the one already described—is that it is the services of *investable funds* required to purchase and finance the holding of capital goods. The fact that capital goods services can be used in general only by acquiring in advance of use accumulated stocks of such services means that funds must be invested in capital goods if the services are to be available. Such funds must be spent in advance of use of the capital goods in return for a postponed earning or return, and the service or use of such funds is therefore essential to production. Creating capital goods requires an expenditure of productive services now to get something which will bring in an income only later, and someone must in effect assume the burden of rewarding these currently expended productive services now and then waiting for some reimbursement.[2]

Suppose that a machine is to be used for stamping out automobile fenders over a period of five years, and costs $500,000. Someone must supply this amount of money in advance—"put up," let us say, $500,000 now against a future return. Having done so, he is presumably in a position to recover his investment, perhaps at the rate of $100,000 a year, over the five years.

Further, the need for investable funds is, in general, not intermittent or attached only to the initial acquisition of some type of capital good. If capital goods are steadily used in production, they will be replaced as they wear out or are used up (and almost uniformly they do wear out or are depleted), so that funds must continually *remain invested* in a continuing production process at every moment in time. Rather than being repaid the original funds they have supplied, suppliers of funds as a group in general will "leave their money in" or allow it to be repeatedly *reinvested* in replacements. Thus, usually, a quantity of more or less permanently invested funds, which as a whole are not withdrawn (although individual suppliers of funds may withdraw and be replaced by others), is essential to the continuing use of capital goods in production.

These funds will be periodically recovered within the enterprise from sales receipts as given capital goods are used up, and then respent to buy other capital goods to replace them. As respent each time, they provide pay-

[2] This will be the explicit pattern in almost all cases, since in a market economy the typical situation will be that those rendering the productive services necessary to make it are currently paid by another party who purchases or pays for the building of the capital good. In the more unusual case where basic factor suppliers—e.g. a group of laborers owning some land—simply build a capital good for their own use in production without selling it, no explicit investment of funds takes place, but merely an acceptance by the basic factor suppliers of postponed rewards for their services. In this case, however, there is an implicit investment of funds in the capital good in that the factor suppliers have done the equivalent of paying to acquire the good the amount of money they could have received had they sold their services to others instead of building the capital good.

ments to the productive services making new capital goods, advanced against a delayed return. The return of the principal amount invested to the suppliers of funds may be indefinitely delayed, however, as their funds remain invested through time. As a consequence, some reward for surrendering the services of their funds on this basis must ordinarily be paid to the suppliers of funds—other than or in addition to the return of funds—to compensate them for leaving them invested over either a finite or an indefinite interval. This payment for the services of funds is ordinarily called *interest,* and such interest qualifies as a distributive share paid for the use of investable funds. It should be noted that this income payment is logically distinct from and in addition to the payment made for capital goods services in the form of the cost of capital goods at the date of their creation. As long as suppliers of funds require such a payment to attract the supply, an interest payment will constitute a distributive share in addition to wages and rents.

The components of the funds invested in any enterprise may be determined by an examination of its balance sheet, or financial statement of assets, liabilities, and so forth. Ordinarily funds invested in the firm will include (1) those invested in "fixed" assets, like buildings and machines, (2) those invested in stock or inventories of raw materials and partly completed goods, (3) those invested in inventories of completed goods awaiting sale and delivery, and (4) liquid funds or cash awaiting expenditure on investment or reinvestment. (Some of the last, in turn, may be temporarily invested by the firm in other enterprises, thus making investors in the firm indirect investors elsewhere.) In general, all of these categories of investment require some funds if the enterprise is to operate.

There are several measures of the use of funds for acquiring capital goods which may be relevant for various purposes of analysis. First, there is *net investment* in capital goods, or the addition to the aggregate amount invested in capital goods which occurs in any time interval. This measure is necessarily a time rate, or amount per unit of time. It is evident that the initial adoption of the use of any sort of capital good requires a net investment, and that any present aggregate investment in capital goods must be an accumulation of past net investments. Second, there is *reinvestment* in capital goods, which represents the respending in any period of time of previously invested amounts on new capital goods to replace old ones which are worn out or used up. This measure is also a time rate. Third, we may designate as *gross investment* in capital goods the sum of net investment and reinvestment in any time period. This is also a time rate. Finally, we may recognize as *aggregate funds invested* the total amount of funds invested in capital assets on hand at any moment in time. (This is an instantaneous magnitude rather than a time rate of expenditure.) It will result from aggregating all past net investments and deducting all net disinvestments and losses.[3] It is the aggregate funds invested which will be of main interest to us in our consideration of capital as a productive factor, since it is this monetary amount which at any moment in time measures in its monetary dimension the amount of capital which is in use and which stands to receive an interest payment as a share of total income.

It is thus established that investable funds are essential to production which employs capital goods, and that these funds constitute a third productive factor which may be able to command a share in income. Where do these funds come from, or by whom are they supplied? In a monetary exchange economy like ours, goods are bought and sold for and incomes received in money. A first obvious source of investable funds is thus the current incomes of individuals however earned, part of which they may divert to purchasing capital goods or to loaning to or participating in enterprises which purchase capital goods. With money a circulating medium, some people will also accumulate balances of money—liquid balances—and hold them long after the money in question was received. Thus, a second source of investable funds is such liquid balances, which may be drawn upon to finance investment in capital goods. Although such balances may in general represent accumulated past incomes, they are a source of funds distinct from current incomes. Third, modern banking institutions are generally so arranged that banks can create new money. Money is in large part made up of deposit credits on the books of banks (liabilities of banks to pay), and banks as a group can create added money by making loans which create added deposit credits in excess of the amount of the funds invested in the banks by their owners and deposits of funds entrusted to the banks by their customers. If banks increase their loans, giving borrowers credit by means of checking accounts and thus creating deposits, new money is created. Thus, investable funds may in effect be created by banks as they make loans to finance the purchase of capital goods. (In addition, banks may of course act as middlemen in supplying for investment the accumulated balances of individuals.) In sum, there are three distinguishable sources of investable funds: current incomes, liquid balances, and new bank credit. All participate in determining the supply of investable funds and its relation to the interest rate. One of the major problems of a theory of income distribution is to analyze the character of the supply of investable funds, which interacts through time with the demand for them to determine the level of aggregate investment in capital goods and the changes therein.

[3] The computation at any moment of a value of *aggregate funds invested* would be actually very complicated because of the problem of identifying losses which wipe out capital goods and the claims of investors to them and of the problem of valuation of old investments, but this need not trouble us for purposes of an initial survey of the character of capital.

Before we go further with this problem, however, we must return to the capital goods in which funds are invested. We have seen that investable funds constitute a sort of third factor of production whenever capital goods are used, and can command an income share for their services. But what of the capital goods themselves, and *their* services? It has been noted that the services of capital goods also have some of the attributes of a productive factor, in that they are productive services distinct from and imperfect substitutes for those of either land or labor and in that their purchase may represent a distinct sort of immediate income payment. Does it follow that capital is really two connected productive factors—the physical services of capital goods and the services of invested funds—and that capital goods services per se, aside from funds invested in them, constitute in a meaningful sense a separate productive factor and command, in addition to the interest on funds, a separate share in income? Let us turn to these issues now.

THE ROLE OF CAPITAL GOODS IN THE PRODUCTION PROCESS

The issues posed may be resolved by seeking answers to the following questions. First, are capital goods services actually a third and independent sort of productive service, in addition to those of labor and land, and correspondingly are capital goods a third and independent source of productive services? Second, do the services of capital goods actually tend to gain a separate additional share in income, in addition to wages, rents, and the interest paid on invested funds, or is all income distribution other than enterprise profit accounted for in the shares just mentioned? Each of these questions may usefully be viewed as referring alternately to the process of economic activity over past as well as present and future time, and to the current and future flow of economic activity beginning as of any contemporary date.

Let us first examine the place of capital goods in the processes of economic activity extending from the very beginnings of production to the present and into the future. It is fairly clear from this standpoint that capital goods services do not constitute a separate basic factor of production with a source of supply independent of that of other productive factors. And in this respect they are clearly distinguished from the services of both land and labor.

We have seen that both labor and land are basic factors of production in the sense that they are originally available in nature, in quantities beyond the control of those organizing production, and that they themselves cannot be produced by the combination of any still more fundamental productive services. The services of land flow from natural resources which have emerged in a form and quantity determined by the processes through which the planet evolved, and they cannot be produced by human effort from other components. Labor services are available from human beings only, the quantity in which they are available is determined by the congeries of forces which determine the level of population, and they cannot be produced from any more fundamental constituents. The labor supply is beyond the control of those organizing production under modern institutional arrangements, or under any such arrangements except those of slavery or of very extreme totalitarian government. Moreover, it is true that both labor and land have independent supplies, in the sense that neither can be produced by conversion of the other. In essential respects, therefore, labor and land correspond to the "basic natural commodities used in all production" which we assumed as productive factors in Chapters 11 and 12.

Capital goods, on the other hand, are by definition produced goods used in further production. They did not originally exist in nature, but are man made. And since the only visible factors of production prior to the creation of any capital goods were labor and land, it must follow that all capital goods must result ultimately from the combination of the services of labor and land. To put it in other terms, capital goods represent the embodiment of labor and land services in the form of "intermediate" goods used in further production. Therefore, the services of capital goods are in a sense the services of labor and land supplied by an indirect route and in a transmuted form. This is not to say that any capital good created today is simply a combination of currently rendered labor and land services; it obviously is not. Once capital goods began to be accumulated, the services of one capital good contributed to the creation and periodic replacement of another, in a sort of chain effect through time, so that any currently produced capital good combines the services of currently used labor and land with the services of existing capital goods, which were made with the aid of other capital goods services, and so on backward through time. But since all relevant capital goods from the first one on must have come ultimately from the labor and land which were available prior to the beginning of production, every currently produced capital good is the embodiment indirectly—though perhaps very indirectly indeed and through many intermediate steps—of labor and land services alone.

It thus appears that if we view the whole history of production as a sort of unit for analysis, capital goods and their services are not basic and independent factors of production in the same sense as labor and land are. They are not basic commodities existing in nature, and their supply is not independent of those of labor and land. On the contrary, they are nothing more than the embodiment of labor and land services in altered form, and their services thus do not constitute an independent productive factor at all. This is the only plausible view if we are considering the process of production through time as a whole.

The use of capital goods over time thus does not involve the introduction of an independent substitute for labor and land. It involves, rather, the use of the services of labor and land in a particular way—to produce goods for further use in production. In effect, the use of capital goods, rather than substituting for the services of labor and land, involves a special routing of the flow of these productive services through the process of production, and it reflects a demand for these productive services in a special and generally indirect form. By using more or less capital goods in combination with labor and land, the economy is essentially routing a smaller or larger proportion of the basic productive services of labor and land through the production of capital goods and thence to the production of final goods for consumption. As far as time is consumed in employing labor and land services to make capital goods before getting around to producing consumers' goods, and as far as the procedure is technically circuitous, we may say that the use of capital goods involves a "roundabout" use of labor and land services. Depending on whether the capital stock is being used down, just maintained or augmented, we may correspondingly say that the "degree of round-aboutness" in production is being decreased, maintained, or increased.[4]

Since the use of capital goods involves the indirect use of productive services otherwise available for more direct use, the analytical problem with respect to the use of capital goods is not that of simple substitution of one factor for others. It is one of the determination of the relation of the demand for productive services devoted to making capital goods to the demand for these services devoted to making other goods—of the proportion of productive services devoted to indirect as opposed to direct use.

If capital goods and their services are simply an indirect form or embodiment of the services of labor and land, is it also true that capital goods services per se command no share in income other than the shares previously identified—the wages of the labor and the rent of the land they embody, the interest payment on invested funds, and (possibly but not necessarily) ordinary enterprise profits? Suppose an enterprise annually employs $10,000 worth of labor services, $5,000 worth of land services, and a machine with a life of ten years and an original cost of $200,000 in which the average in-

---

[4] This last idea has sometimes been expressed by introducing the idea of the "structure of production," which refers generally to the pattern in which land and labor are employed in the economy as a whole—how much directly in the production of consumers' goods, how much in the production of capital goods used in producing consumers' goods, how much in the production of capital goods used in producing other capital goods, etc. The structure of production then is "elongated," generally in the direction of increasing the proportion of resources employed in the latter two categories, when more capital goods are used, or is "shortened" if fewer capital goods are used in production. Although "lengthening" and "shortening" are oversimplified one-dimensional concepts as applied to an essentially multidimensional structure of production, the general validity of the idea is clear. It is quite clear that in industrial societies since 1800, for example, there has been a progressive and rapid "lengthening" of the structure of production, as an increasing proportion of resources has been devoted to the production of capital goods.

vestment over its life is $100,000. Suppose also that the interest rate on invested funds is 5 percent per annum. Now we know that the firm will distribute annually in income $15,000 for labor and land and $5,000 in interest (.05 of $100,000). But is any part of the $200,000 it paid for the machine, or the $20,000 part of this allocable to each of its ten years of use, also a distinct income payment? Or does any special income share, other than interest, necessarily emerge because of the use of the machine?

There is no apparent necessity that the income received by the enterprise from the output produced by its capital goods and by land and labor should exceed its total costs as made up of wages, rent, interest on invested funds, and the original cost to the enterprise of the capital goods purchased. No automatic surplus apparently need accrue to the enterprise by reason of its use of capital goods. Under purely competitive equilibrium, or any other market adjustment which drives price to the level of average total cost, it appears that sales revenues would tend exactly to equal total costs as made up of the components just mentioned. If for one reason or another the enterprise should make a profit in excess of these total costs, this profit surplus is apparently no more attributable to capital goods than to labor and land employed, but is simply an enterprise profit residual above the income payments which make up the costs of the enterprise. The particular enterprise using capital goods, therefore, will not receive an income above the cost of the goods plus interest paid on funds invested in them which is especially attributable to capital goods. Any profit it may make above all costs seems not necessarily allocable to particular productive services.

The next question is whether the amount the enterprise pays out to acquire capital goods, which is a separate income payment from the standpoint of the enterprise, results in any sort of income payment to others which is in addition to income shares already identified—that is, wages, rents, interest on invested funds, and enterprise profit. When the enterprise purchases a machine for $200,000, does a second enterprise receiving this $200,000 get anything other than the previously identified distributive shares?

Evidently it does not. The enterprise supplying the capital goods to the other is essentially receiving a reward distributable as its wage and rent payments, its interest payments on invested funds, its purchase cost of the capital goods it uses to make other capital goods, and its profits, if any. This will be true, in turn, back through any chain of enterprises in which each supplies the one above with capital goods. Then all income payments, if we trace the processes of production and exchange sufficiently far back through time, are fully accounted for by wages, rent, interest on invested funds, and ordinary enterprise profits.

This finding is consistent with the one that all capital goods services are the indirect embodiment of labor and land services alone. The principal thing in addition which is discovered by looking at income flows rather than flows of physical services is that, since one capital good is made by using another and since one enterprise sells capital goods to another, the indirect income payments resulting from the purchase of any capital goods include not only wages and rents but also interest and possibly enterprise profits. In other words, all of the recognized income payments may be made indirectly by the purchase of capital goods by any enterprise. These payments, however, fully account for any income derived from capital goods, so that there is no separable share attributable to capital goods service per se.

A second thing which appears is that incomes currently received from capital goods (by either firms selling them or firms using them) have been indirectly distributed in part *in the past,* so that the outpayment of the wages, rent, interest, and profits which equals the cost of capital goods or their services has significantly preceded in time the receipts of income from the sale of outputs made by using their services. In fact, some part of these indirect income payments may have been made very long ago, since one capital good has been contributing to the manufacture of another for a long time. This is perhaps not a matter of consequence if we are viewing the whole history of production as a unit for analysis. But if we shift our attention to the contemporary production process, and to the contemporary distribution of the income of the present time period, the time lag between the basic income payments made to acquire capital goods and the current receipts of income from selling them or their services may be a matter of consequence.

We have seen that all current incomes are allocable to wages, rent, interest, or enterprise profits made at some present or past time. Is it, nevertheless, conceivable that those now possessing capital goods will be able to command some separate share of *current* income, other than interest, for themselves—that, in effect, the share of the current income of the economy they command is systematically greater than their profits as calculated by deducting past costs from current income? We must now analyze this possibility by centering attention on the contemporary process of production and the contemporary distribution of incomes, past events being provisionally neglected.

CAPITAL GOODS AND CONTEMPORARY INCOME DISTRIBUTION

If we view the contemporary production process as a going thing, and concentrate attention upon how goods are produced today and from now on, it is clear that, wherever it came from and whatever it embodies, there is a very large stock of capital goods in being—several hundred billion dollars' worth in the United States, for example. The economy has been a long time accumulating these capital goods, and the origins of many of them, if we

take into account the long chain of capital goods in which one has contributed to emergence of the next, are in the distant past. Even though their
services represent the embodied or transmuted services of labor and land
rendered previously, as of this time capital goods are the source of a distinct sort of productive service other than the services of labor and land,
and of a sort of service which could not immediately be had from labor and
land were these capital goods not in existence. (Much time would have to
be consumed in recreating this capital stock "from the ground up," as countries which have suffered only a fractional destruction of their capital stock
through war have discovered to their distress.)

This much is clear. But is it clear that the flow of capital goods services
from the existing stock of such goods is truly available to the economy *in
addition to* the full flow of the services of labor and land? Do we have at
our disposal to produce outputs all of the services of currently available
labor and land *plus* the services of all of the available capital goods? The
answer to this question is that in one sense we do but that in another and
more significant sense we may not.

With a large stock of capital goods available, we obviously do have a
gross supply of productive services greater than those of all available labor
and land alone; we have all the services of labor and land plus those of all
available capital goods. Correspondingly, we are able to produce a *gross
output* substantially larger than if the capital goods were not present, not
only because currently available labor and land services are more productive
when assisted by capital goods, but also because capital goods services as well
contribute to output.

But we do not necessarily have a *net supply* of productive services equal
to the sum of all labor and land and all capital goods services, or a *net output* of goods as large as the aforementioned *gross output. This is the result
of the fact that capital goods in general wear out or are used up as they
contribute to production, and as a consequence have to be replaced unless
the stock of capital goods is to waste away and eventually vanish.* As a consequence, a part of the current total output of the economy will have to be
made up of items designed to replace existing capital goods if the capital
stock is to be maintained, and a corresponding share of the gross available
supply of productive services will have to contribute to such replacement.
The economy then receives as a *net output,* or addition to its total wealth
in the form either of consumers' goods or of *additions* to the stock of capital
goods, only its gross output minus the share of that output used to replace
previously existing capital goods. Correspondingly, the net supply of productive services is the gross supply of such services less the proportion of
them devoted to making replacements for existing capital goods.

Of what does this net supply of productive services consist? In general,
existing capital goods services as a whole will be used, in combination with

labor and land services, partly to create net outputs (consumers' goods or additions to the capital stock) and partly to create replacement goods to maintain the quantity of existing capital goods. Correspondingly, parts of currently available labor and land services will be used in these two directions. The net supply of productive services to the economy will then equal total capital goods services rendered minus the share of such services devoted to replacing capital goods, plus the total supply of labor and land services less the share of them devoted to replacing capital goods.

To put this in other terms, by having capital goods on hand we get as a part of the net supply of productive services *some* capital goods services which contribute to net output, the remainder simply being "self-consumed" by the complex of capital goods as it works to maintain itself. And in order to get this net supply of capital goods services, we *give up* that share of currently available labor and land services which also contributes to replacement. There is an explicit offset to the contribution which the services of existing capital goods make to current net output—namely, the part of current labor and land services which contribute to replacement. *We thus do not in the net have capital goods services as an addition to the full flow of currently available labor and land services.* We have them *instead of* that part of labor and land services which currently contribute to the replacement of capital goods. These latter services constitute a *current cost* of using capital goods for net production, just as the past labor and land services actually embodied in existing capital goods constitute a past cost.

What can be said of the relative sizes of the current benefits and costs of using capital goods? This will obviously depend on the extent to which current production is replacing the existing stock of capital goods. If the existing stock of capital goods is currently being fully maintained, so that at the end of each time interval there is on hand an aggregate stock of such goods with just as much stored-up service-providing power as at the beginning of the interval, then there is a maximum offset of labor and land services used for replacement against net capital goods services rendered for other purposes. (The offset cannot be greater than that necessary for full replacement, since any greater use of services results in a net addition to the stock of capital goods available and thus a net output for the economy.) Thus, if we have a complex of capital goods with an average life in use of ten years, suitable both for producing net outputs and for reproducing itself, an average annual use of labor and land services sufficient (when used with a part of the capital goods services) to replace one tenth of the capital stock annually constitutes the maximum offset against the capital goods services yielded by this complex for the production of net outputs.

If the economy should not maintain its capital stock fully for some period of time, of course, then during that interval a larger net flow of productive services and a larger current net output could be secured, essentially by depleting the existing capital stock.[5] In general, however, the tendency in the history of modern industrial organization has been to maintain any existing capital stock fully and to add to it, so that a full offset of labor and land services used for replacement is to be made against a net flow of capital goods services which remains after full replacement.

Let us view this as the usual or normal situation. A net supply of capital goods services contributing to net outputs is offset by a sufficient diversion of land and labor services to replacement to maintain fully (when assisted by the remaining supply of capital goods services) the existing stock of capital goods. Does the economy then gain in the net, or is it true that the net supply of capital goods services is in some sense greater than or more productive than the supply of land and labor services diverted to replacement, so that there is a net addition to productive services currently available because of the existence of a stock of capital goods?

This is not strictly a sensible question if it implies comparison of physical quantities of capital goods services with physical quantities of labor or land services, since the two are not intercommensurable. That is, if we simply know that by having a stock of capital goods we are able to use 100,000 hours of service from machines each working day for the production of net output in return for giving up 40,000 hours of labor service and 70,000 hours of land service for maintenance of the stock of machinery, we do not know whether the sacrifice is greater than the gain. We do not even have a direct conversion ratio between labor and land services on the one hand and capital goods services on the other— such that 40,000 labor hours and 70,000 land hours create by themselves 100,000 hours of stored-up machine services—since the labor and land services devoted to replacement will be used with that part of available capital goods services which have not gone to produce net output in order to create replacements. Two things only are evident. First, a certain quantity of labor and land services is used for replacement as an offset to a certain net supply of capital goods services. Second, the ability to produce both replacements and net outputs is evidently enhanced by the existence of capital goods and by the resultant availability of this "put-and-take" sort of productive process.

A more sensible question concerns the *values in exchange* of the net capital goods services rendered and the labor and land services used for their

---

[5] Such intervals may be encountered. During World War II, for example, production in the United States was controlled so that replacements of many capital goods were deferred or held below the rate necessary to maintain capital goods fully, with the purpose of securing a larger current net output of munitions. When this is done, of course, the economy is essentially using down its store of accumulated labor and land services rendered in the past and now embodied in capital goods, so a larger net output is to be expected. Correspondingly, it cannot do this forever; the procedure will rapidly deplete the store of capital goods and necessitate a subsequent reduction in net output.

replacement. That is, we may meaningfully ask: Will the current incomes received by capital goods owners as a whole, and resulting from the net supply of capital goods services contributing to net output, tend systematically to exceed, equal, or fall short of the payments made for labor and land services currently devoted to replacement of capital goods as a whole?

With one exception, there is no systematic reason that the current incomes of capital goods users should either exceed or fall short of their current outlays on land and labor used for replacement—that is, that they should receive a current profit share in income just because they are using capital goods. The exception is that current incomes will tend to include an interest payment both to funds invested in capital goods supplying net productive services and, as a part of current net replacement costs, to the funds invested in the capital goods which are used in their own replacement.

If we consider all capital goods users as a group (and thus neglect any incomes paid by one to another for use of each others' capital goods services for replacements, since these give rise to no net income or cost to the group) their net costs of current replacements to maintain the capital stock are made up only of current wages and current rents paid to secure replacement plus current interest charges on funds invested in capital goods used for replacement. Their net incomes are those resulting from the sale of their net outputs (other than replacement outputs)—or the value of these outputs as far as they hold them for their own use. There is no evident reason that these net incomes should tend systematically to exceed (or fall short of) their current costs of replacement plus those current wages and rents which are costs of net output plus interest on capital goods investment contributing to net output. Excess earnings to capital goods users will emerge in those situations which permit enterprises to make excess profits generally, and they will be eliminated where market structure and the condition of entry force the elimination of all excess profits. A full competitive adjustment would equate the current earnings of capital goods with their current wage and rent costs of replacement plus interest on invested funds. In other words, although enterprises may make excess profits while using capital goods or not, there is nothing peculiar about the introduction of capital goods into production which makes excess profits necessary.

It is of course conceivable that capital goods may have been created in such a limited quantity that their earnings may systematically exceed both their current costs of replacement and their original costs, or more generally that the current incomes from the net outputs they help produce will systematically exceed all current cost payments. This, however, would simply be evidence of monopoly in production which uses capital goods or supplies them to others. If those holding an existing capital stock did not compete and were able to forestall its expansion by others, they might continually reap from selling their net outputs excess profits essentially attributable to their control of scarce capital goods. Then not only would the original costs of individual capital goods as held by individual enterprises generally include the profits paid to other enterprises in the past, but the current income flow would also continually be diverted in part toward a current income share above current payments to wages, rent, and interest.

But if there were competitive conditions in all markets, with numbers and the condition of entry such as generally to drive out excess profits, any such income share would tend to be eliminated in long-run equilibrium by the expansion of output by existing firms and by new entrants, with a corresponding expansion of the capital goods stock and upward adjustment of wages and rents, until no excess-profit share remained. In effect, the earning power of enterprises using capital goods depends on the size of their outputs and the quantity of capital goods they employ, and if both of these are subject to free competitive adjustment then in equilibrium the current earnings from the use of capital goods will not exceed interest on funds invested in them plus their current replacement costs in terms of current wages, rent, and interest. Having established this, we should hasten to add that in the real economy a certain share of current income generally does pass as excess profits to enterprise employing and supplying capital goods.[6]

ANALYTICAL PROBLEMS CONCERNING THE USE
OF CAPITAL GOODS

Given the preceding general appraisal of the role of capital goods and of investable funds in production, our next task is to elaborate our previous simplified theory of income distribution to take account of the use of capital and to explain the effects of this use on income distribution.

From our discussion to this point, it is clear that the primary theoretical problem involving capital goods is not the determination of the price of their services when they are supplied in some given amount or according to some given supply curve from a given stock of capital goods. That is indeed the character of the general problem with both labor and land, since they are basic and independent productive factors with independent supplies. Capital goods, however, are not a third independent productive factor with an independent supply, but are produced goods made from labor and land (and from other capital goods). As such the supply of these goods and of their services to the economy is freely variable at the discretion of

---

[6] The preceding refers to equilibrium tendencies. It is of course possible that systematic changes through time in the cost of replacing capital goods may be accompanied by lags in competitive adjustment which result in "windfall" profits or losses. It may be that there is some tendency for a secular decline in replacement costs with continual technological change and with accretion to the total capital stock which favors the persistence of some windfall gain of this sort.

enterprise as various proportions of land and labor services can be channeled toward net production by incorporating them first in capital goods. It follows that the primary problem with respect to capital goods concerns the quantity in which they will be used in production—the extent to which enterprise will elect to embody labor and land services in capital goods in order to produce net outputs.

Solution of this problem involves analysis of the determination of the costs of making capital goods and of the relation to these costs of the prices of these goods to enterprises acquiring them. It also involves an analysis of the determination of the interest rate on investable funds, which determines the "cost of money" invested in capital goods to the enterprises using them. Analysis of the simultaneous determination of the quantity of capital goods used in production, of their costs and their prices, and of the interest rate on funds should permit us finally to explain, for any given level of employment, the quantity of invested funds which will be used in connection with capital goods and the size of interest share in total income which suppliers of these funds can command.[7]

D. THE DEMAND FOR AND PRICING
OF CAPITAL GOODS

THE QUANTITY OF CAPITAL GOODS REQUIRED
IN PRODUCTION

Let us attack these issues by considering first the determination of the quantity of capital goods required for production in a drastically simplified situation. Let us suppose the following relevant conditions. There is an economy with a given quantity of land and of labor, each with a supply perfectly inelastic to price, so that a constant quantity of the services of each—namely all the services available—will tend to be offered for employment regardless of real factor prices. Second, there is always an adjustment of the flow of aggregate money purchasing power in the economy to factor

[7] If indeed the supply of capital goods and their services were arbitrarily given and not freely variable, the explanation of the prices which capital goods and their services could command would be our main problem, and it would require no significant elaboration of our earlier theory. Suppose we were to postulate the existence of an arbitrary amount of capital goods, the services of which would be supplied in a certain unique relation to their price, and were to neglect the problem of replacement. Then capital goods would represent for purposes of analysis simply a second species of land, and we could deduce the equilibrium price their services would command (and thus the price at which capital goods would sell) and the portion of their available services supplied from assumptions stating their substitutability for labor and land and the shapes of the independent supply curves for their services and those of labor and land. In effect, the analysis of Chapter 11, which assumed three independent basic factors each available

prices such as to assure their full employment. Third, there is a given list of consumers' goods to be produced, with given interrelated demands as determined by the tastes of consumers.

Fourth, investable funds for use in acquiring capital goods are available at a *zero* rate of interest (there is no positive or negative interest rate on funds), with only the proviso that the principal amount invested be fully recoverable from the sale of the consumers' goods outputs. Enterprises can thus borrow or otherwise secure all the funds they want to invest in capital goods without paying any interest provided they can recover their total costs from their sales revenues.

Fifth, there is a given state of knowledge concerning productive techniques, which implies the knowledge of how to make and use in given ways a strictly given group of capital goods. Sixth, there is pure competition in every industry producing either consumers' goods or capital goods, and in every factor market. In this situation, what will determine the quantities of these capital goods employed, and the proportion of basic resources routed toward the production of consumer goods by supplying capital goods first?

A first question encountered is why enterprises producing consumers' goods will wish to use *any* capital goods in production. (If they did not capital goods production would never begin.) It is observed that in general they do use some, and the reason must be that the use of capital goods permits them to lower their costs of production. By using the services of capital goods in conjunction with those of labor and land, their costs of producing any given output, including the costs of the capital goods, will be lower than if capital goods were not used. There must be some virtual advantage in the use of capital goods which is not fully offset by the price of their services.

The character of the virtual advantage of capital goods presumably is derived from the general law of substitution between productive services. As between labor and land, for example, we have seen that a given output may be produced with various proportions of the two factors, but that as any one factor is increased at the expense of the other, its marginal rate of

in given and limited quantity, would serve to explain capital goods pricing as well as labor and land pricing. Such an analysis is in fact appropriate for the explanation of *short-run* pricing of capital goods services. Even if we extended the analysis to encompass successive replacements of capital goods, it would not be substantially altered as long as the quantity of capital goods to be maintained were taken as arbitrarily given. The price of capital goods and their services could still be explained along the same lines, although the steady conversion of labor and land services into wasting capital goods, with the possibility of accompanying profit, would have to be recognized. But capital goods are not independent in supply or given in quantity outside the short run, and as a consequence an adequate long-run analysis must look to the more complicated range of issues outlined above.

substitution for the other factor increases. Thus, the isoquant in Figure 58 shows the various proportions of labor and land which may be used to produce a given quantity of product. The quantity 100 of product may be produced with all the indicated proportions of labor and land, including, at point *a*, 78 labor and 28 land, and, at point *b*, 26 labor and 82 land. But as the amount of labor is increased (moving, for example, from point *b* to point *a*, the marginal rate of substitution of labor for land increases progres-

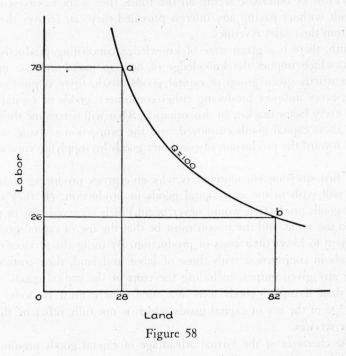

Figure 58

sively. At point *b*, a very little labor will replace a unit of land; as we approach *a*, more and more labor is required. We have also seen that the firm in competition will use these factors in such proportion that the marginal rate of substitution of labor for land is equal to the ratio of price of land to that of labor.

Precisely the same principle applies to substitution between capital goods services and other factors. The substitution relationship between "machine hours of service" (which we shall take as a representative measure of the services of capital goods) and "labor-and-land" hours of service [8] for a firm should follow a similar pattern, as shown in Figure 59. Machine hours may be substituted for labor-and-land hours at a virtually very advanta-

[8] Labor and land may be provisionally viewed as a single "composite" factor against which capital goods services may be substituted.

geous ratio at point *b* or to the right of point *b*. That is, if the firm is at the outset using little or no machinery, it can replace many labor-and-land hours with a few machine hours. But as it sucecssively adds machine hours (moving toward point *a*) the marginal rate of substitution of machine for labor-and-land hours progressively increases.

Does this relationship make it inevitable that the firm will be able to reduce its costs through using machinery (or, generally, capital goods) and

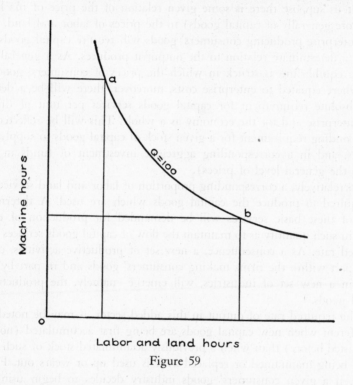

Figure 59

will thus employ at least some machinery? If so, how much will it employ? The immediate answer to both of these questions is that it depends on the price of machine hours of service, and thus of machinery, or, more precisely on the relation of this price to the prices of labor and land. It is conceivable that the price of machine hours of service might be so high relative to labor-and-land prices that any substitution of such service for labor-and-land services would increase production costs. If the machinery price is less than this, however, some machine hours of service will be combined with hours of labor and land service in order to minimize costs. Machine service will be substituted for other service up to the point where the marginal rate of substitution of a machine hour for a labor (or land) hour is equal to the ratio of the price of a labor (or land) hour to the price of a machine hour.

With any relation of the machinery price to labor-and-land prices other than one so high as effectively to exclude all use of machinery, therefore, the enterprise will employ some determinate quantity of machine services in the production of any given output. As the ratio of the prices of machine services to those of labor-and-land services is smaller, the firm will obviously tend to employ a larger quantity of machine services to produce any given output.

Let us suppose there is some given relation of the price of machinery (or, more generally of capital goods) to the prices of labor and land. Then each enterprise producing consumers' goods will require capital goods services in a determinate relation to the output it produces. As a general competitive equilibrium is struck in which the prices of consumers' goods are everywhere equated to enterprise costs, moreover, there will be a determinate absolute requirement for capital goods services per unit of time by each enterprise and for the economy as a whole. This will be reflected in a corresponding requirement for a given stock of capital goods to supply these services, and in a corresponding aggregate investment of funds in them (given the general level of prices).

Correlatively, a corresponding proportion of labor and land services will be required to produce the capital goods which are used. A determinate share of these basic services will be demanded for production of capital goods in such quantity as to maintain the flow of capital goods services at the required rate. As a consequence, a new set of productive activities, carried on in part within the firms making consumers' goods and in part by other firms in a new set of industries, will emerge—namely, the production of capital goods.

The required rate of output in this added sector, it may be noted, may be different when new capital goods are being first accumulated (not having existed before) than when a previously accumulated stock of such goods is just being maintained or replaced as it is used up or wears out. For example, if a given consumers' goods industry decides to begin using machinery in a given process and will require the services of 1,000 machines, capital goods production may have to supply all 1,000 machines within (let us say) two years. If the machines have an average life of twenty years, however, so that on the average only 50 per year wear out, *continuation* of the indicated rate of use of services, "forever after," may require machine production only at the rate of 50 per year. The quantity of basic services required per unit of time for *reinvestment* to maintain an existing stock of capital goods may exceed the quantity required for *net investment* when the stock is first acquired (depending, of course, on how rapidly the net investments take place).

For analysis of the *equilibrium* requirement for capital goods, however, we shall momentarily neglect the production adjustments entailed in net investment, and center attention only on the organization of production needed to sustain a given pattern of use of capital goods services, continually through time, once the requisite stock of capital goods has been initially accumulated. That is, we shall "skip over" analysis of any net investment process and look only at the process implied for maintaining a given rate of use of capital goods services after the requisite net investments have been accomplished. Referring to this process, it is clear that through time a determinate rate of production of capital goods will be required to replace the wasting and wearing capital stock and maintain the required flow of capital goods services, and this will require the continual diversion of a determinate share of basic labor-and-land services to this pursuit.

Actually, the resulting requirement for capital goods production may be rather complex. It will not in general be true that capital goods will be used only by industries producing consumers' goods and will be made by them or for them just by combining basic labor and land services. Those producing capital goods for use in consumers' goods production will require other capital goods, and those producing the latter capital goods will require still others, etc. Thus, if automobile makers require steel and machinery as capital goods, steel makers require blast furnaces and coke ovens and openhearth furnaces, machine makers require steel and other machinery, makers of blast and open-hearth furnaces require other capital goods, and so forth. In each case, the quantity of capital goods services used in production will be determined by the prices of capital goods services and their substitutability for land and labor. The initial requirement for capital goods in consumers' goods production creates a number of derived requirements for the production and use of determinate amounts of other capital goods.

Whatever the details of the organization of production, a determinate requirement per unit of time for capital goods services in consumers' goods production will call forth a complex of supporting capital goods production at corresponding rates to supply this requirement. Further, this complex of capital goods production as a whole will, in order steadily to maintain the required stock of capital goods at each level, regularly convert a determinate share of basic labor-and-land services into capital goods in each time period.[9]

[9] Suppose, for a simple example, that production of ashtrays, representing consumers' goods output, is at an equilibrium rate of 10 million units a year. This requires annually, if costs are minimized at given factor and capital goods prices, 2.5 million labor hours, 40,000 land-acre hours, a quantity of machine hours supplied by 100 identical type A machines each with a useful life of ten years, and 500 tons of steel. Direct capital goods requirements for ashtray production are thus 10 machines per year (10 of the 100 wear out each year on the average) and 500 tons of steel. Let us suppose that ashtrays are produced by firms A_1 to A_n.

The type A machines required each year are produced by firms B_1 to B_n. Their

THE PRICES OF CAPITAL GOODS AND THEIR SERVICES

This determinate requirement for capital goods production to sustain a determinate rate of use of capital goods services in consumers' goods production, however, is derived so far from some arbitrarily given relation of the prices of capital goods and their services to the prices of labor and land. The next question is how these capital goods prices will be related to those of the basic factors, and whether the relation will be such as actually to induce the use of capital goods in production.

In the situation supposed for purposes of initial analysis—which includes pure competition in every line of production and a zero rate of interest—the determination of the prices of capital goods and their services is very simple. In every line where capital goods are used in further production, the relevant current prices of their services to firms using them will be the cost of replacing these services, and this will be determined by the current prices of capital goods required for replacement. In turn, these prices, however, will in long-run equilibrium be equal to the current costs of producing the capital goods. With no profits in a competitive equilibrium and

production consumes, for minimized costs, 50 tons of steel, 500,000 labor hours, and 10,000 land-acre hours.

The steel required each year by both A and B firms is produced by firms C_1 to C_n and requires for minimized costs 50,000 units each of ore and coal (types of land), 1 million labor hours, and the use of 10 type C machines, each with a ten-year life. One of these machines must be supplied each year to maintain the stock of machinery, and is supplied by the B firms at a minimized cost of another 10 tons of steel (already included in the production of C firms), and of 50,000 labor hours and 1,000 land-acre hours.

Adding up capital goods requirements, we find that:

1. Ashtray-producing firms (A) require 10 type A machines and 500 tons of steel per year to sustain a given rate of ashtray output.
2. Machine-producing firms (B) require 60 tons of steel per year.
3. Steel-producing firms (C) require 1 type C machine per year.

The *gross* output of the complex of firms will be made up of 10 million ashtrays, 560 tons of steel, and 1 type C and 10 type A machines. The *net* output of the complex is simply 10 million ashtrays. It is the result essentially of converting 2.5 million labor hours and 40,000 land-hours *directly* into ashtrays, *plus* converting the equivalent of 1,550,000 labor hours, 11,000 land-acre hours, and 50,000 units each of ore and coal (also land) *indirectly* into ashtrays. That is, ashtray producers, by using up 10 machines and 500 tons of steel a year create a demand for the preceding amounts of *indirectly* applied labor and land, as used in B and C firms, to replace the machines and steel used on ashtray production and to replace the capital goods used in making those machines and steel.

It will be noted that the circular exchange between B and C firms—of steel made with machines for machines made with steel—does not vitiate this observation, although it makes it complicated to establish the ultimate full labor-and-land cost of either machines or steel separately.

no interest charges, the current costs of producing any given capital goods (to which their prices are equated) will be equal to their direct wage-and-rent costs plus the costs of replacing any further capital goods used in producing the first-mentioned capital goods. But the latter are equal only to current direct or indirect wage and rent payments made to secure such replacements, so that the entire current cost of any currently supplied capital good is equal to the sum of current payments made for labor and land used in producing it (either directly, or indirectly to replace other capital goods used). Now, since current capital goods prices are equated throughout to the current direct or indirect wage-and-rent costs of these goods, and since the prices of capital goods services to users are their replacement costs as determined by current capital goods prices, the effective prices of capital goods services to every user—in a competitive equilibrium and with no interest charges—will be equal to the costs or prices of the labor-and-land services directly or indirectly required to replace them. The ratio of the prices of capital goods services to the prices of labor and land will thus be reducible to a ratio between the prices of labor and land *indirectly used* (representing the current costs of replacing capital goods used) and the prices of labor and land *directly used,* the wages and rents presumably being the same or approximately so in both cases. It is this price ratio which, in purely competitive long-run equilibrium and with a zero interest rate, would determine the degree of substitution of the services of capital goods for labor and land and the aggregate requirement for capital goods.

THE ADJUSTMENT OF CAPITAL GOODS REQUIRED
TO CAPITAL GOODS PRICES

Will this price ratio (or something approximate to it) be such as to induce some use of capital goods? Very evidently it has; capital goods priced less than this favorably relative to the prices of labor and land have come to be used very extensively indeed. The possibilities of substituting capital goods services for labor and land are evidently such that costs can be reduced by using many capital goods with prices even very roughly equal to their costs.

In what proportion would capital goods services be combined with direct labor-and-land services in production if the competitive price ratio described ruled throughout the economy? (That is, what proportion of labor-and-land services would be devoted to making capital goods and what size stock of capital goods would be held relative to a given supply of labor and land?) It is not possible to answer this question in quantitative terms without knowing the precise conditions of substitution of the services of potentially available capital goods for labor and land. However, it is clear that in a purely competitive economy producing a given range of consumers' goods and with a given and unchanging range of potentially available capital goods, capital goods services in every line would be substituted for direct labor and land up to the point where their marginal rate of substitution for each other factor equaled the ratio of the price of that factor to the price of capital goods services.

This would also in effect be the point at which the marginal rate of substitution of a unit of labor and land services *indirectly used* (in the form of capital goods) for a unit of direct labor and land services equaled the ratio of the price of a unit of direct labor and land to the price of a unit of indirect labor and land. Now if labor and land received the same prices whether employed in making capital goods or otherwise, the last price ratio would necessarily be 1 to 1. Therefore, capital goods would be used down to the point where the marginal rate of substitution of *indirect* for *direct* labor and land was 1 to 1. This is where in effect an indirectly used hour of labor or land will just replace a directly used hour, or where costs cannot be reduced or output increased by shifting further labor or land from direct to indirect use. Under the assumed conditions, the proportionate use of capital goods services necessary to reach this point would be the determinate equilibrium rate of use of such services.

Of course, the individual firm which considers acquiring a capital good does not necessarily inquire why a machine costs what it does. But taking the price of machine hours as given, together with those of labor and land, it will consider the substitution relation (as illustrated in Figure 59) between machine hours and other factor services, and undertake substitution of capital goods services for other factors up to the point where the marginal rate of substitution of capital goods services for other factors is in balance with the price ratios. The substitution relations between capital goods services and labor and land, for example, might appear as follows in a typical instance:

100 UNITS OF PRODUCT PRODUCIBLE WITH THE FOLLOWING COMBINATIONS

Machine hours	Labor-and-land hours
10	5
9	5.75
8	6.62
7	7.62
6	8.87
5	10.37
4	12

For successive discrete movements from 4 to 5, 5 to 6, etc., of machine hours, the marginal rate of substitution is successively 1:1.63; 1:1.5; 1:1.25; 1:1; 1:0.87; 1:0.75. If the price of a machine hour were $1 and that of a labor-and-land hour also $1, so that the price ratio were 1:1, the firm would substitute capital up to the point where the marginal rate of substitution became 1:1—to where between 7 and 8 machine hours were employed per 100 units of output, since at this point cost would be minimized. If, on the other hand, machine hours were $1.25 whereas labor-and-land hours were $1, the price ratio being 1:25 to 1, the firm would substitute only up to the combination where the rate of substitution of machine hours for other services was 1:1.25 or in the neighborhood of 6 to 7 machine hours, since this would now minimize cost. Each firm's employment of capital goods relative to other factors is strictly determinate according to the usual principles if only the relative price of capital goods is given. If it is given as equal to the price of the labor-and-land services embodied, however, and if indirectly used labor-and-land services receive prices identical to those of directly used labor-and-land services, then each firm and the economy of firms as a whole will in effect employ capital goods services in such an amount that an hour of labor or land indirectly used via capital goods will just replace an hour directly used.

The preceding indicates the character of the determination of the proportionate use of capital goods services under the assumed conditions. What of the quantity of capital goods on hand which will be required to supply the indicated flow of services?

Capital goods per se represent essentially stocks of accumulated capital goods services. The quantity of capital goods required to supply any given flow of such services per unit of time will be determined by certain technological conditions, such as the durability of machinery and tools and the ratio of raw material and other inventories to the amount used per unit of time necessary to maintain an uninterrupted flow of production. Thus, if a firm requires certain machine services at the rate of 10 machine days of service per day, it will need to acquire 10 machines, and if each of these has a useful life of 5 years, it will have to acquire 18,250 machine days of service (365 days × 5 years × 10 machines) in advance in order to supply the needed flow of services, or have half this amount accumulated on the average over time. Or, if the firm uses 50 tons of steel daily, it may find that because of relevant shipping and delivery conditions, it needs to carry on the average a 20-day supply in stock, necessitating a regular investment in a stockpile of 1,000 tons of steel. Or, if a firm produces 100 refrigerators a day and each refrigerator takes 3 full days to complete, it must at a minimum have an investment in a work-in-process inventory of 300 partly finished plus just-finished refrigerators on hand at all times.

Given such controlling conditions of technique, then, a determinate amount of capital goods will be required to sustain each given rate of flow of capital goods services required. This will in turn imply, given the prices of the capital goods, a corresponding determinate requirement for funds to be invested (and remain invested) in capital goods. Thus, given the controlling conditions in the form of the supplies of basic productive services in the economy, the range of consumers' goods to be produced, the character of capital goods potentially available, and the structures of all markets, a determinate requirement for the rate and composition of the flow of capital goods services, for the stock of capital goods to be maintained, and for the amount of investable funds needed to finance their maintenance may be deduced for any enterprise and for the economy as a whole. Correlatively, we deduce the structure of production which will tend to emerge, as defined by the proportion of labor-and-land services which will be indirectly used in supplying capital goods services and the shape of the pattern in which they will be used.

THE EFFECT OF USING CAPITAL GOODS ON PRODUCTIVITY
AND ON WAGES AND RENTS

There are two implications of the preceding analysis which are of considerable significance in the appraisal of economic activity. One is that the use of capital goods in production tends to increase the aggregate output of the economy. The other is that it tends to increase the real wages and rents received by labor and land. In a competitive equilibrium with a zero interest rate, in fact, it would increase them by the same amount by which output is increased.

The reasons for this are readily apparent on short consideration. Enterprises evidently substitute capital goods services for direct land-and-labor services because they can thereby reduce their costs of production; if some considerable amount of capital goods are in use, therefore, we may take it for granted that the firms using them have attained lower costs.

The general rule is that they will substitute capital goods services (C) for land-and-labor services (L) down to the point where the marginal rate of substitution C for L equals the ratio of the price of L (P_L) to that of C (P_C). If this is done, it is clear that the last or marginal unit of C substituted for L results in practically no change in a firm's costs of any given output. If *at the margin* one unit of C replaces two units of L and P_C is twice P_L, costs are unchanged.

Substitution of all the *inframarginal* units of C for units of L, however, will have reduced the costs of a given output. The marginal rate of substitution of C for L increases as C is successively substituted for L. Therefore, if at the margin this rate is equal to P_L/P_C, *inside the margin* it has been smaller than P_L/P_C, and costs have been reduced by substituting C for L down to this point.

Thus, suppose we start production of a given output with 15 labor-and-land (L) hours only, such hours being priced at \$1 each, and consider substituting machine hours (C) for them, machine hours also costing \$1 each.

We may find that $1C$ will replace $3L$ (giving us a constant output with $1C$ and $12L$); that a second C will replace $2\frac{1}{2}L$ (giving us the same output with $2C$ and $9\frac{1}{2}L$); that a third C will replace $2L$ (so that we now require $3C$ and $7\frac{1}{2}L$ for an unchanged output); that a fourth C will replace $1\frac{1}{2}L$ (so that we now require $4C$ and $6L$); that a fifth C will replace $1L$, so that we now require 5 machine hours (C) and 5 labor-and-land hours (L) to produce the same output. Pursuing a profit-maximizing and cost-minimizing policy, we shall presumably substitute C for L down to where the marginal rate of substitution of C for L equals P_L/P_C—in this case to where it is 1 to 1.

This will imply using $5C$ and $5L$, since it is in the movement from the $4C$-$6L$ to the $5C$-$5L$ combination that the marginal rate of substitution becomes 1 to 1. And, indeed, this will minimize costs of the given output at $10. Now it will be noted that for the last or marginal unit of C substituted for L, costs are unchanged; the fifth machine hour used costs a dollar and replaces only one unit, or a dollar's worth, of labor and land. But the *inframarginal* machine hours—the first, second, third, and fourth—have reduced costs. Thus, if we used no machine hours at all, but simply 15 units of labor and land, costs of the given output would be $15 instead of $10. This is clearly implied by the existence of a range, on the isoquant which shows substitutability of capital goods services for labor and land, over which the marginal rate of substitution of C for L is less than the ratio of P_L to P_C. Any use of capital goods implies that the enterprise has taken advantage of such a range, and, by moving through it to the point where *further* use of capital goods in place of labor and land will not lower costs, attains lower costs of any output than if no capital goods had been used. The enterprise can thus reduce its money costs of producing any output by using capital goods in place of direct labor and land to a certain extent, given the prices of both.

It will follow in general also that any given output is therefore produced with a smaller total quantity of labor-and-land services, directly and indirectly used, than if capital goods were not employed. That is, the sum of direct labor-and-land hours used and the labor-and-land hours required to supply or replace capital goods services employed will be smaller than the direct labor-and-land hours required if no capital goods were employed. We have seen that in using capital goods, the enterprise is effectively substituting indirectly used for directly used labor-and-land services. The price that it pays for capital goods services will in general be at least as large as the price of the indirect land-and-labor services which they embody, or which are required to replace them. Under competitive equilibrium and with a zero interest rate the capital goods service price will be the same as that of indirect labor and land represented; with positive interest charges or profits included in the cost of capital goods, it will be larger. Now if the indirect labor-and-land services embodied in capital goods services (or required to replace them) command as high a price per unit as direct labor-and-land services, it must follow that whenever the firm can reduce its money costs by employing capital goods, it must also be reducing its total requirement for labor-and-land services. If capital goods services worth $5 will replace direct labor-and-land services worth $10, if the indirect labor-and-land services required to supply the capital goods services cost as much per unit as direct labor-and-land services, and if the capital goods service price is at least as high as the labor-and-land costs of such services, then the money saving must be reflected in at least an equivalent saving in total labor-and-land services used directly and indirectly for production. If interest changes or profits are included in the price of capital goods services, the real savings of labor and land may be greater proportionally than the money savings.

It may be demonstrated that under the conditions so far assumed—universal competitive equilibrium with a zero interest rate—capital goods will be used just to such a point as to minimize the total real cost in terms of labor and land for any output. Under such conditions, the marginal rate of substitution of C for L is expressible as the marginal rate of substitution of units of indirectly applied labor and land for units of directly applied labor and land. Similarly, the equilibrium price of capital goods services may be expressed as the price of units of indirect labor-and-land services embodied in or required to replace the capital goods services used, and the strategic price ratio, P_L/P_C may be expressed as the ratio of the prices of directly and indirectly applied labor-and-land units. When the enterprise uses capital goods to such an extent that the marginal rate of substitution of capital goods services for direct labor-and-land services equals the inverted price ratio, then, it is also equating the marginal rate of substitution of indirect for direct units of L to the ratio of the price of direct to that of indirect units of L.

Now if the same prices prevail for both direct and indirect units of labor and land, and if there are no interest charges or profits, the last price ratio is necessarily 1 to 1. Each indirect labor or land hour has the same price as each directly applied labor or land hour. If then the enterprise proceeds to the point where the marginal rate of substitution of indirect for direct labor and land equals the ratio of the price of direct to that of indirect labor and land, it necessarily reaches the point where this marginal rate of substitution (of indirect for direct hours of L) is 1 to 1.

This then is the point at which, *at the margin,* one hour of indirectly applied labor and land just replaces one hour of directly applied labor and land. The marginal application of capital goods services saves no labor or land. But from the fact that it does not, two things follow.

First, for all *inframarginal* applications of capital goods services, the marginal rate of substitution of indirect for direct L will have been smaller than 1 to 1, so that for each such application less than an hour of indirect labor and land will have replaced a full hour of direct labor and land. There has thus been a reduction of the amount of real resources required to produce any given output.

Second, since the substitution of C for L has been carried to the point where an hour of indirect just replaces an hour of direct labor and land (and beyond which a unit of indirect labor and land would replace less than a unit of direct labor and land), the total real costs in terms of labor and land producing any output will have been effectively minimized.

In effect, if we can reduce money costs by hiring labor and land to produce capital goods and then using the capital goods instead of direct land and labor, and if we pay the same amount for units of land and labor either way, we must be able to use less total land and labor by using capital goods. Further, if we use just such an amount of capital goods as to minimize money costs, and if there are no added charges of using capital goods, we must minimize the total requirement for labor and land to produce any output.

What of situations in which the price of capital goods services to enterprises using them is greater than the prices of the labor-and-land services embodied because of interest charges or because firms supplying the capital goods make profits? Then obviously, with a lower ratio of P_L to P_C, fewer capital goods services will be used, since a lower marginal rate of substitution of C for L will put the firm in a position to minimize money costs. Real costs in terms of land and labor will have been reduced by all inframarginal applications of capital goods services, *and also by the marginal application* (since P_C now overstates the real cost of the marginal application), so that costs are lower by reason of the use of capital goods. But the addition of interest and profits to P_C will have checked the use of capital goods somewhat, so that not enough capital goods will be used to minimize total real costs in terms of labor and land. We shall return to this argument later.

The use of capital goods, then, economizes on the total quantity of labor-and-land services needed to produce any given output, and, in the case of universal competitive equilibrium with a zero interest rate, would minimize this quantity. By using capital goods, we can have all the final output we could get without using them and still have some land and labor left over. If now labor-and-land prices (and with them capital goods prices) adjust relative to money income to permit full employment, we shall obviously get a larger total output for the economy as a whole by using capital goods, since thereby each unit of labor and land produces a greater output. In the case of universal pure competition with a zero interest rate, we would get the maximum attainable output (since real costs are truly minimized); the appearance of interest and profit charges in the prices of capital goods will result in a somewhat less than maximum attainable output. But the use of capital goods will in any event tend to increase the aggregate productivity of the economy, giving us more net output from a given supply of the basic factors. It is in this sense that the "roundabout" process of production, involving the use of a portion of basic resources indirectly to provide capital goods services, has a superior productivity. The degree of superiority is in fact very, very great.

What effect does the use of capital goods have on the distribution of income; in particular, to the earnings of what income recipients is added that increase in aggregate output which results from using capital goods? The precise answer depends upon the structure of the industries using and producing capital goods and on whether or not there is a positive interest rate, although it is generally true that either some or all of the increase in output due to the use of capital goods will go to augment the real earnings of labor and land.

In the simplified situation which we have so far assumed—with pure competition in every market and a zero rate of interest—the entire net income from production would in long-run equilibrium be distributed to land and labor, and therefore any increase in net output resulting from the use of capital goods would be added to real wages and rents. If every industry were in pure competition, long-run equilibrium for each firm in each industry would find the selling price of output exactly equal to average costs of production, and aggregate revenue from sales exactly equal to aggregate costs of production. Every producer of *net output,* therefore—that is, of output in addition to that required to replace existing capital goods—would incur costs to produce this output equal to the selling price of the output. These costs would be equal to the wage and rent payments by the enterprise to labor and land used either directly in producing the net output, or in replacing through its own production capital goods used up in producing that output, plus payments to other enterprises to purchase capital goods for similar replacement. Its price would thus be exactly equal to the direct current payments to labor and land necessary to get the output and maintain the stock of capital goods plus current replacement-cost payments to other enterprises for capital goods needed for replacement. There would be no interest payment, the interest rate being zero. Each enterprise producing net output would thus distribute in current payments to others an amount just sufficient to purchase that net output, and retain no profit share which would permit it to purchase any of it.

Except as far as this enterprise purchased capital goods for replacement, this payment would go only to labor and land. What of its payments to other enterprises for replacement capital goods? This would also go in its entirety indirectly to labor and land. Each enterprise producing replacement capital goods—that is, gross output above or in addition to net output —would also under the assumed conditions be producing with its prices equal to current costs. Therefore, it would distribute its total receipts from selling capital goods entirely to direct labor and land, or to others for further replacement capital goods. These "others" would in turn do the same until all payments made for replacement capital goods were fully matched by current wage and rent payments made to produce replacements. If this were the case, the total payment for replacement capital goods made by producers of net output would be exactly exhausted by the wage and rent payments made by the suppliers (as a group) of replacement capital goods. In effect, the difference between the sales value of net outputs and the direct wage and rent payments made by their producers would exactly equal the indirect wage and rent payments necessary just to replace the existing stocks of capital goods in the hands of all enterprises as they were used up. Then total current wage and rent payments would precisely equal the sales value of current net output, and the suppliers of labor and land would command the entire net output of the economy. Thus, the total net product, including all increases attributable to the fact that capital goods were being used, would be distributed to labor and land, and real wages and rents would be raised by the total of any increment to net production.

Of course, it is true that the *gross output* of the economy (net output plus all replacement capital goods supplied) would exceed net output, and that enterprises as a group would receive the excess in order to replace the capital goods used up in providing net output. Similarly, gross income payments would exceed net income payments to labor and land by just enough to permit them to do this. But the excess of gross over net income payment would essentially reflect a sort of double counting as suppliers of replacement capital goods received and then paid out to labor and land the wage and rent costs of replacement capital goods. Net income payments, after the deduction from gross income of enough to purchase all replacement capital goods sold, would all go to labor and land and exactly equal the value of net output.

By what mechanism of adjustment would labor and land come to receive the increment in net output attributable to using capital goods? As capital goods are brought into use, the costs of supplying outputs are reduced, in the sense that the total requirement for labor and land, directly and indirectly applied, become smaller than if capital goods were not used. Therefore, the money costs of given outputs will be smaller with any given money prices of labor and land. Competition would force enterprises to reduce the prices of their outputs to equality with their costs, and thus the ratio of output prices to labor and land prices would be reduced. Then real prices of labor and land would increase proportionally, as the outputs purchasable, for example, with the wage of an hour of labor, were increased.

Suppose that prior to the use of capital goods, 100 units of output A have a cost of 10 hours of labor paid $1 an hour and 10 hours of land service paid $1 an hour, thus having a money cost of $20 and an equilibrium price of 20 cents per unit. Then the real wage of an hour of labor or land will be 5 units of output A. If now, by using capital goods, the cost of 100 units of output A is reduced to 5 units of labor plus 5 units of land (directly and indirectly used), the money cost with the same money prices of labor and land will be $10 for 100 units and the equilibrium price per unit will be 10 cents. Then the real wage of an hour of labor or land will be 10 units of output A.

Thus, if cost reductions due to using capital goods are passed on fully in lower prices, real wages and rents rise sufficiently to appropriate the entire advantage for suppliers of labor and land. And if money income adjusts to wages and rents so as to permit maintenance of full employment, the total resultant increment to output is added to wages and rents.

The preceding refers strictly to the case of a universal purely competitive equilibrium with a zero interest rate, where all net output necessarily goes to labor and land. What of the situation where there is a positive interest rate, or a departure from competitive equilibrium permitting of excess profits? If a positive interest rate exists, as we shall see, the substitution of capital goods services for direct labor and land services will be somewhat restricted because of the resultant increase in the relative price of capital goods services (which must be compensated by the superior productivity of capital goods services at the margin), and some share of income will be paid as interest on funds invested in capital goods. Costs will have been reduced (and output increased) by more than the income share paid as interest, however—because the savings of inframarginal applications of capital exceed the interest cost—and the entire remainder of the corresponding output increase would in competitive equilibrium go to labor and land.

If profits are earned on final or net outputs, these of course reduce the wage and rent share in income, but they would do so with or without the use of capital goods. If profits are made by the producers of capital goods, these are added to the prices of capital goods services and tend to restrict the use of such services exactly as a positive interest rate does. Correspondingly, a further share of income goes to profit receivers rather than to labor and land. However, the reduction in costs (and increase in output) due to using capital goods will again tend to exceed the income share paid as profits of capital goods suppliers—again because inframarginal applications of capital cut costs by more than enough to pay the profit share in question—and the remainder of the corresponding increase in output will tend to go to labor and land. We thus see that although the emergence of interest charges and profits on capital goods tend to reduce the share which labor and land receive of the increment in total output due to the use of capital goods (and also to reduce this increment somewhat), they still tend to leave to labor and land some share of the increment.

THE COMPOSITION OF NET OUTPUT IN EQUILIBRIUM
AND DISEQUILIBRIUM

In the preceding sections we have spoken primarily of the determination of an *equilibrium* requirement for the use of capital goods services (and of capital goods and investable funds) in an imaginary situation of a highly simplified sort. We have assumed a zero interest rate, and in addition we have assumed (1) given (and inelastic) supplies of labor and land, (2) automatic full employment of them, (3) a given list of consumers' goods to be produced, (4) given productive techniques, which implies the potential availability of a strictly given variety of capital goods and a given state of knowledge as to how to use them, and (5) either a competitive or some other given relation of the prices of capital goods to their costs. For such a situation, we have deduced the determination of the quantity or rate of flow of capital goods services which will be required in production once enterprises have made an equilibrium adjustment to the given opportunities, of the corresponding quantities of capital goods which will continually be held by enterprises once such an equilibrium is reached, of the proportion of current labor and land services which will then be regularly required for replacing these capital goods, and of the quantity of funds which will be continually kept invested in capital goods.[10]

Our analysis has referred directly and only to the situation which should persist after all desired capital goods have once been acquired by enterprises, and in which therefore the only demand for capital goods is a replacement demand. The situation to which we have referred is thus one in which there is no *net investment* demand for capital goods to add to the stock already in existence, and in which net output is composed entirely of consumers' goods. Thus, we have "skipped over" the analysis of any other period, prior to the reaching equilibrium, during which capital goods are being accumulated and net investments being made, and during which a part of net output is therefore made up of capital goods.

Before considering the character of situations in which net investments in capital goods are going on, let us note one further property of the equilibrium situation so far imagined. We have seen that in this situation there

[10] The quantity of funds invested will assume a value which corresponds to the equilibrium stock of capital goods, but which depends for its magnitude in dollars also on the money price level, as governed by the relation of the aggregate flow of money purchasing power to the quantity of basic factors. Regardless of the money price level the quantity of funds invested should stand in a given determinate relation to the rates of flow of gross and net income.

is a determinate stable requirement for capital goods services as a flow through time, and thus a determinate stable requirement for a stock of capital goods and for investment of funds therein. New capital goods will be produced through time at a rate just sufficient to replace already existing capital goods as they are worn out or used up, so that the quantity of funds invested in capital goods will not tend to increase or decrease. Correspondingly, the funds required to secure replacements at the indicated rate will be fully supplied by the cost payments through which enterprises selling net outputs of consumers' goods distribute their sales receipts from these net outputs, and no funds for investment will need to be supplied from the net incomes which result, directly or indirectly, from these cost payments.

We have seen that the sales receipts of enterprises producing net outputs will be fully distributed (after profit net incomes to these enterprises, if any) in cost payments which will go in part as net incomes to the direct labor and land these enterprises employ and in part to purchase replacement capital goods from other enterprises in just such quantity as to maintain the existing capital stock devoted to producing net output. Conversely, the funds required to secure such replacements are fully supplied by the sales receipts from net output. Further, the amounts spent for these replacement capital goods are in equilibrium entirely respent (one or more times) in such a way as (1) to finance replacement of any further capital goods used by capital goods producers, and (2) to result in payments, directly or indirectly, of net income to labor and land (and possibly to profit receivers) just equal to the replacement cost payments of net output producers. Therefore, the expenditure of the sales receipts of net output producers is ultimately sufficient to finance all replacement costs of capital goods and to create in addition a total of net income payments just equal to the sales receipts from net output. (The passage of part of the receipts from net output *through* enterprises supplying replacement capital goods provides a net income equal to the sales receipts from net output and generates a sufficient added gross income to finance all replacements.)

It follows that none of the net income generated (which is just sufficient to purchase a net output equal to that the sale of which generated it, at unchanged prices) is required for current investment in capital goods. All of this net income is available for the purchase of net consumer-good outputs, and none will be demanded to finance the acquisition of capital goods. The use of existing capital goods results in the earning of such an income from net output that there is enough of it to reinvest, after paying other costs as net incomes, to maintain the stock of capital goods. And this reinvestment generates sufficient additional net income that total net income equals the sales value of net output and is all available for spending on net consumer-good output.

For example, enterprises producing consumer-good net outputs may have total sales receipts of $100,000 per period of time. Assuming there are no profits, this $100,000 may be distributed as $75,000 in net income payments directly to labor and land, and $25,000 for the purchase of a sufficient amount of capital goods to replace those used up in producing the net output. The firms supplying these capital goods receive this $25,000 as gross income and distribute it fully as $25,000 in net income payments to labor and land used in producing the replacement capital goods. Now $100,000 of net income payments are available for the purchase of consumer-good net outputs, and none of this amount is needed to purchase capital goods, since these have been financed by the passage of $25,000 through the capital goods-producing firms on their way to land and labor.

The fact that in such an equilibrium there will thus be no call for the expenditure of net income on capital goods of course reflects the fact that there is no net investment demand for added capital goods, or for additions to the amount of funds invested in capital goods. There is thus no demand for *saving* from net income, if by saving we mean not spending on consumption. If total net income is spent on consumers' goods, a sufficient part will be respent by the enterprise on replacement capital goods, and respent again through payments which create net income, to permit both maintenance of the capital stock and re-creation of a constant amount of net income in each period of time. And factor prices will adjust relative to the prices of net outputs so that all this can happen while enterprises at least break even.

What would happen if indeed a part of net incomes *were not spent on consumption,* but saved? Then it is clear that, as long as enterprises continued to use their sales receipts in the same quantity to purchase replacements (rather than shifting them to spending on consumers' goods in counterbalancing amount), spending on consumers' goods would decline from period to period, and the sales receipts of enterprises from net output would become insufficient to sustain a constant rate of output at unchanged prices. Therefore, either employment would tend to decline at given prices, or prices would have to fall fluidly and indefinitely with money income (if they fell with any lag, unemployment would result), and a stable equilibrium with full employment could not be maintained.[11] It is thus seen (and will be argued further in the succeeding chapter) that if an economy should reach a stationary equilibrium with no net investment demand for capital goods, there *must* be a spending on consumers' goods equal to net income when income is at a full-employment level (zero saving at full-employment income) if full employment is to be automatically maintained. The assumption that there will be a continuously stable economy with full

[11] Unless after some finite fall in prices, savings declined to zero with full-employment incomes. This possibility will be analyzed in Chapter 14.

employment when there is no net investment demand, thus necessarily implies the assumption that saving out of net income will be zero at full-employment income, or become so after some price-level adjustment. The latter assumption has thus been implicit in our analysis of equilibrium capital requirements and income distribution assuming full employment; if it is not a valid assumption, that analysis will require modification to explain the determination of the level of employment and the determination of capital requirements at other than full-employment levels. We shall consider this problem in the succeeding chapter.

All the preceding refers to an equilibrium situation in which there is no *net* investment demand and in which, therefore, all net output will be made up of consumers' goods. Such an equilibrium might be reached and held, given a certain behavior of saving, under the assumed conditions of an unchanging list of consumers' goods to be produced, unchanging basic factor supplies fully employed, and unchanging techniques of production. These conditions, however, are not generally fulfilled in fact.

Changes in technique involving the introduction of new types of capital goods or new ways of using them, the development of new types of consumers' goods, and increases in population or in the quantity of known resources have been occurring regularly over long periods of time, with the net result that the flow of capital goods services and the quantity of capital goods which enterprises require has tended to increase progressively through time. As a consequence, the equilibrium quantity of capital goods is a moving quantity, generally moving in the direction of increase. Therefore, enterprises tend never to achieve a stable equilibrium stock of capital goods, but in each successive period of time tend to demand some net additions to the pre-existing stock of capital goods, in order to reach the new and larger equilibrium quantities of capital goods required which are continually emerging. In short, the economy tends to be continually in the process of pursuing a moving equilibrium with respect to the quantity of capital goods required, and thus tends to demand net additions to the capital stock required in each successive period.

If this is the case, a certain portion of the net output of the economy in each period will tend to be made up of "new" capital goods, representing net investments or net additions to the total stock of capital goods. To what extent does the emergence of this phenomenon alter our previous conclusions concerning the effect of the use of capital goods on the distribution of income through time?

Some of the same generalizations hold. That is, the producers of net output—which now includes some "new" capital goods as well as consumers' goods—incur current costs made up of direct land and labor payments plus payments for the replacement of previously existing capital goods used in the production of these net outputs. And there is a virtual *general* tendency for the quantity of such previously existing capital goods to have approached an equilibrium level, and for the total sales receipts from the sale of current net outputs to be paid out—if there is a zero interest rate—either directly to labor and land (and possibly profits), or indirectly to them for replacing the pre-existing capital goods. If there is in addition universal pure competition, all net income will tend to go to labor and land.

On the other hand, the fact that net investment demands are present—demands for addition to the stock of capital goods—is clear evidence of the fact that in some lines of production at least there is a current *disequilibrium,* in that enterprises have not yet acquired the stock of capital goods consistent with minimizing their costs and maximizing their profits. In some enterprises producing consumers' goods, or capital goods for replacement, or capital goods for net investment, a change in the rate of use of capital goods services must be going on, involving a current virtual shortage of capital goods and a process of adding to them. It is thus inconceivable that all enterprises will be in a situation of stable equilibrium with respect to the use of capital goods. Some of them are out of equilibrium, but pursuing it by increasing their capital stock as they modify their production processes to accommodate the use of the added or net investment capital goods.

If this is the case, it follows that it will not be true, even with pure competition, that every enterprise in every line will have an ideal capital stock or that its current sales receipts must equal its total costs. Nor will it be true that the current payments for labor and land plus payments for replacements of existing capital goods will just exhaust current sales receipts.

The net investment demand for capital goods reflects a shift in demands for outputs or in attainable costs to which a full competitive equilibrium adjustment has not yet been made, and therefore current discrepancies between receipts and costs (in addition to any monopoly profits of stable equilibrium) are clearly possible. If costs are falling as added capital goods are brought into use, for example, the first firms to acquire added capital goods will tend to enjoy a temporary excess profit as price declines more slowly, while laggard firms may make temporary losses, until the total stock of capital goods and total number of firms is adjusted to a new equilibrium. Or early investors in the production of a newly developed consumers' good may reap extra profits until sufficient net investments have accumulated to permit production to bring price down to cost. Thus, transitory profits of innovation, together possibly with some net losses, may frequently be a concomitant of the situations which create net investment demands.

A second consideration is that if net investment is regularly taking place, so that the capital stock is continually growing, the rate of spending necessary just to maintain by replacement the stock of capital goods accumulated up to any moment (as it is used up or wears out) will be smaller than the amount of sales receipts recoverable as a return of its original cost. Therefore, even if sales receipts equaled total costs (that is, current labor and land costs plus allocated past costs of capital goods used), not all sales receipts above current labor and land costs would be distributed to secure current replacements, and a share of current net income would accrue to capital goods users as an accumulation against future replacement costs or a return of a part of past net investments. This is because capital goods are durable, and because in effect a growing stock of them tends always to be "young" or relatively new on the average, so that current replacement costs never equal the sum of the past costs allocable to a particular period.

If, for example, a firm is employing three machines each with a life of three years, costing $300 apiece, as a stationary stock of capital equipment, its annual machine depreciation cost, or allocation of past cost, will be $300. It will also need to purchase one new machine each year for $300, so that current replacement costs match the allocation of past costs, and sales receipts sufficient just to cover total costs will be fully distributed currently to secure replacements. But, if an enterprise acquires each year one additional machine of the same type (with a three-year life and $300 original cost) and replaces all previously acquired machines in the year that they wear out (their third year), it is demonstrable that full depreciation costs, presumably recovered in sales receipts, will tend persistently to exceed current replacement costs. In successive years, starting with one new machine and adding one at the beginning of each year, depreciation costs over a period of fifteen years would be as shown in column (3) below, whereas current replacement costs, assuming any machine is replaced during the year at the end of which it wears out, would be as shown in column (4).

(1) Year	(2) Number of machines in use	(3) Depreciation costs	(4) Replacement costs	(5) Excess of depre- ciation over replacement costs
1	1	$100	0	$100
2	2	200	0	200
3	3	300	$300	0
4	4	400	300	100
5	5	500	300	200
6	6	600	600	0
7	7	700	600	100
8	8	800	600	200
9	9	900	900	0
10	10	1,000	900	100
11	11	1,100	900	200
12	12	1,200	1,200	0
13	13	1,300	1,200	100
14	14	1,400	1,200	200
15	15	1,500	1,500	0

There is a persistent tendency for there to be a positive excess (column 5) of depreciation over current replacement costs as long as the capital stock keeps growing—in this case an excess in the average amount of $100 a year —although the excess of course becomes smaller percentage of cost as the percentage rate of increase of the capital stock declines. Such a tendency for some share of net income to fall systematically to enterprise as a return of past costs not required for current replacements further tends to distinguish economies with continual net investments from those with a stationary equilibrium capital stock.

In sum, the tendencies of income distribution—even with pure competition and a zero interest rate—tend to be somewhat different if net output is composed partly of new capital goods for net investment than if there is a stationary equilibrium capital stock, and this because of the implications of the disequilibria which give rise to net investment demand.

An equally important aspect of situations where net investment is going on is that a part of current net income may be spent on the purchase of capital goods rather than consumers' goods. Although replacements of pre-existing capital goods are still financed by enterprise spending out of the sales receipts of net outputs (which when respent create net incomes), the demands for additions to the stock of capital goods, reflected by the inclusion of new capital goods in net output, carries with it a corresponding demand for added funds to finance their acquisition. Therefore, a share of current net incomes may be "saved"—that is, not spent on consumption— and yet find an outlet for expenditure in the purchase of new capital goods.

It is possible that total net income at full employment will be either spent on consumer goods, or saved for spending on new capital goods in just the quantity that such capital goods are demanded, so that "saving" equals net investment spending. Then total net income at full employment (equal to the sales value of net outputs the sale of which generated it) will always be exactly spent, sales receipts from net output will remain constant through time, and full employment can be maintained at unchanged prices. If saving from a full-employment net income does not equal net investment, however, then our previous assumptions of a stable money income flow and automatic full employment cannot be legitimate. We are then required to analyze the determination of the levels of income and employment, and the effect of the level of employment on investment and saving, a task to which we shall turn in the succeeding chapter.

Postponing consideration of this problem, and assuming a spending behavior such as to maintain an unchanging flow of money purchasing power and automatic full employment, we see that, assuming away an interest share, the use of capital goods in stable equilibrium amounts does not necessarily result in any net income shares other than wages and rents, although monopoly profit shares are, of course, possible. We note also that the use of capital goods in progressively increasing amounts, involving regular net investments in new capital goods, tends also to increase wages and rents but in addition probably is associated with the emergence of further shares in current net income—profits of disequilibria and recoveries of past costs in excess of current replacement costs.

E. THE USE OF CAPITAL AND THE INTEREST RATE

THE EFFECT OF THE INTEREST RATE ON INVESTMENT AND INCOME DISTRIBUTION

We have so far analyzed the requirement for capital goods services, for capital goods, and for investable funds, together with the effects of using capital goods on productivity and income distribution, while assuming away any interest cost of investable funds. That is, we have supposed for purposes of simplification that there is a zero interest rate, and thus no interest charge on funds invested in capital goods, and have thus inquired how the capital goods requirement and the distribution of income would be determined if this were so (and if in addition spending behavior were such as to permit automatic full employment). Let us now relax this assumption, and see to what extent the requirement for capital goods and the distribution of income will be altered (as compared to those already predicted) because of the existence of a positive interest rate.

In general, the existence of a positive interest charge for the use of investable funds will have two effects. It will tend to raise the prices of capital goods services to enterprises and thus tend to restrict somewhat the quantities of capital goods services, capital goods, and investable funds required in each line of production. And it will result in the payment of a certain share of net income as interest to those who have supplied the funds invested in capital goods. Let us consider these two effects in turn, looking first at the effect of the interest rate on the quantity of capital goods used.

In the example on page 596, we supposed the following substitution relation between capital goods services and direct labor-and-land hours in some typical line of production:

100 Units of Product Producible with the Following Combinations

Machine hours	Labor-and-land hours
10	5
9	5.75
8	6.62
7	7.62
6	8.87
5	10.37
4	12

The marginal rate of substitution of machine hours as they are successively substituted for direct labor and land hours (reading up the table) is successively 1:1.63, 1:1.50, 1:1.25, 1:1, 1:0.87, and 1:0.75.

We further supposed the cost per machine hour, exclusive of interest, to be $1. Such a cost is presumably calculated, if there is no interest charge, simply as the original cost of the machine [12] divided by the number of machine hours rendered over the economic life of the machine. If, in this example, the unit machine (rendering 1 machine hour per hour) originally cost $60,000, would provide 3,000 hours per year, would last 20 years, and would have no scrap value at the end of 20 years, the cost per unit of service, U, could be calculated at:

$$U = \frac{\$60,000}{20(3000)} = \$1.$$

If $1 is the price of a machine hour, and if labor-and-land hours are also priced at $1, we have seen that the firm would substitute machine hours for labor and land up to the combination of 8 machine hours and 6.62 labor-and-land hours, thus using 8 machine hours to produce each 100 units of output. Correspondingly, a rate of output of 100 units per hour would require an investment in 8 machines; of 1,000 units per hour, an investment in 80 machines.

Suppose now that there is a positive interest rate, so that the firm must each year pay to suppliers of investable funds a given percentage of the quantity of funds invested, and must add this payment to the cost per machine hour. On a $60,000 machine, the average annual interest charge would be (*to a rough approximation only*) the annual interest rate times one half of the original cost of the machine, or the interest rates times $30,000. (The interest rate will be calculated on the average on half the original cost because over its life about this much will be invested, as the cost is progressively recovered from sales revenues from the date of acquisition to the date of replacement.) Then, if the interest charge on investable funds were 4 per cent per annum, the average annual interest charge on a $60,000 machine would be ($30,000 × .04) or $1,200, and the cost per machine hour, assuming the same life and rate of output, would be calculated as:

$$U = \frac{\$60,000 + 20(1200)}{20(3000)} = \$1.40.$$

In effect, the price of capital goods services would be raised from $1 to $1.40 per machine hour by the inclusion of an average annual interest charge per machine of $1,200 for each 3,000 machine hours of service obtained.

---

[12] Viewed either as a past cost or a replacement cost.

If the price of machine hours were thus raised to $1.40 apiece, labor-and-land hours remaining at $1, the firm obviously would use less capital goods. In the example above, it would substitute machine hours for labor-and-land hours only so long as the marginal rate of substitution was less than 1:1.40, and it would thus use machine hours and labor-and-land hours in the proportion of 6 to 8.87, thus employing 6 machine hours for each 100 units of output produced. It would, therefore, require only 6 machines to produce an output of 100 units per hour, or 60 machines to produce 1,000 units per hour.

A first evident effect of a positive interest rate is therefore to raise the relative price of capital goods services, and thus to induce firms to employ less capital goods services to produce any given output, hold fewer capital goods, and require less investable funds than they would with a zero interest rate. This is because the marginal rate of substitution of capital goods services for labor-and-land services must be kept low enough to compensate for the increased ratio of capital goods service to labor-and-land prices. This restriction on the use of capital goods will be accentuated by the fact that, with fewer capital goods employed, the aggregate net output of the economy will be reduced, requiring fewer capital goods services with any given rate of their use relative to output.

It is further obvious that increases and decreases in the interest rate should tend to induce corresponding decreases and increases in the quantity of capital goods and investable funds required. Whereas the basic prices of capital goods are more or less tied to their wage and rent costs, the rate of interest is potentially a free and independent price and may move independently of wages and rents. If it does, the demand by firms for the services of capital goods will be influenced by the rate of interest.

A rate of interest of 6 percent in the preceding example would raise the price per machine hour to $1.60, and a rate of 2 percent would drop it to $1.20. A rate of interest of zero would drop the price to $1. As the interest rate became progressively lower, larger amounts of capital would tend to be employed for the production of any given output (and total output would tend to increase with enhanced productivity) so that correspondingly larger amounts of investable funds would be demanded. Thus, in the example on page 612, we have seen that with a zero interest rate the price of machine services might be $1 per hour, labor-and-land services also being $1 per hour. At this rate, 8 machine hours would be employed to produce 100 units of output, and thus 8 machines to produce 100 units per hour. Investment, at $60,000 per machine, would be $480,000 per 100 hourly units of output as the original cost of the required machines, or $240,000 on the average if in equilibrium the average machine is 50 percent depreciated with half the initial investment recovered. At the rates of interest of 2, 4, and 6 percent, however, fewer machine hours would be used—respectively 7, 6, and 5 per

100 hourly units of output. For the firm in question, therefore, average investment in machines per 100 units of hourly output would vary as follows (at $60,000 new or $30,000 half depreciated per machine) in response to changes in the interest rate:

Interest rate	Average investment
.06	$150,000
.04	180,000
.02	210,000
.00	240,000

It thus appears that for any firm—and consequently in general for the economy as a whole—the quantity of capital goods services, of capital goods, and of investable funds required to produce any given output will tend to be a function of the rate of interest on funds, increasing as the interest rate falls. Any positive interest rate tends to restrict the use of capital goods and the total investment of funds therein, but the smaller the interest rate the smaller is the restriction. There is thus in effect an economy-wide aggregate demand schedule for funds to be invested in capital goods, which in general shows increasing demand with lower interest rates or prices on the use of funds, assuming full employment throughout.

At any given interest rate, however, the economy at full employment will tend, in the absence of dynamic changes in techniques, products, etc., to require some determinate amount of capital goods and of funds invested therein, and to reach a stable equilibrium where just this amount of capital goods are held and regularly replaced. This stable equilibrium will differ from that already attributed to an economy with a zero interest rate only in that the quantity of capital goods held and of aggregate funds invested in them will tend to be somewhat smaller. Otherwise, the picture will be the same, in that in the stable equilibrium a determinate share of labor-and-land services will be devoted to replacing the equilibrium stock of capital goods, in that net output will be composed entirely of consumers' goods, and in that current replacements will regularly be financed by the expenditure by enterprises of a share of sales receipts from net output (subsequently distributed as net incomes). With pure competition everywhere, all income from the sale of net output would be exhausted by cost payments to enterprises producing it.

The major difference in such an equilibrium is that the suppliers of investable funds will necessarily receive a share of net income. We have seen that enterprises employ capital goods services in such restricted quantity that their marginal rate of substitution for labor and land is low enough to compensate for the inclusion of an interest-charge in the price of the services. It will also be true that the sales receipts from their outputs in equilibrium will be large enough to cover their total costs (will equal them in a purely competitive equilibrium), and that these total costs will now include an interest payment made for the use of funds invested in capital goods—either payable to creditor suppliers of funds outside the enterprise or imputable to owner-investors within the enterprise. For any enterprise, this aggregate interest cost will equal annually the quantity of funds invested in capital goods times the annual market rate of interest at which they have been supplied (or could earn elsewhere), and this will be recovered in sales receipts and paid as a share of net income to suppliers of funds.

We have seen that in an economy-wide purely competitive equilibrium with a zero interest rate, with all enterprises holding equilibrium stocks of capital goods, the following would be true. Each enterprise producing net outputs would currently pay out its entire current sales receipts as costs, with a part going to the direct labor and land it employed and the entire remainder to suppliers of capital goods purchased to replace those used up or worn out in earning the sales receipts; the suppliers of these replacement capital goods (and of the replacement capital goods they in turn use, etc.) would be in exactly the same position and do exactly the same; therefore, all sales receipts from net output would be distributed to labor and land either directly employed in producing net outputs or indirectly employed in replacing existing capital goods. If now there is a positive rate of interest, the equilibrium situation will be altered as follows. Enterprises producing net outputs will pay out their entire current sales receipts to direct labor and land, to suppliers of replacement capital goods, *and to suppliers of the funds invested in the capital goods devoted to producing net outputs*. Suppliers of these replacement capital goods will pay out their entire sales receipts (received directly or indirectly from producers of net outputs) to direct labor and land, to other suppliers of replacement capital goods, *and to the suppliers of funds invested in capital goods they devote to producing replacement capital goods for others*. This will be true of each supplier however long or complex the chain of enterprises supplying one another with replacement capital goods. Therefore, all sales receipts from net output will be distributed as cost payments, but instead of them all going to labor and land a part of them will go to suppliers of investable funds as interest. Looking at the distributive picture from the standpoint of producers of net outputs, they continually make from their sales receipts a certain amount of *direct* interest payments to suppliers of funds invested in capital goods they hold, and a certain added amount of *indirect* interest payments, as the interest costs of the suppliers of replacement capital goods are included in the prices of those goods which producers of net output pay. The interest share in income distribution emerges as an additional amount, separate from wages and rents, whenever there is a positive rate of interest on investable funds. The size of the share (relative to total income) will obviously depend on (1) the rate of interest and (2) the size of the equilibrium stock of capital goods, as influenced by the interest rate, by technical conditions such as durability of capital goods, and by the substitution conditions between capital goods services and other factors.

However, as has been suggested (pages 598 to 605), the interest share in income will not tend to be sufficiently large that labor and land receive none of the addition to total output attributable to the use of capital goods. In effect, the interest earning on *each* unit of capital good service used tends to be equal to the reduction in cost and to the increase in product attributable to the use of marginal units of such service in the various lines of production. But the reduction in cost and increase in product attributed to the use of inframarginal units is greater than this amount, and the difference tends to be added to wages and rents.

The preceding refers explicitly to the determination of the interest share in income at full employment when there is universal pure competition and when the economy has attained an equilibrium stock of capital goods. But the same tendencies should be observed if there are monopoly excess profits earned on net outputs or on replacement capital goods, or if there is a disequilibrium associated with a regular progression of net investment in capital goods. If departures from competition permit excess profits, a further income share is created, and the prices of capital goods services may be raised, thus further restricting the use of capital goods. But whatever quantity tends to be used, the suppliers of funds invested in them will tend to command a corresponding share in income. If a progression of net investment reflects certain disequilibria within the economy, as a moving equilibrium is pursued, there may be further departures from equilibrium income distribution, but suppliers of investable funds will again tend to command a share in income based on the current total quantity of investment. The principal differences here are that in some sectors profits of disequilibrium may be added to their interest incomes, whereas in others losses of disequilibrium may be offset against or wipe out their interest earnings.

The preceding analysis, however—both of equilibrium and disequilibrium situations—has been simplified by the tacit assumption so far adopted that there is simply "an interest rate" at some arbitrarily given level, at which any amount of investable funds required may be obtained and, in equilibrium, retained. This has been equivalent to supposing that there is a perfectly elastic supply of investable funds at a given interest rate, so that any equilibrium stock of capital goods may be attained or, in disequilibrium, pursued, without altering the fixed price per annum charged for the use of each dollar of invested funds. It has been implicitly assumed concurrently that there is a behavior of spending at this interest rate such that saving equals net investment at a full employment income and that a stable money income with full employment can thus be continually maintained. Then the only problem involved in explaining the interest share in income is that of the determination of the quantity of capital goods required by enterprise at full employment (and its response to shifts in the level of the interest rate)—a problem on which we have so far centered attention.

Since this assumption of a perfectly elastic supply of funds at a given interest rate may not be entirely valid, there is an important set of unanswered questions concerning the use of capital goods and investable funds to which we must now turn. These are what determines the level of the interest rate at which investable funds are supplied, how high it will be, and to what extent it will vary with variations in the demand for investable funds. In brief, we must undertake to explain, along with the determination of the total requirement for capital goods and investable funds and the income share receivable at any given interest rate, the codetermination of the rate of interest which investable funds will command.

In explaining this, moreover, we shall be concurrently required to explain whether and under what conditions spending behavior will be such that full employment will automatically be attained. We must, therefore, develop explanations not only of what the interest rate will be when full employment does prevail (as so far assumed) but also of what it will be—and what capital requirements and income distribution will be—when it does not.

THE DETERMINATION OF THE INTEREST RATE

The general way in which the interest rate paid on investable funds is determined is fairly obvious. We have seen that enterprises as a group will require the use of investable funds to finance the acquisition and holding of capital goods. With a given state of techniques, given consumer-good variety and design, a given level of employment of basic factors, and given relative prices of capital goods (relative to wages and rents), they will require or wish to hold a determinate stock of capital goods. With a given level of basic factor prices, this will be translated into a corresponding requirement for funds to be invested in capital goods. But both the capital goods and investable funds requirement are dependent on the interest rate. Enterprises as a group will tend to require fewer investable funds as the interest rate is higher, and more as it is lower, other things being equal.

There is thus virtually a sort of over-all demand schedule for investable funds, relating the total funds sought for investment in a given situation to the rate of interest on funds. Like other demand schedules, it will shift if the surrounding situation changes—for example, if techniques change or new products are introduced or if there is a change in the level of employment of basic factors.

This demand (fixed or potentially shifting) will presumably in some way interact with the supply of investable funds to determine an interest rate. Before we turn to the character of this supply, however, we must note a certain peculiarity in the character of the demand. Any given total requirement for investable funds at a given interest rate will necessarily through time have been expressed in two forms. Prior to the acquisition of the capital goods involved and to obtaining funds to purchase them, it will have been a net investment demand—that is, a demand for funds not previously supplied to business for the purchase of additional capital goods. Once the funds have been supplied, and the capital goods purchased, it will be recurrently expressed as a reinvestment demand—that is, a demand for the retention of previously invested funds, presumably recovered from the sale of outputs to the production of which capital goods contributed, and for their reinvestment in the replacement of previously acquired capital goods. From this, several observations of importance follow.

First, the net investment demands necessary for the build up of any required quantity of investment in capital goods will in general not have been expressed all at once—at any moment or over any short period of time. This is generally true because any given total requirement for capital goods will have accumulated from a long series of successive changes in techniques, products, factor supplies, and so forth, so that in each year an added net investment demand emerged to be satisfied. No single time period will see or will have seen a net investment demand comparable to that necessary to acquire *de novo* the total amount of capital goods required at any given rate of interest. Second, any given total demand for funds at a certain interest rate, once it has been satisfied initially by net investments, will be reflected subsequently *only* in reinvestment demands for the respending of amounts which have been previously invested and presumably recovered from the sale of outputs. In an equilibrium, therefore, where enterprises were already holding all the capital goods they wanted at a given interest rate, the entire current demand for funds would be a reinvestment demand, and would exceed this only if the interest rate fell (thus leading toward another equilibrium).

Third, when such an equilibrium has not been reached—and a moving equilibrium is being pursued with consequent recurrent net investment requirements, the bulk of the current demand for funds in an economy which has already accumulated a huge capital stock will be a reinvestment demand, and a minor share will be new or net investment demand. Fourth, if capital goods are on the average durable, so that the average item in which funds are invested lasts over a substantial time interval, then in any shorter time interval the current demand for reinvestment of funds to replace capital goods already acquired will be less than the total amount of funds invested. Thus, if capital goods have previously been acquired requiring investment of $5 billion, and if they have an average life of five years, then the annual reinvestment demand corollary to maintaining $5 billion invested will be only $1 billion. Fifth, this current reinvestment demand plus any net investment demand will be the *gross current demand* for investable funds at a given interest rate. Finally, the position of any current *gross investment demand schedule* will shift with changes in technique, the level of employment, the price level, etc.

The interest rate in each successive period of time will be determined in general by the interaction of such a current gross investment demand schedule (which related current gross demands for new investment plus reinvestment of funds to the rate of interest) with a corresponding gross supply schedule for investable funds. This interaction, or a series of such reactions through successive time intervals, will determine the rate at which net investment proceeds through time, the corresponding rates of reinvestment which emerge, and the amount of funds to be finally invested in capital goods in any stationary equilibrium which might be reached, together with the stable interest rate which would prevail in that equilibrium.

A crucial determinant of the interest rate at any time is thus the character of the supply schedule for investable funds. And the crucial determinants of the movement of the interest rate through time, and of its value in any stationary equilibrium reached, are the characters of the successive supply schedules which will emerge in successive time intervals in response to successive demands. If we are interested primarily in the properties of a stationary equilibrium, the crucial supply schedule for investable funds will be that found in periods after an equilibrium stock of capital goods has been reached.

It is difficult, however, to dispose at all quickly of the character of the supply schedule for funds and of its interaction with a corresponding demand schedule for investment in capital goods.

On a general level we may first point out that, in any time interval, the relation of the supply of investable funds to the interest rate will depend on the character of four component responses to the interest rate, those of: (*a*) amounts supplied from current net income, (*b*) amounts supplied from current returns from the use of pre-existing capital goods—i.e., current gross income over and above net income—(*c*) amounts supplied by banks or other credit institutions through creation of added money, and (*d*) amounts supplied from previously accumulated cash balances of individuals and enterprises. We may also point out that the total supply schedule and the components will shift systematically with shifts in the price level, the level of employment, etc. Roughly, two tasks would then seem necessary. First, we should describe and explain the shapes and shifts of each of these component supplies of investable funds—and then of the total supply—in each of a succession of time periods in which there may be alternatively or successively either net investment and a growing capital stock or only reinvest-,ment and an equilibrium capital stock. Second, we should anaylze the interaction of these successive supply schedules with the demand schedules to which they correspond, with some special attention perhaps to their interaction at the point that an equilibrium stock of capital goods is reached.

Unfortunately, a realistic analysis of the determination of the interest rate cannot be so simple, and for this there are two principal reasons.

First, the determinants of the rate of interest are not confined to the supply of investable funds from all sources (that is, current net or gross incomes, banks, and cash balances) and the demand for funds for net investment and reinvestment in capital goods. Other sources of demand for funds may be periodically or persistently operative, with a corresponding influence on the interest rate—in particular, demand for funds by banks (which may withdraw money from circulation instead of supplying it for investment), the demand for funds to be added to cash balances, and the demand for loans by consumers to finance current purchases. The interplay of all types of demand and supply of funds must be considered in explaining the interest rate, and in this interplay the demand for funds to acquire or replace capital goods is not the only demand. Generally, the interest rate is determined by the demand for and supply of *money*—for whatever purpose money is desired—and all types of demand and supply must be taken into account. This implies, as we shall observe in the succeeding chapter, that the interest rate will not necessarily—except under special conditions—fall at such a level as to equate the demand for funds to invest or reinvest in capital goods with the supply of funds in general or from any particular source. Actually, explanation of the rate of interest involves explanation of the destination of money flows in the economy through time, and of the determination of the level of money income.

Second, the determination of the rate of interest involves the simultaneous determination of the relation of the rate of investment (roughly, spending on capital goods) to the rate of saving (roughly, current income minus current consumption spending). We cannot properly analyze the question of what the interest rate will be, that is, without analyzing what the relation of investment to saving will be, since the interplay of these two quantities is involved in the determination of that rate. And this forces us to consider an issue which we have so far deliberately neglected by assumption—the determination of the level of employment.

In the preceding analysis in general, we have assumed that money factor prices will adjust relative to the flow of money purchasing power so as to permit maintenance of full employment (that is, no involuntary unemployment) of all factors. This assumption has been carried into the analysis in this chapter of the determination of the equilibrium stock of capital goods and of the interest share in income at given zero or positive interest rates, and we have correspondingly analyzed the determination of rates of net investment and reinvestment on the assumption of continuous full employment. That is, we have supposed that the required increments to investment will be those required if full employment is being continuously maintained, and that equilibrium rates of reinvestment will be those necessary for the maintenance of that stock of capital goods which is an equilibrium stock under conditions of full employment.

But this assumption of automatically maintained full employment can be fulfilled only if there is an automatic maintenance of a certain relation of investment to saving. In effect, saving must not exceed investment (and for stability of the price level must also equal it) when the economy is operating at full employment. If saving does exceed investment in this situation, money income will tend to decline relative to factor and commodity prices, creating unemployment, or, more generally, the ratio of money income to money prices will tend to be insufficient to maintain full employment unless a finite decline in factor prices should eliminate this excess.

The analysis of the determination of the interest rate thus calls into question our implicit assumption that savings will no more than equal investment at a full-employment level of income. This is because it asks whether in this situation the interest rate, together with interacting variables such as prices and the level of money income, will tend to arrive at levels where this is true. In turning to the analysis of the interest rate it is therefore necessary to open the question, so far neglected, of the determination of the level of employment. This can best be explored in a separate chapter, which will consider together the codetermination of money income, employment, investment, saving, and the interest rate.

In the terms of the foregoing analysis, this will involve recognition of the possibility of total requirements for capital goods which are not those of full employment, and of investment demand schedules (net or gross) which are correspondingly those of an underemployment situation. Correspondingly, it will involve recognition of shifts in the supply schedule of investable funds as money income, employment, and prices change, and analysis of the interaction of these interdependent and shifting schedules toward the determination of an equilibrium level of income, employment, prices, and interest rate. The conclusion will not necessarily be that the economy always approaches or pursues a full-employment equilibrium with a corresponding equilibrium stock of capital goods.

What then is the meaning of our foregoing analysis of the determination of the rate of use of capital goods on the assumption of continuing full employment, with emphasis on the total capital goods and investable funds requirement and on the interest share in income when equilibrium is reached with full employment? In general, we may say that the situations previously referred to (either equilibrium situations or those where net investment is going on) are conceivable situations so long as, through the interaction of the demands for and supplies of investable funds, the interest rate (other variables responding as they will) is determined at such a level that savings will not exceed investment when full employment is being maintained. For these situations to be attained, it will further be necessary that if there is less than full employment, adjustments will be set in course which will bring the economy toward this full-employment level. This will mean in general that with full employment gross saving must not exceed gross investment at the determined rate of interest. It will mean in particular that with full employment net saving (out of net income) must not exceed net investment, and that in stationary equilibrium, where there is no net investment but only reinvestment demand, there must be no net saving at the determined rate of interest. The source of these propositions will become clear in the succeeding chapter.

In short, our analysis of the use of capital under conditions of full employment is valid for a category of situations in which the relation of demand to supply for investable funds is such (given the interaction of other variables) that the interest rate will be determined so that savings do not exceed investment at full employment. Such situations, it will be seen, are quite conceivable as long as a substantial rate of net investment is going on, although there is considerable doubt about the specified conditions being met once an equilibrium stock of capital goods had been attained. Rather than analyzing separately the determination of the interest rate in these potentially special situations, let us turn now to the general analysis of the simultaneous determination of the interest rate and the level of employment and money income, discovering thereby among other things the character of its determination under full-employment conditions. Our preceding analysis of capital use and income distribution under full employment will then appear to be directly applicable to a certain range of situations, whereas it will require some modifications in order to predict corresponding phenomena in situations of underemployment.

MONOPOLY AND THE USE OF CAPITAL GOODS

Before turning to the analysis of the rate of interest, a few remarks may be added on the significance of monopoly in the production and sale of capital goods.

From the preceding analysis, it is clear that monopolistic selling of capital goods would tend to raise their prices relative to competitive levels, unless their direct and indirect wage, rent, and interest costs were sufficiently depressed by the virtual pressure of monopolistic restriction to offset this effect. If these costs are not so depressed, as they will not be with factor mobility, then the prices of monopolized capital goods and their services will be higher relative to the prices of direct labor and land employed by their users. Then their use will be correspondingly restricted, as they will not be substituted for direct labor and land to the same extent. Thus, the equilibrium quantity of capital goods required at any interest rate, and the equilibrium rate of use of their services—both as measured in physical units —will be reduced as compared to a situation with competitive selling of capital goods. Correspondingly, the net investment demand for capital goods—again in physical units—will tend to be smaller at any interest rate when any given change in techniques, products, and so forth, takes place.

Unless efficiency in the production of capital goods has been substantially reduced as an incident of monopoly, this will also mean that a smaller amount of labor and land will be diverted to the production of capital goods, either for net investment or for reinvestment for the maintenance of a given capital stock, and that excess profits will emerge. It will also mean that the total productivity of the economy tends to be reduced, since the use of capital goods has been held short of the output-maximizing ratio of universal pure competition by the monopolistic increase of capital goods prices.

It will not necessarily mean, however, that the proportion of income paid for capital goods services or the total requirement for investable funds will be reduced at any given interest rate. This will depend upon the elasticity of demand for capital goods services, which will in turn depend primarily on the substitution conditions between capital goods services and other factors. It is thus possible that monopolistic pricing of capital goods services will either increase, decrease, or leave unchanged the proportion of income paid for capital goods services and the requirement for funds for investment in capital goods at a given interest rate.

In general, of course, monopolistic capital goods pricing will tend to create an excess-profit margin to the producers of these goods. As in the case of other monopoly, however, it is possible that the increase in price (and possibly in total receipts) will be fully dissipated in increased costs of producing capital goods, and thus fully distributed as the wage, interest, and rent costs of the capital goods. If this is so, of course, more basic factor units will be used to provide a unit of capital goods because of monopoly.

We shall not pause to trace in detail the possible impacts of monopsony in capital goods purchase, which will in general tend to reduce capital goods prices and to restrict their employment below the competitive level. Application of analyses previously developed will enable the student to answer any essential questions here. Let us turn at once, therefore, to the problems of interest, income, and employment.

SUPPLEMENTARY READINGS

J. R. HICKS, *The Theory of Wages,* London: Macmillan & Company, Ltd., 1932.

JOHN T. DUNLOP, *Wage Determination under Trade Unions,* New York: The Macmillan Company, 1944.

ALFRED MARSHALL, *Principles of Economics* (8th ed.), Book V, Chaps. 6-11; Book VI, Chap. 9.

ARTHUR M. ROSS, "The Trade Union as a Wage-Fixing Institution," *American Economic Review,* XXXVII, Sept. 1947, pp. 566-588.

IRVING FISHER, *The Theory of Interest,* New York: The Macmillan Company, 1930, Part II.

EUGEN VON BÖHM-BAWERK, *The Positive Theory of Capital,* London: Macmillan & Company, 1891.

KNUT WICKSELL, *Lectures on Political Economy,* New York: The Macmillan Company, 1934, vol. I, Part II.

INVESTMENT, INTEREST, MONEY, AND EMPLOYMENT

In this chapter two primary problems remain to be attacked—the determination of the rate of interest and the establishment of the level of employment. We have just seen that the first cannot be meaningfully discussed apart from the second, since the interplay of the demands for and supplies of funds which fixes the rate of interest also helps determine the level of employment, which in turn affects the interest rate. Analysis of the equilibrium tendency of the interest rate thus involves explanation of the equilibrium tendency of employment.

Actually, further matters are involved in the analysis of interest and employment. The level of employment is immediately determined by the level of money purchasing power or income and by the general level of prices— or by the interaction of these two. Similarly the rate of interest, depending as it does on the demand for and supply of investable funds, is determined in part by money income and prices. Therefore, our analysis of interest and employment must include an analysis of the determination of the levels of money income and of prices. Finally, a leading determinant of all of the magnitudes so far discussed—income, employment, interest, and prices—is the rate of net investment spending in the economy through time. Especial attention must, therefore, be devoted to the determinants of investment spending in the modern economy.

How shall we attack this complex of problems? We shall attempt to simplify the analysis by dealing with the various issues piecemeal in the following order.

First, we shall analyze the determination of the rate of interest in a single period of time—not necessarily an equilibrium period—under the simplifying assumption of a substantially given level of money income, prices, and employment, and of "neutral" banks which neither demand nor supply any funds. This will enable us to identify the major immediate determinants of the interest rate other than bank policy. It will also enable us to establish the superficial characteristics of both equilibrium and disequilibrium situations, and to see how the latter may lead to changes in interest, income, prices, and employment.

Second, we shall relax the assumption of neutral bank policy and inquire how the policies of the banking system may influence the rate of interest.

Third, we shall trace the establishment of an equilibrium level of income, employment, and interest through a succession of time periods, retaining the simplifying assumptions of a given price level. This will give us, among other things, a provisional explanation of the determination of the level of employment on the supposition that it is unaffected by price-level changes.

Fourth, we shall discard the assumption that the level of prices is fixed and given, shall inquire to what extent the price level affects employment and interest, and shall analyze the simultaneous determination of interest, money income, prices, and employment.

Fifth, we shall discuss the determinants of the behavior through time of that strategic determinant of all the magnitudes in question—the demand for funds for net investment. Finally, we shall consider some closely related matters bearing on the determination of income and employment—the incidence of risk to enterprises and the fiscal policy of the government.

Let us now turn at once to the first stage of our analysis, concerning the determination of the interest rate in a single period.

A. THE INTEREST RATE IN A SINGLE TIME PERIOD

ASSUMPTION OF THE ANALYSIS

A full analysis of the determination of the interest rate is complicated because it involves explaining the codetermination of money income, employment, and prices. All of these things are determined together, that is, and the interest rate cannot seek an equilibrium or provisionally stable value without inducing responses in these other magnitudes which in turn influence the interest rate.

We may temporarily abstract from the complexities in question, however, by first analyzing the determination of the interest rate for a single time period which is by definition short enough that significant movements in money income, prices, and employment cannot take place, and thus first establish the very short-run tendency of the interest rate with *given* income, employment, and prices. Thereafter, we may extend our analysis to embrace a succession of such time periods through which all interacting magnitudes may adjust.

THE UNIT TIME PERIOD

This single time period which will serve as a framework for the immediately succeeding analysis requires careful definition. We shall define it in general as the time interval required for money to "circulate" once through the economy. Let us make this definition explicit.

In a monetary exchange economy like ours, the production and sale of outputs are elicited and the offering of factor services attracted by a continuous flow of money payments. Thus, consumers and investors buy outputs of consumers' goods and of capital goods for net investment by paying money to enterprises; enterprises as a group in turn make wage, interest, rent, and profit payments which secure factor services to produce the outputs delivered or to replace the capital goods used up in producing them (some of these payments possibly being retained in the enterprise if the enterprise owners make profits or are also factor suppliers); the income payments so created are spent again by the income recipients who are also the consumers and investors, and so forth endlessly. A flow of money payments thus proceeds continuously in a circular flow, from income recipients (who are also factor suppliers) through the system of enterprises and thence back to factor suppliers (who are also income recipients).

We shall define our unit period generally as the time required for money —precisely, the average dollar in circulation—to move in this flow "through the economy" once; that is, for it to circulate from where it has just been received as income, through the enterprise system, and back to be received as income again. There are several alternative definitions of income to which the definition of this unit period might be related, however. For present purposes we shall define the unit period with reference to *net income*—as the time required for the average dollar to pass from net income payment back to net income payment again.

Net income in any time interval may be defined as the total of payments received for services by the suppliers of the services of labor, land, and money (as wages, rent, and interest) plus the net profit (excess of sales receipts over the total cost of output delivered) of enterprises. Most of this will be paid by enterprises to individuals, but some of it will be retained undistributed by enterprises, so far as their managements elect to retain some of the profit, rent, interest, or wage earnings of the services of factors placed in the control of the enterprise by its owners. This is what net income includes. It excludes enterprises sales receipts per se, since these reflect the passage of net income *through* enterprises *to* final net income recipients; to add the sales receipts to the total of wage, interest, rent, and net profit payments would involve double counting of net income. It does not include as a separate item the gross income received by enterprises as a return for capital goods (including inventories) used up in production, and then either retained or paid to other enterprises to secure replacements. In the former case, old assets are converted into cash and the receipts are not scored as income. In the case of simultaneous replacement, the value of replacement outputs is not a net income (being offset by the depreciation or depletion of old capital goods), and the money paid for replacements is properly viewed as passing through the enterprise system to create net income payments in the amount only of final wage, interest, rent, and net profit payments resulting.

The definition of net income may be made clear by the following example. Suppose that at the beginning of some interval of time we find Enterprise A with accumulated capital goods worth $500, Enterprise B with goods worth $200, and Enterprise C with goods worth $100. During the period considered let us suppose that total expenditure on consumption goods plus that on additions to capital stock before deducting any disinvestment is $1,100, all paid to Enterprise A. Suppose that Enterprise A delivers $1,100 of output, in turn using up capital goods worth $400, paying $600 in wages, interest, rent, and net profits to individuals, retaining $100 of undistributed net profits, and paying $400 to Enterprise B to replace its capital goods. Suppose that Enterprise B receives the $400 and delivers output, uses up $200 of capital goods which it replaces by purchasing from Enterprise C, and pays out $200 in wages, interest, rent, and net profits. Suppose further that Enterprise C receives the $200, uses up its $100 of capital goods *which it does not replace,* and pays out $100 in wages, interest, rent, and profit, retaining the $100 realized from unreplaced capital goods.

The total of payments for the interval may now be summarized as follows:

ENTERPRISE A

Sales receipts...................................	$1,100
Payments:	
To net income recipients.........................	600
To Enterprise B, to replace capital goods used.......	400
Retained net profit..............................	100
Total......................................	$1,100

ENTERPRISE B

Sales receipts...................................	$ 400
Payments:	
To net income recipients.........................	200
To Enterprise B, to replace capital goods..........	200
Total......................................	$ 400

ENTERPRISE C

Sales receipts...................................	$ 200
Payment to income recipients.......................	100
Retained realization of capital goods used up and not replaced....................................	100
Total......................................	$ 200

Now in this interval, we may note the following. First, consumption plus net investment expenditure is $1,000—or $1,100 initial expenditure of this sort less a $100 disinvestment by Enterprise C, which $100 must be offset against the $1,100 in deriving consumption plus net addition to capital stock. Second, total net income payments are also $1,000 (the same as consumption plus net investment), the total of $600 such payments by A, $200 by B, and $100 by C, plus $100 of net profit retained by A. Third, total sales receipts (value of gross output) are the sum of the sales receipts of the three enterprises—$1,700. Fourth, gross income is $1,600—calculated as the net income of $1,000 plus the value of replacement capital goods of $600, or as gross sales receipts of $1,700 minus $100 retained by Enterprise C and classified as conversion of old assets into cash. The major points to note in this example are that net investment (after deducting any disinvestment) plus consumption expenditure generates an identical amount of net income; that this expenditure passes *through* enterprises to reach final net income recipients; that interenterprise payments to replace capital goods do not result in added net income but only in a two-step passage of the money flow into net income; and that enterprise sales receipts resulting in a retention by the enterprise of the value of capital goods used and unreplaced constitute disinvestment (a negative item in calculating net investment) and are not counted as net income.

So much for the moment for the definition of net income. The unit time period has been defined as the length of time required for the average dollar in circulation to move from being received as a net income payment, through the enterprise system as expenditure, and back as net income payment again. Let us now specify what is meant by "dollars in circulation." At any given time, there will be some given amount of money, or number of dollars, in existence and available for expenditure within the economy. This stock of dollars may be provisionally subdivided into two parts—active or "working" dollars which are regularly in circulation in buying goods and making income payments, and idle cash balances which are simply held as liquid balances for whatever reasons people hold such balances. (We shall arbitrarily suppose that some clear division can be established between active and idle money.) "Dollars in circulation" refers to the quantity of active of working dollars. The unit time period for analysis refers to the interval required for the average active or working dollar to circulate once from net income recipients, through expenditure on goods, and through factor payments back to income recipients as net income.

The length of this time period may be calculated for any given year by dividing the total number of working dollars in existence by the total of net income payments for the year—the fraction thus obtained representing the fraction of a year required for the average working dollar to circulate· once. For example, if total net income for the year is $300 billion, and if there are $100 billion working dollars in existence, it is clear that the average dollar circulates through net income payments once each one third of a year, or every four months. This is our unit time period.[1]

In employing this time period as a concept in analysis, we shall assume arbitrarily and somewhat artificially—though with no *significant* distortion of reality—that all dollars have the same period of circulation as the average and that they all circulate synchronously. That is, if the average period of circulation is four months, every dollar makes one circuit in exactly four months. And furthermore, each dollar reaches any given point in the circuit at the same time. That is all net income recipients get their incomes at a single date rather than in a staggered fashion through time; all spending for goods (including enterprise-to-enterprise spending) occurs during a suc-ceeding interval; and all dollars come back again in the hands of net income recipients at once. This assumption will greatly simplify the succeeding anal-ysis without altering any fundamental significantly.

Given this assumption, we shall make the definition of the unit period quite precise by specifying when it begins and ends. Each such period may be defined as beginning, *just after* net income recipients have received a round of income payments, with their making consumption plus net in-vestment expenditures out of the net income just received. It includes the production and delivery by enterprises of outputs elicited by this expendi-ture, and the production and delivery of replacement capital goods induced by the current use of capital goods, with the money flow passing through the enterprise system. It ends as the expenditure of the beginning of the period arrives back as net income payments in the hands of factor sup-pliers and net profit recipients.

Each period thus begins with a certain *disposable net income* just re-ceived, in the hands of potential buyers. Each period ends with the receipt of a new round of net income, generated solely by expenditures during the period, which income will be disposable in the following period. During the period the passage of expenditures through the enterprise system not only creates an equivalent net income, but also elicits an equivalent production of enterprise net outputs and an equivalent employment of resources.

We shall center attention in analysis first upon such a single time period. For this time period we shall take the size of the money flow as determined by the total of expenditures from disposable net income, and we shall fur-ther take all prices of goods and factor services as given for the period. We shall further suppose that the banking system is neutral, in the sense that it neither demands nor supplies investable funds. In this setting we shall first inquire into the provisional determination of the interest rate for a single period.

---

[1] The reciprocal of this period—which is the number of times per year the aver-age dollar circulates—may be designated as the *circuit velocity* of active money.

THE DEMAND FOR INVESTABLE FUNDS—CAPITAL GOODS

The rate of interest in any one time period will tend to be determined by
the interactions of the demand for and supply of investable funds which
are effective in that period. A formal explanation of this rate therefore must
begin with an identification of the components of such demand and supply
and with a specification of their principal characteristics. We shall first consider the demands for investable funds.

In general, if any positive activity by the banking system is assumed
away, the demands for investable funds may be grouped under these main
headings—demands by enterprises for net investment in capital goods, demands by individuals for funds to finance consumer purchases, and demands
by either enterprises or individuals for money to add to their idle cash balances. These three types of demand may be designated briefly as *capital
goods net investment demand, consumer finance demand,* and *demand for
hoarding.* Of these three types of demand, we have so far only mentioned
the first—capital goods investment demand. It will thus be necessary not only
to examine this major component of demand for funds further but also to
inquire for the first time into the character of the consumer finance and
hoarding demands which supplement it.

The sources and determinants of the demands for funds to invest in
capital goods have been discussed in the preceding chapter, and they need
not be reviewed here. Suffice it to say that at any moment in time the enterprise system will have accumulated a given stock of capital goods, and a
corresponding aggregate investment of funds therein, and that the amount
of the capital goods and corresponding dollar investment accumulated will
depend upon the list of consumers' goods being made available and the
relative demands for them, the techniques of production in use, the supplies of labor and land and the rate of employment of each, the relative prices
of capital goods, the level of money prices, the going rate of interest, and
the extent to which an "equilibrium" stock of capital goods has been attained
relative to all of these determining data.

In any current unit time period, some of these capital goods will be
depreciated or used up in delivering net output demanded; machines will
use part of their useful lives or accumulated inventories of raw materials
or processed goods will be used up. Correspondingly, a demand for replacement is created—potentially at least, and certainly unless the determining data have shifted to require fewer capital goods—and a coordinate requirement for funds to purchase replacements emerges. The size of the requirement in any period for sufficient funds to replace capital goods used
will depend upon the size of the accumulated stock of capital goods at the
beginning of the period, their prices, their average durability (which de-

termines the proportion used in a single period at a given output), and the size of the current net output demanded for consumption and net investment, which determines their rate of use. Given these things, a determinate amount of funds will be required to purchase sufficient capital goods replacements to maintain total investment in the face of current use. This is an equilibrium reinvestment demand for funds during the current period.

In addition, there will ordinarily be in any period a demand to add to the stock of capital goods, deriving from technological changes, the introduction of new consumers' products, the discovery of new natural resources, population growth, and so forth. (We shall examine the mechanism by which net investment requirements are created in a succeeding section.) This net investment requirement will create a corresponding added requirement for investable funds to finance their acquisition. Since net investment is by definition an addition to pre-existing total investment in capital goods, it is properly defined as investment of funds in addition to the equilibrium rate of reinvestment necessary to maintain pre-existing total investment. The total requirement for funds for investment in capital goods thus has two components: (1) the equilibrium rate of reinvestment, as determined, and (2) the demand for funds for net investment.[2] In addition, there may be a demand for funds to hoard by selling old capital assets not replaced, but we shall turn to this later.

In one sense both the net investment and reinvestment requirements for funds constitute demands for investable funds, and we might refer to their sum as the gross investment demand for funds. The equilibrium reinvestment requirement, however, tends in general to be automatically supplied by a matching flow of sales receipts through enterprises, so that they currently receive in any period as revenues generated by net consumer and investment spending an amount exactly sufficient to finance reinvestments. Thus, in the example on page 629, the $600 requirement for funds for reinvestment is fully met from the sales receipts generated by the initial expenditure of net income. Since there tends to be a gross supply of funds (as sales receipts received to cover use of capital goods) which exactly matches

[2] The sum of equilibrium reinvestment and net investment demand—that is, gross investment demand—is necessarily calculated as net of any disinvestments accomplished by selling previously accumulated capital goods, *not* replacing them, and holding the proceeds. For example, if a group of investors spend $2,000 in replacing old capital goods and $1,000 in acquiring added capital goods (increasing the value of their investments by $1,000), but if another group reduces their investment by selling $500 worth of old capital goods which they do not replace (holding the cash instead), the gross investment of the two groups combined is $2,500, and the net investment of the two groups combined is $500. The difference—that is, the $500 received and held by the disinvestors—represents a demand for "hoarding," or for additions to cash balances. This hoarding forestalls the intended investment of the first group, and diverts $500 of intended investment demand into demand for hoarding.

the reinvestment demand for funds, we may legitimately omit both the supply and the demand from analysis, as self-canceling, and discover no net demand for funds in reinvestment demand per se. The enterprise thus expresses a net demand for investable funds only if it spends on capital goods an amount different from that required to replace capital goods currently used up. If it spends more than this on capital goods, it expresses a net investment demand for funds. If it spends less than this (not replacing capital goods fully), it disinvests—the disinvestment being deducted from others' net investments in calculating aggregate net investment for the economy— and expresses a demand for additions to its cash balances, or hoarding demand. The only net demand for investable funds for investment in capital goods is thus the aggregate net investment demand as defined—a demand for funds to add to total investment in capital goods.[3]

The current demand for funds for net investment will in general be responsive to the rate of interest, increasing as the rate declines. As we have seen in the preceding chapter (pages 612 to 618), in any given state of investment opportunities more capital goods will be required at lower interest rates because reduction of the rate will lower the cost of capital goods services and encourage their substitution for the services of labor and land. Therefore, any new opportunities for net investment will be more fully exploited as the interest rate falls, and less fully as it rises. In addition, previously exploited opportunities already registered in investments will be exploited more fully if the interest rate falls below the pre-existing level, whereas disinvestment (deducted in calculating current net investment) will tend to be induced if it rises above the pre-existing level.

It is therefore apparent that in any unit time period there will be a demand schedule for funds for net investment in capital goods of the usual negatively sloping sort, showing the relation of the quantity of funds demanded to the interest rate, such as I_n in Figure 60. This shows that certain alternative amounts of funds will be currently demanded for net investment in capital goods at various alternative interest rates. The *position* of this schedule—that is, the distance it lies from zero funds demanded (the vertical axis) at various interest rates—will depend of course on the character and pace of current and immediately past changes which create net investment opportunities (technological and product change, change in level of employment, and so forth) and which we shall discuss in a succeeding section.

[3] The preceding is strictly and uniformly true so long as all enterprises recover from sales receipts a sufficient amount to cover the cost of maintaining total investment —that is, so long as they do not suffer net losses from operations. So far as they do suffer losses, expenditures on replacement of more than is currently recovered from sales receipts involves a net demand for investable funds; correspondingly, failure to replace capital goods the value of which has not been recovered in sales receipts should not lead to an offset against net demands for investable funds and does not involve a net hoarding demand for funds.

It will also depend on the rate of interest in immediately previous periods, which will determine the extent to which past investment opportunities have been exploited. It is sufficient to indicate at the moment that the position of the net investment demand curve may be quite variable over time, fluctuating either from unit period to unit period or over longer time intervals. At some times it may indicate a substantial demand for funds per period at any conceivable interest rate, as it does in Figure 60. At other times

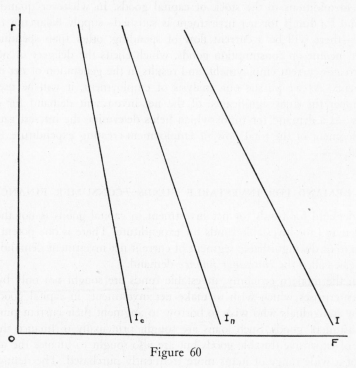

Figure 60

it may show a very small demand, and it may cross the vertical axis at a fairly low interest rate, indicating that at this rate there will be zero net investment and that above it there will be net disinvestment (equivalent to no net investment together with hoarding of money spent on consumption goods by those "selling off" their capital goods without replacing them). Ordinarily, however, there will be some positive net investment demand, large or small, at attainable interest rates, reflected in a demand curve such as I_n in Figure 60, although this curve may lie close to or far from the vertical axis. For the analysis of a single unit period, we shall take the position of this curve as given at some point.

What is the significance of this net investment demand curve? Let us re-emphasize first that it refers to a single unit time period. It states that during this period an amount of money which depends on the interest rate

will be demanded for use in adding to the total investment in capital goods
—in addition to funds drawn from sales receipts for reinvestment to maintain previous investment. Given some interest rate, the corresponding amount
of money shown on the curve will be taken from whatever are the sources
of supply (other than funds for reinvestment drawn from sales receipts)—
that is, borrowed or drawn from savings out of net income, dishoarded from
cash balances, or borrowed from banks—and spent currently on the purchase of additions to the stock of capital goods. In whatever quantity the
demand for funds for net investment is satisfied—supply balancing the demand—there will be a current flow of spending, other than spending out
of net income on consumption goods, which elicits the delivery of net output, creates current employment, and results in the generation of net income
payments. As we pursue our analysis of employment, it will be useful to
remember the dual significance of the net investment demand for capital
goods—as a demand for funds which helps determine the interest rate, and
as a segment of the total flow of employment-creating expenditure for net
output.

THE DEMAND FOR INVESTABLE FUNDS—CONSUMER FINANCE

The demand for funds for net investment in capital goods is not the only
net demand for investable funds for expenditure. There is one potential addition to or distinguishable segment of current net investment demand, what
might be called the *consumer finance* demand.

In the modern economy, investable funds are sought not only by business enterprises which wish to make net investments in capital goods, but
also by individuals who wish to borrow to augment their current purchases
of consumers' goods. Such loans are sought principally to finance the purchase of expensive durable goods but are also sought to finance the acquisition of a wide range of items more frequently purchased. The demand for
such loans may be viewed as expressing itself as a schedule of amounts
sought, per period of time, at various rates of interest.

The psychological origin of such a demand is presumably a preference
by the borrowers for present goods as compared to future goods. They are
willing to pay a rate of interest, thus somewhat reducing their eventual
total spending power, in order to have money to spend now, when they
borrow, instead of later, when they repay. The demand for consumer loans
is thought not to be very sensitive to the rate of interest, but there is nevertheless presumably some interest elasticity, so that the demand for funds for
consumer finance, I_c, might appear in any period as in Figure 60. This would
show that, in the period of reference, certain amounts of dollars for consumer
loans would be demanded at various rates of interest. The position of this
schedule will be primarily dependent on the level of income—shifting right

with increasing income and left with declining income. It will also of course depend on the price level and on the relative prices of consumers' goods.

The significance of this demand is similar to that for net investment in capital goods in that it represents an added draft on the supply of funds (other than those drawn from enterprise sales receipts for financing reinvestments) and that as satisfied it will represent a flow of current spending, other than consumption spending out of net income by the recipients of this income, which elicits current net output and employment. In short, it is a true net investment demand for funds.

It should be noted, however, that corresponding to the consumer finance demand for funds in any period will be some corresponding supply of savings, generated by the repayments out of income which past consumer borrowers are contractually obligated to make to finance companies or others who have made consumer loans. If the rate of consumer borrowing has proceeded at an even pace for a number of periods, this "automatic" saving may tend to balance the demand at a customary interest rate, although changes which influence the consumer finance demand may temporarily upset this balance. In analyzing the supply of investable funds, we must therefore give explicit attention to that segment of the saving supply which emerges in response to contractual obligations to repay past consumer loans.[4]

THE TOTAL CURRENT NET INVESTMENT DEMAND FOR FUNDS

Taking the consumer finance demand with the net investment demand for capital goods, we now have two components of the net investment demand —I_n and I_c. These together constitute the total current demand for investable funds to be spent on net output. This combined net investment demand $I(= I_c + I_n)$, as shown in Figure 60, will constitute the entire net demand for investable funds to be spent on the current net output of commodities and services.

There are, of course, added potential demands for investable funds, for *hoarding,* either directly from the income of the hoarder, or expressed through offering for sale of securities or of old assets not currently replaced, in order to acquire cash to hold idle. These must be added to the combined net investment demand (I) to obtain the aggregate "demand for investable funds" current at any time. We will now turn to such demands. By and

[4] Consumer finance demand is identified primarily with the demand for loans. In order to minimize the number of categories for analysis, however, we shall consider it to include also: (1) any individual's demand for his own accumulated cash balances to extend his current consumption beyond his current disposable income (that is, borrowing from oneself to finance consumption spending, and (2) any individual's sale of securities or old assets to secure funds to finance current consumption (see p. 640, n. 5).

large, they are distinguished from investment demand (I) in that they do not lead to the expenditure of the funds acquired on current net output of either consumption or investment goods, but are basically demands for liquid balances. Such demands for investable funds tend to result in the acquisition of money to be held idle, and they are potentially quite different in significance from investment demands.

CASH BALANCES, LIQUIDITY PREFERENCE, AND HOARDING

Let us now consider the demand for *hoarding*. During a given unit time period, individuals or enterprises may demand investable funds not for spending but simply to increase their holdings of idle cash. Alternatively, they may *dishoard* by supplying funds from previously accumulated cash balances. For the moment, we shall emphasize the demand side of the picture—the demand for additions to idle cash balances.

The phenomena of hoarding and dishoarding of course stem from the existence of *cash balances* and from the facts that they can be increased or decreased and that in certain frequently recurring circumstances people will wish to increase or decrease them. At any time there is some amount of money in circulation—currency, coin, and bank credit, or whatever is freely accepted in payment for goods. (We have supposed, by holding banks hypothetically neutral, that this amount of money is provisionally fixed for the economy.) This money circulates as payments for commodities and factor services through the economy, resulting in a flow of money income. But not all of it circulates all the time. Individuals and business firms throughout the economy regularly hold balances of money in "idle" form—maintain certain average unspent balances of money.

Thus, John Jones has a monthly salary of $500, which he regularly spends for various purposes. But he maintains a minimum cash balance of $750 more—his cash account never falls below $750, and fluctuates between $1,250 immediately after he receives his salary down to $750 just before he receives it again. If this is true for John Jones, it can be true for the economy.

When an economy has a certain fixed amount of money in existence, M, it should be at least hypothetically possible to identify a certain proportion of it which is currently circulating, M_1, and a remainder which is idle, M_2. That part which is circulating will have a certain circuit velocity (number of times per year which the average dollar enters into net income payments), which will tend to be relatively stable through time. This circuit velocity, the reciprocal of which defines the unit time period (see pages 627 to 631), may be measured as net income per year divided by the stock of circulating money. The remaining or idle money may be viewed as not circulating at all.

Suppose that an economy has $60 billion of money in existence, of which

$40 billion may be currently identified as circulating and $20 billion as non-circulating. Suppose further that total net income payments per year are $120 billion. Then the $40 billion of circulating money evidently has a circuit velocity of 3 per year (so that the unit time period is ⅓ of a year or four months) whereas $20 billion is idle.

This situation may be represented in an alternative fashion, without attempting to distinguish idle from circulating money, by measuring the average rate of circulation of all money. In the preceding example, we would find this by dividing annual net income payments by the total amount of money in existence—that is, by dividing 120 by 60 and obtaining 2. This figure 2 might be called the *income velocity* of all money, and is evidently a good measure of the *relative idleness* of money balances in an economy. That is, if there is some given circuit velocity for active or circulating money (3 in the example above), the income velocity of all money will be larger as a smaller proportion of all money is idle and smaller as a greater proportion of it is idle. We could simply neglect the distinction between idle and active money and look directly to income velocity as a fully equivalent measure of the relation of the rate of income payments to the total stock of money.

Now it is obvious that, if there are idle balances of money at all times (or alternatively if money is circulating at less than an infinite rate), the economy as a whole can either increase or decrease its idle balances (can spend a given total money supply less or more rapidly). We have supposed above that the economy had an annual net income of 120, active balances of 40, with a circuit velocity of 3 per year, idle balances of 20, and an income velocity of all money of 2 per year. It is certainly possible that the economy may hoard and add 10 to its idle balances, leaving only 30 in circulation. If it does and if the circuit velocity of money remains at 3, annual net income payments will drop to 90. This hoarding phenomenon might be expressed alternatively as a decline of the income velocity of all money from 2 per year (120 divided by 60) to 1½ (90 divided by 60), due to a slower rate of spending of all money. Alternatively, dishoarding could occur if idle balances were reduced to 10, in which case net income would become 150 per year if active balances, now 50, circulated with a circuit velocity of 3. The income velocity of all money would then have risen to 2½ per year.

How may hoarding (or dishoarding) take place? In general, net hoarding occurs for the economy as a whole if people add to their stock of idle money, while spending active money no more quickly after its receipt, or, what is the same thing, if their rate of spending of all money is reduced by holding all dollars a longer time on the average between receipt and expenditure. Net dishoarding occurs if they reduce the stock of idle money or increase their rate of spending of all money by holding all dollars on the average a shorter time between receipt and expenditure.

If we view the flow of money as proceeding by unit periods of a given length, with each period beginning with disposable net income just received and ending with the receipt of a new round of net income, so that all active money is spent exactly once each period, hoarding will appear as follows. Neither net hoarding nor dishoarding will occur if total current spending on consumption goods plus net investment in capital goods just equals the disposable net income available at the beginning of the period. In this case exactly the same amount of money which entered into net income payments in the previous period—and became the disposable income of the present period—is circulated to become net income once more; idle balances are therefore neither increased nor decreased in the net. Net hoarding will occur if the total current consumption plus net investment spending of the period is less than disposable net income, so that in effect some dollars which entered into net income in the previous period are not spent on net output currently and thus are added to idle balances. It will result from net income recipients as a group spending less on consumption and net investment than their disposable net incomes, while at the same time this virtual reduction of spending is not fully offset by the consumption plus net investment spending of others who may spend from previously idle balances or may borrow otherwise unspent money and spend it. It will be reflected in a decline in net income (the circuit velocity of active money remaining unchanged) and in the increase of idle cash balances either in the hands of those having disposable net incomes at the first of the period or in the hands of others who in the net acquire dollars of disposable net income by selling securities or other assets to net income recipients and then holding the money acquired idle.[5]

Net dishoarding will occur if total current spending on consumption plus net investment exceeds the disposable net income available at the beginning of the period, so that dollars which were idle in the previous period become active by spending in the present period. It will result from people spending from some previously idle balances and from this not being offset by others' use of disposable net income to augment idle balances. It will be reflected in an increase in net income and in a decrease of idle cash balances accomplished either by direct consumption plus net investment spending

[5] "Gross" hoarding (possibly offset by dishoarding elsewhere) obviously occurs if an income recipient fails to spend or to loan to another a part of his disposable net income. It also occurs, however, if another party sells a security—that is, an intangible claim on future earnings such as a stock share or bond or promissory note—and then holds the proceeds idle. So far as the sellers of securities in turn during the period spend the proceeds on consumption, of course, hoarding does not result, and such sales are implicitly already included in the consumer finance demand for investable funds. And so far as they use the proceeds for current net investment spending, hoarding does not result, and such sales are implicitly already reflected in the net investment demand for funds to invest in capital goods. But simple security sales (whether

from them by those who hold the balances or by their acquisition for current net investment or consumption spending by others who borrow from or sell securities to the balance holders.

We have referred so far to the phenomena involved in *net* hoarding or dishoarding—that is, in a net shortage or excess of current net income-creating expenditure as compared to disposable net income. It is obvious that any net tendency to increase or decrease idle balances will be the result of offsetting *gross* tendencies. In any period, some persons or firms may tend to hoard or increase their cash balances, others to dishoard or decrease their balances. The gross hoarders will be those who spend less on all purchases than the total of their disposable net incomes and any money acquired by selling securities or assets, and thus increase their idle balances. The gross dishoarders will be those who spend more on consumption plus net investment plus securities and old assets than the sum of their disposable net incomes and any proceeds of asset and security sales and thus decrease their idle balances. Net hoarding or dishoarding will be the difference, if any, between gross hoarding and gross dishoarding. We may analyze the effects of changes in cash balances by referring to a gross hoarding demand as a component of the demand for investable funds, and a gross dishoarding supply as a component of the supply of investable funds.

What can be said of the demand for funds to hoard and the supply of dishoarded funds? The fact that hoarding and dishoarding do occur implies that individuals and businesses holding cash balances may wish to increase or decrease them. Under certain circumstances, that is, people may prefer to add to their cash holdings instead of continuing to hold assets or securities or instead of spending their incomes on goods or securities, and thus may hoard. Under other circumstances they may prefer to give up some of their previous idle balances in return for more goods or securities and thus may dishoard. What is the rule governing this sort of behavior?

The ruling motive has been aptly described as the psychological attitude of liquidity preference.[6] Money is *the* liquid asset, freely exchangeable

of old or newly issued securities), if unmatched by corresponding current consumption or net investment spending of the security seller, result in gross hoarding.

Similarly, the sale of old assets—previously acquired capital (or durable consumers') goods, land, and so forth—results in gross hoarding unless the seller in turn during the period spends the money on replacement of the goods sold or on consumption. Otherwise, the passage of money toward inducing the production of current net output and the creation of current net income is short-circuited by those who supply assets not currently produced to purchasers without undertaking an offsetting expenditure. So far as sellers of previously produced capital goods (or their services) currently spend the proceeds on replacement, neither hoarding nor net investment takes place as the gross supply of funds obtained in sales receipts is passed on to create net income. But if the sellers do not replace, gross hoarding occurs.

[6] For the basic development of this notion, see J. M. Keynes, *op. cit.,* Chaps. 15 and 17.

for all goods, and no other good or security "can make this claim." To use other assets for spending power they must first be converted into cash. This liquidity attribute of money gives it a certain premium over other assets for individuals and business firms—other things being equal (that is, if they did not need goods to consume or if capital assets and securities did not yield an income) they would rather hold money than other assets. They have, moreover, certain definite demands or needs for liquidity—for working balances to be held between the time income is received and the time it is convenient to spend, as "reserves" against emergency expenditures or unforeseen reverses, and also, speculatively, against the possibility of a fall in the price of goods or securities.

But the need for liquidity is not a need for an indefinite or for a certain absolute amount of money; it is a variable need or desire, which can be more or less completely fulfilled. Correspondingly, balance holders have not only a liquidity preference for cash balances, but a marginal rate of liquidity preference for additions to cash balances which will vary as the size of cash balances varies, in general decreasing as the balances are increased.

This marginal rate of liquidity preference may be represented as the interest rate of return, obtainable by holding other assets, which balance holders are willing to forego to secure a small addition to any given amount of cash balances, or which they demand if they are to give up a small amount of balances in return for claims on future payments in the form of securities or other earning assets. In any given income situation, the marginal rate of liquidity preference will decrease as balances are increased, showing that additions to balances are worth successively less in terms of interest return foregone.

The rational balance holder should then adjust his cash holdings so that his marginal rate of liquidity preference is equal to the going rate of interest return on earning assets—so that the psychological "yield" of liquidity is on the margin equal to the cost of having it in terms of interest return foregone. If the rate of return on all such assets is equated to a market rate of interest, the balance holder will then adjust so that his marginal rate of liquidity preference equals the market rate of interest.

If this is so, there will be a negatively sloped demand schedule for liquidity which shows, for any given income and price situation, the amounts of balances which people will hold at each rate of interest. There will correspondingly be additions to existing cash balances as the interest rate falls below a certain rate and decreases in cash balances as it rises above this level. In effect, an economy of people who have a desire to hold cash balances which is related to the rate of interest will hoard (add to) balances if the rate of interest is "too low," will hoard less if it rises, will hoard nothing at some intermediate rate, and will dishoard (subtract from) balances above this rate. *This is because they will increase or decrease their idle cash holdings to bring their marginal rates of liquidity preference into balance with any going rate of interest.*

The *net* incidence of hoarding or dishoarding for the economy as a whole in any unit period can be summarized in a single "net hoarding" curve, as in Figure 61. The net hoarding curve *h* shows that in a given time period cash balances would be held constant at the rate of interest *r*,

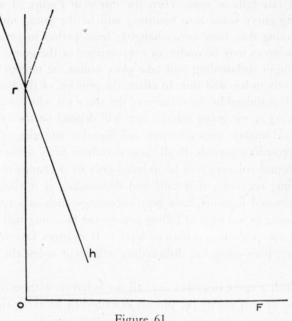

Figure 61

that below this rate there would be net demand for hoarding in the amounts shown, and that above this rate negative hoarding or net dishoarding (as shown by the dotted line) would take place in the indicated amounts. The amounts shown on the solid line *h* below *r* would be subtracted from disposable net income and hoarded; the amounts on the dotted line above *r* would be spent in addition to all disposable net income.

What determines the position of this hoarding curve? The demand for liquid balances is contingent not only upon the general psychological attitudes toward liquidity and upon the interest rate, but also upon the levels of money income, output, and prices. In general, more liquid balances will be desired at any given interest rate if prices and money income are higher at a given output level and less if they are lower; variations in output at given prices will also have some similar effect on the demand for liquidity. Differing amounts of liquid balances will therefore be desired at any given interest rate depending on income, output, and prices.

In any unit time period with some given income, output, and price level, and some prevailing set of liquidity attitudes, there will be a corresponding schedule of amounts of liquid balances desired at various alternative interest rates. If the determining data of this period are the same as those of several immediately preceding periods, the desired or equilibrium amount of balances as of the going rate of interest will probably already be held, and no net hoarding or dishoarding will occur during the period unless the interest rate falls or rises. Then the rate r in Figure 61 at which the net hoarding curve reads zero hoarding will be the going interest rate. If the determining data have been changing from period to period, then the desire for balances may be under- or over-satisfied at the going interest rate; and hoarding or dishoarding will take place unless the interest rate rises or falls sufficiently to forestall this. In effect, the position of the hoarding curve in Figure 61, as judged by the relation of the rate r (at which zero net hoarding will occur) to the going interest rate will depend on the relation of the current period income, prices, output, and liquidity attitudes to those of immediately preceding periods. If all these data have been stable over time, a change in liquid balances will be induced only by a change in the interest rate—hoarding occurring if it falls and dishoarding if it rises. If changes favoring increased liquidity have been occurring—such as a rise in income or an increasing expectation of falling prices—net hoarding will occur unless the interest rate rises to a sufficient level r. If changes favoring decreased liquidity have been going on, dishoarding will occur unless the interest rate declines.

Since such a curve describes over-all net behavior without indicating its components, we may clarify the process described by breaking the net hoarding curve into two component parts—a demand curve for investable funds for gross hoarding and a supply schedule of investable funds from gross dishoarding. The latter can be best discussed when we have first considered saving; for the moment we shall turn to the gross hoarding demand schedule as the third component of the demand for investable funds.

THE DEMAND FOR INVESTABLE FUNDS—GROSS HOARDING

Gross hoarding, as we have seen, may result either from persons with disposable net income spending less than this on consumption plus net investment (hoarding rather than investing a part of the income saved or not spent on consumption) or from persons selling securities or assets (or their services) and not spending the proceeds. In either case, their idle cash balances increase during the unit period. We may aggregate the two tendencies and classify as a gross hoarder any individual who spends less (including security and asset purchases with replacements of any old assets sold) than the sum of his disposable net income and the proceeds of the current sales of any assets and securities sold. The difference will be the amount of his gross hoarding.

The tendency of any individual to hoard will presumably be dependent on the rate of interest. Individuals will be led to hoard income not spent on consumption instead of investing in capital goods or of buying securities (thus supplying funds to others) increasingly as the rate of return on securities or on capital goods investment declines. If all the income not spent on consumption can be invested in capital goods with a high enough yield, or used to purchase securities with a low enough price relative to interest or dividend earnings (that is, a high yield)—then the individual may be disinclined to hoard any of his own disposable income. But as the yield on capital goods declines or the prices of securities relative to their earnings rises, the individual is more inclined to hoard a part of his income than to invest it in capital goods or securities. Similarly, persons holding securities and assets will be more inclined to sell them and hold the proceeds idle (rather than either continuing to hold them or selling and currently replacing them) as the interest rate falls, which is to say as the prices of the securities or assets rise relative to their earnings, thus reducing the advantage of holding earning assets instead of cash.[7] This is all consistent with the phenomenon of a positive liquidity preference on the part of the individual which declines as a marginal rate as liquid balances are increased.

For each potential gross hoarder, therefore, we may construct a gross hoarding demand curve, showing the amount he will demand to add to his idle balances, either from his own income or from asset and security sales, at each possible rate of interest. This curve will slope downward to the right like the usual demand curve, showing increasing gross hoarding at lower interest rates. At some critical interest rate it will intersect the vertical axis, showing zero gross hoarding, and above this rate dishoarding will presumably occur so that the individual becomes a supplier rather than a demander of liquid balances.

The horizontal summation of all individual gross-hoarding demand curves (adding all individual demands at each interest rate[8]) will constitute an aggregate demand curve for gross hoarding. This curve will include successively more individual gross hoarders as the interest rate falls and converts more and more dishoarders into hoarders. Such a curve is shown in Figure 62, relating the aggregate gross hoarding demand to the market rate of interest. We label this demand curve H to designate gross hoarding—

[7] The increased demand for liquidity as the interest rate falls competes in the case of replaceable assets with the stimulating effect on investment of a lower interest rate, as reflected in the net investment demand curve for funds.

[8] But not subtracting supplies from dishoarding, which we shall represent in a gross dishoarding supply curve.

that is, the gross demand for additions to balances out of net income or from security and asset sales. The position of this curve in any unit period will be determined by the same considerations which determine the position of the net hoarding curve in Figure 61, although the entire hoarding picture cannot be shown until we establish the corresponding position of the gross dishoarding curve.

The gross hoarding curve, *H*, will operate with the net investment demand curve, *I*, as the second major component of the demand for investable

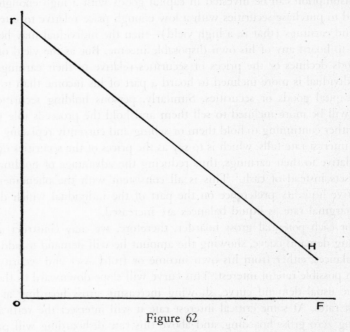

Figure 62

funds in the determination of the interest rate. One major difference is the significance of the *I* and *H* curves should be emphasized at this point. The former (*I*) refers to a demand for funds which will be spent on consumption or net investment and generate net income and employment in the current period. The latter (*H*) refers to a demand for funds to be held idle, and except so far as offset by gross dishoarding, will result in channeling disposable net income into idle balances and thus in reducing net income and employment.

Let us now turn to the supply of investable funds.

THE SUPPLY OF INVESTABLE FUNDS—SAVING

If banks are assumed neither to demand nor supply funds, as they are for the moment, the nonbank sources of supply of investable funds are two:

savings out of net income and gross dishoarding of previously accumulated cash balances. It is upon these sources only that those demanding investable funds for net investment or gross hoarding can draw, and it is the interaction of the two corresponding supply curves—that is, relations of amounts of funds supplied to the interest rate—with the demand curves I and H for investable funds which will immediately determine the interest rate. We shall consider these two sources of supply in turn.

The most obvious source of supply of investable funds is *saving*. But the meaning of "saving" is often obscure, and our first task is to define it precisely. In general, the most meaningful definition of saving is "disposable net income not spent on consumption by net income recipients." If all net outputs which may be purchased are divided into two categories, consumption goods purchased by net income recipients and net investment goods plus financed consumer purchases, the proportion of disposable of net income spent by net income recipients on consumption goods is readily measured. The remainder of such income, not spent on consumption by net income recipients, is by definition saved. Whether or not it is then spent on net investment goods or enters consumer expenditure via consumer finance is of course a matter for analysis. What we are doing in effect in defining saving in this way is to segregate that expenditure from disposable net income which is oriented directly to satisfying the consumer wants of net income recipients from the sum of expenditure on net investment goods (oriented to business profit) and consumer finance expenditure; and to analyze the relation of net income not spent on consumption by its recipients, as a virtual supply of investable funds, to such other spending.

If we view spending activity as proceeding by unit periods as previously defined (pages 627 to 631), saving is measured with reference to the disposable net income of all income recipients in each period. So far as during a period any income recipient spends on consumption as much as (or more than) his disposable net income as received at the end of the previous period, he has not saved. If he spends on consumption less than his disposable net income, he has by definition saved the difference between his disposable net income and his consumption spending. Aggregate saving for the period is then the sum of all of the savings of individual net income recipients.[9] If income recipients in the economy have a total of $1 billion of disposable net income at the beginning of a period, and if expenditure on consump-

[9] It may be noted that we do not deduct from the aggregate saving of all savers as defined the excess of the consumption spending over disposable net income of those who spend more on consumption than disposable net income. Such excesses appear as gross demands for consumer finance (resulting as fulfilled in added expenditure) and are met either by borrowing from suppliers of investable funds or by gross dishoarding by those who are "living over their incomes" and thus borrowing from their own accumulations to finance consumer purchases.

tion (exclusive of that financed by consumer loans and personal dishoarding) is $800 million, then saving during the period has been $200 million.

It will be noted that saving is thus defined here as "net saving"—as a difference between disposable net incomes of a period and expenditures on consumption by income recipients—and not as "gross saving," which would include also sales receipts which are received during the period by enterprises as a return for the use of accumulated capital goods and which are generally not spent on consumption but are either spent currently on replacements or are hoarded. This component of gross saving supply is neglected for analysis. So far as the money is respent by enterprise on replacements, the supply is matched by a corresponding gross investment-demand (also neglected, see pages 633 to 634). So far as any gross hoarding occurs, due to a failure to replace capital goods, the enterprise is viewed as a demander of funds for gross hoarding, and the purchaser of the unreplaced capital goods as a supplier of investable funds (from either saving or dishoarding) when he purchases them. Business gross saving thus does not enter as a separate item in the demand-supply complex as established for analysis.[10]

Net saving being thus defined, it evidently has two components: business net saving and individual net saving. At the end of any unit period, business firms will in general retain undistributed a part of the net income generated during the period, in the form undistributed net profits, interest on owners investment, rent of land owned by the enterprise, and so forth. This becomes a disposable net income at the beginning of the succeeding period. (This disposable net income does not include any amounts realized from selling capital assets not replaced, since this is counted as an addition to cash balances rather than to net income.) Such undistributed disposable net income is almost certain to be saved—that is, not spent on consumption —in the period in which it becomes available for spending.

What will determine the amount of such saving? In general, it will depend upon the size of the net income over which enterprises have control (net

---

[10] We assume for simplicity in analysis that all current purchases of old previously produced goods which are not currently replaced—which are viewed precisely as involving a gross hoarding demand by the seller and a supply of funds by the purchaser —are capital goods and not consumers' goods. Thus, only investment expenditure has to be corrected (deducting these purchases)—in arriving at a net investment figure when gross hoarding is taken into account, and consumption expenditure does not, since it is assumed that no expenditure on consumption goods is short-circuited by the hoarding of enterprises which sell consumption goods inventories and keep the proceeds. Correspondingly, saving is simply calculated and all consumption expenditure becomes by definition net-income-generating. If more complex and realistic assumptions were adopted—so that the existence of some gross hoarding by sellers of accumulated inventories of consumers' goods were recognized—then we should wish to define consumption spending as net of purchases of unreplaced inventories of consumers' goods—and register such spending as a part of saving supplied to meet the gross hoarding demand of those who sold the goods.

profits, interest earnings, and so forth), which will in turn depend (among other things) upon the level of money income and employment, and upon the existing policies of enterprises with respect to the retention and distribution to owners of such net income. It will thus tend to shift from period to period with shifts in income and employment so far as these shifts affect business net income. The proportion of available net income retained and saved by enterprise, however, will probably not be significantly responsive

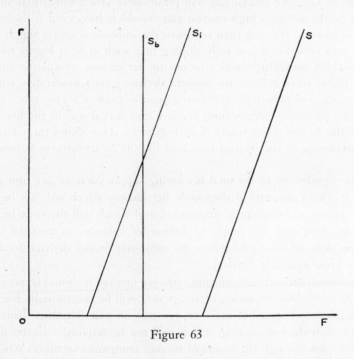

Figure 63

to the rate of interest being paid on funds, since enterprise policies with respect to retention of earnings are normally rather institutionalized and inflexible. We may, therefore, provisionally represent the business net saving supply curve of any unit period as a vertical straight line (perfectly inelastic to changes in the interest rate) such as S_b in Figure 63. This curve states that in a given unit period a certain amount of net income will be saved by business enterprise, and that this amount will be insensitive to the market rate of interest. The position of this curve, in terms of the placement of its origin along the horizontal axis, will depend, of course, on the level of income, on business policy, and so forth.

Individual saving is the second component of total net saving, and represents the share of disposable net income received by individuals (total disposable net income less that retained undistributed by enterprises) not spent by income recipients on consumption goods. It will also presumably be responsive to the level of income and employment, as we shall see immediately. In any given unit time period, with a given level of income, it will probably also be responsive to some extent to the interest rate. That is, people will consume less and save more so far as the interest rate on investable funds (receivable on loans or investments or imputed as the value of additions to cash balances) is higher. But savings will not be greatly affected by the interest rate, and individuals will presumably save a substantial amount, relative to the saving a high interest rate would induce, even if the interest rate falls to zero. We may then represent the individual saving supply curve in any unit period as a positively sloping line, such as S_i in Figure 63. This indicates that individuals will save out of net income alternative amounts at alternative interest rates, the amount declining only moderately with the interest rate, and potentially remaining positive even at a zero rate.

The total saving supply curve for any unit period will be the horizontal sum of the S_b and S_i curves, or S in Figure 63. This shows the relation of total net saving to the interest rate, and like its S_b component is positively sloped.

The significance of the total net saving supply curve in any unit period is that it shows amounts of disposable net income which will not be spent by net income recipients on consumption, and which will therefore be made available, along with any supply of dishoarded balances, to meet the net investment demand for capital goods, the consumer finance demand for funds, and the gross hoarding demand.

In connection with the consumer finance market, it should be noted that a part of individual net saving of any period will be contractually forced, as individuals are obligated to make repayments on past consumer loans. This share of individual net saving, which will not be responsive to the interest rate, will pass through the hands of finance companies or others who have made past consumer loans, and will thus become available either for current consumer finance (or net investment) demand or to meet the gross hoarding demand of those to whom repayments are made.

The position of the total net saving supply curve in any unit period will depend, as noted, on the level of employment or of real net income, and on the level of money prices, shifting as these shift. In general, there is a relation of net saving to real income such that saving will increase with increases in real net income and decrease with decreases in real net income, provided always that other things influencing saving remain equal—in particular that money prices remain unchanged as real income varies. That is, if money prices are constant, so that every variation in net real income is matched by a corresponding variation in net money income, there will be a direct positive relation between money saved and money-and-real income.

Such a relation is shown in Figure 64, which may be read as showing dollars of net saving increasing as real income increases, the money price level and the interest rate remaining constant. In addition, saving as measured in dollars will increase with increases in the money price level, or decrease with decreases therein, real income remaining constant.

The first fundamental relation envisaged is that of *real* net saving to real net income. That is, there is thought to be a virtual positive relation of net savings as measured in dollars of constant purchasing power (that is,

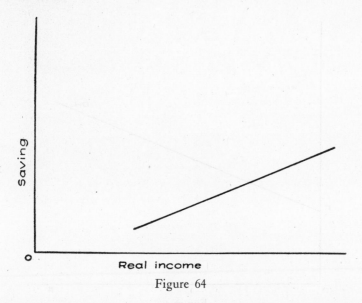

Figure 64

adjusted for price-level change) to net income as measured in dollars of constant purchasing power, given the interest rate. This relation is shown by Figure 64, which also shows the relation of saving in unadjusted dollars to real and money income as long as we assume a constant level of money prices. The second relation is that of saving to money prices; it will presumably change in direct ratio to the money price level at any real income level. Savings thus respond through time to both real income changes and price-level changes, as well as to the interest rate. Such responses will be reflected in shifts of saving supply curve (*S* in Figure 63) as real income and price-level changes occur from period to period.

One characteristic of the saving supply curve, as represented in Figure 63, is worth re-emphasis. This is that it is thought to be relatively "interest-inelastic"—savings are not very responsive to the interest rate—and shows substantial positive savings (relative to those which a high interest rate would induce) even at a zero rate of interest. The importance of this will appear in the succeeding analysis of income and employment.

THE SUPPLY OF INVESTABLE FUNDS—GROSS DISHOARDING

The second component of the nonbank supply of investable funds is the dishoarding of previously idle balances for expenditure during a current period. Individuals may dishoard either by spending on consumption and net investment more than their disposable net incomes (in which case they by definition save nothing), or by purchasing assets and securities from others in amounts which exceed their current net saving. We may aggregate the two

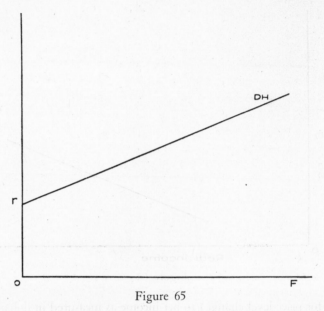

Figure 65

tendencies and count as any individual's dishoarding the excess of his current expenditure on consumption plus net investment plus securities (including any obligations received by loaning to others) plus other assets over his disposable net income plus the proceeds of the sales of any securities or assets (or asset services). Any individual with such an excess is a gross dishoarder, who decreases his idle balances to make a virtual addition to the flow of spending.

The tendency to dishoard is governed by the same liquidity preference considerations which govern gross hoarding. Accordingly any individual may be a gross hoarder—demanding funds to hold idle—in decreasing amounts as the interest rate on securities and assets rises up to a certain point; above this critical rate he will tend to become a gross dishoarder—supplying funds from idle balances to meet the various demands—in increasing amounts as the interest rate goes higher. Thus, the potential dishoarder has, above some critical rate of interest, a positively sloping supply curve of funds supplied from idle balances, indicating his willingness to supply larger amounts of such balances as the rate goes higher. The reason for the positive slope of his supply curve is, of course, that at higher rates the relative attractiveness of holding securities and earning assets is compared to holding cash increases.

For the economy as a whole, an aggregate gross dishoarding supply curve may be constructed, representing the horizontal sum of all individual gross dishoarding curves, and showing the aggregate amount of funds which will be dishoarded from idle balances at each alternative interest rate. This aggregate curve will include successively more individual dishoarders as the interest rate goes higher and converts more and more individuals from hoarders to dishoarders. Such a curve is represented as *DH* in Figure 65. It shows that at some low rate of interest *r* there will be no gross dishoarding, and that above this rate the amounts of investable funds shown on the supply curve *DH* will be supplied (gross) from idle balances. The significance of this curve is that it represents amounts of funds, *in addition to saving,* which will be made available in the current period to meet the demands for funds for net investment in capital goods, for consumer finance, and for gross hoarding. With this we conclude our catalogue of components of the demand for and supply of funds, and may turn to the determination of the interest rate in a single unit period.

THE DETERMINATION OF THE INTEREST RATE—
ARTIFICIALLY SIMPLIFIED CONDITIONS

We shall analyze first the determination of the interest rate in a single unit time period. For this analysis, we take as given (1) the level of employment of the immediately preceding period, (2) the net income payments of that period, which are the disposable net income of the present period, and (3) the level of money prices. Current net expenditure out of disposable net income, together with the assumed given level of prices, will determine the level of employment of the present period. In such a period, how is the interest rate determined?

In general, it will obviously be determined by the interaction of the demands for and supplies of investable funds. Assuming the banking system to be neutral, these are the demands and supplies described in the preceding sections. The process of interaction will be more easily understood, however, if we first consider how the interest rate would be determined in two alternative artificially simplified situations.

First, let us suppose that there is in a period no hoarding or dishoarding —no individual or enterprise either adds to or subtracts from his cash balances, and no funds are demanded or supplied for these purposes. Then the entire demand for investable funds is the net investment demand, represented in the curve *I*, composed of demands for funds for net investment in capital goods plus demands for consumer finance funds to spend on consumption, whereas the entire supply of investable funds is net saving, represented in curve *S*. The gross hoarding curve *H* and the gross dishoarding curve *DH* do not exist. The interest rate will then be determined by the interaction of the net investment demand *I* and the saving supply *S*. These curves are placed in juxtaposition in Figure 66.

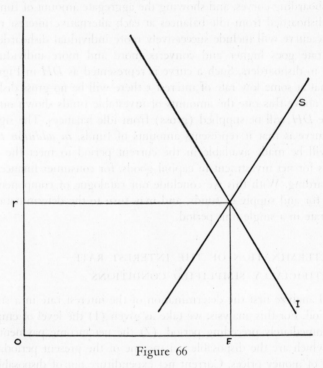

Figure 66

The demand curve *I* states that the alternative amounts of funds shown along the curve will be demanded for net capital investment plus consumer finance expenditure if supplied at the various alternative interest rates. The supply schedule *S* states that the alternative amounts of saving shown along the curve will be saved (that is, not spent on consumption by income recipients and supplied to those demanding investable funds if demanded) at the various alternative rates of interest. There is only one source of supply to meet the demand for funds—saving—and there is only one type of demand to absorb supply—net investment demand.

In this event, the market rate of interest will find equilibrium for the period at the rate *r* in Figure 66, at which demand and supply are equated. Saving will be made in the amount *OF*, and will equal net investment in the amount *OF*.

If the interest rate were so simply determined, several interesting corollaries would be observed. First, since neither hoarding nor dishoarding would be present to complicate the picture, the interest rate would automatically move, through the interplay of I and S alone, to such a level that net investment (in capital goods plus consumer finance) exactly equaled net saving. Second, since this would be so, the net income generated during the period would be exactly equal to the disposable net income available at the beginning of the period, and thus equal to the net income of the previous period. This would be true since exactly the amount of disposable net income which was not spent by income recipients on consumption would be spent on net investment plus financed consumer purchases; therefore, the sum of a current expenditure for net output, which generates net income, would equal disposable net income, which equals the net income received in the previous period. It would thus necessarily be true that net income payments would remain indefinitely constant from period to period—there would be a constant self-sustaining flow of money net income through time. We thus see that our provisional assumption that the income flow is constant through time, as adopted throughout from Chapters 2 through 13, would be automatically fulfilled if there were no hoarding or dishoarding phenomena ever encountered.

Third, if the net money income flow were self-sustaining and constant, with S always equal to I at any level of employment, full employment always *could* be attained, since money prices could adjust relative to the constant income flow until it was secured. It is thus evident that the possibility of hoarding under certain circumstances must be the key to the persistence of underemployment over many time intervals. Fourth, we have implicitly discovered the condition for the maintenance of a constant flow of money net income through time—net saving must equal net investment from period to period. Correspondingly, if full employment is to be automatically maintained, investment must not be less than saving at full-employment levels of income—there must be no systematic tendency to hoard a part of disposable net income when there is full employment. We shall return to these propositions in the next major section.

Let us now consider an alternative simplified situation for the determination of the interest rate. Suppose that there is no net investment demand whatever (zero net investment regardless of the interest rate) and absolutely no net saving, which would mean that every net income recipient spent every dollar of his own disposable net income on consumption. Suppose, however, that there is a gross hoarding demand for and a gross dishoarding supply of funds. Since no person saves in order to hoard his disposable net income, the gross hoarding demand must be entirely expressed as an offer for sale of old assets or securities to obtain cash to hold idle; since no net investment (including consumer finance) demand exists, no person dishoards in order to spend on consumption or net investment beyond his disposable income, and all dishoarding supply must be expressed as an offer to purchase securities or old assets with money from idle balances. Understanding the restricted content of the demand for and supply of idle cash in this setting, we may represent the demands for and supplies of investable funds as *H* and *DH* in Figure 67.

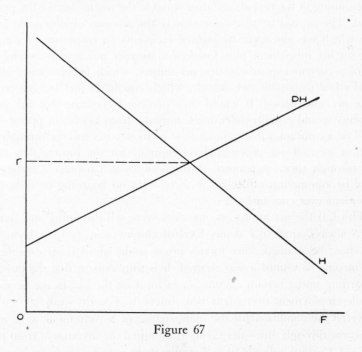

Figure 67

In this case, the rate of interest would be determined at *r* in Figure 67, at such a level as to equate gross hoarding with gross dishoarding. That is, the interplay of offers for sale of old assets and securities, *H*, with the offers to purchase these old assets and securities, *DH*, would result in an equilibrium rate of interest or at which gross hoarding as accomplished by the sale of such assets and securities exactly equaled gross dishoarding as accomplished by their purchase with money drawn from idle balances. *Net* hoarding will be zero, and additions to or subtractions from the total of idle balances will not subtract from or augment the flow of net income.

It follows that in this simplified situation also the net income generated in the period would equal disposable net income (all spent on consumption); money income would remain constant from period to period; and full employment could be automatically attained and maintained by price-level adjustments.

How then is it possible that money net income may *not* remain constant from period to period, and that a full-employment level of income may not necessarily sustain itself? It is clear that this must be the result of the juxtaposition of the gross hoarding demand on saving supply, and of net investment demand upon gross dishoarding supply, so that in the net funds saved may be hoarded or funds dishoarded may be spent on consumption or net investment, thus decreasing or increasing money net income. In other words, net hoarding or dishoarding may subtract from or add to the disposable net income of a period in determining the net income payments to be generated. Let us now see how this may take place.

THE RATE OF INTEREST IN A SINGLE UNIT PERIOD

If we relax our simplifying assumptions, it is clear that (still assuming away any positive bank action) the rate of interest in a single period will be determined by the interplay of two components of the demand for investable funds, net investment demand and gross hoarding demand, and two components of supply, net saving supply and gross dishoarding supply. It should be noted that in this situation gross hoarding H may represent not only sale of old assets or securities to others who supply funds by purchasing either from their savings or idle balances, but also a demand for the hoarders' own savings. Similarly, gross dishoarding may represent not only purchase of old assets or securities from others out of idle balances, but also the supplying from idle balances of one's own funds for net investment or for consumption purchases in excess of net disposable income. Understanding this, we may represent in Figure 68 the component demands for investable funds I and H, and the component supplies S and DH.

If we aggregate the two component demands by adding the curves horizontally, we obtain, as the sum of I and H, an aggregate demand curve for investable funds for the period, $\Delta\Delta'$. And if we aggregate the two component supplies, we obtain, as the sum of S and DH, an aggregate supply curve of investable funds, $\Sigma\Sigma'$. It is evidently the interaction of $\Delta\Delta'$ and $\Sigma\Sigma'$ which will determine the interest rate for the period. The rate will tend to fall at r in Figure 68, at which rate the aggregate demand for investable funds equals the aggregate supply, with the amount OF being supplied and demanded.

This much is simple—the interest rate will move, like any price, to an equilibrium level which equates aggregate demand with aggregate supply. It is the implications of this performance of the interest rate which are interesting.

The most interesting implication is that the rate of interest which equates aggregate demand with aggregate supply need not be such as to equate net investment I with net saving S, nor such as to equate gross hoarding *H* with gross dishoarding *DH*. In fact, these results could be accomplished only if the interest rate which would equate *I* and *S* were the same as that which equated *H* and *DH* (or at which there would be zero net hoarding or dishoarding). Otherwise, net hoarding or dishoarding will take place at the equilibrium interest rate for the period, and investment will fall short of or exceed saving. There will be a discrepancy between investment and saving, positive or negative, which will be balanced by an identical amount of dishoarding or hoarding of balances.

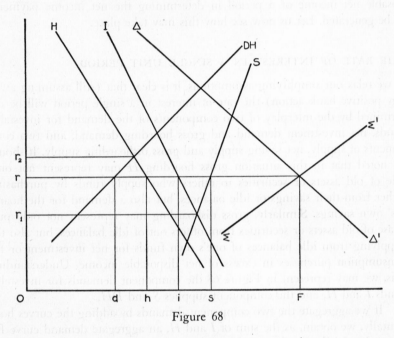

Figure 68

This is easily demonstrated as follows. In any unit time period, we have a given net investment demand schedule, *I*, representing amounts of funds to be invested and spent for net output in this period, and also a given saving schedule, *S*, representing amounts of disposable net income not spent on consumption by income recipients and thus available for net investment or hoarding in this period. *Alone,* these schedules would determine an interest rate r_1 in Figure 68 (*r* in Figure 66), and saving and investment would be equal. Further we have a demand schedule for funds, *H*, representing amounts of funds to be demanded in this period not for spending but for additions to balances, and a supply schedule of funds, *DH*, showing amounts of funds to be supplied from cash balances in addition to saving. This latter pair of schedules *alone* would determine an interest rate r_2, in Figure 68. The aggregate demand for funds, however, is the net investment plus the gross hoarding demand (*I* + *H*) or ΔΔ'. And the aggregate supply of funds is saving plus dishoarding $(S + DH)$, or $\Sigma\Sigma'$. The equilibrium interest rate for the period is evidently determined at the intersection of the Δ and Σ schedules. This rate, r, necessarily falls between r_1 and r_2. At the higher rate supply exceeds demand (here S exceeds I while H equals DH) and at the lower rate demand exceeds supply (here H exceeds DH while I equals S).

At this rate of interest, r, although the aggregate demand and supply for funds will balance, it is not necessary that investment, I, be equal to saving, S, nor that gross hoarding, H, equal gross dishoarding, DH, since the interest rates which would balance the respective demand-supply pairs are not necessarily identical. In the case illustrated, for example, saving (os) is greater than investment (oi) by the amount is, at the equilibrium interest rate, and this excess is exactly counterbalanced by the difference (dh) between gross hoarding (oh) and gross dishoarding (od). In the example illustrated, an amount equal to the excess of saving over investment is hoarded in the net (by savers and by sellers of old assets and securities), their demands for liquidity being sufficient to keep the rate of interest from falling to a level which would equate S and I.

In general, there may be, at the equilibrium interest rate for a unit period, an excess of S over I, an excess of I over S, or, coincidentally, equality of I and S. A somewhat larger net investment demand (I) in the example in Figure 68 (or smaller saving or a lesser net tendency to hoard) would bring investment equal to saving and result in no net hoarding. A still larger investment demand would make investment greater than saving and result in some net dishoarding of cash balances. The fundamental reasons for possible differences between saving and investment lie in the existence of idle cash balances, which may be drawn upon or augmented, and in the liquidity preferences of those holding balances, which will induce them under certain circumstances to dishoard and under others to hoard. The immediate reason for hoarding or dishoarding in any unit period will be that desires for cash balances are in the net virtually either under- or over-satisfied, in the sense either that net hoarding tends to occur at the interest rate which would equate I and S, and thus raises the interest rate above this level, or that net dishoarding tends to occur at such a rate, and thus brings the rate below that which would equate I and S. The rate of interest at any given level of income thus does not necessarily operate to equate saving and investment.

The reason for our repeated emphasis on the possibility of the inequality of investment and saving may be re-emphasized here once more. If the rate of interest were determined at such a level that net *saving* (that is, amounts of disposable money net income not spent on consumption by income recipients) would be exactly equal to net *investment* (that is, amounts spent on net output in addition to this consumption), then the total expenditure on net output of each new period (which equals consumption plus net investment) would be exactly equal to the money net income of the previous period. Total disposable net income would always be exactly spent for net output, on one thing or another, since all net savings would be so spent. Since expenditure on net output generates net income, this in turn would mean that net income would remain constant from period to period through time, and that there would be no additions to or subtractions from cash balances.

If net investment is different from net saving, however, then money net income will change over time—that is, the expenditure on net output and resultant net income of the period in which the discrepancy between investment and saving occurs will change from the income of the preceding period. If investment exceeds saving, money income will increase; if investment is less than saving, money income will fall. (The increase or decrease will be matched by a fall or rise in cash balances.) Correspondingly, the interest rate will tend to change from period to period as the shifting level of money income being generated with a given money supply alters the need for cash balances and thus the relative positions of the hoarding demand and dishoarding supply curves.

Furthermore, *money net income will move from period to period until it reaches a level at which saving equals investment.* And concurrently, prices, real net income, and employment will also tend to move, since changes in money income must induce corresponding changes in either prices or physical output. If money prices are given, as temporarily assumed, employment will tend to move directly with net money income—declining as it declines and rising as it rises at least until a point of full employment is reached, above which point constant money prices would no longer be tenable. Given the level of money prices, equilibrium at less than full employment is possible if net hoarding with I less than S tends to force a decline of net income whenever full employment is attained; progressive price inflation is possible if net dishoarding with I exceeding S persists at full employment. Correspondingly, the rate of interest will not reach a stable equilibrium value until money income and employment reach a stable level. The latter level will necessarily be such that money income has moved relative to the money supply to such a point that the interest rate which will induce zero net hoarding is the same as that at which investment equals saving.

The preceding is important for two reasons. First, out of the interaction of saving and investment there may be determined, after a number of periods, an equilibrium level of money net income and of employment. The process of money income, price, and employment adjustments must be traced to determine the character of such an equilibrium. Second, the rate of interest itself cannot be viewed as having reached more than a very temporary equilibrium until money net income has reached a stable resting place. As long as saving and investment are unequal from period to period, continued net income movements will produce changes in the rate of interest, and the equilibrium value of this rate cannot be said to be fully determined until net income reaches an equilibrium value.

Therefore, a next task is to trace the determination of the interest rate through a succession of periods toward a stable equilibrium value, and concurrently to analyze the determination of an equilibrium level of money income and employment. First, however, let us elaborate our single period analysis by admitting the banking system as a potential demander or supplier of investable funds.

B. THE BANK RATE OF INTEREST

THE FUNCTION OF THE BANKING SYSTEM

To this point we have argued on the assumption that the amount of money (which we may designate as M) was fixed in the economy. By so doing we have abstracted from a principal aspect of the operation of the banking system, which is to supply additional money in the form of bank credits to the economy, or alternatively to reduce the amount of money in existence by canceling such credits.

The banking system of course acts in part as an agent for individuals or enterprises in holding their cash balances for them and making them available for expenditure as required, and in placing their savings with investors. Such functions have been implicitly recognized in the preceding analysis. In addition, however, it may either create new money or reduce the supply of money. Money or credit creation is accomplished by the banks by making loans or by buying securities, in return for which they set up new credits or "deposits" on their books which pass as money; retraction of the money supply is effected by "calling" loans for repayment or by selling securities, thus canceling out an equivalent amount of credits or deposits. The banks are thus potential suppliers of investable funds in addition to those supplied from saving or dishoarding; alternatively, they may demand funds in addition to those demanded for nonbank hoarding or for investment. So far as they supply or demand funds, moreover, they increase or decrease the amount of money available for spending or holding idle by individuals and enterprises.

How do the banks affect the determination of the rate of interest? The general effect of bank action is revealed by inquiring what the effect is upon the interest rate in a given period if the banking system succeeds in increasing or diminishing the supply of money. Suppose the current equilibrium interest rate, with given M, is at the rate r shown in Figure 68. An increased amount of money would tend to reduce this rate. With more money in circulation the liquidity needs of persons, relative to the going money income, would be more fully satisfied, and therefore the supply of funds from balances DH would shift outward and down and the demand for hoarding H would be decreased. This would result in a fall in the rate of interest and a new equilibrium with larger investment and smaller saving. Correspondingly, a decreased M would mean that liquidity needs were less fully satisfied; the supply of balances would be decreased and the demand for hoarding increased, and the rate of interest would tend to rise. By changing the amount of money in circulation, the banking system may thus affect the rate of interest and also the relation of saving to investment.

BANK INTEREST-RATE POLICY

The banking system cannot operate, however, by simply adding or withdrawing money to or from the economy. It operates by setting a bank rate of interest and by making loans available at this rate or by purchasing or selling securities at prices which are consistent with this rate.

It is conceivable that by doing this it could make the interest rate it set effective for all transactions involving investable funds in the economy, and thus fix the market rate of interest relative to which all nonbank demands and supplies would adjust. That is, it could keep the interest rate obtained by any nonbank suppliers from being any higher than the bank rate by offering to supply any demands at that rate by loaning or buying securities, and could keep the interest rate obtained by nonbank suppliers from being any lower than its rate by absorbing any excess of supply over demand at that rate by selling securities or recalling loans. It could thus make an interest rate it set effective for the whole economy.

Actually, the usual banking system does not actually accomplish this. It declines to supply "all comers" who demand loans, being restricted by law and policy to selected types of borrowers and securities, so that it influences the interest rate on rejected categories of loans rather indirectly and imperfectly, and it "rations" credit to some categories of borrowers it supplies by refusing to loan all funds desired at a given interest rate. For these reasons, and because there is also credit rationing by nonbank suppliers of funds, it does not actually succeed in making the bank rate fully effective as the interest rate for all transactions in funds.

The banking system does, however, have considerable influence on all interest rates, either directly by acting as a direct supplier or demander of funds or indirectly by augmenting or reducing the cash holding of nonbank suppliers of investable funds with consequent effects on the nonbank supply of funds. Thus, in this country the Federal Reserve System establishes an interest rate, and makes it roughly effective as the rate to be charged by various commercial banks of the banking system by regulating the amount of "reserves" that they have to serve as backing for loans to individuals; it does this, for example, either by buying or selling securities with the effect of increasing or decreasing the amount of central-bank deposit credit in the hands of commercial banks, which credit is usable as reserves, or by fixing the rate of interest at which added reserves can be acquired through commercial-bank borrowing from the central bank. Further, by direct participation in security markets it can establish an interest rate on securities it trades in.

By the combination of these and other actions, the central bank does strongly influence (though not actually set) all commercial-bank and nonbank interest rates, so that they tend roughly to conform to a single central-bank rate of interest. For purposes of a simplified analysis, therefore, no great distortion of reality will be involved if we assume simply, for the purposes of a provisional approximation only, that "the central bank" controls the banking system in such wise that commercial banks as a group set a rate of interest and make it effective throughout the economy by supplying all otherwise unsatisfied demands for funds which emerge at this rate or, alternatively, by absorbing all otherwise unabsorbed supplies of funds. By this drastic simplification we may be enabled to identify clearly the fundamental character of the influence of the banking system on the interest rate and on investment, saving, and hoarding.

Supposing that the banking system operates in this way, let us see what is implied.

THE EFFECT OF BANK INTEREST-RATE POLICY

In an economy with a given net income and provisionally given money supply, we shall suppose for one unit time period the existence of the primary nonbank determinants of the current interest rate, I, H, S, and DH, as shown in Figure 68. We reproduce such a family of demands and supplies of investable funds in Figure 69. The interest rate which will prevail in the absence of bank borrowing or lending here is r, where the aggregate demand for and supply of funds are in balance.

Now if the banking system sets r as its own rate, there will *currently* (at this income) be no net movement of funds in or out of the banks—they will be called upon neither to buy nor sell securities, neither to loan nor recall loans in the net, and will in effect pursue a "neutral" policy. Suppose, however, that by design or accident the banks are not neutral, and set a lower or a higher rate.

If the banks set and support a lower rate r', they will be called upon, in the current period to which the demand and supply schedules refer, to supply funds by lending or by buying securities, in the amount ab, the discrepancy between the aggregate nonbank supply and aggregate nonbank demand for investable funds at this rate. In effect, they would have to add the amount cd to the net hoarding of cash balances, plus the amount ef to investment, in order to sustain the rate r'.

If I and S are unequal at the bank rate r', as shown, income will, of course, move, and the banks will face a somewhat altered situation in the next period. If the banks set and support a higher rate than r, at r'', the opposite situation prevails. The supply of funds from nonbank sources will ex-

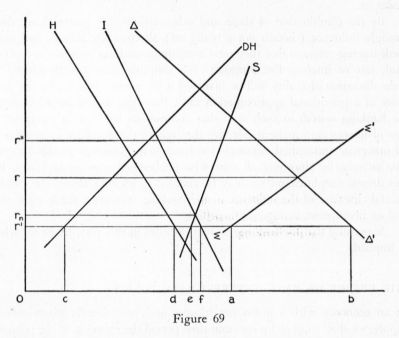

Figure 69

ceed demand, and the banks will be obliged to buy securities or retract loans in the amount of the difference, thus restricting the amount of money in circulation.

In general, the banks can support any rate of interest as a fixed price in the economy so long as they are able and willing, from period to period, to buy or sell sufficient securities to support this rate. When the rate of interest is fixed by the banks, the amount of money becomes a variable which adjusts to the prevailing conditions of nonbank demand for and supply of funds.

It will be well to remember that we have referred explicitly so far only to a single time period of bank operations. A succession of periods with changing income and a changing amount of money introduce additional problems. While we are considering a single period, however, we may as well inquire whether the banks may not, by setting their interest rate appropriately, *stabilize* net income by equating saving and investment. In the case illustrated in Figure 69, for example, cannot the banks set their rate at r_n, at which S would be equal to I, and thus insure a stability of net income from this period to the next, from that period to the following, and so forth?

Assuming that the banks wish to do so, they should be able to stabilize net income from one period to another in a situation where there will be an unsatisfied demand for hoarding at r_n (as in Figure 69) as long as they can continue to supply loans or buy securities sufficiently to meet all unsatisfied liquidity demands at this rate of interest so long as they persist. Conversely, if I tends to exceed S at the equilibrium rate of interest (r) as determined by exclusively nonbank demand and supply, and a higher rate of interest which will induce an unabsorbed supply of dishoarding is required to equalize them, the banks can support such a rate and stabilize income so long as they are willing and able to sell securities demanded at this rate sufficiently to relieve people of the "excess" liquidity they are willing to supply as funds so long as they wish to do so.

In effect, the banking system must be able to supply or absorb securities and loans in sufficient quantity to absorb or make available the difference between gross hoarding demand and gross dishoarding supply at the interest rate which equates I and S if it is effectively to support that rate. And it must be able to do so from period to period so long as unabsorbed supplies of or unsatisfied demands for liquid balances persist if it is to maintain an equality of I and S through time.

LIMITATIONS ON THE BANKING SYSTEM'S CONTROL
OF THE INTEREST RATE

Is it reasonable to suppose that the banking system is generally able to maintain and make effective an interest rate at which I equals S, and thus stabilize net income if it so chooses? The answer is not necessarily affirmative. As for reducing the interest rate to correct a situation where S exceeds I, the banks may be unable to do this, either for the given period or over a succession of periods. If I and S can be equated only at a negative or zero rate of interest, the banks will be practically unable to equate them, since at zero or negative interest rates the demand for loans would be unlimited. Similarly, they may also be unable to equate S and I if the interest rate at which they balance is quite low, and if at this rate the demand for liquid balances becomes insatiably large.

It is possible, that is, that below some certain low positive interest rate the demand for liquid balances (by those who would borrow from or sell securities to the banks) becomes *very elastic,* so that the banks would be unwilling or unable (perhaps because of legal reserve requirements) to supply enough funds to support this rate. Regardless of how much money they pumped into the system from period to period, the demand for balances would still exceed the nonbank supply, and the banks would eventually reach the limit of their resources and have to raise the rate. Thus, unless the saving and investment curves are sufficiently interest-elastic to intersect at some rate above such a positive "psychological minimum" rate, the banks may be unable to keep them in balance and to prevent indefinitely the decline of net income. There is thus a definite theoretical limit on the power of the banking system to curtail the downward movement of the level of income. This is a very important limit if both saving and investment are relatively interest-inelastic.

Suppose, conversely, that at the current interest rate as determined without bank participation, I exceeds S. Are the banks always able to raise the interest rate sufficiently to bring savings and investment into balance? They may again be powerless if at very high rates of interest there is a very large supply of liquid balances which it will be called upon to assume, by selling securities or by calling loans. Thus, if the supply of balances becomes *very elastic* above a certain interest rate, the banks may not be in possession of sufficient callable loans and salable securities to support a higher rate indefinitely. Then if I and S intersect above this rate, the banks will be literally unable to forestall a rise in income, unless the government is willing to create high-yield securities specifically for the purpose of obtaining funds to impound or to withdraw from circulation. There is thus in effect also some maximum interest rate which the banking system can ordinarily support, and this also potentially limits its power over the movement of income. It should be noted, however, that the upper *theoretical* limit is less likely to be tested in practice than the lower, if only because investment is likely to respond in a rather elastic manner to very high rates of interest.

Within the limits indicated, the banking system, as regulated by the central bank, is in a position to set the rate of interest. When it does so, *the interest rate becomes a fixed price, and the quantity of money becomes a variable which will move so long as nonbank demands for investable funds are not equal to nonbank supplies at the bank rate of interest.* Similarly, net income will be a variable which moves until I becomes equal to S at this rate. It seems a reasonable corollary that the range of interest rates which the banking system can effectively sustain will be such that, after adjustments of the money supply and possibly of income over a *limited* succession of periods, nonbank demands for and supplies of funds will at least roughly balance at the bank rate, so that the banking system is not committed to a prolonged rapid expansion or contraction of the money supply.

How can one characterize the rates of interest ordinarily set by a banking system, like our own Federal Reserve System? The determination of the general level of interest rates is a matter of deliberate governmental policy, ordinarily designed to create favorable business conditions—that is, with reasonably full employment, stability, and an avoidance of price inflation. It follows that, within limits, the central bank will tend to adapt its interest rate to the current level of income and employment. In periods of low employment, the aim of governmental policy will ordinarily be to generate an increase in money income, which may be expected, if money factor prices are fairly rigid, to induce a rise in employment and output. The appropriate bank rate in this situation is a very low one, to stimulate investment and restrict saving as much as possible. Cyclical depressions and periods of stagnant employment will thus ordinarily find a low rate of interest supported by the central bank. In periods of rising employment, the bank rate may be adjusted upward somewhat to limit the excess of I over S and to retard the rate of rise of income. When full employment is reached and if income is still rising (investment exceeding saving), a high rate of interest is generally indicated. In conditions of relatively stable income and high employment, the bank will ordinarily attempt to manipulate the rate of interest to maintain an equality between S and I, and to decrease the interest rate when income begins to fall off. The rate of interest under modern central bank conditions is thus likely to respond, because of policy decisions, to the current business situation.

There are, of course, definite limits on the efficacy of bank interest policy to accomplish the desired results on income. In the first place, as we have noted, there are theoretical maximum and minimum limits upon the bank rate of interest, set by the character of liquidity preferences. These limits may be narrowed if there are legal limitations on the amount of credit which the banking system is allowed to create. Further, it must be remembered that the central bank can only *guess* at any current time what the proper rate of interest is—it may well err in this regard in spite of the best intentions.

Three other practical limitations should also be noted. First, the banking system can fully control rates on all types of securities only so far as it deals in all of them. If it is limited to buying and selling only short-term securities, its influence on the yields of long-term securities will be only indirect. Then loans for long-term purposes may carry different rates than the bank rate if the market anticipates rising or falling interest rates in the future. Second, the central bank, as an agent of the government, may find it inexpedient to change the interest rate—especially to raise it—because of the effect of such increases on the government debt. A marked rise in the rate of interest would depress the price of publicly held fixed-yield government bonds, and might thus lessen confidence in the government. Finally, since increases in the interest rate adversely affect those holding all fixed-yield securities, so far as they may wish to sell them (a rising interest rate means falling security prices), the unpopularity of an increase in interest rates above conventional levels may operate to discourage such an increase.

In practice, therefore, and especially when a large government debt is held by the public, the bank rate of interest may tend to be rather inflexible at some level not much exceeding the yield rate on government securities.

THE THEORY OF INTEREST RECONSIDERED

It is now time that we consider the broader implications of our analysis of banks and the interest rate for a satisfactory theory of interest. We have seen that in the absence of active bank participation in the markets for funds, the interest rate would be determined by the interplay of investment and gross hoarding demands for funds with saving and gross dishoarding supplies. But if active banking participation in the money markets is admitted, we have seen that, to a rough approximation, we may simply say that the rate of interest is determined by the central bank. Is it therefore true that we have gone to an undue amount of trouble in analyzing nonbank determinants of the interest rate, when an entire theory of interest might have been contained in a single declarative sentence?

The answer is negative. So far as a theory of the interest rate per se is concerned, we have seen that although it is literally true, in a rough sense, that "the banks set the interest rate," they may set it only within limits, and that these limits are set by the character of nonbank demands for and supplies of funds. Therefore, a "banks set it" theory of interest is misleading and cannot be properly understood without concurrently analyzing the nature and significance of nonbank demands for and supplies of funds.

When we turn to the implications of interest-rate determination for the behavior of money income and employment through time, it is clear that these can only be understood by an analysis of the responses of nonbank demanders and suppliers of funds to a bank-determined interest rate. A full analysis of interest and related phenomena thus requires attention to much more than what interest rate the banking system establishes.

We have now pursued the analysis of the determination of the interest rate in a single period. Let us turn then directly to an analysis of the movement toward equilibrium of money income and employment, together with the movement of the interest rate so far as it is permitted to vary.

C. THE DETERMINATION OF INCOME AND EMPLOYMENT—FIXED PRICES

CONDITIONS FOR MOVEMENT AND STABILITY
OF MONEY INCOME

The determination of the interest rate in a single unit period having been considered, our next task is to analyze the interaction of the demands for and supplies of funds over a succession of periods, in order to ascertain the longer-term equilibrium tendencies of money income, employment, and interest which may develop with any given general conditions of demand and supply for funds.

The analysis may be best undertaken first under the simplifying assumption that money prices are fixed and given over any succession of periods in spite of adjustments in the flow of money income, so that every change in money net income tends to induce a proportional change in the level of net output and of employment. It may be conducted under either of two assumptions about the interest rate: that the rate is freely moving as determined by nonbank demands for and supplies of funds or that it is simply fixed throughout by the banking system at a rate which the system is able to support, the banks therefore varying the supply of money from period to period as necessary as they supply unsatisfied nonbank demands or absorb unabsorbed nonbank supplies at the interest rate they fix. The latter assumption being by far the simplest and reasonably realistic, we shall adopt it for purposes of analyzing income adjustments through time, commenting later on what would happen to the interest rate if it were permitted to adjust freely at the same time as money income. In effect, the problem of the movement of the interest rate per se from period to period ceases to be a problem if the banking system more or less fixes and maintains the rate; the central problem becomes the responses of investment, saving, and hoarding to the bank rate and their implications for the adjustment of income.

Let us then return directly to the problem of money income and its movements. Before examining bank policy, we saw that in any initial unit time period, with a certain going level of money and real net income and with a given amount of money in existence, a balance of the nonbank demand and supply of investable funds would be struck. In this balance, net saving would not necessarily equal net investment. For any unit time period the amount of money saved and thus subtracted from the flow of net income need not be equal to the amount of money invested and thus added to the flow of net income. This would be true even though the money supply were fixed and the interest rate freely adjustable; inequality of S and I is possible by virtue of net hoarding or dishoarding of cash balances.

The supposition of a fixed money supply and a freely moving interest rate may now be replaced with the more realistic assumption that there is a relatively fixed bank rate of interest and a correspondingly flexible money supply. In this situation also the amount of money saved in any initial period need not be equal to the amount invested. It would not be, for example, in Figure 69 on page 664, if the bank set any rate other than r_n.

In general, there will be a given investment demand curve I and a given saving supply curve S, which intersect at some rate of interest r_n, as in Figure 70. This rate of interest may conceivably be high, medium, low, or negative. The demand for and supply of idle balances may now be provisionally neglected, on the supposition that any discrepancy between them is made up by the banks. In this situation, the bank rate may be viewed alternatively as being set equal to or greater or less than the rate at which saving will equal investment. A higher or lower rate might be set by design, or by accident, or because of the inability of the bank (theoretically or practically) to set the rate r_n. In any event, in the absence of the ability

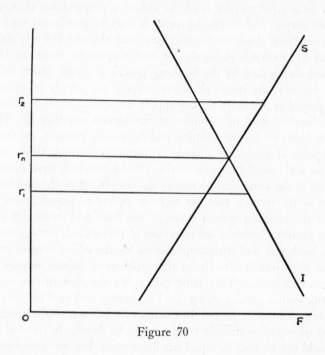

Figure 70

plus the inclination of the banking system to support a rate equal to r_n, S will not be equal to I in any initial income situation. Let us view the rate of interest as set by the banks alternatively at r_n, r_1, and r_2, in Figure 70, and consider the consequences.

Support of the bank rate at the level r_n will result in an equality of S and I and therefore in the stability of money net income from the first period to the next. The reason for this is that net saving subtractions from and net investment additions to net income are just in balance at r_n. Suppose that the total net disposable income flow of a period is \$80 billion. Out of this, net saving is \$15 billion and spending on consumption by income recipients is \$65 billion. If now the rate of interest which the bank has set, and which at given level of income has elicited \$15 billion of net saving, also induces \$15 billion of net investment demand for funds which are in turn spent on new capital goods and financed consumer purchases, all dollars saved will be invested. Then total spending on net output will be $80 billion, and net income generated will be the same as the disposable net income available for spending at the beginning of the period; disposable net income of the *following* period will be the same as that of this period, and so on indefinitely. We thus see that so long as, from period to period, the bank can and does maintain an interest rate at which I equals S, money net income will remain constant over time. And, if all money prices are given, net output and employment will remain constant.[11]

Suppose, however, that the bank rate is set at a lower rate, r_1 in Figure 70, perhaps because the bank wishes to generate a rise in net income, or perhaps because it is practically unable to raise its rate. Then I will exceed S. Net saving will be lower, let us say at $10 billion, while net investment of all sorts will be higher at $20 billion. Now the consumption expenditure from the disposable net income of $80 billion is $70 billion, and it is augmented by an investment expenditure of $20 billion. Net income will rise to $90 billion. An excess of I over S causes a rise of income, accompanied probably by an increase in the amount of money in circulation as the banks meet the difference between the total demand for funds and the total supply from nonbank sources.[12] And, if money prices were fixed, net output and employment would rise correspondingly.

Conversely, a bank rate set at r_2 would result in an excess of S over I and a decline in money net income. Such a rate might be set deliberately, or because I and S intersected at a lower rate than the bank could maintain. If net saving were higher at $20 billion, and net investment lower at $10 billion, consumption out of $80 billion disposable net income would be $60 billion, plus $10 billion of net investment expenditure, so that net money income generated and passed on to the next period as disposable income would decline to $70 billion.[13]

Generalizing, it is obvious that if, at the going interest rate, S equals I, money net income remains constant; if S is greater than I, money net income falls; if I is greater than S, money net income rises. Inequality of S and I causes money income to move; equality allows it to remain stable.

It follows that money net income will tend to move until saving becomes equal to investment. Moreover, a free-moving rate of interest will not prevent such money income movements, and a bank rate of interest may by necessity or by choice be set so as to allow them.

[11] Of course, it is quite possible that at the rate which equates I and S the banking system will be required for some succession of periods to supply a net hoarding demand or absorb a net dishoarding supply of funds from nonbank sources, until the money supply is adjusted to where there is zero net hoarding at the bank interest rate.

[12] This would be true unless there were net nonbank dishoarding of at least $10 billion at the rate r_1.

[13] And bank credit would be contracted unless there were a sufficient nonbank net hoarding demand at the bank rate of interest to absorb the unspent disposable income.

Our first step has been to observe the conditions which will begin a movement of money net income. Where does this movement end? If the money income generated at the end of period 1 and available as disposable net income in period 2 is $80 billion, and if in period 2, $70 billion is consumed and $20 billion invested, the net income of period 2 and disposable income period 3 becomes $90 billion. But what of periods 3 and 4—what is the saving-investment relation there? Can S and I be expected to become equal after a succession of net income movements, and if so at what point?

The analysis from this point forward is complicated by the fact that movements in money net income (set off by inequality of S and I) may cause changes in both S and I and (in the absence of fixed bank policy) in the interest rate. Supposing the interest rate to be held fixed by the bank throughout, we must take account of the response of the investment demand schedule and of the saving supply schedule to the movement of money income. What is the character of these responses?

Movements in money net income will cause I and S to change because of the resultant changes in employment and real income in the economy, and also because of resultant changes in money prices.[14] (For short-term analysis account must also be taken of investment changes based on the anticipation of or speculation on further real income or price changes, but we shall neglect this here.) When money net income increases (because I initially exceeds S) this must induce a rise either in employment or in money prices or in both; a decline in money net income will elicit a decline in either or both, and these induced changes will in turn affect I and S.

For simplicity of analysis, we shall consider separately the effect upon saving and investment of induced price changes and of an induced change in employment and real income. Let us first abstract from the effect of money net income changes on prices, and center attention entirely on their effects on real income and employment.

Let us explicitly assume an economy with given *rigid* money prices which will not change in response to changes in money income. This would involve given money factor prices and given commodity prices. The assumption is logically tenable so long as money income does not continue to rise after full employment is reached. In this economy we begin with some initial disposable money net income, to which there corresponds, at the given prices, a certain level of employment and real net income, registered in the immediately preceding period.

At this money-and-real income level, the current period has a given supply curve of money savings and a given money demand curve for invest-

---

[14] The resultant change in money prices involves a change in money factor prices, and some corresponding change in money commodity prices, which may also involve some change in the relation of commodity to factor prices and in profits.

ment, and also a bank rate of interest, at which saving and investment are by supposition unequal. Money net income therefore changes, money prices remaining fixed and employment changing in response. How, now, will money saving and investment respond in succeeding periods to the resulting identical changes in money-and-real income? This is a useful question because in many situations money prices are in fact relatively rigid and also because answering it may allow us to determine the *net* effect of *real* income movement on saving and investment of funds.

The response of saving to a change in real income is thought to be fairly predictable; that is, money saved as measured in dollars of constant purchasing power will be positively associated with real income (which is money income as measured in dollars of constant purchasing power).[15] Net saving so measured will increase as real net income increases and decrease with real net income decreases; or at any given rate of interest it tends to follow a relationship to net real income about like that described in Figure 64 (page 651). That is, it will increase directly with real net income (although not necessarily in the linear relation shown in Figure 64), so that net income recipients always tend to save a part of any increment to their real income. At very low levels of real net income, net saving will approach and perhaps reach zero, although with savings defined as amounts of net income not spent on consumption by the income recipients (not deducting consumer finance spending from saving) some net saving may persist at very low income levels.

So much for the presumed relation between net saving as measured in dollars of constant purchasing power and real net income. Under the special simplifying assumption of constant prices adopted in this section, the purchasing power of the dollar cannot vary. As a consequence, actual dollar amounts of saving do not have to be adjusted for a changing value of the dollar, as every change in real income is implemented by an identical change of money income. In this special context we may say simply that, given the rate of interest, there is a direct relation of money saving to real-and-money income of precisely the sort shown in Figure 64 and described in the preceding paragraph. The relation of unadjusted money net saving to money-real net income is identical to that which holds more generally between adjusted saving and real income.

Under these assumptions, the response of the supply curve of net money saving (which relates saving to the interest rate) to changes in the level of money and real net income is illustrated in Figure 71, where the net saving supplies for three successively larger levels of income are represented by S_1, S_2, and S_3. The supply curve shifts rightward (along a path suggested by Figure 64) in response to shifts in money-and-real net income (as measured on the horizontal axis in Figure 64).

[15] This relation was discussed on pp. 649-651.

The response of net investment to the same net income change may be analyzed along similar lines. The net investment demand, as a demand for a number of dollars to be spent on current net capital goods output plus consumer finance purchases, represents a certain basic real demand for a given physical quantity of goods, and this is reflected in some specific money demand determined by the going level of money prices. Net investment demand will respond to changes in real income in a presumably positive fash-

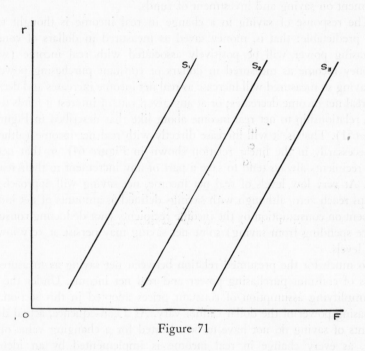

Figure 71

ion. The amount of real output demanded for net investment will increase as real income increases and decrease as real income decreases, and this means that the demand for investable funds as measured in dollars of constant purchasing power will respond positively to changes in real income. If the money price level changes, the actual money investment demand will vary also in response to this change, but the investment demand in adjusted dollars will not necessarily be affected. Under the special assumption that the money price level is constant, however, no adjustment need be made for price changes. It follows that there will then be a direct relation, at any given interest rate and with a constant price level, between actual dollars of money demanded for net investment and the level of real-and-money income.

Why will net investment increase with the level of real income? We have seen that the rate of net investment, or position of the net investment

demand schedule, depends generally upon the accumulated investment opportunities offered by technological change, product development, and so
forth. Net investment demand will increase in response to increasing money-
and-real income for two reasons. First, any going opportunities for net investment at an initial level of income will be somewhat greater at a higher
income level. For example, if introduction of a new machine offers a net
investment opportunity, it will tend to offer a larger opportunity—for the
installation of more machines—if there is a full-employment level of real income than if the level of income and employment is smaller. This will account for some shift in the investment demand schedule in response to increasing income. Second, investment in all lines, including those previously
exploited, will tend to be increased as money-and-real income increases, to
adapt the stock of capital goods (and consumer finance) to a higher level
of output. This will cause an added net investment demand *while income
is increasing,* but this source of net investment demand will vanish once
income stops increasing and simply remains at a higher level. Thus, at a
money-and-real income level of $100 billion, the economy may require $200
billion as a total accumulation of investments in capital goods, and at $150
billion income it may require $300 billion of accumulated investment. While
the economy moves from $100 to $150 billion income, then, there will be a
net investment demand of $100 billion. Once it is stabilized at the new
higher income level, there will be no such net investment demand remaining.

An increase in money-and-real income will thus cause any existing net
investment demand to be somewhat larger, and at the same time create an
additional but quickly satiable net investment demand to adjust the supply
of capital goods to the larger income. As a whole, net investment demand
will respond positively to changes in net income, but part of this response
will be transitory and tend to vanish when income approaches stability at
a higher level. Net investment is thus positively related to net income, but,
except for periods of income *movement,* it is relatively inflexible.

It has been frequently suggested, moreover, that net investment is less
responsive to net income changes than is net saving. If we neglect transitional and temporary effects of income movement on net investment, the
increase in net saving supply corresponding to any increment in real income will tend to be larger than the accompanying increase in net investment demand. This is presumably because many long-range net investment
opportunities (excluding transitional ones) are relatively insensitive to the
going income level, whereas saving responds immediately and directly to
income. Although this belief is not positively verified, we shall accept it
tentatively for purposes of analysis.

This brief and somewhat sketchy survey of the relation of investment
to income suggests that if we were to trace the movement of income in

detail, we should have to take into account short-run *fluctuations* in investment engendered by income movements as well as longer-run ultimate shifts in investment. It is not our intention here to examine this and other aspects of the theory of fluctuations. We shall therefore be content with the *general* observations on the relation of net saving and net investment to movements in real net income:

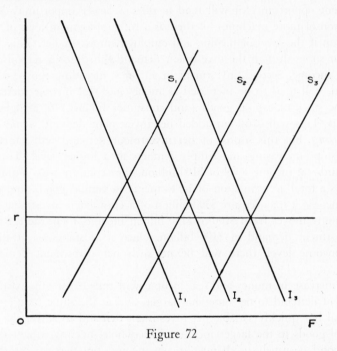

Figure 72

1. that net saving will increase and decrease directly with increases and decreases in money-and-real net income.
2. that net investment will also increase and decrease with money-and-real net income, but ordinarily by smaller amounts.

Let us now return to our initial question—the process of adjustment of money-and-real income (with given money prices) to an initial inequality of saving and investment. Suppose that, in a given situation and with the bank rate of interest r, net investment (I_1) exceeds net saving (S_1), as in Figure 72. Money-and-real income therefore increases. But as income rises, period by period, saving increases, and at the same time investment increases, though on the average at a lesser rate. Thus in a second period the curves shift to I_2 and S_2, where the investment still exceeds saving, but by a smaller amount. Income continues to rise until, in some period 3, saving (S_3) becomes equal to investment (I_3) at the going interest rate. When this point is reached, money-and-real income will tend to be stable so long as investment demand remains at the same level.

In effect, money-and-real income moves until saving out of income becomes equal to investment. This is equally true of situations where there is an initial excess of saving over investment—here income will decline, and with it saving (rapidly) and investment (less rapidly), until at some lower income saving is equal to investment.

We thus have two essential propositions. One, which is obvious, is that an inequality of saving and investment will result in a movement in money-and-real income *until* saving and investment become equal. The second, perhaps less obvious, is that some movement in money-and-real income (given money prices) will tend to bring them into equality, *so long as saving is more responsive to income than is investment.* From the two propositions we derive the idea of *an equilibrium level of real income,* which real income would tend to reach with any given set of money prices. Given such prices, money-and-real income tend to move to this equilibrium level, where saving out of income is equal to investment.[16]

The argument that this is so has been developed on the supposition of a fixed bank rate of interest, with reference to which equalities and inequalities of S and I occur. Obviously then, the equilibrium level of real income would be at least somewhat influenced by the level of the bank rate, lower rates favoring larger real income. The proposition that real income will move to a level which equates S and I will also hold, however, if there is a variable interest rate determined by nonbank demands for and supplies of funds. In this case, as we have seen, the interest rate will not generally move to equate S and I at every income level—the hoarding phenomenon interfering. Therefore, real income will again adjust to equate S and I although in this case the interest rate will adjust concurrently.

The process of establishing an equilibrium income may be illustrated by means of an arithmetical example in the form of a "model sequence" development of income through time. Suppose money prices are absolutely given, and also the rate of interest. Suppose, also, that the rate of net income (Y) is initially $100 per period, and that the rate of net investment (I) is $50 per period. Suppose that at the $100 level of income, people consume $60 and save $40. This gives us initially an inequality of saving and investment. As income moves, let us suppose: (1) that investment is totally insensitive,

---

[16] It should be clear that if investment responded to income change *more* rapidly than saving, then an equilibrium real income would not be attained at a given interest rate, and either progressive decline or progressive expansion of money income would occur, depending on the direction of the initial discrepancy between I and S. Furthermore, if investment exceeded saving at full employment, further income rises would presumably increase saving no more than investment (both being affected alike by price rises). Then stability would not tend to be attained, and progressive price inflation at a full-employment level would tend to ensue.

remaining at $50 per period, but (2) that saving changes with real income so that saving is always 40 percent of the disposable income of a period. Now, letting Y stand for the disposable net income at the beginning of each period of time, I for investment, C for consumption, and S for saving during the period, we can trace the movement of net income, period by period, toward equilibrium.

Period	Y	$C(= .6Y)$	$S(= .4Y)$	$I(= 50)$
1	100	60	40	50
2	110	66	44	50
3	116	69.6	46.4	50
4	119.6	71.8	47.8	50
5	121.8	73.1	48.7	50
6	123.1	73.9	49.2	50
n	125	75	50	50
$n + 1$	125	75	50	50

Beginning with the first period, with a disposable income of 100 available for expenditure, consumption is 60 and investment 50, creating a net income of 110, which is available for expenditure in period 2. Out of the latter income, consumption (after 40-percent saving) is 66, and with investment remaining at 50, total expenditure, and hence the disposable income for expenditure in period 3, is 116. We then progress from period to period with income rising as long as investment exceeds saving. But with stable investment (entirely insensitive to income), saving overtakes investment as income rises, until in period n income approaches the level 125. This is the income out of which saving equals investment—in this case, the income 40 percent of which is equal to $50. When this income is reached, no further income movements will occur so long as (1) investment remains at 50 per period, and (2) people's saving habits remain unchanged. Thus, the income 125 is an *equilibrium level of income* (given certain money prices)—income moves to this level, which is defined as the income the saving from which is equal to investment. There is always potentially some such equilibrium level of income corresponding to (1) the rate of investment, and (2) the relation of saving to income.[17]

[17] The student will note, for example, that in the preceding sequence, if investment were 40 per period, the equilibrium income would be 100; if it were 30, the equilibrium would be 75; if it were 60, the equilibrium income would be 150. Conversely, if investment were 50 and people saved 25 percent instead of 40 percent of their incomes in general, the equilibrium income would be 200 instead of 125.

If, of course, investment is not totally insensitive to income but responds in some degree to income movements, the process of adjustment will be prolonged and the equilibrium level of income altered. In the sequence just developed, for example, the eventual equilibrium might involve an investment per period of 60 (up 10 because of higher income) and an income of 150. But the general principle holds that, with given money prices, income will move to that level at which saving equals investment.

THE SIGNIFICANCE OF MONEY INCOME EQUILIBRIUM

Now that this general principle has been stated, let us examine a few of its implications. First, it is true that, on the assumption of given money prices, the equilibrium level of money net income involves some corresponding equilibrium of real net income and hence an equilibrium level of employment. What we have said in effect is that in this case *employment and output move to such a level that saving equals investment.* By abstracting from price movements, we have made all money net income movements equivalent to movements in real net income and employment, and have argued toward an equilibrium level of employment. The basic determinants of this equilibrium of employment are the relation of saving to real income, the behavior of real investment demand, and the rate of interest. Assuming given money prices, we explicitly trace the adjustment to equilibrium of money income in response to money saving and investment. But the saving and investment adjustments rest basically on real income changes (as opposed to price changes), and the equilibrium money income reached carries with it a corresponding equilibrium level of employment.

Second, this equilibrium level of employment may be less than full employment, at any rate if prices are fixed. Full-employment income can be sustained only if at the interest rate established the net saving from such income is not greater than the currently corresponding rate of net investment. Suppose that at a level of income sufficient to sustain full employment (for example, a money net income of 200 with given prices) the economy will save 25 percent (50 in money at the same prices). Then net investment must be at least 25 percent of income (50 per period) at the full-employment income of 200, or that level of employment cannot be sustained. If net investment will not rise above 20, employment and income will decline to that level where saving is 20, and involuntary unemployment will occur. The level of the interest rate will of course have some influence on the equilibrium employment level, since a lower rate tends to encourage investment and discourage saving. But, as we have seen, the banking system may be practically unable to establish a rate low enough to equate I and S at a full-employment income level because of an unsatiable demand for hoarding at very low rates—and for the same reason a free interest rate (fixed without bank interference) would not go so low. Therefore, underemployment equilibrium, reached because income adjusts to equate S and I, may occur in spite of the maximum feasible manipulation or free movement of the interest rate.

Why cannot full employment *automatically* be sustained? There are two reciprocating reasons. First, net investment does not automatically emerge in sufficient amounts to absorb the savings from income at minimum attainable interest rates. The general rate of net investment is in considerable part for new capital goods, and this in turn emerges mainly in response to dynamic change in techniques, products, and so forth. In the absence of a sufficient pace of such change, net investment demand may be small for any level of real income and not strongly responsive to the interest rate. Second, the rate of saving is linked in definite fashion to the level of real income. With the given bank interest rate assumed, the economy will save a relatively high proportion of a full-employment income, and diminishing amounts from smaller incomes, and its tendency to save at any given income level will not be greatly affected by decline of the interest rate to minimum attainable levels. Then a shortage of investment opportunity does not lead to a restriction of saving *at a high income level,* as the lowest attainable interest rate will not cut saving or expand investment enough to equate S and I, and the demand for liquidity keeps the interest rate from going lower. Rather it leads to a reduction of income. With a reduced investment demand, the economy cannot sustain full employment because it insists upon saving "too much" of its income at that level of employment.[18]

A third implication of the general principle is that an excess of investment over saving at the income where full employment is reached means that the assumption of rigid money prices is no longer tenable. In effect, if such a discrepancy continues at full employment, a rise in money income must continue and will be matched by a corresponding rise in money prices —by inflation.

In this case, if investment and saving are similarly influenced by price increases, no equilibrium of money income may be reached. And again the banking system may be unable to impose a high enough interest rate to check the inflationary tendency. It should be noted, however, that a balance of investment and saving may very often be reached short of full employment, so that the *necessity* of changing money prices is not encountered.

[18] The argument as presented explicitly assumes a fixed rate of interest. It should be noted that it may apply equally well with a variable rate of interest as determined by nonbank demands for and supplies of funds. That is, interest-rate reductions may not balance saving and investment at full-employment income because (1) saving and investment may respond in rather inelastic fashion to interest-rate changes, and (2) the total demand for liquidity will tend to prevent the reduction of the interest rate below a certain positive minimum, which minimum may be too high to equate S and I at a full-employment level of income.

Fourth, an investment demand which changes over time will tend to induce a changing level of employment. New net investment demands arise principally from dynamic changes in techniques and the like, but each additional demand is satiable and as time passes must be supplanted by others. With a varying pace of dynamic change in the economy, investment demand and the rate of investment will fluctuate. If there is a relatively fixed relation of saving to income and if saving and investment are both relatively insensitive to the interest rate, then income and employment will tend to fluctuate also. In periods of a higher rate of investment, employment will tend to be high; if investment is small, employment will be low. Given the relation of saving to income (and assuming given money prices), the rate of investment determines the rate of employment.

Fifth, movements of money income as it adapts to a changing state of investment demand (given money prices and with a given bank rate of interest) will be accompanied by variations in the amount of money in circulation, as the banks buy or sell securities to maintain the balance between the total demand for and supply of investable funds. Thus, a rising money income and employment will be matched by some corresponding rise in bank loans or by security purchases by banks, and a decline in income by some decline in bank loans or by security sales by banks. It is not necessarily true that the exact difference between investment and saving must be supplied or retracted by banks in each period, since there may be also some net hoarding or dishoarding of balances. But this difference will be in large part counterbalanced by expansion or contraction of the money supply.

Even with a fixed supply of money an equilibrium level of employment would be struck in much the same fashion, so as to equate saving and investment. Income would still move until these two became equal. But with a fixed money supply, the interest rate would also move as the ratio of money income to the money supply varied (thus changing marginal liquidity preference)—it would rise with an increasing income and fall with a declining income. This adjustment of the interest rate would cooperate with the adjustment in income to equalize saving and investment, and would thus tend to reduce the amplitude of income movements. Money income changes would then be accomplished entirely by variations in the income velocity of the given money supply.

Summarizing our argument to this point, we have pointed out that, with given money prices, saving need not necessarily equal investment at all levels of money-and-real income. This is true either with a fixed supply of money and a free interest rate, or with a fixed interest rate and a variable money supply. If saving and investment are unequal, money income, and with it real income and employment, will tend to move until they become equal. There may then be some *equilibrium* real income and employment, the level of which is determined, given the rate of interest, by the relation of saving to real income, and by the size of investment demand and its response to real income changes. With given money prices, money income and employment move to such a level that saving equals investment. This level may (or may not) involve involuntary unemployment. With the bank rate of interest also given, the equilibrium level of money income will be matched by some corresponding amount of money as supplied by the banks. We have seen, moreover, that the banking system may be effectively unable to adjust the rate of interest sufficiently to preclude income movements or to stabilize income at the full-employment level.

The preceding analysis has clearly forecast the character of the determination of an equilibrium interest rate. If the banking system establishes and is able to maintain a given rate while an equilibrium of money income and employment is reached and perpetuated, this bank rate, of course, becomes a stable equilibrium rate of interest. As such a rate is maintained long enough to be regarded as tenable for an indefinite length of time, however, two processes will take place. First, as we have seen, money income and employment will tend to move to an equilibrium level at which saving is equal to investment. Second, during this process of adjustment the banking system will supply or demand funds sufficient to close the gap between the changing total nonbank supplies of and demands for funds at the interest rate it sets, correspondingly reducing or expanding the money supply. Even after income has moved to where saving equals investment, moreover, gross dishoarding and hoarding may not balance at the bank's interest rate, and in this case it must continue to supply or demand funds sufficiently to offset net hoarding or dishoarding over a number of periods until the resultant change in the money supply has changed hoarding demands and dishoarding supplies enough to produce zero net hoarding at the bank interest rate, at which point the money supply will become stable and the banking system "neutral" in the market for funds. The ability of the banking system to maintain a given rate of interest will be contingent on the rate's falling within a range for which hoarding demands are not insatiable and dishoarding supplies not indefinitely large. In this connection, it may be noted that if investment continually exceeds saving at full employment, given the bank's interest rate (thus generating progressive price inflation), the bank will be able to maintain the rate only by regularly adding to the money supply to meet otherwise unsatisfied investment and net hoarding demands.

If the money supply is fixed and the interest rate freely moving as determined by nonbank demands for and supplies of funds alone, the interest rate, of course, will move at the same time as income and employment toward a mutual equilibrium level. If there is an initial excess of investment over saving and a corresponding net dishoarding at the interest rate established in an initial period, the succeeding expansion of income will tend to be accompanied by a rise in the interest rate and a reduction of net dishoarding as the larger money income creates a larger demand for cash balances and increases gross hoarding relative to gross dishoarding. The equilibrium interest rate will be reached when investment equals saving and there is zero net hoarding at the interest rate which effects this equality. Conversely, an initial excess of saving over investment with net hoarding will produce not only a decline of income and employment, but also of net hoarding and of the interest rate as liquidity needs become more fully satisfied, until the same equilibrium situation is reached. In this connection it may be noted that, with a fixed money supply, progressive inflation at full employment may tend ultimately to increase the demand for liquidity enough to raise the interest rate to where saving equals investment and thus end the inflationary spiral. This would not be so, however, if a rapid rise in prices induced a progressive flight from liquidity.

The preceding covers the adjustment of money-and-real income on the supposition that there are given and fixed money prices. On this assumption, it is possible to reach fairly definite conclusions concerning the simultaneous equilibrium of saving, investment, income, and interest. In what respects is our analysis altered if we recognize that money prices may rise under the influence of increasing money income and fall with declining money income or because of severe unemployment? This is an important question, since, until the effect of money price changes is admitted, a *true* equilibrium of money income and of employment is hardly established.

D. THE DETERMINATION OF INCOME AND EMPLOYMENT—VARIABLE PRICES

THE EFFECTS OF MONEY PRICE CHANGES

The principal impact of money price changes upon the determination of money income and employment stems from their effects on money net investment and money net saving. A general rise or fall in money prices will cause some change in the amount of money investment corresponding to a given real investment demand, and in the amount of money saving corresponding to a given real income.

If we are initially in a period where disposable income is 100, consumption 80, saving 20, and investment 30, money income necessarily rises, reaching a level of 110. If this rise in income results entirely and only in a price increase (of 10 percent), real income and employment and the interest rate remaining the same, and if the real demand for investment goods remains the same, money investment should now be 33. If people's saving habits relative to real incomes are unaltered, saving should be 22. The rise of money income would then continue, since money investment and money saving have responded directly and in the same proportion to changes in the price level.

We may expect in general that a rising money price level (rising in response, ordinarily, to an increase in money income) will elicit some corresponding upward shifts in money investment and saving, and that a declining money price level will have the opposite effect. As the economy moves through time, and as money income is changed because of inequalities of saving and investment, the movements of money income and employment are much complicated by this fact. Money prices are ordinarily not rigid, and money saving and investment thus change in response *both* to real income changes *and* to changes in the price level. When we can no longer assume rigid money prices, we must appraise in detail the effects of changes in these prices.

Precise appraisal of the effects of money price changes on investment and saving requires that we distinguish between the effects of a changed price level per se, and the effects of anticipations of further price change, as they may arise from changes already experienced. A higher general price level, if it is expected to be maintained, tends to cause an upward adjustment in the money dimension of everything—more money is paid for given goods, a higher money wage corresponds to a given real wage, and investment and saving are similarly affected. Except so far as the *structure* of prices is altered by alteration of the price level and if the interest rate is inflexibly given, the changed price level may imply nothing further than a changed money income. There is no necessary *resultant* alteration in output or employment, and no necessary resultant change in the *relationship* of saving to investment, even though the money dimension of both may be increased. If this is true, a higher price level per se (with given interest rate) does not alter any pre-existing tendency of employment to rise, and a lower price level does not overcome a pre-existing tendency of employment to fall. Changing price levels accentuate the tendency of *money income* to change but tend to be neutral in their effects on employment, *so long as we overlook anticipation of further price change, or speculation on price changes.*[19]

This was the position taken by J. M. Keynes[20] when he held in effect that, speculative matters aside, the money price level is neutral in the determination of equilibrium employment—that real income and employment will move to a determinate level regardless of the level of money prices with any given interest rate. This is essentially because employment depends upon

[19] This is provided the supply of money is perfectly elastic at the going rate of interest, so that a changing price level does not alter the interest rate or the marginal rate of liquidity preference—a situation which holds as long as the bank supports a certain inflexible rate of interest.

[20] *General Theory of Employment, Interest, and Money,* Chaps. 19-21.

the relation of saving to investment, and because money price changes tend to affect both saving and investment proportionately, leaving their relationship unaltered.

If in a given situation investment is invariant at 40 per period, income is 100, and saving is 20 percent of any income, then in the absence of any money price changes, money income would rise to 200 per period. At this income, saving would become 40 and equal investment. This 200 of money income we shall suppose sufficient to support an employment of resources of 1,000; thus the equilibrium employment is 1,000 with given money prices. Suppose, instead, that as money income rises from the initial situation just described, money prices also rise for some reason, eventually doubling their previous values. This will tend to cause money investment per period to rise to 80, since the same real investment will require twice the money at doubled capital goods prices. Money income will therefore rise to 400, at which money saving will equal 80. But at doubled money prices, an income of 400 will support only 1,000 of employment, and the employment equilibrium is unaltered. The only effect of the rising price level is to accentuate the increase in money income, and, at a given bank interest rate, to elicit the creation of more credit money. The determination of the equilibrium level of employment and real income is *as if* there had been a rigid money price level—only *money* income levels and movements are affected by price changes. The economy tends, given the interest rate, to move to a determinate level of employment regardless of what happens to the money price level. This is the Keynesian argument, in general followed here.

THE CASE OF FALLING PRICES

The application of this argument to falling money prices is perhaps the most interesting. We have already indicated that with given money prices and a given interest rate an underemployment equilibrium can occur. That is, the rate of investment can be insufficient to absorb saving from full-employment income, and income and employment decline until saving does equal investment. The question naturally arises whether a fall in money prices can now increase the level of employment.

Consistent with the preceding argument, the answer is no. A decrease in prices causes a proportionate decline in money investment and a proportionate decline in saving at a given interest rate; hence money income declines proportionately to the drop in prices, and employment is unaffected. So long as there is some given level of real investment demand (so that money investment simply varies directly with price changes) and so long as there is some given relation of saving to real income, money price reductions will not cause an alteration of the relation of saving to investment or an increase in employment. They will lead only to declines in money income, and, with a fixed bank rate of interest, to a contraction of the money supply.

This argument is perfectly valid as far as it goes. Higher or lower money price levels per se will not affect the level of employment, *unless* they influence the real investment demand or the fundamental relation of saving to real income. Perhaps it may be well to emphasize also that money price changes *do* influence the level of money income.

For example, the rise in money income generated by an initial excess of investment over saving would ordinarily be fairly limited if money prices were rigid. But if money prices rise with rising income, the increase of money income is accentuated and may proceed to a much higher (theoretically unlimited) point. Correspondingly, where investment is less than saving, successive declines in money prices may lead to an indefinitely declining money income. The consequences of a rising money price level are particularly significant when such a rise is virtually forced by an excess of investment over saving after full employment has already been reached. Of equal importance, however, is the tendency of employment and real income to seek an equilibrium level largely regardless of associated movements in money prices.

LIMITATIONS ON THE ARGUMENTS CONCERNING EFFECTS
OF MONEY PRICES

This general conclusion concerning the effect of money price changes is potentially deficient, however, in three respects. It overlooks the effects of speculation on price change; it assumes a given bank rate of interest; and it neglects associated changes in the price structure.

Speculation on future price change may, of course, have a considerable effect on the current amount of investment. The expectation of higher money prices over some future interval will generally stimulate current investment, as buyers acquire capital goods before their prices rise. This applies both to durable equipment, like machinery, which may be bought "in advance," and to inventories, which may be bought and held for a price increase. Conversely, the expectation of lower money prices over some future interval will reduce current investment, as the purchase of capital goods is postponed. It follows that a part of the immediate importance of money price changes, as they result from changing money income, will stem from the anticipations they create with respect to further changes.

These effects, however, are not always easily predicted. When prices are rising with rising money income, some anticipation of further price increases is ordinarily created, and this will tend currently to induce a greater than proportionate increase in money investment; thus a 10-percent price increase might lead to a 20- or 30-percent increase in money investment because of advance buying. Conversely, a decline in prices may lead to a greater than proportionate decrease in money investment. So far as this is true, money price movements, as they respond to money income movements, will tend to accentuate the current discrepancies between investment and saving and to lead to more severe and prolonged movements of both money income and employment. On the other hand, a continued rise of money prices to an unaccustomed high level may create the anticipation of an eventual decline, and a decline of money prices to abnormal lows may cause investors to anticipate an eventual price rise. When these "contrary" expectations become operative, price movements tend to narrow the gap between investment and saving and to arrest further movements of money income and employment. It is partly because of such contrary expectations that a progressive inflation or deflation of money income and prices may tend ultimately to be self-stopping. It is also for this reason that severe declines in money factor prices may provide some stimulus to investment and employment. Our conclusions concerning the neutrality of the price level in the determination of equilibrium employment must thus be modified to allow for the effects of "speculation" on investment.

A second assumption limiting these conclusions is that of a fixed bank rate of interest and its concomitant, a flexible money supply. This is not a serious limitation, since the interest rate is maintained rather inflexibly by the banking system under most circumstances. If, however, the money supply should be rather inflexible beyond certain limits, so that the interest rate moved freely, the following amendments to our argument would have to be introduced. Rising money prices, generating additions to money income, would create increasing pressure in the form of increased demand for liquid balances and cause the rate of interest to increase, thus putting some drag on the increase of investment and income. Falling money prices would release money for balances and depress the rate of interest, thus tempering the decline of investment and income. The amplitude of movements in money income and employment is thus less augmented by price changes when the money supply is fixed than when it is flexible.

Could falling prices increase employment, via the increase of liquid balances, except by depressing the interest rate? *Not unless the accumulation of balances alters the relation of saving to real income, causing people to save a smaller proportion of a given real income.* There is some disagreement on this point. The Keynesian view is that saving, or the relation of saving to real income, will not be much altered by liquidity, except via changes in the interest rate. Then no conceivable drop in money prices could overcome an underemployment equilibrium, except so far as increased liquidity might reduce the interest rate to a psychological minimum level and thus stimulate investment and reduce saving somewhat. An alternative view is that great price declines, accompanied by greatly increased liquidity relative to needs therefore, would reduce saving (so that a smaller proportion of any real income would be saved at any interest rate) and thus permit a larger employment level to be attained, since I would then equal S at a larger real income. There has been no conclusive empirical test of these conflicting hypotheses, and it is unlikely to occur when governmental authority opposes considerable price declines. Suffice it to say, in an economy which is likely to have either rigid or rising prices only, that the potential effects on employment of large price declines are of strictly academic interest.

Attention must also be paid to the possible effects of a changing price structure as money factor prices change. So far we have assumed that a money factor-price change is accompanied by proportionate changes in all other prices—in effect, we have neglected the effects of connected changes in the price structure. In a complete theory of income and employment these effects are potentially important enough to be taken into account. This is particularly true of changes in profits which result from price and income movements. For present purposes, we shall simply point to the desirability of such elaborations of the theory, which, although they would not greatly alter our main conclusions, would make for quite significant amendments in detail.

INTEREST, INCOME, AND EMPLOYMENT

Let us now condense our preceding arguments concerning the rate of interest and the level of money income and employment. In any initial situation of money and real income, it will be true either (1) that, with a given amount of money, the rate of interest will be so determined as from period to period to equate the demand for and supply of investable funds, or (2) that, with a given bank rate of interest, banks will add to or subtract from the money supply sufficiently to balance the demand for and supply of funds. In either event, saving may be greater or smaller than investment at the initial level of income, and this inequality may not be subject to correction by rates of interest which the banks can support. Where saving initially equals investment, money and real income will remain stable. Where they are unequal, the initial level of income is untenable, and money income will change until investment and saving become equal. (If there is a fixed money supply and a freely moving interest rate, equality of saving and investment will require that there is zero net hoarding.)

Adjustments of money income to such a point of equilibrium may involve changes both in money prices and in employment. But of these, money price changes will probably not serve to overcome an inequality of saving and investment, since these are primarily determined as proportions of real income; as money amounts, S and I tend to respond together to price changes. If this is so, employment must move until saving and investment are equated by virtue of real income changes. We thus derive the idea of an equilibrium level of employment, such that saving out of the corresponding real income is equal to investment. This equilibrium employment may be high or low, depending upon the volume of investment demand current at the time.

The Keynesian thesis, in general followed here, is that movements in the money price level will not affect the equilibrium level of real income and employment (speculative phenomena aside) except by making prices higher or lower relative to the money supply, thus influencing the state of liquidity, and thus affecting the interest rate. If there were a fixed bank interest rate and flexible money supply, the price level would not affect employment at all. Then we could say that there is always a determinate level of employment, but that the money price level and the level of money income per se are not so determinate, depending upon various institutional forces. It should be remembered, however, that there is a dissenting view which would hold that the money price level may further affect employment by affecting the relation of saving to real income via effects on liquidity. If this anti-Keynesian position is correct, the determinants of employment equilibrium are much more complex, and underemployment equilibrium may be escapable by large price reductions.

The outstanding conclusion of the Keynesian argument, of course, concerns the tendency of the economy toward an equilibrium level of employment, possibly involving underemployment. This tendency results from the fact that employment moves until real investment and real saving become equal, and that money price movements have negligible effects on the process. The principles underlying this conclusion are the key to a widely accepted interpretation of transient or chronic unemployment, and of fluctuations in employment generated by fluctuations in investment. The argument is traced only in outline here, and should be pursued in much more detail. Detailed analysis of a period-by-period sequence of changes through time will reveal many phenomena not touched upon here, so that the preceding should be viewed only as a sketchy introduction to the analysis of the dynamics of income and employment.

Let us now consider the broader implications of the foregoing theory of employment for the theories of commodity pricing and income distribution developed from Chapters 2 through 13. In these chapters we did not analyze the employment problem, pointing out only (1) that full employment would always ensue if competitive adjustments of money prices took place and if these adjustments did not cause offsetting adjustments in money income, and (2) that unemployment might ensue if an appropriate adjustment between money prices to money income did not take place because either of money price rigidity or of a tendency of money income to move downward proportionally with money prices, thus canceling the potential effect of any price adjustment. The analysis of commodity and factor pricing was then pursued on the first supposition, of automatic full employment. We have now seen that, if the Keynesian argument is correct, the employment of resources does not, even under competitive conditions, automatically move to the full-employment level. Rather, employment tends to move to such a level that saving from the corresponding real income equals investment, and this may not be a full-employment level. The level of employment depends primarily on the rate of real investment (which may be variable over time) and on the relation of saving (as defined) to real income. Employment cannot rise above the level where saving equals investment.

This implies that the ratio of money prices to money income does not adjust to insure full employment. Movements in money prices, if we follow the Keynesian argument, generally will not alter the equilibrium level of employment except so far as they engender speculation and thus influence investment, or as they influence liquidity and the rate of interest. Money income will tend to adapt itself to any ruling level of money prices, and to change as prices change, in such wise as to maintain the same equilibrium level of employment—a level determined by real investment and the relation of saving to real income. Implicitly, therefore, price-level movements fail to affect employment because they induce hoarding or dishoarding, or contraction or expansion of the money supplied by banks, rather than changing the ratio of prices to the level of money income. The rigidity of money prices is thus not a significant cause of unemployment, except so far as flexibility might bring speculative forces into play.

There may be full employment, if investment is large enough to balance the saving from full-employment income. It is also possible that progressive inflation of money income and prices at full employment may result because of an excess of investment over saving at a full-employment level. But it is also possible that there may be an equilibrium with involuntary unemployment, in which reductions of money prices will reduce money income but will not reduce unemployment.[21] A tentative explanation of the level of employment is thus developed, in terms of the determinants of real investment and of the relation of saving to real income. This relation determines in general the ratio of money income to money prices, and thus the level of employment. The absolute level of money income, on the other hand, is determinate only if movements in money prices are effectively explained.

The equilibrium level of employment just described may be influenced by the rate of interest on investable funds, as ordinarily set by the banking system. Employment may be somewhat increased or decreased by lowering

---

[21] Unless via reductions in the interest rate or by engendering speculation.

or raising the interest rate, and by thus influencing saving and investment. But the bank rate operates theoretically within a range set by a positive theoretical minimum and some positive theoretical maximum, and practically within a narrower range. Moreover, neither saving nor investment may be particularly elastic to the interest rate within this range. Thus, the rate of interest, even when supported by a reasonably flexible money supply from the banks, probably cannot be used to alter seriously the character of a given employment equilibrium.

To the preceding it is necessary to add that employment "equilibrium" is not intrinsically a stable thing which tends to be perpetuated at a single level over time. It is an expression of the tendency of employment in response to any current rate of investment, given the relation of saving to real income and given the bank rate of interest. Since investment moves or fluctuates over time, employment equilibrium is inclined to be a moving or fluctuating equilibrium.

It follows, of course, that to be fully satisfactory, the theories of commodity and factor pricing must be adapted so as to apply directly not only to full-employment situations but also to situations of less than full employment. We shall comment on the character of necessary adaptations in the succeeding chapter.

E. THE BEHAVIOR OF NET INVESTMENT DEMAND

THE ISSUES WITH RESPECT TO NET INVESTMENT

In the preceding analysis of employment, the demand for funds for net investment, including that for additions to the stock of capital goods and that for consumer finance funds, plays a strategic role. We have suggested that there is a more or less fixed relation of net saving to real income, such that saving increases with real income and is a significant fraction of real income when there is full employment, and that at any level of income saving is relatively insensitive to the interest rate and will not be greatly diminished even by an interest rate of zero. If this is so, then for full employment to be maintained, net investment demand must be large enough to absorb the savings out of a full-employment income at an interest rate which is at or above the minimum level where a demand for additions to cash balances will become unsatiable and thus preclude further interest-rate reductions. If net investment demand is not this large, then an underemployment equilibrium will tend to result. If, conversely, it is so large as to exceed full-employment saving at interest rates which because of dishoarding cannot be exceeded, price inflation will result.

It follows that great importance attaches both to the general size of net investment demand from period to period over time (that is, to the position of the net investment demand curve relative to that of the saving supply curve at various income levels) and to the interest-elasticity of the investment demand curve (the responsiveness of this demand to changes in the interest rate). Will the net investment demand in general be large enough, and sensitive enough to the interest rate, to permit maintenance of full employment at attainable interest rates? Will it conversely tend to be so large as to propagate progressive inflation?

THE SHIFTS IN NET INVESTMENT DEMAND

We have seen (pages 605 to 608) that in an economy which had a strictly stationary situation with respect to techniques of production, consumers' products and consumers' tastes, and supplies and employment of labor and land, there would be a finite and limited demand for capital goods at each rate of interest. Consequently, the demand for funds for investment in capital goods would be fully satiable, and once the equilibrium amount of capital goods had been acquired, and the corresponding equilibrium amount of funds invested, there would be no demand for funds for net investment unless the interest rate went below previous levels. There would be a reinvestment demand for funds in each period, but this would be matched by a corresponding amount of enterprise sales receipts available as gross saving for reinvestment, so that there would be no demand on net saving. Should we encounter a truly stationary economy, therefore, net saving (except that absorbed for consumer finance) would have to be zero at full-employment income if full employment were to be maintained.

It follows from this that the recurrent emergence of a net investment demand (except for consumer finance) must be attributable to *change* in the things which affect the size of the requirement for capital goods—to changes in techniques, in consumers' products or tastes, in the quantity of available labor or land or in the level of their employment. In a very general way, moreover, we may say that the size of demand for funds for net investment in capital goods depends at any time on the current *pace* of change in these respects, and furthermore that the pace of change may vary through time and thus that the level of net investment demand may vary correspondingly.

The matter is a little more complicated than this in actuality, and we might wish to inquire in detail by what process and to what extent each sort of dynamic change contributes to the creation of net investment demand. For example, under what conditions and why will an increase in population create net investment demand, what sort of technological change does so, etc.?

The exploration of these issues, however, must be left for works presenting detailed and specialized treatments of the theory of employment.

For present purposes, we shall content ourselves with a few brief observations.

First, the combination of dynamic changes in techniques, in consumers' products and tastes, and in population and the quantity of known resources, continually creates some net investment demand as of any given level of employment of resources, giving rise to a corresponding net investment demand curve for funds to invest in capital goods at any given price level.

Second, the pace of such net-investment-inducing dynamic changes varies over time, with variation in the rate of population growth, in the rate of discovery of new resources, in the invention and introduction of new production techniques or consumers' products. These variations may be short-term or long-term, and are difficult to predict a priori. Correspondingly, the net investment demand curve, as of any level of employment of resources, will shift over time. In some periods or series of periods it may lie far to the right, showing large investment demands relative to savings. In others it may lie far to the left, showing relatively small demands.

Third, the current level of employment of available resources will have some influence on the size of the net investment demand resulting from a given pace of other dynamic changes (see pages 674 to 675). This effect will probably be such that net investment demand will not change by as great a proportion as the level of employment. The effects of a change in the level of employment, however (as distinct from the effects of having the economy operate at one level rather than another) will have substantial temporary effects on the rate of net investment, as the entire capital stock is adjusted to produce a different rate of output. Thus, an increase in the level of employment may create large temporary net investment demands for a period of a year or two only, and a decrease may produce severe temporary offsets to any going rate of net investment. For purposes of an analysis of long-run general tendencies, we have neglected this transitory type of net investment demand induced by the process of change in the level of output and employment.

Fourth, changes in the money price level will tend to change the demand for funds for net investment more or less in proportion, and thus will not tend to alter the relation of money net investment to either money income or money saving in any systematic fashion, except so far as price changes induce temporary speculative investment or disinvestment. (This is on the assumption that the relation of real saving to real income is also substantially uninfluenced by money price changes.) The predicted variation over time in real investment demand is thus substantially uninfluenced by money price-level changes, and reflects itself in a demand for an amount of dollars for net investment which depends on the price level.

We thus conceive of a demand for funds for net investment in capital goods which, aside from the effect of price-level changes and changes in the level of employment, will fluctuate over time. In some periods or succession of periods the demand will be large relative to saving, in others moderate or small. This demand will respond moderately to current changes in the level of employment (neglecting transitory effects of the process of employment change), and will vary more or less proportionally with the price level (as saving will also).

Added to the demand for funds for net investment in capital goods will be the demand for funds to finance consumer purchases (see pages 636 to 637). Ordinarily, however, this will not be such as to alter very much the relation of total net investment demand to saving. Like other net investment demand, the consumer finance demand will be temporarily affected by the process of change in employment, but this we may neglect for present purposes. Otherwise, any recurring amount of consumer finance demand for funds will rapidly come to be matched by an equal amount of saving in the form of contractually forced repayments of past loans out of current income, so that the balance between saving and investment is little affected. Only when the introduction of some new durable consumers' good leads to a drastic alteration in the level of consumer loans will this component of net investment demand contribute strongly to the long-run dynamic tendency of total net investment demand.

Now if all the preceding is generally true, we see that net investment will have a potentially varying relation to net saving supply over time. Whereas saving responds more or less regularly to real income and employment, so that with any given real income we have a more or less given saving supply curve, the investment demand curve may stand in quite different positions at different times at the same level of employment. It follows that, as we have seen in preceding sections, the equilibrium level of employment at any given interest rate may be different at different times, as income moves to different levels to equate saving and investment. Underemployment equilibrium is possible at any attainable interest rate if net investment demand is very low; inflationary tendencies are possible if it is very high. The variability of net investment demand is thus of crucial importance.

THE INTEREST ELASTICITY OF NET INVESTMENT DEMAND

Of similar importance, however, is the interest-elasticity of net investment demand. We have seen that the reason that income movements take place to produce an equality of saving and investment—and thus set up systematic equilibrium employment tendencies rather than permitting any going income and employment level to be self-perpetuating—is that the interest rate will not move, or cannot be moved by the bank, to a level which will equate saving and investment at every going level of income. Underemployment tendencies emerge when the rate of interest will not fall or cannot be lowered to a rate which will equate investment with saving at a full-employment income; inflationary tendencies emerge when it will not rise or cannot be raised far enough to equate them at this employment level. (The barrier to sufficient movements in the interest rate in each case is essentially the liquidity demands or supplies of balance holders.) Now in this case it is clear that the efficacy of the interest rate as a stabilizer will be greater, and the probability of large income and employment adjustments to secure equality of S and I will be less, the greater the responsiveness of both saving and investment to the interest rate. If both were very responsive —that is, very interest-elastic—relatively small administered changes in the bank rate of interest would suffice to stabilize income and employment within a narrow range at any desired level, and such small changes would not tend to be blocked by liquidity adjustments of balance holders. Similarly, a free-moving interest rate with various money prices would tend to produce stability without any great movements away from the full-employment level. On the other hand, if both investment demand and saving supply are unresponsive to the interest rate—that is, interest-inelastic—large movements in the interest rate will be required to overcome any initial inequality between I and S; these may be blocked by liquidity adjustments; and large income and employment adjustments will then ensue, involving possibly either considerable unemployment or substantial price inflation.

Substantial importance thus attaches to the interest elasticity of both saving supply and investment demand. We have noted (pages 649 to 650) that the net saving supply curve is generally thought to be rather inelastic to the interest rate, reflecting the fact that individual plus business net saving at any income level will not be greatly affected by the interest rate of earning obtainable on investments. This insensitivity of saving to the interest rate is held to be explained in part by the fact that individual net savings generally constitute remainders of disposable income left after fulfilling the habitual consumption demands of net savers, and that these consumption demands are not much affected by the rate of earnings receivable on income not spent on consumption. In further part, it is explained by the fact that business net savings are made as a matter of relatively inflexible tradition or policy and not related to the interest rate. The saving supply curve may therefore be tentatively viewed as relatively interest-inelastic.

The net investment demand curve is likewise generally thought to be relatively inelastic to the interest rate. As we have observed (pages 612 to 615) the interest rate affects the demand for capital goods because a corresponding interest charge is in essence added to the price of capital goods services, and because this results in such services being substituted for those of labor and land to a lesser degree. Now the effect of the interest rate on the price of capital goods services—and, given the substitution conditions between these services and others, on the use of capital goods—will depend on the durability of the capital goods in question, or on the ratio of the total investment required to the annual value of services. With very long-lived capital equipment (for example, machines or other installations with fifty-year lives) the interest charge per unit of service will be substantial compared with that resulting from the initial purchase cost of the good; with short-lived equipment it will be a minor portion of the total cost of use.

Given this, it may be observed generally that the typical capital good in which net investment takes place is sufficiently short-lived that the interest rate does not greatly affect the price of its services, the extent to which it will be substituted for other factors, or the rate of investment in it. In other words, the interest rate, given the typical durability of investment goods and the character of the substitutability of their services for other factor services, has only a moderate or minor effect on the rate of net investment. This observation seems well substantiated by experience.

If now both the net investment demand curve and the net saving supply curve are relatively inelastic to the interest rate—and as far as we can tell they are—the shifts of position of the net investment demand curve over time will tend to have substantial effects on the level of real income and employment, since attainable interest rate adjustments will not suffice to equate saving and investment at relatively unchanged levels of employment. Therefore, underemployment or inflationary tendencies will tend to result from broad swings in the position of the net investment demand curve.

F. FURTHER MATTERS CONCERNING INTEREST AND EMPLOYMENT

THE SHARE OF INCOME EARNED AS INTEREST

Let us now turn to certain further matters concerning interest and employment which we have hitherto neglected—namely, the interest share in income, the place of risk in the determination of investment and the earnings therefrom, and the effect of governmental fiscal policy on income and employment.

The share of the net income stream going to capital goods—for their initial purchase and periodic replacement—is largely an indirect payment of wages to labor and rents to land. This is because capital goods are essentially commodities produced with labor and land. This income stream reaches labor and land as they are used to produce capital goods for net additions or replacement. If there were no cost of capital goods other than the wage and rent payments directly or indirectly involved, all income under competitive conditions would go to wages and rents, as prices were driven by competition to the level of costs. A certain proportion of land and labor would be employed in indirect or roundabout fashion to produce capital goods, depending upon the character of production techniques, but all income would in any event go to wages and rents. There would in long-run equilibrium be no profits, and there would be no net or additional return on capital goods.

Any net or additional payment arising from the use of capital goods must be in the nature of *interest,* and this emerges as a share of income because funds must be acquired for investment in capital goods, and because there is an interest charge or cost which must be paid to secure funds for investment. Interest must be paid to acquire funds for investment and to keep them invested; this payment is included in costs of production; prices tend to be adjusted under competition to equal total costs inclusive of interest; and a part of the income stream thus flows to the suppliers of investable funds. The total share of income which flows as interest will thus evidently depend upon the supply price of investable funds and on the total volume of funds invested.

What the supply price of investable funds is or would be under various circumstances can be analyzed, but the primarily relevant circumstance is that of the modern economy with a highly developed central banking system. Here and today, the rate of interest is an arbitrary rate set by the banking system and supported by a flexible supply of money. It will not be lower than some positive minimum at which the demand for liquidity would be unlimited, or higher than a maximum at which the demand for securities would be greater than the banking system can meet, and thus it is limited ultimately by the liquidity preference attitudes of the populace. But between these limits it tends to be an arbitrary rate set by banks in line with over-all economic and political policy.

In recent years, bank rates in the larger nations have ranged from 1½ to 5 percent per annum. Given some prevailing bank rate the supply of investable funds tends to be very elastic or even perfectly elastic at that rate of interest. That is, funds will be supplied in any amount ordinarily demanded at the rate the bank is supporting, the banks standing ready to meet demands not met by nonbank sources or to absorb supplies not taken by nonbank demands. Funds in the aggregate thus tend to be in very elastic supply, and investors will tend to earn, net of risk premiums paid to counterbalance defaults on principal, the same bank rate of interest, more or less regardless of the level of total investment. Given this relatively fixed price of funds—say 2 percent—all invested money will tend to earn a net 2 cents per dollar per annum. The total *amount* of income going as interest will then depend mainly on the amount of funds invested, and the *share* of income will depend upon this and upon the ratio of total accumulated investment to total income.

Investment of funds occurs primarily in capital goods, and secondarily in consumer loans. Either will yield a rate of interest and provide the supplier of funds with a share of income while his funds are invested. The quantity of investment in consumer loans is not easy to appraise analytically, but it would appear to vary roughly with the level of income. Some relatively stable though small proportion of total income thus flows as interest on consumer loans. The quantity of investment in capital goods tends to reach a limit in any given state of techniques, products, population, etc.— and within such a state it will vary somewhat with income and employment. Currently, the quantity of investment is very large, and the share of business income paid as interest is sizable.

With progressive changes in techniques, population, and so forth, total investment in capital goods has tended historically to increase. But because of corresponding increases in total income, resulting from increases in efficiency and in amounts of other factors, the ratio of accumulated investment to income has not increased indefinitely, and apparently tends after a point to become relatively stable. Although the continually increasing use of capital goods has raised the amount of income paid to interest, it has been matched in part at least by corresponding increases in wages and rents, so that the share of income going to interest has not increased in proportion. Summarizing, it is true, with a relatively fixed interest rate, that the share of income going to interest at any current time is substantial but limited by the limitation on the demand for capital goods and consumer loans, and that the increase of the interest proportion of income as accumulated investment increases over time is retarded or entirely checked by the associated increase in total income.[22]

In any event, a certain share of income in a capitalist economy flows as interest paid to investors for the investment of their funds, and this payment tends on the average to be at a rate on invested funds corresponding to the bank rate of interest. Does this mean that every investor receives every month a rate corresponding to the current market or bank rate on the current valuation of his investment? This would be true if the amounts of capital goods would be currently adjusted without lag to changing interest rates, and if all investment contracts and loans were continually rewritten from day to day as necessary to adjust for changing market conditions.

In fact, of course, neither of these conditions is fully observed, and as a consequence the amounts "earned" by capital goods may vary from the current market rate of interest on original investment value, and the

[22] Additional interest returns are of course earned by those who buy nonwasting assets (land) at the discounted present value of future rents. We must add these to interest returns from capital goods and consumer loans to arrive at the full total for the economy.

amounts received by investors as interest payments may vary from the current "earnings" on their investments. Investments in capital goods which have been made to "earn" a 2-percent rate of interest will continue to yield at this rate even though the market rate of interest later drops to 1 or rises to 3 percent, until the amount of capital goods can be adjusted. Thus, the enterprise may currently realize from its capital goods an earning different from the current market rate, and this discrepancy can be corrected only in the long run.

Further, the money earning on capital goods may vary in response to price and income variations in the economy, so that the investment yields more or less than was anticipated at the time it was made. Thus, a 100-percent increase in the price level might double the imputed money earning of a $5,000 original investment in a machine—might double its annual earnings (say from $150 to $300) actually raising its "value" to $10,000. If, in addition, the investor who supplied the funds holds a $5,000 3-percent bond, he will continue to receive annual interest of $150, and the enterprise will receive the balance of current interest as a "profit." The current flow of earnings on capital goods may thus deviate from the current rate of interest on original investment. Further, the amounts received by investors, and especially by creditors on fixed interest contract, may deviate from current earnings. These discrepancies arise respectively from deviations from a previous equilibrium adjustment, which influence the income flow, and from fixed investment contracts, which put the enterprise in a position to pay to investors more or less than current economic interest and to absorb the difference. Subject to such qualifications, our generalization concerning the interest share in income is substantially accurate.

Who receives the interest share? This is more than a needlessly obvious question, because funds are supplied by banks as well as by individuals. The interest share of income, then, flows in the first place to individuals who have supplied funds for investment, or to their descendants who inherit their accumulations. These accumulations originally tend to result from savings out of income, although the income may be variously earned, and, if it is large, saving may not result in any perceptible degree of privation on the part of the saver. Such interest is a reward to individuals for accumulating and making available funds for investment; it is "needed," if not to induce saving, at any rate to induce investors to part from liquidity. In the second place, however, an interest share of income also flows to banks, in return for the supply of funds which they create by expanding their credit. Under modern conditions, a bank is a special sort of private business enterprise, licensed and controlled by the government, one of whose functions is to create credit. Banks are essentially franchised to "manufacture" money, albeit under strict limitations, and to make it available in return for an interest payment. A part of interest is thus a payment to investors in banking enterprises, received in connection with the performance of this special function. It is worth re-emphasizing that the government, through its central-bank organization, undertakes to regulate this rate of earning, and thus also the rate of interest on individual accumulations of funds.

RISK, RISK PREMIUMS, AND INTEREST

In the preceding discussion of the determination of the interest rate, and concurrently of investment, employment, and so forth, we have implicitly abstracted from the phenomenon of risk or uncertainty concerning future yields on investments and correspondingly concerning recoveries or repayments of funds supplied.

To be sure, uncertainty has been recognized in a general way as accounting for liquidity preference; we have seen that people wish to hold cash balances in part because they wish to have cash on hand to meet unforeseen (and therefore a priori uncertain) contingencies of an adverse sort, and because they may anticipate (though presumably with less than complete certainty) declines in the price of goods and securities. Such rather broad uncertainty concerning certain types of future events has thus been recognized as one of the determinants of the interest rate on money; its effect is reflected in the shapes and positions of the gross hoarding demand and gross dishoarding supply curves which interact with investment demand and saving supply to determine this rate.

What we have not recognized at all is the uncertainty of those supplying funds for investment or for purchasing old assets or securities as to whether the promised yield or interest return will actually be earned or paid, and as to whether the principal amount supplied will be repaid (if this is promised) or maintained available for repayment if continued investment of the funds is contemplated. And we have not recognized the effects of this sort of uncertainty on the rate of investment or on the returns to those who supply funds.

In effect, we have spoken as if there were something like complete certainty concerning the future yields on investment and promised returns to suppliers represented in the demand curves for investable funds, so that funds were always supplied with the complete assurance on the part of the supplier that he would receive the promised interest return and recover or maintain his principal, and complete assurance on the part of the demander that he would earn the anticipated amount (if investment for future earning be involved) and thus not suffer losses, insolvency, or bankruptcy.

If the implicitly assumed certainty just described existed, then the rate of investment (and of supply of funds) would be unaffected by the riskiness of investment, and the rate of interest determined and paid to suppliers of investable funds would be essentially a *pure* rate of interest payable for the use of funds in the absence of any risk as to the receipt of promised interest payments or the recovery or maintenance of principal. It is the determination of such an interest rate which we have analyzed in this chapter. Correspondingly, the determination of the rate of investment and associated matters has been described as if there were no risk in investment or to suppliers of funds.

An entirely satisfactory analysis of investment, interest, income, and so forth should therefore elaborate the foregoing analysis by introducing appropriate assumptions concerning the phenomenon of risk. Full development of the theory along this line, however, would be a very complicated task, and would consume more space than is available in an introductory basic treatment. Therefore, we shall confine ourselves here to a brief statement concerning the principal ways in which the conclusions of our simplified theory would be modified by a recognition of the risk phenomenon.

First, the rate of investment will tend to be sufficiently restricted that, on balance and in view of risks, investors have at least an even chance of receiving pure interest returns and recovering or maintaining principal. If each investment or category of like investments in general can have any of many results as to yield, ranging from complete loss of principal and no earnings at one extreme to very large returns at another, and including many intermediate outcomes in between (each outcome having some relative probability in the minds of investors), it will tend to be carried to the point where the probability of gain over and above the pure interest rate required at least balances the probability of loss. (We could omit the "at least" if we were sure investors in general were willing to gamble at even odds; if they are supercautious as a group, they might insist on the average on the odds favoring them.)

For a very simple example, suppose that twenty-one similar investments can be made to yield the pure market rate of interest of 2 percent on $100,000 per investment, to yield 7 percent on $75,000 per investment, and to yield 10 percent on $50,000 per investment. Suppose furthermore that these promised yields are subject to a one-to-twenty chance of complete loss of principal. That is, there is on every investment one chance in twenty-one that nothing will be earned and the principal will be completely lost, and twenty chances that the investment will be successful and earn the anticipated yield. The odds favoring a successful investment are thus twenty-to-one. (We suppose for sake of simplicity only two possible outcomes—"success" at the anticipated yield, with twenty-to-one odds in favor, and complete failure with one-to-twenty odds against.) Investable funds are available by assumption in return for a pure interest rate (net of risk) of 2 percent. Now in this case, investors will (if they are even-odds gamblers) presumably invest $75,000 apiece in the twenty-one opportunities in question. At this rate, each investment promises to yield (1) a 2 percent pure interest rate if successful, plus (2) a 5-percent extra return if successful. This 5-percent extra return in case of success outweighs the one-to-twenty chance of loss of principal, so that an even-odds gambler would be satisfied. He would have an even chance of recovering the principal and earning 2 percent pure interest on it. If, of course, investors were unwilling to gamble at even odds, they might invest less—for example $50,000 per opportunity.

In terms of demand and supply curves for funds, the preceding phenomenon would be reflected in either of two ways. The supply curve for funds might be raised by adding to the pure interest rate required a "risk rate," receivable by the supplier of funds if the enterprise were successful. This would tend to be the case if the suppliers were creditors entitled to a limited fixed return (in case of success), and if the owner of the capital assets acquired were a borrower obligated to pay the return and maintain principal if possible. Or the demand curve for funds might be effectively shifted backward (to the left or down) so as to reflect anticipated rates of return net of the risk of loss involved. This would tend to be the case if the investors were owners with an equity interest in the assets acquired, entitled to receive whatever the investment earned or take any losses. They would thus restrict their investment of their own funds so as to compensate for risk. The preceding applies strictly to the simple case of only two alternative anticipations (success at a given level or complete loss); if there were numerous alternative anticipations, the picture would be more complex. In all cases, however, the general principles stated apply.

It should be noted that in general not all categories of investment will be equally "risky"—some will have relatively certain returns and some may be highly speculative in character. Consequently, the risk rates added to the pure interest rate in determining investments in different lines may be considerably different.

The second effect of the risk phenomenon is that the returns of suppliers of funds will be affected by the variation of actual returns around the mean expectation of returns. We have seen that creditors faced with risk will be contractually guaranteed a rate of return in addition to the pure rate of interest to compensate for the possibility of loss. If the risk calculations have been correct, this will mean that creditors of successful enterprises will receive an extra risk premium, whereas creditors of failing enterprises will incur losses. In the example above, assuming even-odds gambling, twenty creditors might receive a 5 percent risk premium reward (in addition to 2 percent pure interest) in a given year, whereas the twenty-first lost his principal entirely. Similarly, twenty successful equity investors would receive a gross return of 7 percent, whereas the twenty-first would lose all.

If investors effectively gamble at even odds, and if their probability calculations concerning future returns are on the average correct, risk premiums should not constitute a separate share of net income. That is, actual losses should then occur frequently enough and in sufficient volume to offset the risk premiums paid on investments which succeed. The aggregate net earning for risk-taking would then be zero, although some would lose and others gain superior returns. On the other hand, "conservative" investors who refused to gamble at even odds might earn a net risk premium on the average, and consistent failure to calculate probabilities correctly could lead to "windfall" gains and losses to those in a position to receive residual profits. In assessing actual returns to investment, however, it is important to remember that returns in excess of a basic interest rate may include monopoly profits as well as risk premiums.

A third effect of risk is actually to restrict the volume of physical investment. The fact that every investment is restricted because some investments may lose means that total investment is restricted. In effect, the money and real cost of losses from unsuccessful and unproductive investments is added to the cost of successful or productive investments via the mechanism of risk rewards, and this retards the rate of productive investment accordingly. Risk (and the thing it reflects—periodic loss of investment) is a real cost to the economy and a retardant to total investment. It is obvious, however, that in a dynamic economy risk and its cost are unavoidable.[23]

[23] The present treatment of risk is extremely simplified and omits certain significant phenomena arising from uncertainty. For suggestions of a more advanced treatment, see A. G. Hart, "Risk, Uncertainty, and the Unprofitability of Compounding Probabilities," *Readings in the Theory of Income Distribution,* Chap. 28.

A further required amendment in our interest theory as developed to this point results from the fact that we have pursued our discussion of interest and investment on the assumption that there is for the whole economy a single "competitive" market for funds, unaffected by monopoly power on the part of suppliers or monopsony power on the part of borrowers. Funds would thus be secured for investment throughout the economy at the same basic pure rate of interest. To what extent do these assumptions lead us into inaccurate conclusions concerning interest and investment? A full analysis of banking operations and of money and security markets, which would be essential to the answering of this question, lies outside the scope of this volume. Nevertheless, it may be useful to comment briefly on the potential importance of monopoly and monopsony in the market for investable funds.

The meaning of a "competitive" price or interest rate for funds is rather special, since it is essentially a rate dictated by the central-banking system according to broad principles of policy. The central bank endeavors in general to support an interest rate and to provide a perfectly elastic supply of funds at this rate throughout the economy. All other suppliers of funds are in a general way in competition with this rate and tend to be forced toward it so far as funds originating with the central bank effectively compete with them in supplying particular borrowers. The competitive rate is thus the rate supported by the central-banking system. Monopoly power in supplying funds would consist of the ability to charge a higher than competitive rate; monopsony power would consist of the ability either to secure a lower than competitive rate or to negate monopoly power and secure a competitive rate in spite of monopoly. What

GOVERNMENT FISCAL POLICY, INVESTMENT, AND INTEREST

We have so far referred to the use of investable funds entirely in terms of private or nongovernmental investment, undertaken by business enterprises for a profit or by individuals to increase their current purchases of consumers' goods. This is the appropriate emphasis in a capitalist economy, where the bulk of investment activity is privately conducted and based on motives of individual advantage. Nevertheless, the governments under which capitalist economies operate may also borrow funds, potentially in very large amounts, to finance routine or emergency expenditures. Government debts tend to increase most in times of war, when it is politically more expedient to finance armament expenditures by borrowing than by taxes. Govern-

we are basically interested in, then, is deviations of particular interest rates throughout the economy from the rate supported by the central bank.

Monopolistic deviations may stem potentially from two facts. First, the market for funds is not a single unified market accessible to all borrowers. Rather it is made up of one or more central markets accessible to large borrowers or to securities issued by these borrowers, and of a large number of small submarkets each with a group of small borrowers who because of geographical and institutional barriers do not have full or direct access to other submarkets or to the central money markets. Second, the various submarkets are not directly supplied by the central bank but are only indirectly influenced by it. The specific suppliers in submarkets may be a few commercial banks or other lending institutions which have some monopoly power over the borrowers in these markets and can exact what is implicitly a higher than competitive rate of interest. For such local markets the central bank may attempt to influence the interest rate by supplying the commercial banks with funds at the competitive rate. But these and other lending institutions may exploit their local monopoly position and charge a higher rate to borrowers.

For many small borrowers in local markets—especially for businesses too small to establish a "credit" or risk rating in the central markets and for consumers who wish to borrow to finance purchases—there may thus be interest rates somewhat in excess of the "competitive" level. Such monopolistic pricing of funds is restrictive of investment (or may tend to divert investment opportunities to large business firms) and is also a potential source of extra earnings to monopolistic suppliers of funds.

Large borrowers, on the other hand, are not limited to a single submarket and generally have access to the central money markets of New York. For them, the danger of monopolistic exploitation in the supply of funds is decidedly less, both because they have access to a variety of suppliers, and because in many cases they are big enough that their monopsony buying power serves as a protection against exploitation. Nevertheless, it may be noted that in the organization of investing institutions and investment banking in the central markets there are possibilities for the monopolistic control of very large amounts of funds, and that automatic adherence to the "competitive" rate is not a foregone conclusion. Viewing the picture as a whole, we must take some account of deviations of the interest charge from the competitive level on specific loans or classes of loans. Such deviations are probably not persistent enough or large enough to require any serious alteration in our general conclusions. But a detailed study of money and interest would reveal a great many matters which we have overlooked.

mental agencies may also borrow to finance peacetime expenditures, however, such as those on public works, or on aid to foreign countries. Under the pressure of prolonged wars, the government debt may easily become comparable in magnitude to the total private debt, and its accumulation, maintenance, and possible repayment may have considerable effects on the level of activity in the private economy.

Additions to the government debt—current government expenditures financed by a deficit—constitute an addition to the current flow of "investment" in the economy. When the government borrows (from individuals or banks or both) and spends $10 billion, this is a gross addition of $10 billion to expenditure in the economy; so far as the government borrowing operation has not caused any curtailment of private investment or increase of saving or consumption, it is a net addition to expenditure. If the government is maintaining a fixed interest rate through the central bank, and if it does nothing to encourage saving, most of the addition should be net. Government deficit-financed spending, with corresponding *additions* to government debt, thus tends to create income in much the same fashion as private investment. Income for a period will tend to move to the level where saving from it is equal to private investment of the period plus the government deficit of the period. The possibility of using governmental deficit finance to create larger income suggests its use as a means of lessening unemployment in times of depression or chronic stagnation, and it was so used in the period from 1933 to 1941. Wartime deficit-financed spending has the same general income-generating effect, but often the wartime deficits are so large as to keep income rising (with investment above saving) after full employment is reached, and thus to propagate considerable price inflation. This may also occur in peacetime if government deficits are added to an already adequate flow of private investment. Since at least a part of additions to the government debt will ordinarily go to the banks, the rise in income which it generates will be matched by some corresponding rise in the amount of money in circulation, and possibly by increased liquidity relative to income.[24]

Additions to the government debt thus tend to have the same general effect on current income as does private investment. What of the effect of the maintenance or "servicing" of the debts through interest payments? Here we must draw one distinction. So far as the government has invested in revenue-producing projects, such as hydroelectric plants or toll bridges, its operation is very much like that of a private enterprise, in that it collects from users of the service and disburses interest payments along with other costs. So far as its investments are not revenue-producing, however, either

[24] For a discussion of the issues raised above, see A. H. Hansen, *Economic Policy and Full Employment.*

because the expenditure results in no lasting assets—as in the case of munitions—or because it is not expedient to collect directly for the service—as in the case of many educational or recreational projects—then the debt must be serviced from tax revenues. In this case, a share of income is diverted from taxpayers and paid as interest to government bondholders. Since World War II, an important portion of the total "interest" share in income is so collected and paid to bond-holding individuals and banks. The burden of this interest payment is borne by people not necessarily in proportion to benefits accruing from the original investment, but in such proportions as are determined by the principles of taxation in effect. The "cost" is borne in a manner determined by governmental decision rather than by a free market. Large government debts thus tend to introduce an important inflexible element into the pattern of income distribution, and to make taxation an important instrument in redistributing income in accordance with a rather fixed pattern.

The repayment of the principal of a government debt is by no means inevitable, since it may be "refunded" indefinitely over the future. When repayments are undertaken, they may tend in general to have the reverse effect from additions to debt. That is, tax revenues which in part at least tend to reduce consumption spending are used to redeem bonds as they mature, and the former bondholders (including banks) will tend not to spend most of their redemption payments on consumption. Thus, debt repayment tends in general to be a deflationary or income-destroying operation and is best undertaken in periods of superabundant income.

It should be added that governmental fiscal policy with respect to taxing and spending may be by no means neutral in its effect on income and employment. When it collects tax receipts and spends them, the government may influence the flow of money income in two principal ways. First, it may tax away money which would otherwise be saved, thus reducing the private supply of saving and diverting it to spending, with a resultant stimulus to the flow of income in the economy, since the relation of a given private investment demand to saving will thus favor increased income. (If, of course, it taxes away money which would otherwise be spent on consumption, it will not affect income; if it reduces spending by taxes which it uses to repay debts, and if the repaid creditors hoard the proceeds, it will reduce income.) Second, the collection of taxes on income may effectively reduce the net income from investments remaining to investors, and thus reduce the private demand for investable funds. As this occurs, taxation may have a dampening effect on income and employment unless it reduces saving by as much as private investment. Whether this is desirable or not of course will depend in part on whether or not there are inflationary tendencies present in the economy.

The preceding few remarks do not constitute a thorough review of governmental fiscal operations; for this we must refer the student to more specialized works.

SUPPLEMENTARY READINGS

JOHN MAYNARD KEYNES, *The General Theory of Employment, Interest, and Money*, Chaps. 8-10, 13-21.

ALVIN H. HANSEN, *Fiscal Policy and Business Cycles*, Chaps. 1-3, 11-14.

GOTTFRIED VON HABERLER, *Prosperity and Depression* (2d ed.), Geneva: League of Nations, 1939, Chap. 8.

ERIK LUNDBERG, *Studies in the Theory of Economic Expansion*, London: King, 1937.

HOWARD S. ELLIS, "Monetary Policy and Investment," *Readings in Business Cycle Theory*, Philadelphia: The Blakiston Company, 1944, Chap. 20.

FRIEDRICH A. LUTZ, "The Structure of Interest Rates," *Readings in the Theory of Income Distribution*, Philadelphia: The Blakiston Company, 1946, Chap. 26.

FRANK H. KNIGHT, "Capital and Interest," *ibid.*, Chap. 21.

15 INCOME DISTRIBUTION UNDER DYNAMIC CONDITIONS

The bulk of this volume, prior to the treatment in the preceding chapter of the level of income and employment, was devoted to an analysis successively of the pricing of commodities and of factor pricing and income distribution. This analysis was conducted generally, whenever the operation of the economy as a whole was contemplated, on the assumption of stable full-employment conditions, which would emerge presumably from a self-sustaining constant flow of money income relative to which all prices could freely adjust.

We have now seen that stable full employment is in fact not automatically attained in an enterprise economy. It may be attained if the interest rate adjusts or can be adjusted to equate saving and investment at a full-employment level of income, for in this case the ratio of factor and commodity prices to money income will remain such as to employ all resources offered for use. But it also may not be attained. Investment may exceed saving at full-employment income, in which case progressive inflation (probably with full employment, but without stability) will tend to ensue. And investment may be less than saving at full-employment income. In this event an underemployment equilibrium will be approached, and money prices will be unable to adjust relative to money income to secure full employment, but will rather be able to reach only a somewhat higher ratio to income which permits a lower level of employment.[1] We thus have three distinct sorts of possible employment-income tendencies to be considered: full employment with stable money income and price level, rising money income and price level probably with full employment, and less than full employment with either stable or declining money income and prices.

The theories of commodity pricing and income distribution developed through Chapter 13 apply directly only to the first of these situations. There-

[1] This is because money income will tend to adjust downward with every price decline so that the employment or real income equilibrium at underemployment levels is not overcome (see pp. 683 to 688). It will hold generally as long as progressive price declines do not, by building up liquidity relative to needs, eventually affect the relation of saving to real income.

fore, a question is now posed as to how much and in what way these theories must be amended or elaborated in order to give adequate predictions of pricing and income distribution under other than stable full-employment conditions.

Unfortunately, pricing and income distribution theories have not as yet been fully and formally developed on the assumptions of underemployment or of inflationary tendencies. It is not our purpose here, moreover, to develop a new body of theory to fill the gap. Therefore, we shall confine ourselves to a series of comments on the major evident directions in which the pricing and income distribution theories previously developed would be modified if we relaxed our assumption of stable full employment in the economy. To this we shall add some summary remarks on profit as a distributive share.

A. COMMODITY PRICING UNDER DYNAMIC CONDITIONS

NECESSARY AMENDMENTS TO THE THEORY OF
COMMODITY PRICING

Since the theory of commodity pricing is actually concerned largely with the explanation of price-cost relations (that is, the relation of commodity to factor prices) and with the allocation of resources among uses with given income and factor prices, its conclusions do not tend to be fundamentally modified by the assumption of other than stable full-employment settings. If we assume *any* relation of money income to factor prices to be given or determined, commodity prices will tend to be determined relative to factor prices and relative to each other according to the same principles which govern this determination under stable full employment. No general revision of commodity pricing analysis is therefore required.

The following specific amendments in the conclusions of price theory, however, may be suggested. First, under conditions of underemployment equilibrium there may be a tendency toward lower utilization of productive capacity than expected under full employment, lower prices relative to average costs, and lower profits. This will be true, however, only if the enterprise system (or significant parts of it) has adjusted its plant capacity to supply the outputs of a larger level of employment and thus faces what is essentially a short-run excess-capacity problem during an underemployment period. If underemployment should persist long enough for enterprises to make a full long-run adjustment to the restricted level of employment (with its inadequate ratio of money income to factor prices), this equilibrium should have the same properties as those ascribed to full-employment equilibrium in all essential respects. The same adaptation of firm and industry marginal and average costs to prices should tend to emerge at the restricted level of aggregate demand for goods and with a restricted total output.

A further aspect of economies with underemployment is that money prices may fall progressively as factor prices are adjusted downward in an unsuccessful attempt to increase employment. If this phenomenon is encountered, enterprise profits will be favorably or adversely affected depending on whether factor or commodity prices lead the price decline. Prediction of which prices in general will lead the decline, however, would require a very complex analysis into which we shall not enter here.

Second, suppose there are conditions of progressive inflation, resulting from the fact that, after full employment is reached, investment exceeds saving in every period, thus propagating a rise in money income and money prices which does not overcome the excess of investment. In this situation the analysis of commodity pricing with stable full employment should apply with the following amendment. With rising factor and commodity prices, enterprise profits will be favorably or adversely affected depending on whether commodity or factor prices lead the general price increase. A long-accepted view here has been that commodity prices tend to lead an increase (presumably since commodities feel the first impact of rising money demand), with the result that enterprises enjoy extra "windfall" gains from price inflation. With the combination of strong and aggressive labor unions which continually push wage increases, and of business concerns which may be under pressure by the government to go slow on increasing prices, any net tendency of commodity prices either to lead or to lag factor-price increases is hard to establish. In specific lines of production, however, distinct leads and lags may be found, with corresponding effects on profits line by line.

Third, under conditions of fluctuating income and employment, there will of course be corresponding fluctuations of enterprise outputs and profits. The short-run price analysis previously developed (pages 130 to 142), however, seems to predict the behavior expected here reasonably well.

EFFECTS OF COMMODITY PRICING TENDENCIES
ON THE LEVEL OF EMPLOYMENT

In addition, some recognition should be given to the influence which commodity pricing tendencies may themselves have on the level of income and employment. Two major sorts of influence may be mentioned here.

First, the size of enterprise profits, as determined by the relation of prices to average costs, may have some influence on the equilibrium level of employment, both by affecting the relation of saving to real income and by affecting the rate of investment. In general, higher profits will lead to a more unequal distribution of income for the economy as a whole, since profit receivers are generally relatively few and of higher-than-average income to begin with. This increased inequality of income will tend to increase saving at any given level of income, since more income will now be in the hands of persons whose consumption needs are fully satisfied with less than their entire incomes, and who tend to save the bulk of any increments thereto. This will mean that any given level of net investment will generate a smaller level of real income and employment. We may say, therefore, that higher profits tend, via their effect on the relation of consumption and saving to income, to reduce the ratio of money income to prices and to retard employment. It would follow from this that increasingly monopolistic pricing tendencies have a deflationary impact, whereas competitive pricing tendencies have a reverse effect.

Unfortunately from the standpoint of simplified predictions, there is a potentially offsetting effect of profits on employment. Higher profits tend in general to stimulate investment, and this tends to stimulate employment. We are not currently in a position to assesss the net effect on employment of monopolistic high-profit tendencies.

A second effect of commodity pricing tendencies on employment arises from the pricing of capital goods. It is clear that the higher the prices of capital goods relative to the minimum attainable costs of their production, the smaller will be the quantity of these goods which is acquired for investment, since the substitution of their services for those of directly used labor and land will be accordingly retarded. The effect of a higher price on investment spending, however, will depend on the elasticity of demand for capital goods. If this demand is inelastic, higher prices will increase the demand for investable funds; if it is elastic, they will reduce it. Monopolistic pricing of capital goods therefore tends to retard or increase investment demand depending upon whether the demand for capital goods is elastic or inelastic.

B. FACTOR PRICING UNDER DYNAMIC CONDITIONS

FACTOR PRICING WITH UNDEREMPLOYMENT

The conclusions of our factor-price analysis as developed under assumptions of stable full employment (Chapters 11-13) should apply, with one exception to be noted, to any situation wherein investment equals saving at a full-employment income level. They need not be reviewed here. Some amendments to the theory are required, however, for the situation of underemployment equilibrium.

When there are underemployment tendencies in an economy, saving exceeds investment at full employment, and income and employment tend to decline to such a level that saving out of income equals investment at some lower level. When this tendency is present, three results are possible.

First, money factor prices generally may remain rigid (or relatively so), and money income and all money prices may then become stable (or relatively so) at a determinate underemployment level. Thus, money income will move relative to eventually fixed money prices to an equilibrium level with a corresponding equilibrium of employment. Second, some strategic major money factor price may remain rigid, while money income and all other money prices adjust downward and reach an equilibrium level involving underemployment of the rigid-priced factor. Third, all money factor prices may progressively decline or be reduced in order to overcome the unemployment of resources, but the reduction will fail to eliminate unemployment because money income will always decline in proportion.[2] Then money income and prices will fall indefinitely, with persistent unemployment unless they fall (as they will not) fluidly, without lags, and at great speed.

In the last event—progressive decline of all factor prices with progressive deflation of money income and prices generally—the *relative* prices of employed factors may well be different than they would at a full-employment equilibrium. Although all of them are falling, some may fall more rapidly or quickly than others, and in this event the less flexible factor prices will maintain higher relative prices than under full-employment equilibrium. If they do, the effect in the shares of total income they receive will of course depend on the elasticity of demand for their services. The same observations apply as among the various subdivisions of a given factor supply—for example, as among different parts of the total labor supply.

In the event that *all* money factor prices are rigid, their relative prices will of course depend on the potentially arbitrary levels at which they remain unchanged. Suppose, however, that only one major factor price is rigid (or relatively so), whereas the others fall relatively freely in order to seek full employment. Then money income will not decline indefinitely, but will seek an equilibrium level at which (1) saving equals investment, (2) there is a given unemployment of the rigid-priced factor, and (3) there is full employment of the flexible-priced factors. (The "full-employment" level of the flexible-priced factors will be less than if all of the remaining factor were employed, since their relative prices will be lower and will attract fewer of them into employment.) In this case, it is obvious that the pattern of relative factor prices will be quite different from that associated with over-all full employment, and the shares of the reduced net income will also be different depending on relative elasticities of demand for the different factors. In this setting the seller of any factor is in a position to practice monopolistic pricing simply by holding a rigid money price while other factor prices decline.

  [2] Unless the rise in liquidity eventually results in reduction in saving in relation to real income (see p. 687 above).

FACTOR PRICING UNDER INFLATIONARY CONDITIONS

If investment persistently exceeds saving at a full-employment income, the increase of money income tends to induce a rise of all factor prices. Competitively determined factor prices would rise automatically; administered or monopolistically set factor prices (and those set by bilateral monopoly bargaining) will tend to be raised. Each factor-price increase, moreover, sets the stage for another, since the excess of investment over saving will not tend to be corrected thereby.

In this setting, the relative prices of the different factors will be altered from those found in stable full employment if some rise or are administratively raised more rapidly than others. Greater lags in the competitive increases of some than of others will have this effect, as will more aggressive monopolistic price-raising policies in some sectors than in others.

It should be noted, moreover, that in such an inflationary situation, inflation may be accentuated by administered factor-price increases more rapid than would be induced under competitive pricing by the rise of money income. If money income tends to adjust to a given ratio to factor prices (this ratio being determined by the relation of real net investment to real saving) regardless of the money level of factor prices—and this because money investment and money saving at a given employment level move proportionally with the price level—then *any* administered increase in factor prices will tend to generate a corresponding money income and price increase, with no net effect on employment. Thus any administered general factor-price increase (such as a general wage rise forced by unions) will tend to produce a more or less proportionate inflation of income and all prices. It is interesting to note that, *after the rest of the economy has adjusted to such a factor-price increase,* the factor sellers who have hiked price will be no better off than before, with unchanged employment and all prices having risen in proportion. By leading the process of price increases, however, they may enhance their real prices and (given appropriate elasticity of demand for their services) their shares of total income during the period of adjustment. If they raise their prices frequently enough to keep the economy "always adjusting," they may remain perpetually ahead of those whose prices rise in a lagging fashion. Factor monopoly is thus likely to be effective (aside from counteracting monopsony) mainly in altering the relative factor prices of some fraction of factor suppliers at the expense of others, or in permitting some or all factor prices to lead an inflationary movement while other prices lag.

The possibility of inflation being induced by administered factor-price increases has so far been associated with a setting which is in any event somewhat inflationary—where investment exceeds saving at full-employ-

ment income. It is also quite conceivable with conditions of stable full employment, and not unconceivable with underemployment equilibrium tendencies, that factor monopolies might propagate inflationary tendencies by
successive administered increases in their factor prices. (So far as money
income will adjust to factor prices so as to maintain a given equilibrium
employment level, this is certainly true). And factor monopolists may have
a definite incentive to do so once they have learned or sensed the fundamental truth that they can stay ahead of other income recipients whose prices
will lag their own in the inflationary process. Such propagated inflationary
processes, moreover, are undesirable for many reasons, not the least of which
is that there is a large class of income recipients whose salaries or other incomes rise only with great lags when prices generally increase, and that they
are subjected to severe inequities by inflation. Higher and yet higher wages
for the working man—if their result is progressive inflation and only the
gains of inflationary change to the worker—are far from self-justifying.

C. PROFIT AS A DISTRIBUTIVE SHARE

THE EMERGENCE OF PROFIT

Net income is distributed in capitalism as it flows through a system of producing enterprises and is paid out by these enterprises as they acquire productive serivces from labor, the owners of land, and the suppliers of investable funds. Thus, the purchasing power which enters firms as sales receipts
finds its way around the circuit to emerge as purchasing power again. The
bulk of the net income flow at any time is evidently distributed as wages,
rent, and interest. Most of those income payments are made to *hired* factors—to individuals not identified with the enterprise ownership, or to employed labor, rented land, and borrowed capital. But a share of wages, rent,
and interest is ordinarily received by the enterprise ownership for the services
which it supplies itself. A fair portion of the funds invested in enterprise is
ordinarily owner-supplied and stands to earn an interest return for the
owners, and the owners may also supply managerial or other labor as well
as land.

For the share of wages, rent, and interest receivable by enterprise ownership, no definite contract may be written. The ownership may receive its
imputed labor, land, and capital earnings simply as an undifferentiated aggregate left over from sales receipts after making payments to hired factors
and allowing for the use of capital equipment. Such an aggregate difference
is "accounting profit"; it is this difference which accountants compute periodically and designate as the "net profit" of the enterprise. Yet, so far as
this "accounting profit" is made up of wage, interest, or rent payments imputable to services supplied by the enterprise ownership (taking these serv-

ices at their market value), there is logically no additional share of net income discovered, but only a distinction between contractual wages, rent, and interest and imputed wages, rent, and interest.

A question, therefore, arises whether enterprise ownership is generally able to claim any share of income in addition to the market value of the labor, land, and capital it supplies. The enterprise owners in general take a residual share, or accounting profit, representing the difference between sales receipts and amounts paid to hired factors.[3] Does this accounting residual include more than imputed wages, interest, and rent? Any such additional share would generally be referred to as an economic profit, true profit, or *pure profit*. Let us draw together various suggestions from our preceding discussions and consider the probable existence and the sources of a true profit share of income.

THE ABSENCE OF PROFITS IN PURELY COMPETITIVE EQUILIBRIUM

The discussion of equilibrium tendencies in purely competitive industries or economies (Chapters 4 and 11) revealed that in these instances pure profits would move toward zero. With free entry to all industries and market-controlled prices not subject to direct influence by any seller, prices and outputs would move in long-run equilibrium to a point where all sellers produced with selling price equal to the minimum average costs of production. These average costs would be made up directly or indirectly of contractual wages, interest, and rents plus similar shares imputed to ownership at competitive market prices. When these costs were paid, the entire sales receipts of enterprise would be distributed and no true profit share would remain. The accounting profit or residual received by enterprise owners would be composed only of competitive interest on owners' invested funds and competitive wages and rent imputed to owner-supplied labor and land.[4] Such an accounting residual has been referred to as a "normal profit" or an earning including "no excess profit"; it corresponds to having true or pure profits equal to zero. Such zero profits would characterize long-run purely competitive equilibrium, although short-run adjustments toward this equilibrium might permit of positive or negative profits for transitional periods.

It will thus appear that if pure profits do arise, this will be because of departure either from pure competition or from long-run equilibrium. Profits must in general result from monopolistic or monopsonistic tendencies in pricing, from a process of dynamic change in which long-run equilibrium is not persistently attained, or from both.

[3] After setting aside as a depreciation allowance an amount sufficient to maintain wasting capital goods.

[4] See the qualified exception stated where the enterprise has a growing capital stock (pp. 609 to 611).

Before turning to these sources of profit, however, we should refer again to the so-called rewards of risk bearing. It was pointed out in Chapter 14 (pages 700 to 703) that where any risk is involved, the explicit yield on investable funds is calculated to include a premium for the assumption of this risk. Where the basic interest rate is 2 percent, for example, capital goods may be substituted for other factors only down to a point where their yield in the event of success over cost should be 6 percent, on the theory that there is a 4-percent chance of losing the investment entirely. Any successful enterprise may thus earn, in addition to basic wages, interest, and rent, an extra amount representing a premium for risk of loss successfully avoided. Part of this may be paid to creditors in addition to interest, so far as creditor securities have had to yield a premium rate. And part will ordinarily accumulate in the residual going to owners as a return on their investment.

This is an apparent extra profit in the successful enterprises. For the system of enterprises as a whole, however, such risk-bearing rewards should total zero, with the actual losses incurred tending to counterbalance the gains, if investors "gamble at even odds." Then no additional share of aggregate income results, since the losers' loss of assets (deducted from income) equals the amount of extra purchasing power that the winners gain. For the winning enterprises total receipts exceed total costs by a certain amount, but for the losers total costs exceed total receipts by the same amount. The net relative income position of all those in a position to bear risk is thus unaffected, although risk does retard the rate of investment, and investments resulting in loss do reflect a certain unavoidable social loss in real output. The rewards of risk bearing for the system as a whole may thus tend toward zero, and may not represent a source of pure profits for economy, so long as systematic over- or under-estimation of risk, or insistence on better than even odds by investors does not occur. But the existence of risk and the adaptations to it do affect the distribution of income as among enterprise and result in true profits or losses for individual enterprises.[5]

Such risk-bearing rewards for successful enterprise could result even in purely competitive equilibrium (so far as this was consistent with the existence of uncertainty) and as well under monopolistic conditions. And "excessive" caution by all enterprise could result in an excess-profit share for the economy as a whole. Where the rewards of excessive caution ended and the monopolistic profits of impeded entry began, however, would be an almost impossible question to answer except in pure abstraction. Correspondingly, it may be very difficult empirically to analyze the residual reward of any single enterprise or group of enterprises in such a way as to distinguish risk-bearing rewards from monopolistic or other excess profits.

[5] See F. H. Knight, "Profit," *Readings in the Theory of Income Distribution*, Chap. 27, for further comments on the risk problem.

The tendency of true profits to zero in a purely competitive economy has long constituted a sort of ideal, and also on occasion a justification of the essential fairness of income distribution in an enterprise economy regulated by competition. There is a serious question, however, whether the realization of such a tendency would be consistent with the effective functioning of capitalism. A system which is driven by profit-seeking motives, but in which no profit-seeker can succeed in making profits except by gambling on risk at even odds, may be a scoiological impossibility. Certainly, it is apparent from the history of capitalism that the efforts of enterprisers are likely to be turned principally toward escaping the profit-constricting bonds both of competition and of equilibrium. This leads us to the primary considerations of monopoly and of dynamic change as the source of pure profits.

MONOPOLY AND MONOPSONY PROFITS

The discussions of noncompetitive pricing of goods in Chapters 5 to 9 and of noncompetitive factor pricing in Chapter 12 have suggested that monopolistic and monopsonistic market structures may permit enterprise to earn an excess or pure profit reward more or less persistently. Even in long-run equilibrium, the selling firms may be able to maintain a gap between price and full average cost and thus to divert a share of total purchasing power to themselves in return for "nothing." This could hold in either single-firm monopoly or oligopoly selling, and in monopsony or oligopsony buying. In any instance, however, the ability to earn monopoly profits depends primarily on impediments to the entry of additional enterprises into the affected industry. Free entry would tend to eliminate monopoly or monopsony profits. But the existence of legal, institutional, and economic impediments to entry [6] permits the maintenance of at least some excess profits in many fields. Such profits, which may also be referred to as the earning power of whatever it is that firms possess which discourages entry, are a distinct income share and identifiable as pure profits. They will ordinarily be reflected in an accounting net profit which when expressed as a percentage of owners' investment is larger than the interest rate plus a normal risk premium. Even this will not appear, however, if the investment has been so valued as to include the capitalized present value of monopoly earnings attributable to existing blockades to entry.

It is an almost inevitable tendency of capitalist enterprise to seek monopoly positions continuously through time by securing buying or selling market positions protected from the ultimate in free entry. The possibilities of resource monopolization, the patent laws, the issuance of monopoly franchises by governments, and the development of product differentiation

[6] Cf. pp. 193-197.

advantages all offer avenues for gaining monopoly positions. But since blockades to entry are seldom completely effective, since the antitrust laws oppose them in some degree, and since dynamic change permits new monopolies to destroy old ones, the accumulation of monopoly may not continue indefinitely but may instead reach a peak or limit. At any current time, however, monopoly excess profits are a perceptible share of total income.

DYNAMIC CHANGE AND PROFITS

Monopoly is not the only source of pure profit, however. Dynamic changes in income and innovations of either technique or product may also give rise to a distinct share of income to enterprise.

The potential effect of a fluctuating aggregate money income is quite apparent. As money income expands, even from an initial profitless equilibrium of prices and costs, the money prices of both commodities and productive factors tend to rise, since their supplies in general are less than perfectly elastic. If in general commodity prices tend to rise more rapidly than factor prices, a transitional margin between prices and costs is created. As a consequence, excess profits may tend to arise in periods of secularly or cyclically expanding money income and inflating prices. Conversely, periods of contracting money income and deflating prices may tend to produce losses, or a reduction of monopolistic excess profits which would otherwise be earned. If earned, these profits and losses are essentially of a short-period variety, accountable as the result of a process of adjustment in pursuit of new money price equilibria. It may be argued that in the long run the losses of downswings would exactly counterbalance the gains of upswings, so that on the average no genuine profit share is created. This would be true only if the downswings were just as great as the upswings—if there is neither progressive deflation nor progressive inflation—and if the lag of factor prices behind commodity prices was the same in upswing and downswing phases. Otherwise, a systematic average profit or loss for enterprise might be created. And there would at any rate be a tendency to periodic distortion in the pattern of income distribution. Whether the distortion referred to occurs at all, however, obviously depends on whether there is a significant lag of factor prices behind commodity prices as prices generally change, and of this we can no longer be very certain.

Since individual enterprises are generally unable to control the fluctuations of aggregate money income which occur, any profits and losses arising from this source may be appropriately characterized as *windfalls* outside their control. This is not so, however, of profits created by dynamic changes in product or technique, since these are in general purposefully introduced by enterprise precisely in pursuit of a pure profit.

The long-run equilibrium to which an economy would tend rests on the assumption of given techniques of production, from which emerge given costs curves for all goods, and of a given regimen of goods for production. With these things given, a long-run general price equilibrium would eventually be reached, at which, with universal pure competition, all profits would tend to zero. With monopolistic elements present, this general price equilibrium might permit of excess profits in certain sectors of the economy, but each monopoly profit would have distinct limits.

If, now, the techniques of production are changed in one or more lines, the real costs of production there are presumably reduced. Output therefore tends to expand in the affected lines and to be adjusted elsewhere, as the economy seeks a new general price equilibrium corresponding to the new technological data. When the new equilibrium is finally attained, competitive profits should again be zero, and monopolistic profits not necessarily larger than before. But during the process of movement toward a new equilibrium—and this process takes time—the initial innovators who first reduced their costs should enjoy a period during which they can earn excess profits. Until there is sufficient imitation of or entry into the use of the new technique, and until prices are thus driven down to the level of the new costs, the innovators tend to reap an extra reward as a result of their pioneering.

Under universally competitive conditions, the period during which they could thus receive extra profits might not be too long. But when patent monopolies can be obtained for a period of years, innovators may be able to create temporary monopoly positions which exclude entry and preserve their advantages for a considerable time span. The combination of dynamic change and of blockade of entry to new techniques may thus create a distinct extra profit share. So far as enterprise will continually be engaged in developing and protecting technical improvements, this share may persist regularly through time, as the economy pursues an ever-moving equilibrium tendency. Here is the outstanding example of systematic and successful effort by enterprises to escape competitive equilibrium.

The same general argument may be applied to innovations of new products, which change the structure of demand for various goods, give rise to a new general equilibrium tendency, and create a transitional opportunity for excess profits to the innovators.

The profits of dynamic change forced by innovators are probably the principal source of a genuine and distinct profit share of income in a capitalist economy. Together with monopoly and monopsony gains they make up most of the total of such profits, the remainder representing any net windfalls resulting from income movements (some of which may be generated by the investment associated with innovation). It is also clear that profits to monopoly and to innovation are interrelated, in that innovation may open the road to new monopoly as well as tend to reduce the value of old monopoly. The pursuit of at least transitional monopoly profits may indeed be a primary incentive to innovation.

Innovations of technique and product, whether or not assisted by monopoly positions established through innovation, are a principal source of pure profit in the real economy. This admitted, the question arises whether there is not a fourth sort of productive service or "factor of production" which earns this share of income. The profits of innovations indeed go to the entrepreneur-owner group as a reward for its astuteness in changing techniques and products, and also provide a payment to that special category of labor devoted to devising possible ways of changing products and techniques. They may thus serve as a desirable incentive reward for invention and innovation, and may promote progress in the aggregate output of the economy. Because the relation of effort to reward seems highly unpredictable and erratic in this case, however, the recognition of a "fourth factor of production" is not necessarily appropriate. It is sufficient to recognize that a share of the residual pure profit going to enterprise may result from purposive endeavor on the part of enterprise in changing techniques of production and the design of products, and that some sort of rather uncertain relation of innovation reward to innovation effort may thus result.

When profits are considered in this light, it appears that if they are not a payment for money, land, or labor (except that special human effort involved in innovation), they may at any rate in part be a return earned as a result of potentially constructive human effort. But innovation profit and monopoly profit are almost inextricably intertwined. And although the profits of innovation per se tend to perform a desirable function in promoting progress, their emergence in a setting permitting of well-fortified and long-perpetuated monopoly positions could retard progress and result in a total profit share larger than necessary to stimulate progress.

THE RECIPIENTS OF PROFITS FROM INCORPORATED BUSINESS

The traditional justification of economic profit in a capitalist economy has been that it furnished a necessary incentive for the enterprise system to function. At least the possibility of rewards over and above a normal interest return to funds invested has been held desirable as a means of inducing both rational allocation of resources among uses and progress in techniques and products. In equilibrium, the firm should try to maximize profits, and if the maximum is zero, it should still strive toward it. Dynamically, enterprises should be induced to make innovations of technique or to introduce new products because they promise larger profits. The potentiality of profit and the desire to maximize it should serve as a rationalizing force in enterprise action.

Considerable interest, therefore, has been expressed in the development of business organization to a point where the owner-investors do not make the decisions which affect enterprise profits, and where the managers who do make these decisions are not primarily owners destined to benefit directly from increased profits. In very large corporations, which do over a third of all business done in America today, it is often true that the decision-making management is largely independent of the dividend-receiving share-holders, in that the shareholders, in practice, exercise little influence over the selection and retention of the management. In these cases, the shareholder becomes a passive investor, who receives part or all of the profit reward of the enterprising ability of the entrepreneur-manager; the managers, re-warded principally by wages, do not necessarily receive the pure profit re-wards which should provide them with the incentive to maximize profits. Where this situation obtains, it has been suggested that controlling manage-ments may not be primarily concerned with profit maximization as a guide either to current price-output adjustments or to policy respecting innovation.

The general facts of separation of ownership from control or entre-preneurship are fairly clear. The phenomenon is apparently significant in something like half of the largest corporations. Whether or not the princi-ples upon which management decisions turn have been seriously affected by the separate identity of profit makers and profit receivers is still a subject for speculation and investigation. And the extent to which hired managers are paid a salary plus perhaps a bonus which includes some pure profit earned by reason of innovating ability can also bear investigation.[7]

THE DISTRIBUTION OF INCOME—ETHICAL ASPECTS

With the preceding discussion of profits, the general principles governing the distribution of income among productive factors have been fully out-lined. Under various sorts of market organization, we are able to see the general determinants of the relative rates of pay received by labor, land, capital, and enterprise. The aggregate share received by each factor, whether under competitive or noncompetitive market conditions, will depend, of course, upon the amount of it available and employed as well as upon the rate of pay per unit of service. It is generally found that wages and salaries paid to nonowners constitute from 60 to 65 percent of national income. The imputed wages, rent, interest, and profits of owner-managers make up an-other 20 percent. Contractual rent and interest payments amount to about 5 percent, and corporate profits (which include imputed rent and interest

[7] For a discussion of these matters and also of the analysis of profits generally, see R. A. Gordon, "Enterprise, Profits, and the Modern Corporation," *Readings in the Theory of Income Distribution,* Chap. 29.

as well as pure profits) make up the balance. These are extremely rough proportions, subject to systematic secular and cyclical movement.

Whatever the functional distribution of income under either competitive or monopolistic conditions, it has no necessary a priori ethical content. The fact that a free-enterprise economy distributes income in this way does not mean that the distribution is just or unjust. Accepting the postulates of a capitalist system—principally private property in productive wealth and the right to receive property incomes in the form of rent, interest, or profit —it is perhaps expedient that incomes should be distributed about as they are, in order that the economic system function effectively. But preference for a competitive rather than a monopolistic determination of income shares must result from the essentially arbitrary adoption of a value judgment concerning desirable interpersonal relationships with respect to income. Such value judgments are necessary in social conduct, and are freely, if seldom unanimously, adopted. The ethical evaluation of income distribution within capitalism must thus be rooted in political philosophy rather than in technical economic analysis.

This is equally true of the ethical evaluation of capitalistic as compared to socialistic income distribution. The salient aspect of capitalistic distribution is that property ownership is the basis of personal income in the form of rents, interest, and profits, whereas in full socialism the bulk of personal income should theoretically be in the form of wages for labor, other income shares being arbitrarily allocated by the state. The choice must essentially rest upon complex political value judgments. The property incomes of capitalism are the source of argument principally because the property from which they stem is rather unequally distributed (through chance, inheritance, accumulations of wealth based on prolonged historical discrepancies in personal income distribution, etc.). This unequal distribution of property, in turn, leads to a degree of inequality in the distribution of incomes among persons—in extremes of poverty and wealth—much greater than would result from differences in personal wage-earning ability.[8] And this in turn raises some conflicts with the precepts of political democracy. The resolution of this difficulty is not obvious, and the current complex conflict of ideologies reflects the dilemmas encountered when a real solution is sought.

Modification of personal income distribution via progressive income taxation is a principal expedient measure followed today in capitalistic countries. Inheritance taxes have the effect of checking the progressive accumulation of wealth from one generation to another. And it is felt by many that reduction or elimination of monopolistic profits and monopolistic rents would perceptibly reduce the inequality in personal income distribution. Dis-

[8] See Mary Jean Bowman, "Personal Income Distribution in the United States," *Readings in the Theory of Income Distribution,* Chap. 4.

cussion of the ethical and social problems of income distribution, however, must be left to other works.

SUPPLEMENTARY READINGS

ROBERT A. GORDON, "Enterprise, Profits, and the Modern Corporation," *Readings in the Theory of Income Distribution,* Chap. 29.

FRANK H. KNIGHT, "Profit," *ibid.,* Chap. 27.

———, *Risk, Uncertainty, and Profit,* Boston: Houghton Mifflin Company, 1921.

JOHN T. DUNLOP, *Wage Determination under Trade Unions,* New York: The Macmillan Company, 1944.

16 CONCLUSION

This volume has presented a systematic though elementary analysis of several principal aspects of the function of a capitalist economy. We have investigated the determination of commodity prices and outputs and of the allocation of resources among alternative uses; the determination of the aggregate level of employment and output; the manner in which income is distributed among various functional groups. If the student considers the several phases of the preceding analysis in concert, he will observe a certain body of abstractly derived or a priori predictions of the working of a free-enterprise economy in the respects emphasized.

Yet, it should be very strongly emphasized that these predictions and the analysis from which they arise are extremely simplified and are potentially reliable only within a substantial range of error. In the first place, such an abstract analysis essentially proceeds by setting up certain assumptions concerning human psychology and the market structures within which human action takes place, and then by deducing what should happen in the assumed situation. The assumptions are carefully drawn, and every attempt is made to have in them an accurate if simplified representation of reality. Some of these assumptions, however, may be inaccurate, or so oversimplified as to be unable in a single average to take account of a range of conditions which occur in fact. Thus, the assumption that businessmen always try to maximize profits may be a fair guess at the central tendency, but the actual motivation in specific cases may be different, or at any rate more complex. In the case of monopolistic sellers of labor, we really do not know what to assume concerning motivation and thus can only make alternative guesses. Or in distinguishing among market structures, only the broadest differences are recognized, and other individual differences of potential significance to pricing are entirely overlooked in the assumptions. With both oversimplification and chance of error affecting the assumptions upon which the analysis is based, it is clear that the predictions arrived at cannot be precise estimates of real behavior but only rough indications of a central tendency. Much more detailed abstract analysis, or alternatively detailed empirical observation, would be required to gain a more precise notion of what happens.

There is another reason why recourse to empirical investigation should be essential in many instances. When we encounter oligopolistic markets, or markets with bilateral monopoly or bilateral oligopoly, abstract analysis tells us that the outcome is indeterminate within a significant range. This applies both to commodity price-output determination and to factor pricing in labor and other markets. In these instances, we are presented not with the prediction of a central tendency but with a range of alternative central tendencies and perhaps some reason for believing one to be more probable than another. This dilemma can be resolved best by detailed empirical examination of behavior and its rationale in particular cases. A priori, it would seem that economic activity in a capitalist economy may lack a precisely observed law of behavior and be subject to a certain random tendency.

This leads us to another limitation of the particular sort of abstract analysis followed above. For purposes of argument we have assumed that the significant determining variables or variable relationships—prices, costs, demand curves, cost and supply curves—are known to the principal actors in the scene, or at any rate are estimated with sufficient confidence that they are acted upon. Thus, we have supposed "given data"—given either by foreknowledge or by "reliable" estimate. In actuality, of course, the magnitudes of many strategic variables are highly uncertain; as a result they can be estimated with no great confidence, and the reactions to these estimates may be modified by the recognized uncertainty to which they are subject. In the preceding analysis we have taken substantially no account of the idea of a range of alternative estimates of strategic variables, of the effect of such a range on decision making, or, more important, of the consequences of behavior based on erroneous expectations. This is the province of dynamic process analysis, into which we have not entered here.

A final limitation of the preceding analysis is thus that it is an analysis of equilibrium tendencies rather than of the process of change through time. Most of the preceding indicates little about the process of economic activity through time, but rather emphasizes the equilibria toward which this activity tends over a period of time. It describes the path of the rabbit which the hunter pursues rather than the path followed, step by step, by the hunter. It tells us something, but certainly less than all, of the character of economic activity. Dynamic process analysis is a logical further step in the study of economic theory.

Even in the analysis of stationary equilibria, of course, the preceding is elementary in the extreme, deliberately neglecting many advanced or detailed facets of theory, by-passing entirely alternative formulations, and emphasizing only slightly the formal mathematical aspects of theoretical solutions. It is hoped, however, that the volume will have served as a useful introduction to abstract economic analysis.

INDEX

01
03
44
13
23
23
34

21)‾12‾
5)‾1
7)‾40

706
17)‾120‾
119
100